Huebner School Series

FUNDAMENTALS OF INVESTMENTS FOR FINANCIAL PLANNING
Sixth Edition

Walt J. Woerheide

THE
AMERICAN
COLLEGE PRESS

HS328-6

This publication is designed to provide accurate and authoritative information about the subject covered. While every precaution has been taken in the preparation of this material, the authors, and The American College assume no liability for damages resulting from the use of the information contained in this publication. The American College is not engaged in rendering legal, accounting, or other professional advice. If legal or other expert advice is required, the services of an appropriate professional should be sought.

© 2011 The American College Press
270 S. Bryn Mawr Avenue
Bryn Mawr, PA 19010
(888) AMERCOL (263–7265)
theamericancollege.edu
Library of Congress Control Number 2010910564
ISBN-10 1-58293-039-2
ISBN-13 978-1-58293-039-8
Printed in the United States of America

Individual Health Insurance Planning
Thomas P. O'Hare and Burton T. Beam, Jr.

Financial Planning: Process and Environment
Craig W. Lemoine

Fundamentals of Insurance Planning
Burton T. Beam, Jr., and Eric A. Wiening

Fundamentals of Financial Planning
David M. Cordell (ed.)

Fundamentals of Income Taxation
James F. Ivers III and Thomas M. Brinker, Jr. (eds.)

McGill's Life Insurance
Edward E. Graves (ed.)

McGill's Legal Aspects of Life Insurance
Edward E. Graves and Burke A. Christensen (eds.)

Group Benefits: Basic Concepts and Alternatives
Burton T. Beam, Jr.

Planning for Retirement Needs
David A. Littell, Kenn Beam Tacchino, and Paul J. Schneider

Fundamentals of Investments for Financial Planning
Walt J. Woerheide

Fundamentals of Estate Planning
Constance J. Fontaine

Estate Planning Applications
Ted Kurlowicz

Planning for Business Owners and Professionals
Ted Kurlowicz, James F. Ivers III, and John J. McFadden

Financial Planning Applications
Craig W. Lemoine

Advanced Topics in Group Benefits
Burton T. Beam, Jr., and Thomas P. O'Hare (eds.)

Executive Compensation
Paul J. Schneider (ed.)

Health and Long-Term Care Financing for Seniors
Burton T. Beam, Jr., Nancy P. Morith, and Thomas P. O'Hare

Financial Decisions for Retirement
David A. Littell (ed.)

The American College® is an independent, nonprofit, accredited institution founded in 1927 that offers professional certification and graduate-degree distance education to men and women seeking career growth in financial services.

The Center for Financial Advisor Education at The American College offers both the LUTCF and the Financial Services Specialist (FSS) professional designations to introduce students in a classroom environment to the technical side of financial services, while at the same time providing them with the requisite sales-training skills.

The Solomon S. Huebner School® of The American College administers the Chartered Life Underwriter (CLU®); the Chartered Financial Consultant (ChFC®); the Chartered Advisor for Senior Living (CASL®); the Registered Health Underwriter (RHU®); the Registered Employee Benefits Consultant (REBC®); and the Chartered Leadership Fellow® (CLF®) professional designation programs. In addition, the Huebner School also administers The College's CFP Board—registered education program for those individuals interested in pursuing CFP® certification, the CFP® Certification Curriculum.

The Richard D. Irwin Graduate School® of The American College offers the master of science in financial services (MSFS) degree, the Graduate Financial Planning Track (another CFP Board-registered education program), and several graduate-level certificates that concentrate on specific subject areas. It also offers the Chartered Advisor in Philanthropy (CAP®) and the master of science in management (MSM), a one-year program with an emphasis in leadership. The National Association of Estate Planners & Councils has named The College as the provider of the education required to earn its prestigious AEP designation.

The American College is accredited by **The Middle States Commission on Higher Education**, 3624 Market Street, Philadelphia, PA 19104 at telephone number 267.284.5000.

The Middle States Commission on Higher Education is a regional accrediting agency recognized by the U.S. Secretary of Education and the Commission on Recognition of Postsecondary Accreditation. Middle States accreditation is an expression of confidence in an institution's mission and goals, performance, and resources. It attests that in the judgment of the Commission on Higher Education, based on the results of an internal institutional self-study and an evaluation by a team of outside peer observers assigned by the Commission, an institution is guided by well-defined and appropriate goals; that it has established conditions and procedures under which its goals can be realized; that it is accomplishing them substantially; that it is so organized, staffed, and supported that it can be expected to continue to do so; and that it meets the standards of the Middle States Association. The American College has been accredited since 1978.

The American College does not discriminate on the basis of race, religion, sex, handicap, or national and ethnic origin in its admissions policies, educational programs and activities, or employment policies.

The American College is located at 270 S. Bryn Mawr Avenue, Bryn Mawr, PA 19010. The toll-free number of the Office of Professional Education is (888) AMERCOL (263-7265); the fax number is (610) 526-1465; and the home page address is theamericancollege.edu.

Through The American College's website, theamericancollege.edu, students can access information on a variety of topics including:

- **General Information on Courses:** Course descriptions, chapter or assignment topics, and required study materials for all Solomon S. Huebner School, Richard D. Irwin Graduate School, and the Center for Financial Advisor Education courses are listed.

- **The American College Online Learning Center:** The College provides online study materials for this course, including an interactive version of the sample exam, designed to be used in conjunction with the printed study materials to enhance the learning experience. This material is provided only through password access to students registered for this course. To obtain a password, students should complete the e-mail address section of the course registration form; The College will send the student a password and instructions on how to access these materials.

- **Course Pages/Updates:** New developments in the subject area, important study points, links to other useful governmental and organizational websites, and errata in course materials are included. All information is accessible on The American College Online Learning Center with a password at blackboard.theamericancollege.edu.

- **Course Registration Procedures:** Secure online registration plus registration forms that can be printed and faxed/mailed to The College are available.

- **Examinations on Demand (EOD) Testing Procedures:** The policies and requirements for EOD testing, as well as links to lists of our more than 3,000 test centers, are provided.

- **Educational Policies and Procedures:** The education, experience, ethics, continuing education, and transfer of credit requirements for The College's designation and graduate programs are explained.

CONTENTS

Unlike most textbooks in the field of investments, the target audience of this book is only financial planners. The emphasis is on investment planning, not investments per se. Thus, although the book presents the principles and concepts of investment theory and practice, the focus is always on how a financial planner can use this information to serve his or her client. It is has not been written to help someone pass the CFA®, Series 6, or Series 7 exams.

I am mindful that many people are taking this course in preparation to sit for the CFP® exam. Students with access to the Blackboard materials for this course will note two lists of all the investment-related CFP® Study Points covered in this course. One list indicates the study points and identifies the chapter in which they are covered. A second list indicates by chapter which study points are covered in that chapter. The student must remember that the study points are not intended as an exhaustive or comprehensive listing of material that will be on the CFP® exam. Hence, all of the chapters provide additional coverage relevant to these topics so that the student is more fully prepared to sit for that exam if he or she opts to do so, and to be a better overall financial planner.

This book includes numerous pedagogical features designed to help students focus their study of investments. Among the features found in every chapter of the book are

- *Learning objectives:* Statements at the beginning of each chapter are designed to provide direction to students studying the subject matter in the chapter.

- *Key terms:* In the margins where the terms first appear, as well as grouped together at the end of each chapter, certain terms or phrases are singled out because of their importance to the specific subject matter.

- *Examples:* Problem sets interspersed throughout the chapter are designed to help students see how difficult concepts are applied in specific situations.

- *Review questions:* Essay-style questions and computational problems at the end of each chapter are designed to test the student's knowledge of the learning objectives. For students at The American College, the answers are provided at the course's Blackboard site.

- *Self-test questions:* True-false statements are also provided on Blackboard, along with the answers.

Features located in the back of the book are

- *A glossary:* Key terms found in each chapter are defined and included in the back of the book.

- *An index:* The book has a comprehensive index to help identify pages on which various topics are found.

ACKNOWLEDGMENTS

I would like to thank Ben Branch, professor of finance in the school of management, the University of Massachusetts at Amherst, for the original development of this book, as well as his contributions to the first edition of The American College's version of this textbook. I would also like to thank the following faculty at The American College for their contributions to previous editions: Roger C. Bird, professor of economics and holder of the Frank M. Engle Distinguished Chair in Economic Security Research; the late Thomas A. Dziadosz, associate professor of economics; Paul Hoffman, assistant professor of finance; Barbara S. Poole, associate professor of finance and insurance; Robert S. Graber, assistant professor of finance; C. Bruce Worsham, associate professor of taxation and insurance; and David Cordell, professor of finance. I am grateful to David Nanigian, assistant professor of investments and Chris Woehrle, assistant professor of taxation, for their reviews of this edition.

All of these individuals made this a better book. In spite of their help, however, some errors have undoubtedly been successful in eluding my eyes. For these I am solely responsible. At the same time, however, I accept full credit for giving those readers who find these errors the exhilarating intellectual experience produced by such discovery.

 Walt J. Woerheide, Ph.D., CFP®, is the Vice President of Academics and Dean at The American College. He is the current holder of the Frank M. Engle Distinguished Chair in Economic Security Research and also serves as Professor of Investments. Before joining the College in 2001, Dr. Woerheide held faculty appointments at the University of Illinois at Chicago for 10 years, the University of Michigan - Flint for 6 years, and Rochester Institute of Technology for 11 years. He also worked for a year as a Visiting Scholar at the Federal Home Loan Bank Board.

Dr. Woerheide has served as President of the Academy of Financial Services, an association of people interested in teaching and research in the area of financial planning, and as President of the Midwest Finance Association. He has served as a Judge for both the Financial Frontiers Awards and the Kenneth Black, Jr. Journal Author Award Program given by the Journal of Financial Service Professionals. He also serves as an Associate Editor for the Journal of Financial Service Professionals and serves on the Editorial Board of Financial Services Review, Business Quest, and the Journal of Financial Planning.

In addition to responsibility for several editions of The College's Investments textbook, he has also published Introducing Personal Finance with John Wiley & Sons, and The Savings and Loan Industry: Current Problems and Possible Solutions with Quorum Books. Dr. Woerheide has published over 26 articles in various journals including Journal of Financial Service Professionals, Financial Services Review, Financial Counseling and Planning, Journal of Financial Planning, and Journal of Consumer Affairs. He has refereed articles for 16 different journals, served on multiple program committees for professional associations, reviewed numerous textbooks, and served many times as an outside referee for promotion and tenure cases.

Dr. Woerheide earned his Ph.D. and M.B.A. degrees from Washington University, and he has a B.A. from Brown University many, many years ago.

Learning Objectives

An understanding of the material in this chapter should enable you to

1. Explain the purpose and mechanics of the primary market.

2. Describe the people associated with the secondary market.

3. Describe the institutions of the secondary market.

4. Describe the costs of trading, types of transactions, and types of orders an investor can use, and indicate when it is most appropriate to use which type of order.

5. Describe the mechanics and the risk exposures associated with selling short, and the mechanics of large secondary market trades.

6. Identify the important features of each of the major security laws as they affect investors.

7. Decide whether to own a security in street name or to order it out, evaluate which type of account is appropriate, and measure the volume of trading activity in an account.

A central element of financial planning involves advising on or actually managing a client's financial assets. Therefore, a financial planner needs to be knowledgeable with regard to asset or investment choices, the expected rates of return and risk exposures associated with each asset choice, and the suitability of each asset category for a client. Each investment opportunity has advantages and disadvantages. Each investor has a unique set of needs, goals, attitudes, and resources that influence the relative attractiveness and suitability of particular investments for that investor. The goal of this book is to provide the requisite knowledge to prepare a financial planner to advise clients effectively.

We will start our study of investment planning by exploring the structure of the U.S. securities markets, the mechanics and regulation of these markets, and the mechanics of trading. We will consider first the primary market, which is where companies issue securities to raise cash. Then we will look at the players, the components, and the transactions of the secondary market. We will then consider some of the more critical laws that affect financial services firms and the financial markets today. We will conclude with a consideration of some of the practical issues, including whether or not to hold securities in street name and what type of account to establish.

THE PRIMARY MARKET

When corporations want to acquire cash, they issue new securities. This sale of newly created securities to investors is referred to as the primary market. Investment bankers handle the sale of new securities, and the process is referred to as underwriting the offering.

Investment Bankers

Many large brokerage firms have investment banking divisions; therefore, the names of the major investment banking firms are often the same as the names of the major brokerage firms. An investment banker works with companies to facilitate the issuance of new securities, and with holders of large blocks of shares to facilitate the resale of these securities. Think of investment bankers as wholesalers and brokerage firms as retailers of securities.

initial public offering (IPO)   A private firm that sells a substantial block of additional shares and thereby creates a more active and diverse ownership is said to go public, and this sale of shares is known as an *initial public offering (IPO)*. For 2009, there were only 30 IPOs in the U.S., while in 2000 there were 388 IPOs. When a company that is actively traded in the secondary market wants to sell new securities to raise cash, this is referred to as a secondary or seasoned equity offering (SEO). For example, Microsoft may decide to sell $500 million worth of new common stock. An investor may then buy the stock in the primary market or in the secondary market. Alternatively, the shares sold in an SEO may have previously been privately held (owned by one person or a small number of people).

syndicate   Regardless of whether the offering is an IPO or an SEO, when the issue is large, the investment banker assembles a *syndicate* to underwrite the issue. A syndicate is a group of investment bankers who share the risk and return of a public offering. The number of members in the syndicate is related to the size of the new offering. At some point in the process of a public offering, the investment banker or syndicate will publish an ad about the offering, known as a *tombstone*. This ad gives details about the issue and lists the underwriters involved in the deal in the order of their importance. Sometimes the tombstone is published after the issue has been sold.

To initiate a public offering, the issuing firm and its investment banker compose a registration statement. This is submitted to the Securities and Exchange Commission (SEC) for review. During the review period, the investment banker may distribute this registration statement. Because the front page of the statement contains a paragraph in red ink indicating that the company is not attempting to sell its shares before the SEC approves the registration, the statement is known as a *red herring*. Red herrings are sometimes revised several times before the issue is ready for sale to the public.

Once the SEC gives its approval, the investment banker may proceed with the offering. A final offering price is set, along with the size of the issue. The investment banker must give a prospectus to each potential buyer. The main difference between a red herring and a prospectus is that a red herring omits the selling price and the size of the issue.

firm-commitment basis

best-effort basis

Most offerings are done on a *firm-commitment basis*, which means that the investment banker buys the offering from the firm and resells it to the investors. The investment banker bears the risk if the offering is less than fully successful and occasionally absorbs huge losses in this process. Sometimes the underwriting is taken on a *best-effort basis*, in which case the investment banker acts as an agent for the issuing firm. Best efforts are used when the investment banker feels there is a significant risk that the issue may not sell completely.

Financial Planning Issue

There are three good aspects to having a client subscribe to a primary offering. First, the investor pays no direct commission. Second, one of the investment banker's obligations is to attempt to maintain a floor price for the securities offered, thus reducing the risk of an immediate loss. Third, research shows that, on average, primary offerings are usually slightly underpriced, thus producing a slight gain in the first few days of trading. As a result, there is usually more demand to subscribe to a new offering than there are shares available.

Sometimes the market goes through a period in which IPOs become "hot" commodities. Some IPOs will double in value during the first day or first few days of trading. These are particularly good times to be a participant in an IPO if one can get shares.

Unfortunately, there is also substantial evidence that after the initial jump in stock price that the majority of IPOs experience, these same IPOs do poorly compared to the rest of the market over the next 5 years, and do particularly poorly during the second year after the offering.

Shelf Registration

Although most primary sales are marketed quickly after their registration, the SEC's Rule 415 permits shelf registration, which means that a firm can file one registration statement for a relatively large block of stock and then sell parts of it over a 2-year period. The shelf registration option tends to reduce red tape and expenses, and because the stock can be sold directly to institutional investors, it sometimes eliminates the underwriting fee.

Private Placements

lettered stock   New issues are sometimes sold in large lots to a small group of buyers in a private placement. These placements allow start-up firms to demonstrate viability by successfully raising some capital on their own. The private placements are usually sold below the public offering price; additional shares may subsequently be marketed to the public through an underwriter. In exchange for a favorable private placement price, the initial investors may agree to accept *lettered stock*, which under SEC Rule 144, can be resold only if it has been fully paid for and owned for a period of at least 1 year. However, there are volume restrictions on the number of shares that can be sold if the shares are resold prior to being held for 2 years.[1] Many debt issues are placed privately, usually to large buyers such as insurance companies.

THE SECONDARY MARKET: THE PLAYERS

Once an issue has been sold in the primary market, all subsequent trades are between investors and define what is called the secondary market. It is the secondary market that most people think about when the stock market is mentioned. It takes a variety of people and components to make the secondary market work. In this section, we will consider the key people in this market. In the next two sections, we will look at the institutions that make up the markets and the mechanics of trading.

Brokers, Dealers, and Brokerage Firms

registered representative

The term broker/dealer describes an individual or a company that is licensed to buy investment products for or sell them to clients. A broker or a broker/dealer acting only as a broker buys and sells securities on behalf of investors. Brokers implement their customers' trading instructions and act as the customer's agent. A dealer, in contrast, trades for his or her own accounts and makes markets by advertising a willingness to buy and sell. To be in the securities business, an individual or a company must be a broker/dealer or an individual must be affiliated with a broker/dealer as a *registered representative*. People usually refer to both the individual who handles their accounts and to the firm employing that individual as their broker.

Series 7

Series 6

Brokers must be licensed in their state to sell securities and must have passed the *Series 7* exam, formerly administered by the National Association of Securities Dealers (NASD) and now administered by the Financial Industry Regulatory Authority (FINRA). FINRA was created in July 2007 through the consolidation of the NASD and the member regulation, enforcement, and arbitration functions of the New York Stock Exchange (NYSE). This license qualifies the broker to solicit, purchase, and/or sell all securities products, including corporate securities, municipal securities, options, direct participation programs, investment company products, and variable contracts. Some states also require brokers to pass the Series 63 exam, which tests the

---

1.   http://invest-faq.com/articles/regul-sec-144.html, accessed July 21, 2010.

broker's knowledge of state securities law. Individuals who have passed the *Series 6* exam are licensed to sell mutual funds, initial offerings of closed-end investment companies, and variable annuities, provided the individual also holds the appropriate insurance license. However, these individuals are not registered representatives.

Gramm-Leach-Bliley Act As the financial services industry has become more product integrated, many brokerage firms have added such product lines and services as CDs, life insurance, portfolio management plans, and financial planning. In fact, many of the traditional brokerage firms have urged or required their brokers to obtain a financial planning designation such as the ChFC® or the CFP®. As brokerage firms have expanded into these new areas, other types of financial services firms have penetrated into their areas. Although the lines between brokerage firms and other financial services firms, particularly commercial banks and insurance companies, have been eroding for years, the erosion accelerated with the passage of the *Gramm-Leach-Bliley Act* in 1999 that repealed the Glass-Steagall Act (the Banking Act of 1933). The Glass-Steagall Act prohibited investment banks from operating commercial banks and vice versa.

Floor Brokers and Floor Traders

Floor brokers are employees of firms who are members of a stock exchange and execute trades on an exchange floor on behalf of their firm's clients. Floor brokers receive orders from their firm and execute only these orders. Thus, they are different from floor traders who can buy and sell for their own account. When an investor places an order with his or her brokerage firm, it is transmitted to a floor broker or a floor trader for execution on the trading floor.

floor traders Individuals called registered competitive market makers (RCMMs), or *floor traders*, serve as back-up specialists.[2] RCMMs own exchange seats and trade for their own account. However, they also have "a specific Exchange-imposed obligation to enhance the quality of NYSE markets by injecting their own or the firm's capital into difficult market-making situations. At the request of an Exchange official, an RCMM must make a bid or offer that narrows an existing quote spread or improves its depth. An RCMM may also be asked to assist a commission broker or

---

2.   The RCCM title is used at the NYSE. The Amex uses the title of *registered trader or market maker* for essentially the same function.

floor broker in executing a customer's otherwise nonexecutable order."[3] The failure of an RCMM to enter into trading upon request can result in a financial penalty, a suspension, or even loss of membership in the exchange.

The Specialist

The stock exchanges base their trading on specialists. A specialist is charged with making a market in a particular security, although a given specialist may make markets in a dozen or so securities. This is done through four specific activities. The first is managing the auction process. This means that the specialist defines the opening price for that security each trading day, and then stands ready to trade with anyone in that particular stock at the current bid and ask (or offer) prices.

The second activity is to execute orders for floor brokers. Such trades may be immediate or deferred if they involve price requirements. The specialist will also buy and sell from his or her own inventory, as specialists are also dealers.

The third activity is to serve as a catalyst. The presence of the specialist on the trading floor along with his or her obligation to continuously offer bid and ask prices serves to bring together brokers seeking to execute buy and sell orders.

The fourth activity is to provide capital and stabilize prices when needed. There are times when there are imbalances between buy orders and sell orders that are deemed to be transitory. Under normal circumstances, specialists' firms may be managing a few stocks that are under selling pressure, while others have more public buyers than sellers. The specialist is required to restore balance with appropriate buying or selling using his or her firm's own capital. About 10 percent of all shares traded involve the participation of the specialist.

EXAMPLE

There have been occasions when the need to provide the capital to offset trading imbalances has bankrupted specialists' firms. During the October 1987 crash, almost all of the public orders were on the sell side. Most of the specialists' capital was quickly committed. Some firms were unable to provide an orderly market as they were hit with more and more sell orders at lower and lower prices.

---

3.   http://www.nyse.com/glossary/glossarylinks.html?c=1042235996188, accessed July 21, 2010.

THE SECONDARY MARKET: THE FOUR INSTITUTIONS

Any two people can get together and trade a stock or any other investment, just as they can trade a used car. The one catch with regard to trading securities directly is that the issuer of the security must be notified of the change in ownership. The stronger and more effective the institutional structure for trading securities is, the stronger the economy of that country. Economies that depend on direct trading are extremely weak. The existence of a strong secondary market is crucial to a successful primary market. Most investors will not buy in the primary market unless they are confident they can easily sell in the secondary market.

The Stock Exchanges

New York Stock Exchange

In terms of the market value of trades, as well as the market value of companies listed on an exchange, the New York Stock Exchange (NYSE) has always been the dominant trading institution. Historically, only members could transact business on the exchange, and only listed securities could be traded.

After 212 years as an independent trading organization, the NYSE entered into a merger agreement with the Archipelago Exchange on April 20, 2005. The combined entity was known as the NYSE Group, Inc., and was a publicly held for-profit company. In April 2007, the NYSE Group merged with Euronext, which was the European combined market. The surviving organization is a holding company known as NYSE Euronext, and is the first transatlantic stock exchange. The holding group operates six cash equities exchanges in seven countries, and eight derivatives exchanges. The standards a company must meet to be listed on the NYSE, and the standards to continue to be listed, are higher on the NYSE than in any other market.

American Stock Exchange

For many years, the next largest exchange after the NYSE was the American Stock Exchange or Amex. In 1998, the Amex merged with the National Association of Securities Dealers (NASD), which later became known as FINRA. Although the NASD controlled the NASDAQ stock market, the NASDAQ and Amex markets continued to operate as separate exchanges. In late 2003 the American Stock Exchange regained its independence. In October 2008, NYSE Euronext acquired Amex, and in March 2009, the exchange's operation was branded as the NYSE Amex Equities. The Amex is now considered a specialty market, and has a strong leadership position in the ETF marketplace. It should be noted that the listing requirements to be on the Amex are lower than they are on the NYSE or NASDAQ. However, keep in mind that lower listing requirements only mean smaller companies can obtain listings, not that the quality of the investments is any less.

The Regional Exchanges

The NYSE and NYSE Amex are national exchanges in that their listings are companies from all parts of the country and some are listings from foreign countries. There are four other exchanges around the country that are known as regional exchanges. A regional exchange has even lower listing requirements, and it specializes primarily in companies located in that region.

dual listing Like the national exchanges, the regional exchanges have converted from being mutually owned organizations to being owned by for-profit corporations. Although they have their own listings, they also trade stocks that are not listed at their exchanges, and some of their listings are also listed on the national exchanges. This double listing activity is known as *dual listing*.

The largest regional exchange is the Chicago Stock Exchange (CHX). This exchange has two trading sessions. The normal one runs from 8:30 a.m. CST to 3 p.m. CST. The second session runs from 3 p.m. to 4 p.m., although this session only allows for cross orders (i.e., where there is a match of price and number of shares between the buyer and seller). Another regional exchange is the Boston Stock Exchange (BSE), one of the oldest exchanges in the country. Its trading hours are 8 a.m. to 7 p.m., a really long day!

What was once the Philadelphia Stock Exchange (PHLX) was purchased by the NASDAQ, and is now known as the NASDAQ OMX PHLX. It is the oldest stock exchange in the country. Its trading hours are 9:30 a.m. to 4 p.m. This exchange has a particularly strong role in options trading. The National Stock Exchange (NSX®) used to be known as the Cincinnati Stock Exchange. Although founded in Cincinnati, the exchange subsequently moved to Chicago in 1995. In 1976, it converted from a physical trading floor to an all-electronic market. The leadership for this move was provided by Bernie Madoff, who in recent years became infamous for other reasons.

The Over-The-Counter Market and NASDAQ

over-the-counter (OTC) market

The *over-the-counter (OTC) market* is any trading done by a dealer network. Almost any dealer can decide to make a market in any stock in which he or she thinks there is a profit to be made from such trading. Dealers profit from the bid-ask spread.

The National Association of Security Dealers Automated Quotation System (NASDAQ) was formally organized in 1971 as the world's first electronic market in order to provide price quotations from the OTC market. This NASDAQ Market is divided into two sectors: NASDAQ National Market System and the NASDAQ Capital Market. The Capital Market was known prior to 2005 as the SmallCap Market. The NASDAQ market is now considered a stock exchange, as opposed to just a part of the OTC market, based on its organizational structure.

The NASDAQ Market is reported in financial publications as three markets: NASDAQ National Market issues, NASDAQ NM Issues (NMI) under $100 Million Market Cap, and NASDAQ Small Cap issues. The NMI has higher listing requirements than the Small Cap markets.

Since 2002, the NASDAQ Stock Market has been owned and operated by the NASDAQ OMX Group. The stock for NASDAQ OMX Group is itself traded in the NASDAQ market.

The OTC market continues today for securities that are not listed with the NASDAQ Market. The FINRA OTC Bulletin Board Service (www.otcbb.com) provides quotes for many of these companies. To be included in this service, a company must be required to report to the Securities and Exchange Commission or other regulatory body. Companies that do not qualify for the Bulletin Board Service can be included in the OTC Pink Sheets Electronic Quotation Service, which is not a stock exchange or a regulated entity and where price quotations are provided by OTC market makers and company information is provided by the OTC companies (www.otcmarkets.com). Information posted on pink sheets has not been verified by an external entity or reviewed by any regulatory body.

The OTC market remains the primary market for bond trading. Commercial paper, large CDs, municipal bonds, and other money market instruments trade in similar OTC markets. Unlike the exchanges with specialists, the OTC market is a dealer market. More than one dealer may make a market in a particular security. Thus, when a broker is executing a trade in the

OTC market, he or she is obligated to find the best price among the various dealers. The broker may attempt to negotiate a better price with a dealer, or a broker may end up acting as a dealer for the trade. If the broker acts as dealer, the broker is obligated to provide a price as good or better than he or she could have obtained externally for the customer.

The Third and Fourth Markets

Most trading—and virtually all trades involving individual investors— takes place on an exchange or in the traditional OTC market for unlisted issues. Institutional investors, on the other hand, make significant use of two other markets. OTC trading of exchange-listed stocks constitutes what is called the third market.

The third market grew up back when the exchanges had fixed commission schedules. Exchange-set commissions did not bind third-market dealers. Thus, they tended to charge high-volume institutional traders lower commissions than those charged for trades on the exchanges. By the time the exchanges stopped regulating commissions, the third market was well established. Third-market dealers may well offer a more attractive overall price (stock price and commission) than is available on the exchanges.

electronic communications network (ECN)

The fourth market is an informal arrangement for direct trading between institutions. Both third and fourth markets involve off-exchange trading of what are usually large blocks of exchange-traded stock. The fourth market provides its institutional participants with an even less costly way of trading. Because the institutions trade directly with each other, they incur no commission. Organizations that provide this market are known as *electronic communications networks* (ECNs). To trade NASDAQ stocks, these ECNs must be certified by the SEC and registered with FINRA.

ECNs were originally approved by the SEC in 1997. Although there were only four at the start, there are eight ECNs today. They include: Archipelago ECN, ATTAIN ECN, Bloomberg Tradebook ECN, Brut ECN, Instinet ECN, Island ECN, Market XT, and Redibook ECN. ECNs primarily trade stocks and currencies.

THE SECONDARY MARKET: THE TRANSACTIONS

Transaction Fee Components

There are three major transaction costs associated with trading. One is explicit; and the other two are implicit:

- commission (explicit)
- bid-ask spread (implicit)
- price impact (implicit)

Commission

May Day   When a group of brokers assembled in New York City in 1792 to formalize the origin of the NYSE with the so-called Buttonwood Agreement,[4] they included a rate-fixing clause. Later, the NYSE prohibited exchange-member firms from trading listed securities off the exchange. This restriction stayed in place until the late 1960s. At this time, institutional traders made up a large and growing percentage of stock market volume, and they began to find various ways around the fixed commissions. The NYSE began to make special exceptions to its fixed-rate schedule. Finally, the SEC mandated that the fixed-commission schedule be abolished on May 1, 1975 (known in the industry as *May Day*). It was on this date that the industry splintered into the full-service and discount firms. Because it is always explicitly stated and easy to understand, the commission is the one component of trading costs on which some investors focus. This could be a mistake. The Investment Technology Group estimates that, as of the first quarter of 2010, commissions comprise merely one-fifth of total trading costs in U.S. equities.

Bid-Ask Spread

Everyone making a market in securities, which includes OTC dealers and stock exchange specialists, quotes both a bid price at which he or she will buy and an ask price at which he or she will sell. For example, a dealer in TAC Stock might give quotes of 20 bid and 20¼ ask. This means that the dealer is willing to buy stock from an investor for $20 per share and sell stock to the investor for $20.25 per share. What makes a dealer happy is if someone places an order to sell 100 shares of the stock to the dealer at $20 per share, and then a few seconds later someone else places an order to

---

4.   The agreement was named for the buttonwood tree where the brokers met.

buy the stock at $20.25 per share. In this case, the dealer will make a profit of $.25 per share, or $25 on the 100 shares. This is known as the bid-ask spread, and it is the dealer's sole source of income.

In the OTC market, one has the option of finding alternative dealers who might offer better prices. On the exchanges, there is only one specialist per stock. However, there are frequently other brokers who are looking to trade. Thus, to the extent that brokers can find each other, it is in their mutual interest to agree upon a trading price that is inside the bid-ask spread. Thus, if a specialist quotes 22 bid, 22.10 ask, it makes sense for two brokers to trade at, say, 22.05. Unfortunately, investors have no way of knowing if their brokers paid the ask price or received the bid price, or negotiated a better price. To the extent that an ask price is paid or a bid price is received, the investor is implicitly paying a bid-ask spread. Spreads tend to represent a smaller percentage of the price for higher-priced and more actively traded stocks. Listed stocks generally have smaller bid-ask spreads than those traded over-the- counter. In the OTC market, the number of dealers making a market in a particular stock is a function of the expected volume in the stock. The more volume there is, the more dealers there are, and the smaller the bid-ask spread. The purchase of a thinly traded stock in the OTC market can involve a substantial transaction fee in the form of the bid-ask spread.

paying for order flow

Ethical Issue
An ethical issue in the industry can arise from the practice of *paying for order flow*, which occurs when a dealer pays a firm or a particular broker for the number of orders sent to him or her. The problem is that this dealer may not have the best bid and ask prices from the customer's perspective. The dealer is happy because the dealer makes more money on the trades, the broker is happy because the broker gets the supplemental income in addition to the commission. The customer is usually unaware that he or she has paid a higher price or received a lower price than necessary for the stock.

Price Impact

When a specialist or dealer is asked for quotes, the specialist does not know which way the broker wants to trade (that is, buy or sell). Although dealers and specialists stand ready to provide a bid-ask quote to anyone at anytime, this quote is only for a limited number of shares—for example, an investor wants to sell 10,000 shares but the specialist's quote is good only for the first

1,000 shares. However, when the broker sells 1,000 shares the first time, the specialist then knows that the broker is likely looking to sell a large amount of additional shares. Sooner or later, the specialist will start lowering the price as the specialist's inventory grows beyond the desired number of shares. This adjustment in the price as larger orders are processed is the price impact. Institutional investors' attempt to minimize the effect of price impact that may occur on large trades has led to the dramatic growth of trading in the fourth market, as well as the number of firms who are providing the fourth market.

Types of Orders

Market and Limit Orders

market order
There are only two types of orders that the majority of investors use: the *market order* and the limit order. A market order means an immediate execution at the best available price. If a specialist is quoting a stock at 23 bid and 23.25 ask, a market order to buy should result in a purchase at no more than 23.25 and a market order to sell in a sale at no less than 23, provided that the number of shares to be traded does not exceed the share limits on the bid and ask prices. If the order is placed on an exchange, one always hopes that a matching order arrives on the trading floor at the same time and the floor brokers can make the trade at a price within the bid-ask range.

limit order
A *limit order* to buy sets the maximum price the investor is willing to pay, and a limit order to sell sets the lowest price an investor will accept. A market order ensures a transaction, but the price is uncertain. A limit order ensures the desired price, but only if the trade takes place.

Limit orders that cannot immediately be executed are put on the specialist's book for later execution, if possible.

It is important to remember that there may be more than one limit order placed at a particular price. Suppose that several times during the last week a stock's price bounced between $23 and $24. Several investors interested in buying this stock might all come to the same conclusion that a limit order to buy at $23 might make sense. When this happens, limit orders are placed in a queue. In this case, there may be so many limit orders at this price that even if a few other investors are willing to sell at $23, it is possible that not all the orders in the queue will be executed—particularly if some sort of news develops that means that no one is willing to sell at any price less than $23.50. It can be frustrating to have placed a limit order, see that trading has taken place at that price, and then learn that one's own limit order is still in the queue (albeit the order has moved up in the line).

Financial Planning Issue
Suppose a stock is trading at 23.40 bid and 23.65 ask. An investor notes that the stock has traded as high as 24 in recent days and so places a limit order to sell at 24. If, in fact, the stock rises to 24 in the next few days, the investor will reap an additional $60 for each 100 shares owned. However, if the stock drops to $20 over the next few days, the investor will receive $340 less per hundred shares than he or she would have received with a market order.
Everyone feels like a market genius as long as the limit order is executed and the individual saves a little something on the purchase price or makes something extra on the sale price. However, the first time the limit order causes the investor to miss a bigger profit or take a bigger loss, it will probably be the last limit order the person uses.

Stop-Sell and Stop-Buy Orders

The stop-buy order and the stop-sell order are more complex versions of the market order. These orders are used to limit exposure to adverse price moves. The stop-sell order, also known as a stop-loss order, is the more common of the two. A stop-sell order is a request to activate a market order if the stock trades at or below the designated stop price, which is itself below the current market price. For example, suppose someone owns stock that is trading at $30 per share, and for whatever reason wants to sell the stock if the price drops to $25. One reason might be that the person bought the stock originally at $25 per share and believes that a stop-loss order will guarantee that he or she will at least break even on this investment.

Unfortunately, stop-loss orders do not always achieve their objective. Suppose in the above scenario a rumor starts after trading hours that a company has lost a lawsuit involving its major patent. Not only would its stock likely open at a lower price, but it might also open lower than the $25 price specified in the stop-loss order. As soon as there is a trade at $25 or less, this order becomes a market order and will be executed immediately at the best possible price. Suppose this price is $20 per share! Finally, to add insult to injury, suppose that the company then announces that the rumor is false and it has actually won the lawsuit, causing the price of the stock to jump immediately to $35. Not only did this stop-loss order fail to limit the loss to $5 per share, but the investor also needlessly sold the stock.

Stop-buy orders are used with short sales. The stop price is above the current market price. It becomes a market order once the stock trades at or above the designated price.

Stop-Limit Orders

The stop-limit order is also a variation of the limit order. One can place a stop-limit buy or a stop-limit sell. The difference between stop-limit orders and stop orders is that stop orders convert to market orders and stop-limit orders convert to limit orders once the stop price is hit. When placing a stop-limit order, one must specify both the stop price and the limit price, although they could be the same.

Principal Types of Orders
• Market order: requires immediate execution at the best available price
• Limit order: stipulates the minimum (sell) or maximum (buy) price acceptable for a trade to take place
• Stop-sell order: activates a market order if the stop price is reached
• Stop-limit order: activates a limit order if the stop price is reached

Good-'Til-Canceled, Day, Week, Month, Fill-or-Kill, and All-or-Nothing Orders

Because market orders require immediate execution, specifying how long to keep trying to fill the order is not necessary. Limit, stop-sell, and stop-limit orders, in contrast, may be entered either as good-'til-canceled (GTC) orders or as executable for a specified period. An order can be placed to remain on the books until the end of that trading day (day order), until the end of that trading week (week order), until the end of that month (month order), or for some other period (good through date). These orders are canceled automatically at the close of the designated trading period. Fill-or-kill orders must be either executed immediately or canceled.

Period for Which an Order Is Executable
• GTC order: executable until filled or canceled
• Day order: executable only during the day the order is placed
• Fill-or-kill order: canceled if not immediately executed

Commission charges are based on trades of the same security that take place during the same day. If an order to purchase 500 shares is executed in several pieces throughout the same day, the commission will (or should) be computed for a single 500-share trade. If that same trade takes several days to be executed, however, the commissions will be computed separately on each day's trade. A customer who wishes to trade more than one round lot (that is, 100 shares) may either allow the order to be filled a bit at a time or stipulate an all-or-nothing order. All-or-nothing orders must trade as a unit that incurs a single commission (with any volume discount that applies) but can be executed only when sufficient volume is available. A regular order might be filled in pieces when insufficient volume exists for a single fill. Moreover, all-or-nothing orders are automatically superseded by any other limit orders that other customers place at the same price. Thus, those who consider using all-or-nothing orders need to realize that the potentially lower commission is accompanied by a reduced likelihood of execution.

Selling Short

Most of the time, investing involves buying a security, hoping that the price goes up, and then selling it. This is referred to as taking a long position, or going long. Being long XYZ stock means that one owns XYZ stock. It is possible to reverse this sequence of events—that is, to sell a security one does not own, hope the price goes down, and then buy the security back at a lower price. This is known as selling short, and it is a perfectly legal practice. The short seller borrows the shares from his or her broker and sells them at the current market price. The short seller's broker borrows the shares from someone else's account. The short seller then owes the brokerage firm (actually, the lender) the shorted shares. Being short XYZ stock means one has borrowed and sold the stock and has an obligation to return it in the future.

The customer whose stock is borrowed is just as secure as a bank depositor whose funds are loaned out by the bank. If the lender wishes to sell the loaned stock, the brokerage firm simply borrows replacement shares from another customer or brokerage firm. If a loan of additional shares cannot be made to cover the first loan, then the short seller must buy the shares in the open market and return those shares.

The short seller hopes the price will fall far enough so that when the stock is repurchased, he or she will make a profit after covering trading costs. This gain may be reduced somewhat as the short seller must pay any dividends that accrue on the borrowed stock. Moreover, the short sale proceeds and an additional percentage (margin)[5] of the sale price must be left in a non-interest-bearing account at the brokerage house. If the price of the shorted stock starts going up, the short seller receives a margin call. If the short seller cannot meet the margin call, he or she is forced to buy the stock and return it to the lender's account.

EXAMPLE 1
Shorting 100 shares at 50 and then repurchasing them (covering the short position) at 35 produces a gross profit of $1,500 (100 × [$50 – $35]) minus commissions and dividends. However, if the stock price increases to 65, the seller will show a loss of $1,500 ($100 × [$50 – $65]) plus commissions and dividends.
EXAMPLE 2
If a client goes long a particular stock, the most he or she can lose is 100 percent of his or her investment. If a client shorts a particular stock, he or she may lose many times that amount. Suppose a client shorts 1,000 shares of Obscure Research Labs at $50 per share, and overnight the company announces it has found a cure for cancer. The price of the stock could easily open at $500 or more per share. The client might well be forced into bankruptcy to cover the repurchase and return of these shares!

There is no specific time horizon on short positions (people can be short until they die!). The dividend payment and margin deposit requirements, however, could make this position costly to maintain.

One limit to short selling is the brokerage firm's ability to borrow stock to facilitate the short sale. For widely held stocks, finding shares to sell short is generally not much of a problem. Sometimes, however, the interest in selling a less widely held stock short is so great relative to the shares available to short that brokerage firms run out of available shares. This situation is especially likely for small companies in which only a few people hold the shares and/or when none of the brokerage firm's other customers hold these shares in their accounts. Simply put, it may not be physically possible to short certain stocks.

---

5.   The topic of margin is discussed in a later chapter.

Uptick Rule

bear raid

In the past, unscrupulous investors have tried to use a rapid series of large short sales to force a significant decline in a stock's price, which was known as a *bear raid*. Bear raids are now illegal. To forestall attempts to manipulate the market, exchanges such as the NYSE would allow short sales only if the selling price was greater than the previous trading price. This was known as the uptick rule, and it was abolished on July 6, 2007. In February 2010, an uptick rule was reinstated by the SEC. The new rule is that the uptick rule is only activated when a stock's price has fallen by 10% or more in one day. Short sales can then only take place at a price that is about the current national best bid.

Large Secondary Market Trades

The specialists on the exchanges or the dealers in the OTC market can handle the vast majority of secondary market trades comfortably with today's technology. Other institutional arrangements are, however, used to handle trades that would strain the specialist's or market maker's capital resources. Intermediate-sized trades may go through a block trader or be handled as a special offering. Really large amounts of stock usually require a secondary distribution (sale) or tender offer (buy).

Block Trades

block houses

A block trade is any trade that is too large to fill with standard trading procedures. Attempting an unusually large block trade in the ordinary channels likely results in price concession. Therefore, *block houses* that specialize in handling large quantities in ways designed to minimize market disruptions often implement these trades.

For a large sell order, the block house first obtains buyer commitments for part or all of the shares. It then offers to buy and resell the lot slightly below the current price, charging commissions to both sides of the trade. The block house may purchase some of the lot to facilitate the transaction. This facilitating purchase may ultimately have to be sold at a loss. While block houses are usually given the task of selling large quantities of stock, they sometimes are asked to assemble large blocks for single buyers.

Special Offerings

Special offerings or spot secondaries can also be used to sell relatively large blocks of stock. Brokers who buy the securities for their clients receive a special incentive fee. The exchange must approve the offering, which is then announced on the ticker. It must remain open for at least 15 minutes. The offering price must generally equal or exceed the current bid but not exceed either the last sale price or the current ask price.

Secondary Distributions

Unusually large holdings are generally sold in secondary distributions through an investment banker, and they are handled in much the same way as a primary offering. In a secondary offering, the selling price is set and the buyer pays no direct commissions.

Tender Offers

A tender offer is used when someone wants to acquire all or a large block of a company's shares. If the buyer is an outside party, the purpose is usually to acquire control of the company. If the buyers consist primarily of management, the purpose is usually to take the company private. If the buyer is the company itself, the board of directors believes the stock is significantly undervalued, the company has substantial cash holdings that cannot be profitably invested, or the company is attempting to increase its financial leverage.[6] In a tender offer, the buyer offers to purchase a substantial block of stock for a limited period, usually at a premium price. The buyer pays an additional fee to brokers who handle their customers' trades. Tender offers sometimes contain limits on the number of shares to be bought. If there is such a limit and the offer is oversubscribed, the shares offered may be bought on a pro rata basis if the buyer does not want the excess. If too little is tendered, the buyer may reject all tendered shares or purchase what is offered.

SECURITIES MARKETS REGULATION

Because they are "clothed with the public interest,"[7] the securities markets are regulated. It is important that investors understand the nature and

---

6. Financial leverage will be discussed in the chapter on security analysis.

7. In *Mumm v Illinois*, 94 U.S. 114 (1876), the U.S. Supreme Court approved the state regulation of corporations that have a public interest (in this case, the rates that grain elevators charged to farmers), stating that "[property] clothed with the public interest, when used in a manner to make it of public consequence . . . must submit to be controlled by the public for the common good. . . ." The Court ruled that the reasonableness of rates is a legislative and not a judicial question.

direction of this regulation. Let's consider some of the more significant laws and regulations that affect the investment process today.

The Securities Act of 1933

The first significant modern legislation to protect investors is the Securities Act of 1933, often referred to as the "truth in securities" law. This legislation focuses on the primary market. As part of this act, a prospectus that fully discloses all material information must accompany public security offerings. Essentially, it is this act that prohibits deceit, misrepresentations, and other fraud in the sale of securities.

The Securities Exchange Act of 1934

self-regulatory organizations (SROs)

The next major legislation—the Securities Exchange Act of 1934— quickly followed the first. This law created the Securities and Exchange Commission and charged it to oversee the provisions of the 1933 Act. It empowers the SEC with broad authority over all aspects of the securities industry. This includes the power to register, regulate, and oversee brokerage firms, transfer agents, and clearing agencies as well as the nation's securities self-regulatory organizations. The various stock exchanges are *self-regulatory organizations (SROs)*. NASD (now FINRA, following the merger with NYSE) was an SRO created to oversee the securities markets. The 1934 Act also requires publicly traded firms to file periodic financial statements with the SEC (Forms 10K and 10Q)[8], the exchanges where they are traded, and their stockholders (annual reports). Trading by insiders must be reported to the SEC.

One of the weaknesses of the 1934 Act is that although it prohibits insider trading, it does not define an insider. Various court cases over the years have slowly expanded the definition of who is an insider, to the point that a person receiving advanced information from a newspaper columnist about a future column has been considered an insider. Even Martha Stewart was identified as an insider for a company other than her own, with the SEC arguing that she traded on information her broker gave her regarding the trades of another company's president.

---

8. Form 10K is filed annually. As it contains much of the same information as the annual report, some firms take their annual report to the shareholders, attach a few pages with additional required information, and make that their 10K report. The 10Q report is a quarterly report. It provides unaudited financial results for each of the firm's first three fiscal quarters.

Investment Company Act of 1940

This act requires that investment companies disclose their financial condition and investment policies to investors when shares are initially purchased and, subsequently, on a regular basis. It is because of this act that anyone buying a mutual fund must receive a prospectus at the time of purchase and regularly thereafter.

Investment Advisers Act of 1940

This act requires that firms or sole practitioners compensated for advising others about securities investments must register with the SEC and conform to regulations designed to protect investors. Currently, only advisors who have at least $25 million of assets under management or advise a registered investment company must register with the Commission.

Securities Investor Protection Act of 1970

Securities Investor Protection Corporation (SIPC)

In the Securities Investor Protection Act of 1970, Congress set up the *Securities Investor Protection Corporation (SIPC)*. It is patterned after the Federal Deposit Insurance Corporation (FDIC); its objective is to protect customer property. The SIPC is a nonprofit, non-government, membership corporation funded by member broker/dealers, although it does have the privilege of borrowing from the SEC if its own funds are inadequate to meet its obligations.

Nearly all broker/dealers registered with the SEC are SIPC members; those few that are not must disclose this fact to their customers. The SIPC's power to protect customers of former SIPC members ends 180 days after the member loses SEC registration. The SEC generally does not terminate a broker/dealer's registration if the SEC knows that the broker/dealer owes securities or cash to customers. Customers can therefore better protect themselves and assist the SEC by reporting a broker's failure to return cash and/or securities promptly.

introducing firm

clearing firm

In the securities industry, two separate broker/dealers typically work together to service a customer's account. These firms are known as the introducing firm and the clearing firm. The *introducing firm* employs the individual broker, who takes the customer's order and sees that the order is executed. The *clearing firm* holds the customer's cash and securities and sends out statements describing the assets it holds "on deposit" for the customer. Technically, SIPC protection is for when a clearing firm becomes insolvent. If it does or if it otherwise cannot return the customer's property, it is the SIPC's responsibility, not the introducing firm's, to make sure the customer's cash and securities are returned.

SIPC coverage also includes protection against unauthorized trading in a customer's account. This coverage can include unauthorized trading by persons associated with the introducing firm and may be available even if the clearing firm is still solvent. Because there would be a great temptation for an investor who took a large loss on a trade to later try to claim the trade was unauthorized, strict measures are in place to thwart false claims. Customers must clearly establish that the trades were unauthorized and file a complaint in writing as soon as they become aware of the unauthorized trade.

The SIPC liquidates troubled firms at the SEC's request. Customers are insured up to $500,000, not more than $100,000 of which may be in cash. Any claims above those sums are applied against the firm's available assets during liquidation. Note that the $100,000 protection for cash applies only to cash that is left on deposit incidental to transactions. Cash in a brokerage account for the purpose of earning interest is not covered by the SIPC.

EXAMPLE

If $10,000 is left in an account for 6 months, this is essentially an interest-bearing account and is not covered by the SIPC. If the cash enters the account as the result of a sale or is deposited with the intention of making a trade and is in the account for a relatively short amount of time, then this is cash on-hand incidental to transactions.

Most brokerage firms have purchased additional insurance coverage for their customers. Coverage of $2 million or more per account is not unusual. For clients with large holdings of financial assets, a financial advisor should make sure the assets are with a brokerage firm with adequate insurance coverage.

Banking Act of 1933

Although it does not directly involve the securities market, an equally important piece of legislation involved the creation of the FDIC (Federal Deposit Insurance Corporation) under the Banking Act of 1933. Initially, the amount of deposit coverage was quite low, but it has risen steadily over the years to $250,000, a sum that vastly exceeds what most people have on deposit. The rules of coverage are not well understood. The $250,000 coverage is based on the name on the account, not the account. Thus, a person who has multiple accounts at the same bank is limited to the $250,000 deposit insurance on the combined accounts, not on each account separately. For anyone with substantial bank deposits (that is, more than $250,000 in aggregate), there are several strategies to avoid the aggregate limitation. The first is to put the different accounts at different banks. The second is to use different legal titles on the accounts.

EXAMPLE

A couple has $600,000 in their checking account, savings account, and some CDs, all at the XYZ National Bank, and all of the accounts are joint accounts.[9] The couple are extremely risk averse. What alternatives might a planner suggest to this them?

There are two simple choices. First, they could transfer some of their holdings to at least two other banks, so that each bank has less than $250,000 in total deposits under this joint name. The second is that they could use multiple titles. Thus, one account could be in the husband's name, a second in the wife's name, and the third in the joint title. As long as the sum of accounts under each title is less than $250,000, all their deposits would be covered.

OTHER ISSUES

Street Name

street name

Most investors leave their holdings in their account with their broker (that is, the broker's clearing firm). These securities are referred to as being in *street name*. This is because the name of the brokerage firm is the only name of which the company issuing the securities is aware. Thus, if a client owns 10,000 shares of Home Depot and the stock is in street name, Home Depot is completely unaware that the client owns this stock. Despite the use of street name, it is the investor who legally retains beneficial ownership. Street-name registration offers secure storage. Remember, accounts at most firms are covered by the SIPC as well as additional protection that the brokerage firm purchases to cover the customer.

Street name also allows securities to be traded without having to issue new certificates, and it relieves investors from having to deliver their certificates to

---

9.   Technically, the accounts are joint tenancies with right of survivorship. For more discussion of joint ownership, see *Fundamentals of Estate Planning* by Constance J. Fontaine, published by The American College.

their brokers when they sell a security. (Since June 1995, all trades must be settled within 3 trading days. Thus, an investor who orders out a security must either deliver it before the sale or get it to the broker immediately upon sale.)

Furthermore, an investor who holds a diversified portfolio of securities and changes addresses needs to file only one change of address notice with the brokerage firm, rather than notifying all the companies separately. In addition, investors receive only one Form 1099 from their brokerage firm, rather than separate ones for each stock owned. This can be a tremendous convenience when it is time to file tax returns.

Advantages of Street-Name Registration

- It provides secure storage.
- Securities can be traded without new certificates being issued or investors having to deliver certificates to the broker in a timely manner.
- A customer who moves must file only one change of address.
- An investor receives a single Form 1099.

Street-name registration has a few disadvantages. Assets held in street name may be tied up during a bankrupt brokerage firm's reorganization. Moreover, dividends and interest on street-name securities are sometimes credited to an improper account. The customer must discover and report the error before it is likely to be corrected. The broker in a non-interest-bearing account may retain even a properly credited dividend for a few days before sending it to the shareholder. Finally, some companies send discount coupons and sample products to investors who own the shares directly but not to street-name accounts.

Disadvantages of Street-Name Registration

- Assets may be tied up during the reorganization of a bankrupt brokerage firm.
- Dividends and interest may be credited to an improper account.
- The broker may retain properly credited dividends in a non-interest-bearing account for a few days before sending them to the shareholder.
- Discount coupons and sample products may not be sent to street-name accounts.

Stock Certificates

In this day of computerized accounting and electronic transfers, using stock certificates to prove ownership is similar to using a cash-only payment system. Stock certificates must be issued whenever a stock is ordered out. Virtually all financial institutions and most individuals leave their holdings in street name (even though there are some disadvantages to doing so). As such, appropriately safeguarded bookkeeping entries have largely eliminated the need for paper stock certificates. The National Securities Clearing Corporation (NSCC) minimizes stock certificate reissues. It records all members' transactions, verifies the consistency of their accounts, and reports net positions daily. NSCC members settle within the clearinghouse rather than between individual brokerage firms. Moreover, because the Depository Trust Company (DTC) holds member firms' securities, securities traded between members can be handled internally simply by debiting one account and crediting another.

Types of Accounts

Discretionary and Wrap Accounts

discretionary account

In a *discretionary account*, the investor appoints his or her broker to invest the client's money without consulting the client about the price, the type of security, the amount and when to buy or sell.[10] These accounts may also be known as controlled accounts or managed accounts. There are generally two rationales for opening a discretionary account. One is that although the investor continues to be the primary decision maker, he or she does not want to miss an attractive trading opportunity if the broker cannot reach the investor in a timely manner. The other rationale for a discretionary account is that the investor wants the broker to act as the portfolio manager and to make the trades that he or she deems appropriate for the account. An alternative to a discretionary account is the limited discretionary account, in which the investor gives the broker the authority to make only certain types of trades without prior consent. In discretionary accounts, the only income to the broker is the commission from each trade. Discretionary accounts can be of any size.

wrap account

A *wrap account* is similar to a discretionary account. Some firms also refer to a wrap account as a separate

---

10.   http://www.sec.gov/answers/openaccount.htm, accessed July 21, 2010.

account or managed account (although a managed account could simply mean a discretionary account). In wrap accounts, a set fee known as a wrap fee is charged. This fee is usually paid quarterly and ranges from 2 to 3% on an annual basis. This covers all commissions as well as any other expenses incidental to the account. Wrap accounts can be solicited, whereas discretionary accounts are opened as a matter of convenience to clients. Opening a wrap account always requires a certain minimum amount; many firms require assets of at least $100,000.

churning Discretionary accounts create obvious potential conflicts for the broker in that he or she may make some trades for the primary purpose of enhancing his or her commission income rather than for the benefit of the client, a practice known as *churning*. In a wrap account, churning would be counterproductive because the fee for the account is fixed and independent of the amount of trading activity.

It is tempting to compare wrap accounts to mutual funds. The wrap fee usually appears to be much larger than the management fees paid on a mutual fund. Nonetheless, there may be some advantages to a wrap account, including

- customization. The portfolio can be tailored to an individual's specific needs. Clients may choose not to hold a particular company or industry for personal, ethical, or economic reasons.
- tax efficiency. Optimal tax treatment can be achieved.
- simple fee structure. The single wrap fee makes the cost of the account clear, unlike the complex and sometimes hidden nature of fees in a mutual fund.

Cash vs. Margin Accounts

cash account An account number is assigned upon opening an account. The account is also classified according to what activities the investor is allowed to do. The most basic account is the *cash account*. This is sometimes referred to as a Type 1 account. To buy stock in a cash account, an investor must have sufficient cash already in the account to complete any purchase. Almost anyone can open a cash account, although some brokerage firms require a minimum opening deposit.

margin account The next classification is a *margin account*, otherwise known as a Type 2 account. In a margin account, an investor can borrow money from the brokerage firm to purchase stocks (this borrowing process is discussed in a later chapter). Brokerage firms are fussier about who is allowed to open a margin account. For example, they will frequently run credit checks on a prospective client, as well as require the customer to sign a separate margin account agreement. Anyone with a margin account must also have a cash account. The distinction between the accounts is transparent to the investor, as both accounts have the same account number and are therefore grouped together on the same monthly statement. Short sales can occur only in a margin account. Also, because any securities bought in a margin account serve as collateral for any money borrowed to buy the securities, all securities in a margin account must be left in street name. In fact, when an investor opens a margin account, part of the agreement he or she must sign includes a "hypothecation and rehypothecation" clause that allows the broker to borrow any of the securities and lend them out for short sales by other customers. The investor can also borrow money from the broker for other purposes, pledging the securities in the account as collateral. If an investor has both types of accounts, marginable stocks are usually bought in the margin account and nonmarginable securities are held in the cash account.[11]

There are other types of accounts besides cash and margin, but most people use only these two.

Portfolio Turnover Ratio

A portfolio turnover ratio is an especially important ratio to compute when an investor has a discretionary account. It can also be important to track even when an investor is making his or her own investment decisions. The portfolio turnover ratio measures the trading activity in an account. The ratio is computed in a two-step process. The first step is to add up all of the purchases in an account during a period and add up all of the sales during that same period. The second step is to divide the lesser of these two numbers by the average value of total assets.

The reason that the numerator consists of the lesser of the two sums is that turnover should not be confused with trades that involve an expansion or contraction of a portfolio.

---

11. The Fed sets the rules for which stocks are marginable and which stocks are not. However, the brokerage firm may add its own restrictions as to what is marginable.

EXAMPLE

Suppose an investor has a portfolio worth $100,000 at the start of the year. The investor then adds $50,000 in cash to the portfolio, invests the cash, and makes no other trades during the year. In this case, the sum of the purchases is $50,000 and the sum of the sales is zero. The portfolio turnover ratio would then use zero in the numerator, producing a value of zero. This would be an apt description because the investor has not turned over any of the securities in the portfolio; the investor has simply expanded the portfolio.

In essence, the portfolio turnover ratio shows the percentage of the portfolio that has been sold and replaced by other securities. Thus, a turnover ratio of 100 percent indicates that, effectively, every security in the portfolio was sold during the year and replaced. Of course, this does not mean literally that every security was sold. Some securities may have been held the entire year, while other parts of the portfolio were turned over several times.

The best time frame for this exercise is a year, although one could certainly compute it over a shorter period and annualize the number appropriately. For example, a portfolio turnover ratio could be computed for a 3-month period, and then annualized by multiplying this number by 4.

Finally, after computing a portfolio turnover ratio, one has to consider what value is a reasonable or unreasonable number. Obviously, the value pronouncement depends on whether the portfolio is actively or passively managed. Research on this issue suggests that even professionally managed portfolios might have turnover ratios approaching 100 percent—and could even hit 200 percent.[12] Ratios in excess of 300 percent should be a red flag to an investor that perhaps an unreasonable amount of trading is occurring in an account.

Finally, keep in mind that the portfolio turnover ratio is not intended to include the maturing of bonds as a sale or the purchase of new securities from matured bonds as a purchase.

---

12. Woerheide, Walt, "An Analysis of Mutual Fund Trading Activity," *Akron Business and Economic Review*, vol. 18, no. 3 (fall 1987), pp. 82-93.

EXAMPLE

As you review a new client's brokerage statement, you notice that there are a lot of trades over the last 3 months. You decide to compute the portfolio turnover ratio. The value of the account at the start of the 3-month period is $517,850, and it is $485,219 at the end. The sums of all purchases and sales, excluding bonds maturing, are $65,270 and $57,977, respectively. The 3-month portfolio turnover ratio (PTR) is

$$\text{3-month PTR} = \$57,977 \div [(\$517,850 + \$485,219) \div 2]$$

$$= .1156$$

Annualized, this ratio is .4624 (.1156 × 4), which means that 46.24 percent of this portfolio is being turned at an annual rate. This is not an unreasonable turnover ratio, especially if this is an actively managed portfolio and there are some good reasons for these trades.

REVIEW OF LEARNING OBJECTIVES

1. The purpose of the primary market is to assist businesses and other entities in acquiring new money from investors. The primary market is managed by investment bankers. They use outright purchases, best-effort arrangements, shelf registrations, and private placements to facilitate the sale of new securities.

2. The secondary market is all subsequent trading in the securities issued in the primary market. The key players are brokers and dealers, the brokerage firms for which they work, as well as the floor brokers, specialists, and RCMMs who work on the floors of the exchanges.

3. The key institutions in the secondary market are the national and regional exchanges, as well as the OTC and NASDAQ markets.

4. The costs of trading include the explicit cost of the commissions, and the implicit costs of the bid-ask spread and price impact necessary on large orders. The two most important types of orders are the market and limit orders. An investor should use a market order when he or she wants an immediate trade and is willing to take whatever the price is at the time of the trade. A limit order allows an investor to assure a price, provided the investor is willing to wait for a trade to occur at that price, or even be willing to skip the trade if that price cannot be obtained.

5. In a short sale, the broker borrows the security from someone else and sells it on behalf of the investor. Later, the investor buys the security and the broker returns it to the lender. The biggest risk in a short sale is that there is no limit as to how high a stock's price

might rise. Thus, the investor has a huge a loss exposure relative to the potential gain. The other risk is that the investor might be forced to buy back the security at an undesirable time if the lender wants to sell it and a new loan cannot be found. Extremely large trades generally require a secondary distribution (sale) or tender offer (buy). Intermediate-sized trades may be handled by a block trader or as a special offering.

6. The Securities Act of 1933 sets the rules for the primary market, and the Securities Exchange Act of 1934 controls the secondary market and established the SEC. The Investment Company Act defines the rules for mutual fund operations, and the Investment Advisers Act requires that advisors who have at least $25 million of assets under management or advise a registered investment company must register with the SEC. The Securities Investor Protection Act created the SIPC. The Banking Act of 1933 created the FDIC and deposit insurance.

7. Most investors should leave their securities in street name because of the protection provided under SIPC coverage. Investors should avoid discretionary accounts without a significant reason to open them and a review process to provide protection against abuse. Trading activity can best be measured by the portfolio turnover ratio.

MINICASE

Joe Small has heard that the Cute Gimmick Company (CGC) is on the verge of failure, despite the fact that the stock is trading at a price of $15 per share. Joe has always viewed the stock market as being little different from gambling and has never opened an account. He decides that now is a good time to start making some serious investments, and he would like to begin his investment program by taking advantage of his belief that the stock price of CGC is about to take a major tumble. Joe contacts a stock broker one of his fishing buddies recommended to him. The broker says that he will be happy to handle the account and asks Joe how much he would like to deposit to start his investment program. Joe says that he has $125,000 in cash, but that he really doesn't need to deposit that money because his initial investment will be a short sale. The broker indicates that the short sale is easy to do but that Joe should go ahead and deposit the entire $125,000 so that the money will be on hand to initiate some other investment positions. Furthermore, to allow Joe the opportunity to grab any deals that quickly appear in the market, the broker recommends that Joe designate the account as a discretionary account.

1.   Which of the following statements is correct if Joe would like his initial transaction to be a short sale? [5]

(A) He does *not* need to deposit any cash or other assets when he opens the account because the proceeds of the short sale will bring cash into the account.
(B) He needs to deposit at least enough cash to meet the margin requirements and any minimum account requirements for selling short.
(C) He does *not* need to deposit any cash or other assets because he is starting out with only one transaction.
(D) He needs to deposit at least $10,000 as earnest money.

2.   Based on the size of Joe's initial deposit, which of the following statements regarding Joe's concern about the brokerage firm's financial stability is correct? [6]

(A) Joe should worry because he doesn't know the broker very well.
(B) He need not worry, provided the firm has SIPC coverage and his deposit is for the primary purpose of making transactions.
(C) He should worry because the deposit exceeds the maximum cash coverage.
(D) He should not worry because he can still withdraw the cash if the firm declares bankruptcy and he hasn't bought any stocks yet.

3.   After Joe opens the account and places his order for a short sale, the following prices are noted in CGC's stock: $15.20, $15.17, $15.10, $15.15, $15.10, $15.07, $15.02, $14.99, $15.05. If the uptick rate is in effect for this stock, at what price did he likely sell the stock, assuming he placed a market order for a short sale? [5]

(A) $15.20
(B) $15.17
(C) $15.10
(D) $15.15

4.   What guarantees does the lender of the shares for a short sale have that Joe will return the stock? [5]

I.   The guarantee of Joe's brokerage firm.
II. The cash from the sale, along with an additional margin deposit will be held by Joe's brokerage firm to guarantee Joe has the ability to repurchase the stock to return it.

(A) I only
(B) II only
(C) Both I and II
(D) Neither I nor II

5. In this case, should Joe open a discretionary account? [7]

    (A) Yes. That way, his new broker can move him quickly into promising investment opportunities when he sees a mispriced security.

    (B) Yes. Most people have discretionary accounts.

    (C) No. He doesn't know the broker, and because his own knowledge of investments is obviously limited, he could run a risk of exposing his account to churning.

    (D) No. It will limit the types of orders that can be used in the account.

CHAPTER REVIEW

Key Terms and Concepts

initial public offering (IPO)	market order
syndicate	limit order
firm-commitment basis	bear raid
best-effort basis	block houses
lettered stock	self-regulatory organizations (SROs)
registered representative	Securities Investor Protection
Series 7	Corporation (SIPC)
Series 6	introducing firm
Gramm-Leach-Bliley Act	clearing firm
floor traders	street name
dual listing	discretionary account
over-the-counter (OTC) market	wrap account
electronic communications network	churning
(ECN)	cash account
May Day	margin account
paying for order flow	

Review Questions

Review questions are based on the learning objectives in this chapter. Thus, a [3] at the end of a question means that the question is based on learning objective 3. If there are multiple objectives, they are all listed.

1. The primary and secondary markets are both critical to economic growth and development, but each in a different way. Explain why each is important. [1, 2]

2. Investment bankers facilitate new-issue sales of debt and equity securities. Describe the two underwriting approaches they use to accomplish this objective. [1]

3. Although the distinction is becoming blurry, identify the two major categories of stock brokers and how their services differ from each other. [2]

4.   Identify the four activities of a specialist. [2]

5.   Define the third and fourth markets and describe the benefits each provides to investors. [3]

6.   What is the key difference between the NYSE and any other market? [3]

7.   List the three components that make up the potential cost of a trade, and identify which are implicit and which are explicit. [4]

8.   Explain the difference between the following four buy orders: market, limit, stop-buy, and stop-limit buy. [4]

9.   You have inherited an extremely large position in the Family Heirloom Corporation. You would like to liquidate this position. A traditional sell order will be ineffective due to the size of the holding. What are some methods for disposing of this stock? [4]

10. You have $600,000 in stock and $50,000 in cash sitting in your stock account with the Shaky Standard Brokerage Firm. Should you be concerned about your holdings if the brokerage firm files for bankruptcy, assuming the firm is covered by the SIPC? [7]

Learning Objectives

An understanding of the material in this chapter should enable the student to

1. Compute a holding period return, a per-period return, an arithmetic mean return, and a geometric mean return.

2. Compute an expected rate of return and an effective annual rate of return.

3. Describe the sources of risk and the most common methods of dealing with each source.

4. Describe various measures of risk, and compute the variance and standard deviation for a set of ex post returns.

5. Describe what is meant by a normal, a lognormal, and a skewed distribution, and identify the forms of kurtosis.

6. Explain how a Monte Carlo simulation is performed, and understand its implications in considering an investment strategy.

7. Compute the buying power of a margin account, its equity value, the value at which a margin call will be made, the amount of cash that must be added when a margin call is made, and the amount of additional cash that can be withdrawn from a margin account.

Returns are what provide the joy juice to investing! Although every investment is expected to yield a positive return, the actual return will always be different from the expected rate of return, except for investments classified as risk-free. Indeed, many investments produce negative returns. The potential difference between expected and actual return defines our concept of risk. In this chapter, we will look at the different ways of defining and measuring both return and risk, and we will describe the different sources of risk. We will look first at the various definitions and concepts of investment returns. Then we will focus on the definitions of risk and the common measures of risk.

MEASURES OF INVESTMENT RETURN

The Nature of Return

Returns generally take two forms: current income and price changes. Many investments are structured to provide periodic and relatively dependable income payments (such as interest, rents, royalties, or dividends). Other investments (such as common stock) are structured to provide returns primarily in the form of price appreciation, although there is usually the risk of price decline. Some investments offer both current income and expected price appreciation. The concept of total return incorporates both the periodic payments and changes in market value.

Determining an Investment's Overall Return
• Periodic payments: interest, rents, royalties, or dividends • Changes in market value: price appreciation or decline

Holding Period Return

holding period return (HPR)

holding period return relative (HPRR)

The most basic measure of overall profitability is the *holding period return (HPR)*. The HPR relates the profit on an investment directly to its beginning value. The HPR is the sum of the income received from an investment and the change in market value, divided by the beginning value (or cost) of the investment. This is expressed as

$$HPR = \frac{\text{Income received} + \text{Change in value}}{\text{Beginning value}} \quad \text{(Equation 2–1)}$$

A closely related measure of return is *the holding period return relative (HPRR)*, which is the sum of the income received from an investment and the ending market value, divided by the beginning value (or cost) of the investment:

$$HPRR = \frac{\text{Income received} + \text{Ending value}}{\text{Beginning value}} \quad \text{(Equation 2–2)}$$

Although these two formulas look similar, the key difference is that the HPR uses the change in market value, whereas the HPRR uses the ending market value. Because the change in market value is defined as ending value minus beginning value, we can plug this definition into the HPR formula to see the relationship between the two measures. Simply put:

$$HPR = \frac{\text{Income received} + (\text{Ending value} - \text{Beginning value})}{\text{Beginning value}}$$

$$= \frac{\text{Income received} + \text{Ending value}}{\text{Beginning value}} - \frac{\text{Beginning value}}{\text{Beginning value}}$$

$$= HPRR - 1$$

One way to think about the above formula is that subtracting 1 from the HPRR represents the return of principal on the investment. Sometimes the relationship is also expressed as follows:

$$HPRR = 1 + HPR \qquad \text{(Equation 2-2a)}$$

ex post

ex ante

HPRs can be used in either an ex post or an ex ante calculation. *Ex post* means after the fact and *ex ante* means before the fact. Thus, when you use historical data, you are working with ex post data. When you are using expected values, you are working with ex ante data. Example 1 below calculates HPR and HPRR with expected values, and example 2 below does the same with historical data.

expected HPR

EXAMPLE 1

Suppose an investment costs $1,000, that you expect it to provide a payment of $100 during the holding period, and that you will sell it for $1,500. The *expected HPR* and HPRR can be computed as follows:

$$\text{Change in value} = \$1,500 - \$1,000 = \$500$$

$$HPR = (\$100 + \$500)/\$1,000 = .60, \text{ or } 60\%$$

$$HPRR = (\$100 + \$1,500)/\$1,000 = 1.60$$

Note that we could have just as easily computed the HPRR as

$$HPRR = 1 + HPR = 1 + .60 = 1.60$$

EXAMPLE 2

If an investment was purchased for $10, has paid $1 in dividends, and is now worth $8, what were its HPR and HPRR?

The HPRR was

$$HPRR = (\$1 + \$8)/\$10 = .9$$

and the HPR was

$$HPR = HPRR - 1 = -.10 \text{ or } -10\%$$

This investment has resulted in a loss. When there is a loss, the HPR is negative, and the HPRR is less than 1.

The HPR and HPRR computations must always state the period of the computation. An investment with an HPR of 3 percent is outstanding, for example, if the holding period was 2 days but is poor if the holding period was 2 years.

Per-Period Return

per-period return (PPR)   A better way to measure returns is to compute the *per-period return (PPR)*, where a period represents a standard-length holding period.[13] The universal unit for measuring returns is 1 year. **Thus, it is highly unprofessional to quote a rate of return on any basis other than annual.** An asset's PPR is defined as the sum of that period's income and change in value divided by its beginning-of-period market value:

$$PPR = \frac{\text{Period's income} + \text{Period's change in value}}{\text{Beginning-of-Period value}} \quad \text{(Equation 2–3)}$$

This formula is obviously quite similar to the formula for the HPR. The three differences are that in the PPR formula, (1) the income is for a single period only, (2) the price change is the price change for the single period, and (3) the denominator is the value of the investment at the start of the period and not at the time the investment was purchased. Note that one can also construct

---

13. Many authors bypass this distinction between holding period return and per-period return by always defining their holding periods to be 1 year.

a per-period return relative (PPRR) either by using the ending value rather than change in value in the numerator or by adding 1 to the PPR as follows:

$$PPRR = 1 + PPR \qquad \text{(Equation 2-3a)}$$

EXAMPLE

Cindy Field buys a stock on July 1 for $25. It pays a total of $1 in dividends during the first year, and one year later, the stock trades for $30. During the second year, it pays a total of $2 in dividends, and at the end of the second year, the stock trades for $26. What are Cindy's HPR, her two PPRs, and her two PPRRs?

HPR = ($1 + $2 + [$26 − $25])/$25 = .16, or 16%

PPR$_1$ = ($1 + [$30 − $25])/$25 = .24 or 24%

PPR$_2$ = ($2 + [$26 − $30])/$30 = −.0667, or −6.67%

PPRR$_1$ = 1 + .24 = 1.24, or 124%

PPRR$_2$ = 1 − .0667 = .9333, or 93.33%

Note that there is no clear and obvious relationship between the HPR for the 2-year period and the two annual PPRs.

Simple vs. Compound Return

A return may be either in the form of simple return or a compound return. A simple return is where income accrues only on the principal and not on prior income. Simple returns are also referred to as noncompounded returns. When returns are noncompounded, the ending value of an investment can be computed as

$$Ending\ Value = Beginning\ value \times [\,1 + (rate\ of\ return \times t)\,] \qquad \text{(Equation 2–4)}$$

where t = the number of time periods

compounding   In *compounding* returns, the income for each period is added to the principal so that subsequent income is paid on both principal and accumulated income. When an investment is made for

Fundamentals of Investments for Financial Planning

multiple periods and returns are compounded, then the ending value of the investment is computed as[14]

$$\text{Ending Value} = \text{Beginning value} \times (1 + \text{rate of return})^t \quad \text{(Equation 2-5)}$$

EXAMPLE 1

A bank promises to pay 6 percent on a 5-year certificate of deposit. However, the interest rate will apply only to the principal, not to the accrued interest. If your client deposits $10,000 in the account, the ending value is determined by using equation 2–4, computed as

Ending value = $10,000 x (1 + .06 x 5) = $13,000

Keystrokes:[15] 5, x, .06, +, 1, x, 10000, = (display: 13,000)

EXAMPLE 2

Suppose in the previous example the bank changes its mind and agrees to let the interest be compounded. In this case, ending value is determined by using equation 2–5:

Ending value = $10,000 x 1.06^5= $13,382.26

Thus, the compounding process has increased the ending value by $82.26.

There are two different sets of keystrokes one can use to solve this problem. One approach is to perform the calculations as shown in the above problem, using the exponential (y^x) key. These keystrokes are

SHIFT, C ALL

1.06, SHIFT, y^x, 5, =, x, 10000, = (display: 13,382.26)

The other approach is to note that this formula is simply a future value calculation, as described in Appendix B, and to treat the $10,000 deposit as a present value and use the special keys on the top row to solve for the future value. These keystrokes are

SHIFT, C ALL

5, N, 6, I/YR, 10000, +/–, PV, FV (display: 13,382.26)

---

14. Readers familiar with time value of money will recognize equation 2–5 as the future value equation discussed in Appendix B, equation B-1.
15. Students who are not familiar with a financial calculator should read Appendix A on using an HP-10BII calculator.

Annualized Rates of Return

A recurring problem in investments is the need to translate holding period returns that are for time periods other than 1 year into annualized rates of return. For example, if someone has a 3-month holding period return of 3 percent, what is the effective annual rate of return? Similarly, if someone earned a 20 percent rate of return over a period of 13 months, what is the effective annual rate of return?

The formula to determine the effective annual rate of return is

$$R_{ear} = (1 + HPR)^{\#} - 1$$ (Equation 2–6)

where R_{ear} = effective annual rate

HPR = holding period rate of return

= adjustment factor

The adjustment factor depends on the nature of the holding period. If the holding period is measured in months, the adjustment factor is 12, divided by the number of months in the holding period.

EXAMPLE 1

You note that over the last 3 months, you have earned a 7 percent holding period rate of return. What is the effective annual rate of return you have achieved?

Because your holding period is measured in months, the adjustment factor is 12, divided by your 3-month holding period. Thus, your effective annual rate of return is

$$R_{ear} = (1 + .07)^{(12/3)} - 1 = (1 + .07)^4 - 1 = .3108 \text{ or } 31.08\%$$

Keystrokes: 1, +, .07, SHIFT, y^x, 4, =, –, 1, =

EXAMPLE 2

Now consider a holding period return of 17 percent earned over 14 months. In this case, the effective annual rate of return is[16]

$$R_{ear} = (1 + .17)^{(12/14)} - 1 = .1441 \text{ or } 14.41\%$$

Keystrokes: SHIFT, C ALL, 12, ÷, 14, =, M+, 1, +, .17, SHIFT, y^x, RM, =, –, 1, =

---

16. See Appendix A for a discussion of the keystroke sequence for this type of problem.

If the holding period is defined in terms other than months, then the numerator and denominator of the adjustment factor must be changed. For example, if it is measured in quarters, it is 4. Consider the following two examples.

EXAMPLE 1

You note that over the last 71 days, you have earned a 7 percent holding period rate of return. What is the effective annual rate of return you have achieved?

Because your holding period is measured in days, the adjustment factor is 365 divided by your 71-day holding period. Thus, your effective annual rate of return is

$$R_{ear} = (1 + .07)^{(365/71)} - 1 = .4108 \text{ or } 41.08\%$$

Keystrokes: SHIFT, C ALL, 365, ÷, 71, =, M+, 1, +, .07, SHIFT, y^x, RM, =, –, 1, =

EXAMPLE 2

Assume the same facts as in Example 1, except that now your holding period return is 17 percent earned over 5 quarters. Your effective annual rate of return is

$$R_{ear} = (1 + .17)^{(4/5)} - 1 = .1338 \text{ or } 13.38\%$$

Keystrokes: SHIFT, C ALL, 4, ÷, 5, =, M+, 1, +, .17, SHIFT, y^x, RM, =, –, 1, =

Arithmetic Average Return vs. Geometric Mean Return

As we noted earlier, rates of return should be quoted on an annualized basis. Let's now look at the mechanics of how to compute an annualized rate of return when an investment is held for several years. Suppose an investment is held for 3 years and it loses 12 percent the first year, but it gains 20 percent and 22 percent in the next 2 years. What is the effective annual rate of return?

Many people would approach such a problem by computing the arithmetic average also known as the arithmetic mean return or AMR. The arithmetic mean has the advantage that it is simple to compute, and reasonably accurate when the returns are almost the same from year to year. The disadvantage is that it is wrong!

The arithmetic mean is computed by summing all of the observations and dividing by the number of observations. In formal mathematics, this is stated as

$$\overline{R} = \left(\sum_{t=1}^{T} PPR_t \right) / T \qquad \text{(Equation 2–7)}$$

where $\qquad \overline{R}$ = arithmetic average

$\qquad\qquad$ T = number of time periods

Some readers will look at this equation and say "It's Greek to me." In truth, it is partially Greek, as the summation symbol (which looks somewhat like the capital letter E) is the Greek capital letter called "sigma." $\sum_{t=1}^{T}$ followed by an expression, such as PPR_t, means "the sum of" that formula for each value of t from 1 through T;

$$\sum_{t=1}^{T} PPR_t \qquad \text{means } PPR_1 + PPR_2 + \ldots + PPR_T.$$

. This expression would be read as follows:

> The arithmetic mean is computed by taking the summation of the rates of return for time periods 1 through T, and dividing this total by the number of time periods (T).

Note that in this notation, the subscript used is the letter "t." The subscript "t" will be used whenever the rates of return are based on different time periods. (For additional discussion about the term $\overline{R}$, see the tutorial in the next section.)

geometric mean return $\qquad$ The alternative approach to computing the annualized rate of return when an investment is held for multiple time periods is known as the *geometric mean return (GMR).* The GMR is based on a multiplicative relationship. The GMR for T periods is obtained by first computing the PPRRs for each of the T periods. These T values of PPRRs are all multiplied together and the Tth root is calculated. Remember, taking the Tth root of a number is the same as taking that number to the 1/T power. This result minus 1 is the GMR. Stated as equations:

$$HPRR = PPRR_1 \times PPRR_2 \times \ldots \times PPRR_T$$

where $PPRR_t$ =   per-period return relative for period t

HPRR =   holding period return relative for the entire T periods

$$GMR = HPRR^{1/T} - 1$$

EXAMPLE 1

The arithmetic mean return for an investment that earned successive annual rates of return of –12 percent, 20 percent, and 22 percent equals:

$$(-12\% + 20\% + 22\%) / 3 = 10\%$$

EXAMPLE 2

Using the same three rates of return as in Example 1, the GMR is computed by first solving for the PPRRs, as

$$PPRR_1 = 1 - .12 = .88$$

$$PPRR_2 = 1 + .20 = 1.20$$

$$PPRR_3 = 1 + .22 = 1.22$$

Next, the HPRR is computed by multiplying the PPRs together as

$$HPRR = PPRR_1 \times PPRR_2 \times PPRR_3$$

$$= .88 \times 1.20 \times 1.22 = 1.2883$$

Finally, the GMR is computed as the cube root of the HPRR:

$$GMR = 1.2883^{1/3} = 1.0881 - 1 = .0881, \text{ or } 8.81\%$$

Keystrokes: SHIFT, C, ALL, 1, ÷, 3, =, M+, 1, +.2883, SHIFT, y^x, RM, =, –, 1, = (display: .0881)

If all of the returns are identical, the arithmetic mean and the geometric mean returns will also be the same. For example, if an investment provides a 5 percent rate of return for each of five periods, the arithmetic mean and the geometric mean returns will both be 5 percent. When there is any variation among the rates of return, then the two will diverge and the arithmetic mean will always be a larger number than the GMR. Furthermore, the greater the variation in PPRs, the larger the difference between the AMR and the GMR.

It is logical to question when an investor should compute an AMR and when he or she should compute a GMR to evaluate performance. Unfortunately, the answer is not always clear. If an investor is computing the average past performance in order to predict a rate of return for the next period, the AMR is appropriate. If the investor is computing a rate of return to use in one of the traditional risk-adjusted computations, again, the AMR is appropriate. However, if an investor wants a true measure for the annualized performance over the entire holding period, then he or she should use the GMR. To understand why this is the case, let's reconsider the investment discussed in the last two examples.

Suppose you made an investment of $10,000 and over the next 3 years, this investment provided rates of return of −12 percent, 20 percent, and 22 percent. In dollar terms, the investment would be worth $8,800 at the end of the first period [$10,000 x (1 −.12)], $10,580 at the end of the second period [$8,800 x (1 + .20)], and $12,883.20 at the end of the third period [$10,580 x (1 + .22)]. Now let's ask the question, if all the PPRs were identical, what rate of return would you have had to earn for each and every period to end up with exactly $12,883.20? Let's consider first the arithmetic average, which is 10 percent. If an investment earns a rate of return of 10 percent each period and we start with $10,000, we will end up with $13,310.00 (keystrokes: 3, N, 10, I/YR, 10000, +/−, PV, FV). Now let's recompute our answer and change the interest rate to 8.81 percent. In this case, we will end up with $12,883.20 (keystrokes: 3, N, 8.81144632, I/YR, 10000, +/−, FV). (Note that to achieve the answer to the nearest penny, the GMR is entered with 8 decimal places. This number can be derived in Example 2 by simply changing the display mode to 8 digits.] The point is that it is the GMR number that will generate the actual dollar performance of an investment and not the AMR.

Expected Return

A central question with any investment is always, what sort of future rate of return might I get on this investment? More specifically, what is my expected rate of return? The most common model for expected return is to think of future returns as forming some sort of probability distribution and then to take the probability weighted average of this distribution.

Probability Distribution

Probability distributions can be in the form of either continuous or discrete distributions. In a discrete distribution, each possible future rate of return can be identified and the associated probability can be stated. An example of a discrete probability distribution for an investment's rates of return is as follows:

Probability	Rate of Return
50%	8%
30%	12%
20%	−10%

A continuous probability distribution allows for the possibility of any potential rate of return. *Figure 2-1* illustrates a symmetrical, continuous probability distribution. The probabilities rise to a peak at the expected rate of return and decline thereafter. With a normal distribution, the probabilities for returns equidistant from the expected return are equal. The simple average of these paired returns is the expected return.

A continuous probability distribution is clearly the more realistic way to think about the rate of return on an investment. For example, if I want to think about how to represent the rate of return on Exxon Mobile for next year, it is silly to think about all the possible rates of return and then to specify a probability for each. It is more logical to think about an expected return and how the actual return might be distributed in relation to that number.

Despite the fact that continuous distributions are more realistic, we will use only the discrete model of likely rates of return in this book. The reason is that when we start to do some of the mathematical modeling necessary to understand investments, continuous distributions involve the use of integral calculus, while discrete distributions involve much simpler arithmetic formulations.

Figure 2-1
Probability Distribution of Returns

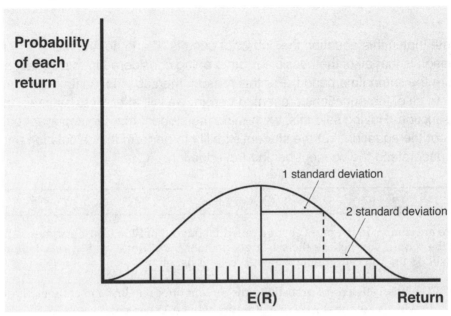

Expected Return with a Discrete Probability Distribution

To compute the expected return with a discrete distribution, multiply each return by the associated probability, and add the products together. In mathematical notation, this is expressed as

$$E(R) = (P_1 \times R_1) + (P_2 \times R_2) + \ldots + (P_n \times R_n) \quad \text{(Equation 2-8)}$$

where $E(R) =$ expected rate of return

$P_i =$ the probability of each rate of return occurring

$R_i =$ each potential rate of return

$n =$ the number of possible rates of return

$1 =$ $P_1 + \ldots P_n$

This equation can be expressed more compactly by using the summation notation (capital sigma) described earlier. The summation notation would reads as follows:

$$E(R) = \sum_{i=1}^{n} P_i \times R_i \qquad \text{(Equation 2–9)}$$

Note that in this equation the subscript used is "i" and not the letter "t." The reason is that all of the possible returns being considered in this equation are from the same time period. For this reason, the subscript shifts from "t" to "i." In all of the equations presented herein, we will attempt to maintain this distinction. Having said this, we remind the student that the important point is not the equation, but the student's ability to perform the calculation and to understand the concept behind the equation.

EXAMPLE

There are rumors in the press about a potential buyout of Blue Goose Airlines. After reading the report, you believe there is a good chance, but not a perfect certainty, the buyout will occur. You can summarize your feelings as follows

- There is a 40 percent probability the buyout offer will bring in another bidder, in which case the stock's rate of return will be 35 percent.

- There is a 30 percent probability the buyout offer will occur as planned, in which case the rate of return will be 20 percent.

- There is a 30 percent probability the buyout offer will fizzle and people will end up dumping the stock, in which case the rate of return will be –10 percent.

The expected rate of return is computed as

$$E(R) = (.40 \times 35\%) + (.30 \times 20\%) + (.30 \times [-10\%]) = 17\%$$

Tutorial

The terms *mean return* and *expected return*, as well as their symbols, $\overline{R}$ and E(R), are sometimes used interchangeably, although they are different. Mean return is used primarily to calculate the average return with *ex post* data. Expected return is used primarily to describe a weighted average rate of return using *ex ante* data. In investments, the most common estimate of expected return is based on the mean return over some historical period of time. Thus, if we calculate that over the past 5 years, a stock has provided a mean return of 8.5 percent, we will likely say that the expected return for this security is also 8.5 percent, and use the two terms of mean and expected rate of return interchangeably.

A Portfolio's Expected Rate of Return

So far, we have talked about the rate of return on an individual investment. Let's look briefly at rates of return when dealing with portfolios. The rate of return on a portfolio can be measured in the same way as the return on a single investment. That is, if one knows the beginning value of the portfolio, the income received on the portfolio, and the ending value, then one can use equation 2–3 to compute the portfolio's PPR.

EXAMPLE 1

You are reviewing the monthly statement of Joan Gitman. At the beginning of the month, her portfolio was worth $158,212. Joan received $1,524 in interest and dividends during the month (which were paid directly to her). The ending value of the portfolio was $161,918. Her PPR for the month is

$$PPR = (\$1{,}524 + [\$161{,}918 - \$158{,}212]) \div \$158{,}212$$
$$= .0331, \text{ or } 3.31\%$$

EXAMPLE 2

Assume the same beginning value and income as in Example 1, except that Joan leaves the dividends and interest in the account. In this case, the ending value of the portfolio represents all of the investments, plus any cash that has accrued in the account. Thus, the ending value is $163,442. Therefore, counting it separately would be double counting. Hence, the HPR can now be computed based only on changes in the account's value, as follows:

$$HPR = (\$163{,}442 - \$158{,}212) \div \$158{,}212 = .0331, \text{ or } 3.31\%$$

In some cases, one might want to compute a portfolio's expected rate of return based on the expected rate of return of the individual securities in the portfolio. In this case, we must first determine the percentage of portfolio value represented by each security in the portfolio. This is obtained by dividing the beginning value of each holding by the value of the entire portfolio, which is referred to as the weight of each holding. Next, we must multiply each weight by the expected rate of return for that particular security, and then sum these products. The sum is sometimes referred to as the weighted average rate of return. In mathematical notation:

$$E\left(R_P\right) = \left(W_1 \times \left[E\left(R_1\right)\right]\right) + \left(W_2 \times \left[E\left(R_2\right)\right]\right) + \ldots + \left(W_n \times \left[E\left(R_n\right)\right]\right)$$

(Equation 2–10)

where $E(R_p)$ =   expected return on portfolio p

W_i =   percentage of portfolio invested in security i

$E(R_i)$ =   the expected per-period return on security i and

1 = $W_1 + \ldots + W_n$

EXAMPLE

You have recommended a portfolio for your clients. This portfolio has three securities.[17] The first security's recommended weight is 50 percent, and the suggested weights for the second and third securities are 25 percent each. If these three securities have expected rates of return of 10 percent, 6 percent, and 9 percent, the portfolio's expected rate of return is

$$(.5 \times 10\%) + (.25 \times 6\%) + (.25 \times 9\%) = 8.75\%$$

Note that equation 2–10 is nearly identical to equation 2–8. Equation 2–8 involves multiplying rates of return with probabilities (where the probabilities add up to 1), and equation 2–10 involves multiplying expected rates of return with weights (where the weights add up to 1). It is the same equation, but a different interpretation is placed on the coefficients.

Also note that if a portfolio is invested equally among different securities, then equation 2–10 reduces to the formula for the arithmetic mean. Thus, in this one special situation, one could simply compute the arithmetic average.[18]

EXAMPLE

Suppose we have a portfolio of five investments that individually have expected rates of return of 3 percent, 7 percent, 9 percent, 11 percent, and 15 percent. If you plan to invest $20,000 in each of these five securities, what is your expected rate of return for the portfolio?

To compute the expected rate of return for this five-investment portfolio, we can add the five separate returns and divide by 5, because the amounts invested in each security are identical. The calculation is

---

17. A three-security portfolio is generally a terrible recommendation because of the lack of diversification. However, we limit ourselves to three securities to keep this example simple.

18. Note that implicit in this observation is the assumption that there is an automatic reinvestment of dividends into the stock of each issuing company.

$$(3\% + 7\% + 9\% + 11\% + 15\%) \div 5 = 45\% \div 5 = 9\%$$

UNDERSTANDING INVESTMENT RISK

Making investment decisions would be incredibly easy if all that was required was to compare the expected returns on the investment choices. The difficulty in investing arises from the presence of risk. There are two steps necessary to better understand risk. The first is to understand the sources of risk or reasons that risk exists. The second is to understand the common techniques for measuring risk. In this section, we will describe the sources of risk; in the next section, we will look at how to measure risk.

What Is Investment Risk?

pure risk
In insurance, risk is viewed as the potential for loss. In this context, a *pure risk* means only the chance of loss or no loss. For example, auto theft insurance is based on the fact that during the term of the policy, either one's car will be stolen (loss) or it will not be stolen (no loss). Thus, the purchase of auto theft insurance will result in compensation for the value of the car if it is stolen, or nothing if the car is not stolen. There is no chance for a profit through the purchase of such a policy. People buy insurance to alleviate the impact of a loss, not because they expect to make a profit. It is agreeing to a small (known) loss (the payment of a premium) to avoid a large (potential) loss.

speculative risk
In investments, assets are acquired with the expectation of receiving some type of gain. It is the expected gain that will cause people to take on the risk of a loss. This trade-off between expected return and the risk of a loss is called *speculative risk*. Speculative risk is commonly defined as the variability in an investment's rate of return. The greater the potential variation in the return, the greater the speculative risk of the investment.

A multitude of factors are responsible for the variability in an investment's returns. Some of these factors affect returns on a daily basis, while others do so less frequently. Some have minor impacts, and others have major ones. Let us consider these different sources of risk.

Sources of Investment Risk

Systematic (Market) Nondiversifiable Risk

market risk   *Market risk* is risk from any events that affect all investments. Inflation risk and interest rate risk are components of market risk. Market risk can also derive from political, economic, demographic, or social events and trends. Market risk is sometimes referred to as systematic risk because it impacts the entire financial system. About the only way to escape market risk is simply to hide one's cash, but even here one is still subject to inflation risk. Some assets are much more affected by market-risk types of events than others.

Financial Planning Issue
A classic example of a specific market risk event is the terrorist attack of September 11, 2001. The attack led people to rethink the risk-expected return relationship, leading to a significant drop in stock prices.

Inflation (Purchasing Power) Risk

inflation risk   *Inflation risk*, sometimes called purchasing power risk, is the variation in real returns caused by changes in the general level of prices. In theory, the general level of prices may rise (inflation), be stable, or fall (deflation). Sometimes the economy will be in a period of disinflation, which is when prices are rising at a lower rate than they were previously. Disinflation is something of a misnomer, as inflation is still occurring, just at a lower rate than it had been. One of the major economic problems in the second half of the twentieth century was inflation.

Inflation can affect investments in two ways. First, to the extent one owns stocks, inflation may affect the profitability of the companies in which one is invested. There has been extensive debate over whether corporations are net gainers or losers during inflationary periods. The results seem to be that it depends on the nature of the company; some businesses benefit from inflation, and some lose.

The second way inflation affects investments is that it has an impact on the purchasing power of one's returns from investments. Regardless of the returns on one's investments, inflation reduces the purchasing power of those returns. However, some investors may benefit from inflation if they own stocks in companies that benefit from inflation. Thus, even though these investors' returns have less purchasing power, they may have higher returns than would otherwise be the case.

It should also be pointed out that investors are not stupid with regard to inflation. During inflationary periods, investors will not make new investments unless they believe there is compensation built into the investment for the expected level of inflation. If the rate of inflation turns out to be lower than what was expected, investors actually benefit from the inflationary expectation.

Where investors truly suffer from inflation is when the actual inflation rate turns out to be higher than the expected inflation rate. The types of investments that are most susceptible to this risk are fixed-income investments such as savings accounts, certificates of deposit, bonds, bond funds, life insurance cash values, and fixed annuities. During deflationary periods (only 2 of the last 65 years have been deflationary),[19] fixed-income investments should provide windfall gains because the income (such as the interest on a bond) typically does not vary with economic conditions; thus, the purchasing power of that income stream rises.

__Real (Inflation-Adjusted) vs. Nominal Return.__ A common technique for analyzing the impact of inflation is to argue that investors start with an expectation of a desired real rate of return, and this is adjusted for inflation to determine the nominal rate of return they need to earn to achieve the desired real rate of return. Nominal rates are the rates we see and work with every day. In equation form, this is noted as follows:[20]

$$(1 + \text{real rate}) \times (1 + \text{inflation rate}) = (1 + \text{nominal rate}) \text{ or}$$
$$(1 + \text{real rate}) \times (1 + \text{inflation rate}) - 1 = \text{nominal rate}$$

(Equation 2–11)

In the second version of the equation, subtracting 1 reflects a return of principal.

---

19. The only 2 years of deflation were 1949 and 1954, and the inflation rates were –2.1 percent and –.7 percent. Source: www.bls.gov/cpi/tables.htm, accessed July 21, 2010.

20. Actually, long-term nominal rates have four unobserved components: the real rate, the inflation compensation, a premium for inflation uncertainty, and a premium for default risk. However, since this third component is so small compared to the others, it is essentially ignored. In addition, this discussion considers only yields on government bonds, so that default risk is also ignored. See *Monetary Trends*, Federal Reserve Bank of St. Louis, February 2004, p. 1.

EXAMPLE

Jeff Robins tells his financial planner that he wants to earn a 10 percent rate of return because he wants a 4 percent real rate of return and he expects a 6 percent inflation rate. The financial planner should advise Jeff that he is mistaken about what he needs to earn. If we plug Jeff's numbers into equation 2–11, we obtain the following:

$$(1 + .04) \times (1 + .06) - 1 = .1024, \text{ or } 10.24\%$$

Thus, Jeff actually needs a 10.24 percent nominal rate of return based on his goal and his inflation expectation.

Some of the time, people approach the relationship between the real and nominal rates in the opposite direction to that expressed in equation 2–11. That is, investors are more likely to inquire about their real rate of return given their achieved nominal rate of return and the observed inflation rate. To answer this question, we can simply solve equation 2–11 for the real rate, as shown in the following equation:

$$\text{Real rate} = \frac{1 + \text{nominal rate}}{1 + \text{inflation rate}} - 1 \qquad \text{(Equation 2–12)}$$

EXAMPLE

A financial planner is meeting with her client to discuss the client's portfolio's performance over the last year. The client is particularly concerned about inflation. The client earned 7 percent on her portfolio and the inflation rate was 3 percent during the same period. Her real rate of return was as follows:

$$\text{Real rate} = \frac{1.07}{1.03} - 1$$
$$= .0388, \text{ or } 3.88\%$$

Note that as a quick and dirty approximation, the real rate of return can be approximated as

$$\text{Real rate} \approx \text{nominal rate} - \text{inflation rate}$$
$$\approx .07 - .03$$
$$\approx .04$$

Financial Planning Issue

Some clients, particularly older ones, are exceedingly worried about the impact of taxes and inflation. This concern about inflation is not inappropriate, as such clients have little or no working years to adjust their investments and investment income to compensate for unexpected rates of inflation. The only way to help clients deal with this issue is to incorporate assets that either benefit from inflation or are at least neutral with regard to inflation. This would suggest TIPS and Series I savings bonds as critical elements of a portfolio.[21] The drawback is that if inflation is lower than expected, TIPS and the Series I bonds will provide lower returns than non-inflation-related bonds.

Interest Rate Risk

interest rate risk

Interest rate risk refers to the degree to which an investment is affected by changes in interest rates. Interest rate risk has two components: price risk and reinvestment rate risk.

price risk

Price Risk. *Price risk* refers to the fact that any change in market interest rates typically leads to an opposite change in the value of investments—when interest rates rise (fall), the value of an investment declines (increases). This inverse relationship is most pronounced for financial instruments that have a contractually specified rate of return and a long maturity, such as bonds.

This potential change in the market price of debt securities takes on importance if a sale of the security is anticipated prior to its stated maturity date. If no sale is planned, changes in the market price are not as critical to the investor unless an unexpected event creates the need to sell. This does not mean to say that the investor sustains no loss. It just means that the losses have taken the form of an opportunity loss.

EXAMPLE

Suppose an investor buys a 3-year CD that pays 4 percent interest, and the following week the bank starts to offer 5 percent interest on these same CDs. The investor sustains no direct dollar loss, as he or she will receive the promised interest and the principal back at maturity, but there has been a substantial opportunity loss.

---

21. All three of these instruments will be discussed in later chapters.

For other instruments, such as common stock or real estate, the relationship is not as pronounced. In fact, as with inflation, some companies actually benefit from higher interest rates. (Banks are often more profitable during periods of high interest rates.)

Many people err by confusing the terms price risk and interest rate risk. Remember, price risk is ONLY ONE COMPONENT of interest rate risk.

Financial Planning Issue

For active management of interest-sensitive investments, decision rules for anticipated changes in interest rates are clear. If interest rates are expected to rise, the investor should sell the debt instruments in his or her portfolio. If interest rates do rise, securities similar to those that were sold can be repurchased at lower prices. If interest rates are expected to fall, the investor should purchase debt securities that can be sold at a gain after the rates decrease. (Typically, longer-term bonds will appreciate most.) Note, however, that these actions are speculative, and there may be tax or other reasons such as trading costs that make them imprudent.

---

reinvestment rate risk

Reinvestment Rate Risk. The other element of interest rate risk is *reinvestment rate risk*, which is the risk related to what the interest rate will be when income and/or principal from investments is reinvested. If interest rates fall, investors will be worse off at the time of reinvestment. Conversely, if interest rates rise, they will be better off when reinvestment occurs. The concept of reinvestment rate risk can also be applied to the principal of bonds when they mature.

Financial Planning Issue

Reinvestment rate risk can be dealt with in several ways. First, if the client lives off of the income and principal returned from investments, there is no reinvestment and no built-in assumptions about future rates of return. Second, clients can focus on zero-coupon types of investments, although they still have to worry about reinvestment of principal at maturity. Third, an investment technique known as immunization (discussed in a later chapter) describes how to trade off price risk with reinvestment rate risk to minimize their combined impact. Fourth, another investment technique known as a laddered portfolio distributes bond holdings equally across a range of maturities, and the investor simply ignores fluctuations in interest rates.

Business Risk or Unsystematic Risk

business risk

Many people use the terms business risk and unsystematic risk interchangeably. *Business risk*, which is also referred to as nonmarket or diversifiable risk, is risk that comes from events that affect a single firm or small number of closely related firms. For example, a corporate treasurer may be accused of embezzling substantial sums of money. In this case, it is only the firm employing this treasurer that is likely to be affected. An example of an industry-related type of risk is a decline in the price of imported steel. The decline would likely be beneficial to industries that use steel as an input to their manufacturing process, but it would clearly reduce profit margins for firms in industries that have steel as an output.

Business (unsystematic) risk can be dealt with only through diversification. That is, if one holds enough securities in different lines of business such that the amount invested in any one company is "small," then the impact from these types of events will be minimal and may, to a large extent, be offsetting.

Financial Risk and Default Risk

Corporations, like individuals, can borrow money to acquire assets. Doing so is just like buying on margin (discussed later in this chapter) in the sense that it increases the variability of the company's rate of return. Companies with heavy use of debt financing will have more volatile rates of return. This is what is meant by financial risk. The more debt a firm has relative to its total assets, the greater the financial risk. Financial risk can be avoided altogether by investing only in firms that use no debt financing. Unfortunately, such firms are nearly nonexistent. The real issue, therefore, is how much financial risk an investor is willing to take with each specific investment.

default risk *Default risk*—the risk that contractual payments on debt securities will not be honored—is closely related to financial risk. If debt principal or interest payments are not made on time, the borrower goes into default. In addition to loss of current and future interest payments, investors often lose some or all of their claims on the principal of the debt. This can occur with investments in both profit-seeking businesses and nonprofit entities such as municipalities. Because all debts must be paid in full before any funds can flow to the stockholders, there is rarely anything left to the owners of profit-seeking firms that have defaulted if the issuer has to be liquidated.

> **Financial Planning Issue**
>
> Investment tactics to minimize default risk include the purchase of investments issued only by organizations that have a high credit rating. Moody's, Standard & Poor's, Fitch, Duff & Phelps, and others provide assessments of the issuer for such securities as bonds, but obtaining the information for other forms of investments, such as limited partnerships, can be difficult. Once again, diversification is the primary strategy to minimize the impact of default risk.

Liquidity Risk and Marketability Risk

liquidity risk   Many people use the terms liquidity risk and marketability risk interchangeably. There is technically some distinction between the two. Liquidity is the ability to quickly convert an asset to cash with little or no price concession. Thus, *liquidity risk* refers either to the inability to sell an asset quickly, or the need for a price concession to sell quickly. Because funds can be withdrawn from a passbook savings account any time with no price concession, this account has no liquidity risk.

Marketability refers to the ease of selling an asset for its fair market value. The fair market value of an investment is defined here as the price that a willing buyer and a willing seller would reach if neither was under immediate pressure to trade. The distinction between liquidity risk and marketability risk is whether there is a high degree of certainty in the selling price. Stocks that trade on the major exchanges are a prime example of assets that are marketable but not liquid. All liquid assets are marketable, but not all marketable assets are liquid.

There are several measures of liquidity risk. One is the magnitude of commission. One reason commissions on real estate are so large relative to most other commission structures is the time and effort typically involved in selling property. Another measure of liquidity risk is the bid-ask spread in the market for a particular asset. The less active the trading activity, the larger the bid-ask spread.

> **Financial Planning Issue**
>
> Liquidity is an especially critical concept when evaluating the appropriateness of investment assets for a client's emergency reserves. Only highly liquid assets–such as savings accounts, short-term CDs, life insurance cash values, Treasury bills, and similar investments–are recommended for emergency reserves.

Political and Sovereign Risk

political risk

sovereign risk

Investments in foreign-based companies and U.S. companies with significant revenue from abroad or assets overseas are subject to additional risks in those countries. This *political risk* includes the effects of trade disputes, wars, political unrest, tariffs, corruption, and expropriation, any of which can cause the value of these investments to drop precipitously. *Sovereign risk* is the risk of a government defaulting on its debt obligations.

Financial Planning Issue
There is basically only one way to deal with political risk, and that is diversification. In this case, clients should not have an undue portion of wealth invested in companies in any one country (with the one partial exception being their own country) or in companies doing business in any one country. However, investments in foreign countries are a major vehicle for diversifying.

Exchange Rate (Currency) Risk

exchange rate risk

Movements in currency exchange rates can be a significant source of risk, called *exchange rate risk* or currency risk. This risk is relevant for individuals investing in foreign companies, because even if the company does well, the value of their investment in dollars can decline if the dollar's value rises relative to the value of the currency in the country where the investment is located. Even investment in U.S. companies is subject to exchange rate risk since virtually all large corporations (and even most middle and many smaller ones) generate considerable revenue overseas, manufacture overseas, or obtain raw materials from overseas.

EXAMPLE
Suppose your client, Glenn, would like to invest part of his portfolio in Genovia because his family is from that country. He has heard that the largest bank in Genovia, the Bank of Genovia, is paying a 10 percent interest rate on 1-year CDs, and he wants to buy a one-year, $100,000 CD at this bank. You note that the current exchange rate is 2 genovas to the dollar. After some research, you conclude that it is likely that the exchange rate in one year will be 2.07 genovas to the dollar. If Glenn plans to bring his money back to the U.S. later, what is his rate of return after adjusting for exchange rates?

This is a three-step problem. Step one is to ascertain how many genovas Glenn will be investing in this CD. With the exchange rate at 2 genovas per $1, the $100,000 will result in a 200,000 genova investment. At a 10 percent rate of return, this will grow to 220,000 genovas at the end of the year. If the exchange rate is, in fact, 2.07 at that time, we have to divide the 220,000 genovas by the exchange rate to convert this back to dollars. After reconverting his currency, Glenn will have $106,280.19 (220,000/2.07). This represents a 6.28 percent rate of return. Not bad on a safe investment, but not as exciting as the 10 percent nominal rate Glenn thinks he is getting.

Financial Planning Issue

To the extent a client has extensive holdings in a particular foreign country (for example, a family's business has its manufacturing plant located in a foreign country), the advisor should consider different techniques for hedging that risk, including the use of foreign currency futures and forward contracts, and possibly foreign currency options. (Hedging is discussed fully in a later chapter.)

Tax Risk

tax risk

Most investments have some tax consequences. The extent to which an investment is exposed to changes in tax laws is its *tax risk*. Income and appreciation in value for most investments will at some time be subject to income taxation, and investment assets may be subject to estate and inheritance taxation as well as gift taxation.

Not only can the government increase tax rates but it can also eliminate tax advantages. When the tax laws remove some favorable, or add some unfavorable, tax consequences, the intrinsic value of the affected investment assets falls. New laws could also penalize certain investments by imposing special tax consequences on income or appreciation. For example, with a few exceptions, withdrawals from Roth IRAs are currently tax exempt. Congress could well decide later to impose criteria to tax some of these withdrawals, just as years ago, Congress made Social Security benefits subject to taxation when they had always been exempt before.

To cope with the effects of this type of investment risk, investments should be based primarily on their economic value and contribution to the investor's goals and should not be based solely on tax advantages. In addition, portfolios should be built around tax diversification so that a change in the taxation of one type of investment does not impact the entire portfolio.

Investment Manager Risk

investment manager risk
Investment manager risk can be characterized as the potential failure of the asset manager to select good investments, effectively anticipate and act on market movements, and/or otherwise execute an investment strategy consistent with the interests of the investors in his or her portfolio. For example, during a particular year, the best performing mutual fund sector might be funds that focus on gold. Let's say that the average gold mutual fund has a 40 percent rate of return during a certain year, while other stock mutual funds are not as successful on average. Nonetheless, within the gold sector, some funds will do better than 40 percent, and others will do worse. Investors in gold funds whose returns were less than 40 percent suffered from investment manager risk.

Financial Planning Issue

There are two ways to minimize investment manager risk. One, again, is diversification. Thus, one might consider holding three funds that are trying to achieve a particular objective, rather than just one fund with that objective. The other way is to invest in index funds whose only objective is to match the performance of a particular index and thus avoid active investment decisions.

Additional Commitment Risk

additional commitment risk
When an investment requires the buyer to put additional money into the investment in the future, it is said to have *additional commitment risk*. This additional funding requirement may arise at an inopportune time for the investor. If funds are not available, the investor might be forced to sell the assets at an unfavorable market price. Investments, such as certain limited partnerships that can require additional contributions, are viewed as being more risky than those that require no further investment.

MEASURES OF INVESTMENT RISK

As mentioned earlier, most people think of risk in the insurance framework as the chance of a loss. This is inapt in investments because of the presence of opportunity loss and the concept that people are willing to take on risk in exchange for an expectation of incremental expected return. Simply put:

- Almost all investments contain risk.

- No one will hold these investments unless there is a reward of an expected return sufficient to compute for this exposure to risk.
- Therefore, earning anything less than the expected return is a form of loss.

In the investments world, therefore, a loss is not just losing money, it is earning less than what one should fairly expect to earn. If one could have earned the same amount or more on an investment that was of equal or less risk, then the investment could be said to have performed poorly.

EXAMPLE

You are reviewing the portfolio of Ashok Lessard, a prospective client. Last year, the broad-based market indices were all up about 10 percent. Ashok holds an aggressive portfolio of mostly common stocks in small- to medium-sized firms. Ashok should have had at least a 10 percent rate of return. His portfolio increased in value by 5 percent. Regardless of Ashok's own feelings about the portfolio's performance, in truth, he lost at least 5 percent from what he should have had, based on his risk exposure.

Risk–Expected Return Trade-Off

There are some people who thrive on speculative risk. They love to gamble even when they know the odds are heavily against them. The vast majority of people prefer to limit their exposure to unpleasant surprises. The profitability and success of the insurance industry illustrates the demand for the reduction of pure risk.

Because investors accept risk in exchange for incremental expected return, modern financial theory is based on the simple premise that this risk–expected return trade-off is linear, as shown in the figure below. Another way to look at this relationship is that most investors are also willing to sacrifice some potential return if they can thereby obtain a sufficiently large reduction in risk. Thus, corporate bonds, which have some risk of default, yield a higher expected return than otherwise similar U.S. government bonds. When an investment offers too low an expected return to justify its risk, the asset's price will fall until the market views its risk to be in line with its expected return. Similarly, if an investment's expected return is more than what is necessary based on its level of risk, the asset's price will rise.

Figure 2-2
Risk-Expected Return Trade-Off

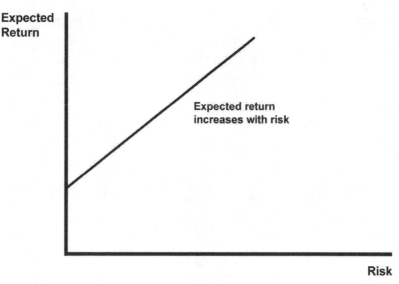

Simple Example of Investment Risk

risk averse Consider the following investment alternatives. Suppose investment A guarantees a return of precisely 5 percent. Now consider investment B with a 5 percent chance of a 0 percent return, a 90 percent chance of a 5 percent return, and a 5 percent chance of a 10 percent return. B's expected return is 5 percent ([.05 x 0%] + [.90 x 5%] + [.05 x 10%] = 0% + 4.5% + .5% = 5%), which is the same as A's. B's actual (or realized) return is less likely to equal its expected return than A's, because 10 percent of the time investment B will not earn 5 percent. Investment A offers an equivalent expected return and lower risk than investment B does. Thus, risk-averse investors would prefer A to B. To be *risk averse* simply means choosing the least risky alternative from investments with equal expected returns. Comparing A to B is straightforward.

Now consider asset C with a 5 percent chance of a 3 percent return, a 90 percent chance of a 5 percent return, and a 5 percent chance of a 7 percent return. Like A and B, C offers an expected return of 5 percent [(.05 x 3%) + (.90 x 5%) + (.05 x 7%) = 5%]. Because C's actual return is uncertain, risk averters would prefer investment A. On the other hand, because C's return variation (or range of possible returns) is less than B's, C is less risky than B. B's actual return could be 5 percent above or below its expected value, whereas C's can differ only 2 percent from its expected return in either direction.

Return possibilities like these are often illustrated graphically, as shown in *Figure 2-3*, as a histogram of investment return possibilities. The vertical axes in *Figure 2-3* report the probability of each possible rate of return; the horizontal axes identify the rates of return.

Figure 2-3
A Histogram of Possible Returns

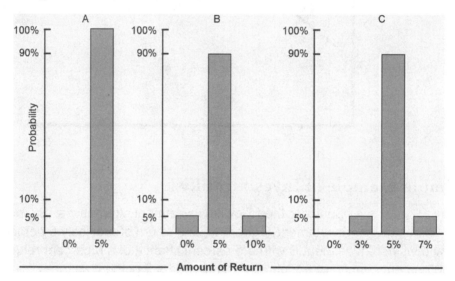

Measuring the Riskiness of a Distribution

Although determining the expected return is rather straightforward as we saw earlier in the chapter, measuring its risk is more complex. Let's consider various possible measures of risk, as well as the benefits and deficiencies of each. In this discussion, we will limit ourselves to discrete distributions.

Range

Range can be defined as the difference between the highest and lowest possible rates of return. In the preceding example, the range for investment B's possible returns is 10 percent (10% – 0%) and the range for investment C is 4 percent (7% – 3%). This technique for measuring risk has the advantage that it is simple, and in this case it clearly and appropriately rates B as riskier than C. However, this approach ignores possible differences in the shape of the distribution of the returns. Consider an investment D with a 50 percent chance of a 10 percent rate of return and a 50 percent chance of a 0 percent rate of return. It has the same expected return and range as investment B (10%), yet it is clearly a riskier investment.

Semivariance

semivariance   A more commonly suggested method for measuring variability is a statistic known as the *semivariance*, and financial analysts occasionally use it. The argument in favor of semivariance is that investors care only about not earning less than the expected return. Potential returns equal to or greater than the expected return are not considered as part of one's risk exposure. An investor who expects to earn a 10 percent rate of return does not lie awake at night worrying that he or she might actually earn a 15 percent rate of return. This argument suggests that risk should be measured by looking only at returns less than the expected return. Potential returns greater than or equal to the expected return are simply ignored in the calculation. The mathematical definition of semivariance is

$$\text{SEMIVARIANCE} = \sum_{i=1}^{n} P_i \times \left[\min(R_i - E(R), 0) \right]^2 \qquad \text{(Equation 2-13)}$$

What this formula says is that if a particular return is less than the expected return, then square that difference and multiply it by the probability of that return. If a particular return is greater than the expected return, then ignore it. Finally, add up all of the squared terms.

EXAMPLE

An investment offers a 30 percent probability of a –2 percent return, a 40 percent probability of an 8 percent return, and a 30 percent probability of an 18 percent return. The expected return is 8 percent, and the deviations from the mean are –10 percent, 0 percent, and 10 percent. If only the negative terms are squared, then only the first differential is used, and the square of –10 percent is 100 percent-squared. When this is multiplied by the associated probability of .30, the semivariance turns out to be 30 percent-squared. The units of this answer, percent-squared, have no relevancy, and can be ignored for practical purposes. For clarification purposes, however, this unit of measurement is discussed in the Tutorial that follows.

Tutorial

As noted in the example showing the computation of semivariance, the units of the answer is "percent-squared." Many students have difficulty with this terminology. The concept of a unit of measurement that is squared is not that unusual. If you have a room in your house that is 15 feet long and 10 feet wide, you could describe the floor area as being 150 feet-square, or 150 square feet. No one has difficulty with this concept because we can envision what a square foot is (it is an area that measures one foot on each side). Similarly, speed can be measured as feet per second. However, when we measure acceleration, it is measured in feet per second-squared. Unfortunately, no one knows what exactly a second-squared is!

If we had shown the semivariance example using decimal notation rather than percent notation for our rates of return, then the expected return and semivariance computations would appear as

$$E(R) = (.30 \times -.02) + (.40 \times .08) + (.30 \times .18) = .08$$

$$\text{SEMIVARIANCE} = (.30 \times [-.02 - .08]^2) + (.40 \times 0) + (.30 \times 0) = .003$$

Both of these answers, 30 percent-squared and .003, are correct; they just reflect the difference between percentage notation and decimal notation when terms are squared. Most people prefer to work with percentage notation rather than decimal because whole numbers are easier to read and enter into a calculator. However, the percentage notation can lead to this awkward set of units when squaring occurs. It is important to note that just as one can move from percentage notation to decimal with rates of return by moving the decimal point **two places** to the left (e.g., 8% = .08), one can move from percent-squared notation to percent by moving the decimal point **four places** to the left. In other words,

$$1 \text{ percent-squared} = .0001$$

The primary defects with the semivariance computation are that it is mathematically difficult to work with, it limits subsequent applications, and nobody knows what is meant by the percent-squared units.

Variance

variance   The measure of variability that turns out to be computationally reasonable AND mathematically tractable for other applications is called the *variance*. As in our discussion earlier on rates of return, the variance can be computed either with ex post (historical) data or ex ante (i.e., a probability distribution) data. For reasons based in statistical theory, the two formulas are different. Because the most common method of computing variance is based on historical data, that is the formula we will discuss in this chapter. The computation of variance when using ex ante data is presented in Appendix C.

To compute variance using historical data, the first step is to compute the arithmetic mean rate of return for the period $(\overline{R})$. The second step is to compute the difference between each rate of return and the mean rate of return. The third and fourth steps are to square these differences and then to total them. The fifth and final step is to divide this sum by the number of observations less 1. The formula can be expressed as:

$$\sigma^2 = \frac{1}{T-1} \sum_{t=1}^{T} \left[R_t - \overline{R} \right]^2 \qquad \text{(Equation 2–14)}$$

The mathematical symbol most commonly used to represent variance is the small Greek letter sigma squared. The term is represented as squared because the differences between each rate of return and its mean are squared.

Standard Deviation

standard deviation
Because the units of the variance term are meaningless (remember, nobody knows what a percent-squared is), and the magnitude of the variance is difficult for many people to grasp, the actual measure of risk used is the *standard deviation*, which is the square root of the variance, shown as follows:

$$\sigma = \sqrt{\sigma^2} = \text{standard deviation} \qquad \text{(Equation 2–15)}$$

Thus, the standard deviation is computed as

$$\sigma = \sqrt{\sum_{t=1}^{T} \frac{(R_t - \overline{R})^2}{T-1}} \qquad \text{(Equation 2–16)}$$

Note that the term $(T-1)$ rather than (T) is used as the denominator in equations 2–14 and 2–16. The variance and standard deviation calculations shown above are called the sample variance and sample standard deviation because they are based on a sample of data, rather than on the universe of possible data points. In other words, the set of future returns is the universe, and the set of past returns we use for our calculation is the sample. Note that equation 2–16 is one of the formulas on the Formula Sheet the CFP® Board provides to students taking the CFP exam. The only differences between its formula and the one provided above is that the CFP® Board uses the letter "s" rather than the small letter sigma and the lower case "r" rather than "R."

EXAMPLE

You note that the returns on a stock for the last 5 years are –15 percent, 5 percent, 10 percent, –3 percent, and 28 percent. You believe these returns are representative of future returns, and you are willing to base your estimate of expected return and standard deviation on these historical data. What are the expected return and standard deviation? The expected return is

$$\overline{R} = \frac{-15\% + 5\% + 10\% - 3\% + 28\%}{5} = 5\%$$

The standard deviation is derived from the variance as follows:

$$\sigma^2 = \frac{1}{5-1} \times [(-15-5)^2 + (5-5)^2 + (10-5)^2 + (-3-5)^2 + (28-5)^2]$$

$$= \frac{1}{4} \times (400 + 0 + 25 + 64 + 529)$$

$$= 254.5$$

$$\sigma = \sqrt{254.5} = 15.95\%$$

HP-10BII keystrokes:

SHIFT, C ALL

15, +/–, Σ+

5, Σ+

10, Σ+

3, +/–, Σ+

28, Σ+

SHIFT, s_x, s_y

(display: 15.95)

We use the s_x, s_y key (the 8 key) rather than the σ_x, σ_y key (the 9 key) because the set of returns is considered to be a sample. Calculating a standard deviation for an entire population requires use of the σ_x, σ_y key. See Appendix C for additional discussion on this last point.

Note that for normal distributions, the semivariances are always proportional to the variances. Thus, if we look at several different return distributions, such as A, B, C, and D described earlier, and rank them by both semivariance and variance (or standard deviation), the rank orders will be identical.

Coefficient of Variation

coefficient of variation

One measure of risk that can at times be quite effective in providing useful information to the financial planner is the *coefficient of variation* (CV). It is computed as the standard deviation divided by the mean return.

$$CV = \sigma / \overline{R}$$ (Equation 2–17)

The CV provides a measure of risk per unit of return. Thus, if one were looking at two investments, E and F, and E had a standard deviation of 1 percent and an expected return of 5 percent, and F had a standard deviation of 3 percent and an expected return of 10 percent, then the CV tells us that investment F has substantially more risk per unit of return than investment E.

Now this does not mean that one would always choose investment E. If one owned investment F, any return that was no worse than one standard deviation *below* the mean return (that is, any return greater than 7 percent) would still be better than any return on investment E that is no better than two standard deviations *above* the expected return (that is, any return no more than 7 percent). This argument makes F a much more tempting investment choice than E, but remember that there is more risk exposure per unit of return in F.

Distributions of Returns

Earlier we talked about the fact that a distribution of future returns could be conceptualized as either a discrete or a continuous distribution. For mathematical simplicity, we have discussed returns and risk in terms of discrete distributions. Nonetheless, we should consider for a moment some of the issues associated with continuous distributions.

Normal Distributions

normal distribution

The most common type of distribution that people use to conceptualize future returns is the *normal distribution*. The traditional description of this distribution is that it is a bell-shaped curve. *Figure 2-1*, shown earlier, is an example of a normal distribution. One of the most important things to remember about a normal distribution is that approximately two-thirds of the time, the actual return will be within one standard deviation of the expected return. Furthermore, about 95 percent of the time it will be within two standard deviations. Finally, about 99 percent of the time the actual return will be within three standard deviations of the expected return.

Note that when we say that two-thirds of the time the actual return will be within one standard deviation of the expected return, by definition we are also saying that one-third of the time the actual return will be more than one standard deviation away form the expected return. Because a normal distribution is also symmetrical, this one-third is split equally between more than one standard deviation above and more than one standard deviation below. Hence, there is a one-sixth (one-sixth is one-half of one-third) probability the actual return will be more than one standard deviation above the mean, and a one-sixth probability it will be more than one standard deviation below. The same concept applies when describing returns more than two or three standard deviations from the expected return.

EXAMPLE

Your client holds a diversified portfolio of common stocks. Based on historical data, you believe the returns on her portfolio will approximate a normal distribution with an expected return of 10 percent and a standard deviation of 15 percent. What can you tell her about her likely rate of return for the coming year?

You can make some of the following points:

- The expected or most likely rate of return is 10 percent.

- Two-thirds of the time, the actual rate of return will be between –5 percent and +25 percent, but one-sixth of the time it will be less than –5 percent and one-sixth of the time it will be greater than +25 percent.

- About 95 percent of the time, it will be between –20 percent and +40 percent.

- About 99 percent of the time, it will be between –35 percent and +55 percent.

Lognormal Distributions

Recent research indicates that even well-diversified portfolios that contain a large number of stocks have negative skewness and are leptokurtic. Nonetheless, using normal distributions to evaluate rates of return on these portfolios is a reasonable approach, especially as most people have some familiarity with bell-shaped curves.

Unfortunately, actual rates of returns for stocks do not seem to conform to a normal distribution. A normal distribution allows for the possibility (albeit a remote possibility) of a rate of return lower than 100 percent. Of course, this is the lowest possible rate of return because it represents a decline in price to zero. Furthermore, substantial research shows that actual rates of return do not conform to the pattern indicated by the standard deviation percentages noted in the example above. It turns out that a lognormal distribution provides a better description for the rates of return on a single stock or an undiversified portfolio than a normal distribution does.

A lognormal distribution is a distribution that becomes a normal distribution if one converts the values of the variable to the natural logarithms, or ln's, of the values of the variable. In our case, let's define the continuously compounded annual rate of return as

$$r_e = e^r - 1 \qquad \text{(Equation 2–18)}$$

where r_e = the continuously compounded rate of return

r = the nominal rate of return

e = the constant 2.7183

The variable r_e will plot as a normal distribution with the added feature that it cannot take on a value less than minus 1 because e^r cannot assume a value less than zero. Using the continuously compounded rate of return to allow for a lognormal distribution is extremely useful in academic research, but has little practical application for the financial planner.

EXAMPLE

If a security has rates of return of –10 percent, 0 percent, and 10 percent, the lognormal rates of return are –.0952, 0, and .1052. The formulas and keystrokes for these three calculations are

$$e^{-.10} - 1 = -.0952$$

$$e^0 - 1 = 0$$

$$e^{.10} - 1 = .1052$$

Keystrokes:

.10, +/–, SHIFT, eˣ, –, 1, = (display –.0952)

0, SHIFT, eˣ, –, 1, = (display 0.0)

.10, SHIFT, eˣ, –, 1, = (display .1052)

Note that the "eˣ" key is the second key from the left on the next to bottom row.

skewed distribution

Skewness. The rates of return on many investments will sometimes exhibit a characteristic known as skewness.

A *skewed distribution* of returns is one in which the tail on one side is longer than that on the other. In the case of discrete data, an example of a skewed distribution is the following:

Probability	Rate of Return
5%	–5%
60%	5%
20%	8%
15%	11%
5%	14%

In the above example, the most likely rate of return is 5 percent. This is referred to as the modal rate of return or *mode*. There is a 5 percent probability of earning less than 5 percent. However, there is a 40 percent probability of earning more than 5 percent. This type of distribution is described as skewed to the right because there is a larger probability of earning more than the mode than of earning less than the mode. This is also described as positive skewness.

As a histogram, the above data looks as follows:

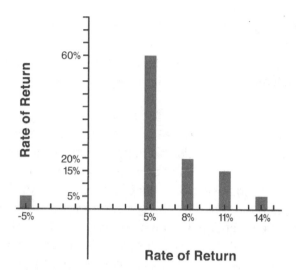

Rate of Return

Figure 2-4 shows skewed continuous distributions. Panel A shows a distribution skewed to the right, as is the discrete example provided above, and Panel B shows a distribution skewed to the left. In Panel A, the expected rate of return is greater than the modal rate of return, and in Panel B, the expected rate of return is less than the modal rate of return. This will always be the case with skewed distributions. The skewness of a distribution can actually be measured, although the calculations are beyond the scope of this book.

Figure 2-4
Skewed Distributions

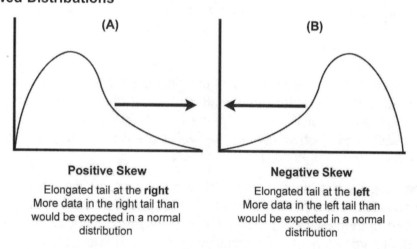

Positive Skew	**Negative Skew**
Elongated tail at the **right**	Elongated tail at the **left**
More data in the right tail than would be expected in a normal distribution	More data in the left tail than would be expected in a normal distribution

The critical question is, does skewness matter to investors? The answer appears to be that it does. Investors prefer positive skewness (skewed to the right) and dislike negative skewness (skewed to the left). Thus, if investors are given investment choices X and Y, and the expected rates of return and standard deviations of returns are identical for both investments but the returns are positively skewed for X and negatively skewed for Y, investors will choose X over Y.

Kurtosis. One final statistic that is sometimes useful in discussing return distributions is known as kurtosis. Kurtosis is a measure of the "peakedness" of a distribution. A distribution may be normal and still have some kurtosis. There are two conditions of kurtosis. One is called *leptokurtic* (shown in Panel A of *Figure 2-5*) and the other is called platykurtic (shown in Panel B of *Figure 2-5*). A leptokurtic distribution will have an unusually high center section to its distribution and unusually thick tails; it resembles the Washington Monument. A platykurtic distribution will have a short center section but negligible tails; it resembles a turtle's shell.

Figure 2-5
Leptokurtic and Platykurtic Distributions

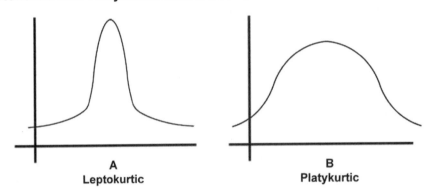

A
Leptokurtic

B
Platykurtic

The reason that kurtosis is important to a financial planner is that research has found that stock returns are leptokurtic. Thus, when we look at historical data, we see more returns that are close to the mean return and more returns that are unusually high or low than we would see if the returns were truly associated with a normal distribution.

Some people argue that the reason stock market returns are leptokurtic is not because of some fundamental economic structure that causes this to be the case, but for a simpler reason. Namely, they argue that the two most important parameters of the distribution of returns—the expected return and the standard deviation—keep changing. Changing parameters would in fact cause the appearance of a leptokurtic distribution when historical rates of return are analyzed.

MONTE CARLO SIMULATIONS

We have heretofore described expected returns with a single number. For example, one can say the annual expected return on a stock or a portfolio is 10 percent. We have also shown how these expected returns are the result of an assumed distribution. We have also looked at the issue of measuring annual average returns over multiple years, and the importance of arithmetic versus geometric mean returns. Another way to discuss returns with a client is Monte Carlo simulation.

Using Monte Carlo to Simulate an Accumulation Portfolio

Simple Monte Carlo simulation is the process whereby one uses a technique of repeated samplings from a probability distribution to ascertain a final distribution of the dollar value of the portfolio.[22] Let's consider a simple example. A planner is presenting a proposed stock portfolio to a client. The planner tells the client that the annual expected rate of return on the portfolio is 8 percent and the standard deviation of the annual return is 15 percent. The client is 45 years old and plans to retire in 20 years. Naturally, the client wants to know not what the expected annual rate of return is or what the standard deviation of return is, but what the dollar value of the portfolio will be at the time of retirement.

Suppose the current value of the client's portfolio is $200,000. If the portfolio achieves exactly an 8 percent rate of return each year for 20 years, its value in 20 years will be $932,191 (C ALL, 200000, PV, 8, I/YR, 20, N, FV [display: –932,191.43]).

However, a good planner knows that it is incredibly unlikely that the portfolio will exactly equal this amount because it is unlikely that it will earn an 8 percent rate of return each year. Thus, it would be more appropriate for the planner to discuss the range of possible ending portfolio values with the client. This range of possible values is where Monte Carlo simulation comes into play.

---

22. For a good discussion on Monte Carlo simulation and similar tools, see "Decision Making under Conditions of Uncertainty: A Wakeup Call for the Financial Planning Profession," by Lynn Hopewell, CFP®, *Journal of Financial Planning*, April 2004, pp. 76–86.

The key to Monte Carlo simulation is looking at a return as being generated by a random distribution process. In the above example, let's simulate the first year's rate of return by randomly selecting a number from a standard deviation distribution table of random numbers. These are numbers that are randomly generated for a normal distribution whose mean is 0 and whose standard deviation is 1. Suppose the number drawn from this table is .625. When we multiply .625 by the standard deviation of 15 percent, we obtain a rate of return that is 9.375 percent above the mean. Adding this to the projected mean of 8 percent results in a simulated first year's return of 17.375 percent. Thus, after 1 year, the portfolio would be worth $234,750 ($200,000 x [1 + .17375]).

To simulate the second year's return, we draw another number from the normal distribution random number table. Suppose the second number drawn is –1.86. Again, we multiply the –1.86 by the 15 percent standard deviation of return to find a rate of return that is 27.90 percent below the mean. We subtract this from the mean of 8 percent to find that the second year's simulated rate of return is –19.90 percent. Thus, after 2 years, the portfolio would be worth $188,035 ($234,750 x [1 – .1990]).

This process is repeated 18 more times to obtain annual rates of return for the projected 20-year period and the value of the portfolio after 20 years. Let's suppose that when this exercise is completed, the ending value of the portfolio turns out to be $910,000. This represents one example of an ending portfolio value. Next, assume that this exercise is repeated a large number of times, say 999 more times. Each of these 999 additional exercises will produce an ending portfolio value. What we are interested in is the summary statistics of these 1,000 different portfolio values.

The most obvious statistic will be the arithmetic mean, but we already know that this number is approximately $932,191. We know this because the mean of the projected distribution necessarily will be about the same as the ending value where we assumed perfect certainty about an 8 percent rate of return every year. The statistics on the range of outcomes are of greater interest. The obvious statistic to compute is the standard deviation of ending portfolio values, and some clients may be able to make sense of this number. For others, a more meaningful representation is portfolio values that represent different likelihoods of outcomes. Think of it as ranking all 1,000 ending values, with the first portfolio representing the largest value and the 1,000th portfolio representing the smallest value. For example, this exercise might produce an outcome in which the 50th portfolio (the lowest portfolio representing the top 5 percent) has a value of $945,000. The 333rd portfolio (the lowest portfolio representing the top one-third) has a value of $937,250, the 667th portfolio has a value of $926,880, and the 951st portfolio has a value of $928,725. These numbers will now give the client a better sense of the risk exposure he or she faces in terms of achieving a desired ending portfolio value.

Financial Planning Issue

The key to Monte Carlo simulation, of course, is whether or not the mean and standard deviation of the hypothesized distribution are correct. Unfortunately, we have no way of knowing what the appropriate numbers are for the future. Thus, most people look at the historical mean and standard deviations of stocks or similar portfolios to see what reasonable numbers are. Because of statistical subtleties (discussed in the previous section), anyone who uses Monte Carlo simulations should have some familiarity with the issues associated with lognormal and leptokurtic distributions. If stock market returns are leptokurtic and the simulation is based on the assumption of a pure normal distribution, the tails of the final distribution will be too small.

Using Monte Carlo to Simulate a Decumulation Portfolio

Monte Carlo simulation has proven to be a particularly effective tool in helping financial planners clarify for clients the effect of various portfolio strategies during retirement. If a retired client plans to live off of the dividend and interest income of a portfolio and never to touch the principal, there is little planning necessary other than to explain to the client the exposure of inflation rate risk. Most clients, however, desire slightly more return from their portfolio than just the dividends and interest. As such, they will slowly but steadily withdraw capital gains and/or principal over time.

The critical issue to clients in planning for their retirement is usually not, what will the value of my portfolio be at the time of my death? Rather, it is, what is the probability of portfolio failure? Portfolio failure is the probability of not having sufficient assets in the portfolio to make a desired withdrawal. The management of a decumulation portfolio involves three decisions. The first is the asset allocation decision. The second decision is the withdrawal rate, which is the dollar amount withdrawn during the first year of retirement as a percentage of the market value of the portfolio at the time of retirement. The third decision is the withdrawal strategy, which is how the amounts withdrawn in subsequent years are determined.

Monte Carlo simulation allows the financial planner to explore different asset allocations, different withdrawal rates, and different withdrawal strategies. The critical output in Monte Carlo analysis of decumulation strategies is the percentage of times that the portfolio fails. Financial planners can then present clients with information about the trade-offs between withdrawal rate, withdrawal strategies, and the probability of portfolio failure.

BUYING ON MARGIN

buying on margin   In addition to all of the other sources of risk discussed earlier, there is a self-induced form of risk: personal financial leverage, also known as *buying on margin*. Marketable securities provide excellent collateral for lenders. The Federal Reserve Board (the Fed) allows most stocks to be bought using borrowed funds for part of the purchase price. This is referred to as buying on margin. The Fed also decides which stocks are marginable (can be bought on margin). However, each brokerage firm can add to the list of stocks that it will not trade on margin. The purchase of stocks on margin is not negligible. The quantity of trades based on margin is substantial.

initial margin rate   An *initial margin rate* of x percent means that a marginable stock can be purchased with x percent cash (called the initial margin) and (100 − x) percent borrowed funds. Thus, a 60 percent initial margin requirement allows the purchase of $10,000 worth of stock with as little as $6,000 in cash. In the past, the Fed raised and lowered the margin requirement on stocks as part of its monetary policy. Since 1974, the margin requirement on stocks has remained at 50 percent. Margin rates are specified by the Federal Reserve Board's Regulation T. Although the actual initial margin rate is 50 percent, in this discussion we will use a different number, usually 60 percent, so that in numerical examples it will be clear to the reader when we are using the margin rate and when we are using the complement of the margin rate, which in this case is 40 percent (100% − 60%).

Note that when a person buys on margin, it is not necessary that he or she use the minimum equity and the maximum loan. Thus, the purchase of $10,000 worth of stock when the initial margin rate is 60 percent requires the investor post no less than $6,000 in cash, but the investor could provide $7,000, $8,000, or $9,000 in cash. These payments would mean loans of $3,000, $2,000, or $1,000. Students should be aware that virtually all problems they will encounter on various exams are constructed to assume the minimum cash payment and the maximum loan value.

buying power A margin account is said to have buying power based on the net equity in the account and the amount of margin borrowing already outstanding. A margin account, as opposed to a cash account, is one in which the investor is allowed to buy on margin. *Buying power* is the amount of additional stock an investor can buy without having to come up with any additional cash. Conceptually, this is accomplished by borrowing cash from the broker using current holdings as collateral, and then using this cash as the equity portion of the purchase price of the new securities.

The buying power of a portfolio of marginable stocks is equal to the net equity of the portfolio divided by the initial margin rate, minus the current account value. In equation form:

$$BP = \frac{E}{IMR} - MV \qquad\qquad \text{(Equation 2–19)}$$

where BP = buying power

E = equity (marginable stocks)

IMR = initial margin requirement

MV = market value of the assets in the account

equity value The *equity value* of an account is the market value of all the securities in an account, minus the loan balance. In equation form:

$$E = MV - LOAN \qquad\qquad \text{(Equation 2–20)}$$

where LOAN = current loan balance

There is a potential difference between the true equity value of an account and the equity value based on marginable securities. In our discussions, we will assume all holdings are marginable. Nonetheless, if there are nonmarginable securities in the account, the equity values in equations 2-19 and 2-20 are based on only the marginable securities. The "true" equity value of the account would, of course, include all securities.

EXAMPLE 1

An investor with $120,000 worth of marginable stocks and no margin debt outstanding could, with a 60 percent initial margin rate, buy another $80,000 worth of marginable stocks with the account's buying power.

$$BP = \frac{120,000}{.60} - 120,000$$
$$= 80,000$$

Note that if the investor buys the $80,000 worth of stock without posting any additional cash, the investor will own $200,000 worth of stock ($120,000 + $80,000) and have a loan of $80,000, which is the maximum loan permitted for a purchase of $200,000 worth of stock with an initial margin rate of 60 percent.

EXAMPLE 2

An investor with $80,000 in marginable stocks, a 60 percent initial margin rate, and an outstanding loan balance of $20,000 would be able to purchase another $20,000 worth of marginable stock with the account's buying power.

$$E = 80,000 - 20,000$$
$$= 60,000$$
$$\text{and}$$
$$BP = \frac{60,000}{.60} - 80,000$$
$$= 20,000$$

Note that in this example, if the investor buys an additional $20,000 in stock without posting any cash, then the investor will own $100,000 worth of stock ($80,000 + $20,000) and have a loan of $40,000 ($20,000 original loan + $20,000 new loan). The $40,000 loan is the maximum loan amount permitted for a new purchase of $100,000 in stock with an initial margin rate of 60 percent.

Margin Calls

maintenance margin percentage

Margin loans may remain outstanding as long as the borrower's equity position does not fall below the maintenance margin percentage. The *maintenance margin percentage* is the minimum amount of equity an investor must have, as a percentage of the portfolio, without having to repay part of the loan. The Federal Reserve Board also sets this rate, but a brokerage firm can set a higher rate.

The current maintenance margin rate set by the Fed is 25 percent. Some brokerage firms set their rates as high as 35 percent. These rates are applied to the portfolio, not to the individual security. Remember, when an investor is buying securities on margin, he or she is borrowing money from the broker and pledging the securities as collateral. Lenders always have the right to set their own loan terms. Maintenance margin rates are always less restrictive (that is, lower) than initial margin rates.

Although interest is charged every month on the loan balance, margin borrowers are not required or expected to make payments according to any particular schedule. In theory, a margin loan has no maturity. The only time an actual cash payment would be due in a margin account is if the market value of the account is less than the loan balance divided by one minus the maintenance margin rate, which is expressed as:

$$MV < LOAN \div (1 - MMR)$$ (Equation 2–21)

where MMR = maintenance margin rate

This inequality can also be expressed as

$$MV \times (1 - MMR) < LOAN$$ (Equation 2-21a)

The underlying concept is that as long as the value of the collateral comfortably exceeds the amount of the loan, the outstanding loan is considered to be secure.

EXAMPLE

An investor bought 100 shares of stock at $50 per share and borrowed $2,000 to help pay for it. If the initial margin rate is 50% and the maintenance margin rate is 25%, what is the lowest price the stock could drop to without receiving a margin call?

Solution:

$$MV = LOAN \div (1 - MMR)$$

100 shares × Price Per Share = $2,000 \div (1 - .25)$

100 shares × Price Per Share = $2,666.67

Price per Share = $2,666.67 \div 100$ shares < $26.67

margin call

house call

Fed call

An investor whose market value fails to satisfy equation 2-21 (counting only marginable securities) will receive a *margin call*. A margin call can be either a *house call* (if the brokerage firm has a higher maintenance margin rate) or a *Fed call*. The brokerage firm has the option of enforcing or waiving the enforcement of a house margin call. However, a Fed call must be enforced.

A margin call may be settled in any of several ways. One way is to deposit sufficient cash into the account to pay down enough of the loan so that the maintenance margin requirement specified in equation 2-21 is met. A second way to settle up is to deposit other marginable securities into the account, thus increasing the equity value of the account. A third way is to sell a sufficient number of shares from the portfolio and use the sale proceeds to pay down the loan until the maintenance margin requirement is met.

Ways to Satisfy a Margin Call

- Add more money to the account.
- Add more collateral (marginable securities) to the account.
- Sell stock from the account and use the proceeds to reduce the margin debt.

In each case, the result must raise the equity percentage above the margin maintenance minimum to satisfy the margin call.

If the investor opts to add cash to the account, the amount of cash needed is the amount necessary to meet the maintenance margin requirement. In mathematical terms:

$$\text{Cash added} = \text{LOAN} - [\text{MV}(1 - \text{MMR})]$$ (Equation 2-22)

EXAMPLE

An investor buys $10,000 worth of stock using $6,000 in cash and a $4,000 loan. The stock falls to a market value of $5,000. If there have been no deposits to offset the loan, what is the amount of the margin call if the maintenance margin rate is 25 percent? (Ignore any interest that might have accrued on the loan.)

Margin call $= \$4,000 - [\$5,000 \times (1 - .25)]$

$= \$4,000 - \$3,750 = \$250$

EXAMPLE

Your client has $50,000 worth of securities in his cash account, and $100,000 worth in his margin account. The values of both accounts are down because of an extended bear market. Unfortunately, the client also has a debit balance on his margin account of $85,000 and the maintenance margin rate is 25%. The maximum loan balance when the market value of the account is $100,000 is $75,000. Thus, he receives a $10,000 margin call. The easiest response would be to deposit a check for $10,000. If the client attempts to meet the call through the sale of securities, he will have to sell $40,000 worth of investments. This sale would reduce the market value of the assets to $60,000, and the loan to $45,000. At this point, the client now meets the maintenance margin requirement. Finally, if some of the stocks in the cash account are marginable, the client need only transfer $13,333 worth of stock from the cash account to the margin account to meet the call. After the transfer, the market value of the assets in the margin account is $113,333 and the loan balance is still $85,000, but the maintenance margin rule has been satisfied. So the three solutions to the margin call are to deposit $10,000 in cash which reduces the loan balance to $75,000, deposit $13,333 in marginable securities, or to sell $40,000 worth of stock.

So far, we have talked only about margin calls when a stock declines. If an investor is short a particular stock, and that stock's price rises, he or she could also face a margin call, or be forced to buy back the shorted security.

Incremental Borrowing

In the previous section, we considered the situation in which the value of the portfolio declines and the investor must meet a margin call. Now let's consider a more pleasant scenario, the removal of cash from a portfolio. In this case, we are not saying that there is actually cash in the portfolio. We are saying that cash is removed as a result of taking out a margin loan, or by increasing one's loan. All that is required to remove cash from a margin account is that the investor's loan balance be lower than what is required under the initial margin rate. The investor can then remove an amount of cash equal to the difference between the maximum loan allowable using the initial margin rate and the current loan balance. In equation form:

$$\text{Maximum cash withdrawal} = \text{MV} \times (1 - \text{IMR}) - \text{LOAN} \qquad \text{(Equation 2-23)}$$

EXAMPLE

Your client, Ted Kowalski, contacts you to indicate he needs $30,000 in about a week and asks you about the easiest way to acquire the cash. You note that the stocks in his portfolio have a market value of $250,000, the initial margin rate is 60 percent, and his current loan balance in the account is $40,000. You compute his maximum cash withdrawal as follows:

$$\$250,000 \times (1 - .60) - \$40,000 = \$60,000$$

This is more than what Ted needs to meet his needs. You need to point out to Ted that if the value of his holdings declines before this loan is repaid, he is at an increased risk of a margin call.

The Leverage of Margin Borrowing

Buying on margin magnifies any gain or loss to the investor, increasing the variability of the returns on the portfolio. To demonstrate these effects, consider the concepts of return on assets (ROA) and return on equity (ROE). In this context, ROA is the equivalent of a holding period return (HPR) for an investment without regard to the use of leverage. ROE is the holding period return actually earned by the investor based on the money invested and the interest expense incurred.

We can present ROA as follows:

$$\text{ROA} = \frac{\text{Ending value of the assets} - \text{Beginning value of the assets}}{\text{Beginning value of the assets}}$$

(Equation 2-24)

Ending value is assumed to include reinvested dividends.

ROE differs from ROA in that it incorporates the interest payments, and uses the out-of-pocket cash invested as the base for measuring the return. The formula is

$$\text{ROE} = \frac{(\text{Ending value of the assets} - \text{Beginning value of the assets}) - \text{Interest charges}}{\text{Initial equity investment}}$$

(Equation 2–25)

The first part of the numerator in equation 2–25 is the same as the numerator in equation 2–24, but then consideration is given to the interest charges paid. Thus, ROE includes the change in the value of the investment and the interest expense, relative to what the investor actually paid for it.

EXAMPLE

An investor buys 1,000 shares at $50 per share. One year later, the shares are worth $55 per share. The ROA (and HPR) are

$$ROA = \frac{\$55,000 - \$50,000}{\$50,000}$$

$$= .10, \text{ or } 10\%$$

If the investor had bought on margin and borrowed 40 percent of the purchase price at an interest rate of 7 percent, then the loan balance is $20,000 ([1 .60] x $50,000), the interest for the year (ignoring compounding) is $1,400 (7% x $20,000), and the ROE is

$$ROE = \frac{\$55,000 - \$50,000 - \$1,400}{\$50,000 \times .60}$$

$$= \frac{\$3,600}{\$30,000}$$

$$= .12, \text{ or } 12\%$$

Thus, one can say that the security provided a 10 percent rate of return (that is, ROA), but the investor received a 12 percent rate of return (that is, ROE).

Of course, leverage entails risk. If the price had risen by only $1 to $51 during the year, the ROA would have been

$$ROA = \frac{\text{Ending value} - \text{Beginning value}}{\text{Beginning value}}$$

$$= \frac{\$51,000 - 50,000}{\$50,000}$$

$$= .02, \text{ or } 2\%$$

and the ROE would have been

$$ROE = \frac{\$51,000 - \$50,000 - (.07 \times [1 - .60] \times \$50,000)}{\$50,000 \times 0.6} = \frac{-\$400}{\$30,000}$$

$$= -.0133, \text{ or } -1.33\%$$

In the above example, the interest rate was applied to the beginning loan balance to compute the annual interest expense and was not compounded. As will be discussed in the next section, the interest rate is actually a variable rate, and if the investor accrues interest charges, the loan balance and interest expense would actually be compounded over time. Hence, the above loan charges are a simplification.

The following table provides a comparison of ROA and ROE for cash and margin purchases with price movements in $5 increments.

Table 2-1 Margin Example: Purchase 100 Shares at $50 Per Share, No Dividends, 7% Borrowing Rate, Holding Period of 1 Year		
	Cash Purchase	**60% Margin Purchase**
Ending Price	**ROA**	**ROE**
$35	–30%	–54.67%
$40	–20%	–38.00%
$45	–10%	–21.33%
$50	0%	–4.67%
$55	10%	12.00%
$60	20%	28.67%
$65	30%	45.33%

The key point to note in Table 2-1 is the same as noted earlier: Buying on margin magnifies the percentage gain or loss the investor achieves and thus increases the variability of the investor's returns. When the investment does well, the investor benefits from buying on margin; when it does badly, he or she suffers even more.

Financial Planning Issue
Because of the increased variability of the returns, only aggressive investors should buy on margin. Margin should not be used as a way to encourage an investor to buy more shares of a stock than he or she would otherwise purchase without the loan.

The Mechanics of Buying on Margin

credit balance

debit balance

broker call-loan rate

Brokerage firms finance some of their margin lending from other customers' credit balances such as those generated through short sales. A positive balance in a customer's account is called a *credit balance*; a negative one (a margin loan) is referred to as a *debit balance*. Brokerage firms also obtain additional funds to lend investors from commercial banks at the *broker call-loan rate*.

Interest charges on margin loans are based on the exact time and amount of the loan. If, for example, $10,000 is borrowed and then $750 is repaid a week later, interest will be calculated on $10,000 for 1 week and on $9,250 thereafter. The margin loan interest rate for a specific customer is usually determined by a sliding scale added to the broker call-loan rate. *Table 2-2* is representative.

Table 2-2 Typical Margin Loan Rates	
Net Debit Balance	Call Rate Plus
$ 0 – 9,999	2.25%
$10,000 – 29,999	1.75%
$30,000 – 49,999	1.25%
$50,000 and over	.75%

Banks generally set their broker call-loan rate equal to or even below their prime rate. Margin loan rates are usually no more than 2 to 3 percent above the prime business rate. Relatively favorable interest rates and flexible payment schedules make margin loans an attractive credit source. Note that rates vary among brokers. Because these rates are unadvertised and often difficult to see, some brokerage firms view the interest rate markup on margin loans as a major profit center. Thus, an investor who uses extensive leverage should certainly shop around for margin interest rates.

EXAMPLE

Your new client, Steve, likes to make about 50 trades per year (about one per week) and carries an average debit balance of $200,000. He is with the National Chain Brokerage Firm. It charges $10 commission per trade and a markup of 1 percent on a loan balance of $200,000. You note that the Local Boutique Firm charges a commission of $15 per trade but has a markup of only 3/4 of 1 percent on a loan balance of $200,000. Should you encourage Steve to switch firms based only on this information?

If Steve switches brokerage firms, he will pay $250 more per year in commissions ([$15 – $10] × 50 trades per year). He will, however, save $500 per year in interest expense ([.0100 – .0075] × $200,000). There are tax implications to both of these numbers, but the main point is that margin interest rates can be an important consideration for investors who carry an extensive debit balance.

REVIEW OF LEARNING OBJECTIVES

1. The HPR is the sum of the income received from an investment and the change in market value, divided by the beginning value (or cost) of the investment. This is expressed as

$$HPR = \frac{\text{Income received} + \text{Change in value}}{\text{Beginning value}}$$ (Equation 2–1)

   An asset's PPR is defined as the sum of that period's income and change in value divided by its beginning-of-period market value:

$$PPR = \frac{\text{Period's income} + \text{Period's Change in value}}{\text{Beginning} - \text{of} - \text{period value}}$$ (Equation 2-3)

   The arithmetic mean return for a security is the per period rates of return divided by the number of observations. A geometric mean return is the nth root of the product of the per period return relatives, minus 1.

2. The expected return for a security can be expressed as the sum of the different future possible rates of return times the associated probability of each return. It can also be measured as equal to the arithmetic mean rate of return using historical data. The formula to determine the effective annual rate of return is

$$R_{ear} = (1 + HPR)^{\#} - 1 \qquad \text{(Equation 2-6)}$$

3. The major sources of risk are systematic risk, inflation (purchasing power) risk, interest rate risk, business (unsystematic) risk, financial and default risk, liquidity and marketability risk, political risk, exchange rate risk, tax risk, investment manager risk, and additional commitment risk. Systematic risk can be avoided only by staying out of the market. Inflation (purchasing power) risk cannot be avoided, but it can be minimized by purchasing securities whose returns are based on the inflation rate. Interest rate risk can be minimized by using the strategy of immunization. Business (unsystematic) risk can be minimized with diversification. Financial and default risk can be minimized by avoiding poorly rated securities and with diversification. Liquidity and marketability risk can be minimized by investing only in highly liquid securities. Political and exchange rate risk can be minimized by diversifying across countries and hedging exchange rate risk. Also, exchange rate risk can be minimized by hedging with currency derivatives. Tax risk is difficult to avoid. Investment manager risk can be minimized with diversification across funds, or limiting oneself to index funds. Finally, additional commitment risk can be dealt with by avoiding investments that might require an additional commitment of cash.

4. The various measures of risk include the range of returns, the semivariance, the variance, the standard deviation, and the coefficient of variation. The formula for computing variance using historical data can be expressed as:

$$\sigma^2 = \frac{1}{T-1} \sum_{t=1}^{T} \left[R_t - \overline{R} \right]^2 \qquad \text{(Equation 2-14)}$$

The standard deviation is the square root of the variance.

5. A normal distribution is the traditional bell-shaped curve that is used to expressed symmetric returns about a mean return. A lognormal distribution is one created by adjusting the return using the value of "e." A skewed distribution has a long tail on one side, and a short tail on the other. Kurtosis means the traditional bell-shaped normal curve is altered so that it either has fatter tails and a taller center (leptokurtic), or a shorter center and thinner tails (platykurtic).

6. A Monte Carlo simulation is performed by using a random number generator to produce various rates of return from a specified

distribution of returns, to see the distribution of possible outcomes over time.

7. Buying power is computed as

$$BP = \frac{E}{IMR} - MV \qquad \text{(Equation 2-19)}$$

where the equity value is computed as the market value of the portfolio or asset, less the loan outstanding. A margin call will be made whenever the market value is less than the loan balance divided by the complement of the maintenance margin rate, which is:

$$MV < LOAN \div (1 - MMR) \qquad \text{(Equation 2-21)}$$

If the investor opts to provide cash when a margin call is made, the necessary cash is computed as

$$\text{Cash added} = LOAN - [MV \times (1 - MMR)] \qquad \text{(Equation 2-22)}$$

Finally, if the investor wishes to borrow from a margin account, the maximum amount of cash that can be withdrawn can be computed as

$$\text{Maximum cash withdrawal} = MV \times (1 - IMR) - LOAN \qquad \text{(Equation 2-23)}$$

MINICASE

You have completed steps one and two of the financial planning process with a new client—defining the terms of the engagement and gathering data. You are now in the steps three and four—analyzing the data and preparing a plan. The client tells you he is quite happy with his broker, as his portfolio has earned 12 percent over the last 18 months. You are not sure this rate of return is as great as the client thinks it is. You would like to help the client understand what the future prospects of his portfolio are. You believe the easiest way to express this is to describe the expected health of the economy as strong, normal, or weak, and to assign probabilities of 40 percent, 30 percent, and 30 percent to each of these outcomes. The associated rates of return in the client's portfolio are 12 percent, 8 percent, and –2 percent. The portfolio is worth $250,000, and is debt-free. Based on the client's overall financial position, you think he should add some more holdings to his portfolio and leverage it. The initial margin rate is 50 percent and the maintenance margin rate is 25 percent.

1. Over the last 18 months, which of the following is the effective annual rate the client has actually been earning? [1]

    (A) 12.00%
    (B) 8.00%
    (C) 7.85%
    (D) 7.70%

2. Based on your economic forecasts, what is the expected rate of return on the client's portfolio? [1]

    (A) 12%
    (B) 8%
    (C) 6.6%
    (D) 6%

3. If you believe that this portfolio's prospective performance can best be described in terms of a normal distribution, with the expected return as defined in the previous question and a standard deviation of 10 percent, then all of the following statements are correct EXCEPT [4]

    (A) There is a 1 in 20 chance the actual rate of return will be greater than 26.6 percent.
    (B) There is a 1 in 6 chance the actual rate of return will be greater than 16.6 percent.
    (C) There is a 1 in 200 chance the actual rate of return will be greater than 36.6 percent.
    (D) There is a 1 in 2 chance the actual rate of return will be less than 6.6 percent.

4. What is the client's current buying power? [6]

    (A) $750,000
    (B) $250,000
    (C) $200,000
    (D) zero

5. Suppose the client bought $100,000 worth of stock, all on margin with no new cash deposited, and the portfolio grew in value over the next year to $400,000. What are the ROA and ROE, assuming an interest rate of 5 percent? (Ignore any compounding of interest each month.) [7]

    (A) 20% and 60%
    (B) 60% and 20%
    (C) 58% and 14.29%
    (D) 14.29% and 18%

CHAPTER REVIEW

Key Terms and Concepts

holding period return (HPR)	tax risk
holding period return relative (HPRR)	investment manager risk
ex post	additional commitment risk
ex ante	risk averse
expected HPR	semivariance
per-period return (PPR)	variance
compounding	standard deviation
geometric mean return	coefficient of variation
pure risk	normal distribution
speculative risk	skewed distribution
market risk	buying on margin
inflation risk	initial margin rate
interest rate risk	buying power
price risk	equity value
reinvestment rate risk	maintenance margin percentage
business risk	margin call
default risk	house call
liquidity risk	Fed call
political risk	credit balance
sovereign risk	debit balance
exchange rate risk	broker call-loan rate

Review Questions

Review questions are based on the learning objectives in this chapter. Thus, a [3] at the end of a question means that the question is based on learning objective 3. If there are multiple objectives, they are all listed.

1. a. Compute the HPRR and the HPR for each of the following: [1]
        i. an investment in land purchased for $5,000 and sold 3 years later
    for $7,000
        ii. a building that is held for 9 months, during which time it generates
    $3,500 in net cash inflows and is then sold for a $30,000 profit. Its original
    purchase price was $195,000
    b. Compute the PPRs and the PPRRs for an investment worth $10 at the
    start of the first period, $11 at the end of the first period, $12 at the end of
    the second period, and $11 at the end of the third period. Assume a $.50
    dividend is paid at the end of each period. [1]

2. Compute the arithmetic mean return and geometric mean return for an
    investment with the following returns over the last 3 years: −22 percent, 7
    percent, and 21 percent. [1]

3. You are considering an investment that you believe has a 25 percent
    probability of a −15 percent rate of return, a 40 percent probability of a 5
    percent rate of return, and a 35 percent probability of a 25 percent rate of
    return. What is the expected rate of return on this investment? [2]

4. You have a holding period rate of return of 4 percent. What is your effective
    annual rate of return if your holding period is [2]
    a. 3 months
    b. 6 months
    c. 9 months
    d. 15 months

5. a. If an investor wants a 5 percent real rate of return, and the inflation rate is
    4 percent, what nominal rate must he or she obtain? [3]
    b. If an investor is receiving a nominal rate of return of 15 percent, and the
    inflation rate is 10 percent, what is his or her real rate of return? [3]

6. Assume XYZ stock has the following rates of return for the last 3 years:
    −15 percent, 10 percent, and 35 percent. Determine XYZ's mean return,
    variance, standard deviation, and coefficient of variation based on this
    historical data. [4]

7. a. What are the continuously compounded rates of return for the annual
    rates of return provided in problem 6? [5]
    b. If an investment can be described as having a 25 percent probability of
    a −5 percent rate of return, a 60 percent probability of a 15 percent rate of
    return, a 15 percent probability of a 60 percent rate of return, is it skewed to
    the right or left, and is it more or less attractive to an investor than a normal
    distribution with the same expected rate of return and standard deviation? [5]

8.   David Gordon buys 100 shares of Uhoh Corp. at $50 per share. The initial margin rate is 60 percent, the maintenance margin rate is 25 percent, and he buys it with minimum margin. [7]
     a.   How much does he initially borrow?
     b.   If the stock rises to $80 per share shortly thereafter (ignore interest charges), how much cash can he withdraw from his account?
     c.   If the stock rises to $80 per share shortly thereafter (ignore interest charges), how many additional shares can he buy without depositing any additional cash?
     d.   If the stock falls rather than rises, what is the lowest price to which it can fall without receiving a margin call?
     e.   Suppose the stock falls to $20 per share. What is the size of the margin call?

9.   Ralph Harrison buys 100 shares of Dynamite Corp. for $30 per share. He purchases the stock with 70 percent margin (that is, he borrows 30 percent of the purchase price). The stock jumps to $35 per share shortly thereafter. What are his ROA and ROE? (Ignore interest charges.) [7]

10.   Assume the broker call-loan rate is 8.5 percent and that the margin loan rates of *Table 2-2* apply. Compute the monthly interest expense in an account for the next 2 months if the initial debit balance is $53,000 and the interest accrues to the loan balance. [7]

Learning Objectives

An understanding of the material in this chapter should enable the student to

1. Explain why the combination of two risky securities can produce a portfolio with less risk than either separately, and compute both the expected rate of return and the standard deviation for any two-security portfolio.

2. Describe how the optimal portfolio for an investor is the tangency between the efficient frontier and the highest possible indifference curve.

3. Show why an investor would prefer as low a correlation coefficient as possible for a two-security portfolio.

4. Explain why the fact that the "new" efficient frontier as defined by the capital market line (CML) dominates the "old" efficient frontier produced by N risky assets alters one's perception of the appropriate portfolio for an investor to hold.

5. Explain the roles of beta and the coefficient of determination in defining the risk of a particular security as part of the capital asset pricing model (CAPM).

6. Describe the arbitrage pricing theory (APT) model.

7. Describe why an understanding of modern portfolio theory (MPT) and its legal implications for a practitioner are important for today's financial planner.

This chapter is about theory! Nobody says that the theory presented herein is a realistic description of how securities are priced. Nonetheless, the theory that follows is critical to understanding how many people think about assets, asset allocation, and the issues associated with constructing and evaluating portfolio performance. This theory, known as modern portfolio theory, is about the concepts of assembling and managing a portfolio of stocks. It is the most commonly accepted theory about stock market returns that currently exists. If a better theoretical model that also seems to be a better description of reality comes along, we will abandon modern portfolio theory and move to the new theory. However, such an alternative theory has not yet been developed, and there is no indication that one will appear anytime soon.

Modern portfolio theory started with the research of Harry M. Markowitz in the 1950s and by the mid-'60s was fairly well developed. It has provided the basic building blocks of financial research for almost 50 years. In this and several of the chapters that follow, we will look at the various issues associated with applications of modern portfolio theory.

INDIVIDUAL VERSUS PORTFOLIO RISK

As discussed in the previous chapter, risk in investments is defined in terms of speculative risk. Thus, simply earning less than one expects to earn, even though the actual return is positive, is considered an undesirable outcome. As long as the possible returns are symmetrical about the expected return (for example, as long as earning 5 percent more than expected is as equally likely as earning 5 percent less than expected), the standard deviation is a useful measure of an individual investment's risk. It is an inadequate risk measure, however, if the asset is part of a larger portfolio. The reason is that if poor performance by some parts of the portfolio tends to be offset by more favorable performance in the rest of the portfolio, the investor's overall wealth position may not suffer. Investors do not know ahead of time which investments will do well and which will not, but they know that some investments will do better than others. The more diversified the portfolio, the more likely individual losses in the portfolio due to a set of events are offset by gains in other investments because of the same set of events. Accordingly, investors should concern themselves primarily with portfolio risk, rather than with the risks of each of the portfolio's individual components. If the values of two investments fluctuate by offsetting amounts, the owner is no worse off than if neither had varied. This following example shows the benefits of diversification.

EXAMPLE

Imagine a sunscreen business and an umbrella business at the beach. Let's say there is a 50 percent chance that it will rain and a 50 percent chance that it will be sunny. The sunscreen business will have a 20 percent return if it is sunny but a 0 percent return if it rains. The umbrella business will have a 20 percent return if it rains but a 0 percent return if it is sunny. Each business will have an expected return of 10 percent (.5 × 20% + .5 × 0%) and a standard deviation of 10 percent. Now imagine a diversified portfolio consisting of equal weights of the sunscreen and umbrella businesses. It will still have an expected return of 10 percent, but the standard deviation is now zero (that is, the portfolio is risk free) because there will be a 10 percent return whether it is sunny or rainy.

As the simplified example above shows, diversification has been used to create a risk-free portfolio out of two risky investments. Note that risk has been eliminated without any reduction in the expected return.

TWO-ASSET PORTFOLIO RISK

The simplest type of portfolio contains a single asset, such as stock in one company. This portfolio is, by definition, totally undiversified. The next simplest portfolio contains two assets, such as stock in two different companies. A two-asset portfolio might be able to benefit from the risk-reduction potential of diversification. As we saw in equation 2-10, the expected return of the two-asset portfolio is expressed as

$$E\left(R_p\right) = W_i\left[E\left(R_i\right)\right] + W_j\left[E\left(R_j\right)\right] \qquad \text{(Equation 3–1)}$$

where W_i = portfolio weight of asset i

W_j = portfolio weight of asset j

The one requirement for the weights is that they add up to 1 (100 percent):

$$W_i + W_j = 1 \qquad \text{(Equation 3-1a)}$$

The fact that they total 1 means the portfolio is fully invested in these two assets. Generally, we think about each separate weight as being bounded by 0 and 100 percent. This, however, is not a requirement. Obviously, if one weight is less than 0, the other will have to be greater than 100 percent. A weight less than 0 implies the person has taken a short position in that asset and used the proceeds from the sale to buy more of the other asset.

EXAMPLE 1

Your client has two stocks, Xylog and PT&A. The expected return on Xylog is 8 percent, and on PT&A it is 12 percent. The client has $3,000 invested in Xylog and $7,000 invested in PT&A. What is the portfolio's expected return?

Answer: The total portfolio's value is $10,000, so the weights are 30% and 70%, and the expected return is

$$E(R_p) = (.30 \times 8\%) + (.70 \times 12\%) = 10.8\%$$

EXAMPLE 2

Suppose your client has shorted Xylog for $3,000, and used that cash and his own $10,000 to buy PT&A. What is the portfolio's expected return?

Answer: The value of the portfolio is still $10,000, $13,000 invested in PT&A, and $3,000 owed to repurchase Xylog, but now the weights are -30% and 130%, so the expected return is

$$E(R_p) = (-.30 \times 8\%) + (1.30 \times 12\%) = 13.2\%$$

The risk of the portfolio depends on both the individual risk of its two components and the degree to which the two components' returns are related. The portfolio variance for a two-asset portfolio is shown in equation 3-2:

$$\sigma_p^2 = W_i^2\ \sigma_i^2 + 2W_iW_jCOV_{ij} + W_j^2\ \sigma_j^2 \qquad \text{(Equation 3-2)}$$

where σ_i^2 = variance of the rate of return on asset i

σ_j^2 = variance of the rate of return on asset j

COV_{ij} = covariance of the rate of return on asset i with the rate of return on asset j

Variance was defined in the prior chapter for a single asset. That definition is used to compute σ_i^2 and σ_j^2 as they appear in equation 3-2. The terms $W_i^2\sigma_i^2$ and $W_j^2\sigma_j^2$ are the squares of each component's weight multiplied by its respective variance.

The remaining term, $2W_iW_jCOV_{ij}$, requires further explanation. The first part of the term, $2W_iW_j$, is two times the product of the weights W_i and W_j. The key–indeed, the central aspect of portfolio risk–is the covariance term COV_{ij}

(the symbol σ_{ij} is also sometimes used), which is defined in the next section. The covariance quantifies the effect of portfolio diversification.

Covariance

covariance The *covariance*, like the mean and standard deviation, is a statistic that is almost always estimated from ex post (historical) values of the relevant variables. It measures the comovement or covariability of two variables. Thus, the covariance of two assets' returns is an index of how they tend to move relative to each other. For example, the market prices of stocks of two similar companies that operate in the same industry probably tend to move together. On the other hand, stock prices of two different types of companies operating in different industries probably tend to move largely independently of each other. Sometimes, there are companies whose stock prices tend to move opposite to each other (like the sunscreen/umbrella example earlier). The first pair of stocks (same industry) has a relatively high positive covariance with each other, the second pair (different industries) has a covariance close to 0, and the last pair (sunscreen/umbrella) likely has a negative covariance. Stocks with negative covariances are the best bet for diversification, but stocks with covariances near 0 are still good combinations. Stocks with high positive covariances are poor vehicles for diversification.

To understand how the covariance statistic is defined, recall that when we computed the variance of a security's returns, we summed the square of the difference between each return and the mean return (see equation 2-14). Because of the squaring process, all of the terms in the summation are positive. Had the squaring process not been used, some of the terms would have been positive and some negative. Now consider the product of the differences between each return and their respective means for assets i and j, namely $[(R_{it} - \overline{R}_i][R_{jt} - \overline{R}_j]$. When the returns of the two assets are either both above or both below their arithmetic mean returns, the product is positive. The product of two positive numbers is positive, and the product of two negative numbers is also positive. The product of these two differences is negative only when one is above its mean and the other below. The covariance is defined as the average of the products $[(R_{it} - \overline{R}_i][R_{jt} - \overline{R}_j]$.

Like variances, covariances can be computed with either ex ante or ex post data. The formulas are slightly different. However, in practice, covariances are computing using historical data and the assumption is usually made that the future covariance will equal the covariance calculated with historical data.

For this reason, the covariance formula used with ex ante data is presented in Appendix C and the formula to use with ex post data is defined as follows:

$$COV_{ij} = \frac{1}{n-1} \sum_{t=1}^{n} [R_{it} - \overline{R}_i][R_{jt} - \overline{R}_j] \qquad \text{(Equation 3-3)}$$

EXAMPLE

Suppose that for the last 5 years we have the following five annual rates of return for securities i and j (expressed in percentages):

$(R_{i1}, R_{j1}) = (5, 4)$

$(R_{i2}, R_{j2}) = (10, 15)$

$(R_{i3}, R_{j3}) = (-7, -12)$

$(R_{i4}, R_{j4}) = (-2, 2)$

$(R_{i5}, R_{j5}) = (19, 16)$

To compute the covariance between these two securities, we must first compute their average returns.

$$\overline{R}_i = \left(\frac{5+10-7-2+19}{5}\right) = \frac{25}{5} = 5$$

$$\overline{R}_j = \left(\frac{4+15-12+2+16}{5}\right) = \frac{25}{5} = 5$$

Note that in computing the average return (that is, arithmetic mean) for each security, we use the number of observations in the denominator. Next, we must compute the values of the differences between each return and its mean, $(R_{it} - \overline{R}_i)$ and $(R_{jt} - \overline{R}_j)$, and their product for each year t:

t	$R_{it} - \overline{R}_i$	$R_{jt} - \overline{R}_j$	$(R_{it} - \overline{R}_i)(R_{jt} - \overline{R}_j)$
1	$5 - 5 = 0$	$4 - 5 = -1$	$0 \times -1 = 0$
2	$10 - 5 = 5$	$15 - 5 = 10$	$5 \times 10 = 50$
3	$-7 - 5 = -12$	$-12 - 5 = -17$	$-12 \times -17 = 204$
4	$-2 - 5 = -7$	$2 - 5 = -3$	$-7 \times -3 = 21$
5	$19 - 5 = 14$	$16 - 5 = 11$	$14 \times 11 = 154$

Finally, we add the values in the right-hand column and divide by (n–1):

$$COV_{ij} = \frac{0 + 50 + 204 + 21 + 154}{5 - 1} = 107.25$$

In this case, the covariance is positive, telling us that these two rates of return tend to move together.

For simplicity of presentation, we have omitted the units from the above numbers. The units for the rates of return are percentages, and the unit for the final answer is percent-squared. As with the case of variances, no one really knows what a percent-squared is. Had we used decimal notation, the answer would have been .010725.

Correlation Coefficient

As indicated above, the covariance statistic is usually difficult to interpret because of the ambiguity of its units. A second problem involves interpretation of its magnitude. In the last example, we computed the covariance as 107.25 (percent-squared). The real question facing a user of this statistic is whether this is a "large" number. The answer is that it depends on the magnitudes of the standard deviations of the two securities. If the standard deviations are 30% or more, then this covariance is "small." If the standard deviations are about 11% each, then this covariance is a "huge" number.

correlation coefficient

The most common way to deal with these two deficiencies of the covariance as a measure of comovement is to use instead the statistic known as the correlation coefficient. The *correlation coefficient* of two securities, i and j, is usually denoted as ρ_{ij} (pronounced rho-i-j). It is defined as the covariance divided by the product of the standard deviations, as shown in equation 3–4.:

$$\rho_{ij} = COV_{ij} / \left(\sigma_i \times \sigma_j \right) \qquad \text{(Equation 3-4)}$$

Sometimes the covariance is defined as a function of the correlation coefficient. In this case, the formula is written as follows:

$$COV_{ij} = \sigma_i \times \sigma_j \times \rho_{ij} \qquad \text{(Equation 3-4a)}$$

If we plug equation 3-4a into equation 3-2, we obtain the following:

$$\sigma_p^2 = W_i^2 \sigma_i^2 + 2\,W_i\,W_j\,\sigma_i\,\sigma_j\,\rho_{ij} + W_j^2 \sigma_j^2 \qquad \text{(Equation 3-5)}$$

It is this version of the equation that is shown on the CFP Board's Formula Sheet provided to candidates during the CFP exam.

Note that although the unit of the numerator in equation 3–4 is percent-squared, the unit for the standard deviation is percent, so the unit of the product of two standard deviations is also percent-squared. Because the numerator and denominator have the same units, a correlation coefficient has no units–it is simply a unitless numerical statistic.

It can be mathematically proven that correlation coefficients will always fall between a maximum of +1 and a minimum of –1. Thus, it is sufficient by itself to indicate the degree of relationship between the returns on any two securities. If the prices of two securities change at the same time in the same direction and are always perfectly proportional, then ρ_{ij} = +1. If the prices change at the same time in the opposite direction and are always perfectly proportional, then ρ_{ij} = –1. If there is absolutely no relationship between the two returns, then ρ_{ij} = 0. Again, the range of possible values for ρ_{ij} is –1 ≤ ρ_{ij} ≤ +1.

Examples of correlation coefficients are shown in *Figure 3-1*. The axes of the graphs are R_i on the horizontal axis and R_j on the vertical axis. Each point on the graph represents one time period's rates of return for these two securities. Whenever investments i and j are both positive, the point is plotted in the upper right-hand quadrant. When they are simultaneously negative, the point is plotted in the lower left-hand quadrant. Investments that tend to vary together in this way will have most of their returns in these two quadrants. Most asset pairs exhibit this positive correlation.

Figure 3-1(A) shows a fairly strong positive relationship between returns on two securities, meaning that there is a strong tendency to move together. The correlation coefficient might be something like +.7. (B) shows a negative and weak relationship between the two sets of returns. Its correlation coefficient might be something like –.2. (C) and (D) both show examples of correlation coefficients of 0. (C) clearly indicates there is no relationship between the two returns. (D) shows a clear relationship, but also that this relationship is not linear; correlation coefficients measure only how closely two returns are to a linear relationship. Finally, (E) and (F) show perfect linear relationships—one positive (E) and one negative (F). Note that proportionality does not imply that returns are necessarily equal, only that they exhibit a constant relationship. If, for example, an asset j always has returns equal to two times those of asset i, the returns are exactly proportional and their correlation coefficient is +1. In this example, the points on the graph will form a line whose slope is 2. The following example illustrates the effects of a correlation coefficient on two-asset portfolios.

Example of a Two-Asset Portfolio's Risk

Returning to equations 3-1 and 3-5, consider a simple example. Suppose securities i and j have standard deviations of 10 and 15 percent, and a correlation coefficient of two-thirds (+.6667). We can form a portfolio composed half of i and half of j. If the expected returns of i and j are 9 and 11 percent, the portfolio's expected return is 10 percent. This is calculated as follows:

$$E(R_P) = .5(9\%) + .5(11\%) = 4.5\% + 5.5\% = 10\%$$

Similarly, the standard deviation of this 50-50 portfolio is 11.46 percent. That is, if we assume the following values ($\sigma_i = .10$, $\sigma_j = .15$, $W_i = .5$, $W_j = .5$, and $\rho_{ij} = .6667$) and insert these values into equation 3-5, we can compute the variance as follows:

$$\sigma_p^2 = (.5)^2 \times (.10)^2 + 2(.5)(.5)(.10)(.15)(.6667) + (.5)^2 \times (.15)^2$$
$$\sigma_p^2 = .0025 + .0050 + .005625 = .013125$$

If percentage notation is used in this calculation, the numbers are

$$\sigma_p^2 = (.5)^2 \times (10)^2 + 2(.5)(.5)(10)(15)(.6667) + (.5)^2 \times (15)^2$$
$$\sigma_p^2 = 25 + 50 + 56.25 = 131.25$$

Figure 3-1
Examples of Correlation Coefficients

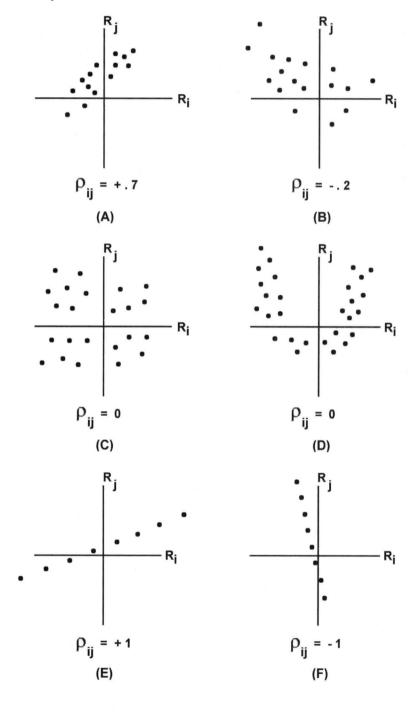

Since the standard deviation is the square root of the variance,

$$\sigma_p = \sqrt{.01325} = .1146, \text{ or } 11.46\%$$

In this case, diversifying the portfolio on a 50–50 basis has reduced the risk below the average of the two components' risks. The average risk of the two components is 12.5 percent ([10% + 15%] ÷ 2).

Three Special Cases

To fully understand the impact that the correlation coefficient has on a portfolio's standard deviation, let us consider three special cases. We will first look at what the combination of all possible portfolios looks like if we combine two assets whose correlation coefficient is +1. Then we will proceed to the more interesting case of what the possible combinations of two securities looks like if their correlation coefficient is -1. Finally, we will consider the case where the correlation coefficient is 0.

Before doing so, it is important to remember that regardless of the value of the correlation coefficient, the expected return on the combination of any two assets is always the weighted average of their expected returns, as defined in equation 3-1.

The general formula for the standard deviation of a two-asset portfolio is

$$\sigma_p = \sqrt{W_i^2\sigma_i^2 + 2W_iW_j\sigma_i\sigma_j\,\rho_{ij} + W_j^2\sigma_j^2} \qquad \text{(Equation 3-5a)}$$

The formula for the standard deviations for the three cases to be discussed is derived by plugging the values of 1, -1, and 0 into this formula for the value of the correlation coefficient.

Correlation Coefficient Equals +1

When the correlation is at its maximum value of +1, the standard deviation formula in equation 3-5a reduces to the following:

$$\sigma_p = W_i\sigma_i + W_j\sigma_j \qquad \text{(Equation 3-6)}$$

Equation 3–6 says that under this scenario, the standard deviation of any portfolio formed by combining assets i and j when the correlation coefficient is +1 is simply a weighted average of the individual standard deviations of assets i and j.

Let's look at a graph of all possible portfolio combinations of these two assets. In *Figure 3-2*, the horizontal axis measures the standard deviation of the portfolios, and the vertical axis measures the expected return. The point on the graph marked i represents the portfolio that has 100 percent invested in security i and 0 percent in security j, and the point on the graph marked j represents the portfolio that has 100 percent in security j and 0 percent in security i. To keep the graph simple, we will consider only combinations of holdings represented by nonnegative weights. One way to think of the graph is that we are plotting 101 different portfolios. The first is invested 100 percent in i and 0 percent in j, the second is invested 99 percent in i and 1 percent in j, and so on. The last portfolio is invested 0 percent in i and 100 percent in j.

Figure 3-2
Two-Security Portfolios: Correlation Coefficient Equals +1

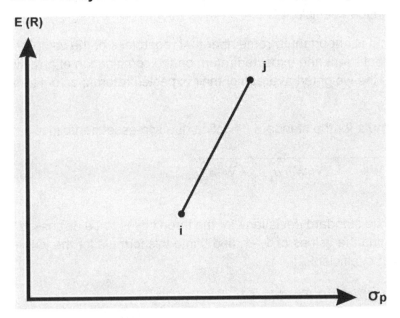

Because all of the portfolios' expected returns and standard deviations are linear functions of the two expected returns and the two standard deviations, the set of possible portfolios formed on our graph will be a straight line connecting the points corresponding to assets i and j. Note that in this scenario, the least risky portfolio is to put 100 percent of the portfolio into the less risky of the two assets.

Correlation Coefficient Equals -1

When the correlation is at its minimum value of -1, the standard deviation formula has two solutions:[23]

$$\sigma_p = \begin{cases} -W_i\sigma_i + W_j\sigma_j \\ \text{or} \\ W_i\sigma_i - W_j\sigma_j \end{cases} \qquad \text{(Equation 3-7)}$$

In *Figure 3-3*, this shows up as two lines. The first line starts at the portfolio that consists of only security i, and moves upward and to the left until in intersects with the vertical axis. The second line then continues moving upward but to the right, until it ends with the portfolio that consists only of asset j.

Figure 3-3
Two-Security Portfolios: Correlation Coefficient Equals –1

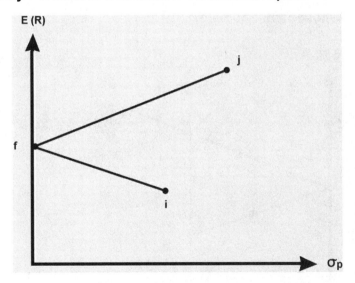

There are two extremely important things about this graph. The first is that when the correlation coefficient is -1, it is possible to create exactly one portfolio so that σ_p = 0. That is, there is one unique combination of the

---

23. There are two solutions because solving for the answer involves taking the square root of a positive number (for example, 4), and the answer could be either a positive number or a negative number (that is, 2 or -2).

two assets that is risk free.[24] On the graph, the point at which the two lines intersect on the vertical axis represents this portfolio. This one special portfolio is marked with the letter f (which stands for risk-free).

The second important point is that no rational person would choose to hold a portfolio on the lower line segment. The reason is that for any portfolio on the lower line segment, there is another portfolio on the upper line segment that has the same amount of risk (as measured by the portfolio's standard deviation) but a higher expected return.

This observation holds true even for the portfolio that consists of only asset i. If we draw a vertical line through asset i, this line will intersect the other line, and thus identify another portfolio that has the same amount of risk as asset i (as measured by its standard deviation) but more expected return, as shown by the dotted line in *Figure 3-4*. In *Figure 3-4*, this other portfolio is noted as P. Thus, no rational person would invest only in asset i, if he or she could hold portfolio P.

Figure 3-4
Portfolios Whose Risk Equals σ_i

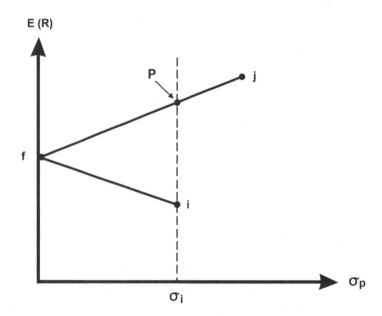

---

24. It is possible to solve for the weights for the risk-free portfolio, but the mathematical complexity of this calculation is beyond the scope of this book.

Another way to understand the inferiority of the lower line segment is to note that the risk-free portfolio has a higher expected return and less risk than any of the portfolios shown on the lower line segment. Thus, the risk-free asset can be described as dominating every portfolio on the lower line.

One portfolio is said to *dominate* another whenever one of the following three observations holds true:

- Portfolio X dominates portfolio Y if the two have equal expected returns and portfolio X has less risk (that is, a lower standard deviation).
- Portfolio X dominates portfolio Y if the two have equal standard deviations and portfolio X has a higher expected return.
- Portfolio X dominates portfolio Y if portfolio X has both a higher expected return and a lower standard deviation than portfolio Y.

It is important to remember that these graphs depict only what the possible portfolios that could be created by combining assets i and j look like in terms of the two fundamental characteristics of expected return and risk. We are not making any judgments as to which of these portfolios an investor should hold, other than identifying some that are dominated by others and thus should not be held. We will return shortly to the topic of which portfolio an investor should hold.

efficient frontier   Because rational investors would only want to choose among portfolios on the upper line segment, and would not want to hold any of the portfolios on the lower line segment, we give a special name to the upper line segment—the *efficient frontier*.

Correlation Coefficient Equals 0

The third special case occurs when the correlation coefficient equals 0. Although this may sound like an intriguing case, actually it is not. The locus of portfolios formed by these portfolios is shown in *Figure 3-5*. Note that unlike the first two cases, this figure is a curved line with its end points at securities i and j.

The formula for the standard deviation of any of the portfolios that can be created when ρ_{ij} equals zero is

$$\sigma_p = \sqrt{W_i^2 \sigma_i^2 + W_j^2 \sigma_j^2} \qquad \text{(Equation 3-8)}$$

It is not a particularly easy formula with which to work.

The two important features in the previous case (that is, when the correlation coefficient equals –1) still apply. First, there is one portfolio that has less risk than all of the other combinations. The difference here is that this portfolio still has some risk to it; it is not a risk-free portfolio. For this reason, we give this portfolio the name MVP, which stands for minimum variance portfolio.

Figure 3-5
Two-Security Portfolios: Correlation Coefficient Equal 0

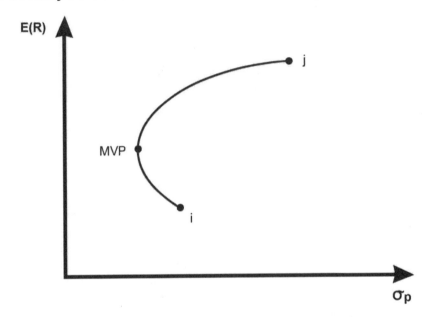

Second, the curved line can be divided into two segments. The upper segment, which starts at the MVP and moves upward to the portfolio that contains only asset j, is the efficient frontier. Investors would only be interested in portfolios on this segment. The lower segment, which starts just below the MVP and proceeds downward to the portfolio that contains only asset i, represents portfolios that no rational person would want to hold.

The relationship between the portfolios formed in all three cases ($\rho = +1$, $\rho = -1$, and $\rho = 0$) is illustrated in *Figure 3-6*.

All Other Cases

Having dealt with three special cases of two-asset portfolios (when the correlation coefficient is +1, –1, and 0), let us now consider all of the other potential values for the correlation coefficient. All correlations between the extreme values of –1 and +1 result in portfolios in the interior of the triangle shown in *Figure 3-6* that is bounded by asset i, asset j, and the risk-free combination of i and j that is marked as portfolio f.

As the correlation coefficient starts to fall from +1, the locus of possible portfolios moves away from the straight line connecting i and j, bowing out slightly to the left of this line. As the correlation coefficient continues to fall, the locus of combinations continues to move to the left. We have already identified the case when the correlation coefficient equals 0. As the correlation coefficient drops below 0, the line of possible combinations continues to move to the left, until eventually the correlation coefficient hits the minimum value of –1, and the locus of portfolios that can be created is the two lines forming two sides of the triangle.

Figure 3-6
Two-Security Portfolios: Correlation Coefficient Equals +1, 0, –1

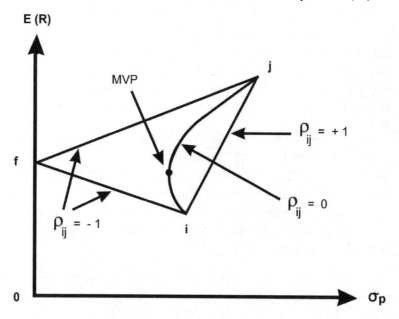

WHICH PORTFOLIO SHOULD BE HELD?

In the previous section we looked at the issue of what portfolios *could* be held when only two assets were available to choose from. The line describing the choices depends on the correlation coefficient for the rates of return of the two securities. Let us now look at the other side of the question—which portfolio *should* an investor hold?

The answer depends on what are known as indifference curves. Each investor has his or her own set of indifference curves. The derivation of an indifference curve starts with what are known as utility functions for wealth.

Utility Functions

utility functions   A *utility function* for wealth reflects the value (or utility) of incremental wealth to a particular individual. Although one of the basic principles of economics is that everyone derives pleasure from incremental wealth (that is, everyone is greedy), the value (or utility or pleasure) of incremental wealth is not equal among all of us. To illustrate this point, let's first consider the question, "Would you like an additional $1,000?" Everyone would answer yes to this question. Next, if you give someone the choice of $1,000 with perfect certainty, or a 50 percent chance of receiving $2,000 combined with a 50 percent chance of receiving nothing, nearly all people would choose the $1,000 with perfect certainty. The reason is that the thought of ending up with nothing when the person could have had $1,000 with perfect certainty creates more pain than the pleasure of possibly receiving the extra $1,000. Note that in this simple example, the expected value of the gamble is $1,000 ([.50 × $2,000] + [.50 × $0] = $1,000).

A person's utility for money can be described by what the probabilities of the gamble would have to be for him or her to prefer the gamble over the perfect certainty. For example, someone with a large tolerance for risk might be willing to take the gamble if the probability of receiving $2,000 were 55 percent versus a 45 percent chance of receiving nothing. A person with a small tolerance for risk might not take the gamble with anything less than a 90 percent chance of winning $2,000.

In the above example, some people might opt for the gamble even with probabilities at 50-50 because the excitement of the gamble may more than offset what they see as a relatively small bet. In such a case, utility for wealth could be better explored by changing the above example to $100,000 with perfect certainty versus a gamble of $200,000 or nothing, or even changing it to $1 million with perfect certainty versus a gamble of $2 million or nothing.

Indifference Curves

**indifference
curves**

Indifference curves are derived from utility functions. The derivation of indifference curves from a utility function is mathematically complex and will not be presented herein.

An *indifference curve* is a locus of portfolios among which an investor is indifferent. For example, an investor is indifferent between the following three portfolios if they all lie on the same indifference curve:

Portfolio	Expected Return	Standard Deviation
X	4.5%	5%
Y	5.5%	7%
Z	8.5%	9%

Each investor has an infinite number of indifference curves. Thus, a figure showing all possible indifference curves will be totally dark because it is filled with an infinite number of lines. Therefore, let us simplify the discussion by presenting three indifference curves in *Figure 3-7*. Each point on an indifference curve represents the same level of utility for the investor, hence the indifference between points on the curve. Each separate indifference curve represents a different level of utility, and because more utility is preferable to less, the investor will choose the highest level of utility available to him or her.

Indifference curves are traditionally thought of as curved lines that slope up as they move to the right. An investor's objective is to find and hold a portfolio on the highest possible indifference curve. The investor depicted in *Figure 3-7* is, by definition, indifferent between holding portfolios A and B because they lie on the same indifference curve. Portfolio C would be preferable to either A or B as it lies on a higher indifference curve, and D would be the most preferred of the four portfolios as it lies on the highest indifference curve. Notice that among the four portfolios, D has the lowest risk. Although portfolio C has a greater expected return than portfolio D, it has too much incremental risk for this investor, and thus lies on a lower indifference curve.

Figure 3-7
Indifference Curves

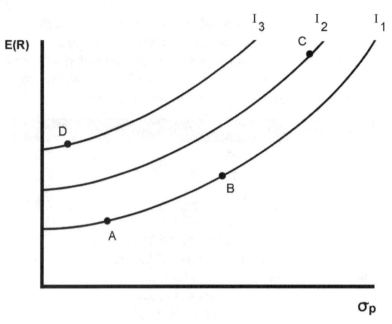

The indifference curves of different investors will vary as to slope and curvature. Let's consider four investors, Timid, Aggressive, Phobic, and Maniac, whose indifference curves are shown in *Figure 3-8* (A) to (D). Timid (A) is extremely conservative and will accept incremental risk only in exchange for a substantial increase in expected return. Hence, his indifference curves are steep. Aggressive doesn't mind risk, and will take on substantial incremental risk for only slight increases in expected return. Her indifference curves, shown in (B), are fairly flat. Phobic cares only about reducing risk. He will always choose the least risky portfolio, regardless of its expected return. His indifference curves are shown in (C) as vertical lines, with the more desirable indifference curves lying to the left. Finally, Maniac is completely oblivious to risk. He will take the portfolio with the highest expected return, regardless of its risk. His indifference curves are shown in (D) as horizontal lines with indifference curves becoming more desirable as we move upward. Of course, no one believes that any investors actually fall into the Phobic or Maniac categories. On the other hand, some investors can clearly be classified as Timid or Aggressive.

Figure 3-8
Indifference Curves for Different Investors

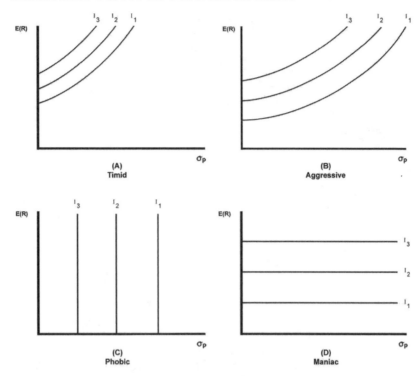

Estimating an investor's indifference curves is one of the most critical components of financial planning. Unfortunately, there is no known technique for mapping these curves for an individual. Nonetheless, in the last chapter of this book we will look at how a financial planner should consider indifference curves in practice.

Combining What Is Possible with What Is Desirable

We are now ready to look at the critical question of investment planning, which portfolio should an investor hold? The answer to this question requires no more than combining indifference curves and the efficient frontier. To illustrate, let's combine the indifference curves of *Figure 3–7* with a locus of possible portfolios. For example, suppose we are considering a portfolio of two securities, i and j, and the correlation coefficient is –1. The combination of indifference curves (what an investor would like to hold) with the locus of what can be held is shown in *Figure 3-9*.

Figure 3-9
Indifference Curves Combined with the Efficient Frontier When ρ = –1

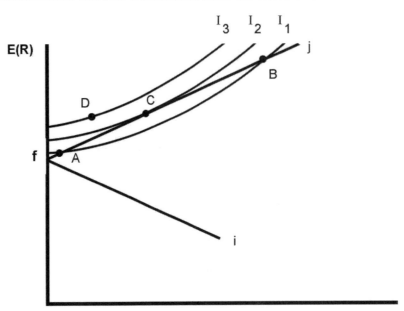

An investor could choose portfolio A or B and be indifferent between these, but would prefer to hold portfolio C because it lies on a higher indifference curve. The investor would love to hold portfolio D, or any other portfolio on I_3, but none of these portfolios are obtainable. *So in this case, the investor should hold portfolio C, because it is the one portfolio that lies on the highest possible indifference curve.*

Why Low Correlation Coefficients are Desirable

By now, the reader should appreciate that if a financial planner could control the correlation coefficient between any two assets, he or she would set it equal to -1. Most people think the reason is that it allows the existence of a risk-free portfolio (portfolio f in *Figure 3-9*). However, the real reason is that the lower a correlation coefficient is, the more it allows an investor to hold a portfolio on a higher indifference curve. Note that in *Figure 3-9*, even though the risk-free portfolio could be held, it is not the portfolio of choice.

THREE-ASSET PORTFOLIO RISK

Interesting things begin to happen when a third risky asset is added to our two existing risky assets. Let us look at the combination of possible portfolios that can be created when we combine securities i, j, and k. The expected return on this portfolio is the weighted average of the three expected returns, as shown in equation 3–9:

$$E\left(R_p\right) = W_i\left[E\left(R_i\right)\right] + W_j\left[E\left(R_j\right)\right] + W_k\left[E\left(R_k\right)\right]$$
(Equation 3-9)

The formula for the variance of any portfolio created from these three securities becomes much more complex than that for the two-security case. For simplicity, let us use the covariance notation again. The formula is

$$\sigma_p^2 = W_i^2\,\sigma_i^2 + W_j^2\,\sigma_j^2 + W_k^2\,\sigma_k^2 + 2\,W_i\,W_j\,COV_{ij} + 2\,W_i\,W_k\,COV_{ik} + 2\,W_j\,W_k\,COV_{jk}$$
(Equation 3-10)

Note that by adding one more security to the portfolio, we have added three terms to the computation of its variance.

To derive the graphical representation of the possible portfolios, we start by considering all of the possible portfolios that can be created on a pairwise basis. That is, we can identify all of the combinations of i and j, i and k, and j and k. There is no additional value in looking at the special extreme cases of the correlation coefficient, so let's consider only the case where the correlation coefficients are between +1 and –1. These three sets of combinations are shown in *Figure 3-10(A);* the figure is scalloped on the right and has a long smooth curve on the left.

The second step in identifying all of the possible portfolios that can be held is to consider combinations of all of the portfolios that can be created by combining any two of the two-security portfolios identified in step one. There will, of course, be an infinite number of combinations that can be created, and these are shown in *Figure 3-10(B).* This figure is tinted to denote a solid figure because of the infinite number of combinations. There are three key features to this infinite number of combinations First, there is still a minimum variance portfolio (shown as the MVP). Second, there is still an efficient frontier. In this case, the efficient frontier starts with the minimum variance portfolio and runs along the perimeter up to the portfolio that consists of holding only security k. A financial planner should consider holding only portfolios that lie on this efficient frontier. Third, the efficient frontier curve will most likely consist of various combinations of all three securities, even though in the figure, it appears that this line is made up of combinations of just i and k; note that the left line in *Figure 3-10(A)* shows the locus of portfolios that can be created with only combinations of i and k. The only way to move to the left of this line in *Figure 3-10(A)* is to add some of security j to the mix. Hence, the left side of the opportunity set in *Figure 3–10(B)* lies further to the left than the left side of *Figure 3-10(A)*.

N-ASSET PORTFOLIO RISK

We are now ready to consider what happens when n risky assets are combined into a portfolio. The expected return on an n-asset portfolio is simply the weighted average of the expected returns on the individual assets, shown as follows:

$$E\left(R_p\right) = \sum_{i=1}^{n} W_i \times E\left(R_i\right)$$

$$E\left(R_p\right) = W_1\left[E\left(R_1\right)\right] + W_2\left[E\left(R_2\right)\right] + \ldots + W_n\left[E\left(R_n\right)\right]$$

The variance and standard deviation for this n-asset portfolio are shown in equations 3-11 and 3-11a.

$$\sigma_p^2 = \sum_{i=1}^{n} W_i^2 \sigma_i^2 + \sum_{i=1}^{n}\sum_{\substack{j=1 \\ i \neq j}}^{n} W_i W_j COV_{ij} \qquad \text{(Equation 3-11)}$$

$$\sigma_p = \sqrt{\sum_{i=1}^{n} W_i^2 \sigma_i^2 + \sum_{i=1}^{n}\sum_{\substack{j=1 \\ 1 \neq j}}^{n} W_i W_j COV_{ij}} \qquad \text{(Equation 3-11a)}$$

Figure 3-10
Three-Asset Portfolios

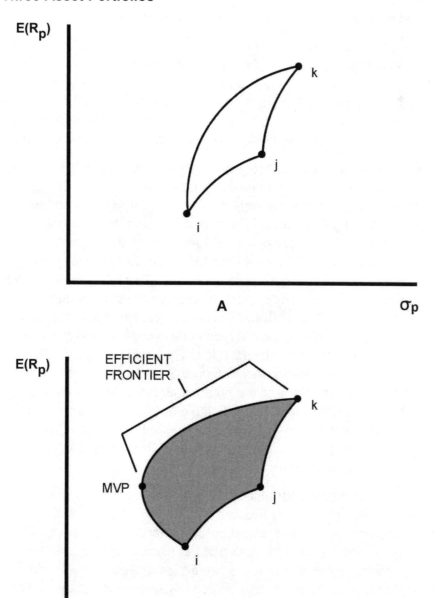

The first summation in equation 3-11 is the sum of the products of the square of each security's weight and its variance. The double summation is the sum of the products of each covariance with the weights of the associated two securities. Note that there are n x (n − 1)/2 covariance terms, and they incorporate the covariance of every asset with every other asset.

The n-asset risk formula demonstrates that the number of covariance terms increases substantially faster than the number of variance terms. This is because each time a new security is added to the portfolio, the variance formula must incorporate a covariance term between that security and each security already in the portfolio. The implication is that diversification benefits increase quickly due to the direct link between covariance and diversification.

Let us now consider the graphical representation of the locus of the various portfolios that can be held when there are n risky assets from which to choose, and n is a fairly large number. As with the three-asset portfolio, we start by considering all of the portfolios that can be held if we look at all possible combinations of two securities. *Figure 3-11(A)* shows this scenario for n = 10. There are a lot of lines, and not all of them have been drawn! Next, let's consider all of the combinations of pairs. This will give us a solid figure. However, looking at pairs of pairs means we are considering only portfolios that hold up to four of the 10 securities. We must continue this process by looking at all of the combinations that could be held, all the way up to all the combinations of all 10 securities. The resulting figure, shown in *Figure 3-11(B)*, looks similar to that in *Figure 3–10(B)*, except that there are more scallops to the right, and the figure is larger. Once again, the three most important features of *Figure 3-11(B)* are that it has a minimum variance portfolio (shown as MVP in the figure), it has an efficient frontier, and the portfolios along the efficient frontier tend to hold most if not all of the available securities.

If the world of investment opportunities were made up of only n risky assets, then financial planners would consider only portfolios that lie on this curved efficient frontier. The actual portfolio that a client should hold would be represented by the intersection of the efficient frontier with the highest possible indifference curve. Hence, different clients would hold different portfolios. Clients with a high degree of risk aversion (that is, clients whose indifference curves are quite steep) would hold portfolios with a lower expected return and lower risk. These portfolios would presumably consist of stocks considered relatively safe such as utilities and large, stable companies. An example of an optimal portfolio is identified as portfolio P_1 in *Figure 3-12(A)*. Aggressive clients (that is, clients whose indifference curves are relatively flat) would hold portfolios with a higher expected return, and higher risk. These portfolios would presumably consist of stocks considered aggressive. An example of an optimal portfolio is identified as portfolio P_2 in *Figure 3-12(B)*.

Figure 3-11
N-Asset Portfolios

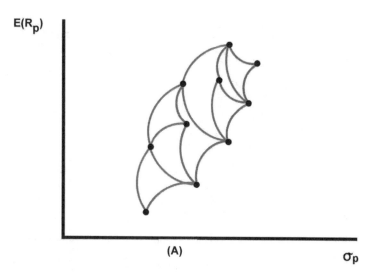

(A)

NOTE: As with the three-asset portfolio, we start by considering all of the portfolios that can be held if we look at all possible combinations of two securities, although all such combinations are not shown above. Figure 3-11(A) shows this scenario for N = 10.

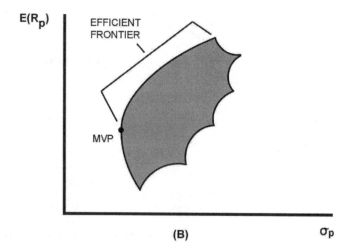

(B)

Figure 3-12
Identification of the Optimal Portfolio for a Risk-Averse Investor in a World of N Risky Assets

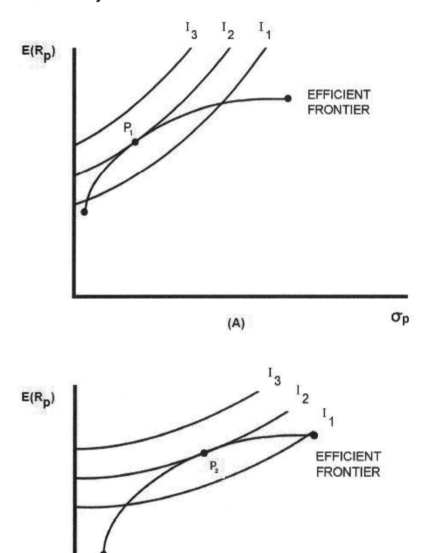

Estimating Variances and Covariances

Covariance and variance statistics can be estimated from past (historical) data. When possible, however, these estimates should also utilize future-oriented information. For example, the stock of a firm whose future environment is expected to be similar to its past is likely to behave much as its historically estimated variance statistic implies. On the other hand, some firms may have recently experienced a major change, such as a merger, new product introduction, different regulatory environment, or large capital infusion. The characteristics of the distribution of returns on these are likely to be quite different than before the change. If the change has a tendency to increase risk, historical risk estimates should be adjusted upward. Similarly, a change that decreases risk should lead to a downward adjustment in the historically based measure of risk.

Mean-Variance Optimization

In practice, financial planners would not actually construct their own efficient frontiers, and they certainly do not compute variances and standard deviations using equations 3-11 and 3-11a. Instead, there is substantial software available that perform these calculations, and even estimate the input values if that is desired. The concept used in constructing efficient frontiers is known as mean-variance optimization—that is, identifying the efficient frontier as the set of portfolios that provides the highest expected return for each given level of risk, or the least risky portfolio for any given level of expected return. It is then up to the financial planner to identify the most appropriate portfolio on the efficient frontier for his or her client.

A BETTER EFFICIENT FRONTIER

In the preceding section, we considered the implications for portfolio management if our choices consist only of n risky assets. In 1958, James Tobin extended the analysis by considering the effects of adding a risk-free asset. We will denote this risk-free asset with the symbol R_f. (Earlier in the chapter, we noted a risk-free asset that could be created by combining two risky securities whose correlation coefficient was -1 with the letter f. In this case, we are defining a new asset that is itself risk free.) In practical terms, many people think of the risk-free asset as a 90-day Treasury bill. Let us consider first the simple case of a two-asset portfolio, where one of the two assets is the risk-free asset and the other asset is a risky asset ("i"). The combination of all of the portfolios that can be created by combining these two assets is shown in *Figure 3-13(A)*.

Figure 3-13
Combinations of the Risk-Free Asset and a Risky Asset

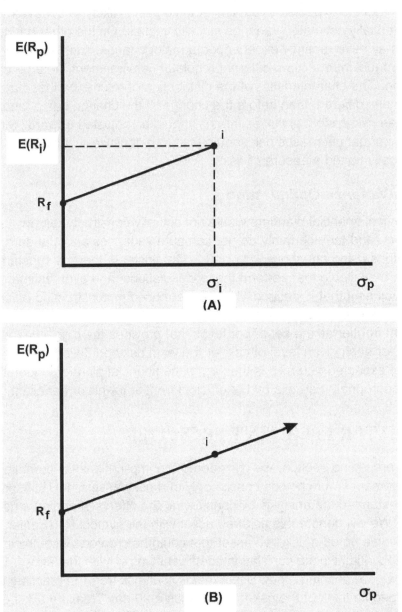

The locus of portfolios is a straight line, running from the risk-free asset located on the vertical axis (by definition the standard deviation of returns for the risk-free asset is 0) to the risky asset i. The reason it is a straight line is that the covariance between any asset's return and the return of the risk-free asset is 0.

By itself, this is not a particularly interesting result, but it has significant implications. Let's start by considering negative weights. When one of the assets from which we can choose is the risk-free asset, a negative weight simply means borrowing money at the risk-free rate rather than investing it at the risk-free rate. The money that is borrowed is used to buy more of the risky asset, because those are the only two assets in the portfolio.

EXAMPLE

Assume a risk-free asset whose rate of return is 5 percent and a risky asset i whose expected rate of return and standard deviation of return are 10 percent and 8 percent. Let us consider two portfolios. One is a "saving" or "lending" portfolio, in which a person puts 50 percent of his portfolio in the risk-free asset and the other 50 percent in the risky asset. It is a lending portfolio because the investor is lending his money to the issuer of the risk-free asset. The other is a "borrowing" portfolio in which the investor borrows an amount equal to 50 percent of his assets and uses the loan to buy more of the risky asset. The weights of the lending portfolio are .50 and .50. The weights for the borrowing portfolio are -.50 and 1.50. The expected returns and standard deviations of the two portfolios are computed using equations 3-1 and 3-2 as follows:

Saving Portfolio

$$E(R_p) = (.50 \times 5\%) + (.50 \times 10\%) = 7.5\%$$

$$\sigma_p^2 = (.50^2 \times .00^2) + (2 \times .50 \times .50 \times .00^2) + (.50^2 \times .08^2)$$

$$= .0016$$
$$\sigma_p = \sqrt{.0016} = .04, \text{ or } 4\%$$

Borrowing Portfolio

$$E(R_p) = (-.50 \times 5\%) + (1.50 \times 10\%) = 12.5\%$$

$$\sigma_p^2 = (-.50^2 \times .00^2) + (2 \times [-.50] \times 1.50 \times .00^2) + (1.50^2 \times .08^2) = .0144$$
$$\sigma_p = \sqrt{.0144} = .12, \text{ or } 12\%$$

Note that in the above example, the expected return on the borrowing portfolio is greater than the rate of return on just the risky asset. This is the benefit of borrowing money at a 5 percent rate and investing it at an expected rate of return of 10 percent. This is the same phenomenon discussed in the previous chapter when we looked at the concept of buying on margin. Note also that the standard deviation of the borrowing portfolio is substantially larger than the standard deviation of the risky asset by itself. In a graphical representation, the existence of lending portfolios means that the line shown in *Figure 3-13(A)* can be extended past asset i. In theory, if there are no limits on the amount the investor could borrow, the extension is unlimited, as shown in *Figure 3-13(B)*.

Let's now consider what happens when a risk-free asset is added to a world of n risky assets. We have already seen that in a world of n risky assets, the only relevant portfolios are those on the efficient frontier. When the opportunity is available to divide assets between any one portfolio on the efficient frontier and the risk-free asset, then the locus of possible portfolios of these two assets is a straight line connecting those two assets. For example, in *Figure 3-14*, the risk-free asset (denoted by R_f) can be combined with the risky portfolio A. The line connecting these two points represents all the portfolios that can be formed by this combination.

Figure 3-14
Efficient Frontier with Lending and Borrowing at the Risk-Free Rate

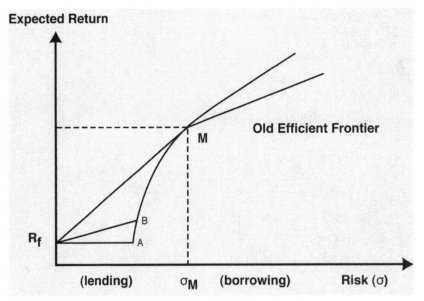

However, we can also combine the risk-free asset with portfolio B. Again, the combination of portfolios created falls on the line R_fB. Note, however, that every portfolio on R_fA is dominated by at least one portfolio on line R_fB.

Hence, no rational investor would hold portfolio A or any combination of R_f and A if he or she could hold any combination of R_f and B.

Note that the combination of R_f and M will dominate all portfolios to the left of M. The line R_fM can be extended beyond M if borrowing at the risk-free rate is allowed and the borrowed funds are then invested in further shares of portfolio M. Portfolios on this extension of the R_fM line will also clearly dominate any of the portfolios on the efficient frontier past the portfolio M. In other words, the addition of a risk-free asset results in a new efficient frontier that consists of a straight line beginning at R_f and passing through portfolio M.

If we now impose an investor's indifference curves on this new efficient frontier, as shown in *Figure 3-15*, we see that a conservative investor (represented by indifference curves I_1 to I_3) will hold portfolio P_1, a combination of portfolio M and the risk-free asset, and an aggressive investor (represented by indifference curves I_4 to I_6) would hold portfolio P_2, also a combination of the risk-free asset and portfolio M.

Figure 3-15
Indifference Curves with Extended Efficient Frontier

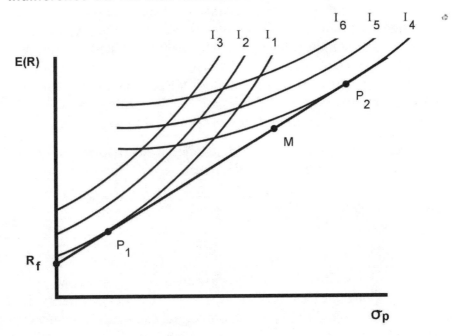

This is an incredible result! It means that M will now be the only risky asset that rational investors will hold. Investors with varying degrees of risk tolerance will attain their desired risk levels by adjusting the relative proportions of R_f and M.

separation theorem   Tobin's insight simplified portfolio choice to selecting the relative proportions of the risk-free asset and a single risky portfolio. This is the essence of the *separation theorem*—that an investor's risk preferences do not affect his or her choice of risky assets, because M is the only rational choice. This was a valuable theoretical innovation, but practical problems remained. The primary one was that the optimum risky portfolio, M, was not specified.

The Capital Market Line

market portfolio   As people considered the nature of portfolio M, it became clear that it could represent only one portfolio, the market portfolio. The *market portfolio* is the portfolio of all assets, with the weight of each based on its market value. As a practical matter, the market portfolio is an unfathomable entity, but it has interesting implications for managing portfolios. The reason that portfolio M must be the market portfolio is that, as noted before, in this model everyone would hold some combination of M and the risk-free asset—nothing more, nothing less. Furthermore, as all assets are owned by someone (there are no ownerless assets), the only way to reconcile these two statements is if M represents the market portfolio. In practice, many people think of the Standard & Poor's 500 Index as a surrogate for the market portfolio. However, it is important to bear in mind that this index covers a small percentage of domestic stocks.

By recognizing portfolio M as the market portfolio, we can specify the equation for the new efficient frontier as follows:

$$E\left(R_p\right) = R_f + \sigma_p \left(\frac{E\left(R_M\right) - R_f}{\sigma_M} \right)$$

(Equation 3-12)

capital market line   This equation is called the *capital market line (CML)*. It is on the CFP Board's Formula Sheet, although on that sheet the lowercase r is used rather than the more formal expectation notation shown above. In other words, the formula sheet equation is stated as follows:

$$R_p = r_f + \sigma_p \left(r_m - r_f\right) / \sigma_m$$

(Equation 3-12a)

The bracketed term in equation 3-12 (repeated below) is the slope of the capital market line:

$$\text{Slope}_{\text{CML}} = \frac{E\left(R_M\right) - R_f}{\sigma_M}$$

This slope represents the market price of risk in our financial markets. It signifies the equilibrium trade-off between risk and return at any point in time. Keep in mind that this slope changes whenever any of the three parameters that define it change.

Figure 3-16 illustrates the capital market line. The CML tells us one thing only-the expected return on a fully diversified portfolio. Remember, the old efficient frontier (made up of n risky assets) constituted the most efficient portfolios that could be constructed. This means they offered the maximum possible expected return for any given level of risk. The new efficient frontier dominates the old efficient frontier. Thus, a portfolio that is fully and effectively diversified should fall somewhere along the CML. Individual securities and inefficient portfolios (that is, those lacking adequate diversification) will fall underneath the CML.

Put another way, we cannot use the CML to evaluate the performance of a single stock. Nor can we use the CML to evaluate the performance of a portfolio that lacks full diversification.

Figure 3-16
Capital Market Line

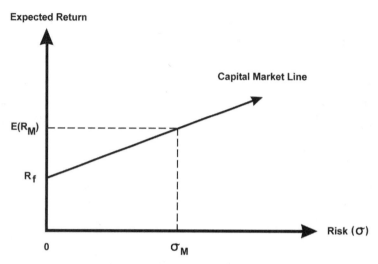

The Capital Asset Pricing Model

capital asset pricing model (CAPM)   William F. Sharpe approached the unknown risky portfolio problem by postulating that returns are related through a common relationship with a basic underlying factor. The foundation of his *capital asset pricing model (CAPM)* begins with six assumptions. These range from everyone having the same expectations about the risk and return of assets, to a market that consists of all assets, to the assumption that all investments consist of only publicly traded securities (for example, there are no private corporations). Many of these assumptions have been relaxed in subsequent research without unduly altering the implications of Sharpe's conclusions.

Proceeding from these assumptions, Sharpe's model enters familiar territory by constructing an efficient frontier for risky assets. Introduction of a risk-free asset leads to a new efficient frontier (a straight line) made up of varying proportions of the risk-free asset and the market portfolio.

Sharpe then posed the question of what would determine the expected return on an individual asset.

beta   Sharpe proved that the expected return was a function of how the individual asset affected the variability of a portfolio's returns. The greater the contribution to a portfolio's variability, the greater the expected return should be. An asset's contribution to a portfolio's variability could then be measured by a term known as the *beta* coefficient (or beta statistic). It can be computed as follows:

$$\beta_i = \frac{COV_{iM}}{\sigma_M^2}$$
(Equation 3-13)

where β_i = market risk of asset i

COV_{iM} = covariance between the returns of asset i and the returns of the market portfolio

σ_M^2 = variance of the market portfolio

There is an alternative method to compute the beta coefficient. In equation 3–4, we noted that the correlation coefficient between the returns of any two assets equals their covariance divided by the product of their standard deviations. Thus, if one of those two assets is the market portfolio, then we can say that

$$\rho_{iM} = COV_{iM} \div (\sigma_i \sigma_M)$$
(Equation 3-13a)

If we solve this equation for the covariance, we obtain

$$COV_{iM} = \rho_{iM} \times (\sigma_i \sigma_M)$$
(Equation 3-13b)

Next, if we substitute equation 3-13b into equation 3-13, we obtain

$$\beta_i = \frac{\rho_{iM} \times (\sigma_i \sigma_M)}{\sigma_M^2}$$

This simplifies to

$$\beta_i = (\rho_{iM} \times \sigma_i) / \sigma_M$$
(Equation 3-13c)

Both equations 3-13 and 3-13c are on CFP Board Formula Sheet.

Based on beta as a measure of risk, Sharpe was able to derive the expected return on any security as follows:

$$E\left(R_i\right) = R_f + \beta_i\left[E\left(R_M\right) - R_f\right]$$

(Equation 3-14)

This equation is also on the CFP Board's Formula Sheet except that it uses a lowercase r to represent expected return and places the beta coefficient as the second term of the product. Hence, it is stated as follows:

$$r_i = r_f + \beta_i\left(r_m - r_f\right)$$

(Equation 3-14a)

security market line (SML)

The graph of the CAPM, known as the *security market line (SML)*, is shown in *Figure 3-17*.

Note that this figure differs from nearly every other figure in this chapter in two ways. First, the vertical axis represents the rate of return on a security i, rather than a portfolio P. Second, the horizontal axis measures risk using β_i rather than σ_i. The SML crosses the $E(R_i)$ axis at R_f and has a slope of $[E(R_M) - R_f]$. There is one readily identifiable portfolio on the SML—the market portfolio. The market portfolio, by definition, has a beta coefficient equal to 1 and an expected return equal to $E(R_M)$.

Figure 3-17
CAPM—The Security Market Line

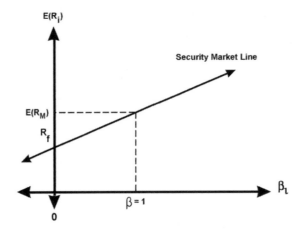

Beta and Expected Return

For a specified beta, risk-free rate, and projected market return, the CAPM defines the expected rate of return of an asset in equilibrium.

EXAMPLE 1

If $\beta_i = 1.3$, $R_f = 5.0\%$ and $E(R_M) = 10.0$ percent, CAPM yields the following:

$$
\begin{aligned}
E(R_i) &= 5.0\% + 1.3(10.0\%\text{-}5.0\%) \\
&= 5.0\% + 1.3(5.0\%) \\
&= 5.0\% + 6.5\% \\
&= 11.5\%
\end{aligned}
$$

Thus, a stock with a beta of 1.3 is expected to return 11.5 percent when the risk-free rate is 5 percent and the market portfolio's return is expected to be 10 percent.

EXAMPLE 2

The expected return on a security is 8 percent, the expected return on the market portfolio is 10 percent, and the risk-free rate is 4 percent. What is the beta for this security?

Answer:

$$
\begin{aligned}
8\% &= 4\% + \beta(10\% - 4\%) \\
8\% - 4\% &= \beta \times 6\% \\
4\% \div 6\% &= .67 = \beta
\end{aligned}
$$

Note that the SML extends to the left of the $E(R_i)$ axis. Since betas are based on the covariance between the asset and market portfolio, they can, in theory, have negative values. Simply put, any asset whose beta is negative will have an expected return lower than the risk-free rate of return. If the beta has a large enough negative value, the expected return will actually be negative! Investors would be willing to hold such assets because the negative betas indicate that these assets will do well when the rest of the market is collapsing. Think of a negative-beta asset as analogous to term life insurance. If you live, the payment of the premiums was a waste of money, but if you die, there is a big payoff (for your beneficiary).

Expected Asset Returns for Different Betas and Market Returns		
Range	Expected Asset Return for Positive Market Return	Expected Asset Return for Negative Market Return
$\beta > 1$	Above market	Below market
$\beta = 1$	Market	Market
$0 < \beta < 1$	Below market	Above market
$\beta = 0$	Risk-free rate	Risk-free rate
$\beta < 0$	Less than risk-free rate, or even negative	Positive

As can be seen in *Figure 3-17* and equation 3-14, return is a linear function of risk. Investors who desire greater expected return must accept greater risk as measured by beta. Correspondingly, investors who desire less risk must accept lower expected returns. In short, an investor's risk preferences determine his or her preferred beta, which in turn determines the expected returns.

The CAPM equation has several important implications. First, if we know the expected rate of return on the market and the risk-free rate, then we can estimate expected returns for all assets once we know their respective betas. Second, an asset's expected return is related only to its market risk exposure, represented by beta. Alternatively, *nonmarket risk* (business and all other types of risk) is not rewarded with higher expected returns because it can be diversified away.

As noted before, the beta coefficient for the market portfolio is 1. This is easy to see if in equation 3-13 we substitute M for i. The numerator of the beta coefficient then becomes the covariance of the market portfolio with itself. The covariance of any security's return with itself is simply its variance. Hence, equation 3-13 reduces to the variance of M divided by the variance of M, or 1.

An important mathematical property of the beta coefficient is that the beta coefficient of a portfolio is simply the weighted average of the beta coefficients of the securities in the portfolio where the weights are based on market values. In equation form:

$$\beta_p = \sum_{i=1}^{N} W_i \times \beta_i$$

(Equation 3-15)

$$\beta_i = W_1 \times \beta_1 + W_2 \times \beta_2 + \ldots + W_N \times \beta_N$$

where N = number of securities in the portfolio

EXAMPLE

A portfolio has three securities in it, with the following market values and betas. What is the portfolio beta?

Security	Market Value	Beta
X	$20 million	1.2
Y	$30 million	1.8
Z	$50 million	-.3

The total market value of the portfolio is $100 million. Hence, the market weights are .20, .30, and .50. The portfolio beta is

$$\beta_p = (.20 \times 1.2) + (.30 \times 1.8) + (.50 \times [-.3]) = .63$$

The CAPM is much more broadly used than the CML. The reason is that it defines the expected rate of return on any security or any portfolio, regardless of whether that portfolio is fully diversified.

The Index Model

Since its unveiling in the 1960s, the applicability of the CAPM has been extended by finding ways to relax Sharpe's original assumptions. The model has thereby gained enough versatility that it can be applied in a great variety of situations. Its utility has garnered it wide acceptance among academics and within the financial industry.

Any uses of the CAPM require knowledge of beta. Unfortunately, there is nothing in the theory that indicates the exact nature of the data that should be used to compute beta. There is no theory to indicate whether daily, weekly, monthly, quarterly, or even annual observations should be used in computing beta. There is nothing in theory to indicate how many observations should be used.

Implicit in the CAPM is the assumption that the beta of a security is either stable (thus allowing us to calculate it from historical returns) or predictable. Alas, these assumption are weak at best. There is no question that the beta of any asset changes over time as the nature of the company represented by the stock changes, and as the nature of our economy changes. The real issue is, how fast do betas change? Early research on the subject showed that if too few observations are used, there is not enough data to provide a good estimate of beta. If too many observations are used, it is likely that they represent different values of beta, as the beta will change over time. In practice, most computations of beta are based on anywhere from 24 to 60 monthly rates of return data, because most people find this reasonable.

index model
characteristic line

Betas are normally calculated by using the statistical technique of regressing an asset's excess returns against the market's excess returns. This is called the *index model*, and the regression line is called the *characteristic line*. It is expressed as

$$R_i = \alpha_i + \beta_i R_M + \varepsilon_i$$ (Equation 3-16)

where R_i =   excess return to asset i

R_M =   excess return to the market in the same period

α_i =   y-intercept value

β_i =   slope of the line

ε_i =   random error term (pronounced "eta")

excess return

Excess return is defined as the actual return less the risk-free rate of return.

As mentioned earlier, a proxy (such as the S&P 500) is used in place of the theoretical market portfolio. The process begins by pairing returns by time (R_{Mt}, R_{it}) where t is the time period. (See *Figure 3-18.*)

Figure 3-18
Characteristic Line

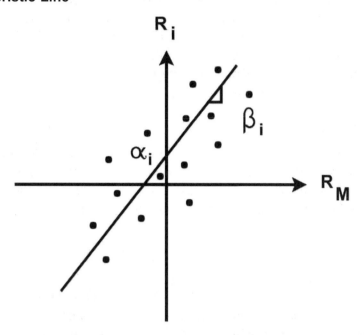

The regression calculations find a regression line that passes through the point that represents the mean market return and the mean asset return $(\bar{R}_M, \bar{R}_i)$ that also minimizes the sum of the squared, vertical distances from data points to the line, which are the error terms. By minimizing the sum of these squared error terms, the process finds the best-fitting line. Beta is the slope of the regression line and alpha (α_i) its intercept with the vertical axis. The market model can be used to estimate asset returns as a function of the market return.

Coefficient of Determination

coefficient of determination
A statistic that is useful in conjunction with beta is the *coefficient of determination (R^2)*. R^2 is a measure of how well the regression line fits the data. R^2 is a percentage and therefore ranges from 0 to 1 (that is, 0 to 100 percent). In relation to betas, R^2 can be interpreted as the percentage of a stock's variability in return that can be attributed to the variability in the market's return. It is therefore a measure of "relatedness." When there is only one independent variable, as is the case here, the R^2 equals the square of the correlation coefficient between these two variables.

In simple regressions, such as the characteristic line, R^2 equals the square of the correlation coefficient between the dependent variable (in this case, the returns on the particular stock) and the independent variable (in this case, the returns on the market). When R^2 is close to 1, the beta should be a highly reliable estimate of how a particular stock will perform relative to the market. When R^2 is close to 0, the beta would be expected to have relatively little predictive value.

Market Risk and Nonmarket Risk

The market model provides a convenient vehicle to demonstrate one additional aspect of market risk. If we compute the variance of both sides of equation 3-16, as shown in equation 3-17, we see that the total risk of a security (σ_i^2) can be broken down into two components:[25]

$$\sigma_i^2 = (\beta_i^2 \sigma_M^2) + \sigma_\varepsilon^2 \qquad \text{(Equation 3-17)}$$

nonmarket risk   The first component is the product of the square of the beta and the variance of the market portfolio. This product is referred to as market risk. The second term measures *nonmarket risk*, and is unique for each security.

No matter how many securities a person holds, there is exposure to market risk. Beta is sometimes referred to as an index of market risk. The larger the value of beta, the greater the contribution of market risk to the total risk of a security. Remember, the variance of the market portfolio is the same for all securities when we break down total risk into its two components.

Nonmarket risk can be nearly eliminated if the investor holds a large enough portfolio. Market risk can never be eliminated, however, no matter how large a portfolio an investor owns (except, of course, if it is invested exclusively in the risk-free asset). The impact of market risk can be magnified or diminished by adjustments in the portfolio's beta. In theory, if the portfolio beta is 0, then market risk can be eliminated. As a practical matter, nearly all betas are between 0 and 2, and the largest percentage are between 0.5 and 1.5. Assembling a well-diversified, zero-beta portfolio of stocks, therefore, is virtually impossible in practice.

---

25. As with many of the other statistics presented herein, the derivation of equation 3–17 involves mathematical complexities beyond the scope of this presentation.

Errors in Betas

Although the CAPM provides a wonderful model for considering and analyzing securities, the financial planner should be aware that the actual application of the model is always problematic because betas can only be estimated–they are not knowable. A large number of advisory services are happy to sell their beta estimates to investors and portfolio managers. As discussed above, betas are generally estimated by regressing historical security returns on market returns. Investors who use these beta estimates as a guide to sensitivity to market moves need to understand why these estimates are not as precise as we would like.

Individual beta estimates have been found in several different tests to be relatively unreliable. Portfolio betas, in contrast, appear to be much more stable. One of the recurring problems with estimates of betas for individual securities is that there is a tendency to regress toward the mean. This indicates that observations that are above a mean are more likely to be lower in the next period, and observations that are below a mean are more likely to be higher in the next period.[26] For example, in baseball, individual high and low first-month batting averages generally move toward the overall all-player average. Note, however, that this phenomenon describes the behavior of extreme values, not the entire population. Thus, batting averages and betas near the mean tend to move randomly away from the mean with sufficient frequency to repopulate the extremes as the prior-period extremes move in. Several adjustment techniques have been developed over the years to take account of the regression-toward-the-mean phenomenon.

E. Fama and K. French provided the most recent significant attack on the use of betas in an article in 1992.[27] They found evidence that the CAPM does not explain why returns of different types of risky stocks differ, and they argued that beta is not sufficient to describe the risk-return relationship in markets. They examined securities traded on the major U.S. stock exchanges between 1963 and 1990 and concluded that better predictors of stock returns were the size of the firm and the ratio of the firm's book value to its market value. Critics of the Fama-French results argue that investors may simply have a preference for large capitalization firms not explained by economic rationality

---

26. For a more formal discussion of this point, see en.wikipedia.org/wiki/Regression_toward_the_ mean or www.mtsu.edu/~dkfuller/psy628/notes/bivariatereg.pdf.

27. E. Fama and K. French, "The Cross-Section of Expected Stock Returns,"*Journal of Finance*, June 1992, pp. 427-465.

or that investors may not have sufficient capital to diversify risk completely, so that systematic risk may not fully explain market returns.

The Market Index Problem

The market index used in the beta estimating equation is one source of error in the estimation process. The theoretical model assumes that betas are estimated with an index that reflects all capital assets in proportion to their relative contribution to investor wealth. In practice, such indices as the S&P 500 Index or the NYSE composite are usually employed. The NYSE index is broader than the S&P 500, although the latter includes securities from several exchanges.

The acceptability of these major indices as surrogates for the market portfolio declines as the relevant universe expands progressively to include U.S. debt securities, real estate, futures contracts, foreign securities, collectibles, precious metals, and so on. Even though the U.S. equity market influences the returns on many of these assets, correlations are relatively weak for most assets and essentially zero for others. Investments other than U.S. stocks (especially home ownership) represent an appreciable part of most investors' total wealth. Accordingly, using only U.S. stocks in the market index may result in bias in the resulting beta estimates.

Multifactor Models

arbitrage pricing theory (APT)

The advent of the CAPM revolutionized financial theory, but many researchers were not convinced that this single-index model sufficiently explained the variability of asset returns. This led to the development of multifactor models, including the *arbitrage pricing theory (APT)* model. A multifactor model takes the form:

$$E\left(R_i\right) = a_i + b_{i1} F_1 + b_{i2} F_2 + \ldots + b_{iN} F_N \qquad \text{(Equation 3-18)}$$

where a_i = the rate of return on security i if all of the factors equaled zero

b_{ij} = security i's sensitivity to factor j

F_j = the value of factor j

N = relevant number of factors

In this equation, F_1 to F_N are the relevant economic factors influencing R_i. Examples of economic variables that serve as factors include the growth rate of the gross domestic product, the inflation rate, and the spread between short-term and long-term interest rates. For example, if F_2 represents the price of oil, then for an oil exploration company, β_{i2} might be quite large.

However, for a bakery, β_{i2} might be virtually 0.

The APT model then takes this concept a step further to postulate that

$$r_i = E(r_i) + b_{i1}f_1 + b_{i2}f_2 + \ldots + b_{iN}f_N \qquad \text{(Equation 3-19)}$$

where r_i = the actual rate of return on security i

$E(r_i)$ = the expected rate of return if all of the factors turned out to equal their expected values

b_{ij} = security i's sensitivity to factor j

f_j = the difference between the actual value of factor j and its expected value

This model is derived from the economic principle that perfect substitutes must have the same price, or arbitrage profits will be available to traders. Through the action of arbitrage, all prices of financial assets remain in equilibrium.

EXAMPLE

The XYZ company has an expected return of 8 percent, a gross domestic product (GDP) beta of .9, and a 90-day Treasury-bill interest rate beta of 1.2. Assume that the GDP had been expected to increase at the rate of 3 percent, and the interest rate is currently 4 percent. In the morning news, an announcement is made that the GDP is now expected to grow at a 2 percent rate, and that the Treasury bill rate has risen to 5 percent. The actual return on this company's stock should be

$$r_{XYZ} = 8\% + (.9 \times -1\%) + (1.2 \times 1\%) = 8.3\%$$

A significant problem with the APT model is that the theory identifies no specific factors. The theory only hypothesizes that these factors exist and are relevant. Moreover, empirical investigation for relevant factors has been inconclusive. Also, as with the CAPM, the theory provides no way to verify the true value of the betas. The APT model has offsetting positive attributes, such as not requiring the use of a market portfolio and allowing for different expectations of market participants.

The important question in comparing asset pricing models is: Does the greater complexity of the multifactor models add appreciably to our understanding of markets and our ability to explain real-world prices? The initial tests on the APT failed to demonstrate clear superiority over the CAPM, and subsequent research has resulted in mixed assessments. Nonetheless, the APT model continues to generate much interest.

IMPACT OF MODERN PORTFOLIO THEORY

After reading the preceding material in this chapter, a practitioner may be prone to say, "That's nice, but what impact does this theory have on how I do business?"[28] There are several reasons why it is important to understand modern portfolio theory.

The Prudent Man and Prudent Investor Rules

Uniform Principal and Income Act

prudent man rule

One area in which modern portfolio theory has had a significant effect is in the management of trusts. The original law affecting the management of trust assets is the *Uniform Principal and Income Act* of 1931. At that time, it laid out the principle known as the *prudent man rule*. This rule stated that each security or asset in a trust must meet this standard: It must be one in which a prudent man who wanted first and foremost to ensure the preservation of his assets would invest. The significance of the terminology is that the rule applied to each holding separately. Hence, even if there were 100 separate investments in a trust account and 99 of them performed well, the trustee could be held at fault if the 100th asset did not perform well. This legal position had the effect of almost mandating that trustees invest only in the most conservative of investments. This meant that rates of return on such portfolios were low, reflecting the conservative nature of these investments.

Many trusts have two beneficiaries: the income beneficiary who would receive income each year and the remainder beneficiary who receives the principal of the trust at its termination. The best interest of the income beneficiary is maximization of current income. The best interest of the

---

28. This section draws on material presented in "The TRU Debate: The Pros and Cons of Using Total Return Unitrusts," by Gerard J. Monchek, JD, LLM, *Journal of Financial Service Professionals*, vol. 57, no. 3 (May 2003), pp. 41–53.

remainder beneficiary is growth in the value of the assets. The problem is that the best interests of both parties cannot be served simultaneously.

prudent investor This revision now says that the trustee must act as a prudent investor, rather than a prudent man. The difference is that a *prudent investor* can invest using the principles of modern portfolio theory. Hence, what counts now is the total return on the portfolio, which is both income and price appreciation, and not the return on each holding separately. Trustees are allowed to recognize that some assets have low correlation coefficients with other assets, and so holding them in tandem may produce reasonable returns at substantially less risk.

Basic Framework

Portfolio theory is an elegant simplification of complex phenomena. The theory's defenders can make useful explanations of a great deal of stock market behavior, and a huge amount of literature (and correspondingly huge commitment of time, money, and reputations) backs up the theory. A cynic might say that portfolio theory proponents would prefer to preserve as much of that investment as they reasonably can.

The theory offers a useful point of departure. Economists, for example, need to understand the model of pure competition to better understand the economy, even though there are no markets that are perfectly competitive. Similarly, most physicists are quite familiar with the properties of a frictionless world. Such world gives us models that yield interesting insights and testable predictions even though a frictionless world does not exist. A particular nonidealized effect may be observed in the difference between the model forecast and the actual event (ex post forecast analysis) and thereby yield useful information for the next (ex ante) forecast period. Remember, for rational investment, forecasting is unavoidable. Therefore, finance theorists and empiricists are expected to know the implications of portfolio theory even if the real world often behaves differently.

Keep in mind that we still have no better alternative model for the relationship between risk and expected return. If we do not use the portfolio theory framework to consider and analyze security returns, then the investment world becomes nothing but a huge collection of meaningless observations. One of the original reasons for developing portfolio theory, especially the CAPM, was to evaluate the risk-adjusted past performance of professional portfolio managers. Prior to the CAPM approach, there was no formal way to evaluate the performance of a portfolio of securities relative to the risks taken to earn those returns. Thus, the CAPM approach may be best suited to evaluate past performance, rather than as a predictive model. In this respect, the model serves a useful purpose. Until a demonstrably superior theory is devised, therefore, the standard form of portfolio theory presented in this chapter will continue to provide the foundation for the study of investments.

REVIEW OF LEARNING OBJECTIVES

1. The combination of two risky assets can be less risky than either held separately because at times, their prices will move in opposite directions, thus reducing the variability of the portfolio's rate of return. The expected return and variance on a two-asset portfolio are computed as

$$E\left(R_p\right) = W_i\left[E\left(R_i\right)\right] + W_j\left[E\left(R_j\right)\right]$$

(Equation 3-1)

and

$$\sigma_p^2 = W_i^2\,\sigma_i^2 + 2\,W_i\,W_j\,COV_{ij} + W_j^2\,\sigma_j^2$$

(Equation 3-2)

The standard deviation of any portfolio's rate of return is the square root of the variance.

2. The efficient frontier defines the best portfolios an investor might hold. They are best in the sense that for any amount of risk, they provide the highest expected rate of return, and for any given expected rate of return, they provide the least amount of risk. Indifference curves define the optimal risk-return trade-off for an investor. The investor seeks a portfolio on the highest possible indifference curve.

3. The lower the correlation coefficient between the rates of return on any two assets, the further to the left the efficient frontier extends. As it extends to the left, it will create tangency points with higher indifference curves.

4. A "new" efficient frontier, created by taking combinations of the risk-free asset and the market portfolio, dominates the old efficient frontier. This means that every investor should hold a portfolio that consists of some combination of the risk-free asset and the market portfolio, rather than some unique combination of risky assets.

5. In a diversified portfolio, the true riskiness of an asset is defined by its contribution to the variability of the portfolio's rate of return, rather than its own variability. This contribution can be measured by the covariance between each asset's rate of return and that of the market portfolio. When this covariance is divided by the variance of the rate of return for the market portfolio, the ratio is known as the beta coefficient. The CAPM then provides the relationship between each asset's beta and the expected rate of return on that asset. In estimations of the beta coefficients with the market model, the coefficient of determination indicates how much of an asset's returns are determined by those of the market.

6. The APT model defines the expected rate of return on an asset as a function of the values of various economic factors and the associate beta coefficients, rather than just the market portfolio.

7. The Uniform Principal and Income Act now specifies that portfolios should be managed according to a prudent investor rule, rather than a prudent man rule. This means that a financial planner may use the principles of modern portfolio theory to develop and justify the management of trusts.

MINICASE

You are in step four of the financial planning process, which involves preparing a plan for a new client. You are considering a portfolio with only two assets, a stock mutual fund and a bond mutual fund. Based on your analysis of historical data and current economic conditions, you believe the expected return and standard deviation of the stock fund are 10 percent and 16 percent, and for the bond fund, 6 percent and 8 percent. You believe the correlation coefficient between the two funds is zero.

1. If you believe your client is super aggressive, which of the following is likely to be the best portfolio? [1]

    (A) 50 percent stock fund and 50 percent bond fund, for optimal diversification.

    (B) the asset allocation that is a mix of the two funds, but whose standard deviation is the same as the standard deviation of the bond fund itself.

    (C) 100 percent stock fund and 0 percent bond fund because the client's indifference curves are likely to be sufficiently flat that this portfolio gets to the highest curve.

    (D) 90 percent stock fund and 10 percent bond fund because you think stocks will have a strong bounce in the next 3 months, and you want a good market timing mix.

2. If you believe your client is risk phobic, which of the following is likely to be the best portfolio? [2]

    (A) 50 percent stock fund and 50 percent bond fund, for optimal diversification.
    (B) the asset allocation that is a mix of the two funds that provides the lowest possible standard deviation.
    (C) 0 percent stock fund and 100 percent bond fund, because the bond fund is the less risky of the two assets.
    (D) 90 percent stock fund and 10 percent bond fund, because you think stocks will have a strong bounce in the next 3 months, and you want a good market timing mix.

3. If you can find another stock mutual fund with the same expected return and standard deviation as the current stock fund you are considering, but that has a lower correlation coefficient with the bond fund (that is, a negative one), which of the following would be the most prudent action in a portfolio theory framework? [3]

    (A) Stick with the current stock fund because no one likes negative returns.
    (B) Stick with the current stock fund because you don't want to end up second guessing yourself in the selection of funds.
    (C) Opt for the new stock fund over the current one because when it is combined with the bond fund, it will allow you to hold a portfolio that is less risky than the one you would have held.
    (D) Opt for the new stock fund because it will allow you to move to a lower indifference curve than you can achieve with the first stock fund.

4. If you decide to go with a 50-50 asset allocation, the standard deviation of the resulting portfolio will be which of the following? [1]

    (A) 16.00%
    (B) 12.00%
    (C) 8.94%
    (D) 8.00%

5. You note that with a 50-50 asset allocation, the resulting portfolio has a correlation coefficient with the market portfolio of .6. If the standard deviation of the market portfolio is 4.47 percent, what is the beta of this portfolio? [5]

    (A) 2.15
    (B) 1.61
    (C) 1.20
    (D) 1.07

CHAPTER REVIEW

Key Terms and Concepts

covariance	security market line (SML)
correlation coefficient	index model characteristic line
efficient frontier	excess return
utility functions	coefficient of determination
indifference curves	nonmarket risk
separation theorem	arbitrage pricing theory (APT)
market portfolio	Uniform Principal and Income Act
capital market line	prudent man rule
capital asset pricing model (CAPM)	prudent investor
beta	

Review Questions

Review questions are based on the learning objectives in this chapter. Thus, a [3] at the end of a question means that the question is based on learning objective 3. If there are multiple objectives, they are all listed.

1. For each pair of portfolios, identify which one dominates the other or if neither dominates the other. [1]
    a. X (E(R) = 4%, s = 8%); Y (E(R) = 4%, s = 10%)
    b. X (E(R) = 8%, s = 12%); Y (E(R) = 10%, s = 12%)
    c. X (E(R) = 6%, s = 10%); Y (E(R) = 8%, s = 14%)

2. Over the last three years, you note that securities I and J have had the following rates of return:

    I: 4%, 6%, and –1%

    J: 5%, 3%, and –5%

    What were the arithmetic mean return and the covariance of returns? [1]

3. a. After running the statistics for two companies, you conclude that the covariance of returns is .0020, and that the standard deviations of returns are .06 and .08. What is the correlation coefficient? [1]
    b. The correlation coefficient between two securities is -.5, and the standard deviations are .06 and .08. What is the covariance between them? [1]
    c. If the standard deviations for two securities are .06 and .08, what are the minimum and maximum values of the covariance? [1]

4.   Securities X and Y have expected returns of 4 percent and 10 percent, standard deviations of 5 percent and 16 percent, and a correlation coefficient of -.5 percent Compute the expected returns and standard deviations for the following four portfolios: [1]
      a.   100% X and 0% Y
      b.   60% X and 40% Y
      c.   40% X and 60% Y
      d.   0% X and 100% Y

5.   You want to create a two-security portfolio. One of the holdings will be company A. The other will be B, C, or D. All three of these companies have identical expected returns and standard deviations. However, they differ in terms of their correlation coefficient with company A. The three correlation coefficients are .2, .6, and −.2. Which company should you choose and why? [3, 4]

6.   Explain why the SML differs from the CML. [4, 5]

7.   a.   Define the efficient frontier, first without borrowing or lending allowed and then with both allowed at the risk-free rate. [4]
      b.   What does the efficient frontier look like with risk-free lending only (no borrowing)? [4]

8.   a.   Describe what is meant by market risk and nonmarket risk. [5]
      b.   What determines the effect of market risk for an individual security? [5]

9.   a.   Using the CAPM, calculate expected portfolio returns for the following sets of risk-free rates, expected market returns, and portfolio betas. [5]

Expected Portfolio Returns				
			β_P	
Risk-Free Rates	Expected Market Return	0.7	1	1.3
0.07	0.14			
0.09	0.16			
0.05	0.10			

      b.   The Widget Company's stock has a beta of 1.25. If the variance of the market portfolio is 225 percent-squared (.0225 in decimal notation), what is the covariance of the stock with the market portfolio? [5]
      c.   The Fidget Company's stock has a correlation coefficient with the market of .60. The standard deviation for its stock is .20 (20 percent). If the standard deviation of the market portfolio is .15 (15 percent), what is the company's beta coefficient? [5]

10.   What is the difference between a "prudent man" investment objective and a "prudent investor" investment objective? [7]

Learning Objectives

An understanding of the material in this chapter should enable the student to

1. Compute a time-weighted rate of return.
2. Compute a dollar-weighted rate of return.
3. Compute a PPR when there are interim cash flows and convert a sequence of monthly or quarterly rates of return to an annual rate of return.
4. Describe some of the more commonly used indices and their deficiencies.
5. Identify an appropriate benchmark portfolio.
6. Compute the Sharpe ratio to evaluate portfolio performance.
7. Compute the Treynor ratio to evaluate portfolio performance.
8. Compute Jensen's alpha and the Information Ratio to evaluate portfolio performance.

Investors should always be asking two basic questions: what was the rate of return on my investments, and was this performance good or bad? Computing the actual rate of return on a portfolio can actually be quite complicated. Deciding whether this rate of return was "good" or "bad" can be even more complex. Because the process of evaluation of portfolio performance often involves comparisons with indices, we will also review the more popular indices and their strengths and weaknesses.

WHY EVALUATING PORTFOLIO PERFORMANCE MAY NOT BE SIMPLE

What complicates the measurement of portfolio performance is the presence of cash additions and cash removals. To illustrate this, consider a portfolio that was worth $100,000 on January 1 and $118,000 on December 31 and during the period, no cash was added to the portfolio, nor was any cash removed. This rate of return is easily computed as 18 percent. Now, suppose that $3,000 had been added to the portfolio on September 1. The ending value of $118,000 represents a return on the $100,000 beginning value for the entire year and on the $3,000 for four months. The rate of return is clearly no longer 18 percent.

Additions of cash to or removals of cash from a portfolio can be referred to as interim cash flow. Interim cash flows are quite common. For example, investors may contribute regularly to retirement accounts such as traditional or Roth IRAs. Similarly, investors may make annual contributions to Coverdell accounts and 529 plans.[29] Many investors have automatic deposits set up for one or more accounts, particularly with mutual funds and direct-purchase plans. Finally, many investors regularly add and remove money from their nonqualified accounts as they have excess cash or need cash for particular purposes.

Note that the crediting of dividends and interest to a portfolio is not an interim cash flow as long as the cash is kept in the portfolio. That is, whether the cash from these payments is simply left in the form of cash, or is used to purchase another security, it is still part of the portfolio, and would be counted as part of the portfolio's ending value in order to determine performance. The only circumstance under which dividends or interest would be considered an interim cash flow is if the investor withdrew them from the portfolio. Similarly, a monthly interest charge in a margin account would not count as an interim cash flow as long as the amount charged is offset against a cash position or added to the debit balance. If the investor paid the interest with the deposit of additional cash, then this cash deposit would represent an interim cash flow.

EXAMPLE

A client has a portfolio that is worth $122,000 at the start of the month. During the month, the securities in the portfolio are credited with $3,000 in dividend income and $500 in interest income. On the last day of the month, the client withdraws $1,000 from the portfolio. In this case, there is an interim cash outflow represented by a withdrawal of $1,000. There are no interim cash inflows in this example.

---

29. Coverdell accounts were previously known as educational IRAs, and they are used to accumulate assets to pay for educational expenses. A 529 plan is another vehicle for accumulating money to pay for college. Most, if not all, states now offer 529 plans, as do many universities.

MEASURING THE PERFORMANCE OF PORTFOLIOS WITH INTERIM CASH FLOWS

For illustrative purposes, consider two portfolios (A and B) where each has an initial value of $1,000. Let's further assume that over the next 4 years, portfolio A has successive annual per-period returns (PPRs) of 30 percent, 20 percent, 10 percent, and 0 percent, and portfolio B has the same return, but in the opposite order: 0 percent, 10 percent, 20 percent, and 30 percent. Let's assume that equal deposits of $1,000 are added to each portfolio at the end of each of the first 3 years. The values of the portfolios at time zero and at the end of each of the 4 years, including the interim cash flows, are as follows:

	A				B			
	%				%			
Year	Return	Subtotal	Deposit	Value	Return	Subtotal	Deposit	Value
0				$1,000				$1,000
1	30	1,300	1,000	2,300	0	1,000	1,000	2,000
2	20	2,760	1,000	3,760	10	2,200	1,000	3,200
3	10	4,136	1,000	5,136	20	3,840	1,000	4,840
4	0	5,136	0	5,136	30	6,292	0	6,292

Note that although portfolios A and B have had identical rates of return over the 4-year period (just in a different sequence), and both have had the same amount of deposits and at the same points in time, portfolio B nonetheless ends up with a substantially higher ending value. The reason is that portfolio A has its high returns in the early years when fewer deposits have been made, so the higher rates are applied to smaller balances. Portfolio B's higher returns are in the later years, and they are applied to higher balances. The critical issue here is, since portfolio B ends up being worth more, has this portfolio (i.e., its manager) performed better than portfolio A (i.e., its manager)?

Time-Weighted Rate of Return

One method for evaluating the performance of a portfolio is the time-weighted rate of return. The time-weighted rate of return is a geometric mean rate of return (GMR). This is computed first by dividing the investment horizon into periods and computing the rate of return for each period (i.e., the PPR). In the example above, we were given the PPRs. We then convert the PPRs to PPRRs and solve for the geometric mean return (GMR). The GMRs for portfolios A and B are:

$$R_A = (1.30 \times 1.20 \times 1.10 \times 1.00)^{0.25} - 1 = 0.1445, \text{ or } 14.45\%$$

$$R_B = (1.00 \times 1.10 \times 1.20 \times 1.30)^{0.25} - 1 = 0.1445, \text{ or } 14.45\%$$

Note that the calculation is the same for both portfolios. This should not be a surprise as the only difference is the order of the returns, which, of course, does not change the product of the PPRRs or the GMR.

Dollar-Weighted Rate of Return

The other method for evaluating the performance of a portfolio is known as the dollar-weighted rate of return. This is measured as an internal rate of return. The internal rate of return (IRR) is the discount rate that equates the present value of the cash flows and the ending value of the investment with the beginning value. In mathematical notation, the IRR is the discount rate that makes the following equation valid:

$$0 = -\text{Value}_0 + \sum_{t=1}^{T} CF_t/(1+r)^t + \text{Value}_T/(1+r)^T \qquad \text{(Equation 4-1)}$$

where $\text{Value}_0 =$ value of the portfolio today (i.e., at time zero)

$CF_t =$ net cash flow in period t (cash withdrawals from the portfolio are positive, cash deposits to the portfolio are negative)

$r =$ internal rate of return

$\text{Value}_T =$ value of the portfolio at the end of the holding period

For portfolio A, this equation works out to the following:

$$0 = -\$1,000 - \$1,000/(1+r) - \$1,000/(1+r)^2 - \$1,000/(1+r)^3 + \$5,136/(1+r)^4$$

Note that in the above formulation, the initial value of the portfolio is treated like a purchase (i.e., a cash outflow) by the investor, and the ending value of the portfolio is treated like income (i.e., a cash inflow) to the investor. In other words, we are treating the portfolio as if it were purchased at time period zero and liquidated at the end of the time horizon. Neither situation is usually the case. However, both concepts are critical to the mathematical definition of the IRR.

This equation cannot be solved algebraically unless there are only one or two time periods. Hence, to ascertain r, one would normally have to use some software designed for this purpose, or a calculator. For the HP-10BII calculator, the keystrokes for solving for the IRR for the two portfolios are as follows:

Portfolio A	Portfolio B
SHIFT, C ALL	SHIFT, C ALL
1000, +/–, CFj	1000, +/–, CFj
1000, +/–, CFj	1000, +/–, CFj
3, SHIFT, Nj	3, SHIFT, Nj
5136, CFj	6292, CFj
SHIFT, IRR/YR	SHIFT, IRR/YR
(display: 10.25[%])	(display: 18.97[%])

Note that when entering the number "3" to indicate that there are three consecutive deposits of $1,000 each, the "Nj" is the gold lettering on the CFj key. It is NOT the "N" indicated by the white lettering on the far left key of the top row. The purpose of the "Nj" key is to alert the calculator that the previous cash flow entry is repeated a certain number of times. In this case, three. One could certainly enter cash flows separately, and obtain the same answer.

Recall that when the performance of these two portfolios is measured using the GMR, which ignores the impact of the interim cash flows, both provided a 14.45 percent rate of return. When the performance of the interim cash flows (that is, the deposits) is considered, portfolio A's rate of return is 10.25 percent and portfolio B's is 18.97 percent, as measured by the IRR.

One way to think about the above example is that portfolios A and B are each actually four portfolios that are held over the 4-year investment period. The first portfolio consisted of the initial $1,000 portfolio (let's call this portfolio A1). The rates of return on this portfolio were 30, 20, 10, and 0 percent and its GMR is 14.45 percent. The second portfolio (A2) came into existence at the end of the first year with the first deposit of $1,000. Its rates of return were 20, 10, and 0 percent. The next portfolio (A3) came into existence at the end of the second year, and its rates of return were 10 and 0 percent.

The last portfolio (A4) came into existence at the end of the third year, and its rate of return was 0 percent. The IRR can be thought of as the average GMR on these four portfolios, weighted by how long each one was held and the relative size of each portfolio.[30] Note that the GMRs for the other three portfolios are 9.70, 4.89, and 0 percent, respectively.

First Deposit	$1,000	$[(1 + .20) \times (1 + .10) \times (1 + 0)]^{1/3} - 1 = .0970$
Second Deposit	$1,000	$[(1 + .10) \times (1 + 0)]^{1/2} - 1 = .0489$
Third Deposit	$1,000	$(1 + 0)^1 - 1 = 0.00$

Hence, when a portfolio that has a GMR of 14.45 percent is combined with three other portfolios whose rates of return are 9.7, 4.9, and 0 percent, the weighted average rate of return would be expected to be below 14.45. In this case, it is 10.25 percent.

Conversely, the portfolios formed by the additional deposits to portfolio B have rates of return of 19.7, 24.9, and 30 percent.

First Deposit	$1,000 $[(1 + .10) \times (1 + .20) \times (1 + .30)]^{1/3} - 1 = .197$
Second Deposit	$1,000 $[(1 + .20) \times (1 + .30)]^{1/2} - 1 = .249$
Third Deposit	$1,000 $(1 + .30)^1 - 1 = .30$

Hence, the rate of return on the combination of these portfolios would be expected to be higher than 14.45 percent.

As a final point to the computation of the IRR, note that we could multiply both sides of equation 4-1 by a minus one, producing the result:

$$0 = + \text{Value}_0 - \sum_{t=1}^{T} CF_t / (1 + R)^t - \text{Value}_T / (1 + R)^T \qquad \text{(Equation 4-1a)}$$

When we then plug in the values for portfolio A, the equation would appear as:

$$0 = + \$1{,}000 + \$1{,}000/(1+r) + \$1{,}000/(1+r)^2 + \$1{,}000/(1+r)^3 - \$5{,}136/(1+r)^4$$

The keystroke sequence would then be represented by:

---

30. This statement is offered as an approximation to help the reader conceptualize this issue, and is not meant to be a mathematical definition.

SHIFT, C ALL

1000, CFj

1000, CFj

3, SHIFT, Nj

5136, +/–, CFj

SHIFT, IRR/YR

(display: 10.25[%])

Conceptually, one could think of the opening value of the account and the subsequent deposits as cash inflows to the portfolio, and the $5,136 ending value as a cash outflow to the portfolio. *The key point here is whether one assigns a positive or negative value to the initial value of the portfolio does not really matter as long as one assigns the opposite sign to the ending value, and one assigns the appropriate sign to deposits and withdrawals.* If the initial value is positive, the deposits should be positive and withdrawals negative. If the initial value is negative, the deposits should be negative and withdrawals positive. Either approach will produce the exact same dollar-weighted rate of return computation.

Computing the Rate of Return for a Single Period with an Interim Cash Flow

In the above example, the rate of return was provided for each time period. In many cases, a financial planner will have to compute the rate of return. Let's consider four special cases for computing rates of return. The first two involve deposits made just before the end of the period and just after the beginning of the period. If a deposit is at the end of the period, then the formula for the PPR is:

$$\text{PPR} = (\text{Change in value} - \text{Deposit})/(\text{Beginning value}) \qquad \text{(Equation 4-2)}$$

where the change in value is based on the value of the portfolio after the deposit. If a deposit is at the start of the period, then the formula for the PPR is:

$$\text{PPR} = (\text{Change in value} - \text{Deposit})/(\text{Beginning value} + \text{Deposit}) \qquad \text{(Equation 4-3)}$$

Note that the deposit is included in the denominator because the investor will have the entire period in which to earn a return on the deposited funds.

The other two cases involve withdrawals at the end of the period and just after the beginning of the period. A withdrawal at the end of a period would mean the PPR would be computed as:

PPR = (Change in value + Withdrawal) / (Beginning value)   (Equation 4-4)

The withdrawal is added to the change in value because the ending value of the portfolio is determined after the withdrawal has been made. Finally, a withdrawal at the start of a period would mean the PPR would be computed as:

PPR = (Change in value + Withdrawal) /

(Beginning value – Withdrawal)   (Equation 4-5)

EXAMPLE 1

A portfolio is worth $100,000 at the start of the year, and $5,000 is immediately deposited into the portfolio. During the year $3,000 in dividends and interest are accrued in the portfolio, and the ending value is $110,000. What is the PPR?

$$PPR = \frac{(\$110,000 - \$100,000) - \$5,000}{\$100,000 + \$5,000}$$

$$= .0476 \text{ or } 4.76\%$$

Note that the $3,000 in income is not directly incorporated into the answer, as it is part of the ending value of $110,000.

EXAMPLE 2

A portfolio is worth $100,000 at the start of the year. At the end of the year it is worth $115,000, after a year-end withdrawal of $5,000. What is the PPR?

$$PPR = \frac{\$115,000 - \$100,000 + \$5,000}{\$100,000}$$

$$= .20 \text{ or } 20\%$$

Sequence Risk

sequence risk The example above illustrates an incredibly important issue in financial planning known as *sequence risk*. Even though the owners of portfolios A and B had the same returns, because of the presence of interim cash flows, the sequence of returns significantly affects the ending values. If there had been no interim cash flows, the sequence would not have mattered and the dollar-weighted rate of return would have been identical to the time-weighted rate of return (see the following example). Sequence risk is important when people are accumulating wealth, and extremely important when they start taking distributions.

EXAMPLE

A client's portfolio was worth $500,000 two years ago. Last year it was worth $560,000, and today it is worth $540,000. The time-weighted rate of return is

$$PPRR_1 = \$560,000/\$500,000 = 1.1200$$

$$PPRR_2 = \$540,000/\$560,000 = .9643$$

$$GMR = [1.1200 \times .9643]^{1/2} - 1 = .0392 \text{ or } 3.92\%$$

As there are no interim cash flows, the internal rate of return formulation using equation 4-1 is:

$$0 = -\$500,000 + \$0/(1+r)^1 + \$540,000/(1+r)^2$$

The dollar-weighted rate of return is computed 3.92 percent, where the keystrokes are:

SHIFT, C ALL

500000, +/–, CFj

0, CFj

540000, CFj

SHIFT, IRR/YR

(display: 3.92[%])

As noted before, the dollar-weighted rate of return calculation is implicitly weighting each period's performance according to the size of the portfolio for that period. Thus, more weight is given to the performance of the portfolio when it is larger in absolute dollar size, and less weight is given to the performance when the portfolio is smaller. To illustrate this point, let's consider an extreme example.

EXAMPLE

A portfolio has $100 in assets. During the first year, the portfolio has a –10 percent rate of return, and so end ups being worth $90. At the end of the first year, $1,000,000 is added to the portfolio, bringing the total assets to $1,000,090. The next year, the portfolio has a +10 percent rate of return, and ends up being worth $1,100,099.

The time-weighted rate of return is –.5 percent, computed as follows

$$[(1+.10) \times (1 - .10)]^{1/2} - 1 = -.005 \text{ or } -.5\%$$

The dollar-weighted rate of return is defined as the discount rate that makes the following equation true:

$$0 = -100 - 1,000,000/(1+r)^1 + 1,100,099/(1+r)^2$$

The answer is 9.9978 percent, and the keystrokes are:

> SHIFT, C ALL
>
> 100, +/–, CFj
>
> 1000000, +/–, CFj
>
> 1100099, CFj
>
> SHIFT, IRR/YR
>
> (display: 9.9978[%]

In the above example, the fact that the geometric mean provides a rate of return of –.5 percent is about what we would expect given that the arithmetic mean return is 0 percent (that is, the arithmetic average of 10 percent and –10 percent would be 0), and we saw earlier that the geometric mean is always slightly less than the arithmetic mean unless the returns are all the same. We would also expect that because the IRR is dollar-weighted, its value would be virtually identical to the 10 percent rate of return achieved on the portfolio in the second period (that is, 9.9978 percent is virtually the same as 10 percent) because the value of the portfolio during the second time period significantly dwarfs the value of the portfolio during the first time period. If these numbers represented a real situation, the investor would not really care how well the portfolio performed during the first time period, and would care a lot how it performed during the second time period.

Which Rate Should Be Used to Measure Portfolio Performance?

Given that both the time-weighted and dollar-weighted rates of return are legitimate measures of return, it is important to understand why one measure may be more appropriate under certain circumstances than another. Circumstances in which one rate is more relevant than the other involve the answers to the following two questions:

1. How did my portfolio perform?
2. What rate of return did my portfolio manager achieve in managing my portfolio?

Return to an Investor

When an investor wants to know how well his or her portfolio has done, the IRR (that is, the dollar-weighted rate of return) is the true rate of return. Interim cash flows are a real part of most portfolios. Thus, the impact of withdrawals and deposits on the performance of the portfolio is just as real to the investor as the rate of return on the securities in the portfolio. Hence, an investor wanting to know how well he or she has done should use the IRR.

Return by a Portfolio Manager

When the portfolio's performance is assessed to evaluate the performance of a financial advisor, one should keep in mind that the advisor may not have had control over interim cash flows, or the interim cash flows may be the result of other types of decisions and not just the decision of whether now is a good time to add cash to or withdraw cash from the portfolio. For example, a client might be retiring from a job and the advisor recommends moving the money from the client's defined-contribution pension plan to a rollover IRA. Hence, the movement of what is potentially a large amount of cash into a portfolio managed by the financial advisor is a result of the client's decision to retire and the advisor's decision to take more direct control of the pension monies via the rollover, and not a result of how the advisor thinks the market will perform in the next year or two. Simply put, if a financial advisor is deliberately influencing the timing of the movement of cash into and out of a portfolio for the purpose of improving overall performance, then his or her performance should also be dollar-weighted. If the portfolio manager has no control over interim cash flows, his or her results should be based on the time-weighted rate of return.

Converting Monthly and Quarterly Rates of Return to Annual Rates

In some cases, a financial planner will have a set of monthly or quarterly rates of return for a portfolio, and will want to convert these to an annual rate of return. This is a three-step time-weighted rate of return calculation. For monthly rates of return, the first step is to compute the 12 monthly return relatives. The second step is to compute the HPRR for these 12 return relatives. The third step is to subtract one. The only difference with quarterly rates of return is that only four return relatives need to be computed.

EXAMPLE

In reviewing a client's portfolio, you find that the rates of return (PPRs) for each month (after adjusting for cash flows) are: 4%, 3%, –8%, –1%, 10%, 1%, 3%, 5%, –9%, –1%, 8%, and 3%. What is the client's time-weighted rate of return for the year?

The holding period return relative is computed as

$$\text{HPRR} = (1.04 \times 1.03 \times .92 \times .99 \times 1.10 \times 1.01 \times 1.03 \times 1.05 \times .91 \times .99 \times 1.08 \times 1.03) - 1$$
$$= 1.1748 - 1 = .1748 \text{ or } 17.48\%$$

In practice, interim cash flows occur at any point during a period, and it would not be unusual to have multiple interim cash flows during a period, especially if a period spans a year. The effort necessary to calculate the IRR when there are multiple interim cash flows can be tedious without software tailored to this exact issue. However, some software programs, such as Excel, allow an investor to compute a reasonably accurate estimate of portfolio performance in the presence of interim cash flows.[31]

BENCHMARKS

Once one has measured a portfolio's performance, the next question is: "How do I evaluate the quality of that performance?" For example, is it a good or a weak performance if a financial advisor achieves a 10 percent per annum

---

31. Excel's XIRR function calculates an IRR based on cash flows and actual dates. Also, an excellent article on this subject is "How Did I Do This Month?", also by Walt Woerheide, *Journal of Financial Service Professionals*, Vol. 57, No. 5 (September 2003), pp. 56–61.

rate of return over a period of 5 years? To answer this question, one needs benchmarks and a method of comparison. We will discuss benchmarks first.

Benchmarks should be chosen for their similarity in risk characteristics to the portfolio under consideration. For example, a portfolio manager may have a goal of beating the Standard & Poor's 500 Index. If the portfolio has similar risk characteristics to the S&P 500 and outperforms it, then the portfolio has beaten the benchmark. Of course, portfolio theory tells us that if the portfolio has a higher beta than the S&P 500, it should outperform it in an up market. The goal of beating the S&P 500 Index does not necessarily imply that this index is the appropriate benchmark portfolio.

Comparing a bond portfolio to a stock index benchmark would make no sense. Even comparing a bond portfolio of AAA bonds to a broad benchmark of all bonds makes no sense. Good benchmarking means only like-kind comparisons.

It is certainly possible to create benchmarks from multiple indices. For example, consider a portfolio that consists of 60 percent in stocks with a risk profile similar to the S&P 500 and 40 percent in investment-grade bonds similar in risk to the Lehman Brothers Corporate Bond Index. A combined benchmark (.60 × S&P 500 + .40 × Lehman Brothers Corporate Bond Index) can be created. It is possible to match the combined benchmark while outperforming in one sector and underperforming in the other sector. Thus, it is helpful to break down the performance.

MARKET INDICES

A myriad of market indices are available to investors for both benchmarking and general market observations. Each index has its own unique characteristics, and investors should be aware of those characteristics before selecting the appropriate benchmark. Let us consider the characteristics of the major market indices.

Description of Indices

Dow Jones Averages

The Dow Jones Industrial Average (DJIA) is the most widely referenced stock market indicator. It is frequently referred to as "the Dow." and just as often people refer to it as "the market." Thus, when someone says, "How is the market doing?", the answer is usually to indicate the change in the Dow. There are several reasons for this, including the following:

1. Dow Jones and Company owns the index as well as the *Wall Street Journal*, which is arguably the dominant daily business publication.

2. The Dow Jones Industrial Average began in 1884 with 11 stocks and increased to 30 stocks in 1928. It was the first widely published index.

3. Use of widely held and frequently traded companies in the Dow Industrial listing provides an important feature of timeliness—that is, the Dow represents major, frequently traded stocks. Therefore, this average represents the direction of current transactions at any point in time, which may not always be the case with broader indices. The broader indices include less frequently traded stocks or stocks that are not widely owned and therefore include price quotes that are not as timely.

Today, the DJIA still consists of 30 major American companies in multiple industries, with the exception of the transportation and utility industries which are in other indices. These 30 stocks are shown in Table 4-1. The reason so many industries are covered is that so many of these large companies are themselves diversified into a large number of industries. The 30 stocks in the Dow Industrials represent a fifth of the $1 trillion-plus market value of all stock traded, and about a fourth of the value of stocks on the NYSE. Although one might question how an index of only 30 stocks could provide useful information about the thousands of stocks that are publicly traded, research has shown that the Dow closely mirrors broader stock market indicators.

In spite of its dominating presence, the DJIA has serious flaws as a market indicator. It only includes a small percentage of stocks available in the market. Industries are not represented in the same proportions as they are in the overall economy. The thirty DJIA companies are large and mature relative to most companies, and thus the index is not necessarily representative of the market as a whole. Its most significant flaw is that the DJIA is price-weighted. A price-weighted index is one in which the highest-priced stock has the greatest impact and the lowest-priced stock the least impact. Price-weighted indices are computed much like arithmetic averages. Like other indicators, the DJIA reflects that part of the return that relates to price changes; it does not consider dividend yields. To create a portfolio that mimicked the performance of the DJIA, one would have to buy an equal number of shares in each company in the Dow, regardless of the price.

Table 4-1 Companies in the DJIA as of 6/29/2010			
Ticker	Company Name	Ticker	Company Name
AA	Alcoa	IBM	International Business Machines
AXP	American Express	JPM	JP Morgan Chase
T	AT&T	JNJ	Johnson & Johnson
BA	Boeing	KFT	Kraft Foods, Class A
BAC	Bank of America	MCD	McDonald's
CAT	Caterpillar	MRK	Merck & Co.
CSCO	Cisco Systems, Inc.	MSFT	Microsoft
CVX	Chevron	PFE	Pfizer
KO	Coca Cola	PG	Procter & Gamble
DD	E.I. DuPont de Nemours	TRV	Travelers Companies
XOM	Exxon Mobil	UTX	United Technologies
GE	General Electric*	VZ	Verizon Communications
HPQ	Hewlett-Packard	WMT	Wal-Mart Stores
HD	Home Depot	DIS	Walt Disney
INTC	Intel	MMM	3M Corporation

* General Electric is the only stock currently in the DJIA that was in the average when it was originally introduced.

Flaws in the DJIA
• Small number of stocks
• Industries not proportionally represented
• Focuses only on large, mature companies
• Price-weighted
• Ignores dividends

Other Dow Jones averages include the Dow Jones Transportation Average, which represents 20 stocks of the airline, trucking, railroad, and shipping business; and the Dow Jones Utility Average, which includes 15 stocks and is geographically representative of the gas and electric utilities industries.

Standard & Poor's 500 Index

The Standard & Poor's 500 Index (S&P 500) includes 500 large-capitalization companies representing about 75 percent of the total market value of all companies traded on U.S. markets.[32] The index includes almost 400 companies that are listed on the NYSE, about 75 that are listed on NASDAQ, a few that are listed on the Amex. The S&P 500 is a much broader index than the DJIA, represents a much larger portion of the total market, and much more closely reflects the industry allocation that exists in the economy. As recently as 1988, the index was made up of 400 industrials, 40 utilities, 20 transportation companies, and 40 financial institutions. Today, there are no such internal constraints. The current criteria for inclusion are that the stocks of each company be widely held by U.S. investors and that the companies be "leading companies in leading industries." It is intended to be a large-cap index. The S&P 500 and all the indicators listed below, with one exception, are either market-value weighted, or utilize a modified market weighting scheme.

Advantages of the S&P 500 Index
• Large percentage of total market capitalization
• Includes stocks from multiple markets
• Industry representation more typical of economy
• Value-weighted

NASDAQ

The NASDAQ 100 Index is constructed with 100 of the largest domestic and international nonfinancial companies listed on the NASDAQ market, based on market capitalization. Although the index is intended as a broad based measure of market performance, it is dominated by technology-oriented companies, and so is viewed by many people as a "tech index." The index uses a modified market capitalization weighting scheme. The modification is to keep the largest companies in the index from dominating the index changes. The formula for the modification is proprietary.[33]

---

32. http://www.standardandpoors.com/indices/sp-500/en/us/?indexId=spusa-500-usduf–p-us-l–, July 22, 2010.

33. http://www.fool.com/school/indices/Nasdaq.htm, March 23, 2010.

Other Indices

The NYSE Composite Index includes all common stocks listed on the New York Stock Exchange, regardless of whether the company is U.S. based or not. It includes common stocks, American depository receipts, real estate investment trusts (REITs), and tracking stocks that are listed on that exchange. It does not include any closed-end funds, ETFs, or limited partnerships. It is recomputed every 15 seconds during trading hours.

The Russell 3000 Index measures the performance of the 3,000 largest U.S. companies, and represents approximately 98 percent of the U.S. equity market. The Russell 1000 Index measures the performance of the 1,000 largest companies in the Russell 3000 Index, and the Russell 2000 Index measures the performance of the other 2,000 companies. The Russell 1000 consitutes about 90% of the U.S. equity market. Although the Russell 2000 Index represents about 8 percent of the value of the U.S. equity market, it is the most widely quoted measure of the overall performance of small- to mid-cap stocks.

The Wilshire Equity Index measures the performance of nearly all U.S.-headquartered equity securities with readily available price data. This index used to be known as the Wilshire 5000. The 5000 represented the number of component stocks when the index was introduced in 1974. Currently, this index includes substantially more than 5,000 securities, but the number changes on a regular basis. It is the closest we have to a Total Market Index. The price of each issue in the index is weighted by its capitalization as follows:

$$\text{Index} = \sum_{i=1}^{n} \frac{P_i \times \text{market capitalization of company i}}{\text{Market capitalization of all stocks in the index}}$$

where P_i = price of company i in the index

n = number of stocks in the index

The Value Line Index is one of the more unique indices. It contains 1,700 stocks, drawn from multiple markets. The uniqueness is derived from the fact that it is an equally-weighted index constructed as a geometric mean. The daily return relatives for all the stocks in the index are multiplied together and the product is taken to the 1/n power, where n is the number of companies in the index. Because of this difference in computation, the Value Line Index is more indicative of how smaller companies have performed than the larger ones because it gives equal weighting to all stocks. Thus, there are times in the market when the Value Line Index is moving opposite to the rest of the market indices, which means that the smaller companies are performing in a manner different than the larger, better-known ones.

Foreign Indices

Since the investment world is increasingly international, investment returns in foreign markets are followed in the United States. The two most often quoted foreign indices are the FTSE 100 and the MSCI EAFE. The FTSE 100 (pronounced "footsie") is an index of the top 100 most highly capitalized companies traded on the London Stock Exchange.

The MSCI EAFE® index (commonly referred to as "eefee") is based on 21 MSCI country indices including countries in Europe, the Far East, and Australasia. The "MSCI" stands for Morgan Stanley Capital International Inc. The index for each country attempts to capture 85 percent of the market capitalization in each industry group within each country. As of May 29, 2009, there were 981 securities in this index. This is the most common benchmark for foreign stock funds.

Two other foreign indices include the Hang Seng Index, which has 33 companies representing 40 percent of the market capitalization of the Hong Kong stock market, and the Nikkei Index, which includes 225 of the largest market capitalization companies based in Japan. The Nikkei Index, like the DJIA, is a price-weighted index.

Bond Indices

Probably the most commonly watched bond indices are those maintained by Barclays Capital, a global investment bank. The Barclays Capital Bond Index consists of the Barclays Capital Government/Corporate Bond Index, Mortgage-Backed Securities Index, and Asset-Backed Securities Index, including bond issues that are of investment-grade quality or better, have at least 1 year to maturity, and have an outstanding par value of at least $100 million.

EVALUATING PORTFOLIO PERFORMANCE

Risk-Adjusted Return

Comparing a portfolio's performance with a benchmark portfolio is inappropriate unless the risk characteristics of the portfolio are the same as those of the benchmark portfolio. Any comparison of returns is invalid if the risk characteristics are different.

As noted earlier, there are two primary measures of risk that are relevant. The broadest measure of risk is standard deviation which is a measure of the variability of an investment's return. The larger the standard deviation is, the riskier the investment.

Financial Planning Issue
On average, actual portfolios tend to slightly underperform market indices for several reasons.[34] First, indices reflect portfolios that are constructed with absolutely no transaction fees or advisory fees. No individual can obtain such beneficial treatment. Second, most portfolios involve trades over time, and unless the portfolio is in a qualified account (for example, an IRA), taxes will be due. The payment of taxes involves a removal of cash from the portfolio, thus reducing the rate of return.[35] Indices pay no taxes. Third, most indices have a large number of securities in them, making them extremely diversified (except for the sector indices). As such, they are likely to have less volatility than an individual's portfolio. Fourth, most people hold some cash and/or fixed-income securities in their portfolios. Comparing the returns on these portfolios directly with an all-equity index will more often than not be unfavorable.

The other oft-used measure of risk is beta. Beta is a measure of the degree of an investment's co-movement with the theoretical market portfolio. Hence, it is technically a volatility measure, not a variability measure. Volatility refers to the price change on one asset relative to another asset. Variability refers to the degree of price changes of an asset, independent of any other asset. Volatility is measured with the beta coefficient. Variability is measured with the standard deviation. Although beta is not a reliable risk measure for individual stocks, it is more reliable for portfolios and mutual funds.

---

34. Material in this section is drawn from "Fire Your Index," by Len Reinhart, Financial Planning, vol. 34, no. 2 (February 2004), pp. 41–42.

35. In practice, the taxes may be paid from other sources, but the net effect is the same as if the taxes are paid out of the account where the tax liability is generated.

Let's consider first the most commonly used performance measure that is based on the portfolio's standard deviation, and then look at three performance measures that are based on a portfolio's beta.

The Sharpe Ratio

reward-to-variability ratio (RVAR)

The Sharpe ratio, or the *reward-to-variability ratio (RVAR)* as it is sometimes called, is defined as follows:

$$S_p = \frac{R_p - R_f}{\sigma_p}$$ (Equation 4-6)

where S_p =   the Sharpe ratio for portfolio p

R_p =   arithmetic mean return on the portfolio being evaluated

R_f =   average yield over the sample time period of a risk-free asset

σ_p =   the standard deviation of the portfolio being evaluated

This formula is provided on the CFP® Certification Examinations formula sheet.

Note that the numerator of this ratio is the portfolio return in excess of the risk-free rate of return, while the denominator is simply the standard deviation of the portfolio's return. The value of this ratio is best understood in the context of the capital market line (CML). Recall that the CML is the efficient frontier created when n risky assets are held in combination with a risk-free asset. The one portfolio of all risky assets that plots on the CML is the market portfolio, M. Hence, the slope of the CML can be defined as the difference between the expected return on the market portfolio and the risk-free rate, divided by the standard deviation of the market portfolio. The performance of the market portfolio can then be measured ex post by using the actual returns of whatever index is selected to represent the market portfolio. Thus, over any time period, the performance of the market portfolio can be measured with the Sharpe ratio as:

$$S_M = \frac{(R_M - R_f)}{\sigma_M}$$

So, when one computes the Sharpe ratio for a portfolio, one could compare this ratio to that of the market portfolio to conclude whether the portfolio being analyzed has "beaten" the market or underperformed the market. A Sharpe ratio for a portfolio that is higher than that of the market would indicate the portfolio has outperformed the market. Similarly, the Sharpe ratio for any two portfolios can be compared directly to determine which has generated the better performance.

EXAMPLE 1

Although it would not be appropriate to use only five annual rates of return to compute a Sharpe ratio, let's do so for illustrative purposes. Suppose that over the last 5 years, a client's portfolio has achieved the following rates of return: 15 percent, –4 percent, 26 percent, 4 percent, and –10 percent. During this period, the average risk-free interest rate has been 4 percent. The arithmetic mean return of the portfolio is 6.2 percent and the standard deviation of return is 14.50 percent. Thus, the Sharpe ratio for this portfolio is:

$$S_p = (6.2 - 4.0)/14.50 = .15$$

Keystrokes: SHIFT, C ALL, 15, $\sum$+, 4, +/–, $\sum$+, 26, $\sum$+, 4, $\sum$+,10, +/–, $\sum$+, SHIFT, $\overline{x}\ \overline{y}$

DISPLAY: 6.20

SHIFT, $S_x\ S_y$ DISPLAY: 14.50

6.2, –, 4, ÷, 14.50, = (display: .15)

EXAMPLE 2

Suppose in the above example that the mean rate of return on the portfolio was 4.0 percent, and the risk-free rate was 6.2 percent, but the standard deviation was still 14.50. In this case, the Sharpe ratio would now be –.15:

$$S_p = (4.0 - 6.2)/14.50 = -.15$$

Next, suppose that during this same period, a second portfolio (portfolio A) had the same value for the numerator, but had a standard deviation of 20 percent. This would produce a Sharpe ratio of:

$$S_A = (4.0 - 6.2)/20 = -.11$$

Because the second portfolio has a "higher" Sharpe ratio, it technically performed better than the first portfolio. However, most people would find this result counterintuitive that the portfolio with greater risk, when returns are identical, is deemed to be the better performing portfolio!

The Treynor Ratio

reward-to-volatility ratio (RVOL)   The Treynor ratio, also called the *reward-to-volatility ratio (RVOL)*, is defined as follows:

$$T_p = \frac{R_p - R_f}{\beta_p}$$

(Equation 4-7)

where T_p =   Treynor ratio for portfolio p

β_p =   beta of the portfolio being evaluated

This formula is provided on the CFP® Certification Exam formula sheet. Note that the numerator is the same as in the Sharpe ratio, but the denominator's measure of risk is now the beta of the security—which means that only market-related risk is considered. That is, the Treynor ratio looks at the return achieved relative to the amount of systematic risk exposure of the investment.

As with the Sharpe ratio, an easy comparison can be made between any particular security or portfolio and the market index in that the beta of the market portfolio is 1 by definition. Thus, the Treynor ratio for the market portfolio is simply the return on the market portfolio minus the risk-free rate, which is also known as the market risk premium. Any security or portfolio with a Treynor ratio greater than the market risk premium can be considered to have outperformed the market. Treynor ratios with values less than the market risk premium have underperformed the market.

EXAMPLE

Suppose that over the last 5 years the market's arithmetic average return was 12 percent and the average risk-free rate was 4 percent. The market risk premium was 8 percent (12% – 4%). The RFD Fund over the same period achieved a return of 10 percent but had a beta of .8. Did it beat the market?

The Treynor ratios are:

$$T_M = \frac{12-4}{1} = 8\%$$

$$T_{RFD} = \frac{10-4}{.8} = 7.5\%$$

Thus the RFD Fund underperformed the market.

Jensen's Alpha

Jensen's alpha uses the capital asset pricing model (CAPM) to evaluate the risk-adjusted rate of return of a portfolio.

It is computed as the actual return less the return that could have been expected given the risk-free rate and the beta coefficient. The formula is stated as:

$$\alpha_p = R_p - \left[R_f + \beta_p \left(R_M - R_f \right) \right] \qquad \text{(Equation 4-8)}$$

Jensen's alpha has one attractive feature over most of the other measures of performance. Namely, its interpretation is easily understood. For example, if a security or portfolio has an alpha of 2 percent, then one can say that the security or portfolio being analyzed has outperformed the market by 2 percent. Positive alphas are good and negative alphas are bad. It's that simple! The alpha for the market portfolio is always, by definition, equal to zero.

Information Ratio

Yet another ratio that is sometimes used to evaluate portfolio performance is the information ratio. This ratio is defined as the portfolio's alpha divided by the standard deviation of the error term from the estimation of the portfolio's characteristic line. Specifically, recall that in the last chapter, the characteristic line was defined as:

$$R_i = \alpha_i + \beta_i R_M + \varepsilon_i \qquad \begin{array}{l} \text{(Equation 3-16} \\ \text{repeated)} \end{array}$$

It was then noted that one could take the variance of both sides of this equation, producing the following expression:

$$\sigma_i^2 = \left(\beta_i^2\, \sigma_M^2\right) + \sigma_\varepsilon^2$$

(Equation 3-17 repeated)

The expression in parentheses is systematic risk, and the second term is nonsystematic risk. It is the square root of the term σ_ε^2 that is used in the denominator.[36]

The rationale for this ratio is that when a portfolio is actively managed and not fully diversified, then two things are likely to happen. One is that its rate of return will produce an alpha that is different than zero. The second is that it will contain nonsystematic risk. This nonsystematic risk will be measured by the term σ_ε. So the real issue is the magnitude of this incremental alpha relative to the nonsystematic risk that is present. The numerator is a desirable term (i.e., the more alpha in a portfolio the better). The denominator is an undesirable term (i.e., unsystematic risk). Thus, the larger the value of the ratio, the more attractive the performance of the portfolio.

An Example of Performance Measurement

Suppose the following data are available for the 1990–2010 period for several mutual funds. (The S&P 500 Index and the 90-day T-bill rate will serve as proxies for the market portfolio and the risk-free rate.)

Mutual Fund	Average Return	Standard Deviation	Beta	σ_ε
Julia Fund	19.20	18.50	.83	14.91
Drake Fund	31.92	18.57	1.08	11.93
Wong Fund	15.19	9.57	.65	4.26
S&P 500 Index	17.16	13.18	1.00	—
T-Bill rate	8.31	2.56	0.00	—

To compute risk-adjusted measures of performance, we would first need to compute the excess return for each of the three portfolios and the market index:

---

36.   The computation of this standard deviation is beyond the scope of this textbook, and will simply be a given in any problems where it might be needed.

Julia Fund	19.20 – 8.31 = 10.89
Drake Fund	31.92 – 8.31 = 23.61
Wong Fund	15.19 – 8.31 = 6.88
Market	17.16 – 8.31 = 8.85

We can now compute the Sharpe and Treynor ratios as follows:

	Sharpe	Treynor
Julia Fund	10.89 / 18.50 = .59	10.89 / .83 = 13.12
Drake Fund	23.61 / 18.57 = 1.27	23.61 / 1.08 = 21.99
Wong Fund	6.88 / 9.57 = .72	6.88 / .65 = 10.58
Market	8.85 / 13.18 = .67	8.85 / 1.0 = 8.85

To compute Jensen's alpha and the information ratio, we need to first compute what each portfolio should have returned based on the CAPM.

Julia Fund	8.31 + (.83 x 8.85) = 15.66
Drake Fund	8.31 + (1.08 x 8.85) = 17.87
Wong Fund	8.31 + (.65 x 8.85) = 14.06

We can now directly compute Jensen's alpha as the difference between each return and what the return would have been based on the CAPM, as well as the information ratio:

	Jensen's Alpha	Information Ratio
Julia Fund	19.20 – 15.66 = 3.54	3.54 / 14.91 = .24
Drake Fund	31.92 – 17.87 = 14.05	14.05 / 11.93 = 1.18
Wong Fund	15.19 – 14.06 = 1.13	1.13 / 4.26 = .27

The interpretation of these results is that the Drake Fund is clearly superior among the funds on all four measures of risk-adjusted performance. However, the Julia Fund and Wong Fund have different rankings, depending on the measure chosen. When risk is measured by the standard deviation, as with the Sharpe ratio, the Wong Fund is superior to the Julia Fund, and the Wong Fund has outperformed the market while the Julia Fund has underpeformed. When beta is used as the measure of risk, the Julia Fund has outperformed the Wong fund, and both have beaten the market. It is important to note that the Wong Fund did not achieve as high an average return as the market, but because the return it achieved involved less risk, its performance is superior to the market.

Financial Planning Issue

Now that as we have noted several well-accepted measures of performance, and noted that the rank ordering of the performance of portfolios will not always be the same among these criteria, the student should ask the question of which performance measurement should be used under which circumstances. Unfortunately, there is not complete agreement within the industry on this issue. In fact, different sources actually give conflicting advice. All of this said, the student should consider the following recommendations:

- Use the Sharpe ratio when the portfolio being considered represents the client's entire package of financial assets. When the portfolio represents the investor's entire wealth, then what is most important to the investor is total variability, not just exposure to systematic risk.

- Use the information ratio when an investor has divided his or her portfolio into two components, and one is an actively managed portfolio and the other is a passively managed portfolio such as an index fund.

- Use the Treynor ratio when an overall portfolio has been allocated to multiple managers, each of whom is actively managing their share of the holdings.

REVIEW OF LEARNING OBJECTIVES

1. A time-weighted rate of return is the geometric mean rate of return for the individual time periods being evaluated, independent of the size of the portfolio at the beginning or end of any time period.

2. The dollar-weighted rate of return is the internal rate of return that equates the present value of the ending value of the portfolio with the beginning value, after allowing for interim cash flows.

3. A PPR, when there are interim cash flows at the beginning or end of a period, would be computed as:

$$\text{PPR} = (\text{Change in value} - \text{Deposit}) / (\text{Beginning value}) \qquad \text{(Equation 4-2)}$$

---

37. For additional discussion, and a more mathematical treatment of this issue, see *Investments*, 6th Edition, by Bodie, Kane, and Marcus, McGraw-Hill, 2005.

$$PPR = \text{(Change in value – Deposit)} / \text{(Beginning value + Deposit)} \qquad \text{(Equation 4-3)}$$

$$PPR = \text{(Change in value + Withdrawal)} / \text{(Beginning value)} \qquad \text{(Equation 4-4)}$$

$$PPR = \text{(Change in value + Withdrawal)} / \text{(Beginning value – Withdrawal)} \qquad \text{(Equation 4-5)}$$

Monthly or quarterly rates of return are converted to an annual rate of return by multiplying all the PPRRs in a one-year time period together.

4. The DJIA consists of 30 large-cap stocks. It is a price-weighted index, not representative of the overall economy, and does not incorporate cash dividends. The S&P 500 index has 500 securities in it and, like most indices, is value-weighted. The NASDAQ 100 represents a "tech index." The Russell 3000 is a comprehensive market index, with the Russell 1000 representing a large cap index and the Russell 2000 a small cap index. The Wilshire Equity Index is the broadest market index, and the Value-Line index is the only one that uses a geometric mean computation. The two most popular foreign indices are the FTSE 100 and the MSCI EAFE®.

5. A benchmark portfolio should match the risk characteristics of a managed portfolio. Real portfolios tend to underperform market indexes for four reasons.

6. The primary standard deviation-based measure of portfolio performance evaluation is the Sharpe ratio, defined as:

$$S_p = \frac{R_p - R_f}{\sigma_p} \qquad \text{(Equation 4-6)}$$

7. An important beta-based measure of portfolio performance evaluation is the Treynor ratio, defined as:

$$T_p = \frac{R_p - R_f}{\beta_p} \qquad \text{(Equation 4-7)}$$

8. Two other beta-based measures of portfolio performance evaluation are Jensen's alpha and the Information Ratio. Jensen's alpha is

defined as the difference between the actual performance and the expected performance as predicted by the CAPM.

$$\alpha_p = R_p - \left[R_f + (R_M - R_f)\beta_p \right]$$ (Equation 4-8)

The information ratio is defined as the portfolio's alpha divided by the standard deviation of the error term from the estimation of the portfolio's characteristic line.

MINICASE

You are now in step six of the financial planning process, monitoring the plan. You are reviewing data for the last 3 years. When the client first came to you, she had a portfolio worth $200,000. At the end of the first year, the portfolio was worth $250,000. She then added another $50,000 to the portfolio. At the end of the second year, the portfolio was worth only $270,000 (it was a bad bear market). She added yet another $50,000 to the portfolio. At the end of the third year, the portfolio was worth $352,000. There were no other additions or withdrawals from the portfolio. During this 3-year period, the market had rates of return of 15, –20, and 10 percent. The average risk-free rate was 3 percent. The beta for the client's portfolio was 1.2. The portfolio is extremely well-diversified (over 90 stocks) covering many industries, but almost all of the stocks are large-cap securities.

1. The most appropriate index among the following for evaluating the client's performance would be the:

    (A) Dow Jones Industrial Average
    (B) Standard and Poor's 500
    (C) Russell 2000
    (D) MSCI EAFE

2. The time-weighted and dollar-weighted annual rate of return for the client's portfolio over the last 3 years have been:

    (A) 7.36% and 6.55%
    (B) 6.55% and 7.36%
    (C) 7.36% and 12.08%
    (D) 6.55% and 12.08%

3. Based on the Sharpe ratio for your client's portfolio (use the arithmetic average for the rates of return for each time period to compute the average rate of return) and for the market portfolio:

    (A) your client's portfolio substantially outperformed the market portfolio
    (B) the two portfolios performed about the same
    (C) the market portfolio substantially outperformed your client's portfolio
    (D) we can't really tell which portfolio performed better

4. If you used the Treynor ratio to evaluate your client's portfolio, you know that

    (A) your client's portfolio will always come out looking better than if you use the Sharpe ratio
    (B) the results may be better or worse than if you use the Sharpe ratio
    (C) your client's portfolio will always come out looking worse than if you use the Sharpe ratio
    (D) the relative evaluation of the portfolio compared to the market portfolio will always be the same

5. Based on Jensen's alpha (using arithmetic means to compute the average rates of return), your client's portfolio

    (A) had an excess rate of return of about –7 percent
    (B) earned almost exactly what it should have earned
    (C) had an excess rate of return of about 7 percent
    (D) cannot be effectively evaluated under this criteria

CHAPTER REVIEW

Key Terms and Concepts

sequence risk   reward-to-volatility ratio (RVOL)
reward-to-variability ratio (RVAR)

Review Questions

Review questions are based on the learning objectives in this chapter. Thus, a [3] at the end of a question means that the question is based on learning objective 3. If there are multiple objectives, they are all listed.

1. a. Explain why there can be substantial differences between the time-weighted and dollar-weighted rates of return.
   b. If there are no interim cash flows, what is the relationship between the two rates of return? [1 and 2]

2. A portfolio has a value of $235,000 at the start of the month, and an ending value of $260,000.
    a. What is the rate of return for the period if $20,000 had been added to the portfolio on the first day of the month?
    b. What is the rate of return for the period if, instead of the $20,000 being added at the start of the month, it is added to the portfolio on the last day of the month? [3]

3. In reviewing your client's pension plan performance, you note the following quarterly rates of return: 10 percent, –15 percent, 8 percent, and 5 percent. What is the effective annual rate of return for the pension plan? [3]

4. A new client comes to you and provides you with her portfolio information for the last 4 years, as shown in the table below. Assume that all deposits (shown by positive numbers) and withdrawals (shown by negative numbers) occur at the end of each indicated time period.
    a. Compute the rate of return for each period, keeping in mind that the value of the end of the period incorporates any deposit or withdrawal. (Hint: The rate of return for the first period is 10 percent.)
    b. Compute the time-weighted rate of return.
    c. Compute the dollar-weighted rate of return. [1, 2, 3]

Year	Value at Start of Period	Deposit/Withdrawal	Value at End of Period
1	50,000	10,000	65,000
2	65,000	0	60,000
3	60,000	–10,000	55,000
4	55,000	0	55,000

5. Describe the Dow Jones Industrial Average and indicate its weaknesses as a major market index. [4]

6. a. How does the Russell 3000 Index relate to the Russell 2000 and Russell 1000 indices? [4]
    b. What is unique about the Value Line Index compared to all of the other indices? [4]
    c. What is the most comprehensive index of international securities? [4]
    d. Which company provides a large number of bond market indices? [4]

7. Describe the five reasons that actual portfolios tend to under perform or at least perform differently than market indices. [5]

8. Calculate the Sharpe and Treynor ratios for the market index and the three funds in the chart below, and Jensen's alpha for the three funds. Use a risk-free rate of 4.70 percent. Rank the funds according to each method. (Hint: Although the student should calculate at least one of the standard deviations, the four standard deviations are 13.97, 7.31, 31.31, and 14.72.) [6, 7, 8]

	Good Fund	Bond Fund	Go Fund	Market Index
Beta	1.1	0.6	1.3	1.0
Return Year 1	10.5	8.8	17.7	12.5
Return Year 2	−8.5	6.0	−21.6	−5.3
Return Year 3	15.7	11.4	31.4	18.9
Return Year 4	14.3	9.6	23.4	16.2
Return Year 5	−21.3	−9.1	−32.7	−20.2
Return Year 6	12.2	10.3	53.4	24.3
Return Year 7	9.0	11.5	−12.3	14.5

9. During the last year, you have been recommending that your clients invest in the Rocket Science Corporation. During the year, the stock shot up 12 percent. The risk-free rate of return during the year was 3 percent, the stock's beta is 1.5, and the market was up 10 percent. Based on Jensen's alpha, did this stock outperform or underperform the market? [8]

10. As the chair of the investment committee for your college, you are reviewing the performance of your three portfolio managers. The values of α and σ_ε for the three managers are 1.8 percent and 2.2 percent for the first. 1.4 percent and 1.7 percent for the second, and 2.1 percent and 2.4 percent for the third. Based on the information ratio, which one provided the best performance? [8]

Learning Objectives

An understanding of the material in this chapter should enable the student to

1. Explain the three forms of the efficient market hypothesis (EMH).

2. Describe serial correlation tests and filter rule tests, and indicate their significance.

3. Define an anomaly and identify various anomalies that have been tested.

4. Define the common sentiment, flow-of-funds, and market structure indicators, and indicate which are bullish, which are bearish, and why.

5. Describe how bar and point-and-figure charts are constructed, and how one interprets a chart pattern, such as a head-and-shoulders formation.

The development of modern portfolio theory and the assumptions contained therein eventually led researchers to develop what has come to be known as the efficient market hypothesis (EMH). It should be remembered that this is a hypothesis; it is not a statement of fact. The purpose of the EMH is to provide a framework for thinking about the issues of market efficiency and the research that is done to shed light on the empirical question of market efficiency. One can almost think about the EMH as if it is a religion. Some people believe it literally, some people reject all of it out-of-hand, and some people accept some of it and reject other aspects. It is critical that any investments professional understand the EMH and its various implications. After that, each person is, of course, free to approach investments with whatever philosophy he or she wants. However, for an investments professional, that philosophy should be grounded in his or her understanding of the evidence of how the stock market works, where that understanding comes from knowledge of empirical research on the subject.

TYPES OF INVESTMENT ANALYSIS

fundamental analysis
To discuss the EMH in a meaningful fashion, we need a basic understanding of the two primary types of investment analysis: fundamental analysis and technical analysis. *Fundamental analysis* consists of analyzing the factors that affect the amount and value of the expected future income streams provided by a security. Thus, fundamental analysts assess a firm's earnings and dividend prospects by evaluating such factors as its sales, costs, and capital requirements. Fundamental commodity analysts base their forecasts on the relevant demand and supply factors. Fundamental real estate analysts generate price and rental value expectations from anticipated future construction costs and demand growth estimates.

technical analysis
Technical analysis, in contrast, concentrates on past price and volume relationships of a security or commodity (narrow form) or technical market indicators applicable to that security or commodity (broad form). Both types of technical analysis attempt to identify evolving investor sentiment, but neither has a sound theoretical base. Technical analysts are not particularly concerned with a theoretical justification for their method. They argue that results are what matter. A wealth of available data facilitates the application of technical analysis to the security and commodity markets.

One major distinction between technical and fundamental analysis is that technical analysis looks at prices and volume of trade in isolation without concern for the type of company whose stock is being traded (its financial strength, the quality of its management, the nature of its competition, and so on). Technical analysis could be performed on data, without any knowledge of the company with which that data is associated. Fundamental analysis requires a thorough understanding of the specific company, the nature of its products, and its method of operation.

THE EFFICIENT MARKET HYPOTHESIS

The EMH contends that the market is extremely proficient at pricing securities. Thousands of security analysts and portfolio managers, with unlimited computer time, ample resources, and access to corporate management, are well compensated for their ability to identify mispriced securities. As a result of their activity, when new information appears, the market as a whole reacts quickly to incorporate that information by bidding the prices up or down. As a result, for an individual to identify mispriced securities he or she would need to discern important information that has been missed or misevaluated by analysts. This is extremely difficult, possibly futile.

Ironically, the EMH implies that because analysts as a group are so effective, the efforts of an individual in trying to find mispriced securities may be a waste of time. Additionally, the EMH implies that analysts (and especially financial planners) should direct their activity toward selecting securities that are suitable for the client's desired risk-return profile, and not toward constantly trying to buy undervalued securities and sell overvalued ones.

Random Walk Hypothesis

Many natural phenomena follow a random walk, or what the physical sciences call a Brownian motion. When applied to stocks, the random walk concept implies that the next price change is unrelated to past price behavior. Obviously, if prices move randomly, the repeating price patterns that technical analysts claim to observe have no predictive ability.

One can think of Brownian motion in the following manner. Think of flipping a coin, where heads is a buy order and tails is a sell order. If you flip this coin 20 times, then you have what would represent the random arrival of buy and sell orders. Let's further say that the price of a security goes up 10¢ any time there are three heads in a row, and it goes down 10¢ any time there are three tails in a row. Clearly, such a process will produce price changes, but these price changes will be random. It is not obvious that a stock's price in this process would always end up where it started.

Of course, stock prices tend to rise over time, so it might be more accurate to describe their movement as a "random walk with upward drift." That is, in the previous example, think of the coin that is being flipped as having a slight bias to it, such that it comes up heads 52% of the time and tails 48% of the time. In this case, the stock would probably rise over time, but significant downward movements are still possible. In other words, it seems pretty safe, based on historical evidence, to predict that the market will be higher 10 years from now than it is today, but it is unrealistic to argue that one could predict with any certainty that the market will be higher (or lower) tomorrow than it is today.

Price movements need not be precisely random for past price data to lack predictive ability. Marginally associated relations between past and future price changes may be either too small or too unreliable to generate returns that consistently exceed transaction costs. Indeed, commissions, search costs, bid-ask spreads, and price impact would generally offset any expected price changes that are "small."

Weak Form of the EMH

The weak form of the EMH states that current stock prices fully reflect all information based on trading data. This would include historical stock prices, trading volume, and short interest positions. The implication is that knowledge of past price behavior has no value in predicting future price movements. That is, such knowledge cannot be used to construct a portfolio that consistently outperforms the market on a risk-adjusted basis.

The weak form implies that once we know the most recent price quote, we know as much about possible subsequent returns as those who know the full price history up to that point. That is, prices do not move in predictable patterns. Weak-form adherents further argue that, if prices did move in dependable patterns, the reactions of alert market participants would rapidly eliminate any resulting profit opportunities. If a particular price pattern were thought to forecast a rise, many market participants would react to take advantage of the move. Such actions would eliminate the value of any recognized patterns, because the market would very quickly be driven to its predicted value.

EXAMPLE

Suppose a stock sells for $6 per share. Now, suppose that it were possible to use a technical formula to predict that next month the price of the stock will be $10 per share. Other people would also use the formula and make the same prediction. Therefore, everyone would want to buy the stock, and nobody would want to sell it. The stock would move immediately to almost $10 per share. (To be exact, it would move to the present value of $10, discounted one month at the risk-free interest rate.)

Simply put, if it were really possible to find trends and predict future stock prices, the forces of supply and demand would immediately bring present prices in line with expected future prices.

Semistrong Form of the EMH

The semistrong form states that current stock prices incorporate all public information about a firm. Implicit in the semistrong form is the assumption that investors and analysts have an expectation regarding future events and information that would affect a company's stock price. Hence, when that event or information becomes public knowledge, the real question is not whether that information or event is favorable in absolute terms. The real question is how that information compares to the expectations of that information or event. For example, if a company announces that its quarterly earnings are up 20% from the same quarter a year ago, then one might initially assume that this is good news for the stock. However, if everyone had an expectation that because of recent trends in the economy and the industry that earnings were going to be up 25%, then the announcement that they went up only 20% would be considered disappointing news, and thus the stock price would likely decline. Conversely, if everyone had been anticipating only a 15% increase in earnings, then the 20% increase would be considered a highly favorable result.

Another aspect of the semistrong form is the concept of the adjustment process. A strict interpretation of the semistrong form would be that as soon as a new event occurs or new information becomes available, everyone (or at least a large number of people) simultaneously becomes aware of this event or information. Furthermore, either everyone processes this information in the same way, or at least they all process it in an unbiased manner. As a result, the next trade in a stock after a significant event occurs or new information comes out will be at a price that reflects the new value of the stock, as both buyer and seller are aware of the information and its effect on the stock's price.

Strong Form of the EMH

In the strong form of the EMH, current stock prices fully reflect all information, whether it is publicly available or not. This version asserts that the market also incorporates information that so-called monopolists of information (usually called insiders) have about security prices.

Corporate insiders constitute the main group of information monopolists. Corporate insiders–defined as managers, board members, and those who own 10% or more of the stock of a company–certainly have access to information that is not yet made public. However, SEC rules and federal law prohibit them from profiting from that information or sharing it with outsiders selectively prior to a public announcement. Insiders are permitted to trade the stocks of their own companies, but they are subject to some restrictions. For example, they are prohibited from engaging in short-term trading and from selling short. Strong-form efficiency maintains that even the information known by these monopolists quickly gets reflected in security prices, thus eliminating the potential for abnormal gains.

Forms of the EMH
• Weak form: Current stock prices fully reflect all market trading data, including past stock prices, trading volume, and short sales. Future returns are unrelated to past return patterns. (Charting and other types of technical analysis do not produce superior returns.)
• Semistrong form: Current stock prices fully reflect all publicly available information. Future returns are unrelated to any analysis based on public information. (Fundamental analysis does not result in superior returns.)
• Strong form: Current stock prices fully reflect all information. Future returns are unrelated to any analysis based on public or nonpublic data. (Insider trading does not result in superior returns.)

Professional money managers, such as mutual fund managers or investment advisory services, are one group alleged to have special knowledge about the companies they follow. Specialists who make a market in stocks on the organized exchanges are also believed to have special knowledge of their stocks. Since they are granted a monopoly in making a market in specific stocks, they have short-term knowledge about the flow of buy and sell orders on those stocks. In particular, knowing what orders are outstanding may give them insight into future price movements.

The Relationship Between the Three Forms

It is possible that none or that all three forms could be true. If the weak form is true, the semistrong and strong form could still be false. But if the weak form is false, the other two must also be false. If the weak and the semistrong forms are true, the strong form could still be true or false. But if the strong form is true, all three are true. Each form incorporates the prior form. The possible relationships are summarized in the following table.

Table 5-1 Possible Relationships of Three Forms of the EMH		
Weak	**Semistrong**	**Strong**
True	True	True
True	True	False
True	False	False
False	False	False

Market Success and the EMH

There are two issues with regard to market success and market efficiency that need to be clarified:

1. If the EMH is true, does this mean that no one can "beat the market"?
2. If someone "beats the market," does this automatically invalidate the EMH?

It is possible for an investor to earn an abnormally high return, just as it is possible to make money at a gambling casino. Some people make the mistake of thinking that if the market is efficient then no one can earn an abnormally high return. That is not the case. Market efficiency simply means that technical and fundamental analysis should not *consistently* earn an investor an abnormally high return once risk and transaction costs are taken into account. (The costs of obtaining information, including the opportunity cost of forgoing other productive uses of one's time, should also be taken into account when deciding whether to use fundamental analysis techniques.)

To illustrate the fact that some people do appear to consistently beat the market requires only the following illustration. Let's define flipping heads as beating the market, and flipping tails as underperforming the market. Over any time period, one-half of investors would be expected to "beat" the market (that is, perform better than some market index), and one-half of them would be expected to underperform the market (that is, do worse than the same index). Let's say that we start with 1,024 investors and their performance is defined by flipping coins. If all the coins are fair, then we would expect one-half of them (that is, 512 of them) to flip heads and beat the market in the first time period. If those 512 investors flipped their coins again, then we would expect 256 of them to beat the market for a second time period. Similarly, we would expect 128 of them to beat the market three periods in a row, 64 to beat it four periods in a row, 32 for five, 16 for six, 8 for seven, 4 for eight, 2 for nine, and 1 investor to beat the market 10 times in a row. Now, does this mean that this one investor is incredibly skillful? Or does it mean that out of the 1,024 investors who started out, this person was the only one lucky enough to flip 10 heads in a row? Similarly, in the actual market, because of the large number of people who are investing, there will be an occasional few who put together an amazingly large number of consecutively successful years. However, we have no way of telling if they are truly superior investors or if they just happen to be the lucky ones.

It should also be pointed out that many portfolio managers, financial advisors, stockbrokers, and financial planners claim consistent, superior performance but do not provide independently validated evidence of that performance. In addition, as we saw in the previous chapter, there are many ways to evaluate performance. One can compare one's results to a simple benchmark, such as any of the many indices described; one can use a standard deviation-based measure or one can use a beta-based measure. Without knowing how a person is measuring his or her own performance, and whether or not that person is doing it properly, it is impossible to know if claims of superior performance are valid. Finally, even the best portfolio managers have occasional poor years, and even the worst portfolio managers have occasional good years.

TESTING THE WEAK FORM OF THE EMH

Tests of the EMH always boil down to this rather simple concept: Is there a strategy that could consistently be applied that would allow an investor to outperform the market by a statistically significant amount? Unfortunately, any test of the EMH is really a dual hypothesis test. The first is a test of the model that is used to adjust for risk (usually the capital asset pricing model), and the second is a test of the efficiency itself.

To be judged successful, a trading strategy needs to generate returns that, after an appropriate adjustment for risk, exceed in the aggregate the market returns of the corresponding periods. Thus, the techniques of both technical and fundamental analysis need to be tested against real-world data. This testing is done by forming portfolios that one would have selected based on buy signals from a particular tool. The hypothetical portfolios are then compared to an actual market index for the same period. Normally, a stock market index, such as the S&P 500 Index or the New York Stock Exchange

Composite, is used to represent overall market performance. Virtually all academic studies of market efficiency utilize such risk-adjusted returns data.

Two of the most basic tests of technical analysis are serial correlations and filter rules. If past price patterns help forecast future price change, past and future price changes should be related, and filter rules should help identify profitable trading opportunities.

Serial Correlation and Runs

A serial correlation coefficient compares returns for each day to returns for the previous day. If stocks tend to move in the same direction on consecutive days more frequently than they reversed direction, the serial correlation coefficient would be a statistically significant positive number. If stock prices tend to flip back and forth on consecutive days, the serial correlation coefficient would be a statistically significant negative number. The early research on serial correlation coefficients consistently showed that they are not statistically different than zero. More recent research has suggested that these statistics are positive. If that is the case, then one should buy "yesterday's" winners and avoid "yesterday's" biggest losers. Let's say the evidence on serial correlation coefficients is mixed.

Other studies have investigated runs of price changes. A run is an uninterrupted series of price increases or decreases. To understand a runs test, think of designating every trade in a stock with either a '+' if the trade represents a price increase, a '–' if the trade represents a price decline, and a zero if the trade results in no price change. Next, ignore all of the zeros. One is then left with a series of plusses and minuses. Next, count the number of times there are two consecutive plusses or two consecutive minuses, the number of times there are three consecutive plusses and minuses, and so on up to the maximum number of consecutive plusses or minuses. This distribution is then compared to the number of consecutive plusses or minuses that one would expect to see if the sequence of plusses and minuses had been generated by coin flips where a head is a plus and a tail is a minus. Studies have consistently failed to find any significant relationship in successive price changes. Thus, past price changes do not appear to forecast future price movements.

Filter Rules

momentum
Filter rules attempt to capture the momentum/resistance-level factors that technical analysts

claim are important. *Momentum* indicates the tendency of a stock price to continue to rise or fall, whereas resistance level refers to a stock price at which either a large number of sell orders (upper resistance level) or a large number of buy orders (lower resistance level) would be expected to appear. Filter rules mechanically identify supposed buy and sell situations.

The standard filter rule flashes a buy signal whenever a stock increases by x percent from a relative low. After an x percent decline from a subsequent high, a sell signal is given. For instance, a 5-percent filter would signal to buy whenever a stock rose 5% from the previous low. Really small filters actually appear to work. Thus, if an investor set a filter of, say, one-half of 1% (0.5%), then the investor could expect to outperform the market. Unfortunately, these results occur only when transaction fees are ignored. When transaction fees are incorporated into the analysis, trading strategies based on filters result in losses.

Conclusions about Technical Analysis

Most academics and practitioners remain highly skeptical of technical analysis. The main reason for this skepticism is that much of the research on technical analysis techniques has failed to confirm their consistency and validity, given the transaction costs involved, relative to a simple buy and-hold strategy. Furthermore, it seems that every time someone identifies and publishes a mechanical rule that would allow a person to outperform the market, that rule ceases to work from that point onward! Also, as with our 1,024 coin flippers, if enough trading rules are tested, some will be shown to be statistically significant in beating the market, when in fact such rules were just "lucky."

In addition, there are other troubling features of technical analysis. First, several interpretations of a particular technical tool or chart pattern are possible, giving rise to numerous different assessments or recommendations.

A second troubling factor is if a technical trading rule (or chart pattern) proves truly successful and is made public, it will become widely adopted by market participants. If any rule or pattern is widely adopted, it will often prove to be self-defeating. Therefore, stock prices will reach their equilibrium value quickly, taking away profit opportunities from most market participants. Moreover, some market observers may start trying to act before the rest on the basis of what they expect to occur; thus, the prices of affected stocks will tend to reach equilibrium even more quickly. Eventually, the value of any such rule or pattern will be negated entirely.

A third problem with technical analysis is that it implies a form of predestination (here we are back to religion!). If tomorrow's stock price is predictable based on current and past market trading data, then it means that what happens between now and tomorrow is immaterial.

It is impossible to test all the techniques of technical analysis and their variations and interpretations. The techniques are too numerous, and new ones are developed all the time. Therefore, absolutely definitive statements about their validity cannot be made.

EXAMPLE

Despite academic researchers' strong opposition to technical analysis, there are still many businesses anxious to sell it. A current example of such a firm is Channeling Stocks.com. In this case, the firm promises to identify for its customers at least 12 stocks that demonstrate a channeling pattern. A channeling pattern is said to be one in which a stock bounces around within a fairly well-defined range. The strategy appears to be that one should buy at the bottom of the range and sell at the top.

SEMISTRONG- AND STRONG-FORM TESTS OF THE EMH (ANOMALIES)

Potential Causes of Persistent Market Imperfections

Conventional theory assumes that market prices are formed by a homogeneous group of investors who analyze the same sources of information in identical fashions. Although market efficiency does not require perfect homogeneity of investor expectations, marginal investors must behave as if they accurately analyze all relevant public information and are unaffected (or identically affected) by such matters as tax status, costs of trading, risk orientation, borrowing power, liquidity preference, familiarity with local markets, and total available funds. In the business world, however, the resources of investors who are best positioned to profit may be insufficient to eliminate some mispricings.

anomaly General tests of the semistrong and strong forms are difficult to devise and perform. Market efficiency cannot be directly proven. Rather, we can only infer efficiency by showing that specific inefficiencies do not exist. The market pricing process generates so much random movement, or "noise," that prices can stray from their intrinsic values without detection by commonly used tests. Nevertheless, various subhypotheses of the EMH have been examined. Many studies have found market anomalies or imperfections. An *anomaly* is a specific strategy that consistently outperforms the market on a risk-adjusted basis.

small-firm effect   Because investment analysts and the financial press concentrate on the larger, better-known firms, the security prices of many smaller firms may depart from the intrinsic values that a careful analysis would yield. These firms generally trade in localized markets; therefore, few investors are positioned to observe the mispricings. This is known as the *small-firm effect*.

Only investors who can purchase control of a company may exploit some types of mispricings. An investor who acquires control of a firm that is worth more out of business than in business could liquidate its assets for more than the firm's value as a going concern. Such takeovers, however, are not usually easy to accomplish. The effort tends to bid up prices and provoke vigorous defensive efforts by those whose interests are threatened. Investors with the necessary resources to eliminate the mispricing may frequently have inadequate incentives to do so. Still other imperfections (arbitrage opportunities) may require quick and low-cost access to several markets. Only if enough investors are able to take advantage of these imperfections will their actions correct the price imbalances.

A number of studies suggest that stocks with low price-earnings ratios, small market capitalizations, low per-share prices, or related characteristics tend to outperform the market. With so much conflicting evidence, the extent of semistrong-form efficiency is decidedly debatable. Some academicians suggest that, since institutional investors—with all their professional expertise—rarely outperform the market on a risk-adjusted basis, individual investors are unlikely to do better. Others claim that there are enough market imperfections that talented investment analysts can outperform the market. Even if the market eventually evaluates public information accurately, academicians claim that some investors and/or analysts may be able to take advantage of lags in the price-adjustment process.

Many strong-form supporters concede that insider information is sometimes useful, but they contend that such instances are rare and therefore the conclusions of the strong form generally hold up. Research on the profitability of insider information is somewhat mixed. Several early studies found little evidence of excess returns to insiders. More recent studies show that insiders earn more than outsiders on the same purchase or sale transaction in the same company's stock. Results also indicate that as the information becomes public knowledge, excess insider returns decrease as the length of the holding period increases.

These mixed results may be due to different definitions of "insiders." The advantages of professional money managers and specialists may be somewhat limited. However, corporate insiders, such as senior managers and directors, clearly have access to information about a company's prospects that is not available to the general public. In the absence of laws against insider trading, they undoubtedly would be able to reap excess profits from that information.

Dogs of the Dow

One of the more famous strategies for beating the market that has emerged in recent years is known as "the dogs of the Dow." The strategy is simple. At the start of each year, an investor ranks the 30 stocks in the DJIA based on dividend yield (from high to low). The investor then buys the top 10 stocks on the list (that is, the 10 stocks with the highest dividend yields). These stocks are held for one year, at which time a new portfolio is constructed in the same manner.

Research into whether or not dogs of the Dow actually works in beating the market has produced inconsistent results. Unusually high-dividend-yielding stocks are usually considered above average in risk. Thus, a strategy that involves holding high-dividend-yielding stocks would be expected to produce rates of return greater than the market. The real question is whether the returns are sufficient given the higher degree of risk. Research by Domian, Louton, and Mossman[38] found that prior to 1987, the selection criterion truly selected stocks that had performed poorly the prior year; hence they deserved the title of "dogs." After 1987, the selection criterion actually ended up selecting stocks that had done well the previous year, even though their dividend yields ended up being high. Hence, the selection process no longer selected "dogs." Since 1987, this strategy has ranged from being ineffective to an outright failure. Domian, Louton, and Mossman conclude that at the time of publication, this selection rule was consistent with the overreaction hypothesis. Since 1987, the rule has no longer functioned as a surrogate

---

38. D. Domian, D. Louton, and C. Mossman, "The Rise and Fall of the 'Dogs of the Dow',"*Financial Services Review*, 7, no. 3 (1998): 146-160.

for this hypothesis, and has no longer worked. This means the rule had no legitimacy in the first place, but it provided support for the overreaction hypothesis.

The overreactions hypothesis is the idea that investors tend to overreact to information, whether that information is good news or bad news. As a result, a strong return on good news will be followed by a downside correction. Conversely, a negative return on bad news will be followed by an upside correction.

January Indicator

January indicator (January effect)   The *January indicator (January effect)* is a rather simplistic tool that often receives a good bit of attention at the beginning of each year. A market that rises in January is expected to rise during the year; a market that falls in January is expected to fall during the year. Because the market generally rises both in January and for the year, the success of the January indicator may easily be overstated. Several other months seem to do about as well.

Regarding the January effect, Donald Keim[39] found that small stocks outperformed large stocks during the first several weeks almost every year between 1926 and the mid-1970s. One explanation for this is that hard-to-trade small stocks tend to be depressed by investors' tax-related year-end selling. But then small stocks bounce back as investors rebuy them early the next year. However, according to Prudential Securities, small stocks underperformed the market averages each January for the period 1993-1998. One explanation is that fund managers buy stocks of small companies in December in anticipation of the January effect, thus offsetting individual investors' tax-loss selling.

Day-of-the-Week Effect

Unusual price behavior has been found to occur on Mondays and Fridays. In the past, the market was consistently more likely to be up on Friday than on Monday. The frequent practice of withholding unpleasant economic news until the market's Friday close might account for this phenomenon. This

---

39. D. B. Keim, "Size-Related Anomalies and Stock Return Seasonality: Further Empirical Evidence," *Journal of Financial Economics*, 12, no. 1 (June 1983): 13-32; "A New Look at the Effects of Firm Size and E/P Ratio on Stock Returns," *Financial Analysts Journal*, 46, no. 2 (March/April 1990): 56-67.

day-of-the-week price effect suggests that, if no overriding considerations intervene, investors planning to sell something might as well sell on Friday and investors planning to buy something might wait until late in the day on Monday to buy.

Additions to the S&P 500

Additions to Standard & Poor's 500 Index are widely followed by the market. Because the S&P 500 is a much broader-based index than the Dow Jones Industrial Average, and it is quoted in the media almost as frequently, it is the index on which many other financial instruments are based. For example, most stock index futures, options on index futures, and indexed mutual funds utilize the S&P 500. Stocks are regularly added to and deleted from this index by Standard & Poor's in order to preserve or enhance its representativeness. The announcement that a stock is to be added to the index tends to cause that stock's price to rise, whereas a deletion has the opposite effect.

Insider Trading

Often, insider information appears to facilitate a relatively accurate stock evaluation. People who are not insiders must generally wait until the information is publicly released, but traders can observe insiders' trading decisions and act accordingly. The insider trades of CEOs and directors appear to be better predictors of subsequent performance than those of vice presidents and beneficial owners.[40]

Insiders must report their trades to the SEC. Thus, investors can consult SEC records to determine insiders' trading on a particular stock. Moreover, some investment services report SEC insider trading data to subscribers. Certain periodicals, including *Barron's* and *Value Line*, report on insider trades, and insider-trading activity is sometimes discussed in the financial press, at least on an ad hoc basis. However, there can be a time lag of several days or weeks between the time insider trades take place and the time they become known by the investing public. During the intervening time, the market price of the company's stock might change sufficiently so that investors who are not insiders would find it difficult to profit after taking transaction costs into consideration.

---

40. K. Nunn, G. Madden, and M. Gombola, "Are Some Insiders More 'Inside' Than Others?," *Journal of Portfolio Management* (Spring 1983): 18-22.

There have been several cases related to alleged misused insider information by outsiders who made trades based on it. An important Supreme Court decision in 1997 clarified what constitutes illegal insider trading. The decision upheld the so-called misappropriation theory of insider trading, which states that traders may not trade on nonpublic information even if they are not corporate insiders.[41] A recent case of insider trading involved Martha Stewart. Although she was not accused of insider trading, she was accused of lying to investigators about trading on what was effectively insider information. Specifically, she was accused of trading on the tip from her stockbroker that the president and CEO of another company was selling a large block of his own shares in that company. If true, subsequent stock price movement validated that Martha made what most people would consider a huge profit on that trade.

Market Efficiency Debate

Although some academicians hold extreme positions, few who have examined the issue believe that the market is strong-form efficient or is always semistrong-form efficient. On the other hand, most serious finance scholars agree that the weak form of the EMH is correct. The principal disagreements relate to the importance, extent, and causes of the imperfections of the semistrong form.

EXAMPLE

A client approaches you to say he has heard about a technique for beating the market. The technique is to buy the 10 stocks in the DJIA that have the highest dividend yields. He suggests that you adjust his portfolio to hold mostly these stocks. How might you respond?

The empirical evidence for such techniques is always weak at best. Frequently, once a technique that has worked in the past is publicized, it subsequently ceases to work. In addition, none of the techniques for beating the market would work well enough to offset the benefits from appropriate diversification and asset allocation. Nonetheless, if the client truly believes this to be the case, the advisor might as well make some of the future stock selections based on this criterion. After all, even if this technique has no value, if markets are efficient then no harm should come from using it.

---

41. E. Felsenthal, "Big Weapon Against Insider Trading Is Upheld," *The Wall Street Journal* (June 26, 1997): C1.

TECHNICAL INDICATORS

Despite the lack of scientific support, technical analysis is still widely practiced and believed in by many market participants. It is crucial that a financial planner understand the jargon and concepts of technical analysis so that he or she can respond knowledgeably to questions and comments concerning technical analysis. This material is NOT being presented herein as concepts a financial planner should use in his or her practice.

Technical analysis consists of two broad areas of application: technical indicators and the construction of charts (known as charting). Let's look first at some of the more popular technical indicators.

There are many, many different technical indicators that are used to predict the market overall, as well as specific stocks. There are other indicators that can be applied to just the market or to just specific stocks. The trick to studying these indicators is to find a way to classify them based on common themes. A variety of common themes have been suggested over the years, but the common themes utilized today are sentiment indicators, flow-of-funds indicators, and market structure indicators. We will adopt this characterization for our discussion.

Sentiment Indicators

sophisticated-investor rationale

contrarian rationale

Sentiment indicators start with the assumption that the general sentiment of certain groups of investors can be ascertained with different indicators. This measurement is then combined with an identification of each group as either "sophisticated investors" or "naïve investors." The assumption is that sophisticated investors are more sophisticated or knowledgeable than other investors and thus are right more often than they are wrong. Similarly, naïve investors are assumed to lack the knowledge and sophistication of the knowledgeable investors, and as a result are wrong more often than they are right. The idea then is that one would want to mimic what sophisticated investors are doing (a *sophisticated-investor rationale*) or do the opposite of what the naïve investors are doing (*contrarian rationale*).

It would be nice to categorize each technical indicator as being either a sophisticated investor or a contrarian indicator, but that is difficult to do as there are sometimes multiple rationales to support specific indicators. That is, different people will agree that a particular indicator is a good forecasting tool, but they will disagree as to why that is the case. In fact, sometimes the same indicator is treated as either bullish or bearing depending on the rationale used to support the legitimacy of the indicator!

Odd-Lot Ratio

The odd-lot ratio is a classic example of the contrarian rationale applied to a sentiment indicator. The rationale is the assumption that people who trade in odd lots (stock trades of less than 100 shares) tend to be inexperienced and unskilled traders. Thus, when odd-lotters are buying on balance, the market may be about to fall; when odd-lot investors are mostly selling, the market may be ready to turn up.

There are a lot of different ways to measure what the odd-lot traders are doing, but the most common measure is the ratio of odd-lot purchases to odd-lot sales. Both numbers are provided daily in various financial publications. For example, on June 27, 2010, there were 2,815,735 shares purchased on an odd-lot basis, and there were 3,400,480 shares sold on an odd-lot basis.[42] Thus, the ratio of purchases to sales on this date was 0.83. The ratio has fluctuated historically between 0.50 and 1.5, but tends to be above 1.0. The reason is that financially weak investors accumulate holdings through odd-lot purchases until they have a round lot, simply because they lack the cash to make a round-lot purchase. However, when they sell, they tend to sell their entire holding, thus making a round-lot sale rather than an odd-lot sale.

Mutual Fund Cash Position

A second sentiment indicator that is usually interpreted as contrarian is the percentage of cash held in mutual fund portfolios. The most direct measure of this sentiment is the cash in mutual funds as a percentage of total assets. The ratio really only makes sense for the equity mutual funds. One would think that the portfolio managers of mutual funds would be among the most sophisticated in the market place, but the popular opinion is that they are in fact laggard on market movements. Hence, they tend to be building up cash at market bottoms and minimizing cash at market tops. Of course, one could also argue that it is not the managers themselves that are causing this, but the investors in the mutual funds. That is, if the investors in the mutual funds are from the naïve group, then they would be liquidating their holdings at market bottoms and buying at market tops. The portfolio managers would

---

42. online.wsj.com/mdc/public/page/2_3024–oddlottrades.html; accessed June 30, 2010

need to anticipate this movement of cash, which would force them to at least build up cash reserves at market bottoms.

A disadvantage of this indicator is that it is available only on a monthly basis. Hence, by the time investors see it, it represents historical, rather than current data. Most sentiment indicators are available on a daily basis.

Trin

short-term trading index

A measure of overall market sentiment is the trin statistic. "Trin" is an acronym for "trading index." The idea is the upward and downward movements in the market are more sustainable when they are accompanied by heavy volume. The statistic is defined as the average volume of declining stocks divided by the average volume of advancing stocks.

$$\text{Trin} = \frac{\dfrac{\text{Volume of declining stocks}}{\text{Number of declining stocks}}}{\dfrac{\text{Volume of advancing stocks}}{\text{Number of advancing stocks}}}$$

The lower the ratio, the greater the average volume in advancing stocks relative to the average volume in declining stocks. Hence, a low ratio is bullish.

EXAMPLE
On June 30, 2010, the following data was recorded for the NYSE:

Advances	1,433
Declines	2,399
Adv vol (000s)	1,914,034
Decl vol (000s)	3,403,642

The trin ratio was:

Trin = [3,403,642 / 2,399] / [1,914,034 / 1,433] = 1.062

Barron's Confidence Index

The Barron's confidence index (BCI) is a sophisticated-investor sentiment indicator. The belief is that bond investors are more knowledgeable than others, and bullish sentiments will be reflected by relative changes in bond yields. The BCI is the ratio of the average yield on Barron's index of high-grade corporate bond rates divided by its index of intermediate-grade corporate bond rates. For the week ending June 25, 2010, the BCI was reported to be 78.1, up from its value of 66.8 at the same time the previous year.[43]

The ratio will always be less than one. When it is closer to one than usual, it indicates that high-grade yields are relatively close to the yields on more speculative issues. At such times, the market is unwilling to pay much of a premium for quality (or, stated differently, does not require a large premium to hold lower-grade issues). Hence, a high value is bullish. Alternatively, a low ratio implies a substantial premium for quality, and thus is bearish.

Put/Call Ratio

The buyer of a put expects the price of the associated asset (usually a specific stock) to fall in price, and the buyer of a call expects the price of the associated asset to rise. Although many people agree that the put/call ratio is a good measure of sentiment, there is disagreement as to whose sentiment, the interpretation of a high or low value, and even the best way to compute the ratio. Although some people compute it as the ratio of outstanding puts to outstanding calls, the Chicago Board of Options Exchange (CBOE) computes the ratio based on the volume of puts and calls traded. In fact, it is the CBOE that publishes the official put/call ratio statistic each day. Using this latter definition, the average value of this ratio is considered to be 0.8.[44]

A common interpretation of this ratio is that people who invest in options usually lose. Thus, when they are buying puts, the ratio will be high and this would be a contrarian indicator. So a high ratio will be bearish and a low ratio will be bullish.[45] An alternative interpretation is that this ratio measures the sentiment of the broad market. Hence, a high value will be bearish as it

---

43. http://online.barrons.com/public/page/9_0210–weeklybondstats.html, accessed June 30, 2010.

44. www.investinganswers.com/term/putcall-ratio-931, accessed July 22, 2010.

45. J. Summe, "Forecasting Market Direction with Put/Call Ratios." www.investopedia.com/articles/optioninvestor/02/052102.asp, accessed June 30, 2010.

indicates a significant portion of investors think that many individual stocks are more likely to decline.

Traditional Technical Market Indicators
• Odd-lot activity: odd-lot purchases to odd-lot sales; high values are usually bearish (contrarian indicator).
• Mutual fund cash position: cash as a percentage of portfolio assets; high value is bullish (contrarian indicator).
• Trin: average volume in declining stocks divided by average volume in rising stocks; high value is bearish (sophisticated-investor indicator).
• Barron's confidence index: ratio of high-grade to intermediate-grade bond yields; high values are bullish (sophisticated-investor indicator).
• Put/call ratio: ratio of volume in put to volume in calls; interpreted both ways and with both rationales.

Flow-of-Funds Indicators

Flow-of-funds indicators attempt to provide some indication of where cash is going, or where it might go. The two most commonly used flow-of-funds indicators are the short interest and the cash balances in brokerage accounts.

Short Interest

Short sellers sell borrowed stock they hope to replace at a profit. At one time, short sellers were thought to be sophisticated traders who were able to anticipate market turns. Thus, an increase in the cumulative short-interest position (uncovered short sales) was said to forecast a market decline. Others have argued that short interest reflects potential demand from short traders who need to buy back the stock to cover their positions. According to this view, a rise in short interest forecasts a market rally.

A measure of the magnitude of short selling is the short-interest ratio, which is:

$$\text{Short-interest ratio} = \text{Total short interest} \div \text{Average daily trading volume.}$$

Think of this ratio as the number of days of normal trading that would be required for all short sellers to cover their positions.

The short-interest ratio has shown a slight long-term increase in value. The most likely reason is that the growth of options and futures trading has provided the opportunity for more hedging and arbitraging activities. These types of trading frequently include the process of shorting the underlying stock. Short interest data is published both for an entire exchange and individual stocks. For example, on June 15, 2010, there were 39,150,131 shares of Saks Incorporated common stock that were short. The average daily trading volume in sales was 4,817,562 shares. The short interest ratio was 33.7, a really large number.

Cash Balances in Brokerage Accounts

We saw earlier that cash in a brokerage account is insured only if it is there incidental to trading. Many people do in fact leave cash in a brokerage account for this reason. That is, they have sold a stock and have not yet decided how to reinvest the cash, or they have deposited cash in anticipation of making a purchase. Many people view this as a measure of near-term buying intentions. Hence, a large cumulative cash balance is bullish, and a small balance is bearish.

Market Structure Indicators

Market structure indicators look at ways of measuring the recent performance of either a particular stock or the market as a whole, and assuming that this performance will continue.

Moving Averages

A moving average (MA) computes the average price of a stock or index for a specified time period, and then looks at the current price relative to the MA. If the current price is above the MA, then that is bullish, and if the current price is below the MA, then that is bearish.[46] The most common time period for the MA is 200 days. Some people like a 50-day MA and others like a 53-week MA. There are multiple techniques to compute the MA, including: simple MA, exponential MA, smooth MA, and linear-weighted MA.

EXAMPLE

Suppose Standard Widget's daily closing prices are as follows:

---

46.   http://ta.mql4.com/indicator/trends/moving-average; accessed June 30, 2010.

May 1, 2008	$30
May 2, 2008	$31
May 3, 2008	$32
May 4, 2008	$31
May 5, 2008	$31
May 8, 2008	$32
May 9, 2008	$31
May 10, 2008	$30
May 11, 2008	$29
May 12, 2008	$30

Assume we wish to calculate the simple MA for the past five trading days. On May 8, our MA would be based on the closing prices of May 1 through 5, or ($30 + $31 + $32 + $31 + $31)/5, or $31. On May 9, our MA would be based on the closing stock prices for May 2 through 8, and so on. For the second week in May, our daily 5-day MA would be:

May 8, 2008	$31
May 9, 2008	$31.40
May 10, 2008	$31.40
May 11, 2008	$31
May 12, 2008	$30.60

Breadth Indicators

Breadth-of-market indicators attempt to look at how the entire market is doing relative to the common market indices. The most common breadth indicator is the advance-decline index. This is the cumulative sum of the difference between advances and declines for each day. Although most of the time the advance-decline index moves in the same direction as the general market indices, there are occasions upon which the two diverge. In these instances, the assumption is that the advance-decline index is preceding the market indices, and thus is a good short-term predictor. In general, a rising advance-decline index is bullish, and a falling one is bearish.[47]

---

47. http://www.investopedia.com/terms/a/advancedeclineindex.asp; June 30, 2010.

EXAMPLE
Yesterday, the *Wall Street Journal* reported that on the previous trading day there were 3,455 issues that traded on the NYSE. Of these, 1,213 advanced, 2,102 declined, and 140 were unchanged. For someone who is maintaining an advance-decline line, the value of this index would be reduced by 889 (1,213 - 2,102) for this day.

Relative Strength Index

A relative strength index compares a stock's volatility on up days to its volatility on down days. Naturally, there are multiple ways to construct the index, but all incorporate the following nature of relative strength:

$$RS = \frac{\text{Average of x days' up closes}}{\text{Average of x days' down closes}}$$

Large relative strength ratios indicate a stock is overbought and low values indicate it is oversold. Thus, the large values are bearish and the low values are bullish.

Dow Theory

The Dow theory is one of the oldest and best-known approaches to market timing. Its originator, Charles Dow, was also the founder and first editor of *The Wall Street Journal*. Dow developed the key averages quoted widely in the financial pages: the DJIA, the DJTA, and the DJUA. The Dow theory asserts that a continuing trend can be identified by looking first for a new high in an index defined as primary (such as the DJIA), and then seeking confirmation from a second high (such as the DJTA). Thus, if the DJIA reaches a new high at approximately the same time a new high is set for the DJTA, an up-trend is said to be intact. One can think of the Dow theory as suggesting that the stock market moves in waves like the ocean, and like the ocean also has tides. Thus, one wants to buy when the tide is coming in, and sell when the tide starts to go out. Recent variations on this wave concept of stock price changes include the Elliott wave theory and Kondratiev waves. Kondratiev was a Russian economist who argued that the economy moves in waves, each of which lasts an average of about 50 years. Obviously, to test such a theory one would want to have at least 1,000 years worth of data, and 2,000 years worth of data would be even better. So, we will need to wait awhile to see if Kondratiev was on to something!

Three Basic Ideas Behind the Dow Theory
• To make a profit in the stock market, investors should take advantage of the primary market trend, which is the generally upward movement of the market over a period of one to four years.
• Whenever a primary trend is up, each secondary trend (a cycle around the basic trend) will produce a peak higher than the last one (vice versa for a down-trend).
• Any true indicator of a primary market trend will be confirmed relatively quickly by similar action in the different stock price averages.

CHARTING

Charting is used to assess both the overall mood of the market and the market's mood toward specific stocks. Charting is controversial, as many people believe it is analogous to trying to read tea leaves, but it is still widely practiced.

Chartists are people who study charts for patterns in price movements. A chartist would say that the statistical tests discussed earlier look largely for linear relations and that they are much too crude to capture subtleties. Moreover, chartists assert that their "craft" is as much art as science, because it depends heavily on judgment, interpretation, and experience. That is, beneath the apparent randomness of stock price movements is a distinct nonrandom pattern that can be discerned from charts. They argue that these patterns are difficult to quantify by standard statistical methods.

Types of Charts

Bar Charts

A common type of chart is the bar chart. The vertical axis of a bar chart is dollars, usually on a logarithmic scale so that price movements of equal percentage amounts will be the same size. The horizontal axis represents trading days. For each trading day, a line is drawn connecting the high and low price of the day. An example of this is the bar chart shown in *Figure 5-1* (the vertical axis in this chart is arithmetic and not logarithmic). A more elaborate bar chart would show the closing price each day by a cross mark or tic on the vertical line representing each day's price range. Some charts will also add the daily volume at the bottom (using a different vertical axis). The basic format of the bar chart may be supplemented with an MA line or even a relative strength line.

Figure 5-1
Typical Bar Chart

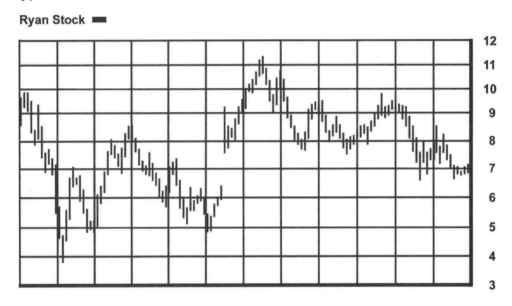

The Head-and-Shoulders Pattern. Technical analysts seek to identify favorable buying and selling opportunities based on repeating price patterns. These patterns include chart formations, such as triangles, coils, rectangles, flags, pennants, gaps, line-and-saucer formations, and V-formations. Perhaps the best-known pattern is the head-and-shoulders formation on bar charts, as shown in *Figure 5-2*. This pattern, which resembles the human form, shows the following stages of development for a bearish signal:

- Left shoulder—The left shoulder builds up on a strong rally, accompanied by significant volume. Thereafter, when a profit-taking reaction occurs, the shoulder slopes downward. Volume is noticeably reduced.

- Head—Rising prices and increased volume initiate the left side of the head pattern, followed by a contraction, or reduced volume. In this configuration, the head always extends well above the left shoulder.

- Right shoulder—A smaller rally and a retreat. Volume action is usually decidedly smaller than it was under the left shoulder and head. The right shoulder tends to be roughly equal in height with the left shoulder and it is always well below the head.

neckline   Note that the bottom of each shoulder is at about the same price. This price is referred to as the *neckline*. As shown in the graph, the formation is complete and the pattern is screaming that an investor should sell. The expectation is that after the right shoulder is completed, the price is expected to drop significantly.

A variation of this pattern is the upside-down head and shoulders. Think of this as a person standing on his or her head. The description of the volume as it relates to each "leg" of this pattern is the same. The only difference is that the upside-down formation is bullish, and the forecast is that there will be a major upward price movement once the price breaks the neckline after completing the right shoulder.

Figure 5-2
Head-and-Shoulders Pattern

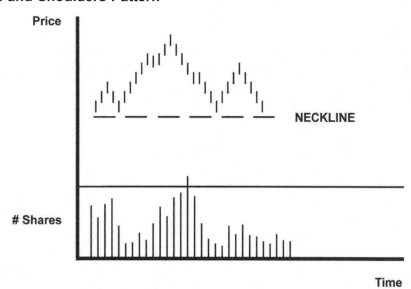

Point-and-Figure Charts

A point-and-figure chart diagrams only stock movements and has no time dimension. The vertical axis measures the stock price, and the horizontal axis is used to note a change in the direction of price movement. To start a chart, one looks for a price movement of a minimum magnitude, usually $3. The initial price movement required to start the chart could be larger or smaller than $3 if the nominal price of the stock is unusually low or high. Price changes are measured based on highs and lows, and closing prices have no relevancy to the chart. Thus, the first column in a chart would be measured either from a low to a high that represents at least a $3 movement, or a high to a low that represents a $3 movement. Using *Figure 5-3*, let's say that the chart is started with an upward price movement that goes from a low of $26 to a subsequent high of $29. Hence, X's are entered in the chart denoting that trading has occurred at $27, $28, and $29. Once this initial entry has been made, then the chartist is looking to see what occurs next, an upward price movement of at least $1, or a downward price movement of at least $3. In other words, no more entries are made on the chart until the stock trades at a high of at least $30, or a low of at least $26. It is certainly possible that both could occur on the same day, and the chartist would have to look at the ending price to see which likely occurred last, the new high or the new low. For the new low to occur, the low of the day must be at least $26 exactly or lower. Thus, a price of $26.05 would be treated as a price of $27, not $26. Similarly, a price of $25.95 is treated as $26, not $25.

If the price of $30 occurs first, then the chartist looks to see whether $31 occurs next (a continuation in the same direction), or $27 occurs next to indicate a reversal in price movement. If the $31 occurs first, the chartist adds another X to the vertical column of X's that has been started. If the price of $27 occurs first, the chartist will start a new column of O's to signal the new price direction.

Figure 5-3
Typical Point-and-Figure Chart

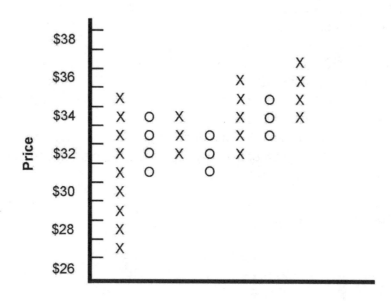

Because several days, weeks, or even months could go by in which there are no entries on a chart, there is no time element to this chart. To a point-and-figure chartist, this simply means that no significant price movement has occurred, and thus there is nothing to record. Put another way, by eliminating time, a point-and-figure chart is meant to provide a picture of only the significant price movements. As with bar charts, there are certain patterns such as triple tops, double tops, triple-top reversal, flags, etc., that have been identified as associated with a "break-out," in which the stock is making a significant price move in a particular direction.

Resistance and Support Levels

resistance level

support level

Underlying most charting techniques is a belief in the existence of resistance and support levels. A *resistance level* occurs when a significant number of investors look to get out when a certain price level is reached and a *support level* occurs as new buyers suddenly emerge when a certain price level is reached.

An alternative way to think about resistance and support levels is as upper and lower price barriers. In other words, suppose a stock trades at around $38 per share. Suppose further that most people believe this is *approximately* a fair price for the stock. Note the emphasis on "approximately." This is because no one knows exactly what the true fair price of the stock is, but many are comfortable that it is around $38. The stock will trade around this price as long as the belief holds that $38 is approximately the fair price of the stock. Because buy and sell orders arrive randomly, the price will move randomly above and below $38. However, if the stock price starts to get too far away from $38, then the "sophisticated" investors will start to enter the market. If the price starts trading significantly below $38, these investors will enter buy orders until the price returns to the $38 range. If it starts trading significantly above $38, these investors will enter sell or sell-short orders until the price again returns to this range. The prices at which these "sophisticated" investors enter the market are the resistance and support levels, as shown in *Figure 5-4*.

Figure 5-4
Resistance and Support Levels

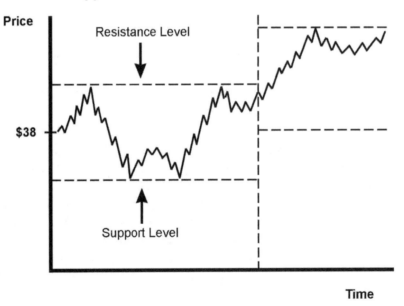

Note that at some point in time, as shown in the previous figure, the belief about the true value will change. In the example in the figure, there is an increase in what is believed to be the fair value of the stock. Hence, at the time of the shift, the price approaches the resistance level, but rather than backing off as before, it moves to a new, higher trading range. Unfortunately, there is nothing in the market place that allows an investor to know when an upward price movement is simply a random movement that will be corrected if it goes too far, or the start of a shift to a new price range.

A Rationale for Technical Analysis

Under any sense of rational economic theory, charting is illogical. Perhaps the best way to provide a defense of technical analysis is to quote an adherent of it:

> The technical analyst believes that the market price reflects all known information about the individual security. It includes all public and insider information. The market price reflects all the different investor opinions regarding that security.
>
> So what's the big deal? Just as fundamental analysis looks at the past, technical analysis also incorporates the past into its analysis. True. However, the technical analyst believes that securities move in trends. And these trends continue until something happens to change the trend. With trends, patterns and levels are detectable. Sometimes the analysis is wrong. However, in the overwhelming majority of instances, it's extremely accurate. Many times, I've successfully traded securities with only the knowledge of its chart behind me. I didn't know what the company did, but the underlying technicals indicated a direction to me. The technicals were right.
>
> Many people believe that buy-and-hold is the right strategy for owning securities. I don't agree with that. ABC might be a company you want to own for the long term. That's great. However, there's nothing wrong with buying at 50, selling at 67, and buying it back at 55 … In the latter, you've made your money work a little more efficiently … Technical analysis can aid in predicting turning points and direction in securities prices.[48]

REVIEW OF LEARNING OBJECTIVES

1. The three forms of the EMH are weak, semistrong, and strong. The weak form says that trading data such as past prices cannot be used to beat the market. The semistrong form says publicly-available information cannot be used to beat the market. The strong form says insider information cannot be used to beat the market.

---

48. About Technical Analysis," Equity Analytics Inc., pages.stern.nyu.edu/~adamodar/New_ Home_Page/articles/techdescr.htm (accessed June 30, 2010).

2. Serial correlation tests examine the relationship between price changes on consecutive days. Filter tests are trading strategies that buy and sell once prices have gone up or down x-percent from relative lows and highs.

3. An anomaly is a strategy that allows an investor to consistently outperform the market on a risk-adjusted basis. Some of the anomalies that have been tested include the small-firm effect, dogs of the Dow, January indicators, day-of-the-week effect, additions to the S&P 500, and insider trading.

4. The common sentiment indicators are odd-lot trading, the mutual fund cash position, trin, Barron's confidence index, and the put/call ratio. High values for the odd-lot trading index, the mutual fund cash position, and the put/call ratio may be either bullish or bearish, depending on which rationale one uses in supporting this indicator. A high value for trin is always bearish and a high value for the confidence index is always treated as bullish. Flow-of-funds indicators include the short interest ratio and cash balances in brokerage accounts. Although there are disagreements about the short-interest ratio, large cash balances in brokerage accounts are bullish. Market structure indicators include moving averages, breadth indicators, relative strength indicators, and the Dow theory. Bullish and bearish interpretations of these are complex.

5. Bar charts are based on vertical lines connecting the high and low trading prices for each day. A point-and-figure chart is constructed with X's and O's to represent significant stock price changes. These charts ignore time. Technical analysts look for well-established repeating patterns on these charts to provide predictions for significant future price moves. A normal head-and-shoulders is bearish, and an inverted one is bullish.

MINICASE

You have been approached by a new client. As you engage in the second step of financial planning, gathering information, you ascertain that the client's personal portfolio has $250,000 in assets. You also note that over the last 12 months, the client's stockbroker made an average of six trades per month. Many of the trades involved selling particular stocks, buying Treasury bills, and then later selling the bills to buy back the same stocks. When you ask the client about the stockbroker's justification for these trades, he indicates he never quite understood the rationale, but the broker always showed him charts with lots of X's and O's on them. Some of the trades were justified by the broker noting that a particular stock had fallen 5% from its peak, and therefore, the client was encouraged to cut short his losses. Your own philosophy is that the client would be best served by focusing on a broad asset allocation model, using mostly mutual funds, but supplemented with some direct holdings of common stock. Your own stock recommendations are based on regularly checking reports on insider trading and then doing whatever the president of the company is doing.

1.   The term that best describes the client's current broker is:

   (A) rabid efficient markets believer
   (B) market timer
   (C) fundamental analyst
   (D) day trader

2.   The type of charting used by the current broker is most likely a:

   (A) point-and-figure chart
   (B) bar chart
   (C) Elliott wave analysis
   (D) efficient market chart

3.   The current stockbroker most likely:

   (A) accepts the strong form of the efficient market hypothesis, but rejects the other two
   (B) accepts the weak and strong form of the efficient market hypothesis, but rejects the semistrong form
   (C) accepts the weak form of the efficient market hypothesis, but rejects the other two
   (D) rejects all forms of the efficient market hypothesis

4.   In addition to charting, the current broker also appears to be using:

   (A) a dogs of the Dow approach
   (B) a serial correlation model
   (C) the Dow theory
   (D) a filter rule

5.   The description of your own set of beliefs suggests that you:

   (A)   accept the strong form of the efficient market hypothesis, but reject the other two

   (B)   accept the weak and strong forms of the efficient market hypothesis, but reject the semistrong form

   (C)   accept the weak form of the efficient market hypothesis, but reject the other two

   (D)   reject all forms of the efficient market hypothesis

CHAPTER REVIEW

Key Terms and Concepts

fundamental analysis	sophisticated-investor rationale
technical analysis	contrarian rationale
momentum	short-term trading index
anomaly	neckline
small-firm effect	resistance level
January indicator (January effect)	support level

Review Questions

Review questions are based on the learning objectives for this chapter. Thus, a [3] at the end of a question means that the question is based on learning objective 3. If there are multiple objectives, they are all listed.

1.   Discuss the three forms of the EMH. What does each imply about the types of investment analysis? Summarize the relevant evidence on each. [1]

2.   Discuss the possible causes of persisting market imperfections. [3]

3.   Discuss the relevance of short interest and odd-lot behavior in market timing. What is the theory, and what is the evidence? [4]

4.   Identify the hypothesized relationships for the following indicators:
   a.   cash balances in brokerage accounts
   b.   mutual fund cash position
   c.   BCI [4]

5.   Compute the BCI for the following values for high-grade and average-grade bond rates: 5.67% and 6.01%; 10.34% and 13.89%. [4]

6. Identify the hypothesized relationships for the following indicators:
   a. advance-decline ratio
   b. short-term trading index
   c. January indicator
   d. Monday-Friday price pattern [3, 4]

7. a. Compare the positions of chartists and those who subscribe to the random walk hypothesis. [5]
   b. What is the role of the market efficiency concept in this discussion? [5]

1. Describe the basic features of common stock.

2. Value common stock using the constant-growth model.

3. Describe the different market-price-based ratios for judging a stock's price.

4. Distinguish between growth and value stocks and their role in portfolio management.

5. Describe the mechanics of dividend payments.

6. Describe the key characteristics of other equity instruments, including ADRs and preferred stock.

7. Describe the key characteristics of rights, warrants, and limited partnerships.

8. Describe the key characteristics of stock-like instruments used in employee compensation, as well as those of nontraditional investments.

Although financial planners often make recommendations regarding securities, these recommendations are frequently based on recommendations of others. Because financial planners may occasionally have to estimate the value of an asset such as a privately held business and because stocks play a significant role in the asset holdings of most clients, it is important that financial planners understand the basics of the valuation process, and specifically how common stocks are valued.

COMMON STOCK

Common stock represents basic ownership of a business entity. Think about a person starting a business. Anyone can wake up one morning and say: I am in business. This would be a sole proprietorship. There is no distinction between the individual and the business in terms of legal or tax issues. If this person is successful in creating some sort of business, he or she may consider taking on one or more partners. **Partnerships** are defined as either limited or general partnerships. A limited partner has a passive interest in the business, and cannot partake in any active duties of running the business. A limited partner is limited in terms of legal obligations. A general partner is essentially the same as a sole proprietor in terms of legal and tax obligations. There is no distinction between the business entity and each general partner. Every business must have at least one general partner, but can have an unlimited number of limited partners.

The most formal form of business is a corporation. In this case, common stock is issued to the owners to recognize their ownership interest. If the business had been a sole proprietorship, then the proprietor would presumably acquire 100% of the newly issued common stock. If it had been a partnership that incorporates, then the common stock would presumably be issued in proportion to the agreed upon ownership interest of the partnership. The major distinction between the corporation and the other two forms of business ownership is that the corporation is now recognized as a separate entity for both legal and tax purposes. Thus, the corporation can be sued and the shareholders not affected other than the extent to which the value of their investment in that firm might be reduced.

When a corporation has 500 million shares outstanding and an investor owns 100 shares, it is easy to forget that, fundamentally, this investor is still a real owner of this firm. Ownership is recognized through the ability of the investor to vote at annual meetings, although most people vote via proxies mailed to them prior to the annual meetings. The proxies normally give the current board the ability to vote the investor's shares as it sees fit, although investors may indicate specific instructions about how their shares should be voted on particular issues. Ownership also means that when the board of directors decides to distribute profits to the owners via dividends, it is to the owners of the shares, where each share has an equal entitlement.

tracking stock   Sometimes companies issue classes of common stock. The most common naming scheme is Class A and Class B shares. Unfortunately, there is no standard as to what each class means. Frequently, both classes have equal claim on earnings and dividends, but one class will have disproportionate powers. For example, Class B might have 10 votes per share, compared to Class A stock having one vote per share.

In such cases, Class B shares are usually held by corporate insiders, and this allows them to retain a disproportionate voting power in the corporation. In other cases, classes of stock are issued wherein one is designated as a tracking stock. A *tracking stock* means that the company promises to tie the dividends on that stock to the performance of a subsidiary of the company, and not the earnings of the entire company. The intent is that the prices of the two classes will be treated almost as if they are ownership interests in two different companies.

STOCK VALUATION

Value Based on Dividends

intrinsic value (stock) The intrinsic value of any security (or asset such as a privately held company) is the present value of the expected net cash flows that accrues to the owner of that security. The intrinsic value is the market value at which a security should trade based on unbiased expectations of future cash flows and the correct discount rate. In the case of equities, there are two sources of net cash inflow: cash dividends and the proceeds from the sale of the stock. Thus, the most general statement that can be said with regard to the price that someone is willing to pay for a share of stock is that it equals the discounted values of each of the projected dividends received during the holding period plus the discounted value of the projected price of the stock when it is sold.

$$P_0 = \frac{d_1}{(1 + r)} + \frac{d_2}{(1 + r)^2} + \frac{d_3}{(1 + r)^3} + \ldots + \frac{d_H}{(1 + r)^H} + \frac{P_H}{(1 + r)^H} \qquad \text{(Equation 6-1)}$$

where:

P_0 = the price of the stock today,

d_t = the dividend during period t,

r = the required rate of return,

H = the holding period, and

P_H = the price of the stock at the end of the holding period.

The above equation is based on somewhat circular logic, in that the price of a share of stock today is defined using its price at a future time period. This raises the rather interesting question, what will determine the price that someone would be willing to pay for the stock at time period *H*? Well, the same concept can be applied, namely, P_H will equal the discounted value at time *H* of all the projected dividends and projected future price during the second owner's holding period. This raises the question of what determines the price that the third owner would be willing to pay for this share of stock. The answer is the same. This scenario can be repeated infinitely. When it is, and the mathematical substitutions are made, we end up with the general model for stock valuation, which is

$$P_0 = \frac{d_1}{(1+r)} + \frac{d_2}{(1+r)^2} + \frac{d_3}{(1+r)^3} + \ldots + \frac{d_\infty}{(1+r)^\infty}$$

$$= \sum_{t=1}^{\infty} \frac{d_t}{\left(1+r\right)^t}$$

(Equation 6-2)

This model is known as the *dividend discount model*, or *dividend valuation model*.

Some people find the above model confusing and even counterintuitive in that selling price is no longer represented. It is critical to understand that selling price is nothing more than a surrogate for the dividends expected to be paid after a share of stock is sold. Thus, if I plan to sell some stock in five years, the selling price will be based on all of the dividends expected to be paid after five years from today. Hence, the above equation does not deny the relevance of the selling price; it simply is looking beyond that to what determines that selling price.

Why Value Isn't Based on Earnings

Some people find the above arguments confusing in that it would seem more intuitive that a stock's price should be based on the profits or earnings of a company, rather than its dividends. The reason that value is not based directly on earnings is that there would be double counting involved. When a company generates earnings, its board of directors must make a choice as to what percentage of the earnings to pay out as dividends, and what percentage to reinvest in the company. Earnings that are reinvested will presumably lead to increased earnings in the future. If one bases value on earnings, then one is giving value to both the original earnings that were reinvested and to the incremental earnings being generated by that reinvestment.

This double-counting argument can be demonstrated mathematically. Let's start with the concept of a company whose dividends are expected to take the form of a perpetuity. The valuation formula for a perpetuity is the annual cash flow divided by the discount rate. Thus, in the case of a company whose dividends are expected to be constant forever, the value of the stock would be expressed as

$$P_0 = \frac{d}{r}$$

where d = the constant annual dividend.

For example, suppose a company was expected to earn and pay a dividend of $1 per year, forever, starting one year from today. Further assume that the appropriate discount for this stock is 10%. Thus, the value of the stock would be $10 ($1/.10). Note that in the above assumption, there is no reinvestment of any earnings. The company is paying out all of its earnings as dividends, and that is why there is no growth in future dividends.

Now let's suppose that an investment opportunity comes along that promises a 10% rate of return, but financing this project will mean that the company will have to skip its dividend for one year. The earnings per share will still be $1, but all of the earnings will be reinvested in the coming year. As a result, there will be no dividend for this year. However, future earnings and dividends will be $1.10 rather than $1 as a result of this project. Remember, this project provides a 10% rate of return. Thus, the one-time investment of $1 per share will provide a return of $0.10 per share forever thereafter.

For purposes of our dividend discount model, there is no dividend for the coming year, but there will be a dividend of $1.10 forever thereafter. To value this stock using the dividend discount model, we need first to consider what the price of the stock will be one year from now. At that point in time, an investor will be looking at a perpetuity of $1.10 forever. Given a discount rate of 10%, this means that the stock one year from today will be worth $11 ($1.10/.10). As there is no dividend to be paid one year from today, the stock price today is simply the present value of the stock price in one year. The present value of $11 discounted at 10% for one time period is

$$\$11/(1 + 0.10) = \$10.$$

Note that the price of the stock has not changed as a result of this investment decision. Nor should it! If investors are requiring a 10% rate of return, and the company invests in a project that pays exactly a 10% rate of return, then there should be no change in the value of the stock. Investors are giving up the $1 dividend they would have received in one year for an increase in future dividends from $1 to $1.10 forever thereafter.

Now, suppose we had argued earlier that the price of stock equaled the present value of future earnings. Before the investment decision, one would say that the value of the stock was $10 ($1/.10). However, after the investment in the new project, one would have to think that the value of the firm had increased. Undertaking the new project does not affect the earnings for the coming year. The earnings will remain at $1 per share. Furthermore, after the investment the earnings will increase to $1.10 each year (at which time the firm returns to paying out all of its earnings as dividends). If we continue to use 10% as the appropriate discount rate, then the value of the stock would be $11 in one year (same computation as with the dividends). However, the price of the stock today would be based on the present value of the price in one year, plus the $1 in earnings the firm would report one year from now. This would produce a stock price today of

$$(\$11 \text{ price in one year} + \$1 \text{ earnings in one year}) \div (1 + 0.1) = \$10.91 \ .$$

In other words, taking the present value of earnings would cause one to believe the stock price should increase in value by $0.91, when in fact the firm's decision to invest in a project that provides exactly the rate of return required by shareholders would have no impact on the value of the firm. The increase in the value results simply from the double counting that has occurred when reinvestment of earnings takes place.

Why Value Isn't Based on Book Value

Sometimes people look to a firm's book value as a measure of value. Book value will be discussed in more detail in the next chapter. However, it is essentially the book value of the assets of the firm less the liabilities. Book value per share is the book value divided by the number of shares outstanding. The problem with book value is that it is based on accounting conventions that are not designed to indicate market valuation. The price of stocks of some firms will be substantially greater than their book value, and the price of other firms will be less than their book value. Book value might be of interest if a firm were going to be liquidated and one believed the book values of the assets represented approximate liquidation values. Thus, if a firm had a book value of $10 million, and someone had an opportunity to buy the firm for $9 million, then this would represent a profitable opportunity to buy the firm and liquidate it if in fact the book value is a good approximation of the liquidation value of the assets. Some people do occasionally buy businesses for the purposes of selling off the assets because they have reason to believe the firm is worth more "dead" than "alive."

The Valuation of Stocks that Don't Pay Dividends

The most immediate objection to the dividend discount model is, how can it make sense for stocks that do not pay dividends? The answer is simple. There has to be an expectation of future dividends. In the prior discussion, we considered a firm that reinvested all of its earnings into a project. For the current year, this firm would have no dividends. But, the expectation that there would be dividend payments starting in two years was sufficient to give the stock value today. In fact, let's rework the above example to show not only why current dividends may not be relevant to valuation, but also why sometimes investors would actually prefer the firm not to pay dividends.

EXAMPLE

The WJC Corporation's dividend is a perpetuity of $1 per year, forever, as the company pays out 100% of its earnings as dividends. The company plans to undertake a project that has a one-time investment equal to $1 per share. The investment pays a return of 20% forever, beginning two years from today. At that time, the firm will resume paying all its earnings on dividends. Hence, if the firm undertakes this project, the value of the stock should change from the current $10 to $10.91. The price in one year, when the dividends return to a perpetuity, is $12 ($1.20/0.10). The present value today of a stock worth $12 in one year (given no dividends will be paid in the coming year) is $10.91 [$12/(1 + 0.10)].

The fact that in the above example the firm is investing the shareholders' money at a rate greater than what the shareholders require creates, for the shareholders, what is tantamount to a windfall gain in the value of their stock. In general, as long as the firm can invest its earnings at a rate of return greater than what the shareholders require, the shareholders are better off and the firm should do so. It is only when the firm is no longer able to find projects that provide rates of return greater than that required by shareholders that it should pay out its earnings in the form of dividends. For a non-dividend-paying company it is these future dividends that are being valued. Thus, a firm may pay no dividends today, and may not be expected to pay any dividends for many years, and still have substantial value. Let's consider a more elaborate example:

EXAMPLE

The WJC Company now believes that it can reinvest all of its earnings over the next 10 years at a rate of return of 20%. Beginning 11 years from today, it will begin paying 100% of its earnings as dividends. If the earnings per share for the year just ended were $1, and if the required rate of return is 10%, what should the price of the stock be?

First, let's figure the earnings of the stock 10 years from today. This is a future value calculation in which $1 grows at the rate of 20% per year for 10 years. At that time, the earnings per share will be

$1 x (1 + 0.20)^{10}$ = $6.19.

Keystrokes: SHIFT, C ALL, 1, +/-, PV, 10, N, 20, I/YR, FV

From this point on, the firm will pay a perpetuity of $6.19 per year, starting in the 11th year. Hence, the price of the stock 10 years from today should be $61.90 ($6.19/0.10). The price of a stock today that will be worth $61.90 in 10 years, based on a rate of 10% is

$61.90/(1 + 0.1)^{10}$ = $23.87.

Keystrokes: SHIFT, C ALL, 10, N, 10, I/YR, 61.9, FV, PV

Thus, this 10-year investment program means that the price of the stock today should be $23.87, rather than $10 without the investment program.

The key in the above example is the investment of earnings at a 20% rate of return when investors are only requiring a 10% rate of return. Clearly, most investors will be happy to see a company omit its dividends when it is able to reinvest the profits at such attractive rates.[49]

Constant-Growth Model

The major problem with the dividend discount model as presented in equation 6-2 is that it is essentially unusable. A literal interpretation says

---

49. The above discussion is oversimplified to the extent that it implies the firm finances its new projects only with profits. Most firms borrow money as part of their financing. Although the interest rate on debt is always less than the required rate of return on equity, the relevant number becomes the weighted average of the cost of debt and the required rate of return on equity. This number is known as the cost of capital. As long as the firm earns more on its projects than the cost of capital, the price of the value of the stock would increase in the manner described herein.

that one should specify the projected dividends of a firm for all eternity, and then take their present value! We were able to use this model in the prior discussion only because we assumed that all future dividends took the form of a perpetuity. For common stock, a perpetuity is wonderful for illustrative purposes. But it is a bust with respect to any attempt to model real situations. What is needed is a model or assumption that is more realistic but is still mathematically easy to use.

Years ago, Myron Gordon popularized just such a model. The one simple assumption of Gordon's model is that dividends are expected to grow at a constant rate, *g*, forever. Thus, the dividend for any year, t, is expected to equal the prior year's dividend times one, plus that growth rate. Thus, $d_1 = d_0 (1 + g)$, $d_2 = d_1 (1 + g) = d_0 (1 + g)^2$, and so on. This relationship can be defined as

$$d_t = d_{t-1}(1+g) \text{ or } d_t = d_0(1+g)^t,$$

where:

d_t =   the dividend in the year *t*,

d_{t-1} =   the dividend in the year prior to year t,

d_0 =   the dividend just paid, and

g =   the growth rate in dividends.

If we are willing to make this one assumption with regard to future dividends, then we can rewrite equation 6-2 as follows:

$$P_0 = \frac{d_1}{(1+r)} + \frac{d_2}{(1+r)^2} + \frac{d_3}{(1+r)^3} + \cdots$$

$$= \frac{d_0(1+g)}{(1+r)} + \frac{d_0(1+g)^2}{(1+r)^2} + \frac{d_0(1+g)^3}{(1+r)^3} + \cdots$$

constant growth model

It turns out that some nifty mathematical manipulation can reduce this complex formula to a rather simple formula, called the *constant-growth model* or Gordon growth model.

$$P_0 = \frac{d_1}{(r-g)} = \frac{d_0(1+g)}{(r-g)} \text{ for } g < r \qquad \text{(Equation 6-3)}$$

In this equation, P_0 is the intrinsic value of the stock today (at year 0), d_1 is the dividend projected for the coming year (year 1), r is the required rate of return, and g is the growth rate. Note that this formula is on the formula sheet provided by the CFP® Board of Standards for its exam.

Based on this constant-growth model, we can make the following statements regarding a stock's value:

- A decrease in the required rate of return (that is, the discount rate) will cause the value of the stock to be higher.
- An increase in the expected growth rate of dividends (g) will cause the value of the stock to be higher.
- An increase in next year's expected dividend (d_1) will cause the value of the stock to be higher.

Bear in mind that this formula applies only when expected growth rate is below the discount rate. Stocks with dividends that have expected growth rates exceeding the discount rate in perpetuity would have theoretically infinite prices. That nonsensical result would occur because each successive expected dividend would have a higher present value than the one before it.

EXAMPLE 1

Assume that Acme Corp. experiences constant dividend growth at a rate of 5% per year. Its required rate of return (discount rate) is 15%. The dividend that was just paid was $2 per share. Using the constant-growth model, we can value Acme common stock as:

$$d_1 = d_0(1+g) = \$2(1.05) = \$2.10$$

$$P_0 = \frac{d_1}{r-g} = \frac{\$2.10}{.15-.05} = \$21.00$$

EXAMPLE 2

Use the same assumptions as in Example 1, except assume that Acme's dividend growth rate is now 7%. The intrinsic value is now computed as:

$$d_1 = d_0(1+g) = \$2(1.07) = \$2.14$$

$$P_0 = \frac{d_1}{r-g} = \frac{\$2.14}{.15-.07} = \$26.75$$

EXAMPLE 3

Use the same assumptions as in Example 1, except assume that now Acme's required return is 20%. The intrinsic value is now computed as:

$$d_1 = d_0(1+g) = \$2(1.05) = \$2.10$$

$$P_0 = \frac{d_1}{r-g} = \frac{\$2.10}{.20-.05} = \$14.00$$

One aspect of the above model that is important to remember (particularly as it shows up on various exams) is that it turns out the value of *g* is also equal to the expected annual increase in the price of the stock. This can be shown in two different ways. First, we can rewrite the constant-growth model to solve for the discount rate. When we do, we obtain the following:

$$r = (d_1 / P_0) + g \qquad \text{(Equation 6-4)}$$

This says that the required rate of return is the expected dividend yield ($d_1 \div P_0$) plus the growth rate of dividends. Note that this formula is also on the CFP® Board of Standards Formula Sheet for its exam.

As an equilibrium condition in markets, the required rate of return will equal the expected rate of return. After all, if the required rate differs from the expected rate, then investors will buy or sell securities until such time as equilibrium is reestablished. The expected rate of return for stock consists of two components, the projected dividend yield plus the price appreciation. That is,

$$\text{Expected return} = (d_1 / P_0) + \text{Percentage price change}. \qquad \text{(Equation 6-5)}$$

If equations 6-4 and 6-5 are then set equal to each other (that is, required return equals expected return), then we get

$$(d_1/P_0) + g = (d_1/P_0) + Percentage\ price\ change.$$

This reduces to the observation that *g* equals the expected rate of change in the price of the security.

A second way to see this same relationship is to compute the percentage change in price, using the constant-growth model. That is, the constant-growth model tells us that the value of the stock now and in one period would be defined as

$$P_0 = d_0 \times (1 + g)/(r - g)$$
$$P_1 = d_0 \times (1 + g)^2/(r - g)$$

Thus, the percentage change in the price of the stock would equal

$$(P_1 - P_0)/P_0 = \{[d_0 \times (1 + g)^2/(r - g)] - [d_0 \times (1 + g)/(r - g)]\}/[d_0 \times (1 + g)/(r-g)].$$

After some mathematical manipulation, we obtain the following:

$$\left(P_1 - P_0\right)/P_0 = g \qquad\qquad\qquad \text{(Equation 6-6)}$$

Again, not only does *g* represent the expected growth rate in dividends, it also represents the expected percentage change in the price of the security.

EXAMPLE

The stock of the Surefire Corporation currently trades at $20. Next year's expected annual dividend is $0.50. If your required rate of return on the stock is 10%, what is your expected annual price appreciation?

We can use the constant-growth model to solve for *g*:

$$P_0 = d_1/(r - g),$$
$$\$20 = \$0.50/(0.1 - g),$$
$$0.10 - g = \$0.50/\$20 = 0.025,$$
$$g = 0.075\ \text{or}\ 7.5\%.$$

For short periods of time, companies may grow more rapidly than their market-determined discount rate. These growth rates are, however, temporary phenomena that exist only when a company is in a stage of rapid growth. In the long run, dividends are always expected to grow more slowly than the rate at which they are discounted. A modification of the constant-growth model, referred to as the supernormal growth model, can be used to price such a security. The supernormal growth model is presented in appendix D.

The discussion so far has used the dividend per share in the numerator and valued for the price per share of the company's stock. The constant-growth model could also be used to value a company in its entirety. All that is required is that one use the total dividends paid in the numerator, and that all other assumptions of our model are met.

EXAMPLE

Your client owns 100% of the stock in a company he started years ago. The company will pay total dividends of \$250,000 next year. If the dividends are expected to grow at a rate of 4% forever, and the appropriate discount rate is 9%, what is the intrinsic value of the company?

$$\text{Value} = \frac{D_1}{r - g} = \frac{\$250,000}{.09 - .04} = \$5,000,000$$

---

d_0 versus d_1

When solving problems using the constant-growth model, many students are confused about what number to put into the numerator. Sometimes, a problem gives the student the value of d_0, in which case the student needs to compute d_1 for the numerator. The rest of the time, the student will simply be told the value of d_1, in which case any attempt to manipulate this number will result in an incorrect answer. The clue is always in the wording. When the student is being given such wording as "the company just paid a dividend equal to" or "the company has paid a dividend of," then these are strong clues that the dividend number being given is d_0, and the student needs to multiply this by one plus the growth rate to obtain the correct value for the numerator. However, when the wording is something like "the company expects to pay" or "the company will pay," then these are strong clues that the dividend number being given is d_1, and the student should plug this number directly into the numerator without any additional computation.

EXAMPLE 1

Assume that Acme Corp. experiences constant dividend growth at a rate of 5% per year. The company's projected dividend is $2 per share and the security sells for $25 per share. What is the discount rate being used to value the stock?

$$d_1 = \$2.00$$

$$r = \frac{d_1}{P_0} + g$$

$$= \frac{2.00}{25} + .05$$

$$= .13$$

EXAMPLE 2

Smith and Daltrey Corp. just paid a dividend of $5.00. The company's projected dividend growth rate is 10%, and the required rate of return is 15%. What is the stock's intrinsic value?

$$P_0 = \frac{d_1}{r - g}$$

$$d_1 = \$5 \times (1 + .10) = 5.50$$

$$= \frac{5.50}{.15 - .10} = \frac{5.50}{.05}$$

$$= \$110$$

Zero-Growth Model

In our earlier discussion in this chapter, we used as an example a common stock whose expected dividend was a perpetuity. The reader should note that the perpetuity is nothing more than a special case of the constant-growth rate model. In this case, the growth rate is zero. Thus, if the student uses a value of zero for g in equation 6-3, the constant-growth rate model reduces to the formula for valuing a perpetuity.

Although the concept of a perpetuity is highly unrealistic for common stock, it is the perfect formula for valuing preferred stock. Preferred shares are usually expected to pay a stream of constant dividends, forever.

EXAMPLE 1

A preferred stock pays a dividend of $1.50 annually. If the appropriate discount rate is 5%, what is the price of the stock?

$$P = \frac{d}{r} = \frac{\$ 1.50}{.05} = \$ 30.00$$

EXAMPLE 2

A preferred stock has an annual dividend of $5. If it trades at a price of $50, what is the expected or required rate of return?

$$r = d/P = \$5/\$50 = 0.10 \text{ or } 10\%$$

Selection of the Discount Rate

In the above problems, the selection of the discount rate to calculate the present value of anticipated cash flows is critical. The investor should select this rate based on the risk of the security as well as the returns available in the market for other securities.

There are two general approaches to selection of a discount rate. The first is based on the use of some formal model that incorporates a specification for risk. The second is traditional security analysis.

The most common risk-based model used to determine an appropriate discount rate is the capital asset pricing model (CAPM), which was presented in an earlier chapter. The model stated:

$$r_i = r_f + \beta_i \left(r_m - r_f \right) \qquad \text{(Equation 6-7)}$$

where:

r_i = the required rate of return,

r_f = the risk-free rate of return,

r_m = the return on the market portfolio, and

β_i = the beta coefficient of the security.

EXAMPLE

After analyzing the LB Corp., you conclude that next year's dividend is likely to be $1.00 and that the long-term growth rate in dividends is 4%. You also conclude that the beta for the stock is 0.8, the risk-free rate is 4%, and the expected return on the market portfolio is 10%. What should be the price of the stock?

We must start by determining the appropriate discount rate, which we obtain by plugging the necessary numbers into the CAPM as follows:

$$r_i = r_f + \beta_i (r_m - r_f)$$
$$= 4\% + .8 \times (10\% - 4\%) = 8.8\%$$

Next, we use this number as the discount rate in the constant-growth model:

$$P_0 = d_1 /(r - g) = \$1.00/(0.088 - 0.04) = \$20.83 .$$

The second approach involves doing a full traditional security analysis of the company and then, with that information, identifying the appropriate discount rate. The basic techniques of security analysis are presented in the next chapter. However, it must be emphasized that there is no formal model that relates the results of a traditional security analysis to a particular discount rate.

MARKET-PRICE-BASED RATIOS

One aspect of security analysis and valuation of publicly traded securities is that the conclusion frequently is seen as already incorporated into the price of the stock. Specifically, when an analysis indicates a company is strong and has high growth potential, then the analyst will usually find that this company's stock is trading at a relatively high price. Similarly, when a company looks dismal and has poor prospects, the analyst will find it to be trading at a rather low price. Therefore, one might like to start the valuation process by knowing which companies are already considered attractive and which are considered "dogs." There are several market-price-based ratios that provide this information. They include the price-earnings, the price-free cash flow, the price-sales, and the price-earnings growth ratios.

Price-Earnings Ratio

The most common ratio used today to get a quick read on how investors like a stock is the price-earnings (P/E) ratio. The more optimistically the market views the prospects for a particular stock, the higher the price of the stock relative to its current earnings. Thus, the stocks of companies with favorable growth opportunities (often called growth stocks) tend to have high P/E ratios. Stocks with less promising earning potentials have lower P/E ratios.

EXAMPLE

Two firms have both just reported earnings per share of $2.00. One of the firms is dominant in its industry, and the $2.00 figure represents a consistent steady growth from prior earnings. There is nothing in the current business dynamics to indicate the firm will not continue to have steady growth in its sales and operations.

The second firm has a relatively new product that just hit the market, but it is too soon to say whether the product will have lasting sales value, and how soon competitors will be able to introduce reasonable alternatives to this product. Thus, next year's earnings could take another jump, or decline substantially.

It is likely that the first firm will have a higher P/E ratio than the second, because of the stability and strength of its earnings.

The P/E ratio can be expressed as follows:

$$P/E = \frac{\text{Price per share}}{\text{Earnings per share}} = \frac{P_0}{\text{EPS}}$$

(Equation 6-8)

In this equation, P_0 represents the price of the security today. The denominator may represent either last year's (actually the sum of the last 4 quarters) earnings per share, or next year's expected earnings per share. If the historical earnings are used, the number is referred to as the past P/E ratio, price-to-current-earnings ratio, trailing P/E, or even the price-to-past-earnings ratio. If the future earnings are used, it is the price-to-future-earnings ratio or future P/E ratio. Most people are sloppy when using this term and simply say "P/E ratio." An investor should always be sure he or she understands which ratio is being described or discussed.

The problem with using the future P/E ratio is that it depends on whose forecast of earnings is being used. Forecasting earnings even one year in advance involves much guesswork. Ample research suggests that anyone who can accurately forecast a company's earnings one year in advance would make an incredible fortune in the market. So if all forecasts of future earnings are suspect, a price-to- future-earnings ratio has to be even more suspect. The preferred P/E ratio is the one that uses the prior year's earnings. There should never be any debate as to what the value of the price-to-past-earnings ratio is at any point in time.

When a brokerage firm reports a future P/E ratio, the number becomes more credible when it uses consensus forecasts prepared by third parties. Several organizations regularly survey security analysts to ascertain their forecasts of earnings per share for various firms, and then publish these numbers. In this case, a future P/E ratio provides some useful information to the investor as to how the market is valuing a stock relative to the consensus expectation of future profitability.

As a practical matter, note that a P/E ratio cannot be computed when earnings equals zero. However, it would be incredibly rare for a company to have earnings of exactly zero, although it surely happens occasionally. Another practice is that the P/E ratio is normally not computed when a company loses money. A negative P/E is a nonsense number. Finally, some companies occasionally report earnings of one or a few pennies per share. Unless the company's stock price is also in this range, its P/E ratio may be extremely large.

There are lots of caveats associated with examining P/E ratios. For example, two companies that are otherwise identical may have different P/E ratios because they have different accounting procedures (both legitimate). One company may use FIFO (first-in, first-out) to value its inventory and cost of goods sold, and another may use LIFO (last-in, first-out). During inflationary periods, these two methods can dramatically alter a company's income statement (as well as their balance sheets).

Blips in P/E Ratios

Another issue associated with P/E ratios is the fact that recognized blips in earnings may affect the ratio dramatically but not really affect the stock's price. Consider a company that has the following sequence of earnings:

2007	$2.45
2008	$2.52
2009	$2.48
2010	$0.22

Let's suppose that the low earnings in 2010 were due to a strike. The strike was resolved before the end of the year, and labor relations are now good at the company. In a situation such as this, the stock price may not adjust much to the drop in earnings, because the drop in earnings is considered unique, with no long-term consequences. If the stock price makes no significant change during the year 2010, then the P/E ratio would likely show a big jump. The jump is not due to investors suddenly thinking the company is a better deal. In fact, their overall opinion of the company may not have changed. The big jump would be due to the transitory drop in earnings. If expectations are correct, and earnings return to their normal level in the following year (2011), the P/E ratio would likely "fall" back to its original level. Naturally, the same scenario would apply in the reverse situation if there were a one-time windfall jump in earnings (say a company won a huge lawsuit settlement) that was not expected to be repeated or have any effect on future earnings. In this case, the P/E would be lower in the current year, and then "rise" back to its normal level as earnings return to the normal level.

Secular Trends in P/E Ratios

Some people like to compute long-term averages for P/E ratios, and then describe the market as overvalued when the average P/E ratio is above this long-term average, and undervalued when it is below this average. Although this method has intuitive appeal, it is also misleading.[50] The reason it is misleading is that two basic ingredients of valuation are not consistent over time. First, there is no such thing as a historically normal interest rate. As we saw earlier, the primary determinant of interest rates is inflation. When there are high inflationary expectations, interest rates will be high. Thus, the discount rates used in valuing stocks will also be high. High discount rates, all other things equal, produce lower stock prices and lower P/E ratios. Conversely, when inflationary expectations are low, interest rates will be low, and P/E ratios will be high. Thus, one expects higher P/E ratios during periods of low inflation, and this would not necessarily mean that stocks are overvalued.

Another feature that is not constant over time is the methodology for computing earnings. The standards for application of accounting methods are constantly evolving. Looser standards will allow firms to report higher earnings, and tougher standards will lead to lower earnings even when the operations of the company are unchanged. Tougher standards mean a better quality of earnings. Hence, a company that reports earnings per share of $2

---

50. Abby Joseph Cohen, "Aristotle on Investment Decision Making," *Financial Analysts Journal*, (July/August 2005): 33.

when accounting standards are tough should have a higher P/E ratio than if it reported the same value of earnings when looser standards permit more manipulation to the earnings number.

Forecasting With P/E Ratios

P/E ratios are sometimes used in forecasting models. One can forecast the entire market with a P/E-based model, or one can forecast an individual stock with a P/E-based model. As the basic idea is the same, let us consider the latter. Simply stated, a P/E-based forecast involves three steps: 1) forecast the P/E ratio, 2) forecast the earnings per share, and 3) multiply these two numbers together.

EXAMPLE

You are evaluating the Natalie Corporation. The current price-to-past-earnings ratio is 10. The average for the industry is 12. However, over the next two years you think the prospects for the Natalie firm will improve, and the P/E ratio will grow to 15. You project earnings at that time to be $5 per share. Your implicit stock price forecast for two years from now will be:

Forecasted P/E × Forecasted EPS = 15 × $5 = $75

Price Cash Flow Ratio

One of the problems with using a P/E ratio to get a sense of the relative value of a share of stock is that earnings can be manipulated, particularly with the use of noncash expenses. Many security analysts argue that what matters more for a firm is the amount of net cash flow the firm is generating, rather than what management says its earnings are. In this case, cash flow is defined as operating net cash flow, and is found on the statement of cash flows (discussed in the next chapter). The cash-flow number in this case is defined as cash flow per share, so it is the operating net cash flow divided by the number of shares outstanding.

The major item that distinguishes earnings from cash flow is depreciation. Thus, many people simply think of cash flow as the sum of earnings plus depreciation. Naturally, any other noncash expenses would also be added to earnings to obtain net cash flow.

Price-Free Cash-Flow Ratio

An alternative to looking at share price relative to cash flow is to focus on share price relative to free cash flow. Free cash flow is defined as operating cash flow net of new investment.

Price-Sales Ratio

Another way of thinking about value that has become popular in recent years is the price-sales ratio, which is share price divided by sales per share (that is, annual sales divided by the number of shares outstanding). The advantages of this ratio over the P/E ratio is, as we noted above, that P/E ratios are meaningless when earnings are negative and earnings can be manipulated. The price-sales ratio is always positive (although in theory it could be negative if a company had more product returns in a year than new sales). The price-sales ratio may also be more meaningful for start-up companies, which typically have negative earnings but a lot of growth potential. For start-up companies, market share may be more important than earnings, especially in markets where there is the potential for huge growth.

The major drawback to the price-sales ratio is that profit margins may vary by industry. Thus, industries with big profit margins would be expected to have higher price-sales ratios than those with smaller profit margins. In fact, it is certainly possible to get a variety of price-sales ratios within the same industry that reflect differences in business strategy rather than differences in value. For example, one firm may have a high-volume, low-margin strategy (such as Wal-Mart), and another firm in the same industry may have a low-volume, high-margin strategy (for example, Neiman Marcus). All other things being equal, one would expect the former to have the lower price-sales ratio. The lower ratio does not necessarily mean it is a better or worse strategy, just different.

Price-Earnings-Growth Ratio

PEG ratio Another popular valuation ratio is the price-earnings ratio to a projected growth rate of earnings (*PEG ratio*). The ratio is somewhat redundant in the sense that over time, dividends are expected to grow at the same rate as earnings. Hence, the same or similar growth rate is showing up in both the numerator (as the growth rate in dividends) and the denominator (as the growth rate in earnings).

VALUE STOCKS VERSUS GROWTH STOCKS

Many people like to use the above valuation ratios to help select stocks for investment consideration. Proof of this is that most stock screening calculators on the Internet include these ratios as some of the screening criteria. An example of what such a calculator might look like is shown in the following table. Of all of the market-price-based ratios discussed in the previous section, the P/E ratio is by far the most dominant in the minds of many people.

Table 6-1 Sample Stock Screening Calculator					
Company Name	**Curr. Price**	**Price/ Book Value**	**Price/ Cash Flow**	**Price/ Free Cash Flow**	**Trailing P/E**	**Forward P/E (Curr. Yr.)**
Meckler Corp.	26.23	7.5	15.73	31.97	19.04	14.65
Remcun Inc.	37.09	4.2	12.87	92.45	14.21	7.78
McLavich AG	13.50	5.2	14.22	51.99	16.45	45.51
Cornine Inc.	6.64	4.9	7.68	11.16	9.77	9.32
Nunwell Corp.	2.34	3.6	4.43	19.03	4.56	4.55

In order to help people understand the nature of a particular company and its stock, a popular paradigm has emerged that classifies stocks as either value stocks or growth stocks. Sometimes an intermediate category is added, known as core stocks, but most people divide the universe of stocks into the two broad categories of growth and value. Unfortunately, as with much of the terminology in the world of finance and investments, there is no universal definition as to how to distinguish a value stock from a growth stock. The ultimate proof of this point is that it is not uncommon for both growth- and value-oriented mutual funds to hold some of the same securities!

The traditional definitions for growth and value stocks focused strictly on P/E ratios. That is, stocks with high P/E ratios were referred to as *growth stocks*, and stocks with low P/E ratios were referred to as *value stocks*.[51] In this definition, growth is sometimes misinterpreted to mean growth in stock

---

51. C. Jones, *Investments: Analysis and Management*, 6th ed. (Hoboken, NJ: John Wiley & Sons, 1998), 401.

price. Technically, it means growth in earnings. Thus, to say something is a growth stock simply means that it is a stock whose earnings are expected to grow at a high rate over the next few years. Because dividends are paid out of earnings, over time the growth rate of dividends must necessarily follow the growth rate of earnings. In this framework, a value stock is one whose assets and earning capacity can be bought cheaply. Such a stock is readily identifiable because it has a low P/E ratio.

A definition that has emerged to distinguish value stocks from growth stocks is to use the book to price ratio as the distinguishing factor. High book to market value ratios denote value stocks, and low ratios denote growth stocks.[52]

Most recently, industry practice has moved to a consideration of multiple factors to distinguish growth from value stocks. The Morningstar organization is a leading provider of information on mutual funds. It attempts to classify stock mutual funds by investment style. To do so, it evaluates individual stocks as to whether they are growth or value, and then looks at the portfolios of each of the mutual funds to see which group of stocks are dominant in a fund's portfolio. Morningstar offers the following as to their methodology:

> To help classify a stock as growth, value, or core, we look at 10 separate factors, including dividend yields, price/earnings ratios… and historical and projected earnings growth.[53]

Performance Comparison

The classification of a value stock and a growth stock is only the first step of an ongoing debate as to the long-term performance for each of these two groups. That is, should investors concentrate on value stocks or growth stocks?

According to such well-known fundamental analysts as Benjamin Graham and John Templeton as presented in many presentations and publications, the market frequently goes to extremes. These two have suggested that the market tends to overestimate the growth prospects and underestimate the risks of some stocks (especially the highly touted growth stocks). As a result, the market accords them higher P/Es than their fundamentals warrant. The stocks of less exciting companies, in contrast, may be viewed by the

---

52. Herbert B. Mayo, *Investments: An Introduction*, 5th ed., (Dryden Press, 1997): 244.

53. Christine Benz, *Guide to Mutual Funds*, 2nd ed., (John Wiley & Sons, 2005): 8.

market as having less attractive prospects than they actually do. Stocks that the market views too pessimistically would then end up with unrealistically low P/Es. Once the market realizes the true potentials of these stocks, the prices of low-P/E stocks should rise at a faster rate than the market averages, whereas the high-P/E stocks should do less well. Those who accept this line of reasoning prefer a portfolio that is heavily weighted toward low-P/E stocks and largely avoid stocks with high P/Es.

Growth-stock advocates, in contrast, have contended that stocks with rapid growth potentials are attractive investments even at relatively high prices. A high current P/E may not seem overpriced relative to future earnings, whereas low P/Es may accurately reflect poor prospects. Therefore, while it makes sense for growth stocks to have higher P/E multiples than other stocks, these multiples should be based on realistic assumptions about the firm's long-term growth prospects. If a P/E ratio appears to be based on the assumption that a company's high-earnings growth rate will persist for many, many years, it seems logical to conclude that the stock is overvalued. The two-stage growth-rate model presented in appendix D shows the mathematics for valuing such a stock.

A recent publication by Chan and Lakonishok (C&L),[54] which reviews past studies on this topic and updates the analysis to more recent time periods, as well as to stocks that trade in other countries, reports fairly strong evidence that although there are a few periods in which growth stocks outperform value stocks, the overwhelming amount of time it is the value stocks that perform better. In their study, to distinguish value from growth stocks, they use a composite model that combines the values of the book-to-market value ratio (BV/MV), cash-flow-to-price ratio (CF/P), earnings-to-price ratio (E/P), and the sales-to-price ratio (S/P). They also present some evidence that the reason for the superior performance over time of the value stocks is behavioral in nature for several reasons.

First, most companies classified as growth companies have recently had a high rate of growth in their earnings. Many investors then have a propensity to overestimate the sustainability of this growth in earnings. Second, the brokerage industry needs to have a constant stream of recommendations in stocks that look like exciting investments in order to convince investors to make trades and thus generate commission income. Growth stocks

---

54.   Louis K. C. Chan and Josef Lakonishok, "Value and Growth Investing," *Financial Analysts Journal*, (January/February 2004): 71-86.

are usually companies in exciting industries for which it is easy to paint glowing pictures of continued company success. In addition, glowing recommendations also lead to investment banking business from the companies most likely to be selling new security offerings. Third, professional portfolio managers like to "window-dress." In this case, window-dress refers to the practice of adding to one's portfolio just prior to a reporting period stocks that have recently done well, and selling those stocks that have done poorly. What portfolio manager wouldn't want investors to see a stock that has doubled in value over the last year in his or her portfolio! Never mind that it was bought just a few days before the end of the reporting period.

C&L argue that all of these factors combined will cause growth stocks to be overvalued and value stocks to be undervalued. Eventually, subsequent earnings announcements will cause investors to realize the misvaluation, and the value stocks will see the higher rates of return relative to the growth stocks. Although no one would deny the wisdom of some diversification even among growth and value stocks, C&L conclude that:

> Because these behavioral traits will probably continue to exist in the future, patient investing in value stocks is likely to remain a rewarding long-term strategy.[55]

In other words, we are back to the arguments offered many years ago by Graham and Templeton!

THE MECHANICS OF PAYING A DIVIDEND

When dividend income is an important component of a client's total income, the financial planner needs to understand the mechanics of dividend payments. Dividends can be paid on common stock only at such time as the company's board of directors declares them. Hence, the first date of note for a dividend payment is the declaration date.

record date

payment date

At the time of the declaration, the board also establishes a record date and a payment date. The *record date* is the date on which the stockholder must own the stock of the corporation in order to receive the dividend. The *payment date* is the date the company pays the dividend. When individuals own stocks directly, it is the

---

55. Ibid., 85.

day the checks are put into the mail. When stocks are held in street name, it is the day the company forwards the payment to the brokerage firm. Even if the stockholder sells the stock the day after the record day and well before the payment date, this stockholder will still receive the dividend payment.

ex-dividend date   There is a fourth date that is critical to dividend payments, and it is the only date not directly controlled by the board of directors. This is the ex-dividend date. Remember, security transactions are settled three days after the trade is made. Hence, to own a stock as of the close of trading on the record date, one must have bought the stock at least three trading days prior to the record date. The next day is the *ex-dividend date*, as it is the first trading date on which one buys the stock without being entitled to the announced dividend.

EXAMPLE

The Ivers Corporation's board of directors has just met on Monday, January 15 and declared the first quarter's dividend. Hence, January 15 is the declaration date. It sets a record date of Thursday, February 15, with a payment date of Thursday, March 15. The exchange on which the stock is traded will then note that to own the stock on the record date, the buyer will have to have bought the stock by the close of business on Monday, February 12. Hence, the exchange will establish Tuesday, February 13, as the ex-dividend date.

The above discussion may make it sound as if dividends are paid haphazardly. This is far from the case. Corporations like for investors to be comfortable about when to expect the next dividend, and what that amount might be. As a result, declaration dates are approximately the same time each quarter, and record and payment dates are almost exactly the same time each quarter, with exceptions usually being made for Saturday, and always for Sunday. Thus, a company whose record date is March 1 will likely have as its other record dates June 1, September 1, and December 1. One could likely project these dates well into the future and be fairly certain about them.

Dividend Increases

Firms like to increase their dividends on a regular basis. Some of the most successful firms like to boast of the number of years of consecutive dividend increases they have had, or at least of the number of years they have paid quarterly dividends without a reduction or an omission. The quarter in which the dividend is increased is usually the same quarter each year. Thus, not only can one predict well in advance the record dates for dividends, one can predict almost as well the date on which the dividend might be increased. Finally, many firms with solid records of steady dividend increases also like to have the dividend increase be the same amount each time. Thus, a firm that increases its dividend by one penny per share in the third quarter of each year for several years will likely be looking to make a one-penny-per-share increase in the third quarter of the coming year. Because of this consistency, the market will sometimes interpret a firm not increasing its dividend in a quarter in which everyone was expecting a dividend increase, or if the firm increases it by a different amount, as a negative signal about its stability or solvency. As a result, there might be a negative price effect associated with such news.

OTHER EQUITY INSTRUMENTS

There are several types of instruments that function essentially like common stock. Some are publicly traded; some are freely traded, but may not have an active market; and some are instruments created solely to facilitate the compensation of employees.

American Depository Receipts

An American Depository Receipt (ADR) comes into existence when the foreign branch of a U.S. bank or its overseas correspondent bank acquires shares of stock of a company based in that foreign country, and then issues certificates that represent claims upon these shares.[56] For example, the XYZ Bank may acquire 10,000,000 shares of the Foreign Corporation, and then issue 5,000,000 ADRs. Thus, each ADR in this case would have a claim on two shares of Foreign Corporation's stock. There is no requirement that there be a specific ratio between the number of shares held and the number of ADRs issued. The ADR is then listed to trade on a U.S. exchange, with the result being that an investor can effectively purchase shares in the underlying stock in U.S. dollars just as easily as any other listed stock can be purchased. ADRs are listed on the NYSE, the AMEX, and trade in the OTC market.

ADRs may be sponsored or unsponsored. Unsponsored ADRs come into existence when a brokerage firm or bank believes there is sufficient demand

---

56. American   depository   receipt,   Random   House   Unabridged   Dictionary.
    http://www.infoplease.com/dictionary/American+depository+receipt, accessed July 22, 2010..

by investors to own shares in the underlying company. No formal agreement is established with the underlying company. The expenses associated with creating the ADRs and listing them on exchanges are passed through to the investors. Due to the high costs of creating and maintaining these instruments, no new ones are being established today.

In a sponsored ADR, the underlying company establishes a deposit agreement or service contract with the bank to create the ADRs, and pays the associated expenses. Sponsored ADRs come in three levels. Level I ADRs are traded only in the OTC market and some foreign exchanges. The underlying company does not have to comply with GAAP (generally accepted accounting principles) or full SEC disclosure. Level II and III involve listing on exchanges and also allow the underlying companies to raise capital in the primary market. SEC registration and reporting, as well as adherence to GAAP are required for both of these levels, with more stringent requirements for Level III. The higher the Level of the ADR, the more attractive it is to an investor in terms of the completeness disclosures.

Other depository receipts are available, including global depository receipts (GDRs), European depository receipts (EDRs), and International depository receipts (IDRs). A GDR is issued in more than one country, and is usually sold through the issuing bank's branches. EDRs are issued when the issuing company is seeking to raise euros. The IDR is a non-U.S. equivalent of the ADR.

Straight Preferred Stock

Although preferred stock is an equity security, it has much in common with debt instruments. For example, a company may issue more than one class of preferred stock, just like it can have a large number of bond issues.

participating preferred stocks   The issuer of the preferred stock is not required to declare dividends. However, the payment of a preferred stock's dividends is required before common stock dividends can be paid. Most preferreds are cumulative, which means that accumulated (unpaid) dividends must be made up before any common stock dividend can be paid. Thus, most companies' preferred stock dividends are almost as dependable as their bond interest. In addition, many preferred stock charters call for the preferred stockholders to gain voting rights if a certain number of consecutive dividend payments are missed, giving preferred stockholders some control over the management of the company. The preferreds of a weak company may, however, be almost as risky as its common stock. Some preferred issues may provide an extra dividend payment if earnings or common stock dividends are high enough, and these are known as *participating preferred stocks*. Each participating preferred stock has a specific formula as to how the extra dividends would be computed.

In the event of bankruptcy, preferred stockholders are residual claimants only one step ahead of common stockholders and behind everyone else. Unless all of the creditors' claims are fully satisfied, nothing will be left for either class of stockholders.

Unlike corporate interest payments, 70% of the dividends received by a domestic corporation (incorporated in the United States) from another domestic corporation are tax exempt. This exemption applies to both common stock dividends and preferred dividends. Moreover, the exemption may be 80% or even 100% of dividends received if the receiving corporation owns a large enough percentage of the common stock of the paying corporation.

This tax-exemption feature has always made straight preferred stock popular with corporate investors. In fact, straight preferred stock usually trades at prices that reflect this tax exemption. Because this tax advantage is available only to corporations, it is typically the case that individual investors should avoid holding any straight preferred stock.

How Straight Preferred Stock Differs From Bonds and Common Stocks

The dividend rate on preferred stocks is usually fixed, with the exceptions of participating, adjustable, and floating rate preferreds. Common stocks always come with an expectation of a growing dividend (if one is currently paid), or of a dividend starting at some point in the future (if one is not currently paid).

Straight preferred differs from bonds first in that bond interest is usually paid semiannually, and almost all preferred stocks pay dividends quarterly. Second, most bonds have a par value of $1,000 and usually start trading at this value. Preferred stocks have par values that most commonly range from $25 to $100, but may take on other values also. For example, Merrill Lynch noted in its 2000 Annual Report that it is authorized to issue 25 million shares of undesignated preferred stock with a par value of $1.00.[57]

---

57. "Note 8. Shareholders' Equity and Earnings Per Share: Preferred Equity, *Merrill Lynch 2000 Annual Report*, 2000. http://www.ml.com/annualmeetingmaterials/annrep00/ar/note8.html (accessed July 2, 2010).

Some companies issue preferred stock with no par value, but then define a liquidation preference value for the stock. In any event, the market prices of these shares will usually be in the same range as their par values.

Traditionally, preferred stock, like common stock, had no maturity date. Today, however, some preferred stocks are issued with maturity dates. Many preferred stocks, like most corporate bonds, are callable.

Rights

rights offering   In some states, corporations are only allowed to sell new stock with a rights offering. In the rest of the states, it is a choice. A *rights offering* to existing shareholders allows a company to raise additional capital and avoid diluting the current shareholders' positions. A rights offering begins with the company simply giving to all current investors a certain number of rights for each share held. Often, this is on a one-to-one basis. Thus, an investor holding 300 shares at the time of a rights offering would normally receive 300 rights from the company.

A right specifies an exercise price (the same concept as the strike price on an option) and an expiration date, after which the rights become worthless. Shareholders who want to maintain their proportional ownership in the company would exercise their rights. For everyone else, the decision of whether to exercise the rights or sell them should be based on their opinions of the attractiveness of the company for additional investment. Thus, some may prefer to sell their rights on the open market, thus effectively reducing their investment in the company. Others will exercise their rights, thus increasing their investment in the company.

When companies issue rights, it is for the explicit purpose of selling new shares of common stock. Thus, the exercise price will be set safely below the current market price. As a result, rights will trade at prices that are about the same as their intrinsic values, which we will define shortly. Rights trading is, however, relatively speculative because most rights have a short lifespan, often only a few weeks.

Although one right is usually issued for each outstanding share, each right typically provides the holder an option to acquire a fraction of a new share of stock. Thus, the holder of 100 shares of the underlying stock might receive 100 rights, the terms of the rights might be that 10 rights are required to buy one new share of stock.

Cum-Rights and Ex-Rights

A rights offering announcement specifies a date of record for people who own the stock to receive the rights. Up to that day, the stock trades cum-rights, that is, with rights attached. After that date, the stock sells ex-rights (no rights attached). Because it takes three business days to settle stock trades (that is, legally transfer the trade), the cum-rights trading stops three days before the record date. The following table shows the typical timing of a rights offer.

Table 6-2 Typical Timing of a Rights Offering		
Date	Day	Event
January 14	Monday	Rights offering announced for shareholders of record on Friday, February 1
January 28	Monday	Last day to buy the shares cum-rights
January 29	Tuesday	Shares go ex-rights
February 1	Friday	Actual record date

Rights Valuation Formula

When a stock goes ex-rights, its market value will adjust for the fact that new shares are being issued at a lower price, but other factors will affect the stock's price. It will rise and fall like any other stock price. At this point, the formula for the intrinsic value of a right is as follows:

$$\frac{\text{Instrinsic value of one right}}{\text{during ex-rights period}} = \frac{\text{Market price of stock} - \text{Subscription price}}{\text{Number of shares needed to subscribe to one share}}$$

EXAMPLE

The Evans Company wants to raise $500 million. It has 250 million shares of common stock outstanding, and each shareholder receives 1 right per share held. The terms require that 5 rights are necessary to buy one new share of stock. Thus, it will be issuing 50 million new shares of common stock. To raise the full $500 million, it must set a subscription price of $10 per share. Finally, suppose the stock is currently trading ex-rights at $20 per share. In this case, the intrinsic value would be:

$$\text{Intrinsic Value} = \frac{\$20 - \$10}{5} = \$2 \text{ per right}$$

Thus, the actual market price of each right would be no less than $2 each.

Financial Planning Issue
Joe Beamer has received 1,000 rights in the Quick Explosion Company in which he owns 1,000 shares. The rights expire in three weeks. He asks your advice on whether he should exercise them, sell them, or forget about them.
The worst choice is to forget about them. If Joe has no interest in them, the financial planner needs to make sure the rights are at least sold lest they die worthless.[58] If Joe has no interest in increasing his investment in the company, then this would be a good time to review if Joe is really interested in continuing to hold his 1,000 shares. If the company is still viewed as a good investment, he should exercise the rights. If Joe lacks the cash to exercise the rights, he should sell sufficient rights to raise the cash to exercise the remaining rights.

Preferred Share Purchase Rights

Many companies have issued preferred share purchase rights. Although these rights provide the investor with the privilege of buying new issues of preferred stock, the rationale for the issuance and their terms are dramatically different than those of the common stock rights discussed above. The purpose of these rights is usually to protect the company from being acquired without the board of directors' blessing.

EXAMPLE
On September 23, 2003, the board of directors of Diamondcluster International, Inc., declared a dividend of one preferred share purchase right for each outstanding share of common stock for the stated purpose of protecting shareholders from what the board might view as coercive or otherwise unfair takeover tactics. Since issuance, the rights have traded as attached to the common stock. Each right allows the owner to buy one one-thousandth of a share of newly issued Series A Junior Participating Preferred Stock for $32.50, once the rights are exercisable. Prior to their being exercised, the right provides no liquidation, voting, or dividend privileges. The rights will become exercisable at such time as someone begins an attempt to acquire the company. The rights will expire on October 15, 2013. They can be redeemed at any time by the board of directors for one penny per right.

Warrants

The motivation for creating warrants is different from that for creating rights. Warrants are usually attached to a bond issue for the purpose of allowing a

---

58. Even if the commission equals the value of the rights, if the client does not want to exercise the rights they should be sold to establish a verifiable record for tax purposes.

company to obtain a lower coupon rate on the bond, and presumably for the purpose of conveniently selling new equity at a later point in time. Frequently, start-up firms or firms with somewhat risky (but optimistic) prospects are the main issuers of warrants. Because pure debt issues would have to carry higher yields, the firm would use the bond-cum-warrants approach to lower its initial financing costs. This approach allows the bondholders to share in the firm's growth while providing a more secure return on capital if the firm does not grow.

Warrants are similar to rights in that a subscription price is paid to the company when exercised and new shares of stock are issued. They differ from rights in that their expiration date may range from several years to perpetual, and at the time they are issued the subscription price is usually substantially above the current market value of the stock. Thus, warrants have value only to the extent the future price of the stock might exceed the subscription price.

EXAMPLE

The Slow-Go Bus Company has issued some bonds with 100 warrants attached to each bond. The warrants expire in 10 years. Each warrant allows a person to buy one new share of stock at $40 per share. The stock currently trades at $25. Without the warrants, the company would have had to pay an 8% interest rate on the bonds; with them, the interest rate is 6%.

Limited Partnerships

Most businesses are organized as corporations. The corporate form of organization provides limited liability for owners (shareholders), but its income is taxed at the corporate level, and its shareholders are taxed again on their dividends and then on any capital gains when the stock is sold.

Some businesses are organized as partnerships. The income of a partnership is taxed only once. Partnership profits, whether distributed or retained by the partnership, are treated for tax purposes as the imputed income of the partners, where the allocation of income is based on the partnership agreement.

The limited partnership is an alternative way of organizing a business enterprise. These partnerships combine the benefits of a corporation's limited liability with the single-taxation advantage of a partnership. A single general partner, who is usually the organizer and may be a corporation, does have unlimited liability. The limited partners, however, are not generally liable for the partnership's debts and obligations beyond their initial capital contribution. Most limited partnerships have one major drawback: Because they are relatively small, their ownership units trade in very thin markets, if at all. In addition, there may be legal or contractual restrictions on the sale of a limited partnership interest. Limited partnerships are particularly common in the real estate industry.

Master Limited Partnerships

The master limited partnership (MLP) is designed to overcome the lack of liquidity of limited partnerships but retain many of the tax advantages of the limited partnership. Most MLPs are relatively large (compared to limited partnerships). The term master is used to signify that these are publicly traded forms of ownership. In fact, many MLPs trade on the NYSE. The majority of MLPs have been organized around oil and gas holdings for tax reasons.

Employee Compensation Instruments

One of the classic problems in the world of finance is what is known as the *principal—agent problem*. This occurs because an agent, hired to represent an employer's best interests, is always tempted to put his or her own interests ahead of the person he or she represents. The oft-suggested solution to the agency problem is to better align the interests of the agent and the person being represented, so that what is best for one is best for the other. Corporate managers are agents for stockholders. In this case, an alignment of interests could be accomplished by providing managers with equity interests in the company. This is accomplished with such instruments as phantom stock, stock appreciation rights and restricted stock.

Phantom Stock

Phantom stock is a promise to pay a bonus based on either the value of company shares or the increase in their value over a period of time. There is no standard formula for the terms of this vehicle. As an example, a company could promise a new employee that it would pay a bonus every five years equal to the increase in the equity value of the firm times some percentage of total payroll at that point. Alternatively, it could promise to pay an amount equal to the value of a fixed number of shares set at the time the promise is made. Phantom stock payments are usually made at fixed, predetermined dates. It is not uncommon that participants in phantom stock plans are required to remain employed by the company for a certain number of years or until retirement. Also, participants must agree not to compete with the employer or to become a competitor's employee after their retirement. Therefore, an executive must carefully weigh the benefits of participating in the plan and the associated decreased career mobility.

EXAMPLE

Employees of Enron Corporation filed a class-action suit after the collapse of their employer, based on Enron's practice of making phantom stock a substantial part of employee compensation. The employees argued that Enron's requirement that the stock not be sold had the dual benefit for the company of keeping stock out of the hands of a potential acquiring firm and greatly reducing the outlay of cash by the firm.

Stock Appreciation Rights

A stock appreciation right (SAR) is a right to a bonus that is granted to an employee, where the bonus is based only on the appreciation in the company's stock price over a specified period of time. This differs from a traditional stock option in that in a stock option, as with any call option, the person exercising the option is required to pay an exercise price. It differs from phantom stock in that phantom stock could be based on either the full value of the stock or the appreciation, and is awarded dividends during the time it is held. With an SAR, the employee simply receives the appreciation as a bonus with no out-of-pocket payment. For example, if an employee is given 200 SARs and the stock price appreciates by $20 per share during the designated period, then the bonus on December 31 would be $4,000 (200 SARs x $20 per share price appreciation).

Although SARs may vest immediately, there is usually a waiting period before SARs fully vest. SARs may be exercised anytime after they become fully vested. Because the majority of stock prices go up most of the time, the usual expectation would be that the SARs would become more valuable the longer one waits to exercise them.

Members of an executive management group may receive the bonus in the form of either cash or stock, but other employees would receive the bonus only in the form of stock. Thus, in the above example, a regular employee would actually receive $4,000 worth of stock. There is no restriction on this stock, and thus it could be sold immediately if the employee actually wants the cash. The reason for the differential treatment is that under the SEC's

Rule 16b, officers of the firm could not sell the stock for the first six months after receipt.

If a person retires before the SARs have been exercised, there is usually an acceleration in the deadline for exercise. An alternative acceleration may apply in the case when the employee departs for reasons other than retirement.

Restricted Stock

Some employers prefer to give restricted stock rather than phantom stock or SARs for the simple reason that to the extent there is an exercise price in the latter two, the award of the bonus may have no value. Restricted stock makes the employee an owner of the firm, regardless of the subsequent stock price performance. Restricted stock is so named because there are restrictions of some sort placed on it. The usual restriction is a vesting period during which the stock would be forfeited if the employee leaves the company during that period. This vesting period may be a specific time period (e.g., three years) or achievement of a goal (e.g., annual sales of $50 million). There are several tax advantages to restricted stock for both the firm and the employee.

NON-TRADITIONAL INVESTMENTS

Equity ownership also includes nontraditional investments such as collectibles, noncollectibles, natural resources, and precious metals. For most, these are not appropriate investments for a number of reasons, including that the price tag for just one unit may be prohibitive, these investments frequently require professional knowledge to evaluate them, they have high carrying costs, the transaction fees may be excessive, and they usually have minimal to no liquidity. There is ample opportunity for fraud and theft in these investments. The marketplace in which they trade is virtually unregulated compared with the stock exchanges. The people who make up these markets also tend to be unregulated beyond rules that apply to all businesses. Nonetheless, for wealthier investors willing to take risks, they may provide substantial diversification as well as nonpecuniary benefits in the form of pride of ownership.

Collectibles

Although a relatively minor investment medium, collectibles have grown substantially in popularity in recent years. Coins, stamps, art, oriental rugs, and antiques have long been of interest to collectors. As an indication of their importance, both Barron's and Forbes report the Sotheby Index of prices on a variety of art, ceramic, silver, and furniture collectibles. Owning collectibles provides the opportunity to combine one's hobby with one's investments.

To be classified as a collectible requires that there be some form of market for these assets. The liquidity of the market depends, of course, on the quantity of any particular item that is traded on a regular basis. Thus, the liquidity of the market for coins may not be too bad, particularly for those coins for which there were a lot minted. Artwork by a particular artist tends to be much less liquid. Many collectibles are sold through auction markets. The seller pays a fee to the auction house that is a percentage of the selling price. Nonetheless, the auction process would normally be expected to attract buyers willing to pay more than an individual could get attempting to sell on his or her own. Also, an auction house will presumably have as good an idea as anyone as to what an item may be worth. Note that not only does the seller pay the auction house, but the buyer will also typically pay a percentage fee that is added to the purchase price.

The prices at which collectibles trade are primarily a function of the demand curve. The supply curve is relatively inelastic, as most collectibles are no longer being produced. The price for any one particular item depends upon who created it (in the case of artwork), the condition of the collectible, and in some cases, the history of ownership (a famous or prestigious former owner will enhance the value).

Noncollectibles

Noncollectibles include such things as Broadway shows, movies, vineyards, racehorses, baseball clubs, and freight cars. In other words, items that are both unique and expensive. Like collectibles, noncollectibles allow a person to combine a hobby or social activity with the investment process. People who own racehorses often like to spend the afternoon at the racetrack anyway. Some people have made fortunes from investments such as these, and others have lost everything. It is clearly prudent that the financial planner be highly knowledgeable in the field of the particular investment, or that the client receive advice from someone who is appropriately informed.

Natural Resources

Yet another investment opportunity is natural resources such as timber and oil. In the case of timber, a person would buy land with trees or would plant trees, and then at such time as the tree sizes seem optimal, have the trees cut and start the process again. One drawback to timber is there are usually some carrying costs in the form of property taxes. In addition, there are risks from such natural disasters as infestations, fires, windstorms, and even from poachers. The price of timber is also primarily dependent upon shifts in the demand curve because the supply is relatively inelastic as it takes trees many years to grow.

depletion
allowance
Some people acquire the mineral rights on land (or land with the potential for oil). They then lease to developers the rights to drill for oil, with the benefit of a royalty on each barrel extracted. There is even a special tax benefit here, in that an investor may take a deduction of 15% of the income as a *depletion allowance*. As with timber, one of the drawbacks to such an investment is the property tax owed each year.

Many people opt to invest in natural resources either by investing in companies whose line of business involves the development of natural resources, or an investment company that specializes in investing in companies in the field of natural resources. Many people invest in natural resources through limited partnerships.

Precious Metals

Although some people might think of the purchase of jewelry as an investment in precious metals, such is really not the case. Although the price of jewelry will reflect to some extent the content of any precious metal such as gold, the price is mainly a function of the exquisiteness of the design. As such, the price of the jewelry will not move in tandem with the price of its precious metal content. In addition, because each piece of jewelry is so unique, there is a high bid-ask spread if one attempts to trade jewelry and the market is extremely illiquid.

Although there are many precious metals in which one could invest, the most commonly used one for investment purposes is gold, and we will focus our discussion on only that metal. Direct purchase of gold usually involves either gold bullion or gold coins. Indirect purchase of gold would mean the purchase of shares in gold-mining companies, shares in mutual funds or ETFs that specialize in stocks of companies in the gold industry, or even options or futures contracts on gold bullion.

Investing in gold coins is as much a numismatic activity as it is a gold investment activity. Thus, the price of a particular coin will reflect not only the gold content, but also the condition of the coin, the rarity of the coin, and the relative desirability of that particular issue of coin.

Beginning January 1, 1975, Americans were once again allowed to own gold bullion, an activity that had been illegal for many years. When gold bullion is purchased, the investor can leave the commodity with the dealer, or take possession. Depositing it with the dealer involves storage and insurance costs. However, taking possession may also necessitate storage, insurance, and moving costs. In addition, if the investor takes possession, then the gold may have to be assayed again to prove its authenticity and purity before it can be sold.

One additional problem with precious metals is these items continue to be produced. Remember, collectibles usually involve items that are no longer being produced and noncollectibles are always unique items. Natural resources are also being produced, but it usually takes a lot longer to change the amount produced each year.

There are some investment advisors who are known as "gold bugs," because their primary investment advice is always to buy gold. Gold is popularly believed to be a good hedge against inflation, as well as an ideal investment in the case of economic collapse. Thus, investors who believe another economic depression is coming might do well to consider investing in gold.

REVIEW OF LEARNING OBJECTIVES

1. Common stock represents ownership of a firm. The two critical features are the right to vote at shareholder meetings and the right to receive dividends.

2. The constant-growth model states that the price of a share of stock today equals the dividend expected to be paid next period, divided by the difference between the appropriate risk-adjusted discount rate for that stock and the expected growth rate in dividends. In equilibrium, the expected growth rate in dividends equals the expected growth rate in the price of the stock. The appropriate discount rate is frequently based on the CAPM.

3. The four common market-price-based ratios to judge a stock's price are the price-earnings ratio (based on either trailing or projected

earnings), the price-cash-flow ratio, the price-sales ratio, and the price-earnings to growth rate (PEG) ratio.

4. Growth stocks are ones where earnings are expected to grow at a faster rate than for the typical company. Value stocks are ones for which the price seems low relative to current measures of value. In practice, the distinction is usually based on P/E ratios, book-to-market value ratios, or other criteria, or some combination of criteria including these two. There is some evidence that the majority of the time, value stocks outperform growth stocks.

5. To forecast with a P/E ratio, one need only forecast the ratio, forecast the earnings of the company, and then multiply the two together.

6. A board of directors declares a dividend, and sets the record date and payment date. The exchange on which the stock is traded sets the ex-dividend date. Dividends are usually paid on the same day of each quarter. Companies try to increase their nominal dividend payment once per year, and it is usually in the same quarter of each year.

7. ADRs are certificates that represent a claim on shares of a foreign stock held by an issuing bank. Straight preferred normally promises a fixed dividend forever, and ranks only ahead of common stock in liquidation priorities. Rights are given to existing shareholders, one right per share, for the purpose of allowing them to protect their pro rata ownership in a sale of new shares and to facilitate the sale of new shares of common stock. Warrants are usually issued in conjunction with a debt issue to obtain a lower interest rate and facilitate the sale of stock at a later date.

8. Employees of corporations are sometimes given phantom stock, SARs, and restricted stock to compensate and motivate them. Nontraditional investments include collectibles, noncollectibles, natural resources, and precious metals.

MINICASE

In reviewing the assets of a major client, you note that the biggest asset is a privately held company. You would like to establish a ballpark figure for the value of the firm. The client pays out 100% of the earnings as dividends to herself. Earnings have been growing at a rate of 4% per year, and are expected to continue to grow at this rate. You note that comparable companies that are publicly traded have betas of 0.75. The expected return on the market portfolio is 9.33 percent, and the risk-free rate is 4%.

1. The appropriate discount rate to use in valuing the firm (ignoring any premium for lack of liquidity or any discount for control) is:

   (A) 4%
   (B) 6%
   (C) 8%
   (D) 10%

2. If the company's projected earnings next year are $1 million, then the approximate value of the company based on the constant growth model is:

   (A) undefined
   (B) $50 million
   (C) $25 million
   (D) $16⅔ million

3. The value of the company would be expected to grow at an annual rate of:

   (A) 4%
   (B) 6%
   (C) 8%
   (D) 10%

4. If you later decide the beta of the company is actually 1.25 rather than 0.75, then the value of the company would be:

   (A) unchanged
   (B) approximately 20% lower than your current estimate
   (C) approximately 36% lower than your current estimate
   (D) approximately 40% lower than your current estimate

5. You decide that the expected rate of return on the market portfolio is 12% rather than 9.33 percent, but all the other parameters are the same as before (beta is 0.75). The value of the company would now be:

   (A) unchanged
   (B) approximately 20% lower than your current estimate
   (C) approximately 33 1/3% lower than your current estimate
   (D) approximately 40% lower than your current estimate

CHAPTER REVIEW

Key Terms and Concepts

tracking stock   intrinsic value (stock)

constant growth model
PEG ratio
record date
payment date

ex-dividend date
participating preferred stocks
rights offering
depletion allowance

Review Questions

Review questions are based on the learning objectives for this chapter. Thus, a [3] at the end of a question means that the question is based on learning objective 3. If there are multiple objectives, they are all listed.

1. Compare and contrast common and straight preferred stock. [1, 6]

2. The American Pig Company (ticker symbol PORK) recently paid a dividend of $3.00 per share, which is expected to rise by $0.25 per share for the next two years. Dividends are normally one-half of earnings. The stock currently sells for $36 per share, a ratio of six times its current earnings. The same ratio of price to earnings is also expected at the end of two years. Compute what the price of PORK stock should be, based on the present value of its dividends and the price of its stock in two years if the discount rate is 8%. [2, 3]

3. a.   A company has just paid a dividend of $0.50 per share. The required rate of return for this stock is 10%, and the expected growth rate in dividends is 5%. What should the price of the stock be? [2]
    b.   Rework part a. assuming dividend growth rates of 0%, 3%, and 8%. [2]

4. The expected rate of return on the market portfolio is 10%, the risk-free rate is 4%. What would be the price of a stock that is expected to pay a dividend of $2 per share next year, if its beta is 1.25 and the dividends are expected to grow at a rate of 6% forever? [2]

5. For the different market-price-based ratios, indicate whether a "high" value or a "low" value is more indicative of a growth stock, or if the value is indeterminate with respect to classification. [3, 4]

6. What are some of the reasons offered for the consistently superior performance of value stocks? [4]

7. After careful analysis, you project that the price-to-trailing earnings ratio of the Worshamatic Corporation will be 15 in three years. At the time, the company will have earnings per share of $3 for the preceding year. What is your implicit stock price forecast? [3]

8. What are the four key dates in the dividend payment process, and what happens on each date? [5]

9. Distinguish between a warrant and a right. [7]

10. XYZ stock is selling ex-rights at $55. The rights entitle the holder to five shares at $47 for every 100 shares owned. What is the intrinsic value of each right? [7]

Learning Objectives

An understanding of the material in this chapter should enable the student to

1. Describe a business cycle, and explain what is meant by leading, coincident, and lagging indicators.

2. Describe the tools of fiscal policy and how they work.

3. Describe the tools of monetary policy and how they work.

4. Describe the goals and the problems in implementing fiscal and monetary policy.

5. Describe the life-cycle of an industry.

6. Interpret a balance sheet, an income statement, and a statement of cash flows.

7. Analyze a company with respect to its liquidity, use of financial leverage, and profitability.

8. Analyze a company with respect to its activity and other ratios, including the use of a Du Pont analysis.

Equity valuation requires estimates of future income and identification of an appropriate discount rate. Estimates of future income and the selection of a discount rate would be the logical outcome of a process known as fundamental analysis, which is the focus of this chapter.

TOP-DOWN VERSUS BOTTOM-UP ANALYSIS

macroeconomic analysis

industry analysis

company analyses

Detailed and comprehensive fundamental analysis is usually prepared within large organizations by well-trained staff, some of whom hold the CFA (Chartered Financial Analyst) designation. When fundamental analyses are performed by such an organization, there are two traditional approaches: top-down and bottom-up. The "top-down" approach starts with *macroeconomic analysis*, which first seeks to identify what the overall economy will look like. Once there is a consensus on what the overall economy will look like, *industry analyses* are then prepared. These reports look at how different industries might perform based on the overall economy. Finally, *company analyses* are developed, which examine the relative strengths and weaknesses of firms within their industry or industries.

These three categories correspond to the three principal influences on stock performance. Clearly, each is important, although studies show that, in terms of both firm profits and stock price performance, industry analysis is not nearly as important as it once was. In fact, recent research shows that company analysis, on average, generates positive returns for mutual funds, but macroeconomic analysis does not.[59]

Three Steps of Top-Down Fundamental Analysis
• Macroeconomic analysis: Evaluates current economic environment and its effect on industry and company fundamentals
• Industry analysis: Evaluates the outlook for particular industries
• Company analysis: Evaluates a company's strengths and weaknesses within its industry or industries

A bottom-up approach simply develops the analysis in the reverse direction. That is, the staff starts with a consideration of how individual companies will perform. These individual performances are then combined to develop industry outlooks, and these outlooks are again combined to ascertain the prospects for the overall economy.

MACROECONOMIC ANALYSIS

As we saw in the previous chapter, stock valuation is based on an assessment of a company's future dividends. Dividends, in turn, are based on a company's current and prospective earnings. Earnings, in turn, are based on a company's sales and expenses. For most companies, particularly the largest ones, the most important factor influencing sales is the general

---

59. Cremers K. J., M. Artign, and Antti Petajisto, "How Active Is Your Fund Manager? A New Measure That Predicts Performance," *The Review of Financial Studies*, Vol. 22, Issue 9 (September 2009), pp. 3329–3365.

level of economic activity. Overall economic activity is most often measured as the *gross domestic product*, or GDP.

Business Cycles

If the economy behaved like the weather in the Sahara desert, forecasting would be easy. The Saharan meteorologist most likely forecasts a hot and dry day every day of the year, and is correct virtually all the time. What complicates forecasting the economy is the existence of business cycles. There are four phases to a cycle: *expansion, peak, contraction,* and *trough.* These are illustrated in the following figure, which shows three peaks and two troughs.

Figure 7-1
Phases of a Business Cycle

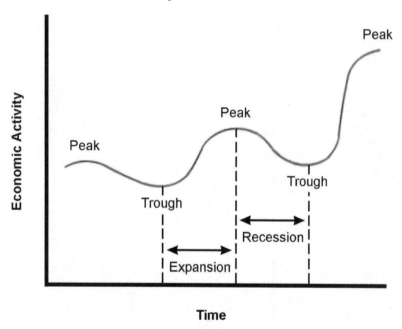

The economy is referred to as being in a recession or contraction when it is moving from a peak to a trough, and in an expansion when it is moving from a trough to a peak.

The forecasting problem arises from the fact that the amount of time for a cycle varies, as well as the extent of fluctuation in economic activity during a cycle. For example, the longest cycle on record lasted 128 months, measured from peak to peak (that is, 10+ years), and the shortest cycle was

17 months (see table below). Cycles are officially defined by the National Bureau of Economic Research (NBER) Business Cycle Dating Committee. The current definition of a recession is "a significant decline in economic activity spread across the economy, lasting more than a few months, normally visible in real GDP, real income, employment, industrial production, and wholesale-retail sales."[60]

Table 7-1 Historical Information on Business Cycles

Business Cycle Reference Dates		Duration in Months			
Peak	**Trough**	**Contraction**	**Expansion**	**Cycle**	
Quarterly Dates Are in Parentheses		*Peak to Trough*	*Previous Trough to This Peak*	*Trough from Previous Trough*	*Peak from Previous Peak*
	December 1854 (IV)	–	–	–	–
June 1857 (II)	December 1858 (IV)	18	30	48	–
October 1860 (III)	June 1861 (III)	8	22	30	40
April 1865 (I)	December 1867 (IV)	**32**	**46**	**78**	**54**
June 1869 (II)	December 1870 (IV)	18	18	36	50
October 1873 (III)	March 1879 (I)	65	34	99	52
March 1882 (I)	May 1885 (II)	38	36	74	101
March 1887 (II)	April 1888 (II)	13	22	35	60
July 1890 (III)	May 1891 (II)	10	27	37	40
January 1893 (I)	June 1894 (II)	17	20	37	30
December 1895 (IV)	June 1897 (II)	18	18	36	35
June 1899 (III)	December 1900 (IV)	18	24	42	42
September 1902 (IV)	August 1904 (III)	23	21	44	39
May 1907 (II)	June 1908 (II)	13	33	46	56
January 1910 (I)	January 1912 (IV)	24	19	43	32
January 1913 (I)	December 1914 (IV)	23	12	35	36
August 1918 (III)	March 1919 (I)	**7**	**44**	**51**	**67**
January 1920 (I)	July 1921 (III)	18	10	28	17
May 1923 (II)	July 1924 (III)	14	22	36	40
October 1926 (III)	November 1927 (IV)	13	27	40	41
August 1929 (III)	March 1933 (I)	43	21	64	34
May 1937 (II)	June 1938 (II)	13	50	63	93
February 1945 (I)	October 1945 (IV)	**8**	**80**	**88**	**93**
November 1948 (IV)	October 1949 (IV)	11	37	48	45
July 1953 (II)	May 1954 (II)	**10**	**45**	**55**	**56**
August 1957 (III)	April 1958 (II)	8	39	47	49
April 1960 (II)	February 1961 (I)	10	24	34	32

---

60. Memorandum, July 17, 2003, NBER's Business Cycle Dating Committee.

Business Cycle Reference Dates		Duration in Months			
Peak	Trough	Contraction	Expansion	Cycle	
Quarterly Dates Are in Parentheses		*Peak to Trough*	*Previous Trough to This Peak*	*Trough from Previous Trough*	*Peak from Previous Peak*
December 1969 (IV)	November 1970 (IV)	11	106	117	116
November 1973 (IV)	March 1975 (I)	16	36	52	47
January 1980 (I)	July 1980 (III)	6	58	64	74
July 1981 (III)	November 1982 (IV)	16	12	28	18
July 1990 (III)	March 1991 (I)	8	92	100	108
March 2001 (I)	November 2001 (IV)	8	120	128	128
December 2007 (IV)			73		81
Average, all cycles:					
1854–2001 (32 cycles)		17	38	55	56*
1854–1919 (16 cycles)		22	27	48	49**
1919–1945 (6 cycles)		18	35	53	53
1945–2001 (10 cycles)		10	57	67	67
Average, peacetime cycles:					
1854–2001 (27 cycles)		18	33	51	52***
1854–1919 (14 cycles)		22	24	46	47****
1919–1945 (5 cycles)		20	26	46	45
1945–2001 (8 cycles)		10	52	63	63

* 31 cycles

** 15 cycles

*** 26 cycles

**** 13 cycles

Figures printed in **bold italic** are the wartime expansions (Civil War, World Wars I and II, Korean War, and Vietnam War), the wartime contractions, and the full cycles that include the wartime expansions.

Sources: NBER; the U.S. Department of Commerce, *Business Cycle Expansions and Contractions*. Reprinted from www.nber.org/cycles.html, July 2010.

Economic Indicators

The primary tools used by the NBER to identify business cycles are the leading, coincident, and lagging indicators. Beginning in the 1940s and based on observations going back to the 1920s, NBER and the U.S. Commerce Department identified 10 monthly data series that tended to lead the business cycle. A coincident indicator series (four components) and a lagging series (seven components) have also been developed. The current components of all three series are shown in the following table.

Table 7-2 The Conference Board U.S. Business Cycle Indicators

Leading Indicators (10 Series)

- Average weekly hours, manufacturing
- Average weekly initial claims for unemployment insurance
- Manufacturers' new orders, consumer goods and materials (inflation adjusted)
- Vendor performance, slower deliveries diffusion index
- Manufacturers' new orders, nondefense capital goods (inflation adjusted)
- Building permits, new private housing units
- Stock prices, S&P 500 Index
- Real money supply, M2 (includes currency and checkable deposits in the hands of the public, plus savings and small-time deposits, repurchase agreements, and money market deposit accounts)
- Interest rate spread, 10-year Treasury bonds less federal funds
- Index of Consumer Expectations, University of Michigan Survey Research Center

Coincident (4 Series)

- Employees on nonagricultural payrolls
- Personal income less transfer payments
- Industrial production
- Manufacturing and trade sales

Lagging (7 Series)

- Average duration of unemployment
- Inventories to sales ratio, manufacturing and trade
- Labor cost per unit of output, manufacturing
- Average prime rate
- Commercial and industrial loans
- Consumer installment credit to personal income ratio
- Consumer Price Index for services

Source: The Conference Board, Inc., "Global Business Cycle Indicators," *The Conference Board*, 2004. www.globalindicators.org

It would really be nice if the leading indicators series were a good predictor of stock prices. This would make sense, as stock prices today are based on future sales, earnings, and dividends. However, stock prices as measured by the S&P 500 index are in fact a component of the leading indicators series. So the real issue might be the simple question, do stock prices predict future economic activity, if in fact they are based on the expectation of future economic activity. The answer is a qualified yes. Stock prices do predict future trends in the economy. However, they also give many false signals. Paul Samuelson, Nobel laureate and one of the most famous economists of the twentieth century, once noted that "the stock market has predicted eight of the last five recessions!"

Anybody can look like a genius who invests at the trough of a business cycle, and nearly everyone looks foolish who invests at the peak. So understanding where the economy is in the cycle is critically important; critically important, but also virtually impossible. Remember, even the NBER defines the business cycle turning points only with clear and sufficient hindsight, and despite this advantage, it occasionally changes its mind later as to the exact dates of the peaks and troughs.

FISCAL POLICY

Complicating an analysis of business cycles is the fact that Congress, through fiscal policy activities, and the Federal Reserve Board, through monetary policy activities, are constantly trying to change what would be the natural course of a business cycle. Hence, they are trying to slow expansions in order to extend them, and to dampen and shorten all contractions. Thus, a financial planner has to have an understanding about what is occurring with regard to fiscal and monetary policy to influence the business cycle, as well as the cycle itself. There are two tools associated with fiscal policy. Let's consider each of them.

Government Revenues and Expenditures

The most common is the adjustment of the government's revenues and expenditures to control the economy. This may happen in several ways. First, when the economy has room to expand, increased government expenditures (whether this is deficit spending or reducing what would have been a surplus) may call forth additional production. Thus, starting a new public works project (for example, a highway, school, or dam) will put people to work to produce the structure and the required inputs (cement, steel, and so on). These newly employed workers will spend their income on consumer goods and services, thereby creating demands that put others to work. These expenditures create income for other people, who also spend a significant portion of their income. This process continues ad infinitum, but with a diminishing effect in each round. This series of income and expenditure effects is referred to as a multiplier effect and the ratio of the final, **combined** increase in consumer spending to the initial government spending **is known** as the multiplier.

Changes in the Tax Code

The second tool of fiscal policy is changes in the tax code. The most fundamental way to change the tax code is to raise or lower the marginal tax brackets. However, other components of the tax code such as the treatment of itemized deductions or tax credits will also have significant and similar economic effects. The effect of a tax decrease (whether through the increase in marginal tax rates or the reduction in allowable itemized deductions or tax credits) is similar to a government spending increase. Lower tax rates and reduced withholding increase households' after-tax income, causing consumer spending to rise. This spending increase, in turn, leads to additional production, employment, and income, which cause further increases in spending. Thus, either a government spending increase or a tax decrease stimulates the economy, whereas a government spending decrease or a tax increase restrains the economy. According to Keynesian theory (the school of economic thought that emphasizes the importance of fiscal policy), a change in government spending has a greater economic impact than a tax change of equivalent size. The multiplier acts on the full amount of the change in government spending to affect the GDP, whereas a portion of the tax change affects savings, leaving the multiplier a lesser amount on which to act.

Tools of Fiscal Policy

- Government spending: More spending stimulates the economy; less spending slows the growth rate.
- Tax revenues: Less taxation stimulates the economy; more taxation slows the growth rate.

MONETARY POLICY

Federal Reserve Board (Fed)

The *Federal Reserve Board* (*Fed*) has primary authority over our nation's monetary policy. The Board conducts its business activity through its 12 regional banks, the most important of which is the Federal Reserve Bank of New York. By largely determining the rate at which the money supply expands or contracts, the Fed exercises a considerable amount of influence over the supply of and demand for credit (that is, loanable funds). Interest rates are the prices paid for the use of such funds. Interest rates are determined by the intersection of these supply and demand functions.

M1

M2

There are multiple definitions of the money supply. The most common is known as *M1*, which is all cash and coin in circulation outside of banks, plus all accounts in depository institutions that are subject to withdrawal by check. The second most common is *M2*, which is M1 plus savings, small-time deposits, and retail-type money market mutual fund balances.

There are three tools of monetary policy. In order of frequency of use, they are open-market operations, changes in the discount rate, and changes in reserve requirements.[61] Before we discuss these tools, let's consider the process by which banks alter the money supply and the role of reserve requirements.

How a Bank Increases the Money Supply

When a bank grants a loan, it funds the loan by creating a deposit in the borrower's account. In effect, it implicitly creates the money that it loans. Checks written against these loan-created deposits will, in turn, be deposited into the accounts of the people or firms receiving the payments, which in turn will be spent and thus transferred to yet other people. This is similar to the multiplier effect from a governmental expenditure. A relatively small portion of the loan money may go into additional cash holdings with each round of expenditures. Thus, most of the new money resulting from granting the loan ends up as deposits somewhere in the banking system.

Reserve Requirements

Most of M1 is held in the form of checkable deposits. Federally chartered banks and state banks with Fed memberships are required to maintain reserves (that is, cash and certain near-cash assets) equal to a certain percentage of their deposits. This percentage is called the reserve ratio

---

61. For additional discussion on the tools of monetary policy, see Federal Reserve Bank of New York, www.newyorkfed.org/education/fed/tools.html, (accessed July 7, 2010). Click on any of the tools listed for additional discussion.

or reserve requirement. The reserve requirements are applied only to transaction balances, not time deposits. They are indexed, and so they change every year. For 2010, the reserve requirements were as follows:

Balance	Reserve Requirements
0 to $10.7 million	0%
$10.7 million to $55.2 million	3%
Above $55.2 million	10%

These three intervals, or trenches, are adjusted based on growth in net transaction accounts and total reserve liabilities at all depository institutions.[62] The reserve requirement percentages rarely change.

EXAMPLE

What would be the required reserves in 2010 be for a bank with $100 million in transactions deposits based on the above balance limits? The requirement can be computed in three steps:

Balance	Reserve Requirement	Reserves
$10.7 million	0%	$0
$44.5 ($55.2 – $10.7) million	3%	$1.335 million
$44.8 ($100 – $55.2) million	10%	$4.480 million

The total required reserves are then $5,815,000, which must be held either as vault cash or deposits at the bank's regional Federal Reserve bank.

Open-Market Operations

Open-market operations consist of the Fed's buying and selling government bonds in the open market. Two things happen when the Fed buys bonds. First, the purchase of bonds will, other things being equal, result in increases in the price of the bonds. Higher bond prices, by definition, mean lower interest rates. Lower interest rates stimulate the economy because consumers and businesses are then more willing to borrow money. This spending, again, creates a multiplier effect. The second thing that happens is those selling bonds to the Fed receive drafts (checks) that increase the

---

62. www.newyorkfed.org/banking/circulars/11996.html (accessed July 7, 2010).

sellers' banks' reserves. In many cases, the seller is a bank, in which case the increase in reserves is direct. When a bank's reserves increase, it becomes more willing to make additional loans that it otherwise might not have made.

If the Fed sells government bonds, the reverse happens. First, the selling causes the prices of the bonds to decline, and thus interest rates to rise. The higher interest rates make consumers and businesses less willing to borrow and spend money. Second, the sales remove cash from the economy, which means consumers, businesses, and banks all have less cash for consumption purchases, business investments, or to make new loans.

What makes open-market operations so effective for the Fed is that they can be done without formal announcement. The Fed buys and sells Treasury securities on a daily basis. In fact, the Fed will sometimes place offsetting buy and sell orders with different bond traders just to create some confusion among market traders as to whether the Fed is a net buyer or seller of bonds at any point in time. Nonetheless, many Wall Street analysts carefully monitor the Fed's open-market operations and the resulting changes in the money supply. The Fed generally prefers to exercise its influence on the banking system through open-market operations rather than changing the reserve requirements because the latter may disrupt the financial markets more than is desirable.

Changes in the Discount Rate

discount rate (monetary policy) One of the activities the Fed engages in is lending cash (reserves) to member banks. The Fed does this because it is charged by Congress to protect the integrity of the banking system. However, borrowing from the Fed is a privilege, not a right. It extends these loans only on a short-term basis and only to applicants that it views as not abusing the borrowing privilege. This lending process is referred to as discounting, so the interest rate the Fed charges is known as the *discount rate*.

Compared with the Fed's other tools, discounting plays a relatively minor role. Changes in the discount rate are used principally to signal changes in Fed policy. At its meeting in February 1994, the Federal Open Market Committee (FOMC) began the practice of immediately disclosing its decisions upon making them, rather than waiting until the next meeting to disclose the minutes of the previous meeting. When the Fed announces a decision that it is lowering the discount rate, it is signaling to the financial markets that it is easing (or continuing to ease) monetary policy in order to stimulate the economy. The lower discount also encourages banks to borrow from the Fed, for the purpose of lending out the money. Increases in the discount rate are intended to slow the growth rate of an economy that is at risk of getting overheated. Overheated economies lead to inflation, which the Fed is intent on avoiding.

The effectiveness of the discount rate is limited by its relationship to the federal funds rate. This is the rate that banks charge each other for overnight use of federal reserves in the so-called federal funds market. Federal funds are deposits that banks hold at Federal Reserve banks. Beginning in October 1997, the Fed announced that its FOMC directive would henceforth specify an explicit target for the federal funds rate. In addition, the directive would express a bias to possible future action in terms of the rate. For a long time prior to the announcement, the Fed had implemented monetary policy by making discrete and frequent small adjustments to its federal funds rate target. Often, changes in the federal funds rate are simultaneous with other changes in the marketplace, such as changes in the various market-determined interest rates.

Changes in Reserve Requirements

excess reserves   The least used tool of the Fed is changes in the reserve requirement. The last change made to the reserve requirement was in April 1992, when it was lowered from 12% to 10% of transaction deposits. If the reserve requirement is decreased, banks do not need the same amount of reserves to support their existing deposits. To the extent that banks loan out this cash that they had previously had to hold as reserves, the money supply expands. The catch is that banks are not forced to lend this money. They may take the freed-up reserves and buy Treasury securities, thus defeating the Fed's attempt to stimulate the economy. An increase in the reserve requirement should have the effect of forcing banks to forgo loans because of the additional cash that must be kept on hand. The problem here is that some banks hold more reserves than are necessary; these are called excess reserves. *Excess reserves* are computed as

Excess reserves = Actual reserves − Required reserves.

For these banks, an increase in reserve requirements may only convert the nature of the reserves from excess to required, and thus have no effect on the economy.

EXAMPLE

Suppose a bank has $5 million in transactions deposits, actual reserves of $300,000, and required reserves of $300,000 (assume that the reserve requirement is a flat 6%). If the Fed lowers the reserve ratio to 4%, the bank is now required to have only $200,000 in reserves ($5,000,000 × 0.04). The bank now has excess reserves of $100,000 and is able to make an additional $100,000 in loans if it desires to do so. If the bank is concerned about the economy and the ability of borrowers to repay, it may opt not to make additional loans, even though it has the capacity to do so.

The Fed's Policy Tools

- Open-market operations: Fed purchases (sales) of government securities increase (decrease) the bank deposits available to support the money supply.
- Discount rate: Decreasing (increasing) the discount rate signals greater (less) willingness to grant discount loans.
- Reserve requirement: Increasing (decreasing) the required percentage reduces (raises) the amount of money that a given reserve base can support.

Why Monetary Policy Is So Important

monetarists

Stock market analysts pay close attention to monetary policy for several reasons. First, monetary policy has different industry effects. This is because some industries are particularly sensitive to changes in interest rates. Second, monetary policy is considered easier to track and perhaps easier to predict than the fiscal policy. The Fed's weekly monetary data releases are intensively analyzed by some members of the financial press, and are readily available on the Internet. Third, an influential group of economists (called *monetarists*, many of whom are associated with the University of Chicago) assert that money drives the economy, while fiscal policy plays a more modest role. Fourth, monetary policy indirectly affects the stock market through its influence on interest rates. We will consider each of these matters in greater detail.

Factors Affecting Likelihood of Shift in Monetary and Fiscal Policy	
A shift toward greater stimulation is more likely if	A shift toward greater restrictiveness is more likely if
• the inflation rate is near its target, or inflation is decreasing;	• the inflation rate is far above its target, or inflation is increasing;
• unemployment is far above its target, or unemployment is increasing;	• unemployment is near its target, or unemployment is decreasing;
• the dollar is strong;	• the dollar is weak;
• the trade deficit is small, or there is a trade surplus;	• the trade deficit is large;
• substantial amounts of capital are flowing into the U.S.	• foreign capital is threatening to withdraw from or slow its flow into the U.S.

Disproportionate Impact of Monetary Policy

Monetary policy works by rationing credit. Restrictive monetary policy not only raises interest rates (at least in the short run), but it also tends to limit availability of credit to borrowers who represent greater credit risks and thereby influences the allocation of funds among the financial intermediaries.

Savings and loan associations and mutual savings banks (thrift institutions) may be particularly hard hit when interest rates increase. The thrifts have historically maintained a large percentage of their portfolios in long-term fixed-rate mortgages (although this has changed somewhat in the last few decades with the growth in popularity of adjustable rate mortgages).

The thrifts' deposits, in contrast, have tended to be available to their depositors on demand or to be represented by CDs with relatively short maturities. This type of situation implies an imbalance between the maturity structure of thrifts' assets (long-term) and their liabilities (short-term). The imbalance has tended to make the thrifts more vulnerable to rising interest rates than other lending institutions that do not have a high concentration of assets in fixed-rate mortgages. As interest rates rise, the costs of funds tend to go up, while the rates that the thrifts earn on existing fixed-rate mortgage loans remain relatively constant. The larger the proportion of their assets tied up in fixed-rate loans, the more vulnerable the thrifts are to rising interest rates. Having experienced the adverse effects of rising interest rates a number of times, the thrifts have sought to limit their exposure. Their sensitivity to increasing interest rates adds to the real estate, construction, building materials, and major appliance industries' vulnerability to tight money.

Relative Ease of Tracking Monetary Policy

Monetary policy is easier to follow than the lengthy, uncertain path of fiscal policy that includes authorizations, appropriation, and implementation of government expenditures. Tax legislation, the implementation tool of fiscal policy, is equally difficult to follow. Moreover, the greater volatility of monetary policy provides more signals than is the case with fiscal policy.

Monetarists versus Keynesians

Keynesians   Since John Maynard Keynes published his *General Theory of Employment, Interest, and Money* in 1936, the monetarists have debated with those who emphasize the importance of fiscal policy (*Keynesians*). Although the Keynesians dominated economic thinking throughout the 1940s and 1950s, by the early 1960s, the debate was again in full swing. The dispute continues, but the issues may be narrowing. During much of the post-1936 period, the Keynesians were far more influential in and out of government. Since the late 1960s, however, both groups have had substantial influence.

In the most recent recession that started in December 2007, Congress has made heavy use of fiscal policy. The best example of this was the $786 billion stimulus package passed in 2009 by the Obama administration.

Direct Effect of Monetary Policy on the Stock Market

Monetary policy indirectly influences the stock market through its effect on the economy and on corporate profits. Moreover, the impact of monetary policy on interest rates has a direct effect on the stock market in three related ways.

First, as seen in an earlier chapter, stock prices reflect the present value of their expected future dividends. The rate at which these expected dividends are discounted is affected by the market rates of interest.

Second, investors find bonds relatively more attractive as their prices fall and thus their yields increase. As a result, some investors will shift from stocks to bonds when interest rates rise (and bond prices fall) and from bonds to stocks when interest rates fall (and bond prices rise).

Finally, higher interest rates mean increased borrowing costs for investors who have bought on margin. These investors will require a higher expected return to justify the greater cost of financing their margin purchases and, as such, may place fewer buy orders than they otherwise would have. Falling interest rates have the opposite effect.

How the Impact of Monetary Policy on Interest Rates Affects the Stock Market
• The market rate of interest affects the rate at which stocks' expected dividend streams are discounted.
• As the yields on bonds increases (fall), some investors may switch from stocks (bonds) to bonds (stocks).
• High interest rates result in increased borrowing costs for investors who have bought on margin, who need a higher expected return to justify their greater financing costs.

MONETARY AND FISCAL POLICY: QUALIFICATIONS AND GOALS

Qualifications

As we have seen, the economy may be stimulated by increased government spending, lower taxes, and an increase in the money supply, and it may be restrained by the reverse processes. Now let us introduce some qualifications.

First, the impacts of changes in tax rates and government spending (fiscal policy) or in the reserve requirement, discount rate, and open-market operation (monetary policy) take time to work their way through the economy. This is particularly true of fiscal policy, because it takes considerable time for Congress to enact a new budget or to change the tax rates.

Second, monetary and fiscal policies are both subject to political pressures. Their degree of sensitivity differs, however. Monetary policy is formulated by the Federal Reserve Board of Governors and its Federal Open Market Committee (FOMC). Members are appointed by the President and confirmed by the Senate for long (14-year), staggered terms. Furthermore, the Fed is not dependent directly on Congressional appropriations. Its own interest income covers its operating expenses. The Fed, therefore, is theoretically able to pursue a relatively independent monetary policy, although Congress and the President, at times, attempt to apply political pressure.

Congress and the President jointly formulate fiscal policy. Many diverse interest groups may affect the decision-making process. As a result, short-term pressures increase the difficulty of implementing long-run fiscal policies.

Third, the stock market already incorporates an expectation of the direction of economic policy. Thus, to obtain an advantage relative to that incorporated in the market, investors need to have a superior understanding of economic policy/economy-stock market relationships. In other words, investors need to be able to outguess the market in its forecast for the economy's future.

Goals

The two primary goals of fiscal and monetary policy are price stability and full employment, although price stability does not mean perfectly stable prices and full employment does not mean everyone has a job. Government policies, including monetary and fiscal policy, also have other goals that need to be kept in mind.

Inflation, Deflation, Disinflation, and Stagflation

price stability

disinflation

Price stability is the absence of either a sharply rising (inflation) or falling (deflation) trend in overall prices.
Inflation is a general rise in the price level. Thus, for example, a 6% annual inflation rate implies that $1.06 is required today to buy the same of goods and services as could have been acquired a year earlier for $1. Inflation of 6% does not mean that *all* prices rise by 6%. In fact, some prices may actually fall, while other prices rise dramatically. An inflation rate of 6% simply means that the cost of a market basket of goods and services that would be acquired by a typical family rises by 6 percent. Deflation, in contrast, is a general fall in the price level. During the twentieth century, actual inflation and potential inflation have been much more of a problem than the threat of deflation. Furthermore, policymakers (especially at the Fed) frequently state the problem of achieving price stability as a matter of lowering the rate of inflation, rather than the complete elimination of all price increases. One sign of a successful monetary policy would be *disinflation*, which means that prices are going up at a slower rate than the rate at which they had previously been going up.

A term that came into existence back in the late 1970s is *stagflation*. Stagflation is inflation during a period of economic stagnation. Normally, inflation occurs during periods of economic growth, when the aggregate demand for goods and services exceeds aggregate supply. When the economy is stagnate, it usually means that the aggregate supply for goods and services exceeds aggregate demand. Stagnation is normally associated with disinflation or deflation. Hence, stagflation represents the worst of both worlds, stagnation and inflation simultaneously.

Full Employment

unemployment rate

It seems logical to think that full employment would be defined as an employment rate of 100% for the current, eligible labor force. Realistically, however, some people will always be unemployed (not necessarily always the same people), even in the best of times. People change jobs (frictional unemployment), work at seasonal jobs (seasonal unemployment), and are unemployed because of location, background, or training (structural unemployment). These various classes of unemployed people create an almost irreducible floor for reported unemployment. In fact, the absence of frictional unemployment would probably not be a good thing. Frictional unemployment often occurs because some percentage of people are looking for better jobs, where their talents, skills, and training can be better utilized and where they can be more productive and earn more money. Society as a whole benefits when individuals work at jobs that maximize their productivity. The level of this irreducible floor, however, changes as the economy evolves. Full employment, therefore, is generally defined as corresponding to some acceptable level of unemployment. The *unemployment rate* itself is defined as the percentage of the labor force that is out of work and actively seeking a job. Sometimes the unemployment rate drops during a recession because some unemployed people become so discouraged that they give up seeking employment. The labor force consists of those who are employed or actively seeking employment. The employment rate, the unemployment rate, and the inflation rate are widely reported every month.

Secondary Goals

balance of trade

The relationship of the U.S. economy to the world economy is increasingly important. As the world economy has grown more interdependent, such matters as the exchange rates, the amount of imports relative to exports (*balance of trade*), and international capital flows (which may take the form of foreigners investing in U.S. securities or U.S. citizens investing in foreign businesses) have become increasingly important to economic policymakers. Moreover, the actions of foreign investors are having an increasingly large impact on U.S. financial markets.

Some of the government's additional economic and quasi-economic goals and concerns include economic growth, freedom, and opportunity; increased productivity; a higher standard of living; environmental protection; energy independence; consumer protection; and product safety. Policies designed to achieve some of these goals may frequently conflict with other goals.

Virtually everyone agrees that price stability and full employment are desirable. Policies to reduce unemployment may, however, accelerate inflation. Similarly, policies to slow the inflation rate may increase the unemployment rate. When the economy is already near full employment and is further stimulated, those bidding for the limited supply of labor will bid up wages, which eventually causes other prices to rise. When inflation is a problem, increases in the interest rate will reduce new spending by businesses, throwing some people out of work.

The international situation adds a further complication. During the 1980s, maintaining the value of the dollar and seeking to attract capital to help reduce the budget and trade deficits led to a relatively restrictive monetary policy. Such a policy raises U.S. interest rates relative to rates abroad. However, higher interest rates usually lead to reduced domestic economic activity. Thus, policymakers may at times have to choose between doing what is best for the domestic economy and doing what is best with respect to foreign trade.

INDUSTRY ANALYSIS

Economic analysis assesses the general environment and its impact on firms and industries. Industry analysis, in contrast, examines the specific environment of the markets in which different industries compete. Not only have different industries provided substantially different returns to investors, but there is also a wide dispersion in the performance of individual firms within industries. Nonetheless, when assessing a firm's financial data, it is important to see how the firm performs relative to other firms in the same industry in order to make a meaningful assessment.

Stages of Industry Development

Industries are thought typically to pass through several developmental stages. Initially, many new firms are established (start-up stage), and growth is rapid. A shakeout then reduces the number of firms (consolidation stage) as the less efficient firms tend to merge or go bankrupt. After the adjustment, growth slows to that of the economy (maturity stage). Finally, new industries begin to grow at the expense of the existing industry (decline stage). Predicting evolution from one stage to another is not easy. Some industries follow different schemes from the typical one just described. For example, the solid waste disposal industry experienced modest performance until the ecology movement brought it to life.

Sometimes, companies or even whole industries reinvent themselves with invention or innovation. Thus, what had been a mature or declining industry may suddenly be an industry that has jumped back to the start-up stage.

Life Cycle of an Industry
• Start-up stage: Many new firms; growth is rapid
• Consolidation stage: Shakeout period; growth slows
• Maturity stage: Growth parallels growth of the economy
• Decline stage: Growth is slower than that of the economy

It is easy to identify a "hot" industry and a mature or dying industry. All we have to do is to look at the P/E ratios for the various industry indexes. The industry indexes with the highest P/E ratios are the hot industries, and those with the lowest are usually the mature and dying industries. The real issue is whether or not the hot industries are over- or undervalued relative to their prospects; the same goes for the mature and dying industries.

Cyclical vs. Noncyclical Industries

Their life-cycle not withstanding, industries are frequently categorized as cyclical or noncyclical. A cyclical industry means that the sales of companies in that industry tend to move with the business cycle. Consumer durables are a classic example of a cyclical industry. People have a greater propensity to buy things like new cars and new washing machines when the economy is performing well. Noncyclical industries are those which involve products that people will tend to buy regardless of how the economy is going. Food is a classic example, with the traditional argument being "everyone has to eat."

Some analysts will at times recommend firms in cyclical or noncyclical industries depending on where the economy appears to be in the business cycle. However, there does not appear to be any research that shows that firms in cyclical industries do better at any one stage of the business cycle than do firms in noncyclical industries. This is what one would expect if the markets were efficient and if investors understood fluctuations in earnings due to business cycle factors.

COMPANY ANALYSIS

Once industry analysis has identified a potentially attractive area for investment, the companies within that industry need to be evaluated. Three important company characteristics are competitive position, management quality, and financial soundness. For our purposes, we are only interested in examining financial soundness, and we look at the basics of how one analyzes financial soundness.

Because accounting data are utilized extensively in financial analysis, we shall briefly review the three principal financial statements: the balance sheet, the income statement, and the statement of cash flows. We will also look at what is meant by a *pro forma* financial statement.

Financial Statements

Balance Sheet

The balance sheet reflects the financial status of a company at a point in time. It is a listing of what the company owns and what it owes. The assets are traditionally listed on the left-hand side of the balance sheet; these are what the company owns. The right-hand side of the balance sheet indicates where the money came from to buy the assets. There are basically two sources of money: debt (money that is borrowed) and equity (money that the owners have provided).

current assets Assets are listed in decreasing order of liquidity. The first assets listed are collectively known as the current assets. *Current assets* are cash and items that are expected to be converted to cash within the next year. They include cash (which encompasses money market instruments), accounts receivable, prepaid expenses, and inventory. For most companies, prepaid expenses is a trivial amount, and we will omit this entry from further discussions.

The remainder of the asset side of the balance sheet is referred to as *fixed assets*. For many firms, the major item here is plant and equipment. Plant and equipment are valued at cost less depreciation, whereas most other assets are valued at the lower of cost or market value.

current liabilities Liabilities are listed first on the right-hand side of the balance sheet. They are listed in increasing order of maturity. Thus, the standard balance sheet has current liabilities first and long-term debt second. The owner's equity is located at the bottom of the right-hand side of the balance sheet. *Current liabilities* are debts due within one year. This includes accruals and payables, such as accrued wages and accounts payable, as well as short-term debt and any payments of principal on long-term debt that are due within the next year.

The equity section is primarily the money represented by the shareholders' purchase of newly issued stock as well as earnings that have been retained in the firm. The purchase of newly issued stock by shareholders is usually broken into two subcategories: par value and paid-in surplus.

par value   Although at one time the par value for stock had legal and practical significance, it no longer does. Hence, some common stock is designated as "no par," and some common stocks have a par value of one cent. When an investor buys stock from the company, the purchase price is allocated to the two accounts based on the amount paid. For example, suppose a company has common stock with a par value of $10, and a new share is sold to an investor for $15. The $15 received shows up on the asset side as an increase in the cash account. In the equity section, $10 is added to the common stock, par value account; the remaining $5 is added to the paid-in surplus account.

The retained earnings account is the sum of the profits the company has accumulated since it was incorporated, less all dividends paid to the shareholders over that same time period. A common mistake is to look at the retained earnings account and assume that it represents a pool of cash. Any cash implicit in the retained earnings account is already a part of the assets. Some of it may be in the form of cash, but the rest of it is invested in the various assets. There is no direct link between most right-hand-side entries (where money comes from) and specific assets on the left-hand-side (how the money is used).

net worth (equity)   The *net worth*, or *equity*, section of the balance sheet is the sum of the common stock, paid-in surplus, and retained earnings accounts. It represents the aggregate of how much money the shareholders have invested in the firm. It is always analyzed as a single number, because it is the total that matters—the breakdown between the individual accounts is immaterial.

The most important fact to keep in mind about the balance sheet is that the sum of the assets always equals the sum of the liabilities and stockholders' equity. This is because all money raised has been invested in one or another asset. Conversely, we could say that all assets owned have some source of financing. Below is an example of a typical balance sheet.

Table 7-3 Balance Sheet Example

Assets		Liabilities and Stockholders' Equity	
Current assets		Current liabilities	
Cash	$10,000	Wages payable	$ 8,000
Accounts receivable	27,000	Accounts payable	29,000
Inventory	61,000	Total current liabilities	$37,000
Total current assets	$98,000		
		Long-term liabilities	
Fixed assets		Note	$ 53,000
Plant and equipment	$187,000	Mortgage	60,000
Less accumulated		Total long-term liabilities	$113,000
depreciation	62,000		
Net fixed assets	$125,000	Stockholders' equity	
		Common stock (parvalue)	$ 40,000
Total assets	$223,000	Paid-in surplus	10,000
		Retained earnings	23,000
		Total stockholders' equity	$ 73,000
		Total liabilities and stockholders' equity	$223,000

Income Statement

earnings before interest and taxes (EBIT)

taxable income

net income

The income statement (see example below) reflects the results of operations for a period of time. It can start with gross sales. In some cases, the first figure listed is net sales or just sales, which is gross sales less returns. From this, the cost of goods sold is subtracted to obtain the gross profit of the business. Next, both cash and noncash operating expenses are totaled. The sum of these expenses is subtracted from the gross profit to obtain *earnings before interest and taxes (EBIT)*. EBIT is frequently referred to as operating income or operating profit. The interest expense is then subtracted from the EBIT to obtain the company's *taxable income.* Finally, income taxes are subtracted from taxable income to produce the net income (or net profit) number. The income statement helps answer the most basic question about the firm: Did the company make or lose money in a particular period, and how much? Every year (unless the company sells or buys back some stock) the company's net worth will change by the amount of net income that is retained—that is, the net income less any dividends paid. The income statement and balance sheet are thus connected by changes in net worth.

Table 7-4 Income Statement Example	
Net sales	$200,000
Cost of goods sold	120,000
Gross profit	$ 80,000
Operating expenses:	
Cash expense	$50,000
Depreciation (i.e., noncash expenses)	10,000
	$60,000
Earnings before interest and taxes	$20,000
Interest expense	8,000
Taxable Income	$12,000
Income taxes	5,000
Net income	$ 7,000

Statement of Cash Flows

The statement of cash flows focuses on where and how cash came into the business, and where and how it left. It shows how the changes in the accounts of the balance sheet contributed to the net change in the cash position for the year. An example is provided below.

A statement of cash flows is divided into three main sections. These are: cash flows from operating activities, cash flows from investing activities, and cash flows from financing activities. The sum of the net cash flows from each of these three activities indicates the net change in the cash position of the firm. The cash position at the start of a fiscal year, plus this net change in the cash position, equals the cash position at the end of the year.

The cash flows from operating activities always start with the net income for the period. To this, one adds the noncash expenses. The primary noncash expense is usually depreciation. One then also adds the changes in the various working capital accounts. Net working capital is defined as current assets minus current liabilities. There are six rules used to define whether a change in a balance sheet account brought in cash (i.e., was a source of funds) or took cash out of a firm (i.e., was a use of funds). These six rules are:

1. Any increase in an asset account is a use of funds.
2. Any decrease in a liability account is a use of funds.
3. Any decrease in an equity account is a use of funds.
4. Any decrease in an asset account is a source of funds.
5. Any increase in a liability account is a source of funds.
6. Any increase in an equity account is a source of funds.

In the statement, sources of funds are noted as positive numbers and uses of funds as negative numbers. As shown below, during the year this firm's inventory increased by $460. Although the inventory presumably was constantly being sold and replaced during the year, by the end of the year this firm has $460 more invested in inventory than it did at the start of the year. Hence, it increased its investment in inventory by $460, and this used funds (i.e., cash).

In the example below, operating activities brought in $28,990. The majority of this consisted of the net income, adjusted for depreciation charges that were added back. Investing activities resulted in a $26,000 cash outflow. The bulk of this went to the purchase of another business (the XYZ Corporation), but a significant portion also went toward the purchase of fixed assets. Finally, financing activities brought in another $7,300. This resulted from the sale of new bonds, with a significant portion of this money going to pay down loans as well as to purchase Treasury stock and pay dividends. (Treasury stock is common stock that has been issued to investors, and then is later repurchased by the issuing corporation.)

Table 7-5 Statement of Cash Flows Example	
CASH FLOWS—OPERATING ACTIVITIES	
Net Income	$16,800
Adjustments to reconcile net earnings to cash provided from operating activities:	
Depreciation	8,200
Decrease (increase) in accounts receivable	(850)
Decrease (increase) in inventory	(460)
Increase (decrease) in accounts payable	5,300
Cash from Operating Activities	28,990
CASH FLOWS—INVESTING ACTIVITIES	
Additions to fixed assets	(13,100)
Sale of fixed assets	5,800
Acquisition of XYZ Corporation	(18,700)
CASH USED FOR INVESTING ACTIVITIES	(26,000)
CASH FLOWS—FINANCING ACTIVITIES	
Net increase (decrease) in loans	(2,700)
New Bonds Issued	25,800
Purchase of Treasury Stock	(7,400)
Dividends paid	(8,400)
CASH FROM (USED FOR) FINANCING ACTIVITIES	7,300
INCREASE (DECREASE) IN CASH AND EQUIVALENTS DURING YEAR	10,290
Cash and equivalents at beginning of year	12,600
Cash and equivalents at end of year	$22,890

Pro Forma Statements

There are occasions when it is important to create pro forma statements. A *pro forma* statement is any hypothetical accounting statement that projects what that statement is expected to look like at a point in the future. For example, when a business applies to the bank for a loan, not only will the bank want to see the firm's recently audited financial statements, it will also want to see pro forma statements for the firm. What is critical for the pro forma statements is that they show that the bank loan will be paid off according to an agreed upon schedule, and that any other conditions specified in the loan (such as a limit on additional borrowings) are also met.

Types of Accounting Statements

- Balance sheet: Picture of resources (assets), obligations (liabilities), and net worth (equity) at a specific point in time
- Income statement: Earnings, calculated as revenues less expenses, over a period of time
- Statement of cash flows: A list of how cash entered and left the firm over a period of time
- Pro forma: Any hypothetical accounting statement that projects what that statement is expected to look like at a point in the future

---

Ratio Analysis

When we look at financial statements, what we see is a lot of numbers. A financial analyst of a firm wants to go to the next step to ask: Are these numbers good? Are they bad? What do they mean? The traditional technique to answer these questions is to create financial ratios. There are hundreds of ratios that can be, and are, used. Many of them are so closely related that they are really not providing additional information. The trick is to identify a relatively small number of ratios that provide critical information, and stick with these. Furthermore, because many of the ratios are closely related, they are always grouped together in terms of the characteristic of the firm on which they focus. Unfortunately, the myriad of books published on the subject of financial analysis do not agree on how many ratios to consider, what the most critical ratios are, how they should be grouped together, or even some of the definitions. Thus, the discussion that follows is representative, not definitive, of ratios, definitions, and classification categories. The classification categories we will use are liquidity, debt, profitability, and activity.

Liquidity Ratios

current ratio The purpose of the liquidity ratios is to evaluate a business's ability to meet its cash obligations in the near future. The most commonly used (and oldest) liquidity ratio is the *current ratio*. It is defined as current assets divided by current liabilities. As with all ratios, the optimal value varies from company to company, industry to industry, and over time. Stable incomes and reliable sources of short-term credit lessen the need for liquid assets and therefore reduce the optimal current ratio level. Indeed, a high current ratio may indicate that resources are being tied up unnecessarily in the form of cash, receivables, or inventory. An excess amount of receivables may mean a firm is either being too generous in its granting of credit, or is not effectively collecting its receivables. An excess amount of inventory may mean the firm is carrying more inventory than is necessary, or the inventory is not selling. Finally, a high current ratio may also mean the firm is not using enough short-term debt to finance its operations. Short-term debt may be an extremely inexpensive source of money.

quick ratio acid test ratio   The *quick ratio*, or *acid test*, focuses on the most liquid of the liquid assets—cash and receivables—and is defined as cash plus receivables divided by current liabilities. Some people define the numerator as current assets minus inventory. The two definitions usually produce the same number, but the presence of prepaid expenses would produce different numerators. The argument for evaluating liquidity without counting inventory is that if the company is having financial difficulties, it may well be that inventory is not selling. Hence, high inventory may be a sign of a liquidity problem, not a source of liquidity. Simply put, a high current ratio and low quick ratio might be a warning sign indicating that the firm is experiencing difficulty moving its inventory.

inventory turnover ratio   The quality of the inventory can be measured directly with the *inventory turnover ratio*. There are several different definitions for this ratio; the most common is the cost of goods sold divided by average yearly inventory.[63] Normally, we would say that a high inventory turnover suggests brisk sales and well-managed inventories. However, a high inventory turnover ratio might also indicate inadequate inventories. A low inventory turnover ratio may reflect idle resources that are tied up in excess inventories and/or a large obsolete inventory component. It might also indicate that the company uses a marketing strategy of assuring customers that there will always be adequate inventory.

One way to interpret the industry turnover ratio is to divide the value into 12 (the number of months in a year). This indicates how long (in months) the

63.   The most common alternative measurement of this ratio is sales divided by average yearly inventory. Also, many people use either beginning-of-year inventory, or end-of-year inventory, rather than average inventory in the denominator. A common way to measure average yearly inventory is to add the beginning-of-year inventory and the end-of-year inventory together and divide by two (that is, take the arithmetic average of the two numbers).

inventory is in the business before it is sold. Thus, an inventory turnover ratio of six could be interpreted as having inventory on hand an average of two months, and a turnover ratio of two would mean that on average the inventory is sitting around for six months.

average collection period (ACP) The quality of a firm's accounts receivable is usually measured by *average collection period (ACP)*, which is defined as the net accounts receivable divided by daily sales. Daily sales is defined as annual net sales divided by 360.[64] The ratio should be compared with the company's stated credit policy. For example, a manufacturer might have a credit policy based on an expectation of receiving payments within 30 days of billing. If the ACP is longer than 30 days, the firm may have a problem with credit extensions. Some firms make easy credit a key part of their marketing program. Such firms would likely have large ACPs reflecting their business strategy. An unusually low average collection period might suggest either that the firm is losing potential customers by maintaining an overly stringent credit policy or that it is selling its receivables to a third party.

Liquidity Ratios
• Current: Current assets/current liabilities
• Quick (or acid test): (Current assets – inventories)/current liabilities or (Cash + Accounts receivable)/current liabilities
• Inventory turnover: Cost of goods sold/average yearly inventory
• Average collection period: Net accounts receivable/daily sales

EXAMPLE
Using the examples above, what are the liquidity ratios for this firm?

---

64. There are, of course, 365 days in a year. However, the industrywide definitions for many of these ratios were established long before the arrival of calculators and computers and thus used 360 for ease of computation.

$$\text{Current ratio} = \frac{\$98,000}{\$37,000} = 2.65$$

$$\text{Quick ratio} = \left(\frac{\$98,000 - \$61,000}{\$37,000}\right) = 1.0$$

$$\text{Inventory turnover} = \frac{\$120,000}{\$61,000} = 1.97$$

$$\text{Average collection period} = \frac{\$27,000}{\left(\frac{\$200,000}{360}\right)} = 48.6 \text{ days}$$

Debt Ratios

debt-equity ratio

equity multiplier
debt ratio

Debt ratios are used to measure the extent to which a company uses debt financing, and the impact of that debt financing on the firm's overall profitability. The four most common debt ratios are the debt ratio, the debt-equity ratio, the equity multiplier, and the times-interest-earned ratio. The *debt ratio* is total debt divided by total assets. It tells the analyst in the simplest possible terms the percentage of assets that are financed by debt. The *debt-equity ratio* is total debt divided by total equity. The *equity multiplier* is total assets divided by total equity. If you know the value of any one of these last three ratios, you can quickly compute the values of the other two. So it is really not necessary in a financial analysis to compute all three of these ratios, one is adequate.

times-interest-earned ratio

The final debt ratio is the *times-interest-earned ratio*, sometimes called the earnings-coverage ratio, which is computed as EBIT (earnings before interest and taxes) divided by interest. Unlike the other three ratios, it relates the company's interest obligation to its earning power. The higher the ratio, the greater the safety of a company's interest payments.

Interpreting the debt ratio can be tricky, because some debt is good, but too much debt is bad. Unfortunately, it is never clear when a business has moved from "some" debt to "too much" debt. There are two reasons that some debt is good. The first is that interest payments are tax deductible for a business. The second is the benefit of financial leverage. Specifically, if a company can borrow at *X* percent and earn (*X* + *Y*) percent on the money, the difference (*Y* percent) is like a windfall gain. Debt becomes a problem as soon as a firm is unable to make its interest and/or principal payments. This failure could force a company into bankruptcy.

debt capacity   A company's appropriate debt ratio varies primarily with its earning stability. A rapid rise in the ratio can suggest potential problems. It is of less concern if the increased debt still leaves the firm with a substantial cushion of equity and the firm has profitable operations; the company may simply be taking advantage of heretofore unused debt capacity. *Debt capacity* is the firm's ability to borrow money. Underutilized debt capacity is a wonderful resource because it means that if a problem or opportunity arises for which a lot of cash is immediately needed, the firm should be able to borrow it. However, underutilized debt capacity would also mean the firm is not currently taking full advantage of the two benefits of using borrowed money.

Debt Ratios
• Debt: Total debt/total assets
• Debt-equity: Total debt/equity
• Equity multiplier: Total assets/equity
• Times-interest-earned: EBIT/interest expense

Debt is not the only type of fixed payment obligation. In particular, leases can complicate accounting statement analysis. Purchasing assets with borrowed funds increases the debt ratio, whereas leasing the same assets does not increase debt *per se*. The long-term obligations are similar, however, whether new assets are leased or purchased with borrowed money. Thus, debt ratios do not always accurately reflect a company's total financial commitments. Investors need to look beyond the debt ratios of companies that lease a large fraction of their assets. Companies must show their capitalized long-term lease obligations on their balance sheets.[65]

EXAMPLE
Using *Table 7-3* and 7-4, what are the debt ratios for this firm?

65. Several ratios have been developed to incorporate the impact of lease payments, but these ratios are beyond the introductory level of this discussion.

$$\text{Debt ratio} = \left(\frac{\$\,37,000 + \$\,113,000}{\$\,223,000} \right) = .67$$

$$\text{Debt} - \text{equity ratio} = \left(\frac{\$\,37,000 + \$\,113,000}{\$\,73,000} \right) = 2.05$$

$$\text{Equity multiplier} = \frac{\$\,223,000}{\$\,37,000} = 3.05$$

$$\text{Times} - \text{interest} - \text{earned} = \frac{\$\,20,000}{\$\,8,000} = 2.5$$

Profitability Ratios

return on equity (ROE)

return on assets (ROA)

net profit margin (NPM)

The three most important profitability ratios are *return on equity (ROE)*, *return on assets (ROA)*, and *net profit margin (NPM)*. ROE is net income divided by total equity, ROA is net income divided by total assets, and NPM is net income divided by net sales.

The net income number should be for a full-year period, as a shorter time frame could allow seasonal influences to distort the results. The total equity and total asset numbers should be for the beginning of the year, rather than the end of the year, because the end-of-the-year numbers would incorporate the earnings that were retained during the year. However, if the beginning-of-the-year numbers are not available, the end-of-year numbers are used. The net sales number should be for the same time period as the net income number.

Profitability Ratios
• ROE: Net income/equity
• ROA: Net income/total assets
• NPM: Net income/net sales

The ROE ratio indicates the profits generated relative to the shareholders' investment. In theory, a firm could pay out all of its net income as dividends.

If it did, then the return on the investors' money would literally be the ROE. The higher the ROE number, the better for the shareholder.

The ROA ratio indicates how profitable the firm is relative to the investment in assets. It provides a measure of operational efficiency. As with the ROE, the larger this number, the stronger the firm is financially.

The net profit margin indicates the percentage of profit in each dollar of sales. Again larger values are always more desirable, all other things equal.

EXAMPLE

Using *Table 7-3* and *Table 7-4*, what are the profitability ratios for this firm?

$$\text{Return on equity} = \frac{\$7,000}{\$73,000} = .096$$

$$\text{Return on assets} = \frac{\$7,000}{\$223,000} = .031$$

$$\text{Net profit margin} = \frac{\$7,000}{\$200,000} = .035$$

Activity Ratios

total asset turnover ratio

fixed asset turnover ratio

The last category is the activity ratios, which are sometimes referred to as efficiency ratios. Activity ratios measure how efficient the business is with certain assets, or with all of its assets. The primary activity ratios are the total asset turnover ratio and the fixed asset turnover ratio.[66] The *total asset turnover ratio (TAT)* is net sales divided by total assets, and the *fixed asset turnover ratio (FAT)* is net sales divided by net fixed assets.

Efficiency Ratios
• Total asset turnover: Net sales/total assets
• Fixed asset turnover: Net sales/net fixed assets

---

66.   Some textbooks include the average collection period and the inventory turnover ratio as activity ratios, but we included them as measures of liquidity as they clearly provide information that is critical in interpreting the current ratio and acid test.

The TAT ratio is interpreted as the amount of sales generated per dollar of total assets. Thus, a ratio of 2.0 means the firm is generating $2.00 in sales per $1.00 invested in assets. Larger ratios mean more efficiency. However, an extremely large ratio may signify a firm is underinvested in assets and would do well to expand its assets.

Similarly, the FAT ratio is interpreted as the amount of sales generated per dollar of fixed assets. Thus, a ratio of 3.5 means the firm is generating $3.50 in sales per $1.00 invested in net fixed assets. Larger values normally mean more efficiency, but too large a value may signify a problem. Remember, the denominator is *net* fixed assets, which means that it is the amount paid for the fixed assets less the accumulated depreciation charges against these assets. Older assets will have substantial accumulated depreciation charges, and thus will tend to produce large FAT ratios. Similarly, new assets (and more technologically efficient assets) will tend to have little in the way of accumulated depreciation, and thus may produce low FAT ratios. Thus, the FAT ratio may say as much about the age of the fixed assets as it says about their efficiency in generating sales.

EXAMPLE

Using *Table 7-3* and *Table 7-4*, what are the efficiency ratios for this firm?

$$\text{Total asset turnover} = \frac{\$200,000}{\$223,000} = .90$$

$$\text{Fixed asset turnover} = \frac{\$200,000}{\$125,000} = 1.6$$

Du Pont Analysis

decomposition analysis   Many people like to use the Du Pont analysis, also called *decomposition analysis*, to analyze a firm's financial statements. The Du Pont analysis can be done in a short-form or long-form version. In the short-form version, the ROE is shown as the product of ROA (operational profitability) and the equity multiplier (leverage).

$$\text{ROE} = \text{ROA} \times \text{Equity multiplier} \qquad \text{(Equation 7-1)}$$

$$\frac{\text{Net income}}{\text{Equity}} = \frac{\text{Net income}}{\text{Total assets}} \times \frac{\text{Total assets}}{\text{Equity}} \qquad \text{(Equation 7-2)}$$

Notice in equation 7–2 that multiplying the ROA by the equity multiplier causes the denominator of the ROA and the numerator of the equity multiplier to cancel out, yielding net income divided by equity, which is the definition of ROE. However, note that calculating ROE from the other two factors is not the point of decomposition analysis. Rather, the point is to break down the ROE value into its critical components.

By breaking down ROE into the ROA and the equity multiplier, we can determine the extent to which ROE is a function of operational profitability—which is a positive concept—and financial leverage—which can be either positive or negative but certainly implies greater risk. In other words, to the extent that a high ROE results from a large equity multiplier rather than a large ROA, it means the firm is taking more risk rather than operating more profitably.

EXAMPLE

You are analyzing a client's business and notice its ROE has been fairly constant over the last few years. However, you decompose the ROE into its ROA and equity multiplier and notice that the ROA is steadily decreasing and the equity multiplier is steadily rising. The implication is that the firm is headed for trouble, as its ability to generate profits with its assets is deteriorating, and there are limits to how high it can increase its equity multiplier.

ROA can be broken down further into the product of the NPM and TAT.

$$\text{ROA} = \text{NPM} \times \text{TAT} \qquad \text{(Equation 7-3)}$$

$$\frac{\text{Net income}}{\text{Total assets}} = \frac{\text{Net income}}{\text{Net sales}} \times \frac{\text{Net sales}}{\text{Total assets}} \qquad \text{(Equation 7-4)}$$

NPM is a measure of profitability, and TAT is a measure of operating efficiency. Again, the point is to evaluate the factors that contribute to ROA, not simply to calculate ROA from them. By plugging the value of *ROA* from equation 7-3 into equation 7-1, we obtain

$$\text{ROE} = \text{NPM} \times \text{TAT} \times \text{Equity multiplier} \qquad \text{(Equation 7-5)}$$

$$\frac{\text{Net income}}{\text{Equity}} = \frac{\text{Net income}}{\text{Net sales}} \times \frac{\text{Net sales}}{\text{Total assets}} \times \frac{\text{Total assets}}{\text{Equity}} \qquad \text{(Equation 7-6)}$$

Equation 7–6 is a longer version of the Du Pont analysis. *Figure 7-2* shows graphically how the Du Pont ratios fit together. Equation 7–6 states that *ROE* is a function of profitability (*NPM*), efficiency (*TAT*), and financial leverage (equity multiplier). Breaking down the critical ROE ratio into the other ratios and comparing them to industry averages allows the analyst to evaluate the sources of performance.

EXAMPLE

Consider the following three firms:

Firm	Net profit margin	Total asset turnover	Equity multiplier	ROE
XYZ	2%	4.0	1.25	10%
JKL	5%	2.0	1.0	10%
PQR	2%	1.0	5.0	10%

All three firms have identical returns on equity (10%). It appears, however, that they have followed three different strategies to achieve this result. The XYZ Company has a low profit margin, but a high turnover ratio. Thus, it is probably a discount type operation, which slashes prices and then makes it up on volume. The JKL firm has a high profit margin, but a low turnover ratio. It is probably charging higher prices so that what it loses in volume, it makes up on profit margin. The XYZ Company might operate like K-Mart, and the JKL firm like Neiman Marcus. Both are retailers, but are dramatically different in business strategies.

The PQR firm has both a low profit margin and a low turnover ratio, but it compensates for these by heavily leveraging the company. The PQR firm is clearly the riskiest of the three firms. It is not completely obvious which of the other two firms is the stronger.

Figure 7-2
Du Pont (or Decomposition) Analysis

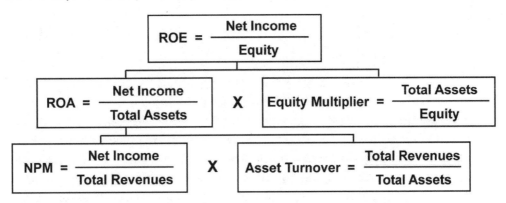

Other Ratios

earnings per share (EPS)

In addition to liquidity, debt, profitability, and activity ratios, investors may find several other ratios useful. *Earnings per share (EPS)* is the company's total earnings (less any preferred dividends) divided by the number of shares of common stock outstanding. Several different earnings numbers are often reported. Fully diluted EPS assumes the exercise of all outstanding warrants and rights and conversion of any outstanding convertible bonds and convertible preferred stock. In other words, to calculate fully diluted earnings per share, we divide net earnings by the number of shares of stock that would be outstanding if all warrants, rights, and conversion privileges were exercised. In a sense, fully diluted earnings per share provides a worst-case-scenario analysis. Earnings figures may include or exclude extraordinary items and the results from noncontinuing operations.

dividend yield

dividend payout ratio

The current annual dividend divided by the price per share is the *dividend yield*. The *payout ratio* is the dividends paid during the year divided by the company's earnings during the year. It can also be computed as dividends per share divided by EPS. A low dividend payout ratio may indicate a desire to finance growth internally, or it may be a sign of a struggling company. A high-dividend payout ratio may suggest a highly profitable company, or one with few attractive investment opportunities.

cash flow per share

Cash flow per share is the sum of net income and depreciation and any other noncash expenses divided by the number of shares of common stock outstanding. The cash-flow-per-share figure reflects an important source of discretionary funds.

book value per share

price-book value ratio

Book value per share equals the company's net worth (after subtracting any equity that is attributable to preferred shareholders) divided by the number of shares of common stock outstanding. The per-share book value is typically compared with the current stock price, and the ratio is known as the *price-book value ratio*. A high book value relative to the stock's price may indicate either unrecognized potential or overvalued assets. For most companies, the book value per share is much lower than the price of the stock. In other words, most firms are worth more than just the combined value of their assets. Book value is based on historical costs and fails to take into account the impact of inflation. It also ignores intangible assets such as the value of well-trained and highly motivated employees or the quality of R&D that the firm is currently undertaking.

Other Useful Ratios

- Earnings per share (EPS): (Net income after taxes – preferred dividends)/number of shares
- Dividend yield: Indicated annual dividend/price per share
- Dividend payout: Dividends per share/EPS
- Cash flow per share: (After-tax profits + depreciation and other noncash expenses)/number of shares
- Book value per share: Net worth attributable to common shareholders/number of shares
- Price-book value ratio: Price per share/(net worth attributable to common shareholders/number of shares)

Sources of Ratios

The value of a ratio by itself provides information, but no perspective. It takes on meaning only when compared to other ratios. There are two sources of comparison. One is to look at each ratio over time. Depending on data availability, analysts look at anywhere from two to five years worth of data. The other source is to compare ratios with those of similar companies. Thus, averages of industrywide ratios are helpful. Robert Morris Associates collects data and computes ratios for a large group of industries. Other sources include Dun & Bradstreet, Standard & Poor's, and Mergent Corporation.

Individual industry ratios may be computed with appropriate data from several similar companies. The most effective comparison may be to compare a company's ratios over time against industry averages over the same time period.

Comprehensive Example

Suppose a client comes to you, and his major holding is a small business for which he is the sole shareholder. Your recommendations for a financial plan for the client will depend, in part, on your analysis of his business. You request and receive his financial statements for the last three years (see *Table 7-6* and *Table 7-7*). Your client indicates that the sales of his firm are growing nicely, the net income was off a little last year, but overall he generates a good dividend income from the business. Despite this summary, you compute the relevant financial ratios and you obtain the industry averages for these ratios.[67]

The current and quick ratios show a slight downward trend, and both are below industry averages at the end of 2010. The inventory turnover has declined significantly from 5.12 to 3.64, which probably means that the inventory is sitting around a lot longer before it is sold. In 2008, the inventory was on hand about two and one-third months (12/5.12), and by 2010, it was sitting around for nearly three and one-third months (12/3.64). Finally, the value of the inventory has risen from $75,000 to $114,000. Unless there has been a deliberate decision to increase inventory, this would suggest a slight problem.

The average collection period has grown from 22.25 days to 41.49 days, well above the industry average of 30 days. In addition, the value of receivables has doubled in two years. Again, unless there was a deliberate decision to give customers more generous credit terms, this suggests a problem with collections.

Overall, this firm is developing a liquidity problem as evidenced by the decline of the current and quick ratios, especially in light of the apparent deterioration of the quality of inventory and receivables.

---

67. For simplicity, we will assume that the industry averages are the same for all three years.

Table 7-6 Client's Balance Sheet for the Last Three Years			
	(All Numbers in Thousands)		
	2008	2009	2010
Cash	50	37	25
Accounts receivable	34	52	68
Inventory	75	92	114
Current assets	159	181	207
Plant and equipment	250	250	250
Less: accumulated depreciation	150	160	170
Net fixed assets	100	90	80
Total assets	259	271	287
Accrued wages	10	10	10
Accounts payable	15	25	35
Notes payable	45	55	75
Current liabilities	70	90	120
Long-term debt	100	100	100
Common stock (par)	20	20	20
Paid-in-surplus	10	10	10
Retained earnings	59	51	37
Total liability and equity	259	271	287

Table 7-7 Client's Income Statement for the Last Three Years			
	(All Numbers in Thousands)		
	2008	2009	2010
Sales	550	582	590
− Cost of goods sold	384	400	415
= Gross profit	166	182	175
− Cash expenses	100	110	115
− Depreciation	10	10	10
= EBIT	56	62	50
− Interest expenses	11	12	13
= Taxable Income	45	50	37

	(All Numbers in Thousands)		
	2008	**2009**	**2010**
– Taxes	9	10	7
= Net income	36	40	30
– Dividends paid out	35	48	44

The firm is increasing its reliance on the use of debt and financial leverage. As noted by the debt ratio, it has gone from financing 66% of its assets with debt to 77%. The firm had more debt financing than the industry average to start with, and the situation has deteriorated. The deterioration in the times-interest-earned ratio indicates that the firm is not doing a good job of supporting the incremental debt financing. If this business needed to find an additional lender for future financing, it would probably not be able to locate one or would have to pay a relatively high interest rate. The increased reliance on debt financing either has exhausted or soon will exhaust the firm's debt capacity. The only source of new financing would be the sale of equity, which means either the owner would have to invest more of his own money in the firm, or he would have to give up part of the ownership of the firm to a new investor.

The strength of the firm is its attractive return on equity, which has remained well above industry average. The return on assets is deteriorating, as is the net profit margin.

The total asset turnover ratio is comparable to the industry average. However, given the deterioration in the quality of the receivables and inventory (as noted by the decline in the inventory turnover ratio and the growth in the average collection period), the TAT ratio is suspect.

The firm is doing a good job with its FAT ratio, but note that the accumulated depreciation is well over one-half of the total investment in plant and equipment. This would suggest aging fixed assets, which itself may be a source of problems. The strong FAT ratio would certainly explain why the TAT ratio is about equal to the industry average despite the overinvestment in accounts receivable and inventory.

Table 7-8 Ratios and Industry Averages				
	(All Numbers in Thousands)			
	2008	2009	2010	Ind. Avg.
Liquidity ratios				
Current ratio	2.27	2.01	1.73	2.5
Quick ratio	1.2	.99	.78	1.0
Inventory turnover	5.12	4.35	3.64	4.0
Average collection period	22.25	32.16	41.49	30.0
Debt ratios				
Debt ratio	.66	.70	.77	.50
Equity multiplier	2.91	3.35	4.28	2.00
Times-interest-earned	5.09	5.16	3.85	6.00
Profitability ratios				
Return on equity	40.4	49.4	44.8	30.0
Return on assets	13.9	14.8	10.5	15.0
Net profit margin	6.5	6.9	5.1	7.5
Efficiency ratios				
Total asset turnover	2.12	2.15	2.06	2.00
Fixed asset turnover	5.50	6.47	7.38	4.00
Other ratios				
Dividend payout	97.2	120	146.7	30.0
Du Pont analysis	NPM	TAT	Eq. Mul.	ROE
2008	6.5	2.12	2.91	40.4
2009	6.9	2.15	3.35	49.4
2010	5.1	2.06	4.28	44.8
Industry average	7.5	2.00	2.00	30.0
NOTE:				
1. Inventory turnover is based on the cost of goods sold and year-end inventory.				
2. Average collections period is based on the year-end balance.				

Because there is no stock price available and we do not know the number of shares outstanding, the only "other ratio" that can be computed is the dividend payout ratio. But this tells an incredible story. In 2008, the owner paid out almost all of his earnings as dividends (97.2%). In 2010, the owner paid out substantially more in dividends than the firm earned (146.7%). These excessive dividend payments are showing up on the balance sheet in two places. One is the dramatic decline in cash, and the other is the steady decline in the retained earnings. (When a dividend is paid, the accounting entries are to reduce cash on the left-hand side of the balance sheet and to reduce retained earnings on the right-hand side.) It is the decline in the retained earnings that is producing a reduction in equity, which in turn creates the rise in the debt ratio.

Finally, the Du Pont analysis emphasizes the above points. Profitability (as measured by the net profit margin) is a little weak, and efficiency (as measured by the TAT) is on the stronger side. The primary reason the firm's ROE is so much stronger than the industry average is the increased financial leverage (as measured by the equity multiplier).

The conclusion should be obvious. The firm is clearly deteriorating. Unless the client is able to get the inventory and receivables under control, improve the profit margin, and most importantly, substantially reduce dividend payouts over the next few years, the firm will likely collapse. This client needs to start worrying about alternative sources of income, as well as about how to straighten out his business.

FUNDAMENTAL ANALYSIS VERSUS MARKET EFFICIENCY

Fundamental analysis of *private* companies is an important skill for many people (for example, a bank loan officer or a financial planner). However, the value of performing fundamental analysis on *publicly* traded companies is not as obvious. After all, if markets are relatively efficient (semistrong form), the (known) fundamental strengths and weaknesses of companies are already accurately reflected in their market prices. Under these circumstances, it could be argued that fundamental analysis of a publicly traded company is a waste of time. If, however, the market at least occasionally misvalues securities vis-à-vis the available public information, fundamental analysis of publicly traded companies may be worthwhile. Although the degree of market efficiency is a controversial topic, whatever level is achieved occurs because some important market participants, such as brokerage firms and other investment houses, analyze fundamentals. In other words, fundamental analysts make markets more efficient than they would otherwise be. Remember, a requirement of market efficiency is that there be a sufficient number of informed investors. Indeed, many investors (both large and small) devote considerable amounts of time and money to undertake or buy such research. Moreover, several firms (for example, Thompson Reuters) regularly publish consensus estimates of earnings by industry analysts. When actual earnings differ from these consensus estimates, the market reacts quickly to raise or lower stock prices, depending on the direction of the surprise.

Several studies have shown that the crucial factor in stocks that enjoyed the best versus the worst price performance during given years is the relationship between expected earnings estimates of professional analysts and the firm's actual earnings (earnings surprise). Invariably, stock prices increase if actual earnings exceed expected earnings (positive earnings surprises), and they fall if earnings do not reach expected levels (negative earnings surprises). Thus, if investors or analysts can do a superior job of projecting earnings and their expectations differ from the consensus, they will probably have a superior investment record.

In analyzing the possible superior returns that might be achieved by performing fundamental analysis, it is important to consider the costs as well as the benefits. Obtaining the information necessary to forecast a company's future sales, profits, and dividends is both costly and time consuming. Even if an investor "beats the market" by performing a detailed fundamental analysis, it might be worthwhile to ask how much time and expense were devoted to that analysis and how much that individual could have earned during that time. It might also be worthwhile to ask whether the investor's methods of analysis result in *consistently* superior returns or whether there have been only a few exceptionally good, perhaps lucky, investments.

REVIEW OF LEARNING OBJECTIVES

1. The two approaches to fundamental analysis are top-down and bottom-up. Top-down starts with an analysis of the economy, then looks at industries, and then finally at individual companies. The bottom-up approach moves in the reverse direction.
2. A business cycle has four components: peak, recession, trough, and an expansion. The leading, coincident, and lagging indicators are devised by the NBER to facilitate identification of where the economy is in the business cycle.
3. The tools that make up fiscal policy are government spending and tax revenues. The basic idea of fiscal policy is to influence the amount of cash that consumers have for spending by adjustment in the tax structure or government spending or the lack thereof.

4. The tools of monetary policy, in order of frequency of use, include open-market operations, changes in the discount rate, and changes in the reserve requirements. Monetary policy works through manipulations of bank reserves.

5. The two primary goals of fiscal and monetary policy are price stability and full employment, although price stability does not mean perfectly stable prices and full employment does not mean everyone is working.

6. The life-cycle of an industry includes the start-up, consolidation, maturity and decline stages.

7. The liquidity ratios include the current ratio, the acid-test, the inventory turnover, and the average collection period. The financial leverage ratios include the debt ratio, debt-equity ratio, equity multiplier, and the times-interest earned. The utilization ratios include TAT and FAT.

8. The profitability ratios include ROE, ROA and NPM. The simple Du Pont formula is ROE = ROA × Equity Multiplier. The more complex version is ROE = NPM × TAT × Equity Multiplier.

MINICASE

You are reviewing your overall strategies for the next quarter, and you are trying to get a take on the direction of the economy. The leading economic indicators are up, the coincident indicators are flat, and the lagging indicators are down. Congress is attempting to modify the tax code to eliminate many of the "loopholes," such as the home mortgage deduction, as well as to raise marginal income tax rates. The Federal Reserve's discount rate has just been lowered for the fifth time in a row. The yields on Treasury bills seem to be falling as the Fed is reportedly buying large amounts of these securities. Finally, the free reserves of commercial banks are growing, but the prime rate is flat.

1. Based on the economic indicators, the phase of the business cycle in which the economy is most likely located is a (an): [1]

   (A) expansion
   (B) peak
   (C) contraction
   (D) trough

2.   If the leading indicators are up, then the most recent change in stock prices has most likely been: [1]

    (A) up
    (B) flat
    (C) down
    (D) indeterminant based on the information given

3.   Congress is using fiscal policy to: [2]

    (A) stimulate the economy
    (B) be neutral to the economy
    (C) retard the economy
    (D) indeterminant based on the information given

4.   It appears that the Fed is using monetary policy to: [3]

    (A) stimulate the economy
    (B) be neutral to the economy
    (C) retard the economy
    (D) indeterminant based on the information given

5.   The information on commercial banks indicates that their actions would: [3]

    (A) stimulate the economy
    (B) be neutral to the economy
    (C) retard the economy
    (D) indeterminant based on the information given

CHAPTER REVIEW

Key Terms and Concepts

macroeconomic analysis	unemployment rate
industry analysis	balance of trade
company analyses	current assets
Federal Reserve Board (Fed)	current liabilities
M1	par value
M2	net worth (equity)
discount rate (monetary policy)	earnings before interest and taxes
excess reserves	(EBIT)
monetarists	taxable income
Keynesians	net income
price stability	current ratio
disinflation	quick ratio acid test ratio

inventory turnover ratio	total asset turnover ratio
average collection period (ACP)	fixed asset turnover ratio
debt-equity ratio	decomposition analysis
equity multiplier debt ratio	earnings per share (EPS)
times-interest-earned ratio	dividend yield
debt capacity	dividend payout ratio
return on equity (ROE)	cash flow per share
return on assets (ROA)	book value per share
net profit margin (NPM)	price-book value ratio

Review Questions

Review questions are based on the learning objectives for this chapter. Thus, a [3] at the end of a question means that the question is based on learning objective 3. If there are multiple objectives, they are all listed.

1. Describe the difference between a top-down and a bottom-up fundamental analysis. [1]

2. Explain how fiscal policy operates through taxes and through government spending. [2]

3. How would the stock market be expected to react to each of the following developments? [2, 3]

   a. The Fed, fearing that a recession is threatening, lowers the federal funds rate and expands the money supply. Long-term interest rates fall by over 200 basis points.

   b. Congress finally gets serious about reducing the budget deficit and raises taxes across the board by $500 billion. The Fed cushions the blow by expanding the money supply. Interest rates fall dramatically, while the GDP continues to grow.

   c. The Third World countries form a debtors' cartel and offer to negotiate. When the bargaining gets nowhere, they announce a total moratorium on interest and principal payments. The creditor nations respond by cutting off all credit.

4. Discuss the Fed's three principal tools and how they are used to affect the economy. Indicate the frequency of use of each method. [2]

5. Why do stock analysts generally give so much attention to monetary (as opposed to fiscal) policy? [3]

6. What are the goals of monetary and fiscal policy? What do these goals indicate is the appropriate action of monetary and fiscal policy during each stage of the business cycle? [1, 2, 3, 4]

7. What is meant by the term "cyclical" company or industry. [5]

8. Briefly summarize the three principal types of accounting statements. [6]

9. Using the balance sheet and income statement provided for this question, find the current ratio, quick (acid test) ratio, inventory turnover ratio (based on average inventory), average collection period (based on average receivables), debt-equity ratio, net profit margin, asset turnover ratio, return on assets, equity multiplier, and return on equity for the fiscal year ended December 2010. [7, 8]

Balance Sheet for Review Question (Amounts in Millions, except Share Data)		
	December 31, 2010	December 31, 2009
Assets		
Current assets		
Cash and cash equivalents	$ 167	$ 168
Short-term investments, including current maturities of long term investments	10	2
Receivables, net	835	587
Merchandise inventories	6,556	5,489
Other current assets	209	144
Total current assets	7,777	6,390
Property and equipment, at cost		
Land	4,230	3,248
Buildings	6,167	4,834
Furniture, fixtures, and equipment	2,877	2,279
Leasehold improvements	665	493
Construction in progress	1,032	791
Capital leases	261	245
	15,232	11,890
Less accumulated depreciation and amortization	2,164	1,663
Net property and equipment	13,068	10,227
Long-term investments	15	15
Notes receivable	77	48
Cost in excess of the fair value of net assets acquired, net of accumulated amortization of $41 at December 31, 2006, and $33 at December 31, 2005	314	311
Other	134	90
Total Assets	$21,385	$17,081
Liabilities and Stockholders' Equity		
Current liabilities		
Accounts payable	$1,976	$1,993
Accrued salaries and related expenses	627	541

Sales taxes payable	298	269
Other accrued expenses	1,402	763
Income taxes payable	78	61
Current installments of long-term debt	4	29
Total current liabilities	4,385	3,656
Long-term debt, excluding current installments	1,545	750
Other long-term liabilities	245	237
Deferred income taxes	195	87
Minority interest	11	10
Stockholders' Equity		
Common stock, par value $0.05. Authorized: 10,000,000,000 shares; issued and outstanding—2,323,747,000 shares at December 31, 2006, and 2,304,317,000 shares at December 31, 2005	110	108
Paid-in capital	4,810	4,319
Retained earnings	10,151	7,941
Accumulated other comprehensive income	(67)	(27)
Total stockholders' equity	15,004	12,341
Total Liabilities and Stockholders' Equity	$21,385	$17,081

Income State for Review Question 9		
(Amounts in Millions, except Per Share Data)		
	Fiscal Year Ended	
	December 31, 2010	December 31, 2009
Net Sales	$45,738	$38, 434
Cost of merchandise sold	32,057	27,023
Gross profit	13,681	11,411
Operating expenses		
Selling and store operating	8,513	6,819
Pre-opening	142	113
General and administrative	835	671
Total operating expenses	9,490	7,603
Operating Income	4,191	3,808
Interest income (expense)		
Interest and investment income	47	37
Interest expense	(21)	(41)
Interest, net	26	(4)

Earnings before Income Taxes	4,217	3,804
Income taxes	1,636	1,484
Net earnings	$2,581	$2,320
Basic Earnings Per Share	$ 1.11	$ 1.03
Weighted average number of common shares outstanding	2,315	2,244
Diluted Earnings Per Share	$ 1.10	$ .99
Weighted average number of common shares outstanding, assuming dilution	2,352	2,342

10.   Consider the following:
a.   Why might a dramatic growth rate in a company's sales, accompanied by an even more dramatic growth in its average collection period, be a bad sign? [7]
b.   Why might an increase in the current ratio accompanied by a decline in the inventory turnover ratio be a bad sign? [7]
c.   What is wrong with a company offsetting a decline in its net profit margin with increases in its equity multiplier? [8]

Learning Objectives

An understanding of the material in this chapter should enable the student to

1. Describe the key nonmarketable instruments available to a client.

2. Explain what is meant by the money market and describe the key money market instruments.

3. Describe the various securities and interest rates related to the money market.

4. Describe the general characteristics of government and government-related bonds.

5. Describe the general characteristics of corporate bonds.

6. Explain the process of corporate bankruptcy.

7. Describe the different features of mortgage-backed securities.

8. Discuss other types of debt instruments, including international bonds, private placements, promissory notes, and insurance-based contracts.

Many of us are introduced to the concept of investing when a savings account is opened in our name. Such an account is a debt instrument—basically an IOU. The bank (or other type of financial institution) holding the account is in debt to the depositor for the balance in the account.

Most loans are accompanied by provisions that constitute a legally enforceable contract. The lender agrees to provide the borrower with a sum of money for a period of time. The borrower agrees to pay interest at a specified rate and repay principal (amount borrowed) according to the terms of the debt contract. The borrower's failure to fulfill any of the contract's provisions (such as missing a scheduled interest or principal payment) constitutes a default. If the default itself is not cured, the lender may take appropriate legal action, which may eventually result in either a seizure of any assets pledged as collateral or bankruptcy.

Debt instruments are classified in several different ways. One is by maturity (short-term versus long-term), another is by issuer (government versus corporate), and yet another is by whether or not a market for the instruments exists (marketable versus nonmarketable). Let's start our discussion by focusing on nonmarketable debt securities.

NON-MARKETABLE DEBT INSTRUMENTS

depository institution

The most commonly owned financial assets are nonmarketable debt instruments offered by the various depository institutions. A *depository institution* is one that accepts deposits. These institutions include banks, mutual savings banks, savings and loan institutions, and credit unions.[68] Although checking accounts technically qualify as nonmarketable debt instruments, they are normally classified as cash. Nonmarketable debt securities offered by depository institutions normally refers to savings accounts, nonmarketable certificates of deposit (CDs), and money market accounts (MMAs).

Deposit Insurance

Depositors at most banks, mutual savings banks, and savings and loans are insured by the Federal Deposit Insurance Corporation (FDIC). Currently a depositor is insured up to $250,000. This limit is set to expire on December 31, 2013, and return to a limit of $100,000 in 2014 for most accounts. The exception will be for certain deposit accounts such as IRAs, for which the limit will remain at $250,000.

Deposit insurance covers all types of accounts including checking, negotiable order of withdrawal (NOW), savings, MMAs, and time deposits such as CDs. The insurance covers principal plus accrued interest up to the date an insured bank closes.

Depositors at most credit unions are insured by National Credit Union Share Insurance Fund (NCUSIF). Accordingly, depositors need not spend time

---

68. For simplification, this discussion will henceforth use the term "banks" in lieu of the more comprehensive term "depository institutions." The rules that apply to banks also apply to all of the competing institutions.

shopping around for a "safe" bank, because their money will be safe as long as the institution is FDIC (or NCUSIF) insured. Instead, depositors should focus on convenience, service, and interest rate.

There is one caveat for financial planners with respect to deposit insurance. Most people think that the insurance is per account. In reality, it is per depositor per bank, based on account title. Thus, if you have two accounts with the same ownership (e.g., a client has a checking account and a CD at the same bank), the coverage is still just $250,000 for the combination of accounts. If the insurance limit is an issue, then the easiest resolution is to move one of the accounts to a second bank. An alternative resolution would be to change the ownership on one of the accounts. If the client is married, he or she could make the second account a joint account, and then each account will be covered for up to $250,000.

Certificates of Deposit

CDs are typically offered with maturities varying from 3 months to 5 years. The interest is usually accrued in the CD, and at maturity, the depositor receives all of the accrued interest plus the original deposit. Although most investors have traditionally purchased CDs through local banks, they can also buy "brokered CDs." Brokerage firms can sometimes negotiate a higher rate of interest for a CD by promising to bring a certain amount of deposits to the institution.[69] Traditionally, CDs paid a fixed rate of interest that was higher with longer term CDs. CD providers today offer CDs with many special features, such as variable-rate CDs, CDs with extremely long terms to maturity, bump-up CDs, step-up CDs, liquid CDs, FDIC-insured CDs denominated in foreign currencies, and callable CDs.

When the depositor is acquiring a variable-rate CD, it is critical to understand the frequency with which the interest rate might change, and how the new interest rate will be determined. Some variable-rate CDs have a predetermined schedule of changes, and others fluctuate according to a specified market rate.

A bump-up CD allows the owner the one-time right to have the bank raise the interest rate on the CD for the remainder of the term, if the bank has raised interest rates on new CDs of comparable maturity. A step-up CD is one where the interest rate increases on a scheduled basis established at

---

69. The FDIC website offers a piece on brokered CDs, "Certificates of Deposit: Tips for Savers" at http://www.fdic.gov/deposit/deposits/certificate/, July 8, 2010.

the time the CD is purchased. A liquid CD allows the depositor to withdraw part of the deposit prior to maturity without penalty.

A callable CD allows the issuer (that is, the bank) to close out the CD at any time during the call period. A callable CD would be terminated if market interest rates fall, and thus the depositor would be forced to redeposit his or her funds at a lower interest rate. Sometimes, depositors confuse the noncallable period with the maturity period.

EXAMPLE

The First National Bank of Everytown offers your client a 10-year CD paying 5 percent that is federally insured and noncallable for 1 year. Because the best alternative security being considered pays only 4 percent, this CD looks attractive. What are the risks?

If interest rates fall, the bank will almost certainly call in the CD after 1 year. The client may then be looking at new CDs that pay less than 5 percent. If interest rates rise, the bank will assuredly NOT call in the CD. The client could be locked in for 10 years to what is later considered an unusually low interest rate. For the first year, this is unquestionably an attractive rate; however, the possible long-term drawbacks make purchasing this CD a difficult decision.

When a CD matures, the depositor should make an active decision as to whether to acquire a new CD or to move the money to other investments (or to spend it!). For CDs with maturities longer than one year, Regulation DD requires the bank to notify the depositor of the maturity date at least 30 days in advance. In cases in which the depositor fails to notify the bank of his or her desired intention, the bank may automatically roll the principal into another CD. In some cases, this new CD is at the market rate but for the same maturity as the original CD. In other cases, the bank may impose the original interest rate as well as the original term.

The penalty for early withdrawal is the biggest drawback to any nonmarketable CD. Although there is a maximum penalty that may be imposed, the actual penalty may vary among providers. It is not uncommon to see advertisements for brokered CDs as not having a penalty for early withdrawal. This is not quite true. What should be made clear by the broker, and is required to appear in the ad's fine print, is an explanation of the purchaser's ability to sell the CD at the then-current rates, which may be higher or lower than the original purchase price. Such a sale may result in a gain or loss on the principal, depending on how interest rates have moved.

Financial Planning Strategy

When CDs are directly purchased from a depository institution, there is an alternative to premature withdrawals. The CD owners may borrow up to the amount of the CD's principal using the CD as collateral. The drawback, of course, is that the rate of interest charged on this loan will exceed the interest rate paid on the CD. Nonetheless, if the differential interest is less than the early withdrawal penalty, such a strategy may be beneficial. This strategy should particularly be considered when the CD principal is large and the term to maturity is short.

Money Market Accounts

As an alternative to CDs, most depository institutions offer *money market accounts (MMAs)*. (These are also referred to as money market deposit accounts, or MMDAs. MMAs are also federally insured up to $250,000, but are limited to a specified number of withdrawals per month and carry a nontrivial minimum balance requirement. The withdrawals can be via check, automatic withdrawal, or telephone transfer. The rates paid on these accounts fluctuate with market rates, such as the yields on Treasury bills (which will be discussed shortly). One drawback to MMDAs is that the interest on these accounts is subject to state and local income taxes, whereas the interest on T-bills is exempt from these taxes.

Savings Bonds

The most significant nonmarketable investments that are not issued by a depository institution are U.S. Government *savings bonds*. The savings bonds currently issued include EE and I bonds. Series HH bonds are no longer issued, but are held by many investors. The rates on these bonds tend to be below but close to the market rates on other short-term instruments.

EE Savings Bond

The EE savings bond, the most popular of the three, accumulates in value over time rather than paying periodic interest. These bonds, which were first issued in January 1980, have denominations that range from $50 to $10,000. The purchase price is always one-half the denomination value. EE bonds will accrue interest for up to 30 years. There is a penalty of loss of 3 months' worth of interest if an EE bond is cashed in within the first 5 years. Furthermore, EE bonds issued since February 2003 have a 1-year minimum holding period, and EE bonds issued prior to that date have a 6-month minimum holding period.

An investor is limited to purchasing no more than $5,000 worth of EE bonds annually. All Series EE bonds issued on or after May 2005 pay a fixed rate set at the time of insurance. For example, Series EE bonds issued between May and October 2010 will earn an annual rate of 1.40%. EEs issued prior to May 2005 are subject to semiannual market adjustments in their yields. Interest accrues on the first day of each month, and there is no accrual during a month. The first interest accrual does not start until the fourth month from the date of issue.

Financial Planning Strategy

Because of the way interest is accrued on EE bonds, such bonds should be cashed in only on the first day of each month. People holding these bonds should regularly check on the current accrued value, which can be found at such sites as www.treasurydirect.gov/indiv/tools/tools_savingsbondscalc.htm. When such bonds are bought for children to help finance their college education (more on this tactic later in the book), it is particularly important that investors not let the 30-year period of interest slip by.

HH Bonds

HH bonds pay a fixed rate of interest income that is set for 10 years at the time the bonds are issued. The rate is then reset for a second 10-year period and the bonds mature at the end of this second period. HH bonds could only be acquired through an exchange for EE or E bonds or by rolling over another HH or H bond. However, effective August 31, 2004, the Treasury is no longer accepting this exchange. Thus, no new HH bonds are being issued, but investors holding them may continue to do so till the normal maturity date.

I Bonds

The interest rate on I bonds is adjusted regularly to reflect the recent rate of inflation. I bonds have many, many similarities to EE bonds. These commonalities include:

- They are issued with denominations that range from $50 to $10,000.
- Interest is calculated monthly and compounded semiannually for up to 30 years.
- The new interest rate dates are announced each May and November based on for the prior 6 months.

- Investors are limited to purchasing no more than $5,000 worth of these bonds each year (between EE bonds and I bonds, one may buy up to $10,000 per year).
- There is a loss of 3 months' worth of interest if these bonds are cashed in during the first 5 years.
- There is a minimum 12-month holding period.
- There is no accrued interest between interest accrual dates.

I bonds differ from EE bonds in that the interest rate is the sum of a low fixed rate (which is supposed to represent a real rate of return) and the inflation rate based on the Bureau of Labor Statistic's CPI-U index. If the inflation rate is negative (that is, deflation), then the interest rate paid would actually be less than the fixed rate.

Nonmarketable Debt Securities
• Savings accounts
• Nonmarketable CDs
• Money market accounts (MMAs)
• U.S. savings bonds (EE, HH, and I)

MONEY MARKET SECURITIES

The major marketable short-term debt securities are collectively known as money market instruments. These securities share the following characteristics: their maturity is 1 year or less, they have negligible risk of default, and there is an active market for buying and selling them. The principal money market instruments are Treasury bills (T-bills), commercial paper, marketable CDs, bankers' acceptances, and Eurodollar deposits. An alternative to directly purchasing these securities is to acquire money market mutual funds and short-term unit investment trusts that invest in money market securities.

The Five Money Market Securities

Treasury Bills

The largest component and most important security in the money market is Treasury bills (T-bills). These are issued at a discount and mature at par (face value). T-bills are issued in $1,000 minimum denominations, and are traded in book-entry form only.[70] An investor might buy a T-bill for $950 and receive $1,000 back at maturity. The $50 difference between purchase price and maturity payoff is the investor's interest income.

New issues of T-bills can be bought through a broker or bank for a commission, or purchased directly from the nearest Federal Reserve Bank at a weekly auction. They can even be bought online by opening an account at www.treasurydirect.gov. Bills with maturities of 28 days, 91 days, 13 weeks, and 182 days (which is 26 weeks) are offered each week, and 52-week bills every fourth week, beginning in 2008 after a 6–year layoff.

Bids may be entered on either a competitive or a noncompetitive basis. The Treasury accepts all noncompetitive bids, and buyers who enter these bids agree to pay the average price of the competitive bids that are accepted. Buyers entering competitive bids state a price they are willing to pay and the Treasury accepts these bids, taking the highest prices first until the issue is sold out. However, the price that all buyers with winning competitive bids actually pay is the same as the price that noncompetitive buyers pay. In other words, once the lowest price that the Treasury is willing to accept is determined, then all buyers (both competitive and noncompetitive) pay that price.

EXAMPLE

Suppose the Fed wants to sell $8 billion of 13-week T-bills. It receives $14 billion in bids, $5 billion of which are noncompetitive. The $5 billion of noncompetitive bids are accepted. The remaining $9 billion in bids are put in order, from the highest price (lowest yield) to the lowest price (highest yield). The Fed then accepts $3 billion worth of these competitive bids (to round out its goal of $8 billion), taking the highest prices first. The last bid in this group determines the price paid by all. All bids are provisional until this final step of the auction when the price is determined.

Dealers in government securities maintain an active secondary market in T-bills. The terms offered by these dealers are reported daily in the financial section of most major newspapers as well as online at the Federal Reserve's Web site. Rather than quote prices in dollars and cents, T-bill prices are quoted in an archaic formula known as the bank discount yield. The yield is defined as

---

70. Book-entry form means that there are no paper certificates denoting the security. Ownership is tracked only by computer records.

$$\text{BDY} = [(10{,}000 - \text{Price})/10{,}000] \times (360/\text{DTM})$$

where BDY = bank discount yield

Price = actual T-bill price

DTM = days to maturity

T-bills are quoted with a bid price and an ask price. The bid price represents the price a dealer will pay an investor who wants to sell his or her holdings. The ask price is the price the dealer wants from an investor looking to buy the T-bills. The difference between bid and ask prices is called the dealer's spread, or bid-ask spread. It is through this spread that a dealer earns his or her living.

A typical T-bill quotation will be presented as follows:

Maturity	Days to Mat.	Bid	Ask	Chg.	Ask Yld.
Jun 01 '07	29	2.64	2.60	0.04	2.64

The maturity date is the day on which the T-bill will be paid off. It is the clearest number in the quotation. The number of days to maturity is always off because there is a 2-day settlement period for T-bill trades. This means that if I buy a T-bill today, I will not legally take ownership until 2 days from now and will not start accruing interest until then. Hence, the fact that the above quotation shows 29 days to maturity means that the quote is for 31 days prior to maturity. Because May has 31 days, this quote is for the close of trading on May 1, and would have appeared in the financial press on May 2.

bid price The *bid price* is the price (as a discount percentage) that a dealer is willing to pay for the T-bill (as of mid-afternoon of the previous trading day). If we plug this number into the above formula,

$$.0264 = [(\$10{,}000 - \text{Price})/\$10{,}000] \times (360/\text{DTM})$$

we can solve for the price as follows:

$$\$10{,}000 - [(.0264 \times \$10{,}000)/(360/29)] = \$9{,}978.73$$

ask price The *ask price* is the price (as a discount percentage) for which a dealer is willing to sell the T-bill for (as of mid-afternoon of the previous trading day). Again, if we plug this number into the above formula,

$$.0260 = [(\$10,000 - Price)/\$10,000] \times (360/DTM)$$

we can solve for the price as follows:

$$\$10,000 - [(.0260 \times \$10,000)/(360/29)] = \$9,979.05$$

bond equivalent
yield (BEY)
"Chg." is the change between the bid price as listed in the bid column and the bid price from the previous trading day. The figure of -0.04 indicates a decrease of 4/100. "Ask Yld." is the *bond equivalent yield (BEY)* for the T-bill based on its ask price. This involves a different formula for converting a yield number to a price. In this case, the formula is:

$$BEY = [(10,000 - Price)/Price] \times (365/DTM)$$

We can verify the BEY by plugging the dollar value of the asked price into the above formula to obtain

$$.0264 = [(\$10,000 - \$9,979.05)/\$9,979.05] \times (365/29)$$

The purpose of the BEY is to make the asked yield into a more realistic measure of the rate of return available to an investor if he or she were to buy the security at that particular price. The BEY will always be greater than the BDY for two reasons. First, the BEY formula has a smaller denominator (price versus par) because T-bills are discount instruments and thus the price will always be less than par. Second, the BEY formula has a larger numerator because it uses 365 rather than 360 for the number of days in the year.

Commercial Paper

Corporations that want to raise short-term financing in the public markets sometimes sell what is called *commercial paper*. Traditionally, this is a short-term IOU issued by large corporations with solid credit ratings. Commercial paper is the oldest of all the money market securities; the earliest commercial paper was issued in the colonial era. However, in recent years enough "lower quality" commercial paper has been issued to cause occasional defaults on commercial paper. This has led the SEC to rule that a money market mutual fund may place no more than 5 percent of its assets into lower quality commercial paper, and that no more than 1 percent of its assets can be in the paper of any one "lower quality" issuer.

Commercial paper can be classified as direct paper or dealer paper. Direct paper is sold by the issuer directly to investors. In this case, virtually all of the issuers are financially oriented companies, and almost all of the direct paper is issued by approximately 50 companies. In fact, the three largest captive finance companies (General Electric Capital Corp., Ford Motor Credit Co., and General Motors Acceptance Corp.) account for 10 to 15 percent of the entire commercial paper market. Dealer paper is sold through dealers by companies who do not raise huge and regular quantities of money through the sale of commercial paper and thus cannot afford to employ a permanent staff to run this financing operation. Normally the yields on dealer paper are higher than those on direct paper (by a few basis points) because the dealer paper issuers are smaller and potentially riskier companies. However, at times the relationship is reversed for various reasons.

The maximum maturity is 270 days, but most commercial paper is issued with a shorter maturity. The most common initial maturities are 7, 15, 30, 60, and 90 days. The issuer usually has a backup line of credit at a bank. This credit line is available to repay the commercial paper issue when due if sale of new paper is not possible in the existing market environment and the cash is not available. Some issuers go so far as to obtain irrevocable letters of credit from banks, because of the possibility that if the company's business starts deteriorating, a bank may cancel its line of credit. Corporations issue commercial paper because they find they can obtain a lower interest rate on such financing than if they borrow the same money directly from their bank, and the interest savings is enough to also pay their banks the fees on their backup credit lines or other guarantees.

Although money market mutual funds are the largest single investor in commercial paper, households directly hold 10 to 15 percent of the paper outstanding. Other buyers include nonfinancial corporations, bank trust departments, small banks, pension funds, insurance companies, and state and local governments. Commercial paper is rated, but as a practical matter, only the highest-grade issues have any liquidity. The minimum denomination of commercial paper is usually $100,000, but most institutional investors prefer to deal in lots of $1 million. Full payment is made at maturity. The secondary market for commercial paper can only be described as "weak" at best. However, given the extremely short maturities of these instruments, most buyers are committed to holding them to maturity. Like T-bills, commercial paper is a pure discount instrument.

Negotiable CDs

negotiable CDs   Earlier we discussed the nonmarketable CDs sold by banks. Banks will sell *negotiable CDs* with a minimum denomination of $100,000. However, trades in negotiable CDs have a minimum denomination of $1 million. Although most of these instruments are issued with maturities of 6 months or less, some have maturities of 1 year or more. These are referred to as term CDs. When the initial maturity is 1 year or less, the interest is paid at maturity. The longer term CDs have coupon payments. It is only these short-term CDs that are a component of the money market.

Several New York–based CD dealers handle most secondary market trading in these securities. They are issued only by the largest and best-known banks. The first $250,000 in principal of a negotiable CD is covered by FDIC insurance. Unfortunately, this means that most of the principal of high-denomination CDs ($1 million or more) is uninsured. Despite the lack of an FDIC insurance guarantee, negotiable CDs are considered essentially as safe as commercial paper. Hence, the yields on these two instruments usually differ by no more than a few basis points (bps), where a basis point equals one-one hundredth of one percent. When talking about differences in interest rates, it is always more effective to use basis points rather than the percentage difference because if one said the yield on CDs was .08 percent higher, then it is not clear if the .08 percent is an absolute value difference or a percentage difference.

Troubled banks generally have difficulty selling uninsured CDs even at high interest rates. Moody's Investors Service rates the quality of some CDs. Trading activity in negotiable CDs ceases when there are 14 or fewer days to maturity. The buyers of negotiable CDs are the same group as the buyers of commercial paper. Also, as with commercial paper, most buyers hold these instruments until maturity.

Bankers' Acceptances

banker's acceptance   A *banker's acceptance* involves an obligation to pay a certain amount at a prespecified time. In other words, it is a time draft. This type of instrument is usually created as a result of international trade. This obligation becomes a bankers' acceptance once it is accepted (guaranteed) by a bank. The acceptance is a liability of both the bank and the company issuing the original promise to pay. As such, the bank is required to redeem it whether or not the issuer funds the redemption. With this possibility in mind, banks are inclined to check carefully the credit standing of the issuers of these obligations. From the bank's perspective, it is similar to a loan to the issuing company.

two-name paper   Once an acceptance is created, it trades at discounts like other money market securities. Acceptances typically trade in multiples of $100,000. A small number of dealers buy and sell acceptances, quoting bid-ask spreads of about 25 bps. Acceptances are also known as *two-name paper* because both the importer and the bank guarantee the payoff at maturity.

Eurodollar Deposits

Eurodollar
deposits   *Eurodollar deposits* are dollar-denominated liabilities of banks located outside the United States (usually in Europe). Eurodollar yields are usually slightly higher than other money market rates. For example, the yield on Eurodollar deposits is only a few basis points higher than on comparable maturity-negotiable CDs. Eurodollar deposits of U.S. investors may occasionally be difficult to repatriate. Moreover, disputes between borrower and lender must be settled without reliance on the protection of the U.S. legal system. In addition, the issuing bank's depositors are rarely as protected by insurance and government regulation as those of U.S. banks. In fact, one reason that many foreign banks can afford to pay a higher interest rate than U.S. banks is that they do not have the reserve requirements and other costs of complying with government regulations that U.S. banks face. Many issuers are subsidiaries of U.S. banks, and others are large institutions with long histories of sound operations. Thus, risks in the Eurodollar market should be considered but not overrated. Defaults have been rare.

Money Market Securities	
Type	Issuer
Treasury bill	U.S. Treasury
Commercial paper	Large corporations
Negotiable CD	Large banks
Banker's acceptance	Export/import companies; bank-guaranteed
Eurodollar deposit	Foreign-based banks

SECURITIES AND INTEREST RATES RELATED TO MONEY MARKET SECURITIES

Although it is the money market securities that the individual investor buys, there are other interest rates and securities with which a financial planner should be familiar. This is because some of these yields provide upper or lower limits to the yields on money market securities. Thus, movements in some of these other rates may signal imminent movement in the yields on the money market securities. Money market rates and related rates and yields are shown in the accompanying table.

Sample Money Market Rates: July 10, 2010	
Prime rate	3.25%
Federal Reserve Board discount rate	.75
Federal funds rate (overnight rate)	.20
Treasury bills (auctions, 3 months)	.165
Commercial paper (120 to 149 days)	.43
Eurodollar deposits (3 months)	.45
Certificates of deposit (3 months)	.53
Banker's acceptances (3 months)	.55
LIBOR (3 months)	.53
Repurchase Rate (Overnight)	.20
Inflation Rate (trailing 12 months, core)	.9
Call Money Rate	2.00
Source: wsj.com/mdc/public/page/2_3020-moneyrate.html?mod=mdc_bnd_pglnk, July 8, 2010.	

Prime Rate

prime rate

The *prime rate* used to be known as the rate that banks charged their largest, safest borrowers. However, in the competition for business, some banks offered their best customers loan rates that were below prime. This created legal problems for the banking community. These problems were resolved by redefining a bank's prime rate as an index rate the bank uses to price its loans. Thus, a loan applicant approaching a bank might be told that he or she would be charged the prime rate plus 1 percent.

Each bank usually has a committee that sets its own prime rate. As with any business entity, banks are free to set their own prices, and the prime rate is the "price" a bank charges for loans. Nonetheless, banks constantly watch each other's prime rates. Any bank charging a lower rate than necessary will attract substantial business with less than appropriate profitability. Any bank charging a higher rate than necessary will find its customers going elsewhere. Certain banks, such as Citibank, have gained a reputation for initiating a change in the prime rate. When a bank announces such a change, most other banks quickly follow. In fact, some banks simply accept the prime rate of another bank as their own prime rate. When one looks at the prime rate over time, it follows along with all of the other money market-related yields. The *Wall Street Journal* publishes a prime rate that some people look to as defining the current value. The *Journal*'s definition of the prime rate is whatever rate is posted by at least 70 percent of the country's 30 largest banks.

Short-Term Municipals

State and local governments have steadily increased their use of the short-term debt market for financing. The three most popular securities they issue are bond-anticipation notes (BANs), revenue-anticipation notes (RANs), and tax-anticipation notes (TANs). The three are similar and differ primarily by the ultimate purpose for their issuance. BANs are issued to raise money for a project prior to the issuance of permanent (long-term bond) financing. In some cases, the reason for the delay might simply be an expectation that interest rates will fall in the near future.

TANs and RANs are both issues to fill the gap between revenue collection dates for state and local governments. For example, a school district normally collects its primary revenue through property taxes, and such taxes are received primarily around a single date each year. When approaching that date, TANs or RANs might be used to cover operating expenses. Local banks are the biggest buyers of these instruments.

Federal Funds, Discount Loans, and Repurchase Agreements

federal funds market   Banks and other financial institutions also participate in several active short-term debt markets. One of these is the federal funds market. As noted in an earlier chapter, banks must have at any point in time a certain amount of reserves. The required reserves are based on each bank's level of deposits. Cash on hand is the primary form of reserve. However, a significant component of reserves is money a bank has on deposit at a Federal Reserve Bank. These funds on deposit are known as federal funds. At times, some banks have more reserves than they need, while others have fewer reserves than are required. The problem of excess and deficit reserves is solved by banks with excess reserves lending some of their federal funds to banks with a shortage in reserves. The exchanging of these deposits is known as the *federal funds market*. The loan of these deposits is an overnight loan, although some banks borrow such funds on a daily basis, and others make it a practice to be a continuous lender. Like the prime rate, the federal funds rate is an indicator of how much a bank has to pay for some of its money. Changes in federal funds rates are a leading indicator of changes in other rates that banks charge on loans and pay on deposits.

discount rate   A key rate that affects the federal funds rate is the *discount rate*, which is the rate that a Federal Reserve Bank charges its members for loans. Simply put, when a bank is short of reserves, an alternative to borrowing federal funds is to borrow cash directly from the Federal Reserve Bank itself. Sometimes the discount rate is above the federal funds rate, and sometimes it is lower. When the discount rate is the higher of the two, banks borrow more federal funds. When the discount rate is lower than the federal funds rate, banks tend to borrow more from the Federal Reserve. Banks always have a slight preference for borrowing federal funds because excessive borrowing from the Federal Reserve may invite additional scrutiny by the Fed in its role as the primary regulator of banks.

Repurchase agreements (repos) are sales of securities with guaranteed repurchase at a prespecified price and date (often 1 day later). The relationship between the purchase and sales prices establishes the instrument's rate of return. This is an indirect way for banks to borrow from other banks, using the security as collateral. Payment is generally required to be in immediately available reserve-free funds transferred between financial institutions. These arrangements are extremely safe. The Fed uses repurchase agreements in its open-market operations on almost a daily basis to manage the federal funds rate.

LIBOR

LIBOR stands for the London Interbank Offered Rate. It is the rate at which London banks are willing to lend money to each other. Thus, it is somewhat analogous to the federal funds rate in this country. LIBOR is frequently quoted on dollar-denominated loans in Europe, and it is the premier short-term interest rate quoted in the European money market. It is frequently used as a reference rate on a worldwide basis. For example, on a floating-rate loan, a bank might agree to charge a borrower an interest rate of LIBOR plus 2 percent.

Money Market Mutual Funds

Money market mutual funds and short-term unit investment trusts (discussed next) were developed in the 1970s in response to interest rate ceilings on bank deposits (known as Regulation Q) coupled with generally higher money market rates. These funds invest resources from many small investors in a large portfolio of money market securities. While some funds have no minimum account size, most set a $1,000 or larger minimum. Still other funds have implemented a rate structure that pays higher rates for larger balances. The net income of the portfolio is distributed to the fund's owners and may be paid monthly or reinvested.

Money market funds can be redeemed in whole or in part on short notice without a redemption charge. Most funds permit several types of redemption: the fund holder can write, e-mail, or call toll free for an immediate check-mailing or wire transfer into the fund holder's bank account. Most funds also permit checks to be written on the shareholder's account. Use of this feature allows the investor's funds to earn interest until the check clears.

The returns paid on money market funds are slightly below the prevailing rates in the money market because of the expenses of the fund. Yields among money market funds differ because of differences in portfolio allocation among money market instruments and in maturities.

Because of the large minimum denominations and transaction fees associated with the direct purchase of the various money market securities, most investors cannot afford direct purchase. Nonetheless, when a financial planner deems that it is appropriate for a client to have liquidity in his or her asset holdings, money market securities are the appropriate choice. The easiest way to reconcile these two facts is to advise the client to own a money market mutual fund.

GOVERNMENT AND GOVERNMENT-RELATED BONDS

Long-term debt securities are broadly categorized as governments, agencies, municipals, and corporate bonds. Preferred stock also competes for the same income-oriented investor dollars that might otherwise go into long-term debt securities.

As you read about all the complexities of bond instruments, keep in mind that all bonds are basically nothing more than formal IOUs. All debt obligations involve the same basic features: amount of the loan, when the loan must be repaid (maturity date), nature of collateral (if any), interest rate, frequency with which interest payments are to be made, what is to happen in case of default, and priority of repayment obligations of a borrower with multiple debts (subordination). Other features that may come into play include whether the borrower has the option of repaying the debt before it is due (call provision), whether the lender has the option of exchanging the financial obligation for an ownership interest (conversion), and whether the lender has the option of demanding repayment prior to maturity (put provision). In this section, we will focus on government, agency, and municipal notes and bonds.

Treasury Notes and Bonds

Treasury notes

Treasury bonds

In addition to the Treasury bills discussed earlier in this chapter, the U.S. Treasury also auctions debt instruments that have intermediate-term and long-term maturities (notes and bonds). *Treasury notes* are issued with maturities from 1 to 10 years; *Treasury bonds* have maturities greater than 10 years at the time of issuance. Both notes and bonds are issued in denominations of $1,000 or more, and both are traded in an active secondary market consisting of dealers in U.S. government securities. Price quotations for notes and bonds in the over-the-counter market are published daily in various publications. Current quotes for a few key bonds may be found at various locations on the Internet. An example of Treasury bond quotations is as follows:

Treasury Note and Bond Quotations (Sample Quotes from the OTC Market)					
Maturity	Coupon	Bid	Asked	Chg.	Asked Yld
2013 Apr 15	1.750	102:08	102:09	–1	.9189
2017 May 31	2.750	101:25	101:26	–8	2.4623
2040 May 15	4.375	106:18	106:19	–26	3.9946

The middle bond in the above quotations matures on May 31, 2017. Virtually all treasuries (the common name for notes and bonds combined) mature on either the 15th or the last day of the maturity month. The coupon rate of 2.750 means that the annual interest payment on a $1,000 bond is $27.50 (2.750% x $1,000). Interest is paid semiannually.

The Bid column shows the price that a dealer is willing to pay for the note or bond. Unlike T-bills, Treasury bond prices are quoted in 32nds and as a percentage of par. The above quote of 101:25 means that the bid price is 101 25/32 percent of par. If par were $1,000, the actual price would be $1,017.81 ($1,000 x 101 25/32%). It is obtained by multiplying the bid price times par value. The Ask column gives the price for which a dealer is willing to sell the note/bond to an investor.

The Chg. column is the change (in 32nds) between the bid price as listed in the bid column and the bid price from the previous trading day. For the first bond shown, the number –8 means that the bid price is 8/32nds of 1 percent lower than on the previous day. On a $1,000 par value bond, this translates into a price decline of $2.50, which is computed by multiplying the price change by the par value.

The Ask Yld. column provides an approximation of the yield to maturity for the note or bond based on its ask price. The concept of yield to maturity will be discussed in the next chapter. This is the single most important number in the quotation.

Prior to 1985, some of the bonds issued were callable at par beginning 5 years prior to the maturity date. They are callable only on the coupon payment dates. Thus, if a callable bond matured on November 15, 2011, then it is first callable on November 15, 2006, then again on May 15, 2007, and so on. Several such bonds still trade in the marketplace, although it takes a little effort to locate them. Currently, they are characterized by substantially higher coupon rates than other bonds of comparable maturity, but yields to maturity that are approximately the same. There is some evidence that at least some of these bonds may be overpriced, but the debate is really over whether the percentage that is overpriced is relatively large or small. [71] When these callable bonds are quoted in the paper, the yield to maturity is based on the call date for premium bonds and the maturity date for discount bonds.

Treasury notes and bonds are traded in an over-the-counter market composed of about two dozen dealers. It is also possible to buy treasuries directly from the U.S. Treasury in the primary market. All Treasury securities (that is, bills, notes, and bonds) will continue to be considered the most secure in the world as long as the government is willing and able to raise sufficient tax revenues to finance the debt.

Treasury STRIPS

In 1985, the Treasury introduced a program call STRIPS (Separate Trading of Registered Interest and Principal Securities). Under this program, a financial institution, government securities broker, or government securities dealer can convert an eligible Treasury security into interest and principal components through the commercial book-entry system. A Treasury bond can be converted into STRIPS at the time of issue or any time thereafter. For example, a 20-year coupon bond could be stripped of its 40 semiannual coupons, and each of these coupons would then be treated as a stand-alone zero-coupon bond. The maturities of these 40 bonds would range from 6 months to 20 years. The final payment of principal would also be treated as a stand-alone zero-coupon bond.[72] In fact, STRIPS are now the dominant zero-coupon bond.

Treasury Inflation-Protected Securities (TIPS)

In 1997, the U.S. Treasury added Treasury Inflation-Protected Securities (TIPS) to its menu of offerings. The goal of TIPS has been to provide inflation protection to investors. Naturally, when a feature like inflation protection is

---

71. Jordan, Bradford, Jordan, Susan, and Kuipers, David, "The Mispricing of Callable U.S. Treasury Bonds: A Closer Look," *Journal of Financial Management*, 1998; Longstaff, F. A. (1992): "Are Negative Option Prices Possible? The Callable U.S. Treasury-Bond Puzzle," *Journal of Business*, 65:571-592; and Edleson, M. E., Fehr, D., and Mason, S. P. (1993), "Are Negative Put and Call Option Prices Implicit in Callable Treasury Bonds?," Working Paper, Harvard Business School.

72. www.treasurydirect.gov/institmarketables/strips/strips.htm, July 28, 2010.

added to a security, something is taken away. In this case, the coupon rate is set lower than what it would be on bonds without the inflation protection. To compensate for the lower coupon rate, the bond's par value is adjusted on a semiannual basis by the amount of the inflation rate, as reported by the Bureau of Labor Statistics in its Consumer Price Index (CPI). The coupon rate is then applied to the par value to determine the interest payment that is due.

Maturity	Coupon	Bid	Asked	Chg.	Yield	Accrued Prin.
2015 Jan 15	1.625	105:00	105:01	+4	.501	1141
2020 Jan 15	1.375	101:12	101:13	+9	1.220	1008
2032 Apr 15	3.375	127:20	127:21	+10	1.829	1228

The only difference between sample TIPS quotations shown above and the quotations on treasuries shown earlier is that the TIPS quotation includes the adjusted (or accrued) principal.

In the event that the CPI declines, the accrued principal would be reduced with one exception. The principal will not be reduced below the original par value.

Let's look at an example of how this would work. Suppose a TIPS is offered with a 1 percent coupon rate. If the inflation rate averages 3 percent during the investment period (1.5 percent per 6-month period), then the coupon payments and principal would rise at that rate. For the first semiannual payment, a client with a $100,000 investment would receive interest on the TIPS of $507.50 ($101,500 principal x 1 percent coupon rate x 1/2 semiannual factor). However, his or her total income during this period is $2,007.50 because he or she receives the interest ($507.50) and the increase in the par value of the bonds ($1,500), although the client will not actually receive the cash associated with the increased principal until the bond matures. If the inflation rate continues to average 1.5 percent per 6-month period, then the interest payment and principal will both increase at this rate.

EXAMPLE

You have a 70-year-old client who has a morbid fear of the impact of inflation. The client indicates that he would like to invest $100,000 in a new issue of TIPS. The coupon rate on the TIPS is 1.0 percent, and the coupon rate on regular Treasuries of comparable maturity is 3.0 percent. Is this a good deal?

The quickest way to get a read on TIPS is simply to look at the difference between the coupon rates on regular Treasuries of comparable maturities and those of the TIPS. In this case, the differential is 2 percent. Hence, if the actual inflation rate turns out to be less than 2 percent, the regular bonds are a better deal. If the inflation rate turns out to be more than 2 percent, the TIPS are a better deal (at least for this investment). TIPS provide an inflation hedge, but at the risk of current income. They make sense as a component of a portfolio, especially where the client has a high degree of anxiety about the inflation rate or when the client has substantive expenses that are tied to the inflation rate.

Agency Issues

A federal agency is an administrative unit of the U.S. government. Some of the agencies are empowered to borrow funds in the open market in order to make loans to private businesses and/or individuals or otherwise subsidize private lending or borrowing. The agencies so empowered can be classified as either government-sponsored enterprises (GSEs) or true federal agencies. The GSEs are privately owned, federally chartered organizations. In some cases, such as the Federal National Mortgage Association (FNMA, pronounced Fannie Mae) and the Federal Home Loan Mortgage Corporation (FHLMC, pronounced Freddie Mac), their stock is publicly traded. The budgets of these GSEs are not part of the federal budget, and many see the existence of these agencies as a way for Congress to get around federal spending limits. GSEs are allowed to borrow from the U.S. Treasury up to a specified limit. Federal agencies are legally a part of the government itself, and their borrowing and lending activities are included in the federal budget.

The critical difference between bonds issued by a federal agency and those issued by GSEs is that the latter are legally not guaranteed by the federal government. Nonetheless, many believe that if a GSE was to be faced with the prospect of defaulting on its debt, the U.S. Treasury would step in. This in fact has happened with both FNMA and FHLMC.

For the sake of analysis, all federal and federally sponsored agencies are lumped together and simply referred to as federal agencies. Most agency securities are short to intermediate term (that is, up to 10 years maturity). Agency securities provide slightly higher returns than Treasury securities of comparable maturity. This is due to two reasons. One is the lack of an absolute full faith and credit guarantee for the GSEs, and the other is their lower marketability. Because the trading volume for most agency issues is less than that for Treasury securities, the bid-ask spreads are wider. This results in greater trading costs for agency issues and forces investors to demand a slightly higher return. Agencies are quoted on the same percentage of par and units of 1/32nds, as are treasuries.

Partial Listing of Federal Agencies and Government-Sponsored Agencies
Federal Agencies:
• Export-Import Bank
• Government National Mortgage Association (GNMA or Ginnie Mae)
• Tennessee Valley Association (TVA)
Government-Sponsored Agencies:
• Federal Farm Credit Banks (FFCBs)
• Federal Home Loan Banks (FHLBs)
• Federal Home Loan Mortgage Corporation (FHLMC)
• Federal Land Banks (FLBs)
• Federal National Mortgage Association (FNMA or Fannie Mae)

Municipal Bonds

revenue bonds

general obligation bonds

State and local government securities make extensive use of the long-term debt security market. The securities issued are called municipals, municipal bonds, or just munis. Municipals may be *revenue bonds* (which are backed by revenues from a designated project, authority, or agency, or by the proceeds from a specific tax) or *general obligation bonds* (which are backed by the taxing power of the issuing government). A subcategory of revenue bonds is the industrial development bond (IDB). An IDB is issued as a municipal bond, but the purpose of the issue is to provide funds to a private business entity. Municipalities do this to encourage local economic development.

In the early 1970s, the insurance industry discovered that there was a market for selling insurance protection of interest and principal payments on municipals. Such protection makes the most sense where the issuer believes that the purchase of such insurance would lead to a sufficient improvement in the bond's credit rating that the issuer could attach a lower coupon rate to the bond than would otherwise have been the case, and the savings in interest expense is greater than the premium for the insurance. Where such insurance exists, the rating agency will focus more on the insurance company's financial strength than on the issuer. Investors should pay attention to who the insurer is on each of these bonds. Alternatives to the purchase of insurance are the acquisition of back-up lines of credit or standby guarantee letters. In this case, the creditworthiness of the supporting bank becomes the substitute for the borrower.

CORPORATE BONDS

Corporations are the largest issuers of bonds. Corporate bonds have all the basic features that government bonds have: coupon rate, maturity date, and maturity or par value. However, corporate bonds can be more complex because they have varying degrees of default risk, a greater variety of collateral, and such interesting features as convertibility. In this section, we will first look at how these bonds are traded in the market. We will then look at the key characteristics of collateral, coupon rate, call feature, maturity, and bond ratings. First, let's review the basic document that defines the details of the bond issue.

The Bond Indenture

indenture   Behind every bond issue is an *indenture*, which is the legal contract between the issuer of the bond and the investor. The indenture describes all of the bond's characteristics, and provides positive affirmations and negative affirmations. The positives are things the issuer promises to do, and the negative are things the issuer promises not to do. These affirmations are intended to ensure that the company remains solvent and able to make interest and principal payments when due. For example, an indenture may specify that a company limit its dividend payments to a specified percentage of its net income. The indenture may also mandate that the company maintain a minimum current ratio or that its debt ratio not exceed a specified value.

The indenture also names a *trustee*, usually the trust department of a large bank, who is appointed to represent the bondholders and ensure that the company abides by the indenture's provisions. The rules defining the trustee's role are defined primarily by the Trust Indenture Act of 1940. The key to this act is that although the trustee is paid by the issuer, the trustee is also personally liable for any losses to bondholders that result from negligence on the trustee's part. Examples of terms found in indentures are shown in the accompanying box.

Typical Indenture Provisions

- Principal and maturity: Specifies amount and timing of principal payment
- Coupon: Specifies amount and timing of each coupon (interest) payment
- Collateral (first mortgage bond, equipment trust certificate, or other collateralized bond): Identifies pledged collateral and specifies obligation of the issuer to maintain collateral's value
- Full faith and credit (debenture): Backs bond with the pledge of the issuer
- Subordination: Gives interest payment and liquidation priority to specified senior debt
- Call provision: Specifies length of no-call protection and call premiums payable over life of the bond
- Dividend restrictions: Restricts dividend payments, based on earnings and/or amount of equity capital
- Current ratio minimum: Requires that the current ratio not fall below a specified minimum
- Me-first rule: Restricts the amount of additional (nonsubordinated) debt that may be issued (usually as a percentage of total assets)
- Trustee: Specifies the institution responsible for enforcing the indenture provisions
- Sinking fund: Provides for periodic redemption and retirement over the life of the bond issue, or for an escrow account to ensure repayment of the principal amount when due
- Grace period: Specifies the maximum period that the firm has to cure a default without incurring the risk of a bankruptcy filing

Trading Mechanics

Most trading of bonds takes place in the OTC market. Bond quotations usually include the name of the company issuing the bond, along with the coupon rate and year of maturity, current yield, volume, closing price, and net change. An example of what corporate bond quotations might look like in a trade publication is shown below.

Examples of Corporate Bond Quotations				
Bonds	**Cur. Yld.**	**Vol.**	**Close**	**Net Chg.**
Att6s20	6.6	4	90 ½	1/8
Hilton5s12	cv	130	82	1
Polaroid11 ½	f	489	14 ½	½

- Bonds: The name of the company issuing the bond, the interest or coupon rate as a percentage of the face or par value (typically $1,000), and the year in which the bond will be paid off (the s that sometimes appears between the interest rate and the year of maturity has no significance other than to separate the interest rate from the year of maturity when the interest rate does not include a fraction—read the explanatory notes given in the financial media for the meaning of other letters used)

- Cur. Yld.: The current yield, calculated by dividing the coupon amount by the current price. Flat bonds show no current yield, and convertible bonds have the letters cv listed here.

- Vol.: The actual number of bonds traded

- Close: The price for the last trade of the day, which is stated as a percentage of par value

- Net Chg.: The difference between the closing price as listed in the close column (see above) and the closing price from whatever day the bond previously traded, which is usually the previous trading day

The buyer of a bond normally pays an amount equal to the sum of three numbers: the price of the bond, accrued interest, and commission. The price quote shows the price of the bond only. The exchange where the bond is traded tracks the accrued interest. The accrued interest involves the buyer paying the seller an amount to reflect the portion of interest that has already been earned but not yet paid.

EXAMPLE

A bond that is quoted at 93 would initially cost the buyer $930 in principal plus the accrued but unpaid interest (plus commission). If the bond has a 10 percent coupon paid semiannually and made its last coupon payment 3 months ago, unpaid interest would have accrued as follows:

$(1/2 \times .10) \times \$1,000 \times 3/6 = .05 \times \$1,000 \times 1/2 = \$25$

That is, because the bond pays interest every 6 months and 3 months have elapsed, half of one coupon payment has accrued. This corresponds to one-half of the semiannual interest payment

As with dividends on stock, interest is paid to the holder of the bond on the day of record. When the issuer makes the coupon payment, the new owner of record will receive the entire amount of interest for that period. In the above example, if the buyer is still holding the bond 3 months later, the buyer receives the full semiannual interest payment. Half of that is a reimbursement for the accrued interest paid to the seller, and the other half is the interest actually earned by the buyer. The accrued interest paid is offset against interest received on the investor's income tax return.

flat
Bonds trading for a net price that does not reflect any accrued interest are said to be trading *flat*. Typically, bonds that are in default or whose interest payments are considered uncertain trade flat. In bond quotations, bonds that trade flat usually have an "f" following their name.

Collateral

Like any large loan, an incredibly important feature of any bond issue is the collateral. Bonds are classified with respect to their collateral. The most common types of bonds are debentures, mortgage bonds, equipment trust certificates, and collateral trust bonds.

Debentures

Debentures do not have specific property serving as collateral but, rather, are backed by the full faith and credit of the issuer. In the event of bankruptcy, holders of debentures are treated the same as any other general creditors of the issuer.

Mortgage Bonds

Mortgage bonds have real property pledged as collateral—specifically, plant and equipment. One of the most critical features of a mortgage bond is whether it is a closed end or an open end issue. A closed-end bond does not permit the property pledged as collateral to be used as collateral on other debt issues of equal status. An open-end mortgage bond would so allow. The problem, of course, is that the quality of the collateral becomes diluted as it is pledged to additional creditors. Closed end bonds are more desirable. Open-end mortgage bonds promise higher rates of return to compensate investors for this potential risk of dilution.

subordination

senior debt

From an investor's perspective, the safest way of dealing with the problem of pledging the same property twice as collateral is subordination. *Subordination* means that the claims of a second set of bondholders are subordinated to the claims of the first set of bondholders. The bonds held by this first set is usually called *senior debt*. The second set of bonds is called junior debt or subordinated debt. Subordinated debt always carries higher interest rates. Subordination is not limited to mortgage bonds. A company can issue two sets of debentures and identify the second set as subordinated debentures. Convertible bonds are frequently designated as subordinated debentures. If a company becomes insolvent, then the holders of any subordinated bonds will not be paid until after the holders of whatever debt is senior debt to those bonds are paid in full.

To protect bondholders from the risk of default, it is not uncommon for an indenture to contain a provision that restricts the amount of additional debt the issuing firm can incur. For example, an indenture might restrict the total amount of long-term debt to a specified percentage of the company's total assets.

Equipment Trust Certificates

Equipment trust certificates function more like a lease arrangement. They are frequently used to finance rolling stock (for example, airplanes or railroad cars). These certificates are actually issued by a trust that is formed to purchase an asset and lease it to a lessee. The lessee pays the trustee, and the trustee uses these payments to pay the interest and principal on the certificates. When the last of the certificates has been repaid, title and ownership of the asset transfers to the lessee. In the event of default, the trustee is the legal owner of the asset, and can thus easily repossess the property and sell it to cover the balance due on the lease.

Collateral Trust Bonds

Collateral trust bonds have stocks, bonds, and other securities pledged as collateral. These securities are deposited with the trustee for safeguarding. Naturally, the market value of the pledged securities should expand or exceed the principal due on the debt issue itself.

Coupon Rate

The interest payments on bonds are technically referred to as coupon payments. This derives from earlier times when bonds were issued with coupons attached. Each coupon had a date and a payment amount. When a payment date arrived, the owner of the bond would clip the coupon from the bond and present it for collection of the interest owed. Most bonds nowadays are registered, which means the issuer tracks who the owner of the bond is and sends out the interest payments automatically. Nonetheless, we still refer to interest payments on bonds as coupon payments, and the rate of interest paid as the coupon rate.

Most bonds come with a coupon rate that is fixed for the life of the bond. Like governments, corporate bonds almost always pay interest on a semiannual basis. The coupon rate for most bonds is pegged at what the issuer believes is the yield to maturity for bonds of comparable risk and maturity at the time of issue. We will see in the next chapter that when a bond's yield to maturity equals its coupon rate, then the bond will trade at par or face value. It is for this reason that most new issues of bonds are sold at par or within a few pennies or dollars of par. There are several variations on coupon payments that have developed over the years.

zeros   **Zero-Coupon Bonds.** Zero-coupon bonds, frequently referred to as *zeros*, provide no explicit coupon payments. They are similar to Treasury bills in this respect. They are different than Treasury bills in that each year there is an implicit interest payment. The implicit interest payment is deductible on the issuers' tax returns for corporate issuers, and it is also taxable for the investor. It is for this reason that most zeros are held, and should be held, in tax-qualified accounts such as IRAs and Keoghs. Investors in zeros know at the outset exactly what the value will be at maturity. In contrast, the end-period value of funds invested in coupon-yielding bonds is uncertain because it depends on the rate earned on the reinvested coupon payments (i.e., reinvestment rate risk). Because of their lack of reinvestment rate risk and relative scarcity, zeros have tended to sell for somewhat lower yields than equivalent-risk coupon bonds.

Like other long-term bonds, long-term zeros lock both the buyer and the issuer into a long-term rate. If rates go up after the purchase, the buyer will end up receiving a below-market return. Moreover, for a given change in interest rates, the prices of zeros change more than those of coupon bonds with comparable maturities. Owners of coupon bonds can at least reinvest their coupon income at higher rates when market interest rates rise.

Original-Issue Discount Bonds. An original-issue discount (OID) bond is a cross between a zero and a regular coupon bond. When an OID is issued, the coupon rate is deliberately set substantially below the appropriate current market interest rate. As a result, the investor receives both imputed interest and a coupon payment. As with zeros, OIDs should be held in tax-qualified accounts so that the investor does not have to pay taxes on the amortization of the discount.

Split Coupon. The term "split coupon bond" is used in four different ways. The first definition is that it is simply another name for a zero. The second definition is that it is a bond that starts out as a zero and then at a specified point in time becomes a coupon bond. These types of split coupon bonds are issued by corporations and are also sometimes called deferred interest bonds. The third definition is that it is a bond that starts out as a zero but converts to a coupon under certain circumstances that would be defined in the indenture. These types of split coupon bonds are issued by municipalities. The fourth definition is that it is a convertible bond that is also a zero.

Floating-Rate Notes (FRNs), Adjustable Rate Securities, and Reset Bonds. Floating rate notes (FRNs) have their coupon payments pegged to a market reference rate such as LIBOR or the federal funds rate with a fixed spread. Although the adjustments are made semiannually, most FRNs have quarterly coupon payments, instead of the more common semiannual. In the U.S., it is the GSEs that are the most common issuer of FRNs, and in Europe it is banks. FRNs are also sometimes referred to as floaters.

The floating rate feature of these bonds generally allows their prices to remain close to their par values, although just how close is a function of how frequently the coupon rate is adjusted, as well as the rate to which it is pegged. Because changes in the interest rate tend to reflect changes in the inflation rate, these bonds keep their *real* rate of return relatively constant. Thus, their prices also can stay relatively stable as interest rates fluctuate.

An adjustable or variable rate note differs from an FRN to only in that its interest rate adjusts no sooner than annually, and there may be several years between adjustment periods.

In a reset bond, or extendible reset bond, the issuer resets the coupon rate at specified points in time so that the price of the bond will move back to par. To avoid a propensity to err on the side of setting the new coupon rate too low, the usual arrangement is that the reset rate is based on the recommendations of at least two investment banking firms. Most reset bonds are of a poor credit quality.

Caps and Collars. When a borrower issues a floating rate security, it exposes itself to potentially catastrophic losses. For example, if a lender issues a floating rate bond with an initial interest rate of 5 percent, and the index to which that rate is tied jumps dramatically and causes the new rate on the reset date to be, say, 30 percent, then the borrower may have difficulty making the interest payment. To deal with this potential problem, some borrowers will purchase caps. A cap is an arrangement to limit the maximum amount of interest paid. A cap is based on a strike rate, which is the price at which an option to buy or sell can be exercised. The seller of the cap agrees that at any time the interest rate on the loan, as determined under the indenture, exceeds the strike rate, the seller will pay the incremental interest expense.

EXAMPLE

Big Chance Corporation has issued some floating rate notes with annual interest payments. The interest rate is 4 percent for the first year, but on the first anniversary, the interest rate will be reset to LIBOR plus 2 percent. The bond issue is for $100 million. The company buys a cap with a strike rate of 6 percent. On the first anniversary, LIBOR is at 5 percent, so the reset rate becomes 7 percent. The seller of the cap will have to pay Big Chance $1 million, which is the difference between the floating rate and the strike rate times the principal of the loan. Big Chance will then owe a net interest payment of $6 million, which is the $4 million on the original rate plus the net increase of $2 million.

To reduce the cost of buying a cap, borrowers will sometimes opt for a collar arrangement. A *collar* combines a cap with an interest rate floor. With a floor, the borrower agrees to pay the seller of the collar any of the interest savings achieved if the floating rate falls below the floor.

EXAMPLE

In the previous example, Big Chance opts for a collar rather than a cap. The price of the collar is lower than the price of the cap. The interest rate floor is set at 3 percent. On the first reset date, the interest rate on the loan resets to 2.5 percent. Because this is .5 percent below the floor, Big Chance owes the seller of the collar $500,000. Big Chance will recoup this money through what it saves on its interest payment to the bondholders.

A collar has the benefit of converting any bond whose coupon rate is indexed to a semi-fixed-rate note. The purchase of a cap is analogous to the purchase of insurance. The purchase of a collar is analogous to the purchase of insurance with large deductibles. In the second example, the buyer of the insurance (that is, the collar) may have to pay some money out of his or her own pocket, but the savings on the premium may more than offset these payments.

An alternative arrangement for a bond issuer to transfer the risk exposure of fluctuating interest rates is to enter into a swap arrangement. Bond swaps will be discussed in more detail later.

Income Bonds. Most bonds must either pay the agreed upon interest or go into default. Income bonds, on the other hand, pay interest only if the issuer earns sufficient monies to pay it. Passed coupons normally do not accumulate. Specific indenture provisions indicate when earned income is sufficient to require an interest payment. Most income bonds originate in a reorganization exchange (that is, bankruptcy) or to replace a preferred stock issue. Some, however, are sold in the primary market. At any given time, there are relatively few income bonds outstanding, and most originate with the railroad industry.

Financial Planning Issue
You have a client who is 60 years old. The client has little need today for investment income, but wants to substantially increase his portfolio income upon retirement in 5 years. He would like to do this without large scale changes in his portfolio. In this situation, split-coupon bonds which start out as zeroes and then become coupon bonds, or step-up bonds, would appear to be natural choices.

Step-Up Bonds. Step-up bonds have a fixed schedule as to changes in coupon rates over the life of the bond. Thus, they differ from the FRNs, adjustables, and reset bonds in that the different coupon rates are not necessarily geared to market rates at the time of the coupon rate change. Such an arrangement allows the issuer to push the bulk of the interest burden to later in the life of the bond. Government agencies are the most common issuer of step-up bonds. Many step-up bonds are callable.

Maturity

When bonds are issued, they have a maturity date. Most bonds are outstanding until the maturity date, at which time the bondholders receive the principal or face value of the bonds. However, bonds can go out of existence in multiple other ways.

Conversion. A relatively simple way for bonds to go out of existence is if they are convertible and the investor elects to convert them. Most convertible bonds convert into shares of the same issuer's common stock. Occasionally, bonds are convertible into other securities such as preferred stock, or the common stock of a different company (such as a subsidiary). Investors will normally convert only at such time as it is in their economic interest to do so.

call price

Call Feature. Most bonds include a call feature. The first component of a call feature is the *call price*, which is the price at which the issuer can buy back the bond from the bondholder. Some bonds are callable from the day they are issued, and others are noncallable initially and then become callable at a later date. The call price is the sum of par value, a *call premium* that is defined in the indenture, and accrued interest up to the day of the call. The call premium is sometimes set at a fixed number (for example, 3 percent of par), and other times it is set at a higher number initially and then the value is amortized over time. Bonds are called in for one of the following three reasons:

forced conversion

- The most common is that the issuer can issue new bonds at a substantially lower coupon rate, such that the issuer can pay the call premium, the costs of processing the new issue, and still save money. This is known as refinancing. It is essentially the same process as a homeowner's refinancing his or her mortgage for a lower interest rate.
- The bond is convertible and the issuer wants to issue the common stock and terminate the interest payments. This is known as *forced conversion*. It can be successful only when the market value of the stock received upon conversion is greater than the call price.
- The terms of the indenture have become a serious constraint for a company, and it wants to get out from under the restrictions imposed by the indenture.

If a bond is called for either of the first two reasons, it is a sure bet that the investor is worse off as a result of the call feature's being invoked. On the rare occasions when a bond is called for the third reason, the investor may receive a windfall gain.

EXAMPLE

A hypothetical bond has an initial maturity of 30 years. The indenture specifies that the issuer may call the bond 20 or more years after the date of issue and that the call premium is 1 percent of the face value for each remaining year until the bond matures. If the company issued a $1,000 bond in 1999, the soonest the bond can be called is 2019, in which case the company will have to pay bondholders $1,100 per bond. If the company redeems the bonds in 2024, the call price will be $1,050 per bond.

Puttable Bond. The puttable bond is almost the opposite of a callable bond. In this case, the bondholder has the privilege of demanding the bond be paid off early. This protects the investor against increases in interest rates. Normally, the put option is exercisable only on pre-set dates. A bond may be both puttable and callable.

sinking fund   ***Sinking Fund.*** Some indentures require a *sinking fund*. Originally, the sinking fund provision called for the issuer to place money in an escrow fund on a regular basis to ensure that there would be sufficient cash to retire the bonds at maturity. The only problem was that sometimes the payments into the fund were not made. Nowadays, a sinking fund arrangement means the issuer agrees to buy back a certain amount of principal at par value on a regular schedule. The buyback may be accomplished either by randomly selecting bonds to be called or by buying the bonds in the secondary market. The buyback program may be designed to retire the entire balance of the loan, or to retire a portion of the issue with the balance due at maturity. Either way, a sinking fund still means more safety for the bond investor because it reduces or eliminates the risk that the issuer will not have sufficient funds at maturity to pay the principal due. However, a sinking fund would also mean that if an investor's bonds are selected for repurchase under this program, the price paid would likely be less than the market price, and would definitely be less than the normal call price.

Serial Bonds. A serial bond issue is similar to a sinking fund provision in that portions of principal will be retired steadily over time. The difference is that in a serial bond issue, the bonds are grouped and assigned different maturity dates. Thus, an investor can select the desired maturity date within the issue. Furthermore, the coupon rate may vary among the different maturities of the serial issue, whereas the coupon rate is the same on all bonds issued with a sinking fund. Serials are issued almost exclusively by municipalities. The major drawback to investors is that by dividing up the issue according to maturity date, the limited amount available for trading in any one segment makes those segments pretty much illiquid.

Consols. All bonds issued in the United States promise to repay principal at some future date. If they did not do so, then the Internal Revenue Service would disallow the interest payments as being tax deductible to the payer on the basis that the bond is really preferred stock. Britain, however, has issued some bonds without maturity, called consols. They can be valued in a manner similar to preferred stock.

Death Puts. Some corporate bonds now come with a special feature known as a death put. A death put allows the executor of an estate to redeem these bonds at par value upon the death of the owner.[73] There is no uniform set of rules that apply to these bonds, but there are some common characteristics. For example, there typically is no constraint upon how the cash from the redemption can be used. There is also usually a restriction that prevents people who are contemplating an immediate death from using this feature. These restrictions might include that the death put cannot be exercised if death occurs during the first year of ownership, or if the investor is known to be terminally ill at the time of purchase. Some companies also place limits on the amount of bonds that can be redeemed for the estate of any one investor.

Bond Ratings

The best way to avoid the uncertainty and potential losses from a default and possible bankruptcy of the insurer is to invest in bonds with low default risk. This strategy requires a method to assess the default risk level. Bond ratings offer just such an assessment. The default risks of both municipal and corporate bonds are rated by several rating services. The best-known services are Standard & Poor's, Moody's Investor Service, and Fitch Ratings. Each service's ratings are based on its evaluation of the firm's financial position and earnings prospects. The following table describes the primary rating categories of these agencies. Pluses and minuses are used to discriminate within a rating category.

---

73. A death put corporate bond may sounds a little like a "flower bond," which was a government bond that, upon the bondholder's death, could be used a face value to pay estate taxes. All government bonds with this feature have been redeemed and are no longer being issued.

Moody's	S&P	Fitch	
Long-term	Long-term	Long-term	
Aaa	AAA	AAA	Prime
Aa1	AA+	AA+	High grade
Aa2	AA	AA	
Aa3	AA-	AA-	
A1	A+	A+	Upper medium grade
A2	A	A	
A3	A-	A-	
Baa1	BBB+	BBB+	Lower medium grade
Baa2	BBB	BBB	
Baa3	BBB-	BBB-	
Ba1	BB+	BB+	Non-investment grade speculative
Ba2	BB	BB	
Ba3	BB-	BB-	
B1	B+	B+	Highly speculative
B2	B	B	
B3	B-	B-	
Caa1	CCC+		Substantial risks
Caa2	CCC		Extremely speculative
Caa3	CCC-		In default with little prospect for recovery
	CC		
Ca	C	CCC	
C		DDD	In default
/		DD	
/	D	D	

From: http://en.wikipedia.org/wiki/Bond_credit_rating, accessed July 12, 2010.

Rating services do not release their specific rating formulas or analyses, but a number of academic studies do reveal a rather predictable pattern. Ratings tend to be stronger with profitability, size, and interest coverage (earnings before interest and taxes, divided by total interest expense). They become weaker with earnings volatility, extensive use of debt financing, and larger pension obligations; they also vary with industry classification. Ratings sometimes differ among the rating agencies; these differences usually reflect a close call on fundamentals.

investment grade

junk bonds

The top ratings categories (which range from AAA to BBB for Standard & Poor's and from Aaa to Baa for Moody's) are referred to as *investment grade* bonds. This is because some financial institutions are restricted to invest only in these better-rated bonds, and other investors also restrict themselves to invest only in these. A financial planner who keeps a client in investment grade bonds is clearly acting prudently with regard to safety of principal. Bonds rated less than Baa or BBB are known as *junk bonds* and will be discussed shortly.

For issues of the same company, a subordinate issue usually receives a lower rating than a senior security. The rating agencies follow the fortunes of issues over time and change ratings on occasion. These rating changes occur relatively infrequently, however, and often take place long after the underlying fundamentals change.

Financial Planning Issue
Bonds worth $50,000 have matured in your client's portfolio. You want to reinvest this money into bonds with a 10-year maturity. Your goal is to have all of the bonds in the portfolio be rated A or better. You have identified three bonds, all rated A, that have yields to maturity of 6.1, 6.2, and 7.3 percent. Which bond is the best deal?
Naturally, an advisor would initially be tempted to buy the issue with the 7.3 percent yield. However, the pricing of this bond suggests that the company is not in as good shape as the others and is at risk of having its bond rating lowered. Although the announcement of a lower rating does not usually have an immediate price impact (the price impact has already occurred), nonetheless you would not want to end up with a lower-rated bond. From a safety perspective, one of the other two bonds might be a better choice.

Junk bonds come into existence in one of three ways. The traditional entry route to junk bond status is as a *fallen angel*. A fallen angel is a bond that was originally rated as investment grade, and then the issuer fell upon difficult times. In more recent years, some investment bankers came to the conclusion that there was a substantial market for junk bonds, and worked with weaker companies to develop new issues that were rated as junk from the start. Finally, some companies discovered that buyouts could be financed through the issuance of junk bonds. Such acquisitions were known as *leveraged buyouts*. In these situations, the buying organizations were willing to pay high interest rates on junk bonds because they believed they could manage the new acquisition in such a way to generate additional profits that would either provide the money to pay the interest or even allow an early retirement of the debt issue.

The NRSRO "Problem"

The bond ratings agencies have been in the news a lot in recent years. The reason is that many highly-rated bonds were ending up in default. Critics naturally ponder what would it take to return integrity to the ratings. One rationale for the failed ratings is that the instruments being rated were just too complex, and the people at these firms didn't really understand what they were rating.

A second rationale is that these three rating agencies are three dominant ones designated by the SEC as *Nationally Recognized Statistical Rating Organizations (NRSROs)*. SEC rules virtually require most bond issuers to obtain ratings only from an NRSRO. These rules give these three firms a virtual monopoly on the bond rating business. Many believe an elimination of this government-granted monopoly would lead to more competition and more effective ratings.

CORPORATE BANKRUPTCY

No investor wants to buy bonds in what appears to be a secure company only to see the company default on its obligations. The bonds might eventually pay off part or all of the principal amount plus accrued interest, but that is uncertain when default occurs. It is even possible that the bondholders will be left with nothing. On the other hand, it is possible for an investor to achieve high yields from investing in a portfolio of risky bonds. Some investors even invest in a diversified portfolio of bonds that are near default because they can purchase these bonds at a substantial discount below their face value, and if enough of these companies recover, the portfolio rate of return may be quite attractive.

Technical Defaults and Defaults

technical default
A firm is in *technical default* whenever any of the indenture provisions of its bonds are violated. Many technical defaults, however, involve relatively minor matters. For example, if the current ratio falls below the stipulated minimum, the firm is technically in

default of the relevant indenture provision. Rarely, if ever, does such a default in itself lead to a bankruptcy filing. The matter may be quickly cured or the trustee may grant an extension or a waiver for the violation.

Even a failure to make an interest payment on time does not necessarily lead to bankruptcy. The firm may rectify the situation within a grace period. In addition, defaults and technical defaults generally result in a mutually acceptable resolution that stops short of bankruptcy and liquidation. Because liquidations ensure maximum losses for all parties involved, everyone may be better off under a resolution than in liquidation.

When a few large creditors (such as banks who have extended substantial loans) can be identified, the troubled borrower may seek direct concessions that will give it a reasonable chance of avoiding a bankruptcy filing. Big lenders have an important stake in their debtors' survival. An interesting oversimplification of the borrower-lender relationship is seen in the following two sentences:

- A borrower who owes $1,000 and cannot pay is in trouble.
- A borrower who owes $1 million and cannot pay puts the lender in trouble.

Accordingly, lenders with large exposures are likely to be asked to accept a payment stretch-out, an interest rate reduction, a swap of debt for equity or tangible assets, a reduction in loan principal, or a change or waiver of certain default provisions. Lenders often agree to such restructurings in the hope of eventually recovering more than they would have in a formal bankruptcy.

Although the stock price of firms that are struggling will already be quite low, when a firm formally files for bankruptcy, there is usually an additional substantial drop in stock value.

EXAMPLE

Enron Corporation, an interstate marketer of natural gas, electricity, and related products, was trading as high as $84.87 in December 2000. The stock's price began a gradual decline in 2001 as bad news about the company circulated. In August 2001, Enron's CEO resigned, and the stock price declined from $42.80 to $36.80 (a 14 percent drop) during the subsequent 11-day period.

The stock price decline continued in October and November as news about the company's financial difficulties hit the market. On October 31, there was a news release to the effect that the SEC had begun an investigation into the company's financial dealings with affiliated partnerships. The decline in stock price accelerated in November.

On November 28, Enron's stock opened at $3.69, which was the low for the year until that point. On November 28, there was news to the effect that Standard and Poor's had lowered Enron's bond rating from BBB (the lowest rating that is still considered investment grade) to B (a speculative grade bond rating).

Enron Corporation formally filed for Chapter XI bankruptcy on November 29. Its stock price reached a low of $.25 on November 30. This was a drop of over 93 percent in just 2 days.

Bankruptcy Filings

Even though bankruptcy should be avoided if at all possible, the reorganization of a financially troubled firm is not always doable without filing for bankruptcy. Bankruptcy proceedings may begin with a petition from a creditor, a creditor group, an indenture trustee, or the defaulting firm itself.

Chapter XI If the firm chooses to file for reorganization under Chapter XI, it intends to emerge from bankruptcy as a continuing entity. Chapter XI permits the firm to retain its assets and to restructure its debts under a plan of reorganization. A *Chapter XI* proceeding can give the firm a respite from creditors' claims because the firm has 120 days after filing the petition to formulate a plan of reorganization.

Reorganizations under Chapter XI, however, are not always successful in salvaging financially troubled firms; they are also very expensive. An unsuccessful Chapter XI reorganization effort usually leads to Chapter VII liquidation proceedings.

Chapter VII If a defaulting firm is thought to be worth more dead than alive, bankruptcy proceedings may begin as a Chapter **absolute-priority-of-** VII liquidation. Under *Chapter VII*, the bankruptcy trustee **claims principle** is responsible for selling the firm's assets and distributing the proceeds according to the *absolute-priority-of-claims principle*. Under this principle, the valid claims of each priority class are fully satisfied before the next class receives anything. The marginal priority group receives proportional compensation. The classes below the marginal priority class receive nothing because the funds available for distribution will have already been exhausted.

Some companies do successfully emerge from Chapter XI bankruptcy proceedings after a careful review of their financial and competitive situation. The process is designed to preserve the potentially profitable elements of their businesses in a recapitalized form. Unproductive assets are liquidated. The bankruptcy trustee and courts seek to retain as much value as possible for distribution to creditors. They also try to minimize the risk that the firm will have to return for court protection or seek additional lender concessions.

Filing for Bankruptcy

• Chapter XI reorganization
 	
    – The proceeding is designed to preserve potentially profitable elements of the business in a recapitalized form.
 	
    – It permits the firm to keep its assets and restructure its debts, provided a plan of reorganization is drafted within 120 days after filing the petition.
 	
    – During that 120-day period, the company is protected from the claims of creditors.
 	
• Chapter VII liquidation
 	
    – A bankruptcy trustee, appointed by the court, is given the responsibility for selling the firm's assets and distributing the proceeds under the absolute-priority-ofclaims principle. Following this principle, the valid claims of each priority class must be satisfied in full before the next priority class receives any proceeds.
 	
    – To regain possession of the company from the trustee, the debtor firm must file an appropriate bond.

Many troubled firms would be financially viable if their debt load were sufficiently reduced. Thus, an objective of many Chapter XI bankruptcy proceedings is to reduce the company's debt load, and because bankrupt firms generally have little or no excess cash to distribute to creditors, most creditors are prevailed upon to accept lower-priority securities of the reorganized firm as payment. Senior creditors may receive subordinated debentures or preferred stock, whereas junior creditors could be given common stock and warrants.

Several factors, however, limit the applicability of the absolute-priority-of-claims principle. The going-concern value of a firm that is experiencing a bankruptcy process is subjective. The securities to be issued by the reorganized firm will not have an established market price until the firm emerges from bankruptcy. Therefore, the relevant values are rather uncertain at the time (in the course of the bankruptcy proceeding) the securities distribution is set. Not surprisingly, the ability of these securities to satisfy claims is often subject to dispute.

Generally, the lower-priority claimants argue for a higher overall valuation for the company and its securities. In this way, they seek to increase the estimated value of the securities that are available for distribution to their priority class. The greater the firm's overall estimated value, the greater the proportion of that estimated value available to satisfy the lower-priority claimants.

EXAMPLE

Suppose a company's high-priority claimants have claims of $95 million and the company's value is estimated at $100 million. The high-priority claimants will be awarded securities representing 95 percent of the firm's value. Only 5 percent will be available to the lower-priority claimants. Now suppose that the lower-priority claimants are able to get the company's estimated value raised to $110 million. At that valuation, the higher-priority claimants will receive about 86 percent (95/110) of the firm's value. The lower-priority claimants will, in contrast, see their share rise to about 14 percent (15/110).

Unless the low-priority claimants are given something, however, they may use various legal maneuvers to delay the proceedings. As a result, most informal workouts and reorganizations ultimately allocate lesser-priority claimants more than what the absolute-priority-of-claims principle requires. In practice, unsecured and subordinated creditors can usually make enough noise to obtain some share of the assets even when senior creditors' claims exceed the firm's remaining asset value. When a company emerges from Chapter XI bankruptcy, the reduced debt burden generally permits it to remain solvent.

SECURITIZATION AND MORTGAGE-BACKED SECURITIES

Securitization

Securitization involves taking assets that heretofore were not easily traded in a secondary market and structuring a marketable security or group of securities from them. The goal of the process is to convert assets with poor marketability into assets with much greater market acceptance. If the effort is successful, one or more of several things will happen. First, the institution doing the converting might be able to sell the new, marketable assets for more than the old, less-marketable assets could be sold for. The difference between the book value of the assets and the market value of the new assets, minus the cost of the conversion, represents the profit earned by the converting institution. A second possibility is that the institution doing the converting might be generating its profit from the creation of the old assets. For example, suppose a bank charges a 1 percent origination on each mortgage loan. After the bank makes $10 million worth of mortgage loans, it then securitizes the loans and sells them for $10 million. The $10 million cash inflow then allows the bank to make another $10 million in mortgage loans and generate another 1 percent origination fee on each loan.

One major benefit of securitization, from the investor's standpoint, is that it effectively creates a diversified pool of loans, thus reducing the overall risk to the investor. While the risk of default would deter most investors from providing a large loan to an unknown individual, investing in a diversified pool of such loans is safer.

Most of the activity in securitization has been based on first-mortgage real estate loans. More recently, however, other types of assets have been securitized. For example, auto loans, credit card loans, second mortgages, sovereign loans to Third World countries, student loans, and a variety of other types of loans are (or are suggested as) the basis for securitization. However, mortgage loans are the most commonly securitized type of asset, and we will focus only on this product.

Mortgages

Mortgages are created as part of the purchase of real estate. The vast majority of outstanding mortgage debt is collateralized by a first claim (first mortgage) on developed real estate, such as single-family homes, apartments, or commercial property. Most such mortgage loans require a minimum initial down payment of 10 to 20 percent. These mortgages are generally amortized with level monthly payments over an extended period (typically 20 to 30 years). Thus, the amount owed would decline over time. Moreover, the property securing the mortgage loan usually (but not always) appreciates as time passes. As a result, the ratio of collateral value to mortgage debt would rise over time as long as the value of the real estate does not also decline. Accordingly, first mortgages are usually declining-risk investments. Even in a default and distress sale of the property, the mortgage holder will usually recover a high percentage of the outstanding debt.

The easiest way to invest in a mortgage is to be a mortgage lender. However, mortgage lending is a complex and expensive process. Thus, individual investors cannot effectively participate in direct mortgage lending. Nearly all mortgages are originated by banks, thrift institutions, and mortgage bankers. Once originated, these institutions will do one of three things with a mortgage: hold it for interest income, sell it to a third party, or securitize it. Some of the buyers then securitize these mortgages.

The two major agencies that buy mortgages are the Federal National Mortgage Association (FNMA, or Fannie Mae) and the Federal Home Loan Mortgage Corporation (FHLMC, or Freddie Mac). These agencies buy only conforming mortgages. A mortgage must meet several criteria to qualify as a conforming mortgage. These include an upper limit on the loan-to-value ratio (usually no greater than 80 percent), a upper limit on the payment-to-income ratio, and a dollar limit on the size of the mortgage. Mortgages that exceed this dollar limit are known as jumbo mortgages. For 2010, the jumbo mortgage has a loan balance of more than $417,000 for property in the continental United States. It is 50 percent higher in Alaska, Hawaii, Guam, and the U.S. Virgin Islands.

Although the above description would seem to suggest that FNMA and FHLMC would be effective vehicles to address an ample supply of mortgage money to credit worthy borrowers, such has not been the case. Many in Congress and the Executive branch started thinking that lower income populations were being underserved in the market for homeownership. They pressured these agencies to lower their quality standards. As a result, lenders began making loans to people who could not afford them. The mortgages were moved to FNMA and FHLMC. Eventually, these two agencies collapsed under the weight of defaulted mortgages. The government is now providing huge securities to these two agencies to prevent bankruptcy.

Most mortgages are conventional, in the sense that they have no special guarantee at the time they are created. The federal government backs some mortgages through the Veterans Administration (VA) guarantee program and the Federal Housing Administration (FHA) insurance program, which add protection for the lender. In other cases, usually where the down payment is less than 20 percent of the purchase price, the lender may require private mortgage insurance, which provides a private guarantee to the lender of the repayment of the mortgage.

Mortgage-Backed Securities

A mortgage-backed security (MBS) is one whose cash flow is dependent on the cash flows of an underlying pool of mortgages. There are three types of mortgage-backed securities: pass-throughs, collateralized mortgage obligations (CMOs), and stripped mortgage-backed securities.[74]

Mortgage-backed securities may be described as agency or nonagency securities. Non-agency mortgage-backed securities are issued by private companies. Each company will have its own underwriting standard as to what mortgages it will buy. The agency securities are not rated, but the nonagency ones are, and the rating depends on the underwriting standards and procedures of each issuer.

Mortgage Pass-Throughs

In a mortgage pass-through, the issuer of the pass-through security collects the payments from the borrowers, deducts a service charge, and then distributes the payments to the holders of the pass-through security. There are three agencies involved in issuing these securities. They are FNMA, FHLMC, and the Government National Mortgage Association (GNMA, or Ginnie Mae). GNMA is a wholly owned government corporation that operates as a division within the Department of Housing and Urban Development.

Collateralized Mortgage Obligations

Collateralized mortgage obligations (CMOs) are similar to a pass-through, with one key difference. The issuer of a CMO sequences the securities with respect to maturities. These sequences are called *tranches*. In a traditional CMO (known as a sequential pay CMO), interest will be paid on all of the tranches as promised, but the initial principal payments are directed to paying off only the first tranche. Once the first tranche has been paid in full, then the principal payments are directed to the owners of the second tranche. The holders of the first tranche have a relatively short-term, low risk security. The holders of the last tranche own a security that has substantial default risk and risk as to the timing of payments. When interest rates rise, people are less likely to move and less likely to be refinancing their mortgages. Hence, the average life of a mortgage grows longer. When interest rates fall, people are more likely to upgrade housing, move, or even just refinance their mortgages

---

74. Fabozzi Frank J., Editor, The Handbook of Fixed Income Securities, Sixth Edition. , McGraw-Hill: 2001, p. 17.

to get a better interest rate. All of these lead to shorter mortgage lives. Naturally, when mortgage rates fall and people pay off their mortgages early, investors in CMOs will get their principal back sooner than expected, but will find their reinvestment opportunities to be much less attractive than their original investments.

CMOs are issued by the same group that issues pass-throughs, including FNMA, FHLMC, GNMA, investment banks, mortgage originators, and insurance companies. The mortgages backing a CMO may be either directly owned by the issuer, or may be a collection of pass-through securities.

Stripped Mortgage-Backed Securities

A stripped mortgage-backed security functions much like a stripped bond. Two securities are issued. One receives all of the principal payments (the PO class) and the other receives all of the interest payments (the IO class). The PO securities are purchased at a substantial discount. If interest rates drop, then principal payments exceed the expected amount and the PO class becomes more valuable. Conversely, when interest rates rise, principal payments slow, causing the PO class to decline in value.

The IO class has no par value. The effect of interest rate changes is the exact opposite for IOs than for POs. When interest rates decline and principal payments accelerate, homeowners will be paying less interest on the remaining balance. This makes the IO class less valuable. Conversely, if rates rise and principal payments slow down, then homeowners will be paying more interest on the existing mortgage than had been expected, making the IOs more valuable.

Financial Planning Issue

If an investor wants to buy these IO and PO securities, then the choice between the two would be based upon the investor's expectations of the change in interest rates. If the investor expects interest rates to fall, then mortgages will have shorter lives, and the PO securities will be more valuable (as the investor gets his or her money back sooner than expected), while the IO securities will become less valuable (as interest payments will cease sooner than expected). A fall in interest rates has the opposite effect of making the PO securities less valuable and the IO securities more valuable.

Asset-Backed Securities That Use Mortgages

There are bonds outstanding that pledge a portfolio of mortgages as collateral, but the payments on the bonds are not a flow-through of the payments made on the mortgages. Although it would seem natural to call these bonds mortgage-backed securities, that is not the common terminology. The term mortgage-backed securities refers only to securities whose payments represent a flow-through from the mortgages themselves. If the mortgages serve only as collateral, the bonds are categorized as asset-backed bonds and not as MBSs.

Personal Mortgages

Sellers of homes will sometimes accept first or second mortgages as part of the proceeds. This was particularly true years ago when mortgage rates were into the teens and some buyers could not qualify to buy homes with a conventional mortgage. To facilitate the sale of the home, sellers would take some form of mortgage as part of the sale. With interest rates at historic low levels in recent years, seller financing has pretty much disappeared. Some entrepreneurs have made a lucrative living by buying these mortgages from the sellers, usually at substantive discounts from their face values. Such mortgages are risky because of the potential legal expenses associated with any defaults. In addition, there is no secondary market.

OTHER DEBT INSTRUMENTS

Domestic, Foreign, and Euro Bonds

The international bond market can be divided into three segments: domestic, foreign, and Euro.[75] A domestic bond market involves bonds issued and traded within a country, in the local currency, under the local regulations, by a borrower also located in that country. Foreign bonds are also issued and traded within a country, in the local currency, under local regulations, but by a borrower located in a different country. Eurobonds are underwritten by an international syndicate and traded in multiple domestic markets. A hybrid form of the foreign bond is the global bond. These are designed to trade and settle in both the Euro and the U.S. markets as Yankee bonds. A *Yankee bond* is denominated in U.S. dollars and issued in the United States by foreign banks and corporations. These bonds are registered with the SEC.

To some investors, the name "Eurobond" may be misleading. The term "Euro" simply means offshore, not that the bond is traded in the current

---

75. Material in this section is derived from *The Handbook of Fixed Income Securities*, Sixth Edition, Frank J. Fabozzi, Editor, McGraw-Hill, 2001.

European currency of Euros. The largest component of the Eurobond market is the Eurodollar bond, which is dollar denominated. The dramatic growth in the size of this market can be traced to several historical events, including restrictions placed on direct investment abroad by U.S. companies in 1968 and the large dollar surpluses acquired by the OPEC countries in the 1970s.

In terms of investor safety, well-rated Yankee bonds are essentially just as safe as well-rated domestic bonds. Eurobonds add a little risk because the issuance process and the markets in which they trade are not as well regulated as U.S. markets. Eurobonds are issued as bearer bonds, which means they are unregistered. There is also no back-up withholding of taxes on the interest payments of Eurobonds. The unregistered nature of Eurobonds combined with the lack of the withholding of taxes has made these bonds attractive for some U.S. investors for the inappropriate reason of tax evasion. In addition, although Yankee bonds adhere to the U.S. bond convention of semiannual payments, Eurobonds pay interest annually.

Investing in foreign-pay bonds is substantially more risky than investing in Yankee bonds and Eurobonds. The major risk is exchange rate risk. If a U.S. investor is buying a dollar-denominated Eurobond or Yankee bond, then the investor need only worry about the two risks of bond investing, default risk and interest rate risk. The complexities of foreign-pay bonds may lead investors consider some form of hedging with forward or futures contracts. Also, the trading hours, settlement procedures, and tax treatment will likely be different for these particular securities.

Private Placements

Approximately one-third of the debt instruments sold are placed privately to a few large buyers (often insurance companies) and publicly announced in the financial press. Announcements are generally referred to as "tombstones" because of the large amount of white space and small amount of lettering. Even if the size (tens of millions of dollars) of typical private placements rules out direct purchases, individuals may participate indirectly through one of the closed-end funds (to be discussed in a later chapter) that specializes in such investments.

Private placements generally yield one-half percent to one percent more than equivalent-risk bonds because they lack liquidity. Private placements offer greater flexibility to issuers. They can be tailored for specific buyers and do not require a prospectus. Moreover, the underwriting cost savings largely offset their somewhat higher coupon. Finally, the relatively small number of owners makes it easier to renegotiate the terms of the indenture if necessary.

Private placements do not have to comply with the standards of disclosure that the SEC requires of public offerings. The absence of disclosure of material risk factors makes the investment more risky to potential investors. Therefore, private placements would be suitable investments only for those with both the know-how and the financial resources to discover risk factors for themselves.

Promissory Notes

Any two people can enter into a loan agreement. If the amount of money loaned is significant, then a more formal promissory note rather than a simple IOU should be utilized. Forms for such promissory notes are readily available on the Internet. Promissory notes are also used in business relationships. A business will sometimes borrow money from an investor and issue a promissory note. Conversely, businesses sometimes lend money to individuals, such as officers and key employees. These loans may be for the individual's personal convenience, or they may be a form of compensation in which particularly attractive loan terms are established. Both the SEC and the North American Securities Administrators Association have warned that some popular scams involve marketing these notes directly to individuals. Promissory notes typically have no specific property pledged as collateral and their maturity may be short-term or long-term. Each promissory note is a truly unique document.

Insurance-Based Investments

An insurance-based investment is one that is issued by an insurance company. It may or may not involve the application of the mortality table. There are two broad categories of this type of investment: guaranteed investment contracts and annuities.

Guaranteed Investment Contracts (GICs)

A guaranteed investment contract (GIC), also known as a stable value contract, is usually an investment option available in a 401(k) retirement plan. More recently, it is available in some profit-sharing plans, and even some IRAs and mutual funds. GICs offer a specified maturity date or dates and a rate of return that is guaranteed through maturity by the insurance company. Neither the FDIC nor any other governmental agency insures these contracts. Employees may make withdrawals against these accounts for a variety of reasons, including: death, disability, attainment of age 59½, financial hardship, bona fide termination of employment, in-service plan withdrawals, plan loans, and participant-directed transfers to noncompeting funds offered through the 401(k) plan.

GICs come in many forms. The simplest GICs are "bullet" contracts under which the funds are returned in a lump sum. Other contracts allow for payouts over time. GICs may be denoted as floating rate. In this case, the interest rate paid would be tied to some benchmark rate, such as a specific maturity Treasury yield. GICs may also be characterized as participating, in which case the interest rate paid is tied to the performance of the portfolio in which the GIC deposit is invested.

GICs also may differ according to deposit methods (lump sum or "window" periods) and maturity (ranging from 1 to 5 years). The primary noninsurance competition for GICs is the bank investment contract (BIC), which is particularly popular for maturities of less than 3 years. BICs have the advantage of being eligible for FDIC insurance coverage.

The rate of return provided on GICs historically has been about the same as intermediate-term, investment-grade corporate bonds. To date, the risk has lessened due to the fact that few insurance companies have completely collapsed.

Annuities

qualified annuity

nonqualified annuity

Annuities are particularly well-designed investments for retirees. An annuity may be designated as qualified or nonqualified. A *qualified annuity* is purchased through a tax-sheltered program, such as a 401(k), a 403(b), or an IRA; a *nonqualified annuity* is purchased outside of any tax-sheltering program. Regardless of the qualification status, the major advantage of a deferred annuity is that the money in an investor's account grows on a tax-deferred basis. If the annuitant dies before starting the withdrawals from the annuity, there is usually a guaranteed death benefit.

Annuities can be grouped into four categories, depending on when the premium is paid, when the benefits start, and how long the benefits last.

1. *Single-premium deferred annuities (SPDAs).* A nonqualified SPDA is appropriate for a client who has suddenly come into a lot of money, such as from the sale of a home or an inheritance, which

he or she would like to apply toward retirement. A qualified SPDA should be seriously considered whenever an individual takes money from a pension plan, IRA, 401(k), or other tax-deferred savings program. This is because such a transfer allows the client to retain the benefits of tax deferral.

2. *Flexible-premium deferred annuities (FPDAs).* A nonqualified FPDA is a form of savings program for retirement. Qualified FPDAs are used for IRAs, 401(k)s, and Teacher's Retirement Plans. FPDAs allow contributions on a monthly basis.

3. *CD-type annuities.* These are similar to SPDAs, but they have guaranteed rates over selected periods of time and a fixed number of payments.

4. *Single-premium immediate annuities (SPIAs).* These are similar to SPDAs, but the benefit payments begin upon receipt of the single premium. They are also referred to as income annuities.

Note that with SPDAs and SPIAs, an investor might elect to do his or her primary saving for retirement in other forms and then, as the investor approaches or reaches retirement, move the money into an annuity program. The alternative is to place the contributions directly into the annuity over the working career (that is, buy an FPDA). With a deferred annuity, two periods are associated with the policy, the accumulation period and the distribution phase or payout period.

An annuity may be either fixed or variable. In the case of a CD-type annuity where the number of payments is certain, the rate of return is fixed and explicit. Such an annuity is usually quoted by its yield. For any other fixed annuity, the dollar payments are certain, but the number of payments is not because of the uncertainty as to how long the annuitant will live. In a variable annuity, the premiums are placed in equity investments and thus there is uncertainty as to both the number and amount of payments.

With a deferred annuity, the investor may choose one type of policy during the accumulation period, and then switch during the payout period. Many people typically choose a variable annuity during the former and switch to a fixed annuity during the latter. In addition, the premiums do not have to be placed into only one policy; investors are usually allowed to split their contract between two policies. An investor might put half of the premium into a fixed-rate policy and half into a variable-rate policy.

Annuities are not insured or otherwise guaranteed by a federal agency; if the insurance company paying the annuity fails, the annuitant could sustain a substantial loss. Such failures do happen. Thus the solvency of the insurance company matters in the selection of a policy. Insurance companies are rated as to financial solvency by several firms, although A.M. Best, an NRSRO who rates only insurance companies, is the best known in this industry.

Some annuity contract holders are protected against loss of deposit due to the failure of the issuing insurance company by state insurance guarantee funds. This raises the question of why all annuity contracts are not similarly covered. In fact, many large companies with solid A.M. Best ratings choose to do business in various states on a "nonadmitted" basis. Nonadmitted companies are not required to seek approval of their rates or coverage forms from that state's Department of Insurance. The underwriting, claims, and financial sections of the Department of Insurance do not routinely audit nonadmitted companies. Finally, should a nonadmitted company fail or go out of business, its policies are not guaranteed by that state's insurance guarantee fund. On the other hand, admitted companies are required to have all rates and forms approved by the Department of Insurance, they are routinely audited by various sections of the state insurance departments, and their policies are backed by the state insurance guarantee funds. The implication here is that if the best annuity contract is offered by an admitted company, then that is the best deal. However, if the best annuity is offered by a nonadmitted company, then the investor has to trade off its risk of default with the extra benefits.

REVIEW OF LEARNING OBJECTIVES

1. The key nonmarketable instruments available to investors include certificates of deposit and money market accounts at depository institutions, as well as Series EE and I savings bonds.

2. The money market consists of extremely safe, highly liquid investments. The key money market instruments are Treasury bills, commercial paper, negotiable CDs, bankers' acceptances, and Eurodollar deposits.

3. Instruments and securities related to the money market are the short-term municipals, federal funds, repurchase agreements, discount loans and money market mutual funds. Interest rates related to the money market include the prime rate and LIBOR.

4. Government and government-related bonds include Treasury notes and bonds, STRIPS, TIPS, agency bonds, and both types of municipal bonds (general obligation and revenue bonds).

5. Corporate bonds include debentures, mortgage bonds, and equipment trust certificates. There are a variety of ways in which bonds go out of existence. They can mature, be retired through a sinking fund, mature in a serial arrangement, be converted, or not mature at all. Bonds also come in many variations with the coupon payment, including zero-coupon, original issue discount, split coupon, and floating rate. Bonds ratings are extremely important to an investor.

6. There are two major chapters for corporate bankruptcy, Chapter VII and Chapter XI. In Chapter XI, the company is given protection from creditors while it reorganizes; in Chapter VII, the company is liquidated.

7. Mortgage-backed securities come as both pass-throughs and CMOs. In the former, all bonds have an equal claim on principal payments. In the latter, the securities are divided into tranches, with the first tranche getting all of the initial principal repayment.

8. The international bond market can be divided into three segments: domestic, foreign, and Euro. Bonds not denominated in dollars create exchange rate risk for the investor. Private placements offer higher yields but lack liquidity. Promissory notes are usually issued to an officer of the firm, or are held by the firm and issued by a key person. Insurance-based contracts include GICs and annuities.

MINICASE

Your client is 66 years old and preparing for retirement. All of his investments in both his pension plans and his directly owned portfolio are in stocks. He realizes he should make his portfolio a little more conservative, and should switch some of his stocks into bonds. This would be more appropriate in his tax-qualified accounts. Although you have not made a final recommendation as to what percentage of the portfolio should be in fixed income securities, you are also starting to think about which bonds would be most appropriate.

1. If the client wants 5 percent of the portfolio to be absolutely safe from any form of risk, have excellent liquidity, and yet still earn a little income, the best selection for this part of the portfolio would be

   (A) Treasury bills
   (B) Treasury notes
   (C) Treasury bonds
   (D) Series I bonds

2. If the client wants 5 percent of the portfolio to provide protection from the general rate of inflation, yet be absolutely safe in terms of default risk, the best selection for this part of the portfolio would be

    (A) Treasury STRIPS
    (B) Treasury bonds
    (C) Revenue bonds
    (D) TIPS

3. If the client wants 5 percent of the portfolio in a money market mutual fund to provide quick access to cash, which of the following securities is most likely to be in the mutual fund's portfolio?

    (A) Treasury bills
    (B) Treasury notes
    (C) Treasury bonds
    (D) Series I bonds

4. Which of the following bonds would make a really safe investment as part of a diversified bond portfolio?

    (A) Westphalia general obligation municipal bonds that mature in 10 years and have a 4 percent coupon rate. They are rated A+.
    (B) Income bonds issued by Solid Corporation. They mature in 25 years and have a 7 percent coupon rate.
    (C) The XYZ Corporation's bonds that mature in 20 years and have a 5 percent coupon rate. They are rated AAA.
    (D) Some "fallen angel" bonds issued by SafetyFirst Corporation that mature in 2 years and have a 6 percent coupon rate.

5. If the client wants 10 percent of his bond portfolio to have a known value in 10 years with a high degree of certainty, then this part of the portfolio should be made up of

    (A) income bonds
    (B) highly rated, 10-year zero-coupon bonds
    (C) revenue bonds
    (D) 30-year Treasury notes

CHAPTER REVIEW

Key Terms and Concepts

depository institution
bid price

ask price
bond equivalent yield (BEY)

negotiable CDs
banker's acceptance
two-name paper
Eurodollar deposits
prime rate
federal funds market
discount rate
Treasury notes
Treasury bonds
revenue bonds
general obligation bonds
indenture
flat
subordination

senior debt
zeros
call price
forced conversion
sinking fund
investment grade
junk bonds
technical default
Chapter XI
Chapter VII
absolute-priority-of- claims principle
qualified annuity
nonqualified annuity

Review Questions

Review questions are based on the learning objectives in this chapter. Thus, an [3] at the end of a question means that the question is based on learning objective 3. If there are multiple objectives, they are all listed.

1. How do the Series EE, HH, and I bonds differ from each other? [1]

2. a. Compute the bank discount yield for a T-bill priced at $9,732 that has 130 days to maturity. [2]
    b. Compute the price for a T-bill with a bank discount yield of .0484 that has 88 days to maturity. [2]
    c. Compute the bond equivalent yield for a T-bill with a price of $9,855 and 120 days to maturity. [2]

3. Name and describe the five money market instruments. [2]

4. For each of the following pairs of rates and securities, indicate which one would normally be lower in rate or yield and indicate why. [3]
    a. T-bill and commercial paper
    b. Prime rate and commercial paper
    c. Bankers' acceptance and negotiable CD
    d. Eurodollar deposit and negotiable CD
    e. Prime rate and negotiable CD

5. a. What are the two general categories of municipal bonds, and how do they differ from each other? [5]
   b. What is the distinguishing characteristic of each of the following types of bonds: [5]
      i. zero-coupon bond
      ii. original issue discount bond
      iii. split-coupon bond
      iv. income bond
      v. floating rate bond with a cap and a collar

6. If you decide that a client's risk tolerance allows him or her to hold bonds rated BB or better, then should you advise the client to invest in the BB bonds with the highest yields? [5]

7. Which of the following indenture provisions would make a bond more desirable, and which would make it less desirable, all other things being equal? [5]
   a. subordination
   b. call provision
   c. restrictions on some of the financial ratios
   d. me-first rule
   e. sinking fund

8. What is the difference between Chapter XI and Chapter VII of the Bankruptcy Code? [6]

9. What is the difference between a mortgage pass-through bond and a collateralized mortgage obligation? [7]

10. Name and describe the four types of annuities. [8]

Learning Objectives

An understanding of the material in this chapter should enable the student to

1. Compute the price of a bond, given the discount rate, and the yield to maturity, given the price.

2. Compute the current yield, the realized compound yield to maturity, the yield to call, and the realized rate of return for a bond.

3. Identify the factors that influence the price volatility of a bond.

4. Compute a bond's duration statistic.

5. Explain how to use the duration statistic as an index number, to estimate bond price changes, and as a tool for immunizing a portfolio.

6. Discuss bond swaps, ladders, bullets, and barbells as strategies for managing a bond portfolio.

7. Describe the term structure of interest rates, and explain the investment implications of the term structure.

8. Describe several factors that affect bond prices and yields.

In this chapter, we will focus on the mathematics of the pricing of bonds as well as ways of computing returns to bond investors. We will also look at strategies for managing bond investments that can reduce investors' risk exposure.

BOND PRICES AND YIELDS

Pricing a Bond

Computing a price for a bond is more complicated than doing a simple present value calculation because a bond provides periodic coupon (interest) payments and then the par or face value at maturity. For most bonds, the par or face value is almost always $1,000. Thus, we will use $1,000 as synonymous with par value in the following discussion. Simply put, the price of a bond is the present value of the coupon payments plus the present value of the par value that is received back at maturity. Although almost all bonds provide interest payments on a semiannual basis, let's start the discussion of bond pricing by assuming that coupon payments are on an annual basis. The computation of the price of the bond can then be represented by equation 9-1.

$$P_0 = \left[\sum_{t=1}^{T} \frac{C}{\left(1+Y\right)^t} \right] + \frac{PAR}{\left(1+Y\right)^T}$$

(Equation 9-1)

where P_0 =   price of the bond today

C =   Coupon payment

T =   maturity of the bond

Y =   appropriate discount rate

PAR =   par or face value of the bond

Most people now solve for bond prices on financial calculators. Therefore, rather than work through the steps of equation 9-1, let's look at the keystrokes for pricing a bond.

EXAMPLE

A $1,000 (par value) bond with a 2.5 percent coupon rate matures in 6 years. Thus, the bond will pay annual coupons of $25 (2.5% x $1,000). Let's assume that the appropriate discount rate is 4 percent. The price of the bond is calculated as follows:

$$P_0 = \sum_{t=1}^{T} \frac{coupon}{(1+Y)^t} + \frac{PAR}{(1+Y)^T}$$

The HP-10BII keystrokes are

SHIFT, C ALL

1000, FV

1000, x, .025, =, PMT

6, N

4, =, I/YR

PV (display: −921.37)

Now let's be more realistic and consider the process of pricing a bond when interest payments are made every 6 months. When this is the case, we must make these three adjustments before we calculate the price of the bond:

- Convert the coupon payment to a semiannual basis, which is done by dividing the coupon rate by 2.
- Adjust the number of time periods to reflect the fact that a time period is now 6 months, which is done by multiplying the maturity of the bond by 2.
- Adjust the discount rate to a semiannual basis, which is done by dividing the discount rate by 2.

In terms of the valuation formula, the price of a bond that pays interest semiannually is defined as

$$P_0 = \left[\sum_{t=1}^{2T} \frac{\left(\frac{C}{2} \right)}{\left(1 + \frac{Y}{2} \right)^t} \right] + \frac{PAR}{\left(1 + \frac{Y}{2} \right)^{2T}} \qquad \text{(Equation 9-2)}$$

Let's consider an example of pricing a bond when interest is paid *semiannually*.

EXAMPLE

A $1,000 (face value) bond with a 5 percent coupon rate will mature in 3 years. Therefore, the bond will pay semiannual coupons of $25 (1/2 x 5% x $1,000). The present value of this income flow at an 8 percent discount rate is

$$P_0 = \left[\sum_{t=1}^{2T} \frac{\left(\dfrac{C}{2} \right)}{\left(1 + \dfrac{Y}{2} \right)^t} \right] + \frac{PAR}{\left(1 + \dfrac{Y}{2} \right)^{2T}}$$

$$P = \left[\sum_{t=1}^{6} \frac{\dfrac{\$50}{2}}{\left(1 + \dfrac{.08}{2} \right)^t} \right] + \frac{\$1,000}{\left(1 + \dfrac{.08}{2} \right)^6}$$

$$= \$921.27$$

The HP-10BII keystrokes are

SHIFT, C ALL

1000, FV

1000, x, .05, ÷, 2, =, PMT

3, x, 2, =, N

8, ÷, 2, =, I/YR

PV (display: –921.37

Note that the prices of the bonds in these two examples are less than their $1,000 face values. Any bond with a coupon rate less than its discount rate will sell at a discount, meaning for less than $1,000. Any bond with a coupon rate exceeding the discount rate will sell at a premium, meaning for more than $1,000. Finally, any bond with a coupon rate equal to the discount rate will sell at par, meaning for $1,000.

Also note in these two examples that the prices of the two bonds are identical. That is, the price of a 2½% coupon, 6-year maturity bond at a 4% discount rate with annual payments is identical to that of a 5% coupon, 3-year bond at an 8% discount rate with semiannual payments. Conceptually, they are identical.

The relationships between a bond's price and its discount rate is curvilinear, as shown in the following figure. The price of the bond is on the vertical axis, and the discount rate is on the horizontal axis. When the discount rate equals the coupon rate on a bond, the price will always be par, regardless of any other features of the bond.

Figure 9-1
Bond Price as a Function of the Discount Rate

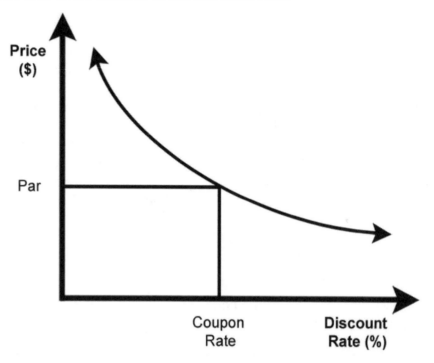

When people discuss and analyze bonds, there are several different rates and yields that may be relevant, depending on an investor's objectives and expectations. The simplest two are the coupon rate and the current yield. The single most important yield is the yield to maturity, followed by the yield to call. Other yields include the holding period yield (or return) and the realized compound yield to maturity. Let's examine each of these.

Coupon Rate and Current Yield

Suppose the XYZ bond pays an annual coupon of $40 and matures at a par value of $1,000 in 6 years. The bond is callable for $1,040 in 3 years. The current price of the bond is $950. (We will assume annual coupons to simplify the calculations and the discussion.)

coupon rate   The *coupon rate* for the bond equals the annual interest payment divided by the par value and is fixed for the life of the bond. Therefore, it is 4 percent for the XYZ bond, calculated as follows:

$$\text{Coupon rate} = \frac{\text{Annual interest payment}}{\text{Par value}} = \frac{\$40}{\$1,000} = 4\% \qquad \text{(Equation 9-3)}$$

current yield   The coupon rate is a descriptive statistic only and has no real relevance for a financial planner. Although the income provided by a bond can be important, knowing the income paid by a bond without knowing the price at which the bond trades is meaningless. This leads us to a more relevant yield: the current yield. The *current yield* is the annual interest divided by the current price. Although the coupon is fixed, the price varies; thus, the current yield will vary during the bond's life. For the XYZ bond, the current yield is 4.21 percent, determined as follows:

$$\text{Current yield} = \frac{\text{Annual interest payment}}{\text{Market price}} = \frac{\$40}{\$950} = 4.21\% \qquad \text{(Equation 9-4)}$$

If a financial planner is creating a bond portfolio for a client when income is important, a critical component is the current yield.

EXAMPLE

George Jones has $2 million in assets and is 73 years old. After extensive discussions with George, you decide to put $1.5 million in bonds and $.5 million in stocks. George would like to generate $100,000 in current income from his investments without any liquidations of principal. You believe that the average dividend yield on his stock holdings will be 1 percent, which, based on $.5 million invested, would be $5,000. What is the current yield you must obtain on the bond portfolio?

If George's stocks generate $5,000 in income, and he needs $100,000 total income, then his bonds must provide current income of $95,000. Based on an investment of $1.5 million, the current yield for coupon rate current yield the portfolio needs to be .0633 or 6.33 percent ($95,000/$1,500,000). If such a holding is not sufficiently safe, then George must adjust his income needs, or an alternative investment plan must be constructed.

Yield to Maturity

promised yield   Yield to maturity (YTM), or *promised yield*, is a much more difficult calculation. It is an internal rate of return calculation. Yield to maturity is the rate that would discount all the future cash flows (coupons and par value) so that their present value equals the market price.

In mathematical terms, it is also stated with equation 9-1. The difference is that in this case the price of the bond (P_0) is given, and we must solve for the discount rate (Y), which we now refer to as the yield to maturity.

$$P_0 = \sum_{t=1}^{T} \frac{C}{(1+Y)^t} + \frac{PAR}{(1+Y)^T}$$

(equation 9-1 repeated)

where Y = yield to maturity

Continuing our example of the XYZ bond that pays $40 interest annually, has a maturity of 6 years, and a current price of $950, the yield to maturity is the discount rate Y that makes the following equation valid:

$$950 = \frac{40}{(1+Y)} + \frac{40}{(1+Y)^2} + \frac{40}{(1+Y)^3} + \frac{40}{(1+Y)^4} + \frac{40}{(1+Y)^5} + \frac{40}{(1+Y)^6} + \frac{1000}{(1+Y)^6}$$

Unfortunately, we cannot solve this equation by simply putting Y on one side and everything else on the other. Although computing yield to maturity requires many iterations, financial calculators make it easy to determine the correct answer, which in this case is 4.98 percent.

The HP-10BII keystrokes are

SHIFT, C ALL

950, +/–, PV

40, PMT

1000, FV

6, N

I/YR (display: 4.98)

To understand why the YTM is also called the promised yield, as well as what is meant by an internal rate of return number, consider the scenario of someone who deposits $950 today into an account that pays an interest rate of 4.98 percent. Let's suppose that this person wants to replicate the cash flows from the bond. To do so, he or she would draw out $40 at the end of each year also for 6 years, and then at the end of the sixth year also draw out $1,000 (the bond's par value). As shown in the following table, this person would have zeroed out the account with the last withdrawal.

Note in the table that this person starts with $950 at time zero. During the first year, he or she accrues $47.35 in interest, which raises the balance to $997.35. The person then withdraws $40 to match the interest payment on the bond. This withdrawal reduces the end-of-year balance to $957.35, which becomes the beginning-of-year balance for the second year. After the sixth and last withdrawal, there is nothing left in the account. To emphasize the above point, one interpretation of a yield to maturity (or any internal rate of return calculation) is that it is the interest rate at which we could invest the price of, or present value of, the cash flows from the asset and exactly reproduce the cash payments from that asset, with nothing left over.

					Balance after With-
Time Period (1)	Begin- ning-of- Period Balance (2)	Interest Accrued for Period (3)=(2) × .0498	Balance before With- drawal (4)=(2)+(3)	With- drawal (5)	drawal (6)=(4) − (5)
0					$950.00
1	$950.00	$47.35	$ 997.35	$ 40.00	957.35
2	957.35	47.72	1,005.07	40.00	965.07
3	965.07	48.11	1,013.18	40.00	973.18
4	973.18	48.51	1,021.69	40.00	981.69
5	981.69	48.93	1,030.62	40.00	990.62
6	990.62	49.38	1,040.00	1,040.00	0.00

Table 9-1 Internal Rate of Return Proof

Finally, note that if we want to price the bond used in this example, and we are given a discount rate of 4.98, then the price would be almost exactly $950. The HP-10BII keystrokes are

SHIFT, C ALL

1000, FV

1000, x, .04, =, PMT

6, N

4.98, I/YR

PV (display: –950.23)

The price is not $950.00 exactly, because the yield to maturity is actually 4.9846 and not 4.98.

Simply stated, given the price of a bond, we can compute its yield to maturity. Given a bond's yield to maturity, we can compute its price. For this reason, people often use the term yield to maturity as the name for the discount rate to use when solving for a bond's price. More important, *price and yield to maturity are interchangeable terms in discussions of bond values.*

Another important aspect of this relationship is that because price and yield to maturity automatically define each other, a change in one automatically defines a change in the other. Hence, it would be silly to say that bond prices fell because interest rates rose; rising interest rates are defined by falling bond prices.

To solve for the YTM on a bond that pays interest semiannually requires the same sort of adjustments, except in reverse, as we made when we discussed how to compute the price of a bond that pays interest semiannually. The steps are as follows:

- Determine the semiannual payment by dividing the annual payment by 2.
- Compute the effective number of periods by multiplying the term to maturity by 2.
- After solving for the YTM, multiply the answer by 2 because the calculator solution is the YTM per 6-month period.

EXAMPLE

The YTM of a bond with a 4 percent coupon rate that pays interest semiannually, matures in 6 years, has a par value of $1,000, and trades for $950 is calculated as follows:

First, compute the semiannual coupon payment to be $20, then compute the number of time periods to be 12, and then enter the FV and PV of the bond as $1,000 and –$950. After solving for the YTM (I/YR), multiply the answer by 2. In this case, the YTM is 4.9841 percent.

The HP-10bII keystrokes are

> SHIFT, C ALL
>
> 1000, x, .04, ÷, 2, =, PMT
>
> 6, x, 2, =, N
>
> 1000, FV
>
> 950, +/, PV
>
> I/YR (display: 2.49), x, 2, = (display: 4.97)

The reason that the last calculation of 2.49 times 2 is 4.97 and not 4.98 is that the 2.49 number has been rounded up. The correct answer is slightly less than 2.49. More precisely, it is 2.4871. When this value is doubled, it becomes 4.9741, which rounds to 4.97.

Relationship between Coupon Rate, Current Yield, and Yield to Maturity

Note that in our example of the XYZ bond, the coupon rate of 4 percent is less than the current yield of 4.21 percent, and both are less than the yield-to-maturity of 4.98 percent. In retrospect, this result was to be expected because the yield to maturity (promised yield) is greater than the coupon rate. When this happens, the bond must trade at a discount to provide the incremental return in the form of price appreciation expected by an investor. Because the current yield is the coupon divided by the price, and the coupon rate is the coupon divided by par, we can make the following statement:

For discount bonds, the yield to maturity will always be greater than the current yield, which in turn will always be greater than the coupon rate.

The reverse will hold for bonds trading at a premium.

The yield to maturity is less than the current yield for premium bonds because yield to maturity considers both the coupon payment and the decline in the price of the bond between now and maturity, at which time the price will equal par. Hence, we can make the following statement:

For premium bonds, the yield to maturity will always be less than the current yield, which in turn will always be less than the coupon rate.

Finally, if a bond trades exactly at par the yield to maturity, the coupon rate and the current yield will be identical. These relationship are shown graphically in the following figure.

Figure 9-2
Relationship between Yield to Maturity, Current Yield, and Coupon Rate

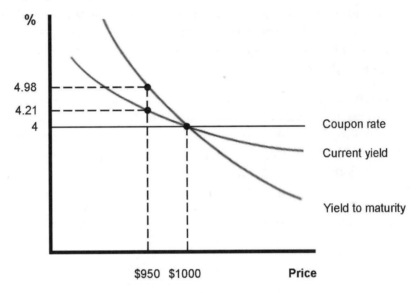

NOTE: The coupon rate is a flat line, but the other two are convex curves.
All these intersect at the single point noted above.

Realized Compound Yield to Maturity

One aspect of the yield to maturity is that it incorporates no assumptions about coupon payments.[76] In general, we can make two assumptions about coupon payments. The first is that they are spent by the investor at the time of receipt. If this is the case, then the YTM is a sufficient calculation of the investor's expected rate of return on the bond.

The alternative is to assume that the coupons are reinvested at a specific rate of return. This reinvestment rate may or may not be the same as the yield to maturity. When an explicit assumption is made about the rate of return on reinvested coupon payments, then the relevant rate of return becomes the

---

76. Some investments textbooks, including earlier editions of this book, make the erroneous statement that the YTM formula assumes that the coupon payments are reinvested at the YTM rate. An examination of the mathematical notation for the YTM clearly shows this not to be the case.

realized compound yield to maturity (RCYTM). The RCYTM is essentially a weighted average of the return on the bond itself and the return on the reinvested coupon payments.

Solving for the RCYTM is a three-step process. The first step is to solve for the future value of what the reinvested coupon payments will be worth when the bond matures. The second step is to add this to the bond's maturity value. The third step is to solve for the internal rate of return that equates the present value of the combined ending values of the bond and the reinvested coupons to today's price of the bond.

Let's continue the previous example of the XYZ bond and assume, for illustrative purposes, that the cash flows (that is, the coupon payments) are reinvested at the yield to maturity (4.9846 percent) until the maturity date (end of year 6). If this is the case, then the terminal value of this investment is $1,271.96, computed as follows:

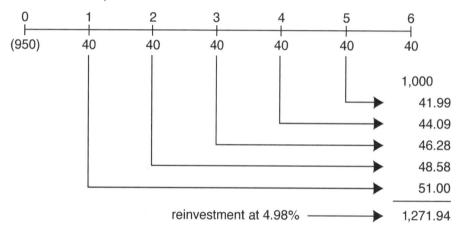

Now imagine a pure discount instrument with a price identical to that of the bond ($950) and a maturity value of $1,271.96—the bond's terminal value with the reinvestment assumptions.

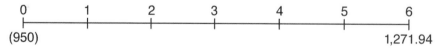

If we calculate the internal rate of return for this synthetic instrument, we find that it is identical to the bond's yield to maturity. The HP-10BII keystrokes are

SHIFT, C ALL

950, +/–, PV

1271.96, FV

6, N

I/YR (display: 4.98)

Recall from earlier discussions that interest rate risk includes price risk and reinvestment rate risk. For example, if the investor buys the bond at $950 and then interest rates fall instantaneously to 4.50 percent, the bondholder would only be able to reinvest the coupon payment at this new lower yield. The ending value of the combined bond and reinvested coupons is then $1268.68.

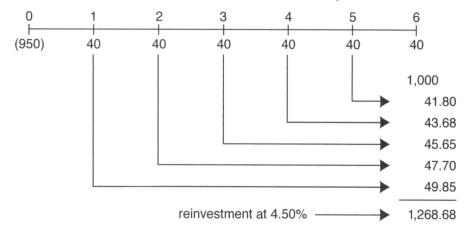

Again, if there were a synthetic, pure discount instrument paying $1,268.68 in 6 years and costing $950 today, the yield to maturity would equal 4.94 percent. This decline in RCYTM by 4 basis points is the consequence of reinvestment risk.

Yield to Call

Yield to call computations are identical to yield to maturity calculations except the call price is substituted for the par value and T equals the number of periods until the earliest call date. Note that because the yield to call is the discount rate that equates the present value of the call price and the coupon payments until the bond is called to today's price, it too is an internal rate of return calculation. The call price equals par plus some type of call premium. Continuing the previous example, the following timeline shows the cash flows for a call price of $1,040 and a period to first call of 3 years.

$$P_0 = \sum_{t=1}^{T_c} \frac{C}{\left(1 + Y_c\right)^t} + \frac{\text{call price}}{\left(1 + Y_c\right)^{T_c}}$$

$$950 = \frac{40}{\left(1 + Y_c\right)} + \frac{40}{\left(1 + Y_c\right)^2} + \frac{40}{\left(1 + Y_c\right)^3} + \frac{1040}{\left(1 + Y_c\right)^3}$$

where T_c = time to earliest call

Y_c = yield to first call

Again, computing the answer of 7.15 percent is made simple with a financial calculator (remember, we are assuming annual payments for simplicity). The HP-10BII keystrokes are

SHIFT, C ALL

950, +/–, PV

40, PMT

1040, FV

3, N

I/YR (display: 7.1529)

EXAMPLE

What is the yield to call on a bond with a maturity of 20 years, that is callable in 5 years at $1,050, has a coupon rate of 4 percent paid semiannually, and currently trades at $1,100?

Compute the semiannual payment to be $20, and the number of time periods to be 10 (10 half-years), and enter the FV and PV of the bond as $1,050 and $1,100. Then solve for the YTM (I/YR), and multiply the answer by 2 to annualize it. In this case, the answer is 2.78 percent.

The HP-10BII keystrokes are

SHIFT, C ALL

1000, x, .04, ÷, 2, =, PMT

5, x, 2, =, N

1050, FV

1100, +/–, PV

I/YR (display: 1.39), x, 2, = (display: 2.78)

Realized Returns

We can use the same approach to calculate an investor's realized rate of return when a bond is sold prior to maturity. For example, suppose our $950 bond investment is sold 2 years later for $980, and the sale is immediately after the (annual) coupon payment. In this case, the internal rate of return is 5.75. We can, again, show the cash flows on a timeline.

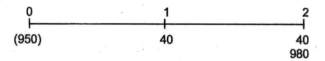

The realized rate of return is the internal rate of return that makes the following equation true:

$$Price = \sum_{t=1}^{T_H} \frac{coupon}{(1 + Y_H)^t} + \frac{selling\,price}{(1 + Y_H)^{T_H}}$$

$$950 = \frac{40}{(1 + Y_H)} + \frac{40}{(1 + Y_H)^2} + \frac{980}{(1 + Y_H)^2}$$

where T_H = holding period

Y_H = realized rate of return

The HP-10BII keystrokes are

SHIFT, C ALL

950, +/–, PV

40, PMT

980, FV

2, N

I/YR (display: 5.75)

BOND PRICE VOLATILITY

maturity effect

coupon effect

There are several theorems about bond pricing with which every financial planner should be familiar. The three most fundamental ones are as follows

- Theorem 1: Bond prices and interest rates are inversely related.
- Theorem 2: The longer a bond's term to maturity, the greater the percentage change in its price for a given change in interest rates. (The is known as the *maturity effect*.)
- Theorem 3: The lower a bond's coupon rate, the greater the percentage change in its price for a given change in interest rates. (This is known as the *coupon effect*.)

The first theorem follows from the mathematical formulation of a bond's price presented in equation 9–1. The second and third theorems are illustrated with the following two examples.

EXAMPLE 1

The Short Circuit Corp. has two bonds outstanding: A and B. Both have a 5 percent coupon rate (with annual payments) and a 5 percent yield to maturity, but Bond A has a 5-year maturity and Bond B has a 20-year maturity. What is the percentage change in each bond's price if interest rates change from 5 percent to 6 percent?

Because the coupon rate matches the YTM, both bonds initially trade at par. At a 6 percent YTM, the price of Bond A is $957.88 and the price of Bond B is $885.30. Thus, the percentage changes in the two bond prices are –4.21 percent ([$957.88 – $1,000]/$1,000) and –11.47 percent. The bond with the longer maturity, all other things being equal, has the greater percentage price change.

EXAMPLE 2

The Live Wire Corp. has two bonds outstanding: A and B. Bond A was issued many years ago, has 10 years to maturity, and has a 3 percent coupon rate. Bond B was just issued, has 10 years to maturity, and has a 10 percent coupon rate. The YTM on both bonds is 5 percent. What is the percentage change in each bond's price if interest rates change from 5 percent to 6 percent?

   The initial prices of the two bonds are $845.57 for Bond A and $1,386.09 for Bond B. After the change in interest rates, the prices are $779.20 for Bond A and $1,294.40 for Bond B. The percentage price changes are –7.85 percent for Bond A ([$779.20 – $845.57]/ $845.57) and –6.62 percent for Bond B. The bond with the lower coupon rate has the greater percentage price change, if all other things are equal.

Note in example 2 above that although Bond A has the greater percentage change, Bond B has the greater change in nominal value. Bond A declines in price by $66.37, and Bond B's price decline is $91.69.

A less common, but still important, bond theorem is as follows:

yield-to-maturity effect

•   Theorem 4: For a given change in interest rates, bonds with lower YTMs have greater percentage price changes than bonds with higher YTMs, all other things being equal. (This is known as the *yield-to-maturity effect*.)

Again, let's demonstrate this with an example.

EXAMPLE

   Bonds A and B each have a 5 percent coupon rate and 20 years to maturity. However, Bond A has a 3 percent YTM and Bond B has an 8 percent YTM. What is the percentage change in each bond's price if the YTMs fall by 1 percent (that is, from 3 to 2 percent for Bond A and 8 to 7 percent for Bond B)? The initial prices of the two bonds are $1,297.55 for Bond A and $705.46 for Bond B. If each YTM drops by 1 percent in absolute terms, the new prices will be $1,490.54 for Bond A and $788.12 for Bond B. The percentage changes are +14.87 percent for Bond A and +11.72 percent for Bond B. The bond with the lower YTM has the greater percent price change.

It is actually easy to visualize theorem 4 by looking at *Figure 9-1*, which showed the prices of a bond as a function of the discount rate. When the discount rate is "large," the curve is relatively flat, meaning changes in the discount rate produce small changes in a bond's price. When the discount rate is "small," the curve is relatively steep, and small changes in the discount rate produce much larger changes in a bond's price.

Financial Planning Issue
This last theorem has two serious implications for the financial planner. First, it means that when market interest rates are low, not only will the client have less income from the portfolio, but the prices of the client's bonds will also be more volatile in percentage terms.
The second implication is that because safer bonds have lower yields to maturity than riskier bonds, it is actually the safer bonds which will have the greater percentage price change when interest rates change.

Based on theorems 2, 3, and 4, we can now pose a simple question: Which of the following three bonds will have the greatest price volatility?

> Bond X: 25 years to maturity, 10% coupon rate, 6% YTM
>
> Bond Y: 10 years to maturity, 2% coupon rate, 6% YTM
>
> Bond Z: 17.5 years to maturity, 6% coupon rate, 4% YTM

Theorem 2 indicates that Bond X will have the greatest price volatility because it has the longest maturity. Theorem 3 indicates that Bond Y will have the greatest price volatility because it has the lowest coupon rate. Theorem 4 indicates that Bond Z will have the greatest price volatility because it has the lowest YTM. In other words, although we have identified three excellent theorems about bond price volatility, they cannot really help us answer the simple question of which of the three bonds will have the greatest percentage change in price for a given change in YTM!

DURATION

Fortunately, there is a statistic for bonds that can be computed, which will answer the question of which of the three bonds, X, Y, or Z, will have the greatest percentage price change for a given change in interest rates. This statistic is known as the bond's duration.

The Duration Statistic

The traditional formula for calculating duration (and one of the ones provided on the formula sheet for the CFP® certification examination) is the following[77]:

$$D = \frac{\sum_{t=1}^{T} \frac{t \times CF_t}{(1+Y)^T}}{\sum_{t=1}^{T} \frac{CF_t}{(1+Y)^T}} \qquad \text{(Equation 9-5)}$$

where CF_t = the cash flow in period t (coupon, principal, or both)
t = the time period when the cash flow is to be received
Y = yield to maturity (discount rate)
T = the term to maturity of the bond

Note that in the above formula, and the one to follow, the term CF_t may stand for a coupon payment, principal payment, or both.

The above formula is more complex than it needs to be. This is because the denominator is the definition for the price of a bond (equation 9-1). Thus, equation 9-5 can be written more simply as

$$D = \frac{\sum_{t=1}^{T} \frac{t \times CF_t}{(1+Y)^t}}{P_0} \qquad \text{(Equation 9-5a)}$$

Macaulay's duration
The value produced by this formula is known as *Macaulay's duration*, in honor of Frederick Macaulay, who first published and promoted this concept.[78] The weight of each promised payment's time to receipt is based on its present value relative to the sum of the present values of the entire payment stream (the bond's intrinsic value). That is, each weight equals the present value of that payment divided by the bond's market price.

---

77. On the CFP Examination Formula Sheet, the bond's maturity is represented by the letter n in this formula, rather than T, and the yield to maturity is represented by the letter i, rather than Y.

78. Frederick Macaulay, *Some Theoretical Problems Suggested by the Movements of Interest Rates, Bond Yields, and Stock Prices in the United States Since 1856* (New York: National Bureau of Economic Research, 1938).

Table 9-2 Durations of Two Bonds Maturing in 7 Years (Assume Annual Interest Payments)

Bond A

(1) Year(s) Until Receipt t Where N = 7	(2) Cash Flow	(3) Present Value at 8%	(4) Year(s) x Present Value [Column (1) x Column (3)]
1	$ 60	$ 55.56	$ 55.56
2	60	51.44	102.88
3	60	47.63	142.89
4	60	44.10	176.40
5	60	40.83	204.15
6	60	37.81	226.86
7	1,060	618.50	4,329.50
Total	$1,420	$895.87	$5,238.24

Duration for Bond A is equal to $5,238.24/$895.87 = 5.85 years

Bond B

(1) Year(s) Until Receipt t Where N = 7	(2) Cash Flow	(3) Present Value at 8%	(4) Year(s) x Present Value [Column (1) x Column (3)]
1	$ 100	$ 92.59	$ 92.59
2	100	85.73	171.46
3	100	79.38	238.14
4	100	73.50	294.00
5	100	68.06	340.30
6	100	63.02	378.12
7	1,100	641.84	4,492.88
Total	$1,700	$1,104.12	$6,007.49

Duration for Bond B is equal to $6,007.49/$1,104.12 = 5.44 years

Consider the durations of two bonds maturing in 7 years. Bond A has a 6 percent coupon, and bond B has a 10 percent coupon; both pay interest on an annual basis. The following table shows the results of computing the durations of both bonds when the yields to maturity on both are 8 percent. Column (1) lists the time period (t) in which a cash flow (that is, interest payment or principal) will be received, and column (2) shows the cash flow (that is, CF_t). Column (3) provides the present value of the cash flow, discounted at the YTM. Note that the total for the third column is the price of the bond. Finally, column (4) is the product of the time until a cash flow is received and its present value (that is, the product of columns (1) and (3)). The duration of the bond is computed by dividing the sum of column (4) by the price of the bond. In this example, the duration for Bond A is 5.85 years, and the duration for Bond B is 5.44 years.

The calculation of the duration statistic can, of course, be done on the calculator, although the process is cumbersome, especially for long periods. To compute the duration for Bond A using the calculator, one first must compute the price of the bond, which is $895.87. Then, the following keystrokes can be used:

> SHIFT, C ALL
>
> 60, FV, 8, I/YR, 1, N, PV, M+
>
> 2, N, PV, x, 2, =, M+
>
> 3, N, PV, x, 3, =, M+
>
> 4, N, PV, x, 4, =, M+
>
> 5, N, PV, x, 5, =, M+
>
> 6, N, PV, x, 6, =, M+
>
> 1060, FV, 7, N, PV, x, 7, =, M+
>
> RM, +/–, ÷, 895.87, = (display: 5.85)

As discussed earlier, most bonds pay interest semiannually rather than annually. If we assumed the above bonds paid interest semiannually, then the table to compute the duration statistics would have to be altered in two ways. First, each semiannual payment would be listed on a separate line. The time until receipt for the first payment would be .5 years. The time column (column 1) would then proceed in increments of .5 years. Second, the discount rate would have to be halved to reflect the semiannual timing of the cash flows. Once these two adjustments are made, one can then proceed to compute the duration statistic.

The "Shortcut" Formula

Fortunately, a "shortcut" formula for computing the duration statistic has been developed. This "shortcut" formula is also on the CFP® Examination Formula Sheet. This formula is

$$D = \frac{1+Y}{Y} - \frac{(1+Y)+T(C-Y)}{C[(1+Y)^T - 1]+Y}$$

(Equation 9-6)

where C =   coupon rate (rather than actual dollars)

Y =   yield to maturity

T =   term to maturity

Students planning to sit for the CFP Exam should be well versed in using this shortcut formula.

Using this alternative formula, the duration statistics for Bonds A and B can be computed as

$$D_A = \frac{1+.08}{.08} - \frac{(1+.08)+7(.06-.08)}{.06[(1+.08)^7 - 1]+.08}$$
$$= 5.85$$
$$D_B = \frac{1+.08}{.08} - \frac{(1+.08)+7(.10-.08)}{.10[(1+.08)^7 - 1]+.08}$$
$$= 5.44$$

The "shortcut" formula is valid only when interest payments are made annually. If payments are made semiannually, then the formula must be adjusted. The modified formula is as follows:

D = [(1 + Y/2)/Y] – [(1+Y/2) + T(C – Y)] / [C{(1 + Y/2)^{2T} – 1} + Y]

EXAMPLE

A bond has a yield to maturity of 7 percent and a coupon rate of 6 percent. It matures in 12 years and pays interest on a semiannual basis. The duration statistic would be computed as

Duration = [(1 + .07/2)/.07] – [(1+.07/2) + 12(.06 – .07)] / [.06{(1 + .07/2)^{24} – 1} + .07]

= 8.56

NOTE: If one had used the formula for the same bond but with annual interest payments, the duration statistic would have been 8.74.

Duration as an Index Number

For anyone who has never heard of the term duration until now, the first question that arises is, what does this number mean? There are several interpretations and uses for the duration number, but the simplest one is that it is an index number. The larger the duration statistic, the greater the percentage change in a bond's price for a given change in interest rates. In our previous example, we can say that the price of Bond A will be more volatile to a change in market interest rates than the price of Bond B because it has a larger duration statistic. We can also say that the difference in the price volatility will not be great because the duration statistics are relatively close. In this particular example, we knew that the duration statistic for Bond A would be the larger of the two because the two bonds have the same term to maturity and the same yield to maturity, but different coupon rates, so all of the conditions of theorem 3 are met.

There is an alternative way to think about the duration statistic. It is that a bond's price volatility will be the same as that of a zero-coupon bond whose maturity equals that duration. A zero-coupon bond will always have a duration equal to its remaining life (T) because it has only one payment, the principal. In other words, because $P_0 = PAR/(1 + Y)^T$ for a zero-coupon bond, equation 9–4a reduces to

$$D = \frac{T \times [PAR/(1+Y)^T]}{P_0} = T \times \frac{P_0}{P_0} = T \times 1 = T$$

This same result can be obtained from the simplification formula if we substitute the value of zero for C, as follows:

$$D = \frac{1+Y}{Y} - \frac{(1+Y)+T(C-Y)}{C[(1+Y)^T - 1]+Y} =$$

$$= \frac{1+Y}{Y} - \frac{(1+Y)+T(-Y)}{Y} = \frac{1+Y}{Y} - \frac{1+Y}{Y} + \frac{TY}{Y} = T$$

Because zero-coupon bonds have no coupons, the only volatility theorem that applies is the maturity effect. Hence, the maturity is an immediate index of bond price volatility for all zero-coupon bonds. In our above example, we can say that Bond A would have the identical duration to a zero-coupon bond whose term to maturity is 5.85 years.

The duration of a bond that has coupons will always be less than its remaining life T because in equation 9-5 the largest value that t can have is T, and since each value of t is multiplied by a weight equal to the present value of the coupon payment divided by the price of the bond, $PV\ (CF_t)/P_0$ (as is done in Table 9–2, column 3), it follows that the duration statistic must be less than the bond's maturity. Another way to see this is in the following figure, which shows the relationship between the duration statistic and 10-year bonds of various coupon rates whose yield-to-maturity is 8 percent. The highest value is 10.0 when the coupon rate is zero, and this decreases at a decreasing rate to 6.74 when the coupon rate is 12 percent.

Figure 9-3
Relationship Between Duration Statistic and Coupon Rate for a 10- Year Bond Whose Yield to Maturity Is 8 Percent

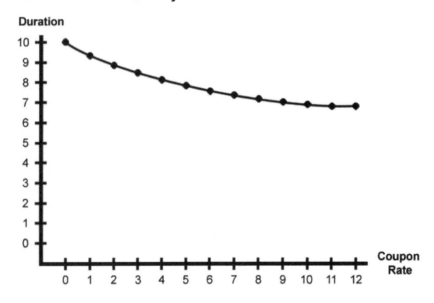

Most of the time, there is a direct relationship between a bond's maturity and its duration statistic. However, this is not a universally true statement because there are some exceptions. Oddly enough, some bonds with low coupon rates, extremely long terms to maturity, and high yields to maturity may actually increase in price volatility with the passage of time. However, these are really obscure exceptions to the concept that a bond's duration statistic is directly related to its term to maturity.

EXAMPLE

Consider two bonds, C and D, both of which have coupon rates of 2 percent, yields to maturity of 10 percent, and terms to maturity of 40 and 50 years. Their duration statistics are

C: $(1+.10)/.10 - [(1+.10)+40(.02-.10)]/[.02(1+.10)^{40}-1]+.10 = 13.13$

and

D: $(1+.10)/.10 - [(1+.10)+50(.02-.10)]/[.02(1+.10)^{50}-1]+.10 = 12.19$

The bond with the longer term to maturity has the lower duration (and therefore less price volatility), despite the fact that all other things are equal. This means that there are some exceptions to theorem 2 (the one on the maturity effect) stated above. Nonetheless, these exceptions are so obscure that a planner will likely never encounter them in his or her career.

Earlier in this section, we considered three bonds—X, Y, and Z—and discussed which would have the greatest price volatility. The answer was complicated by the fact that none of our three basic theorems perfectly applied. The duration statistics for the three bonds are 12.37, 8.96, and 11.99. So the answer is that Bond X would have the greatest price volatility because it has the largest duration, although Bond Z is a close second.

Major Characteristics of Duration

- The duration of a zero-coupon bond is equal to its term to maturity.
- The duration of a coupon bond is always less than its term to maturity.
- There is usually a direct relationship between maturity and duration.
- There is an inverse relationship between coupon rate and duration.
- There is an inverse relationship between yield to maturity and duration.

Estimating a Bond's Price Volatility

modified duration   A second use of the duration statistic is to actually estimate the percentage change in a bond's price. To do this calculation, we must first compute the modified duration. To find a bond's *modified duration*, calculate its duration using equation 9–5 or 9–6, and adjust it for the bond's yield to maturity as follows:

$$D^* = \frac{D}{1+Y} \qquad \text{(Equation 9-7)}$$

where D^* = the bond's modified duration

Having determined a bond's modified duration, it is easy to estimate that bond's percentage price change resulting from a small change in the market interest rate. The bond's modified duration is first multiplied by –1 (to reflect the inverse relationship between bond prices and interest rates) and then by the percentage change in market interest rates. In equation form, this is expressed as follows:

$$\frac{\Delta P}{P} \approx -D \times \left[\frac{\Delta(1+Y)}{1+Y} \right]$$
$$\approx -D^* \times [\Delta(1+Y)] \qquad \text{(Equation 9-8)}$$
$$\approx -D^* \times \Delta Y$$

where P = price of the bond

ΔP = change in the price of the bond

$\Delta(1 + Y)$ = change in bond's yield to maturity

Y = yield to maturity

This formula is also on the formula sheet of the CFP® certification exam.

EXAMPLE

Continuing the earlier example with bonds A and B, Bond A's modified duration would be

$$D^* = \frac{5.85 \text{ years}}{1 + .08} = 5.42 \text{ years}$$

where 5.85 years is Bond A's Macaulay's duration, calculated using a yield to maturity of 8 percent.

Assuming the market interest rate for bonds of comparable risk increases from 8 to 8.5 percent, the price of Bond A would decrease by approximately 2.71 percent. This is computed as follows:

Percent change in bond price $\approx$ –5.42 x 0.5% = –2.71%

The estimated dollar change in the price of the bond can then be computed by multiplying this percentage change by the current price. This is computed as follows:

$$\text{Dollar change in price} \approx -2.71\% \times \$895.87$$

$$\approx -\$24.28$$

$$\text{New bond price} = \$895.87 - \$24.28 = \$871.59$$

If we were to use equation 9-1 to compute directly the new bond price, it is $872.04. Had the magnitude of the change in the discount rate been smaller, the approximation would have been even more accurate.

Convexity

convex   Note in this example that the modified duration formula overestimates the dollar decline in the price of the bond. Had we considered a decrease in interest rates, the modified duration formula would have underestimated the increase in the bond's price. It is important to understand why this happens. The answer can be seen in the following figure, which shows the price of a bond on the vertical axis and the yield to maturity on the horizontal axis. The curved line defines the price of the bond for any given yield to maturity (similar to *Figure 9-1*). Note that this curve is convex. *Convex* means that the curvature of the relationship is away from the horizontal axis.

The other line in the figure is a straight-line tangent to the curved line at the point where the yield to maturity equals 8 percent and the price of the bond is $895.87. The modified duration is the slope of this tangent line. The modified duration formula is a linear approximation of the change in the bond's price, and it is not exact because the true relationship is curvilinear. It is for this reason that all discussions of the use of the modified duration approximation formula emphasize that it works best when the change in yield to maturity is small. "Small" in this case actually means a few basis points. The larger the change in yield to maturity, the greater is the error in the approximation. This is noted by the vertical difference between the approximation line and the curved line in *Figure 9-4*.

Figure 9-4
Why Modified Duration Formula Is an Approximation

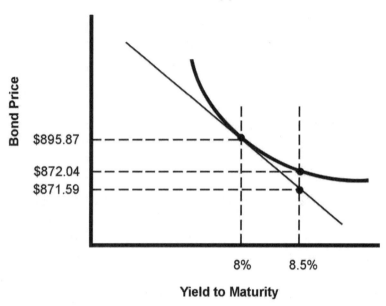

Duration of a Portfolio

From the calculation of the duration of individual bonds, it is a simple matter to calculate the duration of a whole portfolio of bonds. The duration of a bond portfolio is equal to the weighted average of the durations of the individual bonds in the portfolio where the weights are based on market values of the bonds relative to the market value of the portfolio.

EXAMPLE

If a two-security portfolio has one-fourth of its funds invested in Bond A with a duration of 5.85 years and three-fourths in Bond B with a duration of 5.44 years, then the portfolio itself has a duration of 5.54 years [D_p = (1/4 x 5.85) + (3/4 x 5.44) = 1.46 + 4.08 = 5.54 years, where D_p is the duration of the portfolio].

Immunization of a Portfolio

reinvestment rate risk

price risk

As we have mentioned previously, when interest rates change in either direction, there is always both good news and bad news for a bond investor. When interest rates rise, the coupon payments can be reinvested at higher rates (which is the good news), but the price of the bond falls (which is the bad news). When interest rates fall, reinvested coupons will receive lower rates of return, but the price of the bond will rise. The effect of the interest rate change on the yield of reinvested coupon payments is known as *reinvestment rate risk* and this was demonstrated as part of the RCYTM discussion. The effect of this interest rate change on the price of the bond is known as *price risk*.

immunization   The opposite effects of reinvestment rate risk and price risk raise an interesting question: Is there a way to use these opposite effects so that they can be offsetting? The answer turns out to be yes, and the concept is referred to as *immunization*. A portfolio is immunized when the expected benefits from one of these changes exactly offset the losses from the other change.

Components of Interest Rate Risk

- Price risk: The risk of an existing bond's price changing when market interest rates change. If rates increase, the bond's price decreases, and if rates decrease, the bond's price increases.

- Reinvestment rate risk: The risk associated with reinvesting coupon payments as market interest rates change. If rates increase, the coupons are reinvested at higher rates than previously expected, and if rates decrease, the coupons are reinvested at lower rates than previously expected.

An immunization strategy is built on the assumption that an investor has a desired holding period and acquires a bond portfolio in which the portfolio's duration equals the investor's desired holding period. Then, interest rates make a one-time change during the holding period, and that change occurs before the first coupon payment. Interest rates do not change again during the holding period. Under this scenario, an investor holding an immunized portfolio will earn a rate of return exactly equal to the yield to maturity on his or her portfolio at the time the strategy was set up. Mathematical examples of this point are provided in the appendix to this chapter.

Although the theory of an immunization strategy is nice, we know that interest rates are constantly changing. So the real question becomes, how can a person effectively immunize in a world of volatile interest rates?

There are two approaches available to the investor to immunize a bond portfolio. The easier of these approaches is to purchase a zero-coupon bond that matures at the time and in the amount that corresponds to the investor's need for funds. The primary problem with this strategy would be that a zero with the desired maturity date might not be available.

EXAMPLE

Your client has a daughter who will be going to college in 10 years. She has $33,504 in a Coverdell IRA (formerly known as an educational IRA). If this $33,504 were invested in zero-coupon bonds that mature in 10 years with a yield to maturity of 6 percent, then your client would know with certainty that the account would be worth exactly $60,000 in 10 years, provided the issuer does not default on the bonds and the full $33,504 can be invested.

The typical method of immunizing involves assembling and appropriately managing a diversified portfolio of coupon bonds. The portfolio is structured and managed with the objective of keeping its duration equal to the investor's planning horizon. This requires continual portfolio rebalancing because the constantly changing interest rates invalidate the conditions for pure immunization with coupon bonds.

EXAMPLE

Consider Bond B that we discussed earlier, which had a duration of 5.44 years. Suppose that an investor has a planning horizon of 5.44 years. Bond B provides the necessary immunization. However, after 1 year, the investor's planning horizon will be 4.44 years, but the duration of the bond will be 4.85 years. Thus, the investor will no longer be immunized. The reason this occurs is that the bond's duration will go to zero over the term to maturity, which in this case was initially 7 years. To decline from a value of 5.44 to zero over a period of 7 years requires that the reduction in the duration statistic each year has to be less than a full year.

The rebalancing may not be as extensive as one might first think because as cash flows are received from coupon payments, the proceeds can be used to purchase new bonds to maintain the target duration. These cash inflows, however, may not be adequate to rebalance the portfolio fully. To accomplish rebalancing under these circumstances, the investor may have to trade some bonds for bonds with more appropriate characteristics.

Immunizing a Portfolio

- Purchase zero-coupon bonds whose maturities correspond with the planning horizon.
- Assemble and manage a bond portfolio whose duration is kept equal to the planning horizon.

Immunization is only one strategy for managing a bond portfolio; a financial planner should not always seek to immunize a bond portfolio. For example, an investor may not have a well-defined time horizon of when he or she wants to cash out his or her investments. Another possibility is that the investor may want to speculate on interest rate movements. If an investor expects interest rates to fall, he or she should hold a portfolio whose duration is longer than the desired time horizon. Conversely, if an investor expects interest rates to rise, he or she should hold a portfolio whose duration is less than the time horizon. In theory, if an immediate increase in interest rates is expected, then the investor should hold a portfolio whose duration is zero (that is, an all-cash portfolio). After interest rates rise, the investor can then purchase the bonds at a lower price and benefit from higher reinvestment rates.

Uses of the Duration Statistic

- As an index number to compare the relative price volatility of bonds or bond portfolios
- To compute the modified duration, which allows an investor to estimate the percentage change in the price of a bond for a given change in the yield to maturity
- To immunize a portfolio by setting the portfolio's duration equal to the investor's time horizon

---

ASSEMBLING AND MANAGING A BOND PORTFOLIO

Bond portfolios are similar to stock portfolios in that the most important characteristic is diversification. A good portfolio contains bonds that are issued by firms in different industries. Bonds should also be selected to produce the desired level of maturity/duration, default risk/quality ratings, coupon rate/price appreciation, and taxable income.

Bond Swaps

Portfolio managers frequently seek to improve their portfolios by buying a bond with the funds freed up by liquidating another position. These bond swaps may be designed to increase yield to maturity, increase current yield, adjust duration or risk, or establish a tax loss.

Many swaps are not executed simultaneously because bonds are not as marketable as most stocks. Thus, swap traders risk making one side of the swap (say, the sell) only to encounter an adverse price move before the other side of the swap is accomplished. Moreover, transaction costs absorb some of the swap's anticipated benefits. Nonetheless, a variety of circumstances make swaps attractive. Bond swaps generally fall into the following four categories:[79]

- *substitution swap*. In this case, the bond sold and the one bought are considered near-perfect substitutes. The motivation for such a swap might be either recognition of a loss for tax purposes or an attempt to move from a fairly priced or overpriced bond to an underpriced bond. For example, if an investor owns the XYZ Bond and notes that the ABC Bond has the same coupon rate, same maturity, same quality rating, and is in the same industry but trades for $20 less than the XYZ Bond, the investor might expect a $20 windfall gain from selling the XYZ Bond and buying the ABC Bond.

- *intermarket spread swap*. The basis of this swap is the equilibrium relationship in the spreads between yields of bonds in different markets or sectors. For example, suppose the yield on top-rated bonds of utilities tends to be about one-quarter of one percent below that on top-rated bonds of transportation companies, but that currently the two yields are the same. This suggests that either utility bonds are underpriced (the yield is too high) or the transportation bonds are overpriced (the yield is too low). To the extent that the investor holds transportation bonds, an intermarket spread swap involves selling the transportation bonds and buying utility bonds.

- *pure-yield pick-up swap*. In this case, the investor sells a bond with a lower yield and buys another bond with a higher yield. This differs from the intermarket spread swap in that the intermarket swap has an expectation of bond price changes. The pure-yield pick-up swap has expectation of no price changes; it is simply an

---

79. The definitive statement on bond swaps is found in Sidney Homer and Martin Leibowitz, *Inside the Yield Book* (Englewood Cliffs, NJ: Prentice Hall, 1972).

action to increase the yield of the portfolio, even if it means moving into lower-quality bonds.

- *rate anticipation swap.* This trade involves moving money between short- and long-duration bonds in anticipation of a general movement of interest rates. When an investor expects interest rates to fall, the rate anticipation swap entails selling bonds with short durations and buying bonds with long durations. Conversely, when the investor expects interest rates to rise, this swap involves selling bonds with long durations and buying bonds with short durations.

Portfolio Structure

As indicated above, there are a large number of alternatives one can consider when constructing a bond portfolio with a particular duration. Even though the portfolio manager has a portfolio duration in mind, the manager must also decide whether to construct the portfolio as a bullet, barbell, ladder, or other configuration. Let's consider what each of these first three looks like.

Bullet Portfolio

A *bullet* portfolio is one in which the entire portfolio is placed in one maturity. An illustration of this is the earlier example in which a portfolio was created to pay for a daughter's attending college, and the entire portfolio is placed in 10-year zero-coupon bonds. A bullet portfolio may consist of coupon or zero-coupon bonds, or a combination. The one key feature is that all of the bonds in the portfolio have the same maturity.

Barbell Portfolio

A pure *barbell* bond portfolio puts all of the portfolio into two maturities, one short-term and the other long-term. There is no a priori specification as to the weights attached to the two maturities, but most barbell strategies are split about 50-50 between the two maturities. The rationale for a barbell strategy is that the heavy allocation to the short-term bonds increases the portfolio's liquidity, and the heavy allocation to the long-term bonds increases the portfolio's interest income. This is because long-term bonds usually provide higher current yields than short-term bonds (this relationship is discussed in the next section).

EXAMPLE
A classic barbell would be 50 percent in one-year bonds and 50 percent in 20-year bonds. Nonetheless, many variations would still qualify as barbells. Some examples would be: • 40% in 2-year and 60% in 15-year   • 55% in 3-year and 45% in 10-year   • 35% in 4-year and 65% in 12-year

Bond Ladders

The third strategy is known as a bond ladder.[80] A bond ladder spreads the value of the portfolio evenly across a time horizon. If the investor's time horizon is 10 years, a pure bond ladder has one-tenth of the portfolio maturing at the end of the first year, one-tenth maturing at the end of the second, and so on until the end of the tenth year. As each tranche matures, it is reinvested with a 10-year maturity. Note that what had previously been 10-year bonds will now have a 9-year maturity. Rolling over the maturing bonds each year into another set of 10-year bonds keeps the ladder pure.

A bond ladder may also serve a client well if his or her purpose is to liquidate a portfolio over time. A 10-year ladder allows a client to have 10 years' worth of steady cash inflow. Alternatively, the client may simply want the choice each year of whether to liquidate none, some, or all of the maturing bonds. A ladder allows this to occur with minimal disruption to the portfolio.

TERM STRUCTURE OF INTEREST RATES

The relationship between the terms to maturity on bonds and their yields to maturity (assuming all other factors, such as default risk, are equal) is known as the term structure of interest rates.

The Yield Curve

yield curve   The relationship between term to maturity and yield to maturity is illustrated with a yield curve. A *yield curve* is the graphic representation of the term structure of interest rates—that is, the

---

80. For   a   simple   discussion   of   bond   ladders,   see www.fool.com/retirement/retireeport/2000/retireeport000724.htm, accessed July 13, 2010.

relationship between yield to maturity and term to maturity for debt securities with otherwise similar characteristics (default risk, coupon, call feature, and so on). The yield curve takes on different shapes at different times. The most common yield curve is the rising curve (top curve in *Figure 9-5*), in which short-term yields are lower than long-term yields. Occasionally, a falling yield curve will exist (middle curve in *Figure 9-5*), in which short-term yields are higher than long-term yields. On a rare occasion, the yield curve will be flat (bottom curve in *Figure 9-5*), in which case short-term yields equal long-term yields. An extremely rare yield curve is the humped curve, in which intermediate-term yields are higher than both short-term and long-term yields. It is critically important that any investor understand why the yield curve takes on different shapes at different times.

Figure 9-5
Types of Yield Curves

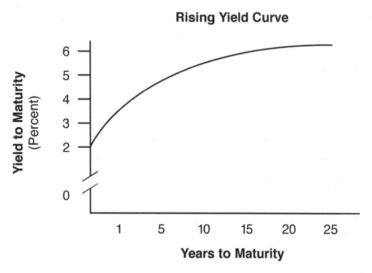

Figure 9–5 (continued)

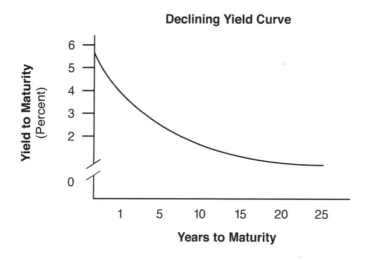

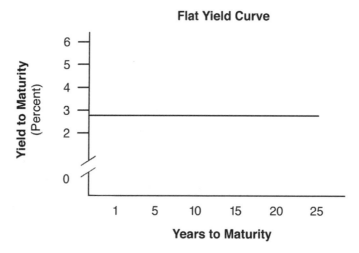

Term Structure Hypotheses

Although there are different yield curves for bonds of different ratings and characteristics, the most commonly discussed yield curve is the one for Treasury bonds. This is probably because Treasury bonds have virtually no risk of default, few are callable, and thus any difference in yield between two Treasury bonds results solely from the difference in their maturities and coupon rates. Hence, this discussion will focus on the Treasury bond yield curve.

Several hypotheses have been developed to explain why the yield curve takes on a particular shape at a particular point in time. The two most significant of these to a financial planner are the expectations hypothesis and the liquidity preference (or maturity premium) hypothesis. Of lesser importance is the market segmentation hypothesis.

Expectations Hypothesis

expectations hypothesis The *expectations hypothesis* starts with the concept of spot and forward rates. A spot rate is one that exists today. The yield curve is a display of spot rates. A forward rate is a rate that will exist in the future. Thus, the yield one observes today on what is today a one-year bond is the one-year spot rate. One year from today, a person could look at interest rates again, and the yield on one-year bonds at that time would probably be different. To distinguish between these two one-year rates, let's use the following symbolism. The letter r represents the interest rate. A pre-subscript could represent the time at which an interest rate is observed, and a post-subscript could represent the maturity of the observed interest rate. Thus, $_0r_1$ represents the interest rate observed today (the zero pre-subscript) on a one-year bond (the post-subscript). Similarly, the rate on a one-year bond that would be observed in one year could be described as $_1r_1$, where the pre-subscript of 1 indicates that the interest rate is one that would be observed in one year, and the post-subscript of 1 indicates that it is the rate on a one-year bond. Similarly, we could describe the rates that would be observed on one-year bonds in 2, 3, ..., T years in the future with $_2r_1, _3r_1$, ..., and $_Tr_1$.

According to the expectations hypothesis, long-term rates are a function of current and expected future short-term rates in a geometric mean relationship, where the expected future short-term rates are the forward rates. For example, the current 2-year rate is a function of the current one-year rate and the expectation of next year's one-year rate, as follows:

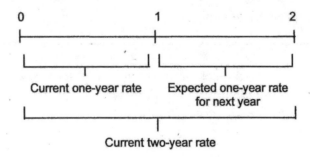

$$\begin{pmatrix} \text{Current} \\ 1 + \text{ 2 } - \text{ year} \\ \text{rate} \end{pmatrix} = \left[\begin{pmatrix} \text{Current} \\ 1 + \text{ one } - \text{ year} \\ \text{rate} \end{pmatrix} \begin{pmatrix} \text{Expected} \\ \text{one } - \text{ year} \\ 1 + \quad \text{rate for} \\ \text{next year} \end{pmatrix} \right]^{1/2}$$

In terms of the interest rate symbols described above, this equation can be expressed more compactly as:

$$(1 + {_0}r_2) = [(1 + {_0}r_1)(1 + {_1}r_1)]^{1/2}$$

Since we can look up the current 2-year rate and current 1-year rate in the newspaper or online, we can manipulate the formula above to solve for the expected 1-year rate for next year.

$${_1}r_1 = (1 + {_0}r_2)^2/(1 + {_0}r_1) - 1$$

EXAMPLE

Consider a current 2-year rate of 10 percent and a current one-year rate of 8 percent.

Using the formula above, we can determine what the market expects next year's one-year rate to be according to the expectations hypothesis.

$$\begin{aligned} \text{Expected one-year rate} & = (1.10^2 \div 1.08) - 1 \\ \text{for next year} & = 1.1204 - 1 \\ & = .1204 \text{ or } 12.04\% \end{aligned}$$

The HP-10BII keystrokes are

SHIFT, C ALL

1.10, SHIFT, x^2, $\div$, 1.08, =, −, 1, =

(display: 0.1204)

One can always make a quick approximation of the expected 1-year rate for next year by treating today's 2-year rate as an arithmetic average of the current and future 1-year rates. Thus,

$${_0}r_2 \approx ({_0}r_1 + {_1}r_1)/2$$

This means that the expected rate in 1 year on a 1-year bond would be approximately defined as:

$$_1r_1 \approx (2 \times {}_0r_2) - {}_0r_1$$

In plugging in the numbers from the above example:

$$_1r_1 \approx (2 \times .10) - .08 \approx .12$$

The basic rationale for the expectations theory of the term structure of interest rates is that if today's long-term rates seem misaligned with expected future short-term rates, investors will move their money between short-term and long-term bonds accordingly. For example, if long-term rates seem too high compared to expected future short-term rates, then some short-horizon investors will sell their shorter-term bonds and buy longer-term issues. Similarly, if long-term rates today seem too low relative to expected future short-term rates, then some longer-horizon borrowers will switch into shorter-term bonds. This activity should quickly drive rates into the appropriate relationship.

EXAMPLE

You have a client who has some significant money to invest and who wants to use that money to buy a house in 2 years. Because bonds seem the most appropriate investment for this client, the only real decision to make is whether to buy bonds or CDs with a 2-year maturity or a 1-year maturity and then buy a new set of 1-year bonds when these mature. Suppose the current 2-year rate ($_0r_2$) is 5 percent and the current 1-year rate ($_0r_1$) is 6 percent.

Based on the expectations formula, the expected rate in one-year is

$$_1r_1 = (1 + {}_0r_2)^2/(1 + {}_0r_1) - 1$$
$$= (1 + .05)^2/(1 + .06) - 1 = .0401 \text{ or } 4.01\%$$

The decision of whether to put the client into 2-year bonds or 1-year bonds now depends on whether the advisor believes that the actual 1-year rate in 1 year ($_1r_1$) will be greater than or less than 4.01 percent. If greater than, the advisor should recommend 1-year bonds that would be rolled over. If less than, the advisor should recommend 2-year bonds today. If the advisor believes 1-year rates will be exactly 4.01 percent in 1 year, then he or she is indifferent between the two strategies.

In the above examples, we have used only a 2-year time horizon. The expectations hypothesis can be expanded to any time horizon. The more general form of the relationship is:

$$(1 + {}_0r_T) = [(1 + {}_0r_1)(1 + {}_1r_1)\ldots (1 + {}_{T-1}r_1)]^{1/T}$$

Again, this equation is a fancy way of saying that under the expectations hypothesis, long-term interest rates are simply the geometric mean average of current and expected future short-term interest rates.

Liquidity Preference Hypothesis

liquidity preference hypothesis

liquidity premium

maturity premium

The *liquidity preference hypothesis* assumes that because price risk (the effect of interest rate changes on a bond's price) increases with maturity, investors demand a premium to hold longer-term securities. Borrowers are willing to pay a premium to borrow for a longer term because it reduces the frequency, and therefore risk, of refinancing at a time when interest rates have increased. Because lenders demand a premium for longer-term lending and borrowers are willing to pay a premium, longer-term rates will overstate the expectation of future short-term rates. For example, suppose the spot rate on 1-year bonds ($_0r_1$) is 5 percent, and the expected rate in 1 year on what are at that time 1-year bonds ($_1r_1$) is also 5 percent. The expectations hypothesis would say that the spot rate on 2-year bonds would also have to be 5 percent ($_0r_2$). However, the liquidity preference hypothesis would say that the spot rate on 2-year bonds would be slightly greater than 5 percent to reflect both the liquidity premium that investors demand for price risk exposure and the premium borrowers are willing to pay to reduce refinancing uncertainty. This difference between current long-term rates and the rate that would be expected based on short-term interest rates is called the *liquidity premium* or *maturity premium*.

Market Segmentation Hypothesis

The *market segmentation hypothesis* asserts that supply and demand within each market segment, as defined by maturities, determines interest rates for that maturity class. According to this hypothesis, the yield curve simply reflects the supply and demand for each maturity class. Because most investors are thought to prefer short-term loans, and most borrowers prefer to borrow long term, we would expect to see upward-sloping yield curves almost all of the time.

Yield Curve Implications of Each Hypothesis

Each hypothesis explains the various yield curve shapes slightly differently and has somewhat different implications. Under the unbiased expectations hypothesis, a rising yield curve exists only when short-term interest rates themselves are expected to increase over time. A flat yield curve indicates neutral expectations—that is, expectations that short-term interest rates will remain constant. A falling yield curve reflects an expectation that short-term rates will fall.

According to the liquidity preference hypothesis, the yield curve's natural shape would be a rising function because of investor risk aversion and borrower preferences. The real issue under this hypothesis in terms of predicting future short-term interest rates is whether a rising curve reflects only the liquidity premium or whether it also reflects an expectation of rising short term rates. The answer to this question would require knowledge of the liquidity premium itself, and this is a number that no one can see. Hence, under this hypothesis, a forecast of future short-term rates is necessarily a forecast of the liquidity premium. The market segmentation hypothesis is also consistent with a tendency for yield curves to rise. Lenders may be relatively more numerous at the short end of the maturity spectrum, and borrowers more numerous at the long end.

Term Structure of Interest Rate Hypotheses

- Unbiased expectations: Long-term rates reflect the market's expectation of current and future short-term rates.
- Liquidity preference: Lenders are risk averse and demand a premium for buying long-term securities. Borrowers would like to tie up a certain cost of funds and are willing to pay a premium to issue long-term securities. As a result, yield curves tend to be upward sloping.
- Market segmentation: Yields reflect supply and demand for each maturity class.

None of the term structure hypotheses have gained overwhelming acceptance or been completely ruled out by research. In general, there is some truth to all of them. Financial planners should most likely act as if both the expectations and liquidity preference hypotheses are correct, and assume a liquidity premium of no more than 25 basis points.

Identification of Misvalued Securities

Yield curve relationships may give bond traders a trading opportunity. First, securities whose yields are substantially above curves plotted with otherwise similar issues may well be misvalued. Thus, bonds whose yields exceed their respective yield curve values may be underpriced. If their market prices adjust more quickly than the curve itself shifts, they could produce an above-market return. Of course, a trader who detects such underpriced bonds will need to act very quickly because other investors will be following the same strategy, thus driving the price of undervalued bonds up to their intrinsic value. Also, the trader should make certain that the underpricing does not represent a risk premium, perhaps for a risk that has only recently been discovered and is not yet reflected in the bond's rating. (This assumes, of course, that the bond in question is not a Treasury bond, which has no default risk.)

Similarly, bonds that plot substantially below the yield curve are bonds that should be avoided, or possibly sold if they are currently held.

Bullet Portfolios, Barbell Portfolios, and Term Structure Changes

If an investor wants a relatively simple bond portfolio, then the obvious choices are a bullet or barbell portfolio. Suppose an investor has a desired holding period of 5 years, would like to be immunized, and the yield curve is flat. Two obvious choices are a bullet portfolio with a duration of 5 years (say a 5-year zero coupon bond) and a barbell portfolio with a duration of 5 years (say 50 percent in a 3-year zero-coupon bond and 50 percent in a 7-year zero-coupon bond). If the yield curve is upward sloping initially, and were to flatten over the next year (that is, if the spread between long-term rates and short-term rates decreases), the investor might be better off with the barbell portfolio. If the yield curve were to become steeper (that is, if the spread between long-term rates and short-term rates increases), the investor might well be better off with a bullet portfolio.

FACTORS THAT AFFECT BOND PRICES AND YIELDS

The discount rate is critical to bond valuation. The appropriate discount rate varies both over time and from investment to investment. Many factors influence discount rates for bond valuation. The general level of interest rates is determined largely by expected inflation rates. The term structure of interest rates is determined primarily by expected future short-term interest rates (which in turn are a function of expected future inflation rates). The discount rate for a specific bond will also depend on such characteristics as default risk, marketability, seasoning, call protection, sinking fund provisions, and "mefirst" rules. Let us consider these features.

Factors That Influence a Bond's Discount Rate

A particular asset's appropriate discount rate depends on the perceived risk of the investment. In general, the lower the probability of default, the lower the appropriate discount rate. Default risk is the risk that the issuer will not fulfill the obligation to pay all coupons and/or the maturity value. The default risk of municipal and corporate debt securities depends on the ability of the issuers producing cash flow and/or the liquidation values of the issuers' assets and on the amount of other debt outstanding.

The federal government guarantee of Treasury-issued securities results in virtually no default risk for these securities. The market trusts the federal guarantee because the government has extensive taxing power, the Fed can facilitate sales of government securities, and Treasury controls the printing press.[81]

Seasoned issues are ones that have traded for at least a few weeks beyond completion of the initial (offering) sale. As with new stock issues, new issues of bonds tend to be priced a bit below equivalent seasoned issues.

Factors Affecting Bond Yields

- General credit conditions: Credit conditions affect all yields to one degree or another.
- Default risk: Riskier issues require higher promised yields.
- Duration: The weighted average of the amount of time until the present value of the purchase price is recouped.
- Term structure: Yields vary with maturity, reflecting expectations of future interest rate changes.
- Marketability: Actively traded issues tend to be worth more than otherwise equivalent issues that are less actively traded.

---

81. One could argue that there is an infinitesimally small default risk to Treasury securities because there is always the possibility that, prior to their maturity, the U.S. government would be overthrown and the successor government repudiate the debt, or that the U.S. government might be unable or unwilling to collect the necessary taxes or borrow additional monies to pay off the current debt.

> - Seasoning: Newly issued bonds may sell at a slight discount to otherwise equivalent established issues.
> - Call protection: Protection from an early call tends to enhance a bond's value.
> - Sinking fund provisions: Sinking funds reduce the probability of default, thereby tending to enhance a bond's value.
> - Me-first rules: Bonds protected from the diluting effect of additional borrowings are generally worth more than otherwise equivalent unprotected issues.

Call protection varies appreciably from issue to issue. Some bonds are callable beginning the day they are sold. Many others may not be called for the first 5 or 10 years of their lives. Callable issues that are likely to be redeemed due to their high yields should be evaluated on their yield to call rather than on their yield to maturity. Callable bonds always trade at slightly lower prices (higher yields) then comparable non-callables.

A sinking fund's presence increases demand slightly and reduces the probability of default. Thus, a sinking fund generally adds modestly to the bond's value. However, to the extent a bond investor might be forced to sell back to the sinking fund bonds that he or she would like to keep, a sinking fund could also be considered undesirable.

Me-first rules are designed to protect existing bondholders. These rules prevent the bondholders' claims from being weakened by the issuance of additional debt with a priority higher than or equivalent to theirs. Research has found that these rules significantly enhance the market values of the protected bonds.

Yield Spreads

flight to quality   As interest rates change over time, the yields on all bonds, regardless of their quality rating, change. However, they do not change at the same rate. The following table provides the annual average yields to maturity on Aaa and Baa bonds from 1976 to 2009. Note that with the exception of 1982, the direction of change from one year to the next is the same for both ratings. Note also that the spread between the two yields varies substantially over the years. The explanation for this varying spread has to do with investors' willingness to accept risk. When investors become more anxious than usual, they want to hold safer securities. Thus, they will sell lower-rated securities and buy higher-rated ones. The result is that the prices of lower-rated bonds fall *relative* to those of higher-rated ones.

This means the yield differential widens. This process is known as a *flight to quality*, which means the movement into less risky securities associated with an increase in the yield differential. The yield differential tends to narrow when the economy is expanding and to widen when the economy is struggling.

Table 9-3 Historical Yields on Moody's Aaa and Baa Rated Bonds			
Year	Yield on Aaa	Yield on Baa	Spread (Baa — Aaa)
1976	8.43	9.75	1.32
1977	8.02	8.97	0.95
1978	8.73	9.49	0.76
1979	9.63	10.69	1.06
1980	11.94	13.67	1.73
1981	14.17	16.04	1.87
1982	13.79	16.11	2.32
1983	12.04	13.55	1.51
1984	12.71	14.19	1.48
1985	11.37	12.72	1.35
1986	9.02	10.39	1.37
1987	9.38	10.58	1.20
1988	9.71	10.83	1.12
1989	9.26	10.18	0.92
1990	9.32	10.36	1.04
1991	8.77	9.80	1.03
1992	8.14	8.98	0.84
1993	7.22	7.93	0.71
1994	7.97	8.63	0.66
1995	7.59	8.20	0.61
1996	7.37	8.05	0.68
1997	7.27	7.87	0.60
1998	6.53	7.22	0.69
1999	7.05	7.88	0.83
2000	7.62	8.37	0.75
2001	7.08	7.95	0.87
2002	6.49	7.80	1.31
2003	5.66	6.76	1.10
2004	5.63	6.39	0.76
2005	5.23	6.06	0.83
2006	5.59	6.48	0.89
2007	5.56	6.48	0.92
2008	5.63	7.44	1.81
2009	5.31	7.29	1.98
Sources: www.federalreserve.gov/releases/h15/data/Annual/H15_BAA_NA.txt, and www.federalreserve.gov/releases/h15/data/Annual/H15_AAA_NA.txt, accessed July 13, 2010.			

High-Yield Corporates

Junk bonds provide substantially higher yields than investment-grade bonds.

Although junk bonds are ill suited to the needs of more cautious investors, many investors with a greater tolerance for risk are attracted to them. Risk and potential return can be comparable to that of many stocks. Indeed, a risky firm's bonds sometimes offer a more attractive way of speculating than its stock does, because the bonds represent a stronger claim on the firm's assets in case of liquidation or bankruptcy. To realize an attractive return, the junk bond investor needs only for the troubled firm to avoid bankruptcy or to maintain substantial value in reorganization. The stockholder's return may not be attractive unless the firm becomes relatively profitable because stocks represent only a residual claim on the firm's assets. In fact, Domian and Reichenstein (2008) find that bond funds with an average credit quality of CCC behave more like stocks than like bonds.[82]

Although it is always an important investment goal, diversification is crucial for junk bond investors. A defaulting issue may eventually pay off, but the wait can be long and nerve racking. Having a diversified bond portfolio substantially dilutes the effect of a single default. Junk bond mutual funds give small investors an effective diversification vehicle. In fact, these funds' growth has encouraged some firms with relatively low credit ratings to return to the bond market.

Transaction Costs for Bonds

When a bond is purchased, the investor will pay the purchase price, accrued interest, commission, and any implicit bid-ask spread. One large brokerage firm posts the following commission schedule on bond trades:

Online Bond Trade Concessions (for all customers)	
U.S. Treasury Auctions, including TIPS Auctions	Free
U.S. Treasury Bills, Notes, Bonds, including TIPS	Free
GSE (Agency Securities), secondary CDs	$1.00/bond
Municipals	$1.00/bond
Corporates (BBB or higher), CATS/TIGRS	$1.00/bond
Corporates (BB+ or lower)	$1.00/bond
Source: personal.fidelity.com/products/trading/Commissions_Margin_Rates/commissions_Margin_Rates.shtml.cvsr?refpr=brk10, accessed July 13, 2010.	

---

82. Domian, D., and Reichenstein, W., "Return-Based Style Analysis of High-Yield Bonds," *The Journal of Fixed Income*, 2008, 17 (4) pp. 72–87.

Depending on whether an investor trades online or through a full-service broker, the commission for a bond purchase can vary substantially, and can be either less or more expensive than a stock purchase of a comparable dollar amount. Note also that the variety of bonds available varies from broker to broker.

As with stocks, the bid-ask spread varies with the volume of trading activity. Actively traded bonds such as most Treasuries have quite narrow bid-ask spreads. Less actively traded securities can carry a significant spread. The accrued interest paid on a bond normally should not be a concern to the investor because this interest will be returned to the investor on the next coupon payment. The exception to this scenario would be when an investor is purchasing a highly speculative junk bond where there is serious concern about a company defaulting on the next coupon payment.

REVIEW OF LEARNING OBJECTIVES

1. The price of a bond is the present value of its coupon payments and its maturity value, discounted at the required rate of return. A bond's yield to maturity is the discount rate that equates the present value of its coupon payments and its maturity value to today's bond price.

2. The current yield of a bond is the annual coupon payment divided by the price. The realized compound yield to maturity is computed by first determining the terminal value of a bond investment, after allowing for the reinvestment of all coupon payments at a specified rate of return, and then by determining the discount rate that equates this terminal value with the price of the bond today. The yield to call is the discount rate that equates the present value of a bond's call price when it is first callable and the present value of the coupons payment till that time to the price of the bond today. The realized rate of return equates the present value of the selling price and coupons received to the purchase price.

3. The major factors that influence a bond's price volatility are its term to maturity (the maturity effect) and the coupon rate (the coupon effect).

4. The shortcut formula for computing a bond's duration statistic is:

$$D = \frac{1+Y}{Y} - \frac{(1+Y)+T(C-Y)}{C[(1+Y)^T - 1]+Y}$$

5. The duration statistic can serve as index number of bond price volatility because the larger the duration statistic, the more volatile the price of the bond. The change in a bond's price per unit change in yield can be estimated from duration statistics by noting that:

$$\frac{\Delta P}{P} = -D^* \times \Delta Y$$

In theory, a portfolio can be immunized when its duration statistic is set equal to the desired holding period.

6. There are four general types of swaps. These include a substitution swap, an intermarket spread swap, a pure-yield pick-up swap, and a rate anticipation swap. In a ladder portfolio, the maturities are spread evenly over a specified time horizon. A bullet portfolio is one in which the entire portfolio has a single maturity date. A barbell portfolio is one in which the entire portfolio is allocated approximately evenly into two maturities, one long and the other short.

7. The term structure of interest rates is the relationship between yield to maturity and term to maturity for bonds of like quality. Most published yield curves are based on Treasury bonds. The two best explanations of why the yield curve takes on a particular shape are the expectations and liquidity preference hypotheses. Different yield curve shapes, combined with which theory one believes is dominant, will lead to different strategies in managing bond portfolios.

8. Factors that influence a bond's yield include general credit conditions, default risk, the duration statistic, the term structure, marketability, seasoning, call protection, sinking fund provisions, and me-first rules.

MINICASE

A client has a $2 million portfolio. The client would like to put $500,000 into bonds. You could invest the money directly into T-bills or T-bonds, or buy one or more bond mutual funds. The purpose of the bond holdings is to fund the payment to a retirement community that the client plans to enter in 10 years. Two bond mutual funds that you are considering, A and B, have Macaulay duration statistics of 8.6 and 10.0 years, respectively. The yields to maturity on both funds are 8 percent. Your client is convinced that interest rates will fall over the next few years, and would like to take advantage of the decline to enhance her returns.

1. If you decide to immunize the bond portfolio, then the best purchase would be: [4]

    (A) Bond Fund A because it allows for extra profit if interest rates fall
    (B) Bond Fund B because its duration matches the intended holding period
    (C) Direct purchases of bonds to create a portfolio whose duration equals 10 years
    (D) Treasury bills

2. If interest rates were to go up rather than down and the client were to liquidate the portfolio in 5 years, then the best purchase among the following would have been: [5]

    (A) Bond Fund A because the shorter duration means less price volatility
    (B) Bond Fund B because its duration matches the intended 10-year holding period
    (C) Direct purchases of bonds to create a portfolio whose duration equals 10 years
    (D) Treasury bills

3. If market interest rates were suddenly to fall by 1 percent, the change in the market value of the Bond Fund B's portfolio would be approximately: [5]

    (A) +8.0 percent
    (B) +8.2 percent
    (C) +9.0 percent
    (D) +9.2 percent

4. The most efficient security to purchase if you were to construct an immunized portfolio would be: [5]

    (A) a 10-year, 8 percent coupon, AAA-rated bond
    (B) a 10-year, 8 percent coupon, government bond
    (C) a 10-year, zero-coupon government bond
    (D) a 10-year, floating rate coupon, AAA-rated bond

5. Whether interest rates go up or down the actual new price of a bond will likely be _____ the price predicted with the duration statistic. [5]

    (A) higher than
    (B) equal to
    (C) less than
    (D) indeterminant based on the information given

CHAPTER REVIEW

Key Terms and Concepts

coupon rate

current yield

promised yield

maturity effect

coupon effect

yield-to-maturity effect

Macaulay's duration

modified duration

convex

reinvestment rate risk

price risk

immunization

yield curve

expectations hypothesis

liquidity preference hypothesis

liquidity premium

maturity premium

flight to quality

Review Questions

Review questions are based on the learning objectives in this chapter. Thus, a [3] at the end of a question means that the question is based on learning objective 3. If there are multiple objectives, they are all listed.

1.   a.   Bonds for the Taylor Corporation have 20 years left until maturity and carry an annual coupon of $40. Comparable bonds have a yield to maturity of 6 percent. What should the price of these bonds be? [1]
     b.   Recompute the price of the above bonds if the interest is paid semiannually rather than annually. [1]

2.   A bond trades at 90 ($900), matures in 15 years, has an 8 percent coupon rate with interest paid semiannually. What is its yield to maturity? [1]

3.   Hayes-L Corporation bonds recently paid the annual interest payment of $35. The bonds mature in 12 years and have a market price of $975. They are callable in 3 years at a price equal to par plus one year's interest.
     a.   What is the coupon rate of the Hayes-L bonds? [2]
     b.   What is the current yield of the Hayes-L bonds? [2]
     c.   What is the yield to maturity of the Hayes-L bonds? [1]
     d.   What is the yield to earliest call of the Hayes-L bonds? [2]
     e.   If the bonds are purchased today and sold for $990 immediately after the coupon payment 5 years from today, what will the investor's realized yield be? [2]

4.   You buy a bond today for 90 ($900). It matures in 10 years, and has a 6 percent coupon rate, paid annually. Assume you believe you will be able to immediately reinvest all coupon payments at a 10 percent rate of return. What would be the realized compound yield to maturity (RCYTM) for this bond? [2]

5. For each of the following pairs of bonds, indicate which bond's price is likely to be more volatile for a given, equal change in interest rates, and indicate why: [3]

   a.

       i. a 15-year, 6 percent coupon bond with a YTM of 8 percent
       ii. a 7-year, 6 percent coupon bond with a YTM of 8 percent

   b.

       i. a 15-year, 6 percent coupon bond with a YTM of 8 percent
       ii. a 15-year, 5 percent coupon bond with a YTM of 8 percent

   c.

       i. a 15-year, 6 percent coupon bond with a YTM of 8 percent
       ii. a 15-year, 6 percent coupon bond with a YTM of 6 percent

6. Recompute the duration for bonds A and B in Table 9-2 using an appropriate discount rate of 20 percent. Compare the results with those derived from the 8 percent rate. [4]

7. What is immunization? Explain the two methods of immunization. [5]

8. a. What should be considered when assembling a bond portfolio? [6]
   b. What are bond swaps? [6]
   c. What are three common strategies for setting up a bond portfolio? [6]

9. Describe the three hypotheses for the term structure of interest rates and how each explains the normal (rising) yield curve. [7]

10. Discuss the effect on yields of [8]
    a. marketability
    b. seasoning
    c. call protection
    d. sinking fund provisions

Learning Objectives

An understanding of the material in this chapter should enable the student to

1. Explain the various characteristics of mutual funds, including their sales fees, benefits, and disadvantages.

2. Describe how closed-end funds work.

3. Decide whether an ETF or an index fund is more appropriate for a client.

4. Describe the differences between REITs, RELPs, and REMICs.

5. Describe the differences between a UIT, a hedge fund, a variable annuity, and a separately managed account.

6. Identify the important characteristics to consider in selecting an appropriate mutual fund for a client.

7. Reconcile the poor average performance of mutual funds with their appropriateness for an investor's portfolio.

An alternative to the direct purchase of stocks, bonds, and money market instruments is the purchase of shares in an investment company. An investment company is an entity in which multiple investors pool their cash and then use this cash to buy securities. The investors own shares that are claims on the portfolio. Investment companies are structured in many different ways.

open-end investment company

closed-end investment company

The major distinction among investment companies is whether they are open-ended or closed-ended. *Open-ended investment companies* are known popularly as mutual funds. The distinction between an *open-ended investment company* (that is, a mutual fund) and a closed-end one is that the only way an investor can buy shares in a mutual fund is from the fund itself through the creation of new shares. The only way an investor can sell shares of a mutual fund is back to the fund through the redemption (that is, liquidation) of shares. Shares in a *closed-end investment company* can be bought only from another investor; they also can be sold only to another investor.[83]

As of year end 2009, the combined assets of the 7,691 mutual funds in the U.S. were $7.7 trillion.[84] They own a significant portion of all publicly traded equities. Because mutual funds are the dominant type of investment company, and because most investors hold at least one if not several mutual funds,[85] we will start this chapter with a comprehensive discussion of mutual funds. Much of what is said about mutual funds applies to the other types of investment companies.

MUTUAL FUNDS

Net Asset Value

Because all trades in a mutual fund's shares can be only with the fund itself, there must be a mechanism that determines the price. The prices for all mutual fund shares are based on the net asset value (NAV) of those shares, which is calculated as follows:

$$NAV = (Total\ assets - Total\ liabilities) \div Number\ of\ shares\ outstanding$$

The total assets of a fund are measured by the market value of all of the securities and any cash held in the portfolio.

EXAMPLE 1
The Holy Grail Mutual Fund reported total assets at the end of the trading day of $322,738,516, and total liabilities of $2,517,683. Prior to the sale of new shares and the redemption of old shares, there are 4,698,245.633 shares outstanding. The NAV at this point in time is computed as $($322,738,516 - $2,517,683) \div 4,698,245.633 = 68.16

---

83. Some closed-end investment companies, such as unit investment trusts, do not have an active secondary market in their shares. Thus, they technically do not trade.

84. www.icifactbooks.org/df/10_fb_table01.pdf, accessed July 13, 2010. .

85. John C. Bogle, "The Mutual Fund Industry 60 Years Later" For Better or Worse," *Financial Analysts Journal*, January/February 2005, p. 17.

Fair-Value Pricing

In theory, a fund computes its NAV at the close of trading each day, and then processes all new purchases and all redemptions using the computed NAV. A problem that has grown as more and more funds expand their holdings to securities that trade in other countries or include thinly traded securities is that the official closing prices of some of these assets may be stale by the time the U.S. markets close. The value of such securities may have already changed in after-hours trading, or news may have indicated how some of these stocks' prices will change on the next day's opening. The SEC has recommended that funds deal with this problem by using *fair-value pricing*, which means that the funds should use what they believe is the appropriate price of securities with stale prices, rather than the official close. It is the failure of funds to do so that has led to the scandals in recent years in which some investors have placed buy orders on funds not using fair-value pricing where the NAV will be undervalued. Sell orders have also been placed on this basis. The losers in this practice, of course, are the rest of the fund's investors.[86] Unfortunately, each fund is currently on its own to ascertain how to impute value to these securities. If a fund does a poor job of imputing fair values, investors may actually be worse off rather than better off.[87]

Types of Mutual Funds

An investment advisor's major task is to make sure the client holds a portfolio whose objectives and risk exposure match the client's objectives and risk tolerance. The great thing about mutual funds (and investment companies in general) is that at least one (if not several) fund can match almost any objective or risk tolerance. Thus, when selecting a mutual fund for a client, the financial planner must ensure that the objective of the mutual fund matches the type of investment that is appropriate for the client, or at least that portion of the client's money. To facilitate this search, many organizations categorize mutual funds according to common objectives. Unfortunately, there is no universal categorization paradigm. So not only does a planner need to know what type of fund he or she is searching for, but which organization's classification scheme will produce the best grouping of funds for that search.

---

86. Tom Lauricella, "SEC May Police Fair-Value Pricing, The *Wall Street Journal*, April 26, 2004, p. C15.

87. Daisy Maxey, "Looking at Mutual Funds in a New Light," The *Wall Street Journal*, December 6, 2004, p. R1.

Stock Fund

common stock funds

mixed portfolio funds

The largest category of mutual funds is the stock fund category. As of May 2010, these funds held $4.80 trillion in assets (44.9 percent of all assets held by mutual funds). Also on this date there were 4,593 stock funds operating.

Stock funds hold portfolios that consist primarily of common stocks and perhaps a small number of preferred stocks. One of the more common schemes today is to categorize a fund in terms of investment style as defined by size of companies and type of stocks of the securities in the portfolio. The popular approach to categorizing investment style for stock portfolios uses the following two descriptive factors:

- *the relative market capitalizations of the companies in which the fund invests.* (Market capitalization is the total market value of a corporation's outstanding stock.) Some analysts divide this factor into three categories: large cap, mid cap, and small cap.

- *the relative emphasis of growth stocks versus value stocks.* Factors used to classify stocks in these two categories include the price-earnings ratio (price per share divided by earnings per share) and the market-to-book ratio (price per share divided by accounting book value per share). Funds are classified as growth-oriented, blended, or value-oriented. Combining these two factors generates a matrix of nine possibilities as shown below:

Table 10-1 Categorization Scheme for Equity Mutual Funds		
large cap value oriented	large cap blended	large cap growth oriented
mid cap value oriented	mid cap blended	mid cap growth oriented
small cap value oriented	small cap blended	small cap growth oriented

Hybrid Fund

As of May 2010, hybrid funds held $648.2 billion in assets, which represented 6.0 percent of the industry's assets.[88] A hybrid fund invests in stocks, bonds, convertible bonds, and cash. Although these funds adjust their portfolios

88. www.ici.org/research/stats/trends.05.10, accessed July 14, 2010..

based on what is happening in the market, on average the plurality of their assets are in stocks. The portfolio objective statement will typically emphasize the fund's flexibility to shift among assets classes. The disadvantage of this category for an investor is that the fund may end up with an asset class composition that is different from that which was originally intended.

Bond Funds

Taxable Bond Fund. Funds that specialize in fixed income securities can be divided into four broad categories, the first being taxable bond funds. As of May 2010, taxable bond funds held $1.92 trillion in assets, which represented 17.9 percent of the industry's assets. For fixed-income portfolios, the most appropriate factors are interest rate risk—primarily the price risk aspect—and credit quality. The interest rate sensitivity can be captured by the duration or weighted average maturity of the bond portfolio and can be characterized as long term, intermediate term, or short term, corresponding to high, medium, and low price risk, respectively. Credit quality can be captured by the average credit rating of the bonds in the portfolio. Presumably, a continuum of credit worthiness is possible, but one simplified approach limits the classifications to high, medium, and low credit quality. Combining the two factors also generates a matrix similar to that for stocks of nine possibilities:

Table 10-2 Characterization Scheme for Bond Mutual Funds		
high quality short term	high quality intermediate term	high quality long term
medium quality short term	medium quality intermediate term	medium quality long term
low quality short term	low quality intermediate term	low quality long term

High quality is synonymous with highly rated corporate bonds. At the other end of the spectrum, low quality would typically mean junk bonds.

Municipal Bond Fund. As of May 2010, municipal bond funds held only $487.9 billion in assets, which represented 4.6 percent of the industry's assets. Of the categories used herein, this is the smallest. As with taxable bond funds, these bond funds can be further subdivided by quality and maturity ranges.

Taxable Money Market Fund. This is the second largest category of funds. As of May 2010, taxable money market funds held $2.48 trillion in assets, which represented 23.2 percent of the industry's assets. Like the other categories of debt instruments, these funds also differ with respect to type of issuer. Simply put, there are variations among the rates of return of these funds that are directly traceable to differences in their portfolios.

Tax-Free Money Market Fund. As of May 2010, tax-free money market funds held $352.0 billion in assets, which represented 3.2 percent of the industry's assets. These funds also exhibit differences in terms of risk exposures and maturity.

Other Categorizations

There are many funds which are typically categorized into much more specific groupings. Some of these funds include the following:

- *Index funds* own portfolios that replicate a market index, such as the S&P 500. Index funds have substantially lower expenses and fees than actively managed funds. They are especially useful in passive investment strategies in which the investor is satisfied to match the performance of an index.

- *Sector funds* concentrate on one investment sector or industry. For example, a fund may limit its portfolio to health care companies, technology companies, or energy companies. Obviously, the emphasis on one sector means that these funds are not well diversified and are appropriate only for relatively small portions of an individual's portfolio.

- *Specialty funds* have a unique focus to them. Both index and sector funds are sometimes categorized as specialty funds, but true specialty funds may be characterized as having a gimmick. For example, there is a "race car" fund that invests in companies tied to the sport of auto racing. This is not really a sector fund because auto racing is not an industry; it is more like a subindustry. Hence, it is a specialty fund.

- *International funds* specialize in investments outside of the United States and help the investor to further diversify his or her portfolio. International funds may specialize in specific countries or regions, such as the Pacific Rim.

- *Global funds* invest in the United States and foreign markets. The general philosophy is that we live in a global economy and capital should flow toward those regions that offer optimal risk-return combinations.

- *Asset allocation funds* allow managers considerable flexibility in allocating the portfolio among the three major asset categories (stocks, bonds, and money market instruments) as market conditions change.

- *Life-cycle funds* are designed to appeal to investors in specific phases of the life cycle by providing different asset allocations. For example, one fund may be oriented toward growth investments and intended for young investors, while another may be oriented toward current income and intended for older investors. Some life-cycle funds come with a retirement date, and the portfolio will steadily move toward a more conservative stance as that date approaches and is passed.[89] These are known as *target dates funds*. Some of these funds invest in specific securities, while others take a fund of funds approach.

- *Socially responsible funds* invest only in corporations or other entities that maintain social and/or ethical principles that are consistent with those the fund advocates. For example, a fund may elect not to invest in any company that produces tobacco products or other products associated with potential health hazards, or in any company that is considered environmentally unfriendly. A problem with socially responsible funds is that it might be difficult to find one that has standards that exactly match the investor's standards. Although these funds eliminate many investment opportunities, compromising their potential to obtain an optimal risk/return profile, there has been no evidence developed to date to indicate that they perform any worse than other funds.

What's in a Name?

Because it is not difficult to tell what a fund's objective is, as well as what the portfolio looks like, just by the fund's name, in most cases the name is quite important. Nevertheless, funds sometimes opt to change their name, their objective, or both. Recent research has examined the effect of funds changing their names to appeal to what are the current, hot investment styles. The research indicates that "the fund experiences an average cumulative abnormal [positive cash] flow of 28 percent with no improvement

---

89. John Markese, "Mutual Funds Allocation Over Time: Life Cycle Mutual Funds," *AAII Journal*, November 2004, pp. 5–9.

in performance."[90] In other words, these funds are not really changing their portfolio or their strategy, but just implying that they are, and it does seem to be tricking some investors.

Price Appreciation, Dividends, and Capital Gain Distributions

When investors buy a mutual fund, they are effectively buying a pro rata share of the portfolio. As with any holding, investors are looking for price appreciation and/or dividend and interest income. If the values of the securities in the portfolio appreciate, the NAV of the fund will rise. An increase in the NAV is analogous to the price of any other security rising. Over time, the securities in the fund will accrue dividend and interest income. On a regular basis (usually quarterly but sometimes monthly, semiannually, or annually), the mutual fund distributes this dividend and interest income to investors on a per share basis. This is known as a *regular dividend*.

regular dividend   Over time, the portfolio manager will trade the securities in the portfolio. Each trade will generate a capital gain or capital loss. In most years, the capital gains exceed the capital losses, and the net capital gain must be distributed to shareholders. This is known as a capital gain distribution.[91] When dividends and distributions are made, the NAV of the shares automatically adjusts for the distribution of cash from the portfolio.

Mutual funds as operating entities do not pay income taxes, provided they operate as a conduit. For tax purposes, a conduit is simply an organization that passes taxable income through to another taxable entity. To be recognized as a conduit, Subchapter M of the Internal Revenue Code specifies that mutual funds must distribute to shareholders at least 90 percent of the dividends and interest received by the fund.

Although dividends and capital gain distributions are taxed to the investor, many mutual fund shareholders direct that these payments be reinvested.

---

90. Michael Cooper, Huseyin Gulen, and P. Raghavendra Rau, "Changing Names with Style: Mutual Fund Name Changes and Their Effects on Fund Flows," *Journal of Finance*, Vol. LX, No. 6 (December 2005), pp. 2825–2858.

91. Some people mistakenly refer to this as the capital gain dividend. It is a distribution and not a dividend because the long-term capital gains component of it is taxed to the investor as capital gain income and not as dividend income.

Note that the reinvestment process does not alter the treatment as taxable income. The reinvestment process is always optional, and investors can elect to implement it or discontinue it at any time.

Financial Planning Issue
Some investors elect to take the dividends as cash and reinvest the capital gain distribution. The appeal of this strategy is that taking the capital gain distribution as cash is analogous to dipping into principal. It is certainly possible to reinvest the dividends and take the capital gain distribution as cash, although this is less appealing intuitively. In addition, the dividends do not fluctuate as much as the capital gain distributions from year to year, and when investors opt for income, they usually prefer stable sources. Note that when there has been a serious bear market, many funds simply have no capital gain distribution because their capital losses have exceeded their capital gains.

Fund Families

One of the most dramatic changes in the mutual fund industry over the last quarter of the 20th century has been the growth in the family structure. A mutual fund family exists any time one management company manages more than one fund. For example, Fidelity currently offers investors over 175 funds from which to choose and Vanguard about 115.[92]

Load Charges

The mutual fund industry can generally be divided into two types of funds: load and no-load. For reasons that will be explained shortly, the distinction is not always clear. The term load is industry jargon for commission. The general idea is that load funds are sold through salespeople who work with the individual investor and generate a commission for their efforts, whereas no-load funds are marketed directly to individuals and thus there is no salesperson to compensate. Traditionally, when investors buy shares in a load fund, they pay the NAV price plus the load charge; when they redeem their shares, they receive back only the NAV price per share. Investors in no-load funds both buy and redeem at the NAV price.

The legal maximum load charge is 8.5 percent. Note that this is 8.5 percent of the total investment, not the investment in the fund's shares. Thus, if an investor writes a check for $10,000 to buy shares in a fund charging an 8.5

---

92. http://personal.fidelity.com/products/funds/mutual_funds_overview.shtml.cvsr; accessed July 14, 2010.

percent load, the salesperson will receive a commission of $850 ($10,000 × .085), and the remaining $9,150 will go toward the purchase of shares at the NAV. Because we traditionally think of the commission as a percentage of the money actually placed in the investment, this 8.5 percent maximum rate actually works out to a 9.29 percent ($850 ÷ $9,150) commission rate. Nowadays, the maximum charged by most equity funds is 5.75 percent, and the maximum charged by most bond funds is 4.75 percent.

Consider the following two examples.

EXAMPLE 1

The Pegasus Mutual Fund has a bid price of $20 and an ask price of $21. The bid price is the price the investor will receive for the redemption of any shares, and the ask price is the price the investor must pay for new shares. The difference in the two prices is a load charge of $1. The load charge as a percentage of the NAV is $1 ÷ $20 = 5.00 percent.

EXAMPLE 2

The Victory Mutual Fund has an NAV of $50. If it has a 3 percent load, the NAV must be divided by (1 − load percentage) to calculate the ask price.

$$P_L = NAV \div (1 - L)$$

where P_L = ask price (NAV + load)

  L = load percentage

Thus, the ask price is $50 ÷ (1 − .03) = $51.55. The load is $51.55 − $50 = $1.55

Breakpoints

Many load funds offer investors what are known as *breakpoints*. These are volume discounts in which a lower load is charged for larger investments. An example of a breakpoint schedule is shown in the table below.

Using the table below, suppose an investor has $24,000 to invest. The load charge is $1,200 ($24,000 × .05). However, if the investor opts to invest $25,000, the load charge declines to $1,062.50. In other words, by putting up an additional $1,000, the investor is *actually saving* $137.50 in commission.

Table 10-3 Sample Breakpoint Schedule	
Investment Amount	**Sales Load**
Less than $25,000	5.00%
at least $25,000 but less than $50,000	4.25%
at least $50,000 but less than $100,000	3.75%
at least $100,000 but less than $250,000	3.25%
at least $250,000 but less than $500,000	2.75%
at least $500,000 but less than $1 million	2.00%
$1 million or more	No rates change
Source: www.finra.org/InvestorInformation/InvestmentChoices/MutualFunds/p011 777; accessed July 14, 2010.	

Ethical Issue in Financial Planning

The January 2004 issue of the *Journal of Financial Planning* reports that in 2001, of all the mutual fund transactions that should have received a breakpoint charge, 20 percent did not. Either some financial planners are deliberately cheating their clients, or planners clearly need to double-check these critical details.

Right of Accumulation

Many load funds provide for a right of accumulation. This means that when an investor is making an additional purchase of a load fund, the load charge is based on the accumulated purchases.

EXAMPLE

Johnnie Johnson has previously invested $20,000 in the XYZ Growth Fund. The load charge schedule is that shown in the table above. Johnnie now wants to invest an additional $10,000. Although her commission rate was 5 percent on the first purchase, with the right of accumulation it will be 4.25 percent on this incremental purchase because the sum of the prior and current purchases exceeds the $25,000 breakpoint

Some funds add the feature that the right of accumulation will be based not only on purchases in one specific account, but also on other accounts the same person owns. For example, if the investor has both a retirement account and an ordinary account, the breakpoint is based on combined purchases. Other funds even allow an investor to include in the right of accumulation other accounts his or her spouse or children own. Finally, some fund families allow the right of accumulation to apply to all purchases of load funds within that family of funds.

Letter of Intent

Certainly, in the above example, Johnnie would have liked to have had the benefit of the breakpoint on her first purchase. Some funds will allow the use of a *letter of intent*. A letter of intent states a schedule of future (planned) share purchases. This letter then allows the investor to receive the commission rate for the total of planned purchases, beginning with the first purchase. In the above example, if Johnnie had signed a letter of intent for the second purchase at the time of the first purchase, her load fee on the first purchase would have been $850 ($20,000 × .0425) rather than the $1,000 ($20,000 × .05) she actually paid. Naturally, failure to make the subsequent purchases specified in a letter of intent will cause the fund to retroactively collect the higher sales charge.

Note that some fund companies will also apply a letter of intent retroactively.

Ethical Issue in Financial Planning

Consider the following five scenarios:

- A husband and wife have $100,000 and want to buy a mutual fund. If you recommend two separate accounts of $50,000, rather than a joint account, you will receive a substantially greater commission.

- A client has a large account invested in a fund with a right of accumulation that includes family members. The client wants to open three small accounts for her children. If you forget to indicate her account on the applications, you will receive a substantially larger commission.

- A client wants to open a small account today but will be receiving a substantial windfall in 6 months. If you forget to mention the letter of intent, you will receive a substantially larger commission today.

- A client has $99,000 to invest in the fund whose breakpoints are shown in table 10-1. If you neglect to mention the breakpoint of $100,000, you will generate nearly $500 in additional commission.

- A year ago, a client invested $200,000 in a load fund. The fund is fine, but if you switch the client to a similar fund with a different company, you will generate what is essentially a double commission.

All of the above are not only morally and ethically wrong, but they are also illegal.

Back-End Loads

contingent deferred sales charge

Although the original load charges were always front-end load charges, many funds now incorporate back-end load charges. The technical name for a back-end load is *contingent deferred sales charge*. Other names include rear load and reverse load. These charges usually decline over time. A typical back-end load is 5 or 6 percent the first year, and then it usually declines by 1 percent per year until it is eliminated in the sixth or seventh year. A contingent load is attached to each deposit in such an account, not just the first deposit. The maximum back-end load that can be charged is 7.2 percent.

Dividends and capital gain distributions are exempt from the deferred sales charge, and some funds actually allow withdrawals each year of up to 12 percent of the principal without triggering the deferred load charge. When an investor does make a withdrawal subject to a back-end fee, the fund normally assumes the withdrawal is on a FIFO (first in, first out) basis so that the lowest possible redemption fee would apply.

Many back-end load funds refer to themselves as no-load funds. This may be technically true in that the load charge is avoidable, but to an investor who ends up paying a sales fee, it would have a really bad smell.

Ethical Issue in Financial Planning

Sally Gardner, a 72-year-old widow, comes to you as a new client. Her biggest asset is $500,000 she invested just last year in the Great Growth Mutual Fund on the recommendation of her stockbroker. She says it is a no-load fund, but when you look up the fund, you find it is, in fact, a back-end load that had a first-year redemption rate of 6 percent. This load is now 5 percent. After analyzing Sally's finances, you believe she needs to cash out most of this holding and buy an annuity for two reasons. One is that based on her age, level of wealth, and risk tolerance, she needs a substantially lower percentage of her portfolio in equities. The second is that she should substantially increase her annual income. How do you explain to her that her "no-load" fund has a $25,000 back-end load?

Redemption Fee

One of the standard features of a mutual fund is the provision of costless liquidity to its investors. To accommodate short-term trading by their investors, mutual funds hold cash or liquidate portfolio holdings. These activities reduce returns to long-term investors due to the relatively low return offered on cash and the trading costs associated with rapidly selling publicly traded securities. Short-term redemption fees have become an increasingly prevalent instrument used by funds to reduce short-term trading by their investors. A short-term redemption fee is a fee of up to 2% imposed on an investor upon the sale of shares if the shares are held for less than a specified time-period (often between 1 and 6 months). Unlike other fees imposed by mutual funds, proceeds from redemption fees are retained by the fund, which transfers wealth to long-term investors, and are not revenue to the investment company that operates the fund. Nanigian, Finke, and Waller[93] find that risk adjusted fund performance is greater among funds with the fee, and that performance increases relative to the size of the fee and the time-period during which the fee is effective. For example, the authors discover that small-cap funds with a 2% redemption fee and an effective time-period of greater than two months generate annualized risk-adjusted returns that are 3.3% greater than those with no redemption fee.

Operating Expenses

All funds, whether they are load or no-load, have operating expenses. These fees are usually deducted from the interest, dividend, and capital gain income before distribution to the shareholders. There are three components to operating expenses: the management (or investment advisory) fee, marketing (12b-1) fees, and other expenses. All of these are computed as a percentage of net assets.

Investment Advisory Fee

The *investment advisory fee* is the fee paid to the mutual fund's managers for portfolio supervision and other managerial activities. Many funds place this on a declining scale whereby a lower fee is charged on incremental assets. For example, the management fee may be 1.50 percent on the first $100 million in assets, 1.45 percent on the next $25 million, and so on. The advisory fee is a function of the nature of the securities in the fund's portfolio and the extent to which the fund is actively or passively managed.

12b-1 Fee

Not all funds charge a *12b-1 fee*, which pays the marketing expenses of the fund. The fee cannot exceed 0.75 percent of average net assets per year plus another 0.25 percent service fee (*trail commission* or trailer) that can be paid to salespeople, presumably for providing ongoing service and information.

---

93. Working Paper, David Nanigian, Michael Finke, and William Waller, 2009, "Redemption Fees: Reward for Punishment."

When the mutual fund industry originally sought approval to charge a 12b-1 fee, it argued that the fee would actually benefit investors. The argument was that such marketing would sufficiently increase a fund's total assets so that the investment advisory fee could be spread over more assets and would be lower for each investor. The reduction in the management fee was supposed to have been greater than the direct cost of the 12b-1 fee. There is no proof this has happened, and there is some proof that investors are actually worse off as a result of the 12b-1 fees.[94] Most mutual funds with 12b-1 fees in excess of 0.25 percent are classified as load funds. A recent trend in the industry has been for funds to lower or eliminate the load charges and replace them with 12b-1 fees.

Other Fees

Other fees include various administrative costs such as keeping shareholder records, sending out financial reports, filing documents with the SEC, and generally paying for the service department.

The sum of all of the operating expenses charged to shareholders divided by total assets equals the management expense ratio. For equity funds, these ratios have averaged over 1.5 percent in recent years. They tend to be lower for bond funds, and they are extremely low for money market funds.

Brokerage Fees

portfolio turnover ratio

Although these fees are readily available in the funds' financial statements, the funds' transaction costs (brokerage fees incurred when buying and selling securities) are not listed as operating expenses because they are netted out in each transaction. However, they can represent a significant drag on performance for funds with high portfolio turnover rates. Portfolio turnover refers to the relative frequency of trading by the fund. The *portfolio turnover ratio* equals the lesser of annual purchases or annual sales (excluding securities with less than 1-year maturities) divided by the average monthly net assets. The average equity fund now has a portfolio turnover ratio well in excess of 100 percent per year. This means the average investment is held for less than 1 year. Funds with turnover ratios of 300 percent or more for several years in a row are spending a substantial amount of investor

---

94. The classic study on 12b-1 fees is "The Effects of 12b-1 Plans on Mutual Fund Expense Ratios: A Note," by S. Ferris and D. Chance, *Journal of Finance*, Vol. 42 (1987), pp. 1077–1082.

monies on brokerage commissions as well as the implicit transaction costs of the bid-ask spread and price impact.

Switching

switching   *Switching* is the process by which an investor moves money from one fund to another. The term switching applies to both inter-family and intra-family switches. If the receiving fund is a no-load fund, then by definition there will not be any load charges. However, if the receiving fund is a load fund, then it makes a difference. In this case, in an inter-family switch the new fund will still charge a load. However, in an intra-family switch, the load will usually be waived provided a load of equal or greater percentage was charged when the original fund was purchased. Thus, if a family offered a no-load money market fund and a load stock fund, one could not bypass the load fee by buying shares in the money market fund first and then switching into the stock fund.

Other Expenses

The Investment Company Act of 1940 requires that each new investor in a mutual fund be provided with a prospectus that details all of the potential expenses associated with fund ownership. Appropriate investment advising requires that the advisor be familiar with the prospectus issued by the fund that he or she recommends. Each fund has the ability to create fees that are unique to it. Although a comprehensive listing of all the different fees an investor might encounter is impossible, some of the other fees that exist in mutual fund investing include

- *exchange fees.* Although some funds do not charge for switching, others do. In fact, because some investors engage in switching trades multiple times per month, and because such fast movements of cash in and out of a fund make it more difficult to manage the fund, most funds impose a fee for a switch, or they place a limit on the amount of switching that is permitted in an account. The purpose of the fee is to discourage investors from using the funds to engage in timing trades.

- *account maintenance fees.* A common practice of mutual fund families is to charge an annual fee for every account the investor holds. This fee, which may be as little as $10, defrays the cost of account record keeping. This fee is usually waived for accounts above a certain size.

- *reinvestment loads.* Some funds charge a load even for automatic reinvestment of dividends.

Classes of Shares

multi-class funds   Once 12b-1 fees started to become common, some funds allowed investors to choose how they would pay for marketing fees by creating classes of shares known as *multi-class funds*. The categorization now used by many funds is that investors can choose between Class A, Class B, and Class C shares.[95] The common distinctions are as follows:[96]

- *Class A shares* typically have a large (front-end) load fee but a minimal or no 12b-1 charge. The average load fee is 5 percent, with most funds in the 4 to 5.75 percent range. The average expense ratio for an equity fund is 1.3 percent.

- *Class B shares* typically have no front-end load but do have 12b-1 fees and back-end loads that typically start at 5 percent and declines to zero over a period of 4 to 7 years. The average expense ratio is 2 percent because of the 12b-1 fee. These shares usually convert to Class A shares after about 5 to 8 years. Finally, these shares are usually excluded from any right-of-accumulation rules.

- *Class C shares* typically have no front-end load, but the back-end load starts at about 1 percent. This load is eliminated after one year. The average expense ratio is about 2 percent because these shares have the highest 12b-1 fees of the three classes, and they typically do not convert. Hence, investors are stuck with the 12b-1 fee for as long as they hold these shares.

Some funds also offer Class I shares, which are for institutional investors only. Because institutional investors typically put substantially larger amounts of money into a fund (for example, millions of dollars versus thousands of dollars), the entire fee structure is likely to be different.

What conditions favor the selection of each class? Class A is favored by investors who intend to make a large purchase (provided there are

---

95. Some funds offer an entire alphabet soup of classes of shares. For example, one fund company's prospectus covers Class L, M, N, H, Z, and E shares. There is no legal requirement for the definition of what is meant by each class of shares, but the nomenclature presented here seems to be nearly universal. The legal requirements with respect to classes of shares are covered in Rule 18f-3 of the SEC, adopted under the Investment Company Act of 1940.

96. *Money*, March 2006, p. 86.

breakpoints), already hold other funds in the same family if there is a right of accumulation, plan to make regular purchases if a letter of intent is allowed, and/or have family members who hold funds in the same family of funds if these can be included in the right of accumulation. Class C shares are usually preferred by anyone with a limited time horizon for the investment, such as no more than a few years. For investors with longer time horizons, Class A or B is preferable, depending on the terms of the shares.

Some fund companies are phasing out Class B shares and other fund companies are limiting the amount an investor can put into Class B shares.[97] This is because they have been the source of some ethical problems that have hit the industry. Some brokers have been known to advise clients that Class B shares are no-load and to place them in these shares when Class A would be more appropriate.[98]

Ethical Issue in Financial Planning
NASD's National Adjudicatory Council (NAC) upheld an NASD Hearing Panel's decision that Wendell D. Belden made unsuitable sales of Class B mutual fund shares. Belden is the sole owner of Southmark, Inc., based in Tulsa, OK. He was fined $40,000, suspended in all capacities for 1 year, and ordered to pay restitution of $55,567, plus interest. Belden was also ordered to requalify as a principal by examination, and assessed costs of the proceeding.
The NAC determined that a registered representative's suitability obligation includes the requirement to minimize the sales charges paid for mutual fund shares, when consistent with the customer's investment objectives. In this case, the NAC found that the recommendations were unsuitable because the purchase of Class B shares, instead of Class A shares of the same fund, resulted in significantly higher commission costs, including the payment of a contingent deferred sales charge upon the sale of the shares.
Specifically, Belden recommended and sold more than $2.1 million in Class B shares rather than Class A shares to his customer, a retired individual. While Class A shares typically involve a front-end sales charge, these fund shares incur lower ongoing charges and there is no contingent deferred sales charge upon the sale of the shares. Class B mutual fund shares generally do not incur a front-end sales charge, but are subject to higher ongoing charges and a contingent deferred sales charge upon the sale of shares. In this case, the customer purchased shares in two mutual fund families. The amount invested in one fund family was more than $1 million, which would have entitled the customer to purchase Class A shares with no front-end sales charge. The customer's investment in the second fund family

97. "To B or Not to B," *Financial Planning*, March 2005, pp. 45–46.

98. Steven T. Goldberg, "Bye-Bye B Shares," *Kiplinger's*, February 2005.

was over $800,000, which would have entitled the customer to receive the largest discount on the front end sales charge offered by the fund.

The NAC stated that over an 8-year period, the ongoing fund charges for Class B shares would have been 64 percent higher than the same charge for Class A shares. The NAC also found that Belden placed his customer in Class B shares to generate higher commissions for himself and explained that its finding was bolstered by Belden's statement that he could not stay in business if he had to rely on the lower commissions for the sale of Class A shares. In this case, Belden and his employer firm earned commissions on the sale of Class B shares of $84,000. The commissions on the sale of Class A shares would have only been $28,000.

Source: NASD Press Release, September 10, 2002.

Benefits of Mutual Fund Ownership

There are benefits and drawbacks to investing in mutual funds. Let's consider the benefits first.

Professional Management

Many investors lack the time to properly select securities and can better delegate this responsibility to others. Professional portfolio managers typically have extensive education in investments and portfolio management. They have ready access to professional analysts and quantitative techniques to evaluate financial statements, market conditions, management quality, research and development, competition, and other relevant factors. Portfolio managers can speak directly to corporate management because of the quantity of shares that the portfolio managers control, and they can also speak directly to competitors, suppliers, and customers.

Years ago, almost all mutual funds were effectively run by an "investment committee." Nowadays, over 80 percent of equity funds are run by "portfolio managers." In fact, the average portfolio manager stays with a fund for about 5 years. Long-term investors in mutual funds can expect to have at least two or more managers running their funds.[99]

Diversification

Small investors are effectively precluded from diversifying their portfolios through purchase of individual securities. They simply lack sufficient assets to make reasonably sized purchases of a large number of assets. In addition,

---

99. Bogle, op cit.

the structure of transactions costs makes diversification more expensive for small investors. Mutual fund portfolios typically include 50 to 200 securities. A recent study by a major brokerage firm found that in an analysis of 150 equity mutual funds, the average number of stocks in the portfolio was 112.[100]

Buying even one mutual fund usually means instant diversification.

Convenience

Almost all mutual funds offer the following services:

- automatic reinvestment programs for dividends and capital gains
- automatic checking account debits (the fund will transfer money from one's checking account on a regular basis to buy new shares)
- check writing privileges for money market funds
- telephone and electronic account transfers between funds in the same family

Another convenience of mutual funds is that an investor does not need to worry about buying full shares to match an exact dollar amount. Funds track shares to at least three decimal places. Thus, when an investor purchases shares, the fund divides the dollar amount of the purchase (less any load charge) by the NAV to obtain the number of shares purchased.

EXAMPLE
Suppose an investor makes a purchase for $5,000 and at the close of business that day, the ask price is computed to be $23.18. The investor will be credited with 215.703 shares (that is, $5,000/$23.18).

Record Keeping

Among the account data provided are the following:

- statements to confirm transactions
- periodic statements (monthly, quarterly, or annually)
- documentation for tax calculations
- shareholder newsletters
- shareholder reports (at least semiannually)

---

100. Arden Dale, "Holdings Show Many Mutual Funds Drift in Investment Style," *The Wall Street Journal Online*, April 5, 2005

- telephone and online access to account information

Other Factors

The following factors also encourage mutual fund ownership:

- *marketability.* Because the account value is based on the NAV, fund balances can be redeemed, and thus converted into cash, on short notice with no concern about affecting the market price. As long as any order to redeem shares is placed at least 30 minutes prior to before the market close, the shares will be liquidated that day at the closing NAV.
- *switching.* Switching provides the only opportunity in the investments world wherein an investor can move substantial sums of money from one large diversified portfolio to another such portfolio with minimal or no transaction fee (provided the investor is not engaging in an inter-family switch to a load fund).
- *minimal investment requirements.* Some investments are sold in denominations that are too large for small investors. For example, the minimum denomination for a bond may be as high as $10,000. However, most mutual funds are available in much smaller amounts, especially for monthly automatic investment plans.
- *regulation.* The recent scandals in the mutual fund industry notwithstanding, the extensive regulation of the industry by FINRA and the SEC should provide some comfort to investors that they will not be abused. Complaints about abuse can be directed to either organization.

Drawbacks of Mutual Fund Ownership

The major drawback to mutual fund ownership is the various fees and expenses. A more subtle drawback is that the investor loses control over the timing of capital gains. When the fund manager declares a capital gain distribution, it triggers a taxable event for the owner of a taxable account. Of course, the investor still has control over the timing of gains generated by the sale of the fund shares themselves.

Another disadvantage, particularly for funds with large portfolios, is that mutual funds sometimes adversely affect the market prices of the stocks that they trade. Large purchases tend to trade above the most recent market price (buying concession), and large sales tend to trade below it (selling concession). Small investors, in contrast, can generally purchase what they want with no price effect. Funds sometimes attempt to counteract this problem by assigning portions of their portfolio to several different managerial groups. Subdividing may reduce, but is unlikely to eliminate, the adverse price effects of their large trades. Furthermore, subdividing may increase management and administrative costs.

The Prospectus

Under the federal laws that regulate security transactions, a prospectus (a document produced by the mutual fund management that provides relevant information about the fund) must be delivered to prospective investors before the purchase. The prospectus offers a large amount of information about the fund, including the following:

- *the fund's investment objectives.* For example, the prospectus may state that the primary objective is long-term growth of capital, and the secondary objective is current income.
- *the fund's investment policies.* The prospectus may state, for example, that the fund invests primarily in common stocks, but that it may also invest in bonds or money market instruments, or even stock futures and options.
- *general information* about the risks of investing in the fund
- *tables showing the loads and other expenses* associated with the purchase, retention, and sale of the fund's shares
- *additional information* concerning performance, management, purchase and redemption procedures, minimum initial purchase and subsequent minimum purchase amounts, and more

With regard to information concerning performance, the SEC requires mutual funds that advertise past financial performance to use a standard calculation method, which is defined in Form N-1A, the registration statement that investment companies must file with the SEC under the Investment Company Act of 1940. Sales loads or other charges, as well as the fund's expenses, are deducted from the average annual total return figure. Dividends and distributions by the fund are assumed to be reinvested.

Governance

Mutual funds are governed pretty much like other corporations. The shareholders elect a Board of Directors, which in turns appoints the managers and generally oversees the fund's operations. Directors are classified as inside or outside directors, depending on whether or not they are an employee of the management company overseeing the fund's operations. Many people, as well as the SEC, are concerned that not enough directors of funds are outside directors, and thus shareholders do not have adequate protection from abuses by the management company. A recent study suggests that a more appropriate criterion for directors is the extent to which they have large amounts of their own money in their fund.[101] The study finds that funds in which directors have significant amounts of their own money invested in the fund perform substantially better than when this is not the case. Furthermore, these same funds have substantially lower fees that are charged to shareholders.

In the case of fund families where a large number of funds are managed by a single company, it would be awkward to have a completely unique board for each fund. In these cases, the same board frequently is elected to many of the funds within that family. The above cited study found that if a director had no money in his or her own fund but had substantial money invested in another fund in the same family, then the superior performance and lower fees still occurred.

OTHER POOLED INVESTMENTS

Closed-End Investment Companies

The second most common type of investment company after mutual funds is the closed-end investment company. At the end of December 2009, there were 627 closed-end funds, and their combined portfolios were worth $228.4 billion. The majority of these assets were in bond funds, and the majority of the bond funds invested in domestic municipal bonds.[102]The number of a closed-end investment company's shares outstanding is basically fixed. The shares outstanding for a closed-end fund change only if the fund has a public offering, a dividend reinvestment plan (DRIP), a direct purchase plan (DPP), or a share buy-back program.

Unlike purchasers of mutual funds, buyers of shares in a closed-end fund do not receive a prospectus when they consider a purchase. Investors buy and sell their shares in the secondary market in the same way as stock in any publicly traded corporation. Like publicly traded stock, their share prices are

---

101. Martijn Cremers, Joost Driessen, Pascal Maenhout, and David Weinbaum, "Does Skin in the Game Matter? Director Incentives and Governance in the Mutual Fund Industry," forum.johnson.cornell.edu/faculty/weinbaum/weinbaum.pdf, accessed March 9, 2007.

102. www.ici.org/research/stats/closed-end/cef_q1_10, accessed July 14, 2010.

determined by supply and demand. The shares may sell for a premium or a discount relative to their NAV. Most of the time, closed-end funds trade at a discount, and sometimes these discounts are not trivial.

Some investors believe the purchase of closed-end funds at substantial discounts is a "free lunch" available in the marketplace. Others believe there are real reasons for these discounts. Some of the more commonly listed reasons for these continuing discounts include the following:

- *embedded tax liabilities.* To the extent that portfolios of closed-end funds contain unrecognized capital gains, a buyer of these shares is buying future tax liabilities. Stated another way, the portfolio cannot be liquidated to net the NAV because of the capital gains taxes the shareholder would owe.

- *lack of marketability of some holdings.* Because closed-end funds do not have to worry about share redemptions, they do not have to worry about the marketability of all of their holdings. This lack of marketability may even extend to the point where they have holdings for which daily price quotations are not available. As a result, the NAV that is computed each day may represent no more than a best guess.

- *general market sentiment.* Recent research found that closed-end fund discounts increased dramatically following the September 11 attacks and then slowly recovered over time as the general markets recovered, suggesting that "discounts reflect the sentiment of small investors, who took their cues from the broader market's overall movement."[103]

- *Increased risk due to leverage.* Closed-end funds, unlike mutual funds, can buy on margin or even issue debt. As long as the borrowing rate is less than the yield on the portfolio, then investors benefit. However, if the borrowing rate exceeds the yield on the portfolio of assets, then the losses can become dramatic.[104]

Many people find it strange that a closed-end company will sometimes trade at a premium. No economically sound explanation appears to have ever been offered in the literature. At best, we could argue that occasionally a closed-end company holds a portfolio that is concentrated in a sector that is "hot" and for which no other sector funds might exist. Hence, this company

103. Timothy R. Burch, Douglas R. Emery, and Michael E. Fuerst, "What Can 'Nine-Eleven' Tell Us about Closed-End Fund Discounts and Investor Sentiment?" *The Financial Review*, Vol. 38, No 4 (2003), pp. 515-529.

104. Donald Jay Korn, "Case Closed," *Finanical Planning*, October 2003, pp. 119–121.

is a unique investment opportunity for which investors are willing to pay a premium. In view of the overwhelming tendency for closed-end companies to trade at discounts, investment advisors should be wary of placing clients in one that trades at a premium.

Conversions and Lifeboat Provisions

Occasionally some closed-end funds convert to an open-end format. There was an average of about 10 conversions per year in the late 1990s,[105] although that was an unusually high rate compared to the rate at most other times. To the extent that the fund's discount was an irrational phenomenon, such a process would generate a windfall gain for the shareholders. One downside to this conversion process is that some funds create an exit fee after the conversion. This fee usually amounts to about 2 percent and typically lasts for about 6 months to one year. The revenue this generates can be substantial, as the average asset decline during the 6 months following conversion is 28.2 percent.[106]

lifeboat provisions

Because of this propensity to trade at discounts, many closed-end funds adopt *lifeboat provisions* for their investors. These provisions usually require that the funds take action to bolster their shares if they sell at a persistent discount, such as for more than 10 percent, for a specified period of time. Such provisions may either be established when a new fund is created or added at a later date.[107] The action may be either to repurchase fund shares in the open market, or to initiate a conversion.[108] The repurchase process is frequently done through a *Dutch auction*, which is an auction process in which the final price is established as the price that is just sufficient to buy the desired number of shares.

Managed Distribution Policies

Some closed-end funds follow what is known as a managed distribution policy. Such a policy sets a minimum percentage yield that will be promised for the year, based on the NAV at the start of the year. For example, a fund

---

105. Aaron Lucchetti, "Scudder Is at Center of Fight over Fees," *The Wall Street Journal* (Eastern edition). New York: July 14, 1999, p. 1.

106. *Medical Economics*, December 14, 1998, p. 24.

107. www.fundaction.com/pdf/FA050905.pdf, accessed July 14, 2010.

108. www.amex.com/servlet/AmexFnDictionary?pageid=display&titleid=3709, accessed July 14, 2010.

might promise a 5 percent yield. If the ordinary dividend distribution and the capital gains distribution equal or exceed this 5 percent mark, then the promise has been achieved. If the dividend and the capital gain distribution fall short of this mark, then the fund liquidates some of its holdings and makes a return of capital distribution. The return of capital distribution will cause a reduction in the fund's total assets. There is evidence to suggest that closed-end funds that adopt a managed distribution policy tend to trade at smaller discounts to the NAV because investors appreciate the certainty of the cash flow that they will receive from the investment.

Dual-Purpose Investment Companies

income share

capital appreciation share

Dual-purpose investment companies (DPICs) are closed-end funds with two classes of shares. One is the *income share*, and the other is the *capital appreciation share*. The income share is like a preferred stock with a maturity date. It promises a fixed rate of return and par value back at maturity. The capital appreciation share promises no dividends during the life of the income shares.

Only nine such companies were publicly traded in the U.S. in the years 1967 to 1985. None are publicly traded now in the U.S., although some are traded in other countries.

Real Estate Based Investment Companies

Mutual funds cannot own equity interests in real estate for several reasons, including the practical ones that daily price quotations are not available and there is a lack of marketability in the event of a large amount of redemptions. For this reason, all equity real estate investing by investment companies is done via closed-end funds. This investing takes several forms, including REITs, RELPs, and REMICs.

REITs

Real estate investment trusts (REITs) are the most common vehicle for pooled investing in real estate. REITs assemble and manage portfolios of real estate and real estate loans. By law, at least 75 percent of REIT assets must be invested in real estate, and no less than 75 percent of income must be derived from real estate. In addition, to be recognized as a conduit and thus avoid taxation, REITs must pay out at least 90 percent of their income annually.

Based on investment objectives, REITs fall into one of three general categories:

- Equity REITs invest in properties that produce income or have growth potential, such as office buildings, apartments, shopping malls, and hotels.
- Mortgage REITs are in the business of making both construction loans and mortgage loans.
- Hybrid REITs are a combination of equity and mortgage REITs.

Equity REITs are the most popular type with investors who want to participate in the growth of real estate values. Dividends should rise if rents increase more than expenses, and share prices generally reflect changes in property values. Mortgage REITs are similar to bonds. Like all interest-rate-sensitive investments, their prices rise when interest rates fall and fall when interest rates rise.

RELPs and Unlisted REITs

More aggressive investors looking for equity positions in real estate might consider real estate limited partnerships or RELPs, and unlisted REITs. RELPs were popular in the 1980s until the passage of the Tax Reform Act of 1986. This act reduced or eliminated many limited partnership holders' ability to deduct partnership losses. Another drawback is that RELPs are often sold with large loads. RELPs usually have a provision that they will be liquidated at a point 8 to 12 years from the time of creation. Similarly, most unlisted REITs today carry a provision that promises the REIT will become listed by a certain date or it will be liquidated. Investors who want out of unlisted REITs or RELPs before a step is taken to provide marketability will probably have to pay a high price to get their cash back. Unlisted REITs have for the most part taken the place of RELPs.

REMICS

Real estate mortgage investment conduits (REMIC) are a complex pool of mortgage securities created for the purpose of acquiring collateral. Unlike traditional pass-throughs such as REITs, the principal and interest payments in REMICs are not passed through to investors pro rata; instead they are divided into varying payment streams to create classes with different expected maturities, differing levels of seniority or subordination, or other characteristics. The assets underlying REMIC securities can be either other mortgage-backed securities or original mortgage loans. In essence, REMICs consist of a fixed pool of mortgages broken apart and marketed to investors as individual securities. GNMA and FHLMC both administer large REMIC programs. REMIC shares are similar to mortgage pass-through securities and collateralized mortgage obligations.

Unit Investment Trusts

There are two key features to a unit investment trust (UIT): The portfolios are unmanaged and they must have a termination date that is established at the time the UIT is created.[109] The minimal management of these trusts means there are negligible management expenses. UITs are typically set up and marketed by a brokerage firm that receives an underwriting fee from the proceeds of the sale and manages the trust until it is liquidated. Investors technically buy units rather than shares. There are two types of UITs: debt and equity.

As of yearend 2009, the number and size of assets held by UITs were as follows:

Type	Number	Assets Held
Tax-free Bond Trust	3,466	$9.89 billion
Taxable Bond Trust	438	$3.67 billion
Equity Trust	2,145	$24.77 billion

So there are more municipal UITs in existence than equity UITs, but the equity UITs have about 2½ times the market value of assets.[110]

Debt UITs

Once assembled, most debt security portfolios can be left unmanaged until the last holding in the portfolio matures. Interest payments and principal payments for maturing securities are passed through to UIT investors as they occur, net of any administrative costs. Once all of the securities have matured, the trust is dissolved. One problem that can occur with such a portfolio is that if there is a default on one of the bonds, it can take years for final resolution. In such situations, the portfolio manager will usually sell the defaulted bond and either distribute the proceeds or reinvest, depending on

109. www.sec.gov/answers/uit.htm, accessed July 14, 2010.

110. www.ici.org/research/stats/uit/uits_05_10, accessed July 14, 2010.

what seems more appropriate. Debt UITs have maturities that range from 5 years to 30 years. The minimum investment in a debt UIT is usually $1,000.

Equity UITs

The termination date means that the portfolio is effectively liquidated on this date and investors are cashed out. Most equity UITs have a termination date of 1 year. There is usually a strategy or theme to an equity UIT. One popular theme has been "dogs of the Dow," which is a strategy based on the belief that the 10 stocks in the DJIA with the highest dividend yields will outperform the other 20 stocks over the next 12 months. These UITs are assembled for 12-month holding periods. Hence, an investor who believes in this strategy could regularly repeat it by buying a UIT based on this theme, then rolling the proceeds over into a similar UIT when the old one matures.

Advantages and Disadvantages of UITs

There are advantages and disadvantages to UITs, although many of these are similar to the advantages and disadvantages of other investment companies. The advantages are

- *convenience.* One purchase allows the investor to obtain a fully diversified portfolio that meets a particular objective.
- *minimum investment size.* The minimum investment requirements are substantially less than if an investor attempted to create such a portfolio directly.
- *portfolio stability.* The investor knows from the date of purchase what the underlying portfolio should be over the life of the investment.
- *tax efficiency.* In the case of debt UITs, there should be minimal capital gains or losses. Equity UITs have a known date on which the capital gain or loss will be recognized.
- *Negligible management fees.* Due to the lack of any active management, there are negligible management fees.

The disadvantages are as follows:

- UITs are not as common as other forms of investment companies. Thus, an investor is less likely to find a UIT that seeks to fill a particular investment goal, especially with equity trusts.
- Front-end loads can be steep.

- The resale market is usually maintained by the trustee (the issuer). Such markets typically lack marketability and thus investors may have to sell their units at substantial discounts.

Exchange-Traded Funds (ETFs)

As of May 2010, there were 468 domestic exchange-traded funds (ETFs) that held $461 billion in assets.[111] This can be compared to the fact that at the end of 2001, there were 102 ETFs with total assets of $83 billion. The portfolio of an ETF is typically, but not always, passively managed. Many are designed to mimic an index that reflects either the broad market, a sector, or an international index. ETFs do not sell individual shares directly to investors.[112] Instead, they issue their shares in large blocks (blocks of 50,000 shares, for example) that are known as *creation units*. These units can only be bought with a basket of securities that mirrors the ETF's portfolio. Naturally, the buyers of creation units are usually institutions. The buyer often resells some of these shares in the secondary market, which is how individuals acquire them. Investors who want to sell their ETF shares can either sell them in the secondary market or, if they have enough shares to form a creation unit, exchange the creation unit for the basket of underlying securities.

An ETF does develop a prospectus, and this is given to anyone buying a creation unit. Some ETFs deliver these documents to secondary market purchasers. ETFs that do not deliver a prospectus are required to give investors a document known as a product description, which summarizes key information about the ETF and explains how to obtain a prospectus. All ETFs will deliver a prospectus upon request.

ETFs come with many intriguing names. The most widely advertised is the SPDR, which stands for the Standard & Poor's Depository Receipt. This was the first ETF, created in 1993, but it did not really become popular until the late 1990s. Other appealing ETFs include DIAMONDS, which tracks the Dow Jones Industrial Average, and iShares, which stands for index shares and tracks indexes used in countries all around the globe.

The most heavily traded ETF is known by the nickname Cubes, because its ticker symbol is QQQQ. Cubes is an ETF that tracks the technology-laden NASDAQ 100 index.

---

111. www.ici.org/research/stats/etf/etfs_05_10, accessed July 14, 2010..

112. www.sec.gov/answers/etf.htm, accessed July 14, 2010.

Although we might think an investor would be indifferent between an index fund and an ETF, there are real advantages and disadvantages to each, and the financial planner should make sure that a client is being placed into the correct vehicle when one of these two investments is selected.

The advantages of ETFs over index funds include the following:

- ETFs are traded on a daily basis like any other stock and thus give investors the ability to buy or sell at any time during the trading day. Index funds can be bought or redeemed only at the end of a trading day.

- The investor can buy an ETF on margin. Index funds require the full purchase price.

- One can sell short an ETF, but not an index fund.

- ETFs can have extremely low management fees because the fund manager does not have to deal with the individual investors' accounts and provide regular mailings to the shareholders.

- ETFs are extremely tax efficient for several reasons, including:

  - the fact that withdrawals are via distribution of shares in exchange for a creation unit means that no shares have to be sold and thus no capital gains recognized, and

  - when shares are distributed, the ETF normally distributes the shares with the lowest cost basis in the portfolio, leaving only shares with the highest cost basis in the portfolio.

- ETFs more closely track an index. It is more difficult for an index fund to track an index due to transaction costs. Each time an index fund has a net cash inflow or outflow, it must incur the bid-ask spread as well as any direct commission costs.[113]

- Because ETFs neither accept cash nor redeem shares for cash, they do not need to hold cash in their portfolio for this purpose. This allows them to hold a higher percentage of their portfolio in the actual securities of the index than can an index fund. This contributes to their ability to more closely track an index.

- ETFs avoid the problems and related scandals associated with late trading and market timing that plague mutual funds.

---

113. Leonard Kostovetsky, "Index Mutual Funds and Exchange-Traded Funds: A Comparison of Two Methods of Passive Investment," *The Journal of Portfolio Management*, summer 2003, p. 81.

This close tracking of indices by ETFs has been recently documented for Cubes. The statistical evidence indicates that most of the time the price of Cubes is extremely close to the NAV. Nonetheless, significant intra-day disparities do occur sometimes, although they appear to be eliminated relatively quickly.[114]

The advantages of index funds over ETFs include the following:

- Most index funds are no-loads, whereas ETFs are normally bought through a broker, thus requiring a commission. This is particularly important if the amount being invested is on the smaller side. In fact, if an investor is acquiring shares through a monthly investing program, it is extremely likely that the purchase of an index fund is more cost effective. Shorter holding periods and smaller investment amounts favor the purchase of an index fund.[115]

- As with stocks, ETF trading involves a bid-ask spread, thus creating an implicit cost to buy and sell these shares.

- Index funds always trade at the NAV, but ETFs will sometimes trade at a discount from the NAV. This discount is good for buyers, but bad for sellers.

Both ETFs and index funds suffer from tracking error problems when stocks in the index being tracked go ex-dividend. This is because most indices assume that the proceeds of the dividend are automatically reinvested on the ex-dividend date. In practice, there are several days if not several weeks between the ex-dividend date and the payment date. Thus, neither the index funds nor the ETFs have the cash available to make the reinvestment that is built into the actual index.

---

114. Richard J. Curcio, Joanna M. Lipka, and John H. Thronton, Jr., "Cubes and the Individual Investor," *Financial Services Review*, vol. 13 (2004), pp. 123–138.

115. Kostovetsky, op cit.

Financial Planning Issue

When should an advisor recommend an ETF, and when should he or she recommend an index fund? If the client (or the planner) wants to engage in market timing trades, then index funds are preferable. Timing involves frequent trades. Although index funds can be bought or redeemed only at the end of the day, the transaction is cost free. The commissions and bid-ask spreads make ETFs less appealing for this strategy, although there are some ETFs that actively solicit this type of investor.

Conversely, investors with long-term objectives should prefer ETFs because the low annual expenses of managing the fund will easily offset commissions over a period of several years.

Holding Company Depository Receipts (HOLDRs)

In recent years, *Holding Company Depository Receipts (HOLDRs)*, a variation of ETFs, have become popular. HOLDRs are analogous to sector funds—that is, they are ETFs that, instead of mimicking an index, hold selected stocks (frequently 20) in a particular industry.

Hedge Funds

Hedge funds are a type of pooled portfolio instrument organized for maximum flexibility for the portfolio manager. They have been characterized as "mutual funds on steroids."[116] For example, hedge funds may invest in derivatives, sell short, use leverage, and invest internationally. Most hedge funds have been organized offshore to avoid the regulations imposed on U.S. funds, and most of them take substantial risks. They are typically organized as limited partnerships and allow only *accredited investors*[117] and large institutions to participate. These investors must demonstrate both the sophistication and the financial resources to understand and take the risks associated with such investments. Unfortunately, it is easy to bypass the accredited investor requirements by buying a mutual fund that invests only in hedge funds.[118]

Hedge funds, unlike mutual funds, do not have to register with the SEC. Because their sale of securities is classified as private offerings, they are

---

116. David Swensen, "Invest at Your Own Risk," *The New York Times*, October 19, 2005, p. A21.

117. The term accredited investor is defined in Rule 501 of Regulation D. There are eight categories of accredited investors, but the two for individuals specify that to be accredited the investor must either individually or jointly with his or her spouse have a net worth of $1 million at the time of purchase, or meet some income requirements.

118. Allan Sloan, "Hedge-Fund Horrors," *Newsweek*, September 26, 2005, p. E34.

exempt from registrations under the Securities Act of 1933. They are also exempt from the reporting requirement of the Securities Exchange Act of 1934.[119]

It is still possible to invest in hedge funds without being an accredited investor or an institutional investor. Some investment companies offer funds of hedge funds, and some of the minimums are as low as $25,000.

Statistics on the returns of hedge funds are always quite exciting, but they are also misleading. Research on hedge funds shows that their returns have a low degree of skewness but a high degree of kurtosis. The problem with this is that investors prefer a high degree of skewness and a low degree of kurtosis.

About 20 percent of the active hedge funds cease operations every year because of poor returns.[120] Two of the more notable biases in the statistics on returns include backfill bias and survivorship bias.[121] Backfill bias starts with the fact that unlike mutual funds, hedge funds are not required to provide their rates of return to anyone. Thus, when new funds start up, they keep their results confidential. If they are successful, then they begin reporting them to the various database publishers. Some funds (presumably the ones with good records) report their earlier results. The rest of the funds, presumably with less attractive results, do not report the earlier rates of return. An analysis of this phenomenon suggests that backfilled returns are more than 500 basis points higher than contemporaneously reported returns, thus making the industry look incredibly more successful than it is.

Survivorship bias refers to the fact that rates of return are reported only for funds still in existence at any point in time. Because these are the funds that have had better rates of return, their records will almost always be better than what the industry as a whole has achieved. Estimates of this bias indicate it causes the rates of returns to be overstated by more than 400 basis points.

It would be nice to think that the better hedge fund managers are the ones able to consistently outperform the other managers, and that it is the weaker managers whose funds disappear. Unfortunately, recent research also

---

119. www.sec.gov/answer/hedge.htm, accessed July 14, 2010.

120. S.J. Brown, W.N. Goetzmann, and R.G. Ibbotson, "Offshore Hedge Funds: Survival and Performance: 1989–1995," *Journal of Business*, vol. 72, 1999, pp. 91–117.

121. "Hedge Funds: Risk and Return," by Burton G. Malkiel and Atanu Saha, *Financial Analysts Journal*, Volume 61, No. 6 (November/December 2005), pp. 80–88.

suggests that the probability of a superior performance in one year being followed by a superior performance in the following years is only about 50-50, which is about the same statistics as for mutual funds, and what we would expect from random chance.

One reason it is difficult to believe the phenomenal returns associated with hedge funds is the typical cost structure associated with these organizations. The average hedge fund charges a management "fee of 2 percent of assets and 25 percent of the profits that the fund makes."[122] Thus, if a fund earned a 12 percent return on assets, the 2 percent fee and 25 percent profit sharing leaves the investor with only a 7.5 percent rate of return. If the investment is acquired through a mutual fund of hedge funds that charges a 1.5 percent management fee, then the investor's return on equity is down to 6 percent!

Investors in hedge funds should be wary of lock-up periods and advanced notice of redemptions. For example, a hedge fund may have a one-year lock-up period, which means none of one's investment can be redeemed during the first year. Thereafter, investors would also have to give advance notice of say, 90 days, of an intent to redeem, and even then such redemptions might be limited to specific days, such as the last business day of each month.

Hedge funds can have a substantial impact on the securities markets. Consider the near collapse in October 1998 of Long Term Capital Management—a large and previously high-flying hedge fund that at its peak value was leveraged to the tune of more than $100 billion in assets against a capital base of $3 billion. Another example is the collapse of the EiFuki Master Fund, which lost its entire $300 million market value in a mere 7 trading days.

Variable Annuities

Yet another form of pooled investing is the variable annuity. An individual buys an annuity with the insurance company, which places the premiums into its own pooled portfolio. The value of the annuity contract then depends on the performance of the insurance company's portfolio. The policyholder may opt for a variable annuity during either or both the accumulation period and the payout period. Some policyholders select a variable annuity during the accumulation period, and then during the payout period switch at least part of the funds to a fixed annuity. For example, upon retirement, an individual

---

122. Sloan, op cit.

might switch from a 100 percent variable annuity to one that is 50 percent variable and 50 percent fixed. This gives the individual some assurance as to a minimum fixed income and an opportunity for income growth. The NAVs of variable annuities are reported in the financial press.

A variation of the variable annuity is the equity-indexed annuity. This product usually offers a guaranteed minimum fixed rate of return. However, it also promises a rate of return tied to a market index. Thus, if the market goes up, the owner receives more than the promised minimum rate of return, and if the market goes down, the owner receives the promised minimum rate of return.

The drawback to a variable annuity is that the sale of the annuity involves a relatively high load, and the individual still has to pay the portfolio's management fees. In addition, if the policyholder is unhappy with the performance of the insurance company's portfolio, there may be a substantial fee to cancel the policy.

Because variable annuities are separate accounts from the issuer's assets, they are considered securities under federal law. This means that the seller must have a life insurance license and be registered with FINRA to sell variable annuities. The seller must also obtain state licensing powers or authorization to sell variable annuities within each jurisdiction in which they are sold. Any potential buyer of a variable annuity must be given a prospectus. The seller must ascertain that a variable annuity is a suitable product choice for the purchaser. Suitability involves assessing a potential investor's investment objectives, time horizon, and risk tolerance.

Reasons to Recommend a Variable Annuity

Whether or not a financial planner recommends a variable annuity depends on the client's risk tolerance and how long the money will be invested before the client plans to start withdrawals. People with short investment time horizons and low investment risk tolerance will generally be happier with a fixed annuity. If they have long time horizons and moderate risk tolerance, a planner might recommend an equity-indexed annuity. The advantage of both the variable annuity and the equity-indexed annuity over the fixed annuity is that they are more likely to keep up with inflation because of their link to the financial markets. An advantage of all annuities is that the assets accumulate on a tax-deferred basis, although the policyholder has to pay income taxes on the gain in value either at the time of withdrawal or as the payments are received during the payout phase.

Types of Pooled Portfolio Funds by Organizational Structures

- Mutual funds: Open-ended; price based on NAV

  - Load funds: Sold through salesperson for a commission
  - No-load funds: Sold directly without an up-front fee

- Closed-end investment companies: Managed portfolio; stock trades on an exchange or OTC, usually at a discount from NAV

- Unit investment trusts (UITs): Unmanaged; self-liquidating

- ETFs and HOLDRs: Have infinite lives; usually passively managed to match an index

- Hedge funds: Typically organized as offshore limited partnerships for qualified investors; maximum investment flexibility

- Variable annuities: Can be used in either the accumulation period or the payout period

---

The variable annuity is for the senior client who realizes that gains and losses may occur, but who wants the investment flexibility that comes from being able to move funds among subaccounts within the separate account. This flexibility allows annuity owners in the seniors market to change their investment focus in response to changes in the financial markets or in their personal situations at the different stages of their retirement.

Other Types of Pooled Portfolios: Pooled Funds, Corporations, and Blind Pools

Many people have personal accounts that are managed by trust companies, trust departments within banks, and insurance companies. It would be nearly impossible for a large trust operation to manage each account separately. To facilitate the management of these accounts, the company creates its own in-house portfolios (that is, mutual funds), which are also known as pooled funds. The assets in a trust account can then either be sold and the proceeds used to buy shares in the pooled funds, or the assets can be given in kind to the pooled fund and allocated shares based on their market value. To facilitate such trades, the pooled funds compute a daily NAV and function pretty much as any other mutual fund, except that they cannot be directly purchased by the public.

Several other types of pooled portfolios are available to the investor. For example, some ordinary companies hold such large portfolios of stock in other companies that they are closed-end investment companies in all but name. Among the better known of these firms is Berkshire Hathaway. Berkshire Hathaway was once in textiles but now is primarily an owner of stocks. Its CEO, Warren Buffett, is highly respected for his adroit portfolio management.

blind pool   Perhaps the most risky pooled portfolio device is the blind pool. With a blind pool, the investor agrees to finance a venture whose precise purposes are to be revealed later. The prospective investor will, however, be told the pool's general purpose (for example, to finance a program of risk arbitrage). Most people who invest in blind pools proceed on the basis of their faith in the investor or group of investors whom they are bankrolling. Blind pools may be organized as shares of stock (usually as a closed-end fund), limited partnership interests, or debt securities (often to be used in as yet undisclosed takeover attempts). Somewhat surprisingly, many people are quite willing to buy these "pigs in a poke."

Separately (Privately) Managed Accounts

The terms *separately managed accounts* (SMAs) and *privately managed accounts* (PMAs) still appear to be evolving, particularly as various firms bring to the market programs that incorporate variations of these names. The majority of commentators on these topics seem to agree that these terms are two names for what is essentially the same product. An SMA is a PMA opened through a broker or financial advisor who uses pooled money to buy individual assets. We will use the term SMA in this discussion as it is the more common.

About 80 percent of SMAs are sold through the major brokerage firms. These were first developed by E.F. Hutton in the mid-1970s. Retail SMAs had $774 billion in assets as of June 30, 2006, which represented an 18 percent increase over the prior year. These assets were distributed over about 4,700 separate accounts. Quotes for all of these accounts are available online and quotes for some of the larger ones may be found in the printed media. Institutional SMAs hold about $7.5 trillion in assets. The institutional accounts include such vehicles as 401(k) accounts that are open to individuals. Our discussion will focus strictly on the retail accounts. One reason brokerage firms like promoting separate accounts is their belief that these assets are less likely to go elsewhere than if they were in a mutual fund.[123]

---

123. Lawrence C. Strauss, "Tailor Made," *Barron's*, February 20, 2006, pp. 27–28, 30.

An SMA can be thought of as a mutual fund with personalized holdings. The following example provides the basic idea of how an SMA works.

EXAMPLE
Let's say 10 investors each open an SMA for $100,000. The $1 million is then invested by a portfolio manager as if it were a mutual fund. However, the shares technically are owned by the 10 separate accounts, rather than the portfolio. Thus, the portfolio manager is managing the aggregate of the SMAs, but the actual assets reside in each of the accounts individually.

SMAs can be thought of as a variation of mutual funds that attempts to deal with some of the perceived deficiencies of mutual funds. The attributes of SMAs include the following:

- SMAs tend to provide updates on their portfolio much more frequently than do mutual funds. Thus, there is more transparency as to holdings

- As noted in the above example, when shares are purchased in an SMA, the cost basis is the purchase price itself because the shares purchased are treated as belonging to the account itself rather than to the fund. When one buys a mutual fund, one may also be buying accrued capital gain whenever the mutual fund holds many substantially appreciated securities.

- With an SMA, an investor can specify certain stock or sectors in which he or she would prefer not to invest. With a mutual fund, the investor can only hope that any stocks the fund buys conform to any constraints stated as part of that fund's objectives.

- An SMA can be managed to optimize an investor's tax situation.

- A key feature of SMAs is that clients pay their administrative, investment management, and brokerage commissions separately. In addition, the fees are usually adjusted for the size of the account, with larger accounts getting a discount. In mutual funds, all investors pay the same management expense fee.

Critics of SMAs are concerned that SMAs have excessive fees relative to the benefits they provide, and that the customization and tax advantages aren't as effective as they are touted to be. Some critics go so far as to suggest that most investors don't really need all of the customization they are, in effect, being sold.

Separately managed accounts should not be confused with wrap accounts. In a wrap account, the client pays an annual fee, equal to a percentage of assets, which covers all of the account's associated expenses. The assets in a wrap account may include separate accounts, mutual funds, or even individual securities. A wrap account allows a customer access to an independent money manager without requiring the client to enter into a direct contract with the money manager.

SELECTING A MUTUAL FUND

Now that we have discussed the nature of mutual funds and other investment companies, we turn to the practical question of how to select a mutual fund or investment company from among the multitude available.[124] As mentioned earlier, the first step in the investment process is to identify the appropriate category of funds to be considered. This is based on understanding the client's objectives and risk tolerance. Once this has been accomplished, then the task becomes one of picking a particular fund within that investment category.

EXAMPLE

Your client is an 80-year-old widow with a portfolio of $700,000. It is clear that preservation of principal is a critical need, which implies safety. However, like most older clients, she worries about the ravages of inflation, and she is willing to forgo some current income if she can feel that she has some inflation protection. Is there an appropriate mutual fund for her?

Safety and low income are automatically synonymous. However, protection from inflation with a willingness to sacrifice current income suggests one particular type of instrument—TIPS (Treasury Inflation-Protected Securities). Bond funds that hold a significant percentage of their assets in TIPS are an excellent investment vehicle for this senior client.

Although it might seem that the past performance of a mutual fund should be considered in the selection of a fund, returns are actually relatively unimportant. The reason is that research consistently shows that past performance has no predictive value relative to future performance, with one notable exception. Carhart's (1997) seminal work on persistence in

---

124. Some of the material for this section is based on "The Art and Science of Mutual Fund Selection," by Nancy Opiela, *Journal of Financial Planning*, vol. 17, issue 1 (January 2004), pp. 36–41.

fund performance showed that funds in the bottom 10% of performance in a given year frequently underperform in subsequent years or cease to exist. However, there was little consistency in year-to-year rankings among most other funds. Subsequent studies have confirmed these results.[125]

Third-Party Evaluation

A good starting point to selecting funds for further consideration is third-party evaluation. This process entails compiling a list of funds in a particular category and seeing what others have to say about these funds. Two of the more popular third-party evaluators are Morningstar (www.morningstar.com) and Lipper, Inc. (www.lipperweb.com/). Morningstar assigns ratings of from one to five stars to each fund, with five being the best. In addition to obtaining factual information on a fund (such as load charge, management fees, portfolio turnover ratios, and so on) from these companies, we can acquire a rating for each particular fund. Blake and Morey (2000) find that funds with one or two stars in a given period tend to perform poorly in future periods.[126] However, the predictive value of the ratings are weak, at best, for the higher rated funds. Additionally the predictive power of the star ratings are only slightly better than alternative performances. In fact, more recent research suggests that basing selections on the management expense ratio works just about as well (with the funds with the lowest expense ratios being preferred). This means it would behoove a financial planner to attempt to keep his or her clients in well-rated funds as a normal part of due diligence, unless there is a particular reason to pick a fund that is poorly rated.

The Morningstar System

Rating schemes by these third-party evaluators may have a substantial impact on cash flows into and out of mutual funds. For example, in 1999, funds rated with four or five stars by Morningstar had a net cash inflow of $223.6 billion and funds rated less well had a net cash outflow of $132.0 billion.[127] The intent of the Morningstar rating is to evaluate the quality of a fund's management, and not the performance of the fund in absolute terms. Each year, certain sectors of the market do better than other sectors, and in

---

125. Carhart, Mark M., "On Persistence in Mutual Fund Performance," *The Journal of Finance,* 1997, 52(1), 57–82.

126. Blake, C., and Morey, M.R. "Morningstart Ratings and Mutual Fund Performance," *The Journal of Financial Quantitative Analysis,* 2000, 35(3), 451–83.

127. "Fund Ratings and Recent Results Diverge," *The Wall Street Journal,* May 3, 200, p. C27.

any given year, a fund manager may find himself or herself lucky enough to be in a well-performing sector. This manager should not be rewarded for the luck of his or her sector performing well.

Morningstar uses what is known as a single scalar measure. A single scalar measure is a unitless number. The Sharpe ratio is a classic example of a single scalar measure. The primary input to Morningstar's measure is the excess geometric mean return (EGMR) over a 36-month period. The EGMR is defined as the geometric mean return based on monthly return relatives divided by one plus the risk-free rate for each month.[128] For each of its many, many categories of funds, Morningstar ranks the funds according to this measure. Finally, the top 10 percent of the funds within each group are given the five star rating, the next 22.5 percent of funds are assigned four stars, the next 35 percent get three stars, and the last 22.5 percent and 10 percent get two and one stars, respectively. Morningstar makes its own assessment of how to categorize a fund, and funds sometimes move among categories. For equity funds, it uses a 3 × 3 matrix, where one side is made up of value, blend, and growth ratings, and the other side is made up of large cap, mid-cap, and small-cap ratings. For fixed-income funds, the 3 × 3 matrix is defined in terms of duration on one side and quality on the other side. The allocation of a fund to a particular box is based on a combination of factors.[129]

Other Selection Factors

Fees and Expenses

Because of the overwhelming documentation of the drag that expenses and fees create in mutual fund returns, an obvious selection factor is to choose funds with minimal expenses and fees. The load fee is perhaps the easiest fee to see and to avoid, although there might be circumstances under which one might buy a fund with a front-end load (see next section). A back-end load may actually be desirable. The reason ties into the recent fund scandals we have discussed wherein market timers attempted to steal returns from long-term investors. The quickest way to kill market timers is with load fees that would affect primarily these types of investors. The nice thing about back-end load fees is that they eventually go away. Thus, they discourage

---

128. "The New Morningstar Rating™ Methodology," *Morningstar Research Report*, 22 April 2002.

129. William Reichenstein, "Morningstar's New Star-Rating System: Advances and Innovations," *Journal of Financial Planning*, March 2004, pp. 40–47.

market timers, but can be avoided by people committed for longer time horizons.[130]

Similarly, a lower management expense ratio is more desirable, as is avoidance of 12b-1 fees and any of the variety of other fees funds may impose. Frequent trading tends to be undesirable because it means more commissions to be paid as well as greater chance of capital gains distributions and greater chance of style drift. If an investor is holding the mutual fund in a tax-deferred account, then the size of the capital gains distribution is immaterial, although the magnitude of trading costs and style drift is still a concern.

Diversification/Concentration

Because one of the main advantages to investing in a mutual fund is diversification, investors should avoid funds that minimize diversification. A quick review of the top 10 holdings provides some indication of concentration. Simply adding the percentages of the top 10 holdings in the portfolio gives a comparative measure of concentration. Looking at the nature of the industries of the top 10 holdings is another indicator of concentration. If the top 10 holdings are in 10 different industries, then there is good diversification. If they are all in one industry, there is a significant lack of diversification. A lack of diversification is not necessarily bad. If the investor wants a sector fund for a particular component of his or her portfolio, a concentrated fund is good. If the fund is meant to provide industrial diversification, however, concentration in a single industry is bad.

Age of Fund and Manager Experience. Two factors that many financial planners seriously consider are (1) the age of the fund and (2) the experience, qualifications, and longevity of the fund's manager. Many planners prefer several years of history before selecting a fund and thus will simply ignore newer funds. In addition, some planners will ignore funds in which the portfolio manager is relatively new to the job. No matter how great that fund's past performance, it is not the performance generated by that particular manager. That manager has little or no track record with the fund; therefore, for all intents and purposes, a fund with a new manager is no different from a new fund. Nonetheless, there is something to be said for newer fund managers. Chevalier and Ellison (1999) find that younger fund

---

130. Johnathan Clements, "How to Pick a Fund That Cares For Its Long-Term Shareholders," *The Wall Street Journal Online*, November 5, 2003.

managers have better performance than "older" managers. The authors speculate that this may be due to career concerns or that talented managers often decide to manage institutional money after developing a track record.[131]

Family Membership. If the fund is in a fund family with a broad selection and solid performance, clients will have a good set of alternatives for reallocation of assets, and they may be able to avoid loads with intra-family switches. Service issues are also important. Funds differ in the timeliness, responsiveness, and clarity of correspondence and statements. Funds also vary in the availability and user friendliness of their online account information and services.

Some financial planners deliberately choose funds from different families. This is not unreasonable when there are no load charges and no breakpoints involved, and there is a certain element of diversification in using funds from different families. For example, if another scandal develops that involves a fund in a particular family, a client who owns only funds in the family may get nervous, and with good reason. Family diversification, therefore, can offer safety from scandals and other forms of inappropriate or illegal activity. In addition, not every family will have what a planner considers to be the best fund in a particular area. It is unwise to opt for a family fund just to "keep it in the family" when another fund appears to be better suited for the client.

Many financial planners visit the offices of various funds to check out their culture and professionalism. Some planners regularly talk to the portfolio manager or at least to some of a fund's analysts to get a feel for the direction of the fund and to see if the decisions the fund is making seem reasonable.

When to Sell a Mutual Fund

style drift   The most obvious signal of when to sell a fund is when there is a style drift. *Style drift* means that the portfolio is drifting away from what had been an established style. The SEC requires that at least 80 percent of a fund's portfolio must conform to the designated style. Despite this, style drift occurs and the investor ends up with a holding different from what the financial planner intended. In fact, Sensoy (2009) finds that around a third of mutual funds have a prospectus-stated

---

131. Chevalier, J., and Ellison, G., "Are Some Mutual Fund Managers Better Than Others? Cross-Sectional Patters in Behavior and Performance," *The Journal of Finance,* 1999, 54 (3) 875–899.

benchmark index that does not match the funds' style.[132] An example of style drift is when a fund manager, in anticipation of a bear market, increases his or her cash holdings from 2 percent of the portfolio to 30 percent of the portfolio. The portfolio manager's forecast may or may not be right, but in the meantime, the manager is altering the investor's total portfolio away from what the investor wants to hold. One indication of a change in style might be if a fund merges into another fund or acquires another fund. Also, if the fund manager is replaced, there is reason to be concerned that the fund's characteristics will change.

Another factor, although not unique to mutual funds, is poor performance over an extended period of time, especially if the poor performance is related to high expenses. It would be inappropriate to sell a fund based on subpar performance over a short period. Most managers feel that at least a 3-year time frame is necessary to validate a manager's performance. If the fund's underlying characteristics are unchanged, switching to a similar fund with slightly better performance in an attempt to "chase returns" frequently generates a tax liability without improving the portfolio.

Why Mutual Funds Usually Underperform the Market

All sorts of research over the last 40 years has consistently shown that the majority of mutual funds provide below market risk-adjusted returns. The primary reason for this is the fees and expenses associated with a fund. A 2004 study by Standard & Poor's examined the performance of nearly 17,000 stock-fund share classes, and found that "over the 1-, 3-, 5-, and 10-year periods ended May 31, 2004, U.S. stock funds with lower-than-average expense ratios performed better than funds with higher-than-average expense ratios in all investment-style categories except one.[133] Outperforming a relatively efficient market (such as the U.S. stock market) is difficult. Still, mutual funds do have the resources to hire the best talent, collect the most useful information, and analyze it with the most sophisticated techniques. Furthermore, their large size should facilitate operational efficiency—especially when securities are bought in quantities that qualify for commission discounts. Why then, with all these advantages, do the funds as a group perform so poorly? There are several reasons:

---

132. Sensoy, Berk A., "Performance Evaluation and Self-designated Benchmark Indices in the Mutual Fund Industry," *Journal of Financial Economics,* 2009 (92), 25–39.

133. "Study Finds Lower-Cost Mutual Funds Prevail," *In the Vanguard,* Autumn 2004, p. 6.

- *Institutional investors constitute a large part of the market.* Outperforming the average would be difficult for any group of investors that makes up a large part of the average. Institutions hold a significant portion of the total value of U.S. stocks; a still higher percentage of the larger listed issues makes up most of the market indexes.

- *Some other types of large investors have advantages similar to those of the institutions.* Each type of institutional investor (e.g., mutual funds, insurance companies, pension funds, college endowments, foundations, and bank trust departments) has access to similar managerial talent, sources of information, and types of analysis. Furthermore, private investment managers, individuals with large sums to invest, and nonfinancial corporations with large stock portfolios all have equivalent advantages. Thus, mutual funds must compete with other similarly positioned institutional and noninstitutional investors.

- *Mutual funds have a number of disadvantages relative to many other types of investors.* Although mutual funds offer several advantages to investors, they also have a number of disadvantages (described earlier) that tend to lower their return by outweighing any likely advantage they may have over small investors. Their primary disadvantage is their fee structure.

Are Mutual Funds Appropriate Investments?

If the average fund underperforms market averages, should individuals invest in mutual funds (other than index funds)? In other words, should they pay for active professional management that on average does not increase the risk-adjusted expected return?

This is a really good question and one over which many planners disagree. Currently, there are 7,618 mutual funds from which investors can choose.[134] Many in the financial services industry believe that in the foreseeable future this number will collapse to something on the order of 5,000 funds, with a good number of these being index funds. There will always be a place for funds with objectives other than indexing, just as there will always be investors who want to specialize in a particular industry or style but do not have a sufficient portfolio to achieve the necessary degree of diversification. Other investors may want diversification but would rather construct it themselves by holding a variety of funds with different objectives.

---

134. www.ici.org/research/stats/trends/trends_05_10, accessed July 15, 2010.

Investors in mutual funds will find relatively few reliable selection guidelines. Even the most avid practitioners of fund selection readily agree it is an art, not a science. For believers in the EMH, there are a few obvious criteria to consider. Clearly, investors should prefer a fund with a risk level corresponding to their preferences. Also, a fund that has a favorable past performance and a low portfolio turnover, a low expense ratio, no load, and no 12b-1 fee may be expected to generate a bit better performance than the average fund. For a point of reference, the average equity fund in 2004 had a portfolio turnover ratio of 112 percent and an average management expense ratio for actively managed funds of 1.52 percent.[135] This turnover ratio means that the average stock was held for a period of less than 1 year. The average holding period can be found by dividing the turnover ratio into 100, so a turnover ratio of 112 means the average stock is held for .89 of an year, which is about 10.7 months.[136]

Most investors should probably give serious consideration to index funds. One type of strategy that involves the use of index funds is "core and explore." The idea is to build the core of one's portfolio around index funds, and then concentrate a smaller portion of the portfolio in sectors that the investor believes might outperform the rest of the market.

EXAMPLE 1
In the November 2005 issue of the *AAII Journal*, John Markese describes some issues to consider when selecting an index fund. He notes two index funds that are both geared to the S&P 500 Index. One has an expense ratio of .52 percent and the other an expense ratio of .15 percent. He also notes that over the prior 5-year period, the difference in the annual average rate of return of the two funds almost exactly equals the difference in the expense ratios.
EXAMPLE 2
Recent research provides some strong evidence that due diligence is critical for a fiduciary, even in something as simple as picking an index fund. Elton, Gruber, and Busse report the following:

---

135. Daniel P. Dolan, "Best of Both Worlds," *Investment Advisor*, April 2004, p. 75.

136. Bogle, op cit.

> *"S&P 500 index funds represent one of the simplest vehicles for examining behavior. They hold virtually the same securities, yet their returns differ by more than 2 percent per year. Although the relative returns of alternative S&P 500 funds are easily predictable, the relationship between cash flows and performance is weaker than rational behavior would lead us to expect. We show that selecting funds based on low expenses or high past returns outperforms the portfolio of index funds selected by investors."*[137]

Should an Investor Buy a Load Fund?

One final question is whether anyone should consider buying a load fund. There is no evidence that load funds perform any differently than noloads (before consideration of the load). After all, the load charge pays the person who sells the shares, not the person who manages the portfolio.

There are several reasons why load funds should not be automatically rejected in any analysis. First, many investors should be in mutual funds, but they lack the knowledge or financial sophistication to get there. To borrow a phrase from the insurance industry, some funds are sold, not bought. This means that a financial advisor needs to educate a client as to the benefits of funds and help the client understand how funds work. Financial planners who do such work are entitled to fair compensation for it. Compensation can be on a fee basis or a commission basis. If it is on a commission basis, then load charges can be fair compensation.

As we saw with classes of shares, some load funds carry little or no 12b-1 fees, and others may have unusually low management expense ratios. Some funds may have relatively low portfolio turnover ratios. In other words, certain load funds may provide other cost savings to an investor that could make paying the load fee a reasonable charge.

Some load funds may have a unique objective that is not available in no-load funds. If the investor really wants this particular objective, then he or she may have to pay the load charge.

REVIEW OF LEARNING OBJECTIVES

1. Mutual funds are open-end investment companies in which new shares are created whenever someone invests new money with a fund, and shares are cancelled whenever someone redeems them

---

137. Edwin Elton, Martin Gruber, and Jeffrey Busse, "Are Investors Rational? Choices among Index Funds," *Journal of Finance*, Vol. LIX, No. 1 (February 2004), p. 261.

for cash. Funds can be load or no-load. The major advantages of mutual funds are the immense diversification they offer, along with convenience and the ability to move large amounts of money from one set of holdings to another with minimal expense in most cases. The major disadvantages are that funds on average underperform comparable indices by an amount equal to the fees and expenses associated with each fund. In addition, shares can only be bought or redeemed at the close of trading each day.

2. Closed-end investment companies have a fixed number of shares that are determined at the inception of the fund. The share price of a closed-end fund is determined by supply and demand; it is therefore generally different from the NAV. The purchase of closed-end shares occurs in the open market, unlike the purchase of open-end shares, which only come from the issuing company. Closed-end companies can decide to become or be forced into becoming open-end companies.

3. An ETF is generally better than an index fund for an investor when the amount traded is larger, the holding period is longer, and either no or minimal additional purchases or sales are planned. The reasons are that normal commissions must be paid on ETFs, but index funds usually trade noload, and there is a bid-ask spread on ETF prices.

4. REITs, RELPs, and REMICs are the vehicles for pooled investment in the real estate sector. The three general types of REITs are an equity REIT, a mortgage REIT, and a hybrid REIT, which holds both equity and mortgage positions. RELPs lost a substantial amount of popularity when changes in the tax code limited the ability of investors to write off the RELP's operating losses against their ordinary income. In addition, the transaction fees tend to be high and there is little marketability in these instruments. REMICs are securities created from mortgage holdings that give different investors different types of claims.

5. UITs are usually self-liquidating portfolios. There is negligible management expense because there is minimal management of the portfolio, with an intention of no trading. There may be a significant load charge. There is usually a minimal secondary market, with the trustee usually indicating a willingness to buy back shares if an investor needs to bail out. Technically, an investor buys units in a UIT, rather than shares. A hedge fund is often located offshore and is not subject to traditional restraints. A variable annuity is an investment in an equity portfolio through an insurance

wrapper. Managed accounts pool the assets of multiple accounts to offer a better portfolio management.

6. Research has suggested that there are several criteria that should be considered in the selection of a mutual fund. Past rates of return are not a significant indicator of future rates of return. Instead, higher rates of return are associated with funds that minimize expenses and fees and provide tax efficiency. Thus, no-loads are preferred over load funds, lower management expense ratios are preferable, 12b-1 fees should be avoided, and funds with lower portfolio turnover ratios are preferred. In addition, funds in which the members of the Board own significant shares in the fund, or at least in the fund family, tend to have better performance due to a lower fee structure.

7. For some investors, particularly those with smaller amounts of capital or those who want to invest on a programmatic basis, mutual funds offer an efficiency that may well offset their poor performance relative to various market indices. For many investors (such as those in company pension plans), mutual funds may be the only vehicle available to them.

MINICASE

The $$$ Mutual Fund had a portfolio valued at $652 million, $2 million in liabilities, and 30 million shares outstanding at the start of the year. At year end, the fund's portfolio value increased to $802 million, liabilities remain the same, and shares outstanding increased by 2 million. In addition, over this 12-month period the fund paid an ordinary dividend and a capital gain distribution of $.70 per share. You have a client with $20,000 to invest in this mutual fund.

1. What was the initial NAV? [1]

    (A) $26.73
    (B) $21.73
    (C) $21.67
    (D) Can't be determined from the data provided.

2. What was the percentage increase in the NAV? [1]

    (A) 15.37%
    (B) 15.34%
    (C) 15.30%
    (D) Can't be determined from the data provided.

3.   Based on the load fees in table 10-1, how much would the client pay per share? [1]

    (A) $22.81
    (B) $22.75
    (C) $21.67
    (D) Can't be determined from the data provided.

4.   What would be the 1-year rate of return for this investor in the $$$ Fund? [1]

    (A) 12.97%
    (B) 12.67%
    (C) 9.6%
    (D) Can't be determined from the data provided.

5.   If the client invested another $5,000 in addition to the $20,000 he intends to invest, what would be the increase in load charge based on Table 10-1? [1]

    (A) $250.00
    (B) $212.50
    (C) $125.00
    (D) $62.50

CHAPTER REVIEW

Key Terms and Concepts

open-end investment company
closed-end investment company
common stock funds
mixed portfolio funds
regular dividend
contingent deferred sales charge
portfolio turnover ratio
switching

multi-class funds
lifeboat provisions
income share
capital appreciation share
Holding Company Depository
   Receipts (HOLDRs)
blind pool
style drift

Review Questions

Review questions are based on the learning objectives in this chapter. Thus, a [3] at the end of a question means that the question is based on learning objective 3. If there are multiple objectives, they are all listed.

1.   Assume that the $$$ Mutual Fund in the minicase is a load fund that charged a 3 percent front-end load and paid a distribution of $.70 per share over the past year. What would the 1-year return for an investor in the $$$ Mutual Fund be? [1]

2.   Compare loads with 12b-1 fees. [1]

3.   Using table 10-1 as the structure for load fees, compute the following: [1]
    a.   If an investor has $495,000 to invest, how many shares would he or she buy if the NAV were $52.76?
    b.   How much more cash would go to buy shares if the investor wrote a check for $500,000?
    c.   If an investor pays $100,000 today to buy shares and signs a letter of intent to buy another $100,000 on each of the next four anniversary dates, how much commission does he or she save over the 5 years, as opposed to making the same purchases but not signing a letter of intent?

4.   Briefly describe and contrast open-end and closed-end investment companies. [2]

5.   Why are there no closed-end money market funds? [2]

6.   A client has $10,000 to invest and wants the money back in 3 years to pay college tuition. The client plans to occasionally add additional monies to this investment, and would like to invest in what is essentially the S&P 500 index. What is probably the most appropriate investment and why? [3]

7.   a.   What are the three general types of REITs? [4]
    b.   Why are RELPs not terribly popular today? [4]
    c.   What is the basic concept behind a REMIC? [4]

8.   What are the common characteristics of a UIT? [5]

9.   Identify whether a high or low value is normally considered desirable among the following attributes of a mutual fund: [6]
    a.   load charge
    b.   management expense ratio
    c.   12b-1 fee
    d.   portfolio turnover ratio
    e.   holdings of shares in the fund by members of the Board of Directors
    f.   number of stars assigned by Morningstar

10.   If the average mutual fund underperforms the market on a risk-adjusted basis, why might a planner nonetheless recommend one? [7]

Learning Objectives

An understanding of the material in this chapter should enable the student to

1. Be conversant in the basic option terminology and the mechanics of the options markets.

2. Describe the two reasons options have value, and compute the value for each reason.

3. Construct a profit function for a person long or short a put or call option.

4. Construct a profit function for combinations of options and stocks.

5. Describe how the variables used in the Black-Scholes and binomial option pricing models and the put-call parity relationship affect the value of a call option.

6. Describe how stock index options, interest rate options, and LEAPS® differ from listed puts and calls on common stock.

7. Explain the advantages and disadvantages of convertibles and compute conversion values and conversion premiums.

People regularly create options. For example, if someone rents a house with an option to buy and the prospective purchase price is clearly defined, the owner and renter have created an option. Whenever someone leases a car with an option to buy, the lessor and lessee have created an option. Options also exist for financial assets.

Although option trading has been around for hundreds of years, options became a significant part of the financial markets when the Chicago Board of Options Exchange (CBOE, pronounced Cee-bow) opened its doors in the early 1970s for the formal trading of options. The trick was to standardize the terms on option contracts so that investors wanting to trade in options had a limited number of choices. This created the necessary marketability to make option trading interesting to a large number of people for a variety of reasons.

This chapter focuses on the two basic option instruments: call and put options. Rights and warrants are variations of call options, but because they have been covered in an earlier chapter, they will not be discussed again here (although most of what is said about call options applies to both, particularly warrants).

It should be noted that there continues to be OTC market trading in options. However, the vast majority of option trading takes place on option exchanges, and all of the discussion in this chapter will focus on exchange-based trading.

LISTED OPTIONS

An option is basically what its name implies: a choice. An option gives the owner the choice of whether or not to engage in a specified transaction, such as buying or selling an underlying asset at a specified price at some future time. The choice itself has value, and people are willing to pay a price in order to have the choice of whether or not to engage in a specified transaction in the future.

Option Terminology

Options come into existence when an order to buy an option is matched on the floor of an exchange with an order to sell an option with the exact same terms that has been placed by someone who does not currently own the option. In this case, the seller is referred to as a *writer* because by selling something he or she does not currently own, he or she is creating or writing the option. Options are contracts. A writer is writing a contract. Buying an is referred to as *going long* that option. Writing an option is referred to as *going short*.

A *call option* gives the owner the privilege (or choice) to **buy** a specified number of shares of a specified asset at a specified price prior to an expiration date. For example, a call option on Xerox stock gives the holder of the option the right to purchase from the writer 100 shares of Xerox at a specified price at any time up until the option's expiration date.

A *put option* permits the owner to **sell** a specified number of shares of a specified asset at a specified price prior to an expiration date. For example, the holder of a put option on Xerox stock has the right to sell 100 shares of Xerox stock to the writer of the put at the specified price at any time up until the option's expiration date.

premium (option) There are three prices associated with an option. To avoid confusion, special names are assigned to two of them.
The first is the price of the option itself, known as the *premium*. Normally, we think of a premium as the price we pay for an insurance contract, and in some trading strategies involving options, the option is used as a form of insurance.

exercise price

strike (striking) price

The second price is the price at which the underlying asset is bought or sold if the option is exercised. This is referred to as the *exercise price* or *strike (striking) price*. It is specified in the option contract, and cannot be changed once the option is created. The third price is the price at which the underlying asset trades. Unfortunately, there is no simple name for this price; it is known as the *price of the underlying asset*.

in the money

out of the money

at the money

An option is said to be *in the money* if it could be exercised immediately to produce a cash inflow. For the call option, this means that the market price of the underlying asset is higher than the exercise price of the option. Conversely, for the put option, it means that the exercise price of the option is higher than the market price of the underlying asset. When the strike price of a call option exceeds the market price of the underlying stock, or when the market price of the underlying stock exceeds the strike price of a put, the option is *out of the money*. When the exercise price of the option is equal to the market price of the underlying stock, both the put and the call option are *at the money*.

The standard trading unit for options is 100 shares. However, due to stock splits and stock dividends, sometimes an option contract will be adjusted to require delivery of other than 100 shares. Also, the premiums are quoted on a per share basis. Thus, a premium of $2 for an option normally means the trading value is $200.

Expiration Dates

It is incredibly important for the owners of options that the options be exercised or sold if they are in the money just before the close of trading on the expiration date. After the close of trading on the expiration date, all options become worthless (it would be like trying to sell tickets to the Super Bowl on the day after the game is played). This need to exercise or sell is so important for in the money options that are about to expire that many brokers demand from their customers the right to exercise these options on the expiration date if the customer has failed to do so. Obviously, this would be one of the benefits to a having a discretionary account.

EXAMPLE
About 3 months ago, RG stock traded at $72 per share. At that time, you bought an RG call option and paid a premium of $2.50 per share. The option has a strike price of $75 per share. The option expires tomorrow; the stock currently trades at $76 per share, and the option trades at $1.06 per share. If you take no action by the close of trading the next day, the option expires and is thus worthless. What should you do?
Answer: You have three choices. First, you could exercise the option and buy the stock for $75 per share (and pay the standard commission for the purchase of stock). Second, you could sell the option today and pay the standard commission for the sale of an option. Third, you could wait to see what happens on the expiration date. If the price of RG goes up, you could make a fantastic percentage gain. If the price goes down (below $75), the option would become worthless.

Option Markets

Before listed options appeared, all option trading was in the over-the-counter market. Now, virtually all option trading takes place on option exchanges, although some unlisted puts and calls still trade in the over-the-counter market. Furthermore, the Chicago-based Options Clearing Corporation (OCC) sets the rules for option trading. The OCC was founded in 1973, and currently provides "clearing and settlement services to 14 exchanges and platforms for options, financial and commodity futures, security futures, and securities landing."[138]

The OCC acts as an intermediary between the two principals in every option trade. Each put and call buyer and seller is actually contracting with the OCC, rather than directly with the opposite party to the transaction. Thus, the writer of a call option who wants to cancel his or her position does not need to go back to the original buyer in that trade to buy back the contract. The writer simply places an order to buy a call option with identical terms, and upon purchase, the OCC cancels the original writer from that contract. Because of the presence of the OCC, no option buyer need ever worry about whether or not the writer will honor the terms of the contract. The OCC ensures the integrity of the traded option-if the writer defaults on its position in the transaction, the OCC stands ready to fulfill the terms of the defaulted

---

138. en.wikipedia.org/wiki/options_clearing_corporations, accessed July 15, 2010.

side of the option contract. The OCC management and guarantee-of-option contracts have dramatically improved the efficiency of the options market.

When listed option trading began in 1973, new option contracts were introduced every 3 months and had an initial maturity (time to expiration) of 9 months. Three sets of expiration dates were traded at any particular time. For example, a company might have options on a January cycle. Its options would be set to expire every 3 months, beginning with January and following in April, July, and October. When the nearest expiration month is January, the other listed options would be April and July. Once the January option expired, a new set of options would be listed for October. Other companies' options were set for February and March cycles.

Some companies' options still expire only every 3 months. Most companies with listed options, however, now have additional expiration times that fill in the 2 nearest months. Consider, for example, a company with a January cycle. In early January, there would be options expiring in January, April, and July. In addition, an option expiring in February might also be listed.

Thus, most companies now have a total of four expiration dates. Two are in the nearest 2 months and two are more distant expirations at 3-month intervals. Listed options are set to expire on the Saturday following the third Friday of their month of expiration. The value of the options traded sometimes exceeds the value of the stocks traded for the underlying shares.

Setting Strike Prices

Strike prices are initially set at levels that are divisible by 5 or 10 (or in some cases 2½), depending on the stock's market price. Thus, a stock trading at 43 would typically have options listed with strike prices at 40 and 45. Similarly, a stock trading at 21 would have options listed at 20 and 22.50. If a stock price moves out of this range on either the up or down side, the listing exchange will usually create new options for trading with additional strike prices. Thus, a stock might be trading at $20 per share, but have call options listed with strike prices all the way up to $75 or more. This would indicate that at one time this stock traded in the $75 range, but its price has since dropped.

Note that when there is a stock split, all contracts are automatically adjusted to incorporate the split. Thus, the announcement that a company was preparing to have a 2 for 1 split would not be cause to buy puts on the company's stock!

American, European, and Bermuda Options

American options

European options

Bermuda options

Options are distinguished by when they can be exercised. Options that may be exercised at any time up to the expiration date are called *American options*. It is primarily the American options that are traded on the U.S. option exchanges. All of the discussion in this chapter will focus on American options. Options that may be exercised only on the expiration date are called *European options*. Options that can be exercised on a multiple set of predetermined dates (the last being the expiration date) are called *Bermuda options*. The typical Bermuda option has an exercise period of once per month.

WHY OPTIONS HAVE VALUE

intrinsic value (option)

Puts and calls always have an intrinsic value. For an in the money call, *intrinsic value* is the difference between the market price of the underlying stock and the strike price. For at the money or out of the money calls, the intrinsic value is zero. Similarly, for an in the money put, this is the difference between the strike price and the market price of the underlying stock, and for at or out of the money puts it is zero. In mathematical notation:

Intrinsic Value of a Call	$= P - X$	if $P > X$, and
	$= 0$	if $X \geq P$.
Intrinsic Value of a Put	$= X - P$	if $X > P$, and
	$= 0$	if $P \geq X$.

where

P = current market price of underlying stock, and

X = exercise or strike price.

An option can never be worth less than its intrinsic value because if it were, then investors would buy it and exercise it immediately.

Options also have a speculative or time value in addition to intrinsic value. To understand this, consider a simple example. Let's say that the price of the stock of Big Fox Corp. trades at $50 per share. Let's further assume that there is an option on this stock with a striking price of $50. At this point in time, the intrinsic value of the option is clearly zero (why would anyone pay for the privilege to buy something for $50 when that item can be bought directly for $50!). However, let's assume that the investor believes that on the option expiration date, the stock will either trade at a price of $60 per share or a price of $40 per share. Let's further assume that these events are equally likely (that is, a 50 percent probability of either price). If this is the case, then on the expiration date, the call option will have an intrinsic value of either $10 (that is, $60 - $50) or zero (if the market prices closes at $40). The expected intrinsic value of the option on the expiration date is then computed as:

$$\text{Expected intrinsic value of the option} = .50 \times \$10 + .50 \times \$0 = \$5$$

The speculative or time value is then based on this expected intrinsic value of $5.

Note in this above example that the expected price of the stock on the expiration date is $50.

$$\text{Expected price of the stock} = .50 \times \$60 + .50 \times \$40 = \$50$$

Recall that the current price of the stock is $50. Hence, the expected rate of return from owning the stock in this case is 0 percent. Despite the 0 percent expected rate of return, the option has value.

Options are a form of leveraged investing, somewhat akin to buying on margin. As such, they provide a magnification of the percentage gain or loss for the investor, compared to what would have been achieved with a direct purchase of the common stock.

EXAMPLE

Assume that an investor can choose between buying a stock outright for $50 per share today and buying a call option for $4 per share with an exercise price of $50. If the stock price falls to $30, the call option would not be exercised, and the $4 price of the option would be a complete loss (-100%). If the investor had purchased the stock outright, the loss would be -40 percent [($30 - $50)/$50 = -40%]. Conversely, if the stock price rises to $70, the option could be exercised for a net gain of $16. The option holder would receive a holding period return of 400 percent [($20 - $4)/$4 = 400%], while the shareholder would earn a holding period return of 60 percent [($70 - $50)/$50 = 40%].

In both the gain and the loss situations above, the percentage return on the option has a larger absolute value than that of the stock, meaning that the option is inherently and significantly more risky than the stock. It is for this reason that most trading in options involves options that are at the money or close to at the money. Options that are deep in the money have little leverage appeal, and options that are way out of the money are unresponsive to changes in the underlying stock price.

Financial Planning Issue

When are options appropriate for clients? Generally, there are three motivations for engaging in option trading.

The first is purely speculative. If a client has a strong belief a particular stock will go up or down, a call or a put are effective ways to speculate on these price movements. There are many variations of this speculative motivation. For example, suppose a client is expecting a cash windfall in the near future, but wants to buy a particular investment today. The client could buy call options at a fraction of the future purchase price, and then use the cash windfall to exercise the options (assuming the stock has gone up). Another possibility is that the client wants to sell a stock, but for tax reasons needs to postpone the sale until next year. If the client is concerned the stock price might fall in the meantime, he or she can buy a put.

A second motivation is hedging activity. Covered call writing trades off incremental income with potential opportunity losses in price appreciation. Similarly, married puts can provide an investor with a sense of insurance protection.

A third motivation is to arbitrage. Arbitrage occurs when an investor believes that one or more options are mispriced relative to other options, and places orders in an attempt to profit from the mispricing. The mispricing belief may be based on a model such as the Black-Scholes or binomial option pricing models, or just on historical relationships between various prices.

PROFIT AND PAYOFF FUNCTIONS FOR OPTION STRATEGIES

Profit and Payoff Functions for Single Positions

It is a lot easier to understand the risk exposure and the return potential of options if one can graph either the profit function or the payoff function for a particular position. The profit function shows the potential prices of the underlying asset on the expiration date (which range from zero to infinity) on the horizontal axis and the profit derived from a particular investment associated with each price on the vertical axis. The payoff function has the same horizontal axis (that is, the price of the underlying asset on the expiration date), but the vertical axis shows the payoff of the option position associated with each potential price.

For simplicity, both functions are usually on a per share basis, and transactions costs, dividends, and taxes are ignored. The difference between the two functions is that the profit function combines the initial cash flows of the investment (that is, the "cost" of the investment) with the payoffs, and the payoff function focuses only on the cash flows on the expiration date.

Because of the similarity of these two functions, some students ask why it is necessary to study the construction of both. The reason is that in practice, the planner will encounter discussions of options and options strategies in both formats.

Payoff and Profit Functions for Being Long and Short Stock

Before looking at options, let's look at the profit and payoff functions for owning stock (a long position) and holding a short position. When we are dealing with only stock, there is, of course, no expiration date, so let's substitute the term holding period for expiration date. For a long position, the payoff and profit functions are defined as follows:

Payoff function (long the stock)	= PS
Profit function (long the stock)	= PS – Purchase price
where PS	= price of the stock on the expiration date

The payoff function, shown in the following figure, will be a line emanating from the origin at a 45-degree angle. Simply put, the payoff for long a share of stock will be whatever the stock price is on the payoff date (that is, the end of the holding period).

Figure 11-1
Payoff Function for Long the Stock

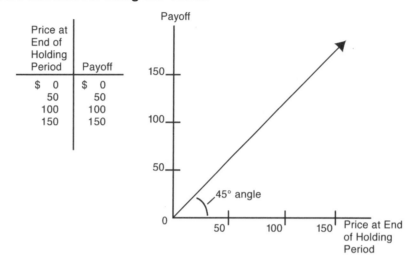

Price at End of Holding Period	Payoff
$ 0	$ 0
50	50
100	100
150	150

Profit functions are usually a little trickier. Although anyone who works with options on a regular basis can visualize these graphs without effort, the rest of us usually require the identification of a few points on the function before we are able to "connect the dots." This is done by arbitrarily picking a few stock prices on the expiration date (or at the end of the holding period) and identifying the payoff or profit associated with that ending price. Let's consider an example.

EXAMPLE

Assume that a stock's current price is $100. If the stock is purchased at this price, the profit or loss equals the change in the price. A future price of $105 equates to a profit of $5; a future price of $95 equates to a loss of $5. The break-even point is at $100, where the future price equals the purchase price. The following figure displays the profit function for this stock's purchase. Notice that, as with the payoff function, the slope of the line is still 45 degrees. The only difference is that this function intersects the horizontal axis at the current price of the stock, and the payoff function intersects it at the origin.

Figure 11-2
Profit Function for Long the Stock

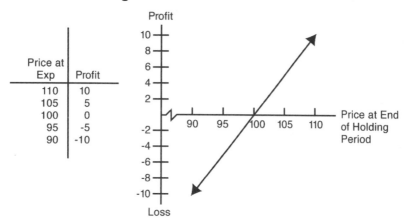

Price at Exp	Profit
110	10
105	5
100	0
95	-5
90	-10

Now let's consider the two functions for a person who is short a share of stock. The equations for the two functions are:

Payoff function (short the stock) $= -$ PS

Profit function (short the stock) $=$ Sale price today $-$ PS

The graph for the payoff function, shown in the following figure, will be a line emanating from the origin at a negative 45-degree angle. In other words, whatever is the price of the stock at the end of the holding period, the short seller must pay out that price to cover his or her short position.

Figure 11-3
Payoff Function for a Short Sale

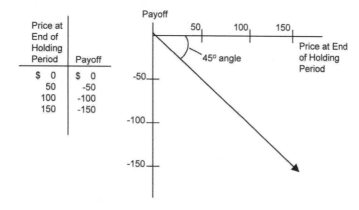

Price at End of Holding Period	Payoff
$ 0	$ 0
50	-50
100	-100
150	-150

The graph for the profit function of someone who shorts a stock, shown in the figure below, is similarly a negative 45-degree angle, but it intersects the horizontal axis at the current price of the stock rather than at the origin.

Figure 11-4
Profit Function for a Short Sale

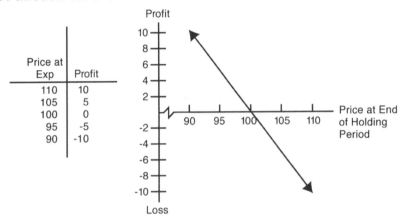

Price at Exp	Profit
110	10
105	5
100	0
95	-5
90	-10

Payoff and Profit Functions for Being Long a Call

Now let's look at the payoff and profit functions for someone who buys a call option (that is, goes long in a call). The payoff function for long a call is the intrinsic value on the expiration date. This can be stated as:

Payoff function (long a call)	$= PS - X$	if $PS > X$
	$= 0$	if $X \geq PS$

The following figure shows this payoff function for a call option with a strike price of $100.

Figure 11-5
Payoff Function for Long a Call with a Strike Price of $100

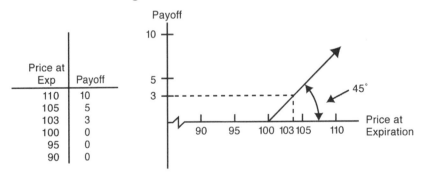

Price at Exp	Payoff
110	10
105	5
103	3
100	0
95	0
90	0

The formula for the profit function for long a call is:

Profit function (long a call)
$= PS - X - C$ if $PS > X$

$= -C$ if $X \geq PS$

where C = the price of the call option

Consider the following example:

EXAMPLE

The premium for a call option with a strike price of $100 for TK stock trades at a $3 per share. If the price of the stock is $100 or less at expiration, the option expires worthless because there is no benefit to the call owner to exercise the call, buying stock for $100 that is readily available in the market at that price or less. Since the premium was $3, the call owner has lost $3. Thus, the maximum loss is the call premium, and the horizontal portion of the function in the figure below shows this. If the price at expiration is between $100 and $103, then the option will equal its intrinsic value, although this value will be less than $3. So the buyer of the option incurs a loss on the holding, but this loss is lessened by the intrinsic value of the option on the expiration date. If the stock closes at exactly $103 on the expiration date, the option holder would break even because he or she could exercise the option for $100 and sell the stock for $103, for a gain of $3. This would exactly offset the $3 premium paid for the option. If the stock price closes at any price above $103, the profit is then the intrinsic value of the option less the premium paid. For example, if it closes at $105, the profit is $2 ($105 - $100 - $3). If the price increases to $110, the profit is $7 ($110 - $100 - $3). Notice in the figure below that the profit function is a 45-degree angle in the right-hand section of the graph-a dollar increase in stock price leads to a dollar increase in profit. The amount of profit is theoretically unlimited.

Figure 11-6
Profit Function for Long a Call with a Strike Price of $100

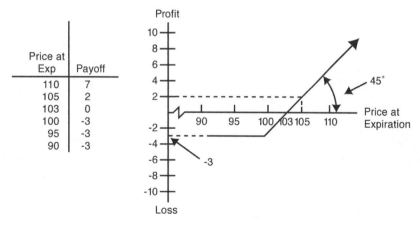

Price at Exp	Payoff
110	7
105	2
103	0
100	-3
95	-3
90	-3

The profit function makes it easy to see why some people like to buy call options. The owner of a call option has a security that provides unlimited potential gain (because there is no upper limit on the stock price), and limited loss (the maximum loss is the premium). Unlimited potential gain and limited loss sounds incredibly attractive! The only drawback is that the limited loss is 100 percent of the initial investment. Many options expire worthless. An analogy would be the purchase of a lottery ticket. If you pay $1 to buy a lottery ticket, you have a limited loss ($1), and almost unlimited gain (big ticket winners get checks of 7 digits or more).

Profit Function for Being Short a Call

covered writer

naked writer

We mentioned above that the person who sells a call option that is not currently owned is known as a writer. The exact description of a writer depends on whether or not the writer owns the underlying security at the time of writing. If he or she owns the underlying security, he or she is referred to as a *covered writer* and the position is known as a *covered call*. If the writer does not own the underlying stock, he or she is referred to as a *naked writer* and the position is known as a *naked call*. It is possible for someone to be a naked writer and then later buy the underlying stock to change the position to a covered call. Similarly, a covered writer may sell the underlying shares while still being short the call, thus converting the position to a naked call (provided his or her account qualifies for holding naked calls).

Let's consider the profit function for a naked call writer. (The reader should now have a good concept of the payoff function and its relationship to the profit function, so we will focus only on profit functions going forward.) The mathematical notation for this function is:

$$\text{Profit function (naked call)} = C \qquad\qquad \text{if } X > PS$$
$$= (X - PS) + C \qquad \text{if } PS \geq X$$

Let's consider an intuitive interpretation of the above equations. The first equation notes that if the stock price ends up less than the strike price, the naked writer pockets the premium, essentially as a windfall gain. The second equation says that if the stock price ends up greater than the strike price, then the writer will incur a loss equal to the difference between the strike price and the stock price, which is offset only by the premium received earlier. On the expiration date, the loss will be the same whether the writer buys back the option or buys the stock in the market and sells it under the option. In either case, the loss will be an amount equal to X - PS. The profit function of the naked writer, shown in the following figure, will thus be a flat line representing the premium income if the stock price ends up between 0 and the strike price. From that point on, the profit function turns down at a 45-degree angle, representing the fact that the writer loses $1 for each $1 increase in stock price.

Figure 11-7
Short a Call (Naked Writer)

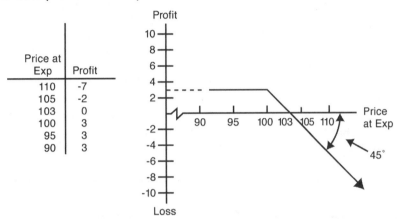

Price at Exp	Profit
110	-7
105	-2
103	0
100	3
95	3
90	3

Why would someone be a naked writer of a call? This is a particularly good question when the graph shows that the profits on a naked call are limited, but the potential loss is unlimited-that is, the maximum profit is the premium income. But as the upside potential of a stock's price is unlimited, the potential loss to the naked writer is unlimited. Clearly, a naked writer is someone who strongly believes that the price of the underlying stock will drop, or at worst will not rise. It is a truly speculative position.

When an investor enters into a position such as a naked writer of a call option where there are theoretically unlimited losses, the brokerage firm will have certain account requirements to ensure that the investor has sufficient assets to withstand a loss and honor the commitment to buy the underlying stock and deliver it.

Long a Call and Naked Writer as Mirror Images

zero-sum game   It is extremely important to note the relationship between figures 11-6 and 11-7. If one rotates one of the figures around the X-axis, one will obtain the other figure. The reason this is the case is that a call buyer and a naked writer essentially have a bet with each other about the ultimate price of the stock, and no other parties are involved. Thus, what one gains on the transaction, the other necessarily loses, and vice versa. The economic term for this process is a *zero-sum game*. (It's a negative-sum game when transaction costs are considered.) Stated another way, the sum of the two profit functions is always zero.

EXAMPLE

Is it appropriate for your clients to buy call options or to engage in naked writing? It depends on the clients' objectives and risk tolerance. Really aggressive clients with high tolerances for risk could reasonably look to be long on *some* call options. However, even these clients should not have an undue investment in these instruments. A sudden downturn in the markets could cause most options to become worthless, thus wiping out most if not all of that part of a client's portfolio. For conservative clients, going long on calls is inappropriate.

Similarly, although some people see naked writing as a chance to enhance the income from a portfolio (when the options expire worthless), every now and then there is a large jump in stock prices and naked writers could get severely burned. Only the most aggressive investors might consider naked writing.

Profit Function for Long a Put and Short a Put

Now let's consider the profit function for purchasing a put option (that is, long a put), shown in the following figure. The formula for this function is:

$$\text{Profit function (long a put)} = X - PS - P \qquad \text{if } X > PS$$
$$= -P \qquad \text{if } PS \geq X$$

Figure 11-8
Long a Put

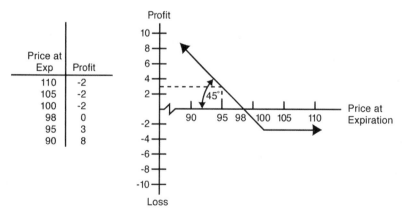

Price at Exp	Profit
110	-2
105	-2
100	-2
98	0
95	3
90	8

EXAMPLE

   Suppose an investor buys a put option with a strike price of $100 and pays a premium of $2. If the price of the underlying stock is $100 or greater at expiration, the option expires worthless because there is no benefit to the put owner to sell stock for $100 if the put owner would have to pay $100 or more to obtain the stock intended for the sale. Since the premium was $2, the put owner has lost $2. Thus the maximum loss on the put purchase is the put premium of $2, as represented by the horizontal part of the profit function.

   If the price falls to $98, the put owner can buy the stock in the market for $98 and sell it to the put writer for $100, a $2 gain. However, the $2 gain is exactly offset by the $2 option premium, so $98 is the break-even point. A market price of $95 equates to profit of $3 ($100 – $95 – $2). A market price of $90 equates to a profit of $8 ($100 – $90 – $2). For every dollar that the market value falls below $98, the profit function increases by a dollar, as indicated by the diagonal part of the function shown in *Figure 11-8*.

Why would anyone want to buy a put? The characteristics of long a put are that it has limited loss (limited to the premium) and large potential gain. As with the position of long a call, there is a bit of an analogy here to buying a lottery ticket. The buyer of a put must strongly believe that there is a significant chance that the price of the underlying stock will decline. We have already noted that one way to profit from an expected price decline in a stock is to sell the stock short. The problem with selling short is that one's loss is potentially unlimited if one is wrong (see figure 11-4). Thus, for anyone betting on the underlying assets declining in value, buying puts may be a less risky way to try to make money on an expected price decline.

The profit function for a put writer can be quickly derived from that for a person long because of the zero-sum nature of options. The writer of the put option has the opposite profit function to the put purchaser's function, as shown in figure 11–9. The equation for the function is:

$$\text{Profit function (writing a put)} = + P \qquad \text{if } PS > X$$
$$= PS - X + P \qquad \text{if } X \geq PS$$

The holder of a put option with a strike price of $100 can sell the stock to the writer for $100 whether the actual value is $99 or $2. Figure 11–9 shows the profit function for a writer of a put with a strike price of $100 and a premium of $2. At $98, the put writer loses $2 on the stock transaction, exactly offsetting the put premium received. At $95, the put writer must allow the put purchaser to put the stock to the writer for $100, for a net loss of $3 ($95 – $100 + $2). For every additional dollar of market price decline, the loss increases by $1, as represented by the diagonal line in figure 11–9. If the market price of the stock rises, the put purchaser will not "put" the stock to the put writer at the strike price because he or she would incur a loss in doing so. Thus, if the stock price rises, the put writer receives the maximum profit of $2.

Because the essence of writing a put is that one can have only limited profit (limited to the premium) and almost unlimited loss (the maximum loss is if the stock price goes to zero), the concept of writing a put sounds extremely aggressive. Clearly, the writer of a put has a strong belief that the price of the underlying asset will go up. If this is the case, the writer would likely be better off buying a call option, which would offer unlimited potential gains on the uptick and limited loss on the downside.

Profit Functions for Combination Positions

combination position

Heretofore, we have discussed the profit functions for six different holdings: long the stock, short the stock, long a call, short a call, long a put, and short a put. Many people trading options actually establish combination positions. A *combination position* is any position wherein more than a single put, single call, or single position in the underlying stock is held. Combination positions can create much more interesting strategies for investors.

Figure 11-9
Short a Put

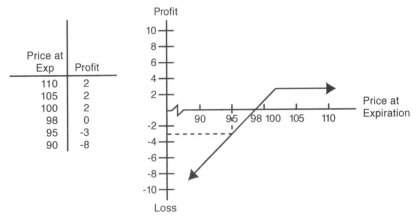

Price at Exp	Profit
110	2
105	2
100	2
98	0
95	-3
90	-8

Financial Planning Issue

Should a financial planner have a client buy puts or write puts? As was the case with calls, a limited program of the purchase of puts may be appropriate for aggressive investors with a good capacity for handling risk. For conservative investors, the purchase of puts is totally inappropriate. Similarly, the writing of puts is sometimes seen as a way to generate incremental income (from the premiums) for investors, but sooner or later, a big price drop in an underlying asset will occur, generating a substantial loss for the investor. Hence, the incremental income is probably not worth the risk, and could easily lead to lawsuits.

Profit Function for a Covered Call Writer

The most common example of a combination position is the covered writer. Recall that a covered writer owns the stock (or simultaneously buys it) on which he or she writes a call option. The profit function for a combination position is simply the sum of the profit functions for the two positions separately. In this case, we would combine the profit function for owning stock with the profit function for writing a call.

To illustrate how this is done, let's again assume a stock has a market price of $100. A call option on the stock has a strike price of $100, and the call's premium is $3. Based on these numbers, the combined profit structure will look like the following figure. As an example of how to plot a particular point on the graph, suppose the stock price were to close on the expiration date at $105. The profit on the stock since the inception of the covered call position would be $5 because the writer either owned at the time of writing or bought the stock for $100 and it appreciated $5 during the life of the option. Unfortunately, the writer will either have to buy back the call option or deliver the stock. If he or she buys back the call option at the expiration date, its price will be the intrinsic value of $5. This is offset by the original premium of $3, so there is a net loss on the option of $2. When this loss of $2 on the option is combined with the $5 price appreciation on the stock, the net gain is $3. If the writer delivers his or her own stock, then the profit on the stock is zero because he or she sells for $100 stock that was originally worth $100 and the profit on the option is the premium income of $3, hence the net profit is $3.

Notice that the upside potential of owning the stock is cut off because of writing the call. On the other hand, if the stock price falls, one is better off by the amount of the premium received than if one simply retained the stock without writing the call.

For example, if you had bought the stock at $100 and it closes at $95, you have a $5 per share loss on the stock. However, if you had written the covered call for a $3 premium, your loss on the combined holdings if the stock closes at $95 is only $2, as you have the cash inflow of the $3 in premium to offset the $5 loss on the stock.

Notice that the profit function for a covered call writer (see figure below) has the identical *shape* as the profit function for writing a put. Thus, the position can be characterized as one offering limited gain and nearly unlimited loss (the maximum loss is if the stock goes to zero). Only someone who is bullish on the stock should consider this strategy.

There are some other ways of viewing covered call writing. Suppose a client were considering selling a stock anyway. Then writing an in-the-money call option might be a way to generate a slightly higher price for the stock than selling it outright. Another issue might be that a client needs to sell a particular stock, but for tax reasons the client needs to have the sale be assigned to next year rather than the current year. In this case, writing a deep-in-the-money call option would normally allow the investor to postpone the sale of the stock until the call option expires and provide some protection against a subsequent price decline.

Figure 11-10
Writing a Covered Call

Price at Exp	Profit on Stock	Profit on Call	Net Profit
110	10	-7	3
105	5	-2	3
103	3	0	3
100	0	3	3
98	-3	3	0
95	-5	3	-2
90	-10	3	-7

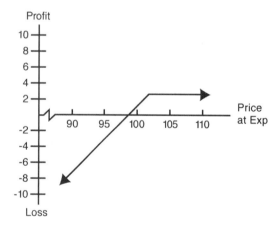

Financial Planning Issue

Should clients be encouraged to write covered call options? There may be some situations where this is an appropriate strategy. Many financial planners see covered call writing as a way to generate extra income for the client. If the alternative to a covered call position is to be long the stock, then the covered call position clearly provides extra income. The only risk from a covered call position compared to long the stock is an opportunity cost. Suppose in the above example the underlying stock were to double to $200 after the call was written. Without the call, the client would have doubled his or her investment. With the covered call in place, the client will receive only the limited gain of $3 per share. The benefit here is that when the planner presents the portfolio returns to the client, he or she will still show a profit. Opportunity losses are never shown on financial statements. So, with a covered call position, if the stock goes down, the client is always better off than he or she would have been without the covered calls, and if the stock goes up, the client will see that he or she has made money, not what he or she could have made.

The real issue is whether a consistent program of covered call writing outperforms or underperforms the portfolio that consists of only the underlying stocks. The answer is probably that just being long stocks should outperform repeated covered call positions.

Profit Function for a Married Put

A *married put* is a combination of long the underlying stock and long the put. This position is also referred to as a protective put. As with the covered call option, we can plot the profit function for a married put by combining the function for owning the stock with the function for long a put. Again, assuming a current stock price of $100, a put strike price of $100, and a put premium of $2, the profit function will look like *Figure 11-11*. Note that a married put profit function has the exact same *shape* as the profit function for long a call (see figure below).

Who buys married puts? Married puts should be analyzed as an alternative to being only long the stock. Many people see the purchase of puts as analogous to buying insurance protection against a price decline. This is not a bad analogy. The real issue is if one made the purchase of puts (insurance premiums) a regular part of one's portfolio over a long period of time, then would the premiums paid for this insurance be worth the safety provided? It may well be that over long periods of time for a diversified portfolio that the losses sustained from price declines would work out to be less than the sum of premiums paid for this insurance protection.

It should now be apparent that for any option position that could be established, the opposite position could just as easily be established by going short wherever one had gone long, and going long wherever one had gone short. Thus, an investor could just as easily take the opposite side of a married put by going short the stock and short the put. The profit function would then be the mirror image of a married put, rotated around the x-axis. It is the same shape as that for being short a call (that is, a naked writer). Thus, being short a married put means one has limited gain if the stock goes down and unlimited losses if the stock goes up.

Figure 11-11
Buying a Married Put

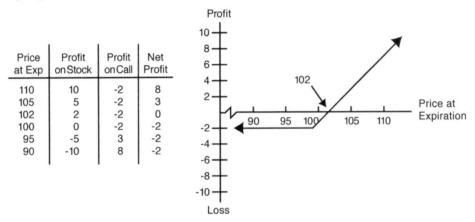

Price at Exp	Profit on Stock	Profit on Call	Net Profit
110	10	-2	8
105	5	-2	3
102	2	-2	0
100	0	-2	-2
95	-5	3	-2
90	-10	8	-2

Profit Function for a Straddle

A popular combination of options is called the *straddle*. In a straddle, the investor simultaneously buys or sells a call option and a put option with the same underlying asset, exercise price, and expiration date. The purchase of both options is called long a straddle, and the simultaneous sale of both is called short a straddle. To generate the profit function for a long straddle position, we merely combine the profit functions of the call and put that make up the straddle.

Continuing the previous examples, consider a stock for which a call has a strike price of 100 and a premium of $3, and a put with the same expiration date and strike price trades for $2. Going long a straddle-buying both the call and the put-will generate the profit function shown in the following figure. It is shaped like a large letter V. It has limited loss (the sum of the two premiums, which is $5 in this case), almost unlimited gain on the downside (the maximum gain is if the stock goes to zero), and unlimited gain on the upside. Note that the break-even points (that is, where the profit function intercepts the horizontal axis) of $95 and $105 equal the exercise price plus or minus the sum of the two premiums.

Figure 11-12
Long a Straddle (Buying a Put and Call)

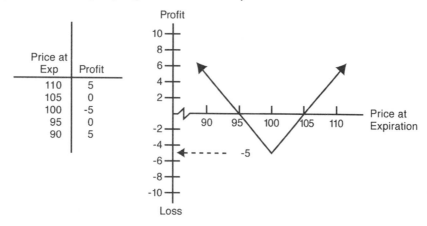

Price at Exp	Profit
110	5
105	0
100	-5
95	0
90	5

As the graph shows, with a long straddle, the investor loses if the underlying asset price ends up near the exercise price of the two options, but gains if the underlying asset price is highly volatile (makes a big jump one way or the other). Investors frequently use this strategy to profit when they expect unusual volatility in a particular stock. For example, suppose a company's stock was getting bid up because of speculation that the company is a takeover target. If the takeover happens, the purchase price will exceed the current stock price. If it does not, the stock price will fall back to its prior level. Thus, one can speculate on this by going long a straddle. However, in such a case, one will usually find that the prices of both the puts and calls have already both increased because other investors have hit upon the same strategy!

Naturally, one can just as easily short a straddle. As may be anticipated from previous examples, it is a mirror image of going long a straddle and is shaped like an inverted letter V. The following figure demonstrates graphically that the straddle writer benefits if the stock stays in a narrow trading range, but loses if the stock moves significantly in either direction. The maximum gain occurs if the stock closes on the expiration date at exactly the exercise price (and thus both options are worthless). In our example, this gain is $5. The break-even points are still the exercise price plus or minus the sum of the premiums, or $95 and $105.

Figure 11-13
Short a Straddle (Write a Put and Call with the Same Exercise Price)

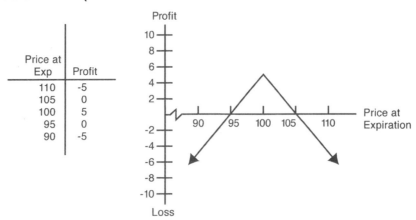

Price at Exp	Profit
110	-5
105	0
100	5
95	0
90	-5

Profit Function for a Strangle

A *strangle* is similar to a straddle, except that the options have different strike prices. Specifically, the strike price of the call option is above the strike price for the put option. A profit function for long a strangle, where the call option has a strike price of $105 and a premium of $2 and the put option has a strike price of $100 and a premium of $1, is shown in figure 11-14. The shape is somewhat like a cereal bowl. It has the advantage over the long straddle in that the maximum loss is less. In this case, the maximum loss is $3, compared to $5 in our long a straddle example. But the break-even points are now wider—$108 (the call exercise price plus the cost of both premiums) and $97 (the put exercise price less the cost of both premiums). As with long a straddle, long a strangle has limited losses and almost unlimited gain on the downside (if the stock price goes to zero) or unlimited gain on the upside. Naturally, one can be short a strangle by writing rather than buying the same two options. This short position has limited gain and large or unlimited potential losses.

Profit Function for a Bullish Call Spread

There is yet another entire class of strategies that can be pursued with options. These are known as spreads. In a spread, one option is purchased and the other is sold, with each option having a different exercise price or a different expiration date. Spreads can be constructed with either two puts or two calls. Let's look at the profit function of a *bullish call spread* that involves two call options with different striking prices.

Suppose a call is available with a strike price of $100 and a premium of $3. Another call is available with the same underlying stock, the same expiration date, a strike price of $110, and a premium of $1. A bullish call spread would involve a long position in the option with the lower strike price, and a short position in the option with the higher strike price. To think about the graph, let's start by considering the profit at two key points: $100 and $110. If the underlying stock closes at $100 on the expiration date, the investor's own option is worthless, and the option he or she sold would also be worthless. The investor paid $3 for the first option and sold the second for $1, so there is a loss of $2. In fact, if the stock price ends up at anything less than $100, the same discussion would apply, and the net loss would be the same, minus $2.

Figure 11-14
Long a Strangle (Long a Put with a $100 Strike Price and Long a Call with a $105 Strike Price)

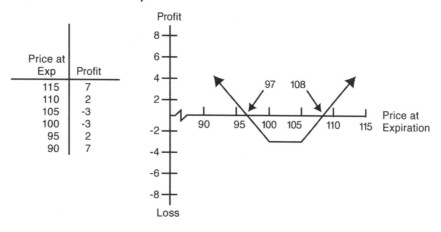

Price at Exp	Profit
115	7
110	2
105	-3
100	-3
95	2
90	7

If the stock closes at $110, the investor can sell his option at its intrinsic value of $10 (or buy the stock for $100, exercise the option, and sell it to the option writer for $110). However, he or she will not have to worry about honoring the shorted call because there is no intrinsic value to it. The net profit at this price is the net gain on the option bought of $7 (the $10 intrinsic value less the $3 purchase price), plus the $1 premium for the option sold that is now worthless, or a total of $8. For any closing price above $110, the incremental profit on the long call will exactly be offset by a loss on the short call, leaving a net profit of $8. For closing prices between $100 and $110, the profit will range from a loss of $2 to a gain of $8. The break-even point will be $102 (see the figure below).

Figure 11-15
Bullish Spread: Buy a Call with a Lower Strike Price, Sell a Call with a Higher Strike Price

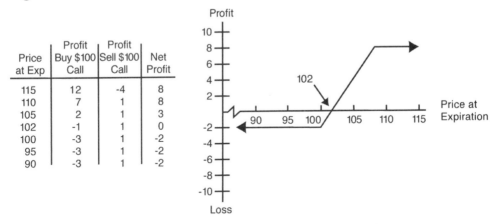

Price at Exp	Profit Buy $100 Call	Profit Sell $100 Call	Net Profit
115	12	-4	8
110	7	1	8
105	2	1	3
102	-1	1	0
100	-3	1	-2
95	-3	1	-2
90	-3	1	-2

Financial Planning Issue

Should a financial planner recommend straddles and/or spreads to his or her clients? For more aggressive clients who are willing to take double or nothing type bets, going long on straddles and strangles would seem reasonable. In fact, they are better than the racetrack because at least the losses are potentially tax deductible. Although one might look at the short side of these positions as an opportunity to generate extra income, especially for conservative, income-oriented investors, the potential risk of loss is so great that taking short positions in either strategy would seem inappropriate for almost any type of client.

Why would an investor go long a bullish spread? This strategy is used by the same investors who would go long a call option but prefer not to pay for the unlimited potential profits of the call option with the $100 strike price. In other words, although the upside potential of the bullish spread is less, the cost of creating the position (which is also the maximum loss) is also less. By itself, the call option costs $3, while the bullish spread costs only $2. The break-even point occurs where the underlying asset price is equal to the lower exercise price plus the difference in premiums between the two options. As with the purchase of an individual call, the downside risk is limited.

bearish spread   Alternatively, the investor who would like to purchase a put option but does not want to pay for the high profit potential of the put option may create a *bearish spread*. The bearish spread can also be constructed with two puts or two calls. The version with two calls can be constructed by buying a call with a higher strike price and selling a call on the same underlying asset and with the same expiration date, but with a lower strike price. This is simply the opposite side of the bullish spread construction.

As an example, let's say that there is another call option with a strike price of $90 and a premium of $11. Since this call is in the money, it will have value at expiration unless the stock price falls to $90 or below. However, the intrinsic value now is only $10. (The $11 premium also reflects the speculative or time value of the option.) Selling this call brings in $11. If the stock price closes at $101, the investor breaks even. For every dollar that the stock price rises above $101, the investor loses $1. If the stock falls below $90, the option will expire worthless, and the investor will gain $11, the cash received from the sale of the call. In the range from $90 to $101, the potential $11 profit declines $1 for every $1 that the stock price rises above $90.

Now, let's complete the bearish spread by buying the call from earlier examples with the $100 strike price and the $3 premium. We have already discussed its profit function. Again, we combine the two profit functions to see the total effect. If the stock price at expiration is below $90, the profit is the difference between what was received for the call the investor sold and what was paid for the call the investor bought, $8 ($11 – $3). The net profit declines by $1 for every $1 of stock price increase between $90 and $100. As the stock price at expiration rises above $100, every $1 of price increase on the call that was purchased is offset by $1 of price decline on the call that was sold. The following figure depicts the profit function for a bearish spread. Similar to the bullish spread, the bearish spread is cheaper than just going long a put option.

Figure 11-16
Bearish Spread: Buy a Call with a Higher Strike Price, Sell a Call with a Lower Strike Price

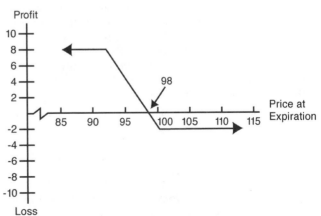

Price at Exp	Profit on $90 Call	Profit on $100 Call	Net Profit
115	-14	12	-2
110	-9	7	-2
105	-4	2	-2
100	1	-3	-2
98	3	-3	0
95	6	-3	3
90	11	-3	8
85	11	-3	8

There are a large number of combinations involving options that produce all sorts of profit functions with all sorts of risk exposures and return opportunities. An entire book can be (and many are) devoted to option strategies. However, our purpose here is only to introduce the reader to option strategies and the appropriate techniques (profit function or payoff function) by which you can understand and analyze these strategies. So far, we have focused only on looking at trading strategies that can be implemented with options. We will now turn to a related question: How does one value an option?

VALUATION OF OPTIONS

Valuation of an Option: Black-Scholes Model

Black-Scholes model

The valuation of options has long intrigued financial theorists. F. Black and M. Scholes wrote the classic theoretical option pricing work,[139] which is now known as the *Black-Scholes model*. Black and Scholes began with the assumption that investors could buy the underlying non-dividend-paying stock and write (sell) calls to maintain a riskless hedge. In this case, a riskless hedge position is defined as one in which an investor would neither make nor lose money. For stock price increases, writing calls is similar to selling short the stock. Thus, one could identify a hedge in which any change in the value of the stock's price would be offset by an equivalent but opposite change in the value of the short position in calls.

EXAMPLE
Suppose that a $1 change in the stock price would be associated with a $.50 change in the call price. Investors could then construct a fully hedged position by writing calls on twice as many shares as are held. If the investor is short two calls, a $1 increase in the stock price would be matched by a $1 decrease in the value of the call position. Similarly, a $1 decrease in the stock's price would be offset by a $1 increase in the value of the call position. In fact, any small move in the stock price would be precisely offset by a change in the value of the option position.

---

139. F. Black and M. Scholes, "The Pricing of Options and Corporate Liabilities," *Journal of Political Economy* (May-June 1973), pp. 637-654.

hedge ratio   In the above example, the ratio of the change in stock price to the associated change in option price is defined as a *hedge ratio*. As time passes and stock and call options prices change, the appropriate ratio for hedging changes. For example, the hedge ratio of two calls to one share of stock might later change to a ratio of three to one. The investor can maintain a fully hedged position by adjusting the ratio of calls to shares whenever necessary. Thus, if the required ratio changes from two calls per share to three calls per share, the hedger can write (sell) an additional call for each share held. The result of this process is called a *riskless hedge*—designed to insulate the investor from market moves in the underlying stock's price. Selling the calls provides a form of insurance against the contingency of market changes in the price of the stock.

In an efficient market, an investment in the combined riskless position should earn the riskless interest rate (that is, the rate on T-bills). Building on these concepts, Black and Scholes developed a call valuation formula that is a function of five variables. The precise form of the model, shown in appendix G, is rather complex, but the most important results are as follows: Call values *increase* with increases in time to maturity, interest rates, the price of the underlying stock, and volatility (or variance) of the underlying stock; they *decrease* as the strike price increases.

Most of these relationships are intuitive, but the two that are probably more difficult to understand are the volatility and interest rate effects. There are two rationales as to why increases in the interest rate make an option more valuable. The first is that the present value of the strike price declines with increases in the interest rate. This makes the cost to exercise the option even cheaper in terms of today's dollars. Hence, the option is more valuable.

The second rationale is that an alternative to buying stock is to buy call options. Thus, an investor might have to choose between buying 100 shares for $5,000 and buying one call option for $500. The difference in cash outlay, $4,500 in this case, could be invested if the option is bought. The higher the interest rate, the more attractive it is to buy the option and invest the difference. Hence, higher rates make options more valuable. The following example demonstrates why an increase in volatility will also increase the value of a call option.

EXAMPLE

At the start of this chapter, we noted that options had value based on both intrinsic value and speculative value. The example at the time was that a stock trades at $50 per share, and has an equally likely chance of going to $60 per share or dropping to $40 per share. Although the expected price of the stock was $50 and the expected rate of return was 0 percent, the option had value. Let's expand upon that example by assuming that on the option's expiration date, the price of the stock would either be $70 or $30. The expected price of the stock on the expiration date and the expected rate of return are unchanged, yet the expected intrinsic value of the option on the expiration date is now $10, double what it was before. Clearly, increases in the variability of a stock's price will increase the value of the option, even if the expected rate of return of the stock is unaffected.

The Black-Scholes formula is more than just an interesting theoretical exercise. Option traders often compute Black-Scholes prices to follow a strategy of buying undervalued options (vis-à-vis the model) and writing overvalued ones. The importance of Black-Scholes and its later extensions, therefore, cannot be overstated. It gave investors confidence in fair values for options.

Five Variables in the Black-Scholes Model

- Time to maturity: the longer the time to maturity, the more valuable the call
- Interest rate: the higher the interest rate, the more valuable the call
- Price of underlying stock: the higher the stock price, the more valuable the call
- Volatility: the more volatile the price of the underlying stock, the more valuable the call
- Strike price: the higher the strike price, the less valuable the call

---

Binomial Option Pricing Model

binomial option-pricing model

There is an alternative to the Black-Scholes option-pricing model, and it is known as the *binomial option-pricing model*. Because this model is mathematically complex when used in a realistic manner, we will use a simple, if unrealistic, presentation of the model.

It starts with the same type of scenario we used for our intrinsic value presentation. Let's assume a stock currently trades at $50 and that at the end of the year it will have a value of either $60 or $40. Let's now value a call option with a strike price of $50. To do so, we need an interest rate at which the investor could borrow money today. Let's assume a 10 percent interest rate and ignore any constraints due to a margin requirement.

Now, in one year the intrinsic value of the call option will be either $10 or zero, and the value of the stock will be either $40 or $60. Let's assume that an individual can borrow just enough money to buy one share of stock so that in the worst-case scenario the price of the stock is the exact amount needed to pay back the loan with interest. As the worst-case price is $40, and as the interest rate is 10 percent, taking the present value of $40 discounted at 10 percent for one year indicates the investor would borrow $36.36 ($40/(1+.10)). Because the stock is trading at a price of $50, the individual would have to put up the difference between the price and the loan amount of $13.64 ($50 – $36.36).

The purchase of stock with borrowed money will result in a value 1 year from now of either $20 (if the stock goes to $60 and the loan is repaid with interest) or $0 (if the stock goes to $40 and the loan is repaid with interest). Note that this is exactly double what the payoff to our call option with a $50 strike price would be (that is, $10 if the stock ends up at $60 and $0 if the stock ends up at $40). Hence, the investor should be able to buy two calls (because the stock payoffs are two times the call option payoffs) for the same out-of-pocket cost of buying one share of stock. The share of stock has an out-of-pocket cost of $13.64; dividing this by two (because there are two options), means each option should be worth $6.82 ($13.64/2).

EXAMPLE

Consider a similar scenario. Suppose the stock trades for $100 today, and the only two possible prices a year from now are $125 and $80. Further assume an interest rate of 8 percent with no restriction on initial margin. What is the value of an option with a striking price of $100?

Answer: The option payoffs are $25 or $0. To replicate the $0 payoff for the option, let's assume just enough can be borrowed so that in the worst case scenario, the sale of the stock just pays off the loan with interest. At an 8-percent interest rate, this means a loan of $74.07 [$80/(1 + .08)]. Hence, one share of stock could be bought for only $25.93 of out-of-pocket cash ($100 – $74.07). The payoffs for the share of stock are $45 or $0. To equilibrate the payoffs, one would need to buy 1.8 call options. This is obtained by dividing $45 by $25. Thus, 1.8 call options must be worth $25.93. If this is the case, then one call option must be worth $14.41 ($25.93/1.8).

As with the Black-Scholes option-pricing model, the binomial option-pricing model provides certain insights into option valuation. Specifically, the five variables we identified as affecting the value of a call option in the Black-Scholes framework will have the exact same effect in a binomial option-pricing model. Specifically, call values increase with increases in these four variables: time to maturity, interest rates, the price of the underlying stock, and volatility (or variance) of the underlying stock; they *decrease* as the strike price increases.

Put-Call Parity

put-call parity   The Black-Scholes and binomial option-pricing models provide insights into the pricing of call options. Unfortunately, they do not directly tell us how to price a put option. However, another concept that allows valuation of put options has evolved along with the option-pricing models. This concept is known as *put-call parity*.

The basic argument for put-call parity is simple. If there are two ways to create profit functions of the same shape, then a position of long one profit function and short the other profit function should provide a risk-free rate of return. This is because investors will buy the less expensive combination and sell the more expensive one until the value of doing so is no more than can be obtained by investing in a risk-free asset.[140]

When we discussed combinations of holdings in the previous section, we noted several instances where different combinations produced the same shaped profit function. For example, a call-like position was created from going long the stock and long a put (that is, a married put). When a simple position can be essentially duplicated with a combination of securities, the combination is referred to as a *synthetic position*. The following table provides six examples of simple positions and their synthetic equivalents, some of which were discussed earlier and some of which were not.

Table 11-1 Simple Positions and Their Synthetic Equivalents	
Simple Position	**Synthetic Equivalent**
Long Stock	Long a Call & Short a Put
Short Stock	Short a Call & Long a Put

---

140. Remember, we are assuming there are no transaction fees or taxes. To the extent that there are transaction fees and differences in tax consequences, then put-call parity is not perfectly achievable.

Simple Position	Synthetic Equivalent
Long a Call	Long Stock & Long a Put
Short a Call	Short Stock & Short a Put
Long a Put	Short Stock & Long a Call
Short a Put	Long Stock & Short a Call

In the above table, a synthetic equivalent of long a call is to be long the stock and long a put. Thus, if a person were to go long a put, long the stock, and short a call, then this person would be undertaking what is essentially a risk-free investment. It turns out that the cost of setting up such a position should be equal to the present value of the strike price on the options. Hence, put-call parity would imply that:

$$\frac{X}{e^{r_f t}} = P_0 + S_0 - C_0$$

where

C_0 = call value

P_0 = put value

r_f = risk-free rate

e = 2.718 (the natural logarithmic constant)

S_0 = initial stock price

X = strike price

t = time to expiration of the option as a fraction of the year

The more common version of this formula is derived by adding the value of the call option to both sides, and subtracting the present value of the strike price from both sides, thus producing:

$$C_0 = P_0 + S_0 - \frac{X}{e^{r_f t}} \qquad \text{(Equation 11-1)}$$

The use of the value "e" for discounting is associated with continuous discounting, a concept we have not addressed herein. For our purposes, the put-call parity formula may be modified to discrete compounding with the following adjustment:

$$C_0 = P_0 + S_0 - \frac{X}{\left(1 + r_f\right)^t}$$ (Equation 11-1a)

One can actually interpret the put-call formula by noting that it says that going long a call (the left-hand side of the equation) should be the same as going long a put, long the stock, and borrowing just enough cash to pay the exercise price at maturity (the right-hand side of the equation).

EXAMPLE

Suppose a stock has a market price of $25, and both put and call options have a strike price of $24 and 6 months to expiration. The annualized risk-free rate is 4 percent. If the put option has a price of $2, the price of the call can be determined as follows:

First, determine the discount factor for 6 months:

$(1 + .04)^{1/2} = 1.0198$

Then plug this factor into the model

$C_0 = \$2 + \$25 - \$24/1.0198 = \$3.47$

Traders normally prefer to buy puts or calls directly, but some people choose synthetic positions. Any time the price of any one of these three securities becomes misaligned with the other two as defined by the put-call parity model, arbitragers will take short positions in what might be overvalued and long positions in what might be undervalued. This arbitrage activity drives the prices back toward their proper parity.

Note that all but one of our observations about the determinants of the value of a call option can also be verified with the put-call parity model. We can see directly that an increase in the interest rate, the time to expiration, and the price of the underlying stock will be associated with an increase in the value of a call option. An increase in the strike price lowers the value of the call. The effect of a change in the variance of the price of the underlying stock can be observed only indirectly. If the variance of the stock's price increases, then the value of the put will increase. This is for the same reason that was shown earlier for call options. In the put-call parity formula, if the price of the put option increases with nothing else changing, the price of the call option must also increase. This is a mathematical certainty, even though it is extremely counterintuitive to think about the values of both the put and call options going up simultaneously.

OPTIONS ON OTHER ASSETS

Options can be developed for any standardized asset, provided enough investors are interested in trading these instruments. Assets on which standardized options are written include the following:

- foreign currencies
- stock indexes
- industry indexes
- interest rates (Treasury securities)
- precious metals
- futures contracts

Stock Index Options

Users of stock index options can buy or sell an entire stock market index, such as the S&P 500 (SPX) or the NASDAQ (NDX) stock exchange index, for the premium paid for the option. Instead of selecting either an index mutual fund (whose portfolio replicates a specific stock market index) or specific stocks (with which to go long if a prolonged market rise seems imminent), the investor "buys" the market by acquiring a calls on the index. Bearish investors can buy puts to profit from an expected decline in a market index.

As with stock options, standardized expiration dates and strike prices have been established for index options. Settlement between the writer and the holder takes place on the expiration date (that is, they are European options). Strike prices are written with 5-point increments on the underlying index. For example, if the SPX (the most popular of the indexes used for option trading) stands at 1441, put and call options at 1440 and 1450 and in ± 5- or 10-point increments from there could be written and traded. When the index rises to new highs or lows, options for new strike prices around those levels are written and traded. The options exchanges will trade index options at strike prices well beyond any recent levels of the indexes (even well above historical highs) as long as buyers and sellers can be matched.

The table below shows sample premium quotations for SPX options from a typical financial page. The actual price of the contract is computed by multiplying the premium quotation by 100. For example, assume that the

SPX trades at 1441 and the premium asked for a December call option with a strike price of 1450 on that specific index is $29. For an index option, the normal lot is 100 units. Therefore, the price for this call option is $2,900 ($29 x 100). Because the index is 1441, this call is currently out of the money and thus the intrinsic value is zero, but it has a time value of $2,900.

Table 11-2 Sample Quotations on Stock Index Options				
S&P 500 Index (SPX)			**Close 1441**	
	Calls		Puts	
Strike Price	Nov	Dec	Nov	Dec
1430	15.50	42.00	3.80	32.00
1440	11.00	35.50	8.50	36.00
1450	4.10	29.00	12.00	39.50
NASDAQ-100 (NDX)				
	Calls		Puts	
Strike Price	Nov	Dec	Nov	Dec
1300	41.00	61.00	1.00	18.40
1375	50.00	18.00	33.50	50.00

As with a company-specific naked call writer, writers of index options place margin deposits with their brokers for the period of the option or until the option position is closed out through purchasing an offsetting contract. Unlike the stock options in which settlement of exercised options includes the delivery of the common stocks to the call holder (or to the put writer), settlement for stock index options is made in dollars. The amount of money that will be paid on the settlement date is based on the difference between the exercise price and the closing value of the index on the expiration date. Multiplying this difference by $100 determines the amount that will be paid by the option writer if it is exercised.

EXAMPLE

Referring to the above table, suppose that on the above date a December call on the SPX with a strike price of $1,430 is purchased at the closing price of $42. Suppose also that the index closes at 1500 on the expiration date-a difference of 75, or approximately 6.4 percent. In this case, the writer's obligation requires payment of $7,000 ([$1,500 - $1,430] x 100) to the holder of the option. As the holder acquired the call at a price of $42 from the writer for a cost of $4,200 ($42 x 100), the buyer's gain is $2,800.

A similar put option at a strike price of $1,430 would not be exercised because the index value in the example above exceeds $1,430. Holders of puts exercise their options only when the strike price exceeds the index value on the day the option expires. However, if the purchaser of the put had bought the put at the same time as the call buyer, the put purchaser would have paid $32.00 per unit and would have lost it all (-100%).

Industry Index Options

Industry options work pretty much the same way as index options. There are at present a large number of industry index options. The semiconductor index option (SOX) probably has the most number of options and volume associated with it of any of the industry index options. Examples of other industry index options include pharmaceuticals, high tech (MS HITECH), and oil service.

Interest Rate Options

Puts and calls on specific U.S. Treasury securities are called interest rate options. For example, the Chicago Board Options Exchange has options in the following:[141]

- 13-Week Treasury Bill
- 5-Year Treasury Note
- 10-Year Treasury Note
- 30-Year Treasury Bond[142]

Usually, these options are written for a relatively large dollar amount of a particular issue, such as $100,000. These options are based on the average yield of the most recently auctioned Treasury bonds, and they are European style.

---

141. http://www.cboe.com/Products/InterestRateOptionsSpecs.aspx, accessed July 30, 2010.

142. Actually, a 30-year T-bond has not been issued for several years, but at the time of this writing, new 30-year bonds have been issued and the intent is to continue such issuances. Presumably, these option contracts will come back into existence.

LEAPS®

Long-term Equity Anticipation Securities (LEAPS)

Puts and calls are normally written for relatively short periods (9 months is typically the longest available); however, a 1990 innovation in the options market called *Long-term Equity Anticipation Securities (LEAPS®)* with expiration dates as long as 39 months from the date of initial listing—and covering both calls and puts—was introduced on the CBOE and the AMEX. They are now traded on all the options exchanges. There are no differences in the terminology or strategy used with LEAPS® as with regular options, other than that LEAPS® can have a substantially longer time to expiration.

There are two types of LEAPS®, Equity LEAPS® and Index LEAPS®. All equity LEAPS® are American style, and typically expire in January of the designated year (actually the Saturday following the third Friday of the expiration month).

Index LEAPS® are long-term index options based either on a fractional value of one-tenth of the value of the underlying index or on the full value of the underlying index, depending on the value of the particular index. Like regular index options, Index LEAPS® are settled in cash based on the difference between the settlement value of the index on the exercise date and the strike price of the option. Some Index LEAPS® are American style, but others are European-style options. Index LEAPS® expire in January, June, and December of each year.

CONVERTIBLES

A convertible is any security that, at the owner's discretion, can be converted into another security. The two most common convertibles are convertible bonds and convertible preferred stock. Sometimes when there are two classes of common stock, one is convertible into the other. Usually, a convertible is converted into the common stock of the same firm, although occasionally the conversion may be into some other security. Almost all of the details involving convertible bonds also apply to preferred stock. In this section, we will focus the discussion primarily on convertible bonds, and talk only about how convertible preferreds differ from their bond cousins.

Convertible Bonds

Companies issue convertible bonds for much the same reasons they issue warrants: it allows them to pay a lower coupon rate on the bond, and it gives them the ability to issue new stock at a later date, provided the market price of the stock rises above the conversion price. Convertible bonds give the owner the option of exchanging the bonds for a fixed number of shares of common stock. The number of shares of common stock received is the exchange ratio or *conversion ratio*. In some situations, people will refer to a conversion price rather than an exchange ratio. The conversion ratio is par value divided by the conversion price. Alternatively, one could say that the conversion price is the par value divided by the conversion ratio.

$$\text{Conversion ratio} = \frac{\text{PAR}}{\text{Conversion price}} \qquad \text{(Equation 11-2)}$$

and

$$\text{Conversion price} = \frac{\text{PAR}}{\text{Conversion ratio}} \qquad \text{(Equation 11-2a)}$$

When considering convertible bonds, an investor needs to be alert not only to the price of the bond itself, but also to the conversion value. Conversion value is the value of the common stock that would be received upon immediate conversion. It is the product of the conversion ratio and the price of the common stock.

$$\text{Conversion value} = \text{Conversion ratio} \times \text{Price of common stock} \qquad \text{(Equation 11-3)}$$

At the time of issuance, the conversion value is always less than par (which also means the market price of the stock is less than the conversion price). Like warrants, convertibles are analogous to out-of-the-money options at the time they are issued.

The difference between the market price of the convertible bond and the conversion value is known as the conversion premium. This number may be stated in absolute dollars or as a percentage of the conversion value. The percentage conversion premium is the conversion premium divided by the conversion value.

$$\text{Conversion premium} = \text{Market price of bond} - \text{Conversion value} \qquad \text{(Equation 11-4)}$$

and

$$\% \text{ Conversion premium} = \text{Conversion premium} / \text{Conversion value} \qquad \text{(Equation 11-4a)}$$

With one rare exception, convertibles sell for more than their conversion value. This exception is if the price of the common stock has risen to such a high level that there is no real distinction between the convertible bond and the stock. In this case, the market price of the convertible is the conversion value.

EXAMPLE

A $1,000 par-value bond trades at $980 and has a conversion price of $20. If the underlying stock trades at $15, what are its conversion ratio and its conversion premium?

Answer: The conversion ratio is 50 (that is, $1,000/$20). The conversion value of the bond is 50 x $15 = $750. So the conversion premium in dollar terms is $230 ($980 – $750), and in percentage terms it is 30.7 percent ($230/$750).

---

straight-debt value

A third value associated with a convertible and the only one that is not directly observable is the *straight-debt value*. This is the investor's estimate of what the value of a convertible bond would be without the conversion feature. It requires ascertaining what the appropriate discount rate for the bond would be if it traded as straight debt.

EXAMPLE

Suppose the convertible bond in the example above has an annual coupon rate of 6 percent and 5 years to maturity, and a straight bond of comparable risk trading at par pays a coupon rate of 7 percent. Using a discount rate of 7 percent and calculating the present value, we find that the straight-debt value of the convertible bond (assuming annual interest payments) is $959.00. The keystrokes are: SHIFT, C ALL, 1000, FV, 60, PMT, 7, I/YR, 5, N, PV (display: –959.00).

The market price of a convertible bond is always at least the greater of its straight-debt value or its conversion value. This is because the holder has the option of either keeping the instrument as a bond or converting it into stock. The price of most convertibles exceeds these floor values for two reasons. The first is the speculative value of the option. Just as call options have value even when the stock is less than the strike price, convertibles trade at a premium to these floor values because of the chance that the price of the stock might increase sufficiently before the bond matures to make conversion worthwhile. Also, as with options, the size of this speculative value is directly related to the time to maturity and the volatility of the price of the underlying stock, and it is inversely related to the spread between the conversion price and the stock's current market price. The second reason for the premiums is that the current yield on convertibles usually exceeds the dividend yield on the underlying stock.

The So-Called Advantages of Convertible Bonds

There are two advantages often cited to investing in convertibles compared with common stock. The first is the above-mentioned current yield relative to the dividend yield. The second is the presence of the floor value defined by the straight debt value of the bond.

The higher current yield is clearly a nice advantage, although it comes with a price tag. The price tag is that if the price of the stock goes up, the conversion premium declines toward zero. Thus, the percentage price appreciation from owning common stock will be greater than the percentage price appreciation in the convertible associated with the stock price movement.

Financial Planning Issue

When analyzing convertible bonds for their clients, financial planners should focus on the bond ratings for safety, but should also consider the relationship between the bond's current yield and the conversion premium percentage. Unfortunately, higher current yields are associated with higher conversion premiums. When faced with a variety of convertibles to choose from, a planner will usually be willing to give up some current yield for smaller conversion premiums.

The second cited advantage, the presence of a floor value, is simply not true! When a company's stock price declines precipitously, it is because the company's prospects have declined. When this happens, the prices of all its securities decline, not just its stock price. Thus, when a company's financial condition deteriorates, the yield to maturity on its debt rises, and so the straight bond value would also decline. This point is illustrated in figure 11-17, which shows the conversion premium as a function of the price of the common stock. A straight line emanating from the origin represents the conversion value, and its slope equals the conversion ratio. The straight debt value also starts at the origin, but steadily rises to the point where it becomes a flat line defined by the company's current bond rating. The actual price of the convertible bond will always be greater or equal to the larger of these two values. Thus, when the price of the stock is "low," the convertible bond's price is determined primarily by its straight-debt value. When the convertible bond's price is "high," it is the conversion value that determines its price. The key point in this graph is that the market value of the convertible bond will go to zero if the price of the common stock also goes to zero. At a price of zero, the company is bankrupt, and so both securities are worthless.[143]

Figure 11-17
Conversion Premium of a Convertible Bond

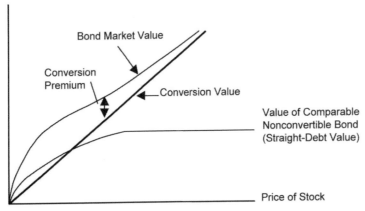

EXAMPLE

Consider again the convertible bond with an annual coupon rate of 6 percent, 5 years to maturity, and a conversion ratio of 50 shares (conversion price of $20). The following table sets forth hypothetical values, conversion values, straight bond values, and market prices for this convertible bond for when the common stock trades at different prices:

Price of Common Stock	Conversion Value	Straight Debt Value	Price of Convertible Bond	Conversion Premium
$5	$250	$400	$410	$160
10	500	600	670	170
15	750	900	950	200
20	1,000	1,000	1,250	250
25	1,250	1,000	1,300	50

---

143. This argument is overstated only to the extent that the firm's assets may have may have liquidation value, and thus the convertible bonds (which are normally subordinated debentures) may have some value in any bankruptcy proceedings.

Call Feature

All convertible bonds are callable. Remember, the call feature allows the issuing company to buy back the bond at a predetermined call price which is always greater than par, but usually equal to or less than par plus 1 year's worth of interest. For straight debt, companies make bonds callable to give them the opportunity to refinance the bonds in the event market interest rates drop sufficiently such that the issuer could refinance the bonds with new bonds that have a lower coupon rate. Although the refinancing option might be a motivation for making convertibles callable, it is not the primary motivation. This is because convertibles have lower coupon rates to start with, and therefore the drop in interest rates would have to be huge to make the refinancing option attractive for the issuer. The real motivation for making convertibles callable is the opportunity to create a forced conversion. After the last date of the call period passes, the investor no longer has the option to convert and will not earn any additional interest. Consider the following example.

EXAMPLE

The King Company has outstanding a convertible bond with a conversion ratio of 100 (a $10 conversion price), a coupon rate of 8 percent, a call price of 110 (that is, $1,100), and 5 years left to maturity. It currently pays no dividend on its stock. The company has had a run of good news recently, and its stock price has risen from $5 per share to $15 per share. The conversion value is now $1,500, and the market price of the convertible bond is $1,505. The reason the conversion value and market value are so close is that everyone knows the company will likely call the bond in the near future to force conversion. A primary reason for forcing conversion is that the company is currently making annual interest payments of $80 per bond (8 percent coupon rate) and by calling the bond, all of the bonds will be converted into the common stock on which no dividends are being paid. After all, the bondholder will be given a choice of taking $1,500 worth of stocks per bond or accepting the $1,100 call price. Thus, the company will save the annual interest payment, and only have to distribute new stock that it would likely have had to distribute anyway.

Convertible Preferred Stock

There are similarities between convertible bonds and convertible preferreds, but there are also some differences. The downside value associated with the straight-debt value of the bond is less certain with convertible preferreds because there is no legal requirement that the preferred dividends be paid. However, preferred dividends must be paid before common stock dividends are paid, so there is still some degree of downside protection.

The pricing of convertible preferreds is similar to the pricing of convertible bonds. When the market price of the underlying stock is close to or above the conversion price, the conversion value influences the price of the convertible preferreds. When the market price is far below the conversion price, the price of the convertible preferreds is closer to the straight preferred stock value.

As with convertible bonds, the number of common shares that can be obtained by converting one preferred share is known as the conversion ratio. The conversion ratio can change over time. For example, an issue of convertible preferred stock may have a conversion ratio of 4:1 for the first 10 years after issue, 2:1 for the next 10 years, and become straight preferred stock thereafter. Convertible preferreds also always have a call feature to allow forced conversion.

> **Financial Planning Issue**
>
> Are convertibles an appropriate investment for clients? The historical rates of return on convertibles are higher than straight bonds and lower than equities, which is what one would expect given the combined equity and debt features of this instrument. Thus, convertibles would make sense for those clients who want to hold both bonds and stocks in their portfolios. Although they should not be pitched to clients as the best of both worlds (equity appreciation with the safety of bonds), neither do they need to be pitched as the worst of both worlds—less price appreciation potential than equities, and lower rates of return than straight debt.

REVIEW OF THE LEARNING OBJECTIVES

1. A call is the privilege to buy and a put is the privilege to sell. The three prices associated with an option are the premium, the strike price, and the price of the underlying security. An option can trade in, at, or out of the money. Option expiration dates are usually in the 2 nearest months, and the next 2 cycle months. The OCC provides the integrity to all option contracts by substituting itself as the other party in all transactions. Strike prices are set as near to the price of the underlying security as possible. The time to exercise an option can be based on the American option, European option, or the Bermuda option approaches.

2. Options have an intrinsic value, which is the greater of zero or the difference between the price of the underlying security and the strike price. They also have a speculative or time value, which is based only on the potential variability of the stock's price, and is the difference between the market price of the option and the intrinsic value.

3. A profit function is derived by combining the payoff function with the price of the premium paid or received. A person long a call has limited loss and unlimited potential gain. A person who is long a put has limited loss and almost unlimited potential gain. A person who is short a call has limited gain and almost unlimited potential loss, while a person short a put has limited gain and almost unlimited potential loss. The sums of the profit functions for a person long and a person short the same option are always zero.

4. Combinations of puts, calls, and the underlying stock can be constructed to create synthetic positions to mimic being long or short a put, a call, or the underlying stock. Straddles and strangles can be created to take advantage of potential volatility or stability in a stock's price, and bullish and bearish hedges can be structured to generate limited potential gains with limited loss exposures.

5. Call values *increase* with increases in: time to maturity, interest rates, the price of the underlying stock, and volatility (or variance) of the underlying stock; they *decrease* as the strike price increases.

6. Index options allow one to hedge against or speculate on the entire market or a specific sector of the market. Settlement is in cash rather than delivery of a specific security. Interest rate options allow one to hedge against or speculate on the direction of interest rate movements. LEAPS® can have maturities of multiple years.

7. Convertibles usually allow one to earn a better current yield than the dividend yield on the underlying stock, and provide some moderation to downward price movements. They don't provide as much price appreciation potential as the stock, and can't protect an investor from significant loss in the case of bankruptcy. The conversion value equals the conversion ratio times the price of the underlying common stock. The conversion premium is the difference between the price of the convertible bond and the conversion value of the bond.

MINICASE

It is December 30. Your client has a $2.2 million portfolio but is really nervous about the market during the next few months. You are considering the purchase of put options on the S&P 500 Index (SPX) to hedge the client's portfolio during this period because holdings in the portfolio closely resemble the S&P 500 index and the changes in the client's portfolio closely parallel changes in this particular index. The current value of the index is 1148.29 and the price of the March put option with a striking price of 1150 is 22.20.

1.   To hedge your client's portfolio, you should [4]

    (A)   buy the put options to give you the privilege of selling the equivalent of an index portfolio at the price of 1450

    (B)   sell the put options to offset the long position in the portfolio

    (C)   go long the put options and long the call options with a similar strike price

    (D)   go short the put options and short the call options with a similar strike price

2.   The dollar value at which the put option contract trades is [1]

    (A) $22.20

    (B) $222.00

    (C) $2,220.00

    (D) $22,200.00

3.   The most appropriate number of contracts to use in the hedge would likely be [5]

    (A)   about 4

    (B)   about 9

    (C)   about 15

    (D)   about 19

4.   The above described hedge using the March options can be maintained [1]

    (A)   only for 1 week

    (B)   until the option expires in March

    (C)   until March 31st

    (D)   indefinitely

5.   One of the drawbacks to setting up this hedge is [4]

    (A)   the client must pay to the person who sold the option all dividend payments made by stocks in the S&P 500 index during the period of the hedge

    (B)   the client will have to recognize any capital gains in his portfolio at the time the hedge is established

    (C)   although this hedge protects the client from losses, it also eliminates any chance for profiting from general increases in stock prices

    (D)   none of the above

CHAPTER REVIEW

Key Terms and Concepts

premium (option)	naked writer
exercise price	zero-sum game
strike (striking) price	combination position
in the money	bearish spread
out of the money	Black-Scholes model
at the money	hedge ratio
American options	binomial option-pricing model
European options	put-call parity
Bermuda options	Long-term Equity Anticipation
intrinsic value (option)	Securities (LEAPS)
covered writer	straight-debt value

Review Questions

Review questions are based on the learning objectives in this chapter. Thus, an [11-3] at the end of a question means that the question is based on learning objective 11-3. If there are multiple objectives, they are all listed.

1. a. Distinguish between a put option and a call option. [1]
    b. Explain the writer's obligations for each. [1]
    c. Why is purchasing a call not equivalent to writing a put? [1]

2. The ASD Company's stock sells for $32; a 6-month option to purchase it at $35 sells for 1 3/4. (Ignore time value and dividends.) [3]
    a. What price must the stock reach within those 6 months for the buyer of the call option to break even?
    b. What are the percentage gains for the buyer of the stock (that is, ROA) and the buyer of the call option if the stock rises to $45?

3. a. What kind of option would an investor purchase to protect a profit in a stock he or she owns? [3]
    b. How would such a strategy differ from simply selling the position? [3]
    c. What factors should an investor consider when evaluating the two strategies? [3]

4. a. What obligation does the writer of a covered call undertake? [1]
    b. What are the risks and prospective returns of a covered-call-writing strategy? [4]

5.   a.   What is a straddle? [4]
     b.   Under what circumstances would an investor be inclined to buy a
     straddle? [4]
     c.   When would a writer be inclined to write a straddle? [4]
     d.   Briefly explain a spread. [4]
     e.   What is the motivation for holding a bullish spread? [4]

6.   a.   Name the five variables in the Black-Scholes option pricing model that
     determine the value of a call option. [5]
     b.   Indicate how an increase in the value of each would affect the value of
     a call option. [5]

7.   XYZ Corp. stock is selling for $30 per share. Both a put and a call option
     are at the money, with exercise prices of $30 and 3 months to expiration. If
     the put option sells for $1 and the risk-free rate of interest is 6 percent, use
     put-call parity to find the value of a call option (assume annual rather than
     continuous compounding). [5]

8.   a.   Why is call risk particularly relevant to convertibles? [7]
     b.   Under what circumstances are convertibles likely to be called?
     c.   What do convertible bond investors obtain and what do they sacrifice
     relative to investors in straight bonds and relative to investors in the
     underlying stock? [7]

9.   A share of convertible preferred selling at $100 might be exchanged for two
     shares of common stock trading at $40. What is the conversion premium
     in dollar and percentage terms? [7]

10. The SOM Company convertible debentures sell for 105 ($1,050), while its
     common stock is priced at $40 per share. The convertible's conversion ratio
     is 20; its annual coupon rate is 10 percent. Its estimated straight-debt value
     is 90. The stock pays a dividend of $2 per share per year. The bonds mature
     in 3 years and are callable at 107. [7]
     a.   Compute the convertible's

     •   conversion price
     •   conversion value
     •   conversion premium (in dollar and percentage terms)
     •   premium over straight-debt value
     •   current yield

     b.   If you purchased the bonds at par ($1,000) and the stock subsequently
     rose to $55 1/2, what is the minimum profit per bond (ignoring commissions
     and coupon payments)?

Of all the major investment vehicles discussed in this book (that is, stocks, bonds, investment companies, options, and futures), most people have the least familiarity with futures contracts. Futures contracts can be broadly divided into three segments: agricultural, mineral, and financial. There are two primary motives for trading futures contracts: speculation and hedging. Financial planners may use financial futures contracts for hedging purposes even with conservative clients. In this chapter we will discuss primarily the agricultural futures markets because they are easier to understand. We will then examine the more complicated issues of the financial futures markets that a planner is more likely to use.

THE SPOT MARKET, FORWARD CONTRACTS, AND FUTURES CONTRACTS

Everyone uses the spot market, even if they don't use that name or think of it in that way. The spot market involves any transaction wherein the purchase price is paid (whether in cash or credit) and the commodity purchased is given to the buyer at the same time (that is, on the spot). For example, when an individual buys something at the grocery store, he or she is buying in the spot market.

The entire nature of the transaction changes, however, when both parties agree to a later delivery and later payment of the item purchased. Such a transaction is referred to as a forward contract. People occasionally enter into forward contracts. For example, if Juanita Rodriguez goes to a new car dealer but can't find the exact combination of color and options she wants, she may sign a contract for delivery of the specified car at a later date. Juanita does not want to pay for the car until she receives it, and the dealer wants assurance that Juanita will buy the car once it is delivered. Juanita resolves this by placing a deposit on the purchase of the car. If Juanita fails to show up, the dealer can confiscate Juanita's deposit as compensation for the lost sale. For her part, Juanita will want as precise a description as possible as to what the car will look like and when it will be delivered. Juanita and the car dealer have created a forward contract. Note that Juanita has bought a product, and the car dealer has sold a product, that has not yet been produced.

If the contract that Juanita and the car dealer had created involved standardized terms, an active market for these contracts, and a third party to guarantee that both parties honor their contracts, then it would be known as a futures contract. As a futures contract, if the car dealer no longer wanted to be responsible for the delivery of the car, or if Juanita no longer wanted to buy the car, either party could sell his or her obligation under the contract to a third party.

There are always two parties to a futures contract, the person who is long (that is, the buyer), and the person who is short (that is, the seller). The person with the long position has agreed to take delivery of the particular commodity described in the contract and pay the agreed upon price at the time of delivery. The person with a short position has agreed to make delivery of the particular product described in the contract and will receive the agreed-upon price at the time of delivery. Each futures contract fully specifies what commodity is to be delivered, where it is to be delivered, when it is to be delivered, and what the consequences are for failure to meet each of the above requirements. Simply put, when one trades in the futures market, one is trading in contractual obligations.

Futures versus Options

There is some similarity between a futures contract and an option. Both involve subsequent events. An option holder has a right but not an obligation to buy (if he or she owns a call option) or sell (if he or she owns a put option) a specified quantity of some asset at a specified price between now and the expiration of the option (assuming it is an American option). The holder of a futures contract, in contrast, has the obligation to accept and pay for a specified quantity of an asset at a specified price at a specified time. Thus, those who own options have a *choice* to do something in the future, whereas those who own futures have an *obligation* to do something in the future.

Difference between Futures Owner and Option Holder

- A futures buyer has the *obligation* to accept and pay for a specified quantity of an asset at a specified price at a specified time.
- A option holder has the *right*—but not an obligation—to buy or sell a specified quantity of an asset at a specified price over a specified time period.

Forward Contracts versus Futures Contracts

As noted earlier, a forward contract is a customized contractual agreement between parties to accept delivery (buy) and to deliver (sell) a specified commodity or financial instrument at an agreed-upon price, settlement date, quantity, and location. The terms of this contract result from direct negotiations between the parties, and both parties must accept the terms. Because these contracts are nonstandard ones, there is no organized exchange for trading forward contracts.

A futures contract is divided into two contracts—one to buy and one to sell—and it contains standardized features that cover the commodity in question. Because the terms are standardized, active secondary markets exist. Indeed, most futures contracts trade on an organized exchange that sets the terms of the contracts, provides the location for their trading, and monitors their settlements.

Futures contracts allow those who expect to have something to sell or need to buy an asset later to establish a price and quantity ahead of time. Standardizing the contract's terms (grade, quantity, delivery location, and date) facilitates active trading. That is, a large number of interested parties can trade the same (standardized) contract.

Unlike forward contracts but like exchange-traded options, futures contracts are actually contracts between each contracting party and a clearinghouse. Therefore, neither the person who is long nor the person who is short has to worry about the other party to the contract defaulting because the clearinghouse is obligated to honor the contract regardless of the actions of the party taking the opposite side of the contract. Thus, the two parties need only worry about the clearinghouse defaulting, and it is the clearinghouse that worries about any one party to a contract defaulting. As we will see shortly, significant safeguards are built into the trading process to minimize the risk of default.

Because of the standardized nature of futures contracts, transaction costs tend to be much lower than those of forward contracts. Forward contracts are private, customized agreements between two contracting parties. As such, there can be considerable transaction costs involved in the negotiation of a mutually acceptable agreement between the two parties.

Differences between a Forward Contract and a Futures Contract
• Forward contract: a nonstandardized (unique) contract between parties to buy and sell a specified commodity or financial instrument at an agreed upon price, settlement date, quantity, and location. There is no organized exchange for trading forward contracts.
• Futures contract: a standardized contract divided into two contracts—one to buy and one to sell—a specified commodity or financial instrument. Futures trade on an organized exchange that sets contract terms, which establish price, quantity, delivery location, and date.

THE INSTITUTIONAL FRAMEWORK

The Commodity Exchanges

Just as we saw that there are multiple exchanges for the trading of stocks, so there are multiple exchanges for futures contracts. The oldest such exchange was the Chicago Board of Trade. In 2007, it was acquired by the Chicago Mercantile Exchange (CMEX) as part of the CME Group, and ceased to exist as an independent entity.

The Professional Traders

A substantial number of commodity traders are professionals. For example, large firms in commodity-related industries (mining, baking, meatpacking, grain, and so on) often maintain representatives on the relevant exchanges. These professionals seek to establish prices for future supplies of new material for future product sales. They make it their business to have access to, and a detailed understanding of, the latest information relevant to their particular commodities. For instance, they may be following the latest crop estimates, cost comparisons, weather reports, possible government policy changes, trade figures, international markets, and a host of other data. Access to all of the relevant and available knowledge gives these professionals a decided advantage over less-informed traders.

Several additional classes of professional commodity traders bear mentioning. They include scalpers, day traders, position traders, and arbitrageurs. Like stock exchange floor traders and specialists, these traders usually have seats on the exchange and trade for their own accounts.

scalpers   *Scalpers* are people who hold positions for a few seconds to a few minutes at most. They stand at the hub of trading activity looking for temporary misalignments in prices. If one contract appears to become slightly overpriced due to a temporary surge in buy orders, scalpers will move in to sell this contract and bring the price into alignment with other contracts. They may make 50, 100, or more trades in a single day, trying to reap small gains of a few dollars on each trade. They thrive on action. Concentration, quick thinking, and reliable, high-speed access to the markets are essential. Timing is everything.

Types of Professional Futures Market Traders
• Firm representatives: hedge needs or outputs of firms that deal with these commodities
• Scalpers: hold positions for a few minutes at most
• Day traders: short-run traders who close their positions each day
• Position traders: may hold positions for several days based on fundamental or technical factors
• Arbitrageurs: seek to exploit departures from expected relative price relationships

day traders

position traders

arbitrageurs

Day traders usually close their positions by the end of each day. They hope to profit from modest price moves. Unlike day traders, *position traders* seek to profit from fundamental or technical forces that may manifest themselves over several days. Finally, *arbitrageurs* try to exploit misalignments of relative prices by simultaneously taking long and short positions. An example of an arbitrage would be if a particular currency contract was trading at one price in the London market and at a slightly different price in the U.S. market. An arbitrageur would go long the lower-priced contract and short the higher-priced contract on the assumption that eventually the two prices will converge. They will likely converge because it is relatively cost-free to move money around the world (especially if you run a business with branches all over the world). Once the prices have converged, the arbitrageur will *unwind* the two positions, which means selling the long position and buying the short position.

Regulation of the Futures Markets

The primary regulator of the futures markets is the Commodity Futures Trading Commission (CFTC). Its mission is "to protect market users and the public from fraud, manipulation, and abusive practices related to the sale of commodity and financial futures and options, and to foster open, competitive, and financially sound futures and option markets."[144]

The Commission is directed by five Commissioners appointed by the President to serve staggered 5-year terms. No more than three Commissioners at any one time may be from the same political party. To facilitate its monitoring of both the markets and the market participants, the CFTC maintains regional offices in the cities that have future exchanges—New York, Chicago, Kansas City, and Minneapolis.

CHARACTERISTICS OF FUTURES CONTRACTS

Different Types of Futures Contracts

Contracts are broadly grouped as agricultural, mineral, and financial. Agricultural futures contracts include the following: cattle, hogs, chickens, wheat, oats, corn, soybeans, barley, sugar, potatoes, coffee, orange juice, and cocoa. To facilitate a convenient grouping of contracts, contracts in

---

144. http://www.cftc.gov/About/MissionResponsibilities/index.htm, accessed July 16, 2010.

lumber, plywood, cotton, and wool are also referred to as agricultural contracts. The minerals traded on futures exchanges include crude oil, natural gas, gasoline, heating oil, copper, zinc, gold, silver, platinum, tin, palladium, and lead. Financial futures can be broken down into three subgroups: interest rate, stock market index, and foreign currency. The primary interest rate contracts are for the federal funds rate, Treasury bills, and long-term government bonds. Stock market index contracts focus primarily on the S&P 500 and the DJIA indices. The currency contracts include the currencies of all of the major trading partners for the United States.

Successful futures contracts possess most, if not all, of the following characteristics:

- a relatively competitive spot market for the underlying commodity
- a meaningful standardized contract (for example, a well-defined deliverable)
- storability or its equivalence (that is, ongoing production) for the underlying commodity
- sufficient price volatility to attract (or require) speculative and hedging interest for the underlying commodity
- a significant business use for the product

For example, no legal or theoretical barriers prevent futures trading in rhubarb or mint, but volume would probably be insufficient to justify these listings because there is not enough business need for these products. When the price of gold was fixed at $35 per ounce by the U.S. Treasury and it was illegal to own gold, there was no futures market in gold for two reasons: delivery could not occur (illegal to own) and there was no uncertainty as to price.

Characteristics of a Successful Contract

All of the commodity exchanges are constantly looking to establish new contracts for trading. For example, contracts for turkeys, shrimp, apples, and diamonds were tried and failed. Many other items such as steel reinforcing bars (re-bars), scrap aluminum, returnable drink bottles, uranium, milk, butter, coal, cement, cinder blocks, sulfur, and nails might or might not support futures trading. Even when all of the above conditions are met, a particular futures contract will not necessarily succeed.

Many Contracts per Commodity

For any commodity that is traded, there are actually multiple contracts. The most common distinction among contracts is the month of delivery. For example, in July 2010, the CME traded 15 different corn contracts. The nearest term contract was September 2010 (delivery can be made any time during the delivery month). The furthest out contract was July 2014. At the same time, multiple wheat contracts were traded on three different exchanges: the CME, the Kansas City Board of Trade, and the Minneapolis Grain Exchange. There were substantial differences in the quality or type of wheat that could be delivered under each contract, as well as the delivery location designated by each contract. Anyone trading a commodity should be familiar with the technical features of the contract traded (that is, quantity of product to be delivered, quality of product to be delivered, time of delivery, location of delivery, penalties for failure to honor each specific term, and so on).

Unwinding a Contract

Although we have mentioned several times now that the person who goes long (that is, buys) a contract is committing to take delivery of the commodity and the person who goes short (that is, sells) a contract is committing to make delivery, deliveries rarely occur. The reason is that few people actually want to make or take delivery because that can be expensive. Instead, nearly everyone with a contract closes out his or her position by entering into an offsetting contract. As described earlier, closing out a contract by placing a sell order if one is long or a buy order if one is short is referred to as unwinding a position. Remember that although a contract is created when a buy and a sell order of two people without prior positions in that commodity are matched on the trading floor, the contract of each party is actually with a clearinghouse. Thus, a futures holder who is long a September wheat futures contract can liquidate his or her position by placing a sell order on that same contract. For someone who enters the contract on the short side (has promised to make delivery), he or she liquidates by placing a buy order for the same contract. Being simultaneously long and short a contract abolishes one's position.

The Clearinghouses

Each futures exchange has its own clearinghouse. Membership in the clearinghouse is composed of well-capitalized members of the exchange. Exchange members who do not join the clearinghouse association must clear their trades through a member of the association. Each clearinghouse member must post and maintain margins, which in turn are posted by their customers (margins will be discussed shortly).

Occasionally two traders will disagree about the details of a specific trade made on the trading floor. This is relatively rare, but it does occur. It is the clearinghouse which requires the two traders to reach an agreement as to the details of the trade. The two traders in the dispute are barred from entering the trading floor the next day until the disagreement is resolved. To facilitate resolution of any disputes, each exchange has a set of rules that can be imposed.

Large Dollar Value

Although stocks and bonds have standard trading units such as 100 shares constituting a round lot, the standard trading unit for each contract is unique. For example, each contract for corn is based on 5,000 bushels, and each contract for soybean oil is 100 tons. Prices are quoted on a per unit basis. Agricultural commodities are usually quoted on a pennies per unit basis. Thus, if corn were trading at 250.00, the trade price is $2.50 per bushel. As there are 5,000 bushels per contract, this means that this particular contract would be valued at $12,500.

Commissions

round-trip fee Since the standard procedure is to close out a position by acquiring an offsetting contract, the transaction cost paid at the formation of a long or short futures contract position is a *round-trip fee* that covers the commission for both ends of the transaction. The size of the commission varies, depending on the contract and the number of contracts being traded.

Margin Deposits

Investors purchase stocks and bonds by paying in full at the time of purchase, although some of the purchase price may come from borrowed money. The amount that is the investor's own money is called margin. Sellers of stocks and bonds receive the full selling price. In the futures market, the term margin has a slightly different meaning. Both the buyer and seller must make a margin deposit, which is *performance bond money* to guarantee the performance by *both* participants in the futures contract. In fact, the margin money must be on deposit with the broker *before* an order is placed. The transaction does not involve any borrowing. The margin deposit stays with the broker (actually, the clearinghouse) through whom the order is placed until the contract is either completed or unwound.

Like margin accounts with stocks and bonds, these margin deposits have initial and maintenance requirements established for each commodity or financial instrument. The margin requirements are set in terms of a fixed dollar amount per contract. These requirements can and do change over time. For example, at the time of writing, the initial and maintenance margin requirements on a corn futures contract, for other than hedging or spreading positions, are $1,148 and $850 per contract.[145] The margin amounts are based on the commodity's price volatility—the greater the potential price volatility, the higher the margin requirements. In general, the margin percentage for each type of contract is set just high enough to limit the risk of default by the buyer or seller, typically 5–15 percent of the contract's value.

Mark to the Market

To maintain the integrity of the margin, the futures market uses a procedure called *mark to the market*. In this process, the futures contract is valued at the close of business each day, and the investor's deposit is adjusted for the full change in the contract's dollar value for that day. Under this procedure, losses in value reduce the investor's deposit, and a margin call is made if the deposit falls below the maintenance margin figure for that particular futures contract. If the investor fails to meet the margin call, the broker will close out the account by unwinding the position, and the investor must then settle any loss on the account with the broker.

If the mark-to-the-market procedure results in a gain to the contract holder, the deposit is increased by the gain. The investor can use the gain, if sufficient in amount, as the initial deposit on additional futures contracts, thus pyramiding his or her holdings in exactly the same manner as used in margin accounts for stocks and bonds. The investor might also be able to remove cash from the account as a kind of early distribution of the profit on the trade.

---

145. www.futuresview.com/margins1.html, accessed July 16, 2010.

EXAMPLE

A December wheat futures contract trades at a price of $6 per bushel. An investor takes a long position (buys one contract) and places the minimum initial margin of $1,500 in his brokerage account. The next day, the price of the contract falls by $.25 per bushel. The value of the contract has declined by $1,250 (5,000 bushels x $.25/bushel) from $30,000 to $28,750. The broker removes the $1,250 from the investor's account, leaving a balance of $250. If the minimum margin requirement is $1,000, the investor is now required to come up with at least $750 to get the account back up to the minimum margin. Failure to do so will result in the broker's selling the contract; the remaining cash in the account ($250, assuming the contract's price has not changed in the meantime) is returned to the investor.

Had the price of wheat risen by $.25 per bushel, the investor would have been able to remove the $1,250 gain from his account.

Price Limits

daily price limit (interday limit)

In the stock markets, there is no limit on the amount the price of a stock can change in a given trading day (other than it cannot fall below zero).[146] Not so for futures contracts. The *daily price limit* rule (sometimes called the *interday limit*) prohibits any trades taking place outside a range defined by the prior day's closing price plus or minus the limit for that contract. Each commodity has a different daily price limit, depending on the price per unit of the underlying commodity or financial instrument.

---

146. Sometimes companies will ask that trading in their securities be suspended before a blockbuster announcement (usually negative). Depending on the amount of time of the suspension of trading, this indirectly places a limit on the price change of a stock during that day.

EXAMPLE
Assume that the daily price limit for wheat is $0.25 and that September wheat futures closed at $5 yesterday. Today's opening price for September wheat futures can be neither lower than $4.75 nor higher than $5.25, no matter what new information might have come to the market between the closing and opening times. For instance, suppose that during the night, a severe storm ravaged the wheat-growing section of the Midwest and early reports describe widespread damage to wheat crops. This information would make many individuals and businesses seek to immediately acquire wheat futures contracts for September delivery in anticipation of sizable price increases. Without the daily price limit, the price of wheat would skyrocket—perhaps unnecessarily— say to as high as $6, but the daily price limit means the opening trade cannot be at a price greater than $5.25. Although buyers at this price of September delivery wheat futures would be numerous, there would probably be no sellers. If there are no sellers, no contracts will trade at $5.25 or less, and no trading takes place for the day. The closing price (called the settle) is set at $5.25 so that all investors can be marked to the market.   The following day, the upper limit of the opening price is $5.50 (lower limit $5). Again, if no one wants to sell, then no trading occurs, and the following day's opening price can be as high as $5.75. Following this procedure, the market will eventually find the price range in which trading will occur. The major benefit of the price limits is that if there are abrupt changes in the contract's trading price, the limit means that the necessary marking to the market will be spread over several days. This gives the losing investors (in this case, those with short positions) more time to come up with the cash to cover their losses.

Differences between the Markets in Commodities Futures and Stocks	
Commodities Futures	Stocks
• Limited term	• Unlimited term
• Maximum daily price moves	• No limit on daily price moves
• Margins of 5% to 15%	• Margins of 50% or more
• Long interest equal to short interest by definition	• Short interest usually small fraction of long interest
• No interest charged on unpaid balance	• Short sales not permitted on a downtick
• Market has no specialist system	• Interest incurred on monies borrowed to buy
• Positions must be opened and closed with same brokerage firm	• Market making by specialists
	• No restriction on opening and closing positions with different firms

TRADING STRATEGIES WITH FUTURES CONTRACTS

Based on the motive of the individual, the trading of futures contracts is divided into two broad categories: hedging and speculating. Speculating can take the form of speculating on the price of a particular contract, or spreading, which involves speculating on the relationship of prices among contracts. Let's look first at the process of hedging, and then at speculating and spreading.

Hedging

Hedging is the practice of offsetting the price risk in the cash market by taking an equal-size but opposite position in the futures market. Let's consider a classic example of a hedge. Suppose Jack Lessard is a farmer who is planting some corn, and anticipates that he will harvest 50,000 bushels of corn in 4 months. The current price of corn in the local cash market (the spot market) is $3 per bushel. Suppose also that there is a futures contract that calls for delivery exactly 4 months from now, and that this contract is trading for $2.90 per bushel. Finally, let's assume that Jack would be perfectly happy to sell his corn at $3 per bushel. This would mean that Jack's gross revenue for his corn would be $150,000.

At this point in time, Jack has two major risks. One is that something might destroy the crops (for example, fire or hail storm), and the other is that the cash price of corn may drop over the next 4 months. Although Jack might consider something like crop insurance for the first risk, that risk is not our concern here. Our concern is the second risk, known as price risk. Futures contracts may substantially reduce the price risk.

short hedge   To do this, Jack takes a short position in 10 corn futures contracts that mature in 4 months (remember, each corn contract is for 5,000 bushels). Jack is committing to deliver 50,000 bushels of corn under the terms of the contract. We can now describe Jack's position as being long the crop (he has or will soon have the crop planted in his field) and short the futures contract, which is known as a *short hedge*. A hedge is defined as long or short depending on the position the hedger has in the futures contract. In this case, Jack has a short hedge because he is short the futures contract.

basis   At the time Jack plants his crop, the cash market price is $3, but he had no corn to sell. When he sells the futures contract, the price is $2.90 per bushel. The difference between the cash price and the futures price is known as the *basis*, **that is**

basis = cash market price – futures market price.

In Jack's case, the basis is $.10 per bushel. Bases can be positive or negative. The key to the success of Jack's hedge is what happens to the basis between now and when the crop is harvested.

perfect hedge   The ideal scenario is that the basis does not change. The cash and futures prices might change, but they change in perfect tandem, leaving the basis unchanged. Suppose that 4 months from now, the cash price is $2.50 and the futures price is $2.40 (thus the basis is still $.10). Jack will then harvest his crop, sell it in the local cash market, and close out his futures position. By selling his crop in the cash market, Jack will receive $125,000 ($2.50/bushel x 50,000 bushels). When Jack closes out his futures contract, he will pocket a profit of $25,000 ($.50/bushel x 50,000 bushels). This is because he will have sold the contracts at $2.90 per bushel and bought them for $2.40 per bushel, thus providing a profit of $.50 per bushel. So, even though the cash market price declined by $.50 per bushel, Jack's gross revenue is the same as what he anticipated it would be when he set up his hedge. It is exactly the same because the basis did not change.

Suppose the cash market price had gone up $.50 per bushel and the basis had stayed the same. In this case, Jack would sell his corn for $3.50 per bushel, taking in gross revenue of $175,000 in the cash market. However, his futures contracts would be trading at $3.40 per bushel. He will incur a loss of $.50 per bushel on these contracts, or a total loss of $25,000. So his net revenue will still be $150,000. Jack would have been wealthier by $25,000 if he had not set up the hedge, but this is the consequence of a hedge—namely, one gives up the chance for a windfall gain in exchange for protection from an unanticipated loss.

One might ask why Jack didn't just deliver the corn under the terms of the futures contract. There could be several reasons. The most common is that it would likely involve substantive transportation expense to ship the corn to the location specified in the contract. Another reason is that the type and quality of corn Jack planted may not have exactly matched the type and quality specified in the contract. It is much easier for Jack to sell in the local cash market.

Basis Risk

In practice, the basis does not always stay the same. Let's revisit the first example above by assuming that the cash price falls to $2.50 per bushel, as before, but that the futures price falls only to $2.50 (same price as in the previous example). The basis is now zero. When Jack sells his corn in the cash market, he will still receive gross revenue of $125,000. When he buys back his future contracts, he will receive a profit of only $20,000, based on the fact that he sold the contracts at $2.90 each and bought them back for $2.50, or a gain of $.40 per bushel. So Jack's net revenue on the sale of the corn is now $145,000, not the $150,000 he had originally anticipated. Jack has been a victim of basis risk, or the risk that the basis changes.

The key point here is that if Jack had not set up the hedge at all, he would have been $25,000 worse off. Instead, he is only $5,000 worse off. So the hedge clearly accomplished something, just not everything Jack had hoped. *The goal in hedging is to substitute basis risk for price risk.* The desire is that the basis risk will be less than the price risk.

There is, of course, the chance that one might gain from basis risk. Suppose in the above example the futures price drops to $2.30 per bushel. The basis has now widened to $.20. In this case, Jack will take in $125,000 from his sale in the cash market, and another $30,000 ($.60/bushel x 50,000 bushels) on the liquidation of the short positions. This totals $155,000. Jack had the benefit of substituting basis risk for price risk, and a gain from the basis risk to boot!

Clearly, when one embarks on setting up a hedge, one needs to be sure that the futures contract chosen for the hedge has the smallest basis risk possible. If an ineffective contract is chosen, the basis risk might turn out to be greater than the price risk.

Long Hedge

Let's now consider the case of a heating company planning for the upcoming winter. The company wants to sign its customers to contracts for the season, but to compete it must guarantee the price per gallon for the heating season. If the company guesses too high, it may not take in much business. If it guesses too low, it could get a lot of business and lose money on all of it.

Let's assume the company wants to make its profit on the delivery of oil, and not on price speculation. It can do so by going long the appropriate heating oil contracts. It will likely have to guess as to the number of contracts (each heating oil contract is for 42,000 gallons), but this is probably an easier guess than having to guess the price of the oil during the heating season. As winter arrives, the company then sells each contract as it buys the heating oil in the cash market. Again, buying in the cash market probably saves substantial transportation costs over taking delivery on the futures contract.

As in the short hedge, the major concern is whether the basis risk will be substantially less than the price risk. If that is the case, then the heating oil company can focus on delivering oil, confident that it has substantially reduced its price risk.

Speculating

Individuals can always speculate on the price of a futures contract. They take a position in which they expect to benefit from the price movement. If a speculator expects the price to rise, he or she purchases futures contracts (goes long). A speculator who expects the price to fall sells (goes short) the futures contract and gains if the price declines.

Spreading

As with options, users of spreading as an investment tactic go long one futures contract and go short a second futures contract that has different terms. The objective in spreading is to look for misaligned prices. There are two types of spreads: intra-commodity and inter-commodity.

EXAMPLE

An intra-commodity spread might start with a December wheat contract trading for $4.50 per bushel, and the subsequent March contract trading for $4.70. A spreader might have reason to believe that this spread is too large. Hence, he or she expects the December wheat contract to rise relative to the March contract. Both may rise or fall in absolute terms, but the key is whether the spread will narrow or not. In this case, the spreader would buy the December contract and sell the March contract. Let's suppose the spreader is correct: the December contract rises to $5.00 per bushel, and the March contract rises to $5.10 per bushel over the holding period. When the spreader closes out his or her positions, he or she will make a gain of $.50 per bushel (buy at $4.50/bushel and sell at $5.00/bushel) on the December contract, and lose $.40 per bushel on the March contract (sell at $4.70/bushel and buy at $5.10/bushel). Thus, the spreader makes a profit of $.10 per bushel.

Because spreading requires knowledge about the product, the contract, and the history of price differentials, it is really an activity for professionals only. Also, because spreading is less risky than speculating, there are special margin requirements for positions that involve spreading that are lower than margin requirements when someone is hedging or speculating.

Hedge Trading Results

We indicated earlier that there are two basic motives for trading futures contracts: hedging and speculating. No market would exist if there were only hedgers or only speculators participating. An active market requires both. So an interesting issue arises. If hedgers use the markets to substitute basis risk for price risk on the belief that the former is much smaller than the latter, and speculators are simply looking to profit from price changes, are the speculators successful? Put another way, if hedging is akin to purchasing insurance, then those who facilitate hedge trading (speculators) might well be expected to earn a risk premium.

Testing this proposition requires identifying those who are seeking to hedge and separating them from those who are speculating. Discriminating between risk takers and hedgers from aggregated data, however, is difficult. Nevertheless, several studies that have attempted such desegregation indicate that professionals (large speculators) may profit at the expense of small traders, and small speculators do not seem to receive a risk premium for their risk taking.[147]

Financial Planning Issue

A new client, Ted Casey, sits down with a financial planner and as a part of the process, the planner is reviewing Ted's portfolio for the last couple of years. Most of the holdings seem normal and appropriate, but the planner notices an occasional commodities trade. There are trades in pork bellies, soybean oil, gold, and natural gas futures contracts. The typical trade is for 2 to 3 weeks. What is an appropriate action for the planner?

The planner needs to ascertain first whether Ted is aware of the trades, and if so, whether he or the broker is the source of the trades. If Ted indicates he is speculating in futures based on "hot tips" he is getting from various sources, then the planner should make sure Ted is aware of the tremendous risk exposure he is

---

147. E. Chang, "Returns to Speculators and the Theory of Normal Backwardation," Journal of Finance (March 1985), pp. 193–208; E. Fama and K. French, "Commodity Futures Prices: Some Evidence on Forecast Power, Premiums, and the Theory of Storage," Journal of Business (January 1987), pp. 55–73.

taking on, and the poor track record of individual speculators such as himself. If Ted is aware of the trades but indicates the broker suggests them, then the planner needs to make sure the broker has fully explained the speculative nature of these contracts and the risk exposure to Ted. If Ted is unaware of the trades, then the broker has clearly been irresponsible and it would be appropriate to suggest that Ted find a new broker ASAP.

FINANCIAL FUTURES MARKETS

So far, the discussion has focused only on agricultural futures because the tangible nature of the examples makes them easier to understand. Most financial planning clients are more likely to use financial futures for hedging purposes. In this section, we will review the basic elements of some of these contracts. Transactions in financial futures deal with contracts for foreign currencies, debt securities (commonly called interest rate futures), and stock indexes (index futures). Many of the characteristics and trading concepts of financial futures are the same as for agricultural futures, but there are a few differences.

Futures on Indexes and Cash Settlement

We have seen that with agricultural futures, if a short position is not unwound by the end of the delivery month, then the seller must deliver the commodity specified in the contract. In the case of some financial futures contracts, delivering the underlying asset would be difficult, expensive, inconvenient, or impossible. Specifically, futures contracts on various market indexes present a serious problem with respect to delivery. Rather than settling by delivery of a physical asset, index contracts are settled with cash. That is, contracts still in existence at the close of trading on the contract's last day are treated as if both parties make the appropriate offsetting trade at the actual closing price of the index on that day. Because of the daily marking-to-the-market prices, this usually requires minimal cash payments. Both parties then have their margins (earnest money) returned to them.

Interest Rate Futures

Trading in interest rate futures began in the early 1970s with the Chicago Board of Trade's Government National Mortgage Association (GNMA) futures contracts and the Chicago Mercantile Exchange's (CME) T-bill contracts. The market subsequently expanded to include long-term Treasury bonds, 1- and 5-year Treasury notes, municipal bonds, CDs, and Eurodollars. Most of the recent trading has been in Eurodollars, T-bills, and Treasury bonds. GNMA futures are no longer actively traded.

Interest rate futures contracts call for delivery of a specific security at the contract's expiration. For example, the CBOT Treasury bond contract specifies the following contract size and deliverable grades:

Table 12-1 Specs for the CME T-Bond Contract	
Contract Size	One U.S. Treasury bond having a face value at maturity of $100,000.
Deliverable Grades:	U.S. Treasury bonds that, if callable, are not callable for at least 15 years from the first day of the delivery month or, if not callable, have a maturity of at least 15 years from the first day of the delivery month. The invoice price equals the futures settlement price times a conversion factor plus accrued interest. The conversion factor is the price of the delivered bond ($1 par value) to yield 6 percent.
Source: www.cmegroup.com/trading/interest-rates/us-treasury/30-year-us-treasury-bond-contract-specifications.html, accessed July 16, 2010.	

Thus, although this is ostensibly a 30-year bond contract, the seller can deliver any Treasury bond that is noncallable for at least 15 years at the time of delivery, or is noncallable and has a maturity of at least 15 years. The coupon rate is specified to be 6 percent, but other coupon rates can be delivered, and an appropriate conversion factor will be used to determine the invoice price. During the time of trading, all traders will consider which Treasury bonds would be the cheapest to deliver under the specifications of this contract because that is what in fact will be delivered on any contracts not closed out on the expiration date.

Individuals in either short hedges or long hedges can use interest rate futures. A short hedge (a short position in a futures contract) would be undertaken by someone concerned that interest rates will rise, and a long hedge (taking a long position in a futures contract) would be undertaken by someone concerned that interest rates would fall. Let's consider two examples.

EXAMPLE 1

Ralph Edwards is looking to buy a home sometime in the next 3 or 4 months. He could afford the home at today's interest rates, but if rates go up, he is concerned he would have to buy a smaller home than he desires, or be squeezed out of the home market altogether. What could Ralph do?

Answer: There is the possibility Ralph could set up a short hedge. One concern is the size of the mortgage Ralph would need, and a second concern is whether Ralph is sufficiently comfortable that a contract exists for which the basis risk is substantially less than the price risk. Let's suppose that Ralph (and the planner) are comfortable that local mortgage rates would move in tandem with the price on the CBOT 10-year Treasury Note Futures Contract. Because the contract calls for delivery of $100,000 worth of principal, Ralph would need to plan on a mortgage of at least $100,000. If interest rates rise, bond prices fall, and so the price of this contract would decline. Ralph could then take the profit from this short position and use it to increase the down payment on his house, thus reducing the size of the mortgage he would need. The smaller mortgage would then help offset the increase in the mortgage rate. The downside to the short hedge is that if interest rates fall, Ralph would incur a loss on the futures contract. However, this loss would be compensated for by the lower mortgage payments Ralph would be making in the future. The worst-case scenario would be if Ralph does the short hedge, interest rates fall (giving him a loss), and then he changes his mind about buying a home or does not qualify for a mortgage.

EXAMPLE 2

Connie James has just learned that she will inherit $600,000 in 6 months. She is elated. However, she likes the interest rates she could invest the money at if she had it today, and she is afraid that rates will decline over the next 6 months. What should she do?

Answer: She can look for an interest rate futures contract that most closely represents the type of security she would buy when she actually receives the money. Let's say this is 2-year U.S. Treasury notes. She could then go long $600,000 worth of principal of this contract. As the contract is based on $200,000 in principal, this would be 3 contracts. Six months later, she can actually take delivery if she wants, or she can sell the contracts and buy the appropriate investments in the spot market. If interest rates do go down over the next 6 months, as she fears, then the value of her futures contract will have risen. She will end up investing the money at a lower yield, but she will be able to offset that with the profit from her futures position. If interest rates instead go up, then she will lose money on her futures contract, but she will be able to invest her cash at a higher rate than she thought she would. Thus, she is hedged in the sense that the gain or loss on her futures contract will match up with an opportunity loss or gain in her cash position (when she actually receives the money). If the contract she buys is for delivery of the exact security she intends to buy when she receives the money, the hedge may be a perfect hedge. The worst case would be if she takes a loss on the futures contract and then it turns out that there is no inheritance.

Stock Market Index Futures

The successful introduction of debt instrument futures contracts spurred interest in equity futures. Popular stock market index futures include the Chicago Mercantile Exchange's S&P 500 Index and its E-mini S&P 500 Index contracts. These equity contracts offer a variety of ways to speculate or hedge on the stock market's movement. In particular, the contracts are an ideal way for portfolio managers to hedge either their anticipated funds needs or their portfolios against anticipated market reversals. As with any other hedging strategy, one has to be careful when working with stock index futures to choose the best contract and the number of contracts to hedge with so that the basis risk is minimal. Selection of an inappropriate index and/or use of the wrong number of contracts could mean that the basis risk is greater than the price risk one is trying to obviate.

There are two techniques to selecting the best contract. One is to analyze the portfolio that is being hedged with regard to the nature of the companies, and then find the index that provides the best match. The second technique is to compute the rates of return from this index and the rates of return on the portfolio to be hedged, and then compute the correlation coefficient for these two series of numbers. The higher the correlation coefficient, the more appropriate the index is for hedging.

Futures Options

A commodity option, or futures option, is an option on a futures contract. As such, it is an abstraction on an abstraction. The futures contract is itself a deferred-delivery agreement that trades and has a life of its own. An option on such an agreement represents the right, but not the obligation, to enter into such a contract. Thus, call and put options on futures contracts are the rights to buy and sell such contracts at specified prices over a specified period. The unique feature of options on futures is that they give the investor the opportunity to make a small dollar investment that can control a sizable position in a particular futures commodity or financial instrument. Currently, futures options are listed on a number of agricultural, mineral, and especially financial assets.

In the various examples given above demonstrating how a client might use futures contracts for hedging purposes, futures options provide an alternative approach. One of the earlier examples dealt with how Ralph Edwards could use a Treasury Note futures contract to alleviate his concern that mortgage interest rates might rise. Ralph could also consider buying a put option on the Treasury Note futures contract. If interest rates rise, Ralph would benefit from the decline in the value of this contract. If interest rates fall, Ralph's option would become worthless. Although he could lose 100 percent of the premium he paid for the option, at least Ralph would know in advance the magnitude of his loss. However, it is much more difficult to make the gain on one position closely match the loss on the other when the premium on the futures option is tossed into the equation.

Similarly, Connie James could have bought a call option on one of the interest rate futures contracts to protect against a decline in market interest rates. The one drawback here is that there are a limited number of contracts for which there are active futures options markets. Hence, it is not as clear that Connie could find a futures call option that would match well with her prospective investment.

Finally, Nancy Gleason could have bought a put option on the S&P 500 futures contract. However, as in Ralph's case, Nancy could end up losing 100 percent of her premium and not having this match up with the gain in her actual portfolio holdings.

REVIEW OF LEARNING OBJECTIVES

1. The spot market is cash paid today for a commodity delivered immediately. A forward contract is a privately negotiated contract between two parties in which they agree to make a trade of a specified commodity at a specified price at a later date. A futures contract is a standardized version of a forward contract for which there is an active market; the contract is actually with the clearinghouse.

2. Futures contracts are traded on many exchanges such as the Chicago Mercantile Exchange. Futures traders are either hedgers or speculators, and speculators may be either price speculators or spreaders. On the floors of the exchanges, there are scalpers, day traders, and position traders, as well as arbitrageurs. The futures market is regulated by the Commodity Futures Trading Commission.

3. Futures contracts are broadly grouped as agricultural, mineral, and financial. There are multiple delivery dates for each contract, as well as variations in contracts among exchanges. Trades are technically with the clearinghouse, which guarantees the contracts. The dollar value of most contracts is large, even though the initial margin

posted may be only a fraction of this amount. Commissions are paid at the time a position is established, not when it is unwound. There are daily price limits on most contracts, which means if the natural price is outside this range, no trading takes place.

4. A short hedge would be used to protect someone who is long a commodity for business reasons, and a long hedge would be used to protect someone who is short a commodity for business reasons. Hedging involves substituting basis risk for price risk. The basis is the difference between the cash price for the hedger and the price of the futures contract. Speculators may speculate on the price of a contract, or limit their risk through spreading.

5. Financial futures can be used to hedge against changes in interest rates or stock prices. The key is to make sure there is a strong, positive correlation between whatever interest rate or portfolio is being hedged and the price of the contract selected for the hedge. Futures on options add another layer of complexity to hedging or speculation strategies.

MINICASE

It is December 30, 2005. Your client has a $2.2 million portfolio but is really nervous about the market during the next few months. You are considering the use of the S&P 500 Index futures contract to hedge the client's portfolio during this period, because holdings in the portfolio closely resemble the S&P 500 index and the changes in the client's portfolio closely parallel changes in this particular index. In fact, the beta of the portfolio when the S&P 500 is used as the market index is almost exactly one. The March 2006 contract has a settle price of 1260.10 on this date.

1. To hedge your client's portfolio, you should [5]

    (A) go long the futures contract to match the simultaneous long position in the portfolio

    (B) go short the futures contract to offset the simultaneous long position in the portfolio

    (C) take both a long and a short position in the futures contract

    (D) go long the futures contract and liquidate the client's current portfolio

2.   The type of hedge you are setting up would be known as a [5]

    (A) long hedge
    (B) short hedge
    (C) intermediate hedge
    (D) unbiased hedge

3.   When setting up the hedge, you note the value of the basis is slightly negative. Your client not only benefits from the risk transfer aspect of the hedge, but could also make profit on it if: [5]

    (A) the basis becomes more negative
    (B) the basis stays unchanged
    (C) the basis becomes a more positive number
    (D) the basis becomes exactly zero

4.   The above described hedge using the March contract can be maintained [5]

    (A) only for one week
    (B) until the first trading day in March
    (C) until the last trading day in March
    (D) indefinitely

5.   One of the drawbacks to setting up this hedge is [5]

    (A) the client must pay to the person who bought the contract all dividend payments made by stocks in the S&P 500 index during the period of the hedge
    (B) the client will have to recognize any capital gains in his portfolio at the time the hedge is established
    (C) the premium paid for the hedge can be rather expensive
    (D) none of the above

CHAPTER REVIEW

Key Terms and Concepts

scalpers	daily price limit (interday limit)
day traders	short hedge
position traders	basis
arbitrageurs	perfect hedge
round-trip fee	

Review Questions

Review questions are based on the learning objectives in this chapter. Thus, a [3] at the end of a question means that the question is based on learning objective 3. If there are multiple objectives, they are all listed.

1. What differentiates the spot market from a forward contract and a futures contract? [1]

2. Explain the motivations and advantages that firm representatives, position traders, and scalpers each possess. [2]

3. A silver futures contract is based on 5,000 troy ounces, and is priced on a per-ounce basis. Suppose you start with $5,000 that you invest in silver futures at $5 per ounce, putting down an initial margin of $500 per contract. [3]
    a.   How many contracts can you buy initially?
    b.   A month later, silver rises to $6 per ounce. What is the dollar profit to the investor?

4. What characteristics are needed for a commodity contract to be traded actively on a futures exchange? [3]

5. What is basis risk, and what is its role in a hedging strategy? [4]

6. A farmer has planted enough corn to produce 50,000 bushels. The spot price for corn is $3 per bushel. The corn will be ready to harvest in 4 months. The futures contract for that delivery date is $3.25. [4]
    a.   What is the current basis?
    b.   What type of hedge might the farmer set up if he would like to lock in (as firmly as possible) the current spot price? What are the positions in this hedge?
    c.   Suppose that at the time of harvest the spot price is $2.50 per bushel and the futures price is $2.60. What are the farmer's proceeds on the sale of the corn (net of the gain or loss on the futures contract)?

7. What is wrong with saying that people hedge in order to eliminate risk? [4]

8. a.   What is unique about stock index futures contract as opposed to agricultural or mineral contracts? [5]
    b.   Some of the stock index futures include S&P 500, S&P Midcap 400, NASDAQ 100, S&P 500/Growth, S&P 500/Value, and the DJIA. How does the financial planner decide which is the appropriate index in which to hedge a client's portfolio. [5]

9. Define a futures option. [5]

Learning Objectives

An understanding of the material in this chapter should enable the student to

1. Explain the basic model of personal taxation, compute a tax liability, and identify the relevant marginal tax rate.

2. Compute the cost basis or adjusted cost basis of an investment.

3. Determine the tax consequences of various equity investments, including the treatment of capital gains and losses as well as qualified and nonqualified dividend income.

4. Discuss the pros and cons of tax-loss harvesting and tax-efficient investing.

5. Avoid subjecting a client to violations of the wash-sale rule for various types of investments.

6. Compute the tax consequences associated with investing in various types of bonds, including a tax-equivalent yield.

7. Describe the tax issues associated with investing in investment companies, options, annuities, LPs and MLPs, as well as futures contracts.

8. Demonstrate the tax advantages of net unrealized appreciation on stock distributions from a pension plan, tax-harvesting losses in an IRA account, and the tax implications of converting assets from a traditional IRA to a Roth IRA.

Although taxes play an extremely important role in the investment process, they have heretofore been ignored so that we can focus on the tax aspects of investment planning as a separate and cohesive topic. The integration of taxes into investments requires a basic knowledge of how our personal income tax system works. The most important concept to derive from this discussion is the concept of the relevant marginal tax rate. A financial planner must always be aware of a variety of marginal tax rates that apply to different forms of income. Unfortunately, the tax code also contains a substantial number of rules with which the financial planner should be familiar. The rules do not always make sense, but they are critical to making sound investment decisions. The purpose of this chapter is to focus primarily on the tax-related aspects of investing, not to serve as a comprehensive overview of taxation.

TAXATION OF ORDINARY INCOME

Personal taxation is based on requiring each individual who meets certain criteria to file the tax return known as Form 1040.[148] The basic outline of this form has not significantly changed since the modern version of the income tax was introduced in 1913. The model for the determination of tax liability has two steps. The first step is the determination of taxable income, which is derived as follows:

> *Total (gross) income*
>
> *– Adjustments to gross income*
>
> *= Adjusted gross income,* or *AGI*
>
> *– Standard deduction* or *itemized deductions* (whichever is larger)
>
> *– Personal exemptions*
>
> *= Taxable income*

Based on taxable income, the taxpayer can determine his or her tax liability according to what is referred to as filing status. Then the following formula is applied:

> *Tax liability* (based on taxable income and filing status)
>
> *– Credits*
>
> *+ Other taxes*
>
> *= Total tax*
>
> *– Tax paid to date*
>
> *= Amount overpaid or amount owed*

---

148. There are alternative versions of Form 1040, namely Form 1040A and 1040EZ. These are shorter, less complex forms that can be used when a taxpayer's situation is relatively simple. The same tax model applies; it is just that the form is much simpler.

Let's consider each component of this model.

Computation of Taxable Income

Filing Status

The first step in filing a return is the declaration of filing status. Although there are four different statuses, the two most common ones are single (S) and married filing a joint return (MFJ). Our discussion will focus only on these two statuses.[149]

Gross Income

ordinary income   The first section of Form 1040 determines the taxpayer's total income, which is frequently referred to as *gross income*. The first line of this section is the summation of all wages, salaries, tips, and any other income. Whenever any other income is classified as *ordinary income*, it simply means that income will be subject to the statutory marginal tax rates discussed below. Other investment income that is treated as ordinary income includes the following:

- Taxable interest
- Dividends other than qualified dividends
- Taxable portion of IRA distributions
- Taxable portion of pensions and annuities
- Net income from rental real estate, royalties, partnerships, S corporations, and trusts.

In addition to the above, net capital gains and losses are included as part of total income even though the tax treatment of the capital gains and losses depends on the time frame and the amount. Thus, if the taxpayer has capital gains, he or she must use a special form to determine tax liability.

Qualified dividends are also part of gross income and are not taxed at the same rates as ordinary income. Like capital gains or losses, if the taxpayer

---

149. We focus on only the two filing statuses for several reasons. First, this chapter is an overview of the topic, and consideration of the other three filing statuses creates a lot of added detail for the students. Second, on tests such as the CFP Certification Exam, these are generally the only two statuses considered. The treatment of material covered in this chapter for other filing statuses can be found in The American College's *Fundamentals of Income Taxation* or at the Internal Revenue Service web site (www.irs.gov).

has qualified dividend income, he or she has to use a special form to determine tax liability.

Adjustments to Gross Income

adjusted gross income (AGI)

Adjusted gross income (AGI) is derived by subtracting certain payments from gross income. Investment-related payments are as follows:

- IRA contribution
- Self-employed SEP, SIMPLE, and qualified plan contributions
- Penalty on early withdrawal of savings

Contribution to a Traditional IRA. Anyone can make a contribution to a traditional IRA account. The maximum contribution to an IRA account beginning in 2010 is the lesser of $5,000 or one's taxable income. People 50 years old and older before 2011 may make an additional $1,000 "catch-up" contribution each year.

Certain conditions must be met for that contribution to qualify as an adjustment to gross income.[150] People without an employer sponsored retirement plan may always deduct their contributions. People who have an employer sponsored retirement plan may fully deduct their contributions only if their modified adjusted AGI are below specified limits. For most people, modified AGI, as defined for this purpose, is the same as AGI. For 2010, this limit is $55,000 for S taxpayers and $89,000 for MFJ taxpayers. IRA contributions are partially deductible on a pro rata basis if the income of the S or MFJ taxpayer exceeds this limit by up to $10,000. MFJ taxpayers have a $20,000 range for a pro rata deduction.

EXAMPLE

To what extent can each of the three following people make a deductible IRA contribution in 2010?

1. Charlie, age 56, is not an active participant in his company's pension plan, and his modified AGI is $250,000. He files as a single person.

2. Rosie, age 32, is an active participant in her company's pension plan, and her modified AGI is $48,000. She files as a single person.

---

150. U.S. Department of the Treasury,*Publication 590: Individual Retirement Arrangements (IRAs).* Internal Revenue Service, 2007. www.irs.gov/pub/irs-pdf/p590.pdf (accessed July 16, 2010).

3. Jamal, age 44, is an active participant in his company's pension plan, as is his wife, age 42. Their modified AGI is $99,000, and they file as MFJ.

Answers:

1. Charlie can make a fully deductible contribution of $5,000, since he is not an active participant, and a fully deductible catch-up of $1,000, since he is over 55.

2. Rosie can make a fully deductible contribution of $5,000 even though she is an active participant, because her income is less than $50,000 and she files as a single person.

3. They can each make a contribution of $2,500, since their income is half way through the phase-out range for people covered by pension plans.

Standard and Itemized Deductions

After computing the AGI, one determines which is larger: the standard deduction to which the taxpayer is entitled based on filing status, or the sum of itemized deductions. For 2010, the standard deduction is $11,400 for MFJ filers and $5,700 for S filers.

The primary investment related itemized deduction is interest expenses. Mortgage interest is almost always deductible, and interest on margin loans is frequently deductible. Taxpayers who own homes (and thus incur real estate taxes) and have a mortgage on that home (and thus have mortgage interest) will almost always find it beneficial to itemize. Those who do not own homes usually find that their standard deduction is larger than the sum of their itemized deductions. There are some limits on the deductibility of mortgage interest.

Net Investment Income

When buying on margin, the interest expenses on the loans may qualify as an itemized deduction.[151] The rule is as follows:

> Interest payments on a nonbusiness loan incurred in the course of an investment activity are referred to as investment interest. Deductions for investment interest expenses are allowed but are limited to the taxpayer's "net investment income" for the year.

---

151. The material in this section is summarized from James F. Ivers, III, *Fundamentals of Income Taxation*, 9th ed., (Bryn Mawr, PA: The American College, 2010): pp. 9.15, 9.16.

Ordinary dividends clearly count as investment income; qualified dividends (to be discussed shortly) do not, unless the taxpayer elects to waive the special lower tax rates applicable to such dividends. Gains on property sold, other than capital gains, count as investment income. An example of a gain on property sold that is not a capital gain is the recapture of depreciation associated with the sale of depreciable assets. Capital gains can be included as investment income, but the taxpayer has to treat those capital gains as subject to ordinary income tax rates, and not apply the lower capital-gains tax rates to them.

net investment income

Net investment income refers to investment income after the deduction of investment expenses. Investment expenses are generally all deductible expenses (other than interest expenses) that are connected with the production of the taxpayer's investment income. An example of an investment expense is a subscription to an investment publication the investor uses in the management of his or her investments.

Note that if a taxpayer has more investment interest expense than can be deducted in the current year, he or she can carry the balance forward to the next year. Any amount not used that year can again be carried forward.

Financial Planning Issue

Your client, Hortense, has $10,000 in investment interest expense she paid during the year. She has $1,000 in investment expenses, $4,000 in qualified dividends, $3,000 in (ordinary) nonqualified dividends, and $8,000 in long-term capital gains. The investment interest and investment expenses give her $11,000 ($10,000 + $1,000) of potential deductions. Because the qualified dividends do not count against investment interest, only the nonqualified dividends ($3,000) can be offset by the investment expenses, leaving Hortense with $8,000 of currently nondeductible investment interest expenses.

Hortense asks about using the $8,000 in capital gains as investment income to take full benefit of this deduction. Although this strategy will work, it has a potentially costly side effect. The capital gains will be taxed at a much lower rate than Hortense's other income. If Hortense carries forward the unused investment interest, she might be able to shield more nonqualified dividends or other interest income next year that would otherwise be taxed as ordinary income. There are, nonetheless, two situations where Hortense might consider using the capital gains. One would be if she expects her investment interest and investment expenses to exceed her net investment income for the foreseeable future. The other is if she expects to die this year. Simply put, getting some tax benefit from the investment interest is better than getting no tax benefit.

Personal Exemptions

The last step to derive taxable income is to subtract personal exemptions. For 2010, the personal exemption is $3,650. Each taxpayer automatically receives a personal exemption, plus a personal exemption for the spouse if electing MFJ status plus an exemption for each dependent claimed.[152] The only exception to claiming a personal exemption is if the taxpayer is claimed as a dependent on someone else's tax return.

Computation of Taxes

brackets
The actual tax liability incurred depends on both the individual's taxable income and filing status. The computation uses a schedule similar to the example below, which shows the relevant figures for 2010 for MFJs and S's. For each filing status, the table is broken down into what are known as *brackets*, which are based on income ranges.

Table 13-1 Individual Tax Rate Schedules for 2010		
Filing Status	**Taxable Income**	**Tax**
Married filing jointly	Not over $16,750	10% of taxable income
	Over $16,750 but not over $68,000	$1,675 plus 15% of the amount over $16,750
	Over $68,000 but not over $137,300	$9,362.50 plus 25% of the amount over $68,000
	Over $137,300 but not over $209,250	$26,875.50 plus 28% of the amount over $137,300
	Over $209,250 but not over $373,650	$46,833.50 plus 33% of the amount over $209,250
	Over $373,650	$101,085.50 plus 35% of the amount over $373,650
Single return	Not over $8,375	10% of taxable income
	Over $8,375 but not over $34,000	$837.50 plus 15% of the amount over $8,375
	Over $34,000 but not over $82,400	$4,681.25 plus 25% of the amount over $34,000
	Over $82,400 but not over $171,850	$16,781.25 plus 28% of the amount over $82,400
	Over $171,850 but not over $373,650	$41,827.25 plus 33% of the amount over $171,850
	Over $373,650	$108,421.25 plus 35% of the amount over $373,650

---

152. Several requirements must be met to qualify as a dependent. The two primary requirements are that there be a familial relationship and that the taxpayer has provided the majority of that person's living expenses. Thus, dependents usually means children, but it can include other people.

EXAMPLE

In 2010, Jan Q. Investor's $50,000-per-year income was the sole support for her family of four. Her four personal exemptions (including one each for herself and her husband, and two dependency exemptions for her children) total $14,600 (4 x $3,650). The standard deduction for married couples filing jointly is $11,400. This gives her and her husband a taxable income of $24,000 ($50,000 – $14,600 – $11,400). Table 13-1 shows that joint filers (Jan and her husband file jointly) with taxable incomes between $16,750 and $68,000 pay $1,675 plus 15% of the amount over $16,750. This formula yields a tax liability of $2,762.50 ($1,675.00 + $1,087.50).

A crucial point to note about the tax rate schedule is that it changes every year. Congress has indexed the brackets to the inflation rate. Hence, unless there is no inflation or there is deflation, the bracket intervals will likely be increased each year. In addition, every few years Congress changes the tax rate associated with each bracket.

Average Tax Rate

There are two tax rate numbers with which each investor should be familiar. The first is the average or effective tax rate. The average tax rate[153] is defined as

$$\text{Average tax rate} = \text{Total taxes paid/Total income.}$$

In the case of Jan and her family, the average tax rate is 5.52% ($2,762.50/$50,000). This means that on average, 5.52¢ of every dollar Jan earned went to pay federal income taxes. This number is useful in preparing budgets. It is also useful in understanding the impact of federal income taxes on an individual's personal situation. In case applications or on test questions, it is often the only tax number given in order to keep tax issues simple. It gives a sense of the relative burden of taxes that an individual is carrying. For example, in Jan's case, she pays a social security tax of 7.65% on her full $50,000 of income. Thus, her burden from social security taxes is actually heavier than her burden from income taxes. However, the average tax rate has no relevancy in financial decision making. Simply put, it is a descriptive number, not a financial planning number.

---

153. An alternative definition of the average tax rate is total taxes paid divided by taxable income. There is no IRS-specified definition for this term. Both definitions are commonly used, but the one with total income as the denominator is more commonly used in income tax textbooks.

Marginal Tax Rate

The relevant number that the financial planner needs when analyzing the impact of taxation on investment decisions is the marginal tax rate. The most common definition is that this is the rate at which incremental income is taxed. The marginal tax rate is the tax rate associated with the income bracket into which an investor falls. In most cases, the marginal tax rate is relatively simple. For example, suppose in the previous example, Jan Q. Investor is considering buying a certificate of deposit that will generate an extra $100 in interest income, which will be taxed as ordinary income for the current year. We only have to look at Table 13-1 to see that this $100 will be taxed at the 15% rate. Thus, Jan will owe an additional $15 in taxes ($100 x 15%) if she buys the certificate. Hence, 15% is her marginal tax rate.

EXAMPLE

The Lyn Hayes family projects a taxable income for 2010 of $137,000. They will use the married filing jointly status. They are considering the purchase of a certificate of deposit that will generate $500 in interest and be taxed as ordinary income. What is the marginal tax rate?

In this case, the income tax bracket changes at $137,300. Thus, the first $300 will be taxed at the 25% marginal tax rate, and the other $200 will be taxed at the 28% marginal tax rate. Therefore, the marginal tax rate for this particular investment is 21%, which is computed as ($300/$500) x 25% + ($200/$500) x 28% = 26.2%.

Marginal tax rates can also be relevant when considering reductions in income. Consider the following example.

EXAMPLE

Hunter is a single person whose taxable income is $500,000. He is considering selling some bonds that have been generating $10,000 per year in interest income (which is taxed as ordinary income). He complains that he uses that $10,000 to pay for a nice vacation each year and really doesn't want to give up the income. The problem here is that Hunter fails to understand that by selling the bonds, he is not giving up $10,000 in cash inflow. The marginal tax rate on this income is 35%. Hence, along with the income is a tax liability of $3,500. In selling the bonds, he will be giving up $6,500 in after-tax dollars, not $10,000.

The Alternative Minimum Tax

Individuals with a large number of so-called tax "preference" items (including certain itemized deductions) may be subject to the alternative minimum tax (AMT). To determine whether the AMT applies, the tax liability is first computed in the regular way, and then it is computed using the AMT schedules. The taxpayer owes the larger of the two tax bills. Investment-related items that can create AMT problems include:

- Mortgage interest
- Exercising (but not selling) incentive stock options
- Tax exempt interest from private activity bonds
- Passive income or losses
- Investment expenses
- Foreign tax credits

When it was first created, the AMT affected few people.[154] However, unlike the regular tax schedule (for example, the table above) where the income brackets are indexed each year, the AMT is not indexed. Hence, with the presence of inflation alone, more and more people each year are finding themselves subject to the AMT. It appears to be one of the least understood aspects of our tax system, and one that comes as a shock to people who suddenly find for the first time that they have to pay additional taxes, even though they set their tax withholding to pay the full amount of taxes due using the regular calculation.

Determining the Final Tax Bill

Note that even after computation of the tax liability as represented in the table above, there are additional calculations. The first adjustment is for tax credits. The two adjustments related to investments are the foreign tax credit and the retirement savings contribution credit.

---

154. The AMT came into existence years ago when members of Congress decided to make an issue of the fact that a certain number of high-income earners were paying zero income tax each year. It was certainly possible for someone to avoid paying income taxes if he or she emphasized avoidance of taxation as the foremost principle of investment planning. Such a strategy may not be a particularly good method for wealth accumulation, but it was used at least by some people. Note that there was no accusation that these taxpayers were doing anything illegal. They were simply following the rules of the tax code that had been created by Congress. Thus, to attempt to ensure that everyone pays at least some taxes, Congress enacted the AMT.

Foreign Tax Credit

The foreign tax credit occurs whenever an investor owns stock in a corporation that is headquartered in a foreign country and foreign taxes are paid out of the dividends received by the investor. Note that if the foreign taxes paid are less than $300 for an S return or $600 for an MFJ return, the taxpayer is usually able to take the full credit. If the foreign taxes paid exceed the $600 limit, the taxpayer must fill out Form 1116 to determine the percentage of the foreign taxes that qualify for a credit.

Savers Credit

The savers credit, formerly known as the retirement savings contribution credit began in 2002, and was made permanent in 2006. It helps to offset the cost of the first $2,000 ($1,000 for an S payer) contributed to IRAs; 403(b)s; and 457, SEP, and SIMPLE plans. For 2010, the credit applies only to individuals with incomes up to $27,750 and married couples with incomes up to $55,000. These limits are adjusted for inflation. In addition, the person claiming this credit must also be at least age 18, not a full-time student, and not claimed as a dependent on another person's return.

The credit is a percentage of the qualifying contribution amount, with the highest rate for taxpayers with the least income, as shown below.

Table 13-2 Savers Credit Schedule		
Credit Rate	Taxable Income for MFJ	Taxable Income for S
50%	Up to $33,500	Up to $16,750
20%	$33,501–$36,000	$16,001–$18,000
10%	$36,001–$55,000	$18,001–$27,750

When figuring this credit, taxpayers must subtract the amount of distributions received from their retirement plans from the contributions they have made. This rule applies for distributions starting two years before the year the credit is claimed and ending with the filing deadline for that tax return. Note, this subtraction rule does not apply to distributions that are rolled over into another plan or to withdrawals in excess of contributions.

The retirement savings contribution credit is in addition to whatever other tax benefits may result from the retirement contributions. For example, most workers at these income levels may deduct all or part of their contributions to a traditional IRA.

EXAMPLE

Consider the case of Betty (MFJ) with an annual wage income of $20,000. As a result of her standard deduction and personal exemptions, her marginal tax rate is 10%. Suppose she actually has enough cash to make a $2,000 IRA contribution, and qualifies to use this as an adjustment to her total income. What is the net contribution Betty will be making?

Betty will receive two tax breaks. The first is the tax break from using the contribution as an adjustment to total income. Based on her 10% marginal tax rate, this saves her $200 in taxes ($2,000 x 0.10). By also claiming the contribution as a tax credit, she saves another $1,000 in taxes ($2,000 x 0.50). Thus, her total tax savings is $1,200. The contribution is therefore a net cash outflow of only $800 ($2,000 – $1,200).

Other Taxes

The last two categories to consider in determining the final tax bill are other taxes and payments. The primary other-tax item related to investments is any tax that might be due in conjunction with qualified plans, including IRAs, and other tax-favored accounts. These would include taxes based on the following:

- Any premature distribution from a tax-qualified account, which carries a tax penalty (generally 10% of the taxable amount withdrawn)
- Any excess contribution that is made to an IRA, a Coverdell educational savings account (ESA), or an Archer medical savings account (MSA)
- Any taxable distribution taken from a Coverdell ESA or qualified tuition program (which normally means a distribution that was not spent on tuition or other designated expenses)
- Any shortfall in a minimum required distribution (MRD) from any IRA or other qualified retirement plan

Payments

Payments include withholding taxes taken out of paychecks, any estimated taxes paid during the year, any overpayment from the prior year that was carried forward, and any excess Social Security contribution made. An excess contribution can occur if a person holds more than one job during the year and his or her combined income exceeds the maximum amount of income that is taxed by Social Security for its retirement program (which is $106,800 in 2010).

Financial Planning Issue
Many taxpayers "enjoy" getting large tax refunds. In fact, the average tax refund in 2010 was about $3,036.[155] The easiest way for taxpayers to obtain a substantial tax refund is to authorize the maximum withholding of taxes from their paychecks. (This is achieved by declaring zero withholding allowances.) Some taxpayers do this because they believe (perhaps rightly so) that if they do not overwithhold, they will simply spend the money as they receive it and never save. They can then save the large refund and use it to buy something that otherwise would not be affordable. The only problem with this strategy is that the taxpayer is lending his or her money to the U.S. Treasury at a 0% interest rate. When clients are overwithholding, a financial planner could encourage automatic payments from the client's paycheck into a savings program (through a bank or a mutual fund). This way, the money is out of the client's reach (the same effect as overwithholding), and the client is earning more than a 0% rate of return.

People with substantial investment income need to do one of the following:

- Make estimated payments during the year.
- Adjust the amounts withheld by employers on wage income.
- Elect to have 20% of their investment income withheld for taxes.

Naturally, a taxpayer may use more than just one of the above methods to assure taxes are paid during the year.

Measurement of After-Tax Returns

Heretofore, we have discussed returns solely on a pre-tax basis. In some situations, that is appropriate. For example, some investors may not have enough taxable income, so their marginal tax rate is zero. Remember, a married couple filing jointly has, at a minimum, a standard deduction and two personal exemptions. This means that the first $18,700 ($11,400 standard deduction + $3,650 husband's personal exemption + $3,650 wife's personal exemption) of income is tax exempt. Furthermore, if this couple is retired and Social Security is a significant portion of their income, they may have substantially more income and still not owe any taxes. Another situation occurs when a taxpayer has a Roth IRA wherein the distributions are tax exempt, provided certain conditions are met.

Nonetheless, for most clients and investors, the tax consequences do matter, and decisions and analysis should be based on after-tax returns, not pre-tax

---

155. www.usatoday.com/money/perfi/taxes/2010-03-22-tax-refunds22_ST_N.(accessed July 16, 2010).

returns. The appropriate adjustment depends on the nature in which the marginal tax rate is applied and when any tax is due to be paid. We will discuss specific examples of tax treatments in conjunction with individual investment instruments.

Note that there is a general formula for relating pre-tax returns to post-tax returns:

$$r_{post\text{-}tax} = r_{pre\text{-}tax} \times (1 - \text{marginal tax rate})$$

In some cases, investors want to convert post-tax returns to pre-tax returns. In this case, the formula is

$$r_{pre\text{-}tax} = r_{post\text{-}tax} / (1 - \text{marginal tax rate}).$$

State and Local Taxes

Most discussions of taxation focus only on income taxation at the federal level. This is somewhat appropriate because it is federal income taxation that accounts for the majority of income taxes paid. Some states have no income taxes and others have minimal income taxation. A few tax only interest and dividend income. A few states, however, have significant marginal tax rates for people in higher income brackets. For example, California's highest marginal tax rate is 10.55%, Hawaii's is 11.0%, and Oregon's is 11%.[156]

Combined Marginal Tax Rate

The impact of state income taxation on the marginal tax rate is complicated by the fact that state income taxes are an itemized deduction if the taxpayer itemizes. In general, the appropriate marginal tax rate to use (defined herein as MTR$_{combined}$) is computed as

$$MTR_{combined} = MTR_{federal} + MTR_{state} \qquad \text{(Equation 13-1)}$$

if state income taxes are not taken as an itemization on the federal tax return. However, when state taxes are itemized on the federal return, the effective combined marginal tax rate is

---

156. Federation of Tax Administrators, "State Individual Income Taxes: Tax Rate for Tax Year 2008," FTA, 2008. www.taxadmin.org/fta/rate/ind_inc.html (accessed July 16, 2010).

$$MTR_{combined} = MTR_{federal} + MTR_{state} \times (1 - MTR_{federal}) \qquad \text{(Equation 13-2)}$$

EXAMPLE

A wealthy client, George, has the good fortune to be in the highest marginal tax brackets for both federal and state taxation. He lives in New York, where the highest tax rate is 8.97%. What is George's appropriate marginal tax rate if he does not itemize his deductions? What is it if he itemizes?

If George does not itemize his deductions (unlikely for people in the highest marginal tax brackets), for taxation of ordinary income the effective marginal tax rate is

$$MTR_{combined} = MTR_{federal} + MTR_{state}$$
$$= 35\% + 8.97\%$$
$$= 43.97\% \ .$$

If he does itemize, his effective marginal tax rate is

$$MTR_{combined} = MTR_{federal} + MTR_{state} \times (1 \ MTR_{federal})$$
$$= 35\% + 8.97\% \times (1 - 0.35)$$
$$= 40.83\% \ .$$

TAX ISSUES FOR STOCK INVESTORS

When an investor buys, sells, or otherwise holds stock, the two major tax issues are the taxation of dividend income and capital gains and losses.

Dividend Income

Dividends always represent the distribution of profits to the owners of a firm. It used to be that all dividend income was taxed as ordinary income, but the current treatment is that dividends are classified as ordinary (or nonqualified) and qualified.

Qualified versus Nonqualified Dividends

In 2010, qualified dividends are taxed at a rate of 15%, except for taxpayers whose marginal tax bracket is 15% or less. For the taxpayers in the two lowest marginal tax brackets (that is, 10% and 15%), the tax rate on qualified dividends is 0% (i.e., they will effectively be tax exempt).

"Qualified" dividends for purposes of the 15% maximum tax rate include dividends from most domestic corporations, whether or not publicly traded. Dividends from certain foreign corporations also qualify, including those paid by companies traded publicly on an established U.S. exchange. Certain dividends are not qualified dividends, including those paid by credit unions or mutual insurance companies. Credit union dividends are classified as interest income, and dividends on participating life insurance policies are classified as rebates of premiums and thus are tax exempt unless the cumulative value of the dividends paid exceeds the cumulative value of premiums paid. Any dividend paid on stock purchased with borrowed funds, if the dividend was included in net investment income for purposes of claiming an investment interest expense deduction as discussed above, is also not qualified. To qualify for the reduced tax rate, a shareholder must own the dividend-paying stock for a minimum period of 60 days during the 121-day period beginning on the date that is 60 days before the stock's ex-dividend date.

Capital Distribution

Sometimes companies will make what are known as capital distributions, or a return of capital. Such a distribution could be a dividend paid at a time when the corporation does not have current earnings or accumulated retained earnings. The good news is returns of capital are not taxed as dividend income. The bad news is that, at the very least, an investor needs to reduce his or her cost basis by the amount of the capital distribution. If the investor's cost basis is at zero or is less than the return of capital, the capital distribution or the differential must be treated as a capital gain.

EXAMPLE
Zsa Zsa owns 10,000 shares of XYZ stock. The company has a capital distribution of $0.10 per share. Zsa Zsa's cost basis in the stock is $400. Because her capital distribution is $1,000 (10,000 shares x $0.10 per share), the distribution will reduce her cost basis to zero and she will have to declare $600 in capital gains, meaning that the capital distribution is being treated as if she has sold some of her stock.

Capital Gains and Losses

Capital Assets

Capital assets are defined under Section 1221 of the Internal Revenue Code as any property the taxpayer owns (whether or not connected with a business activity) except for the following types of property that are specifically excluded from the definition:

- "Stock in trade," also known as inventory
- Depreciable or real property used in the taxpayer's business
- Property for which value is defined solely or primarily by the creator of the property, such as an artistic composition
- Accounts or notes receivable acquired in the ordinary course of business
- Publications of the U.S. government

Financial assets such as stocks, bonds, and mutual funds clearly qualify as capital assets and are treated as such for tax purposes.

Personal assets, such as automobiles and houses, that are owned primarily for the personal use of their owners do not qualify as capital assets if they are sold at a loss. However, if they are sold at a gain, they are then treated as capital assets. Thus, if a person sells his or her car for more than they paid for it, he or she would have to recognize this as capital gain. Currently there is an exemption on the capital gain from the sale of a home. If the capital gain exceeds the amount of the exemption, then the excess capital gain is subject to taxation.

Determination of Basis

The basis of an asset refers to its cost basis. *Cost basis* is normally the price paid for an asset plus any expenses associated with the purchase. Thus, in the case of stock where a commission is normally paid, the cost basis would equal the price paid for the stock plus the commission.

Basis becomes a little more complex when an asset is received as a gift or an inheritance. The cost basis of the giver also passes to the recipient of the gift when as asset is received as a gift. Thus, gifting 100 shares of Exxon Mobile to one's child does not allow the child to change the cost basis from that of the parent. When assets pass as an inheritance, there is normally a step-up in cost basis to the value of the property at the time of death.[157] This is because the estate of the deceased is valued based on the market value of the assets at the time of death. This process is referred to as a step-up in cost basis.

---

157. Under certain circumstances, the cost basis may be set equal to the value of the asset six months after the date of death.

In some cases, a cost basis might be adjusted. Examples of this for financial assets will be noted below.

Unrealized Gains

Unrealized gains (appreciation on assets that have not yet been sold) are not subject to tax.[158] Gains become taxable only if and when they are realized, which would normally occur only if the asset is sold.

Determination of a Gain or Loss

cost basis   Normally, the taxable gain equals the sale price (minus commission) less the cost basis.

EXAMPLE
Suppose 100 shares of the BDC Company are purchased for $25 per share and sold for $35 per share. The commission for each trade is $15. The cost basis for the investment is $2,515, and the proceeds from selling the investment are $3,485 ($3,500 − $15). The capital gain on this transaction is $970 ($3,485 − $2,515).

Determination of Holding Period

short-term capital transaction

long-term capital transaction

The holding period for a capital asset is critical in determining how it will be taxed. All capital transactions are classified as either short-term or long-term. A *short-term capital transaction* is defined as one whose holding period is exactly one year or less. A *long-term capital transaction* is defined as one with a holding period longer than one year.

EXAMPLE
Martha bought some stock on March 17, 2009, and sold it on March 17, 2010. Is this a short-term or long-term holding period?
Trades occurring 12 months apart, but on the same day in both years are treated as being exactly one year apart. Thus, this is a short-term holding period. Martha needed to wait until March 18, 2008 to sell the security to qualify for long-term status.

---

158. The one exception to gains on unsold assets not being subject to taxation is futures contracts.

There are several exceptions to the determination of holding period. For example, property that is acquired as an inheritance is automatically treated as having a long-term holding period, regardless of how long the beneficiary holds the asset. Similarly, the value of appreciated company stock that is taken as a withdrawal from a company pension plan is treated as having a long-term holding period. The holding period for any subsequent increases in value, however, will depend on the time elapsed since the stock was withdrawn from the pension plan (we will return to this topic).

An example of tacking a holding period is when an asset is given to another family member. The cost basis does not change and the holding period includes that of the donor.

EXAMPLE

James gives his adult daughter Jennifer 200 shares of Exxon Mobile. The stock is worth $18,000 dollars, has a cost basis of $4,000, and has been owned for over 20 years. The gift itself escapes gift taxation, because James is married and the gift is classified as a joint gift from him and his wife, thus putting it under the annual gift tax exclusion. Had James sold the stock and given the cash, he would have owed tax based on his long-term capital-gains tax rate of 15%. Whenever Jennifer sells the stock, she will owe tax based on her long-term capital-gains tax rate of 5% because her holding period includes that of James. Note that if James were to die in the near future, he could give the shares to Jennifer through his will, which would eliminate any capital-gains tax, although there might be a risk of an estate tax.

Treatment of a Capital Gain or a Capital Loss

Let's consider the treatment of a capital gain or loss in cases where a taxpayer has only one transaction for the year. There are four possible situations.

Short-term Capital Gain. A net short-term gain is taxed as ordinary income. Hence, the relevant marginal tax rate is the tax rate on ordinary income.

Long-term Capital Gain. For 2010, the long-term capital-gains tax rate is 5% if the marginal tax rate on ordinary income is 10% or 15%; otherwise it is 15%. This is the same treatment granted to qualified dividends.

Financial Planning Issue

Your client, Ralph, bought 1,000 shares of GrowFast Co. one year ago for $10 per share, or $10,000 total (ignore commissions). The stock had been trading as high as $20 per share but has suddenly declined to $15 per share. Ralph calls you to indicate that he really thinks the stock should be sold before it falls further. Ralph is in the 28% marginal tax rate. You note that today is the first anniversary of the stock's purchase. What do you recommend to Ralph?

If Ralph sells the stock today, he will owe $1,400 in taxes ($5,000 capital gain x 28% marginal tax rate). If he waits one more day, he will owe $750 in taxes ($5,000 capital gain x 15% long-term capital-gains tax rate) if he can sell for the same price. In other words, Ralph can save $650 in taxes. Selling the stock today nets Ralph the equivalent of $13,600. In fact, as long as Ralph can sell the stock tomorrow for more than $14.24 per share, he will benefit from waiting one more day to sell it. If he sells at $14.24, he will have a long-term capital gain of $4,240, and he will owe taxes of $636, leaving him with $13,604 after taxes ($14,240 – $636). This is essentially the same as the net proceeds of $13,600 he would receive if he sold today.

Short-term and Long-term Capital Loss. The treatment of a capital loss is much simpler than the treatment of a capital gain. If there is only one capital transaction for the year, and it is a loss, then this loss must be used to reduce ordinary income by an amount up to $3,000 per year. The only exception to the $3,000-per-year reduction is for married taxpayers who are filing separately. In this case, the capital-loss reduction is limited to $1,500 per year. It does not matter if the capital loss is short-term or long-term. A capital loss in excess of $3,000 must be carried forward to the next year. Note that the use of the $3,000 capital loss as a reduction of ordinary income is independent of whether or not the taxpayer has taxable income.

EXAMPLE

You have an older client, John Century. The majority of his income is Social Security. All of John's income, as well as some of the principal of his portfolio each year, is spent on his nursing home bills. Many of John's bills are deductions that can be itemized as medical expenses. As a result, John has zero taxable income. To pay part of his nursing home expenses, John had to sell some stock, and the stock he sold this year caused him to recognize $5,000 in long-term capital loss. John must recognize $3,000 of this capital loss on his tax return, even though he has no taxable income to offset. The remaining $2,000 of long-term capital loss will be noted as a carryforward to next year's tax return.

The Treatment of Multiple Gains and Losses. When a person has more than one capital transaction, the treatment becomes more complex.

The first step in figuring the tax consequences of multiple trades (which are reported on Schedule D of Form 1040) is to aggregate all of the short-term trades and all of the long-term trades. As a result, one of the following eight possible scenarios will apply:

1. Net short-term capital gain, no long-term gains or losses
2. Net short-term capital loss, no long-term gains or losses
3. Net long-term capital gain, no short-term gains or losses
4. Net long-term capital loss, no short-term gains or losses
5. Net short-term capital gain and a net long-term gain
6. Net short-term capital loss and a net long-term gain
7. Net short-term capital gain and a net long-term loss
8. Net short-term capital loss and a net long-term loss

In the first four scenarios, the tax treatment is the same as if the taxpayer had only one such transaction for that category. For example, suppose a taxpayer reports five trades for the year, all short-term gains or losses, and the sum of the gains and losses is a net gain of $5,000. This $5,000 is then taxed as ordinary income, just as if there had been only one trade that resulted in a $5,000 short-term capital gain.

In the fifth scenario, the net short-term gain is taxed as ordinary income, and the net long-term gain is taxed at the long-term capital-gains tax rate of either 0% or 15%.

In the sixth and seventh scenarios, the short-term capital gain and the long-term capital loss, or the short-term capital loss and the long-term capital gain, are combined. The resulting number will then be either a short-term or long-term gain or loss, depending on which number is larger. Regardless of which of the four categories the net number falls into, it is now treated as if it were a single trade.

EXAMPLE 1

Jaime Morales has the following four trades during the year:

- A short-term capital gain of $7,000

- A short-term capital loss of $1,000

- A long-term capital gain of $2,000

- A long-term capital loss of $4,500

When Jaime groups the short-term and long-term transactions, he has a net short-term capital gain of $6,000 and a net long-term capital loss of $2,500. When these two numbers are then combined, Jaime ends up with a net short-term capital gain of $3,500. This is taxed as ordinary income, just as if there had been only one sale that resulted in a short-term capital gain of $3,500.

EXAMPLE 2

Let's reconsider the situation of John Century in the earlier example. John had a $5,000 long-term capital loss as his only capital transaction and was unable to obtain any tax benefit due to a lack of taxable income. In such a situation, an excellent argument could be made in favor of identifying a capital gain of approximately $5,000 in John's portfolio, so the capital gain would be rendered tax-free.

Although the eighth and final scenario is always a sad one for any taxpayer, the result is that the taxpayer will use the capital losses to reduce current income, up to a combined maximum of $3,000 ($1,500 if married filing separately), and carry the rest forward. Although it would seem immaterial as to whether it is the LTCL or the STCL that is used in the write-off against current income, the rules say that it is the short-term capital losses that are used up first.

Note that the LTCLs and STCLs are not combined. The reason is that for most of the twentieth century, the treatment of STCL and LTCL were different. At different times, long-term capital gains have been taxed as ordinary income, taxed at half the ordinary rate, and subject to a 6-month or 18-month (as opposed to 12-month) holding period. Hence, it mattered significantly whether one first applied the STCL to ordinary income, or to the LTCL. Tax practitioners continue to retain the ST and LT distinction for losses, even though it is meaningless under the current rules. Keep in mind that Congress may, at some point in the future, reintroduce rules that result in a differential tax treatment for STCLs and LTCLs. If a person is carrying forward any form of capital losses at the time of the next change in rules, it may matter quite a bit as to whether the loss was a STCL or a LTCL.

EXAMPLE

Juanita Gonzalez has a $2,000 short-term capital loss and a $1,500 long-term capital loss. Juanita, who is filing as a single person, will reduce her ordinary income by $3,000, wherein $2,000 comes from her short-term capital loss and the other $1,000 from her long-term capital loss. The remaining long-term capital loss of $500 is carried forward to next year. In the following year, this carryforward will be treated as a trade in that year in which Juanita incurs an LTCL of $500.

Timing of Capital Gains and Losses

The preceding section should make it clear that taxpayers may want to recognize at least $3,000 per year in net capital losses, if such losses exist in their portfolios (one would never generate a loss on purpose).[159] Efforts to time one's recognition of capital gains and losses is referred to as *tax-loss harvesting*. The savings from a net capital loss equal the taxpayer's marginal tax rate times the amount of the loss. Thus, a person in the 28% tax bracket who takes the full $3,000 capital loss will save $840 ($3,000 x 28%) in taxes. Naturally, it would be better to have no capital losses. Recognizing a capital loss for tax purposes is simply akin to the concept of making lemonade when the stock market gives you lemons.

One of the least enjoyable parts of being a financial advisor is the task of pointing out to clients that they have sustained losses. Nonetheless, when there are losses in a client's portfolio, an advisor should point out that there are several benefits to tax-loss harvesting. The first benefit is the immediate savings in income taxes if the loss is written off against ordinary income. The second benefit is that capital losses also allow a client to take capital gains without paying taxes. This is particularly valuable if the gains are short-term in nature. Thus, if a client has accrued a $5,000 long-term capital loss in one holding and a $5,000 short-term capital gain in another holding, the client can recognize both the loss and the gain and not have to pay any taxes.

Keep in mind, however, that capital losses provide the maximum benefit when they are used to offset ordinary income or short-term capital gains. Capital losses are least effective when they are used to offset long-term capital gains because these gains are usually taxed at a much lower tax rate.

A third benefit of tax-loss harvesting is that it provides the opportunity to rebalance a client's portfolio. As will be discussed in the next chapter, each client's portfolio should have a target asset allocation associated with it. Over time, the actual weights of the categories will change as some of the categories do well and others poorly. Taking capital losses in those categories that have done poorly allows the taxpayer to take capital gains in the sectors that have done well and use the freed-up cash to rebalance the portfolio back toward the target asset allocation weights.

---

159. Some of the ideas in this section are based on Donald Whalen, "Turning Losses to Gains," *Investment Advisor* (November 2003): 107-108, 110.

Note that it is far easier to describe and promote the benefits of tax-loss harvesting than to do it in practice.[160] The reason is that when portfolios have been held for several years, and particularly if those years include a significant bull market, the taxpayer simply runs out of losses to take.

Limits to the Benefits of Tax-Loss Harvesting

Research on the benefits of tax-loss harvesting has provided evidence that the value of these benefits may be somewhat exaggerated.[161] Tax-loss harvesting is most beneficial under the following conditions:

- High coefficient of variation for individual securities
- High dividend yield which allows more new investments
- Low correlation between individual securities
- Low direct and indirect costs of trading
- Low incremental management fees for monitoring the tax situation

Monte Carlo simulations suggest that the incremental benefits from tax-loss harvesting may be roughly 22 basis points per year. This tax savings benefit may come at the expense of loss of diversification.

Tax-Efficient Investing

Tax-efficient investing is a topic related to tax-loss harvesting. Tax-efficient investing means the avoidance of taking of capital gains on which the taxpayer must pay a capital-gains tax. There are two problems with tax-efficient investing.[162] First, when practiced to the extreme (which means no capital gains taken that offset any long-term capital losses, or ensuring that all capital losses taken always exceed capital gains by at least $3,000 per year), a portfolio can become extremely concentrated. If an investor is lucky enough to hold a stock that does extremely well over a period of several years, it can grow from being a small percentage of the portfolio to a significant percentage. At some point, there will be a tough choice to make between paying taxes and retaining diversification. This topic is referred to as the problem of a concentrated portfolio, and is addressed in the next chapter.

---

160. For a more complete discussion of the issues raised in this section, see Robert H. Jeffrey, "Tax-Efficient Investing Is Easier Said Than Done," *Journal of Wealth Management* (Summer 2001): 9-15.

161. Earl D. Osborn, "How Beneficial is Tax Loss Harvesting Using Portfolios of Individual Securities?," *Journal of Financial Planning*, (February 2006): 78.

162. Ibid.

The second problem with tax-efficient investing involves one of appearances. Again, truly tax-efficient investing means a minimal number of trades. If a financial advisor recommends no trades for a portfolio during the year, and then presents the client with a bill for portfolio management services, the client will surely wonder why he or she should be paying the financial advisor!

Financial Planning Issue

Your client, Warren Buffer, started with you 30 years ago. Early on, he put a few thousand dollars into Berkshire Hathaway (BH) and a few thousand more into Microsoft (M). Today, his portfolio is worth $10 million, but BH constitutes 53% of his holdings, and M is another 42% of the portfolio. To achieve an appropriate degree of diversification, he should sell nearly all of both of these holdings (which together are $9.5 million in market value). However, because the cost basis is negligible on both, virtually the full value would be taxed as long-term capital gains. At a 15% long-term capital-gains tax rate, this would mean a tax liability of approximately $1,425,000 ($9.5M x 0.15). Because this would constitute 14.25% of Warren's portfolio, it would be a tough sale to promote the unknown benefits of diversification over the tangible tax bill of $1,425,000. The argument to diversify becomes even tougher if there is a chance that Warren might die soon and his holding could get a step-up in cost bases.

Wash-Sale Rule

When tax-harvesting, an investor might be tempted to sell a poorly performing security at a loss and immediately buy it back if the investor thinks it is ready to bounce back. Unfortunately, the IRS limits the tax benefits from such a strategy with what is know as the wash-sale rule. Under this rule, a loss sustained on the sale of a security is not deductible for tax purposes if the investor purchases a "substantially identical" security within a period beginning 30 days before the sale and ending 30 days after the sale. In other words, there is a 61-day window during which an offsetting purchase cannot have been made.

Although this rule sounds simple, there are two aspects to the wash-sale rule that create problems. First, what happens to the loss if the investor does violate the wash-sale rule? For example, suppose an investor buys 100 shares of Bellcamp stock for $10,000 that is later sold for $7,500. Let's say the investor then buys another 100 Bellcamp shares two weeks after the sale for $8,000. By buying the stock within 30 days, the investor forgoes the $2,500 capital loss. The one compensation to the investor is that the capital loss sustained during the first holding period can be added to the cost basis of the second holding period. Hence, in this example the cost basis of the replacement Bellcamp stock will be $10,500 ($8,000 purchase price + $2,500 capital loss on the first sale).

The second aspect that creates a problem is what is meant by "substantially identical" securities. In the case of a company with one class of common stock, it is clear the investor cannot buy back the same common stock. However, if a company has more than one class of common stock, the wash-rule application depends on the relationship between the class of stock sold and the class of stock bought. Similarly, the purchase of a contract, a call option, or rights to purchase essentially the same stock also creates a wash sale.

Another scenario that constitutes a wash sale is if the spouse or a corporation owned or controlled by the taxpayer or the taxpayer's spouse buys essentially the same stock within the 61-day window. Even the sale of stock in a personal account coupled with the purchase of the same stock in an IRA account also falls under the wash-sale rules.

Convertible securities may or may not constitute a substantially identical holding. Equivalency depends on whether the convertible is indistinguishable from the common stock in terms of ownership and price changes. A convertible bond or convertible preferred stock is considered substantially identical if it meets the following five conditions:[163]

- It is convertible into common stock.
- It has the same voting rights as the common stock.
- It is subject to the same dividend restrictions.
- It trades at prices that do not vary significantly from the conversion ratio.
- It is unrestricted as to convertibility.

As a final item of note, the wash-sale rules do not apply to gains. Thus, if a person sells a stock at $20 per share that was bought for $15 per share and buys the stock back a few days later, then no wash-sale applies. The investor would have to declare a capital gain of $5 per share and apply the normal tax treatment. In other words, the IRS is happy to accept taxes on a sale and immediate repurchase if there is a gain, but will not let the investor obtain tax benefits for a sale and immediate repurchase if there is a loss.

---

163. U.S. Department of the Treasury, *Publication 550: Investment Income and Expenses.* (Internal Revenue Service, 2007): 55.

EXAMPLE
Your client, Hilda Steinman, is in extremely poor health, and may not live out the year. She would like to give away some of her stocks to family members before she dies, but you note that the cost bases on these stocks are quite low and it is these cost bases that will pass to the relatives if she gifts the securities. However, you also note that Hilda has carried forward $50,000 in capital losses from last year—a really bad year! If Hilda dies, the capital-loss carryforward becomes worthless. A tax-efficient strategy in this case would be to sell and immediately repurchase the stocks to be gifted. As these stocks are sold at a gain, there is no problem with the wash-sale rule. If the accumulated gain does not exceed $50,000, there is no tax consequence. If Hilda dies this year, there is no frustration at the loss of the tax benefit of the capital-loss carryforward. The gift of the securities may reduce her potential estate tax. Finally, the beneficiaries will have the current value of the stocks as their cost basis, rather than eventually having to pay a capital-gains tax on Hilda's gain.

Restricted Stock

Restricted stock is sometimes used as part of a compensation package for top management. One of the motivations to awarding restricted stock has been the limitation by Congress on the tax-deductibility to the corporation of salaries over $1,000,000. One way to bypass this is to sell the employee restricted stock, and lend the money to him or her to buy the stock, with the condition that the loan would be repaid when the stock is sold. If the company later forgives the loan, the loan becomes taxable income at the time of forgiveness. Thus, the employer may get the tax deduction then, and the employee defers recognition of this money as taxable income until that time.

There is another advantage to restricted stock. If a manager takes restricted stock today and the company is later acquired, the manager has the potential to take his stock profits as long-term capital gains. If the manager owns options and the company is bought, then the exercise of the options would be followed immediately by the sale of the stock, creating a short-term capital gain.

Stock Splits/Dividends

Companies occasionally declare stock splits and stock dividends. Stock dividends are dividends paid with newly created shares of common stock, as opposed to the cash dividends discussed earlier. There is no taxable event associated with these, other than the treatment of cash in lieu of a fractional share. Thus, if an investor owns 100 shares of a company that declared a 2-for-1 stock split, he or she would end up with 200 shares. The investor needs only to adjust his or her per share cost basis. For example, if the stock previously had a cost basis of $10 per share, the new cost basis is $5 per share. If all 200 shares are sold at the same time, this adjustment is immaterial, because the original purchase price for the 100 shares will be used as the cost basis. However, if only some of the shares are later sold, then the original cost basis has to be prorated based on the number of shares sold. The treatment for a stock dividend is the same as a stock split in that the cost basis has to be prorated.

A problem that sometimes arises with both splits and dividends is the creation of a fractional share. For example, if an investor owns 97 shares of a company, then a 3-for-2 stock split would replace these with 145.5 shares, creating a half share. Similarly, a 5% stock dividend would mean the issuance of an additional 4.85 shares, creating 0.85 of a share. Most corporations automatically pay the shareholder the cash equivalent value of the fractional share, based on the market value of the stock on the day of the stock dividend or stock split. The investor can allocate a portion of the cost basis to the fractional share.

EXAMPLE

Sally owns one share of common stock that she bought on January 3, 1996, for $100. The corporation declared a common stock dividend of 5% on June 30, 2007. The fair market value of the stock at the time the dividend was declared was $200 per share. She was paid $10 for the fractional share stock dividend. Her gain or loss is as follows:

Fair market value of old stock	$200.00
+ Fair market value of stock dividend (cash received)	+ $10.00
= Fair market value of old stock and stock dividend	$210.00
Per share cost basis after the stock dividend ($100 ÷ 1.05 shares)	$95.24
Cost basis of fractional share (0.05 x $95.24)	+ $4.76
Cash received	$10.00
Basis (cost) of stock dividend	$4.76
= Gain	$5.24

Because Sally had held the stock for more than one year at the time the stock dividend was declared, her gain on the stock dividend is a long-term capital gain.

Sometimes an investor might find that the computational effort of allocating the cost basis for the sale of a fractional share is more work than it seems to be worth. Although it is not technically correct, an alternative method of dealing with the sale of fraction shares is to assign a zero cost basis to them. This means the entire sale of the fractional share is a capital gain, and thus would maximize the capital-gains tax owed. However, for most people the nominal value of this tax is so small that it is worth paying to save the computational effort. For instance, in the above example, if Sally simply declared the entire $10 sale as a long-term capital gain, then she would owe $1.50 in capital-gain taxes, assuming a 15% capital-gains tax rate. By pro rating the cost basis, she reduces her capital-gains tax to $0.79 ($5.24 x 15%), a savings of a whopping 71¢ for her computational effort and the additional recordkeeping she must perform!

Warrants

The sale of warrants would be treated the same as the sale of common stock. The sale of common stock and the purchase of warrants to buy that stock within 30 days of the sale is the same as the purchase of an option, and it creates a wash sale. However, the reverse is not necessarily the case. If the taxpayer sells the warrants first and then buys the underlying stock, the wash sale rule is violated only if the warrants qualify as substantially identical under the rules given earlier for convertibles.

If a warrant is exercised, the cost basis of the warrants is added to the exercise price for the stock to determine the new cost basis of the shares acquired. For example, if an investor buys 100 warrants for $500, and later exercises these warrants to buy 100 shares of stock at an exercise price of $20 each, the cost basis for the stock is $2,500 plus any commissions.

Rights

Although the distribution of stock rights may be taxable or nontaxable depending on the nature of the rights, in practice such distributions are almost always nontaxable. If the investor allows these nontaxable rights to expire without exercising them, the cost basis is zero and there is effectively no transaction. But if the investor exercises the rights, then some of the original cost basis of the stock must be allocated to the rights if the fair market value of the rights equals or exceeds 15% of the fair market value of the stock at the time of the distribution. If the fair market value of the rights is less than 15%, the investor has the choice of leaving the cost basis of the original stock unaltered, or dividing it between the rights and the old stock. If the cost basis is divided between the original stock and the rights, when the rights are exercised, the cost basis of the new stock equals the subscription price plus the allocated cost basis of rights.

EXAMPLE

Thomas Johns owns 100 shares of Wolf Company stock, which cost $22 per share. The Wolf Company gave him 100 nontaxable stock rights that would allow him to buy 10 more shares at $26 per share (it takes 10 rights to buy a new share of stock). At the time the stock rights were distributed, the stock had a market value of $30, not including the stock rights. Each stock right had a market value of $0.30. The market value of the stock rights was less than 15% of the market value of the stock, but Thomas chose to divide the basis of his stock between the stock and the rights. The basis of the rights and the basis of the old stock is computed as follows:

100 shares × $22 = $2,200, cost basis of stock

100 shares × $30 = $3,000, market value of stock

100 rights × $0.30 = $30, market value of rights

($3,000 / $3,030) x $2,200 = $2,178.22, new basis of the 100 shares of stock

($30 / $3,030) x $2,200 = $21.78, basis of the 100 rights

If Thomas sells the rights, the basis for figuring gain or loss is $0.218 ($21.78/100) per right. If he exercises the rights, the basis of the stock he acquires is the price he pays ($26), plus the basis of the rights exercised ($2.18), or $28.18 per share ($26 + $2.18). The remaining basis of the old stock is $21.78 per share.

Short Sales

What is different in the treatment of a short sale for tax purposes is that the selling date occurs before the purchase date. Despite this reversal, the distinction between a long-term and short-term classification depends on whether the sale and purchase are more than one year apart. The computation of the gain or loss is still the sale price less the purchase price.

Liquidations

Sometimes companies will sell off part or all of their assets. In the case of bankruptcy, the court may decide to sell all of the assets of the company. Usually when this happens, there is not enough cash after the creditors are paid to distribute to stockholders, but occasionally there is. A partial liquidation of a company is treated as a return of capital, which was discussed earlier. That is, the distribution is applied to the cost basis. If the cost basis is greater than the distribution, the taxpayer can declare a capital loss. It is only when the distribution exceeds the cost basis that the taxpayer has to declare a capital gain based on the difference and the holding period of the stock.

A more interesting situation arises if the investor has bought the stock in multiple batches. Each batch will likely have a different cost basis. For complete liquidations, it is not uncommon for the liquidating dividends to be made in multiple payments. If this is the case, any payment received must be distributed among the batches based on the number of shares in each batch. Once a liquidating dividend exceeds the cost basis of any one batch, the difference becomes a capital gain, even though the cost basis on another batch is still greater than zero.

TAX ISSUES FOR FIXED-INCOME INVESTORS

tax-exempts
All interest income is either taxed as ordinary income (that is, at the same rates as wages and salaries) at the federal level or is tax exempt. Thus, interest income on savings accounts, corporate bonds, and U.S. government bonds is taxed as ordinary income. The one exception to taxing interest as ordinary income is that interest income from most state and local bonds (known as municipals) are not taxed within the state that issues them. Hence, municipals are frequently known as *tax-exempts*. As a practical matter, not all municipals qualify for this tax-exempt treatment. Thus, the buyer of municipals needs to make sure that they are, in fact, tax exempt, although almost all are. The interest income on municipal bonds issued by other jurisdictions is fully taxed in the owner's own state and local residence jurisdiction if there are state and local income taxes. Certain municipal bonds may produce income that is subject to the alternative minimum tax, but not to the regular income tax.

Some states, including New Hampshire and Tennessee, tax only interest and dividend income. The interest income on U.S. Treasury issues is exempt from state and local income taxes. It is obviously somewhat of a misnomer, therefore, to talk about municipals as being tax-exempts and governments as being taxables, when the former might be taxed, and the latter do enjoy some tax exemption. However, because it is the federal tax bite that people worry more about than the state tax bite, discussions of tax treatment are usually limited to the federal tax aspects.

Not only are the securities issued by the Treasury exempt from state and local taxes, but securities issued by government agencies are similarly exempt. However, securities issued by government-sponsored enterprises do not enjoy this special tax treatment. The major government-sponsored corporations are FNMA, GNMA, and FHLMC.

Determination of Cost Basis

Determination of the cost basis on a bond is more complex than for stock. When a bond is traded, the buyer pays and the seller receives accrued interest, provided the company has not announced that it is defaulting on the interest payment. The payment of interest is not part of the cost basis. Rather, it is incorporated into computing the taxpayer's net interest income for the year. The cost basis for a bond is the price paid for the bond, plus the associated commission and any other fees or taxes paid in conjunction with the trade.

EXAMPLE

On July 1, 2006, Tyriq bought 10 Treasury bonds (that is, $10,000 worth of par value). They have a coupon rate of 5%, mature on October 1, 2024, and pay interest every April 1 and October 1. Tyriq paid $9,725 for the bonds, but the payment included $40 for commission and $125 in accrued interest. Hence, he actually paid $9,560 for the bonds. His cost basis for tax purposes is $9,600 ($9,560 + $40). The $125 interest paid will show on his tax return as an offset to any other interest income. If he still owns the bonds on October 1 (the next interest payment date), he will receive six months' worth of interest, which is $250 ($10,000 x 5% x ½ year). On his tax return, he will report his interest income from this holding as $125, based on his cash receipt of $250 in interest, less his cash payment of $125 when he bought the bond.

Tax-Equivalent Yield

Once an investor has decided to buy bonds and has chosen the quality of the bonds (for example, AAA, BAA, and so on), he or she usually needs to determine whether or not to buy taxable or tax-exempt bonds. The primary technique for this analysis is either to convert the yield on a tax-exempt bond to a pre-tax equivalent, or to convert the yield on a taxable bond to its after-tax equivalent.

tax-equivalent yield   The traditional formula for converting the yield on a tax-exempt bond to its pre-tax equivalent, also known as the *tax-equivalent yield*, can be expressed as follows:

$$Y_{TE} = \frac{Y}{1-T} \qquad \text{(Equation 13-3)}$$

where: Y_{TE} is the tax-equivalent yield,

T is the investor's marginal tax rate,

Y is the tax-exempt municipal yield.

EXAMPLE
For a municipal bond with a 6% yield, the tax-equivalent yields for someone with a marginal tax rate of 28%, 33%, and 35% are 8.33%, 8.96%, and 9.23%. Thus, each of these investors would prefer the municipal over a taxable bond with a yield of 8.25%.

In some applications, the analyst wants to go from a taxable yield to a tax-exempt yield. This is done by multiplying the pre-tax yield by (1 -*T*), as shown in equation 13-3a:

$$Y_{pre-tax} \times (1-T) = Y_{after-tax} \qquad \text{(Equation 13-3a)}$$

Longstaff (2010) finds that the average marginal tax rate of municipal investors is 38%. This suggests that perhaps only investors in the highest marginal tax bracket should be in municipal bonds.[164]

The only problem with equation 13-3 is that it is perfectly correct only for bonds that are trading at par. When a bond trades at par, the coupon rate, current yield, and yield-to-maturity are all the same, and so the yield number referred to in the formula is any of these values. If a bond trades at a price other than par, then these three numbers will differ from each other, and the formula becomes ambiguous. If the investor buys a municipal for other than par value and holds the bond to maturity, there will be a capital gain or loss on the price of the bond. This is true even for municipal bonds where the interest income is tax exempt. Because the price change would likely be taxed at the capital-gains rate (depending on the investor's other capital gains and losses), equation 13-3 becomes slightly misleading. If the bond

---

164. Longstaff, Francis A., "Municipal Debt and Marginal Tax Rates? Is There a Tax Premium on Asset Prices?" Forthcoming in *The Journal of Finance*.

trades near par, then the bias is not excessive. If the bond being analyzed as part of a taxable-tax-exempt decision trades at a price substantially different from par, the computation of a tax-equivalent yield becomes more complex, as discussed in the next section.

Ethical Issue in Financial Planning

Your client, Robert Ramig, is 75 years old. His portfolio is worth about $750,000 and has a reasonable mix of stocks and bonds. Robert's taxable income is low enough that he has a 15% marginal tax rate. Robert takes great pleasure in minimizing his federal income tax bill. He has asked you to make sure all of his bonds are municipals so that he can minimize his tax liability. Given Robert's marginal tax rate, it is clear that he should consider only taxable bonds. Should you structure the portfolio as Robert requests, or should you explain to Robert the inappropriateness of his proposal and risk losing him as a client?

Tax Implications of the Coupon Tax Effect

deep discount bonds   The relative amounts of coupon payments and price appreciation in the return on a bond can have significant tax implications. For bonds originally sold at par, capital gains are taxed or capital losses recognized only when they are realized as the bonds either mature or are sold in the secondary market. Thus, the capital-gains income on such bonds is both tax deferred and taxed at a lower rate. The tax benefits of any capital loss are also deferred. An investor in a high tax bracket may therefore prefer to buy bonds that pay a below-market coupon rate of interest and are sold at a discount in the secondary market. The market usually contains some low-coupon bonds that were initially sold at par but are now priced at a deep discount.[165] These are known as *deep-discount bonds*. They are distinct from OIDs which were initially sold at a discount.

coupon tax effect   Accordingly, private investors in high tax brackets often tend to prefer deep-discount bonds to higher coupon issues. As a result, the before-tax yields to maturity on low-coupon, deep-discount issues are usually somewhat below yields on otherwise similar issues trading nearer to par. This relationship is called the *coupon tax effect*.

---

165. The existence of a large number of deep-discount bonds is clearly more common when interest rates have been through a long sustained upward trend, rather than a downward trend.

To figure the after-tax yield-to-maturity on a bond for a particular investor, we have to look at after-tax cash flows and compute the yield to maturity (that is, the internal rate of return) on these numbers. In other words, the after-tax yield to maturity is the discount rate that makes the following equation true:

$$P = \left\{ \sum_{t=1}^{T} \left[(1 - T_{OI}) \times C_t / (1 + i)^t \right] \right\} + \left[PAR - T_{CG} \times (PAR - Cost) \right] / (1 + i)^T$$

(Equation 13-4)

where:

T_{OI} = marginal tax rate on ordinary income,

C_t = coupon payment in period t,

PAR = par or face value of the bond,

T_{CG} = marginal tax rate on capital gains,

Cost = price paid for the bond,

T = term to maturity,

i = after-tax yield to maturity.

EXAMPLE

Mike buys a bond ($1,000 par value) with a three-year maturity for $900. The bond has a 6% coupon rate. Assume the bond pays interest in annual installments starting one year from today. If Mike's marginal tax rates on ordinary income and capital gains are 28% and 15%, what is the after-tax yield to maturity?

We need to solve for the discount rate that makes the following equation true:

$$900 = \frac{(1 - .28) \times 60}{(1 + i)^1} + \frac{(1 - .28) \times 60}{(1 + i)^2} + \frac{(1 - .28) \times 60}{(1 + i)^3} + \frac{[1,000 - .15 \times (1,000 - 900)]}{(1 + i)^3}$$

$$900 = \frac{43.20}{(1 + i)^1} + \frac{43.20}{(1 + i)^2} + \frac{43.20}{(1 + i)^3} + \frac{[1,000 - 15]}{(1 + i)^3}$$

The keystrokes for this problem would be:

SHIFT, C ALL

900, +/–, PV

43.2, PMT

1000, –, 900, x, 0.15, =, +/–, +, 1000, =, FV

3, N

I/YR (display: 7.72%)

Note that in this last example, the pre-tax yield to maturity is 10.02 percent,[166] and the after-tax equivalent using equation 13-3a is 7.22% [10.02 x (1 - 0.28)]. This is different from the correct answer by 50 basis points. As noted before, the accuracy of the approximation formula improves as the price of the bond gets closer to par.

So far in our discussion of after-tax returns, we have focused only on discount bonds. There is an interesting complication that can arise in computing an after-tax yield when dealing with premium bonds. When an investor buys a premium bond and holds it to maturity, he or she has a guaranteed capital loss. For example, if the cost basis of the bond is $1,100, there will a $100 capital loss if the bond pays par value at maturity. The complication arises because we do not necessarily know in advance what the tax benefit of a future long-term capital loss will be. If it is used to offset long-term capital gains, the tax savings is based on the capital-gains tax rate. If it is used to offset a net short-term capital gain or to reduce ordinary income, the tax savings is based on the ordinary income tax rate. There is no simple answer on how to project this tax savings.

Convertible Bonds

If a convertible bond is simply bought and later sold, there is no special tax treatment accorded to it over other assets. If the conversion option is elected, then this is a tax-exempt event. The IRS treats this as an exchange of like assets. The important points for convertibles are that the cost basis for the shares of stock so acquired are based on the cost basis of the convertible,

---

166. The keystrokes would be: SHIFT, C ALL, 900, +/-, PV, 60, PMT, 1000, FV, 3, N, I/YR (display: 10.02%).

and the holding period of the stocks starts with the purchase date of the convertibles.

EXAMPLE

Amy buys 10 convertible bonds for $900 each in January 2007 (ignore commissions). In 2011, she converts the 10 bonds into 500 shares of stock. The cost basis for the 500 shares is $9,000, the original purchase price of the bonds, or $18 per share ($9,000/500). The holding period for the stock is already long-term, because the bonds have been held for more than one year at the time of conversion.

Zero Coupon Bonds

As previously noted, zero coupon bonds pay no explicit interest. The return on these securities is derived from the difference between their purchase price and selling price or maturity value.

imputed interest   For tax purposes, the IRS imputes an annual tax liability for these zero coupon bonds. Determining a zero coupon bond's tax liability requires determining the relevant amount of *imputed interest*, which is based on the bond's yield to maturity at the time of issuance. The imputed interest rate does not change over the life of the bond, regardless of what happens to interest rates. Thus, a zero coupon bond that was sold at an 8% yield to maturity would be treated for tax purposes as if it did, in fact, pay 8% each year. The issuer is allowed to deduct the imputed interest cost each year, while the owner incurs an equivalent tax liability. As a result, the issuer obtains a tax deduction even though no cash is paid, while the owner is obligated for the taxes on this income, even though no actual cash is received.

EXAMPLE

LH Corp. zero coupon bonds, par value $1,000, due to mature in September 2022, were sold to the public for $240 in September 2002. Calculation of the imputed annual interest rate is a simple *present value/future value* problem that uses the following keystrokes:

SHIFT, C ALL

1000, FV

240, +/−, PV

20, N

I/YR (display: 7.40)

Imputed interest in the first year is $240 x 0.074 = $17.76. The owner of a bond must declare this as ordinary income. At the end of the year, the cost basis of the bond increases by $17.76 to $257.76 ($240 + $17.76). The imputed interest rate for the second year is $19.07 (0.074 x $257.76). By the end of the 20th year, the imputed interest will bring the cost basis of the bond to $1,000.

Because many investors find it discouraging to have to declare taxable income when they in fact received no cash, zero coupon bonds are much more attractive when purchased in a tax-qualified account (such as an IRA or Keogh) than in a regular account.

Original Issue Discount Bonds

An original issue discount (OID) bond is one whose coupon rate is set sufficiently below the current market rate for bonds of like quality and maturity that it will be issued at a discount. Like zero coupon bonds, there will be imputed interest income, but the calculation requires an extra step. This is because once the imputed interest payment is calculated, the actual interest payment is deducted from the imputed number. The difference is then reported as the noncash interest income, and it is this difference that is added to the price of the bond to adjust its cost basis.

EXAMPLE

The BW Company issues a five-year, original issue discount bond. The coupon rate is 5% paid annually, and the yield to maturity at the time of issue is 8%. As a result, the issue price is $880.22. The interest for the first year is $70.42 ($880.22 x 0.08). However, investors actually receive $50 in coupon payments. Hence, the imputed interest for tax purposes is the difference, or $20.42 ($70.42 − $50). At the end of the year, the cost basis is adjusted to $900.64 ($880.22 + $20.42). The process then continues for each year, with the last imputed payment bringing the cost basis up to par.

Taxation of TIPS

Because TIPS are Treasury instruments, they are exempt from state and local tax, but the investor will owe federal tax on the interest earned as well as on the increase on the principal value, even though he or she will not receive the adjusted principal value until the bond's actual maturity. In other words, they work like original issue discount bonds. As with zero coupon and OIDs, an investor should attempt to purchase TIPS only in tax-deferred or tax-exempt accounts.

Taxation of EE and I Savings Bonds

Because they are Treasury securities, the interest income on savings bonds is exempt from state or local income taxes. When Series EE and Series I bonds are bought, the owner has the option of reporting the increase in the redemption value of the bonds each year as interest income and paying taxes thereon. (As with other zero coupon bonds, this involves the payment of taxes without an accompanying cash inflow.) Most owners elect to defer the federal income tax until the bonds are redeemed or reach the end of their interest-bearing lives. Savings bond earnings are exempt from federal tax if their proceeds are used to pay the tuition and fees of higher education. In 2010, this tax exclusion was available to S taxpayers with modified adjusted gross income less than $70,100 and MFJ taxpayers with modified adjusted gross income less than $105,100. There is then a phase-out range that extends another $15,000 for S taxpayers and $30,000 for MFJ taxpayers.

Wash-Sale Rule for Bonds

The wash-sale rule is avoided on bonds as long as there is at least one important characteristic that is significantly different, be it issuer, maturity, or coupon rate. Thus, if an investor buys some of a company's 10-year bonds and the bond prices fall, the investor can sell those bonds, and buy 10-year bonds of like quality rating and coupon rate for any other company, and be safe from the wash-sale rule. In fact, the investor can even buy 20-year bonds issued by the same company.

TAX ISSUES FOR INVESTMENT COMPANY INVESTORS

To qualify as a regulated investment company under chapter M of the Internal Revenue Code, an investment company must distribute at least 90% of its gross income (dividends, interest, and capital gains). Accordingly, virtually all mutual funds comply with the income distribution requirements. The investor is liable for income taxes on these distributions, regardless of whether they are accepted as cash payments or reinvested in the account. Because the content of the investment portfolios of these funds is regularly changing, the amounts of these distributions may not always be easy to predict, although the timing is fairly predictable.

Dividend and Interest Distributions

Dividends and interest are distributed as ordinary dividends, and they may be paid monthly, quarterly, semiannually, or annually. They are treated as any other dividend and interest income by the taxpayer and taxed accordingly. When dividends are distributed, they retain their character as to whether they are qualified or nonqualified dividends. Nonetheless, in order for the distributed qualified dividends to be treated as qualified by the taxpayer, he or she must meet the holding period requirement for qualified dividends (i.e., own the investment company shares for at least the 121-day period surrounding the payment date.)

When interest income is distributed, it retains its character as to whether it is taxable or tax exempt. Dividend and interest distributions received in January may be allocated for tax purposes to the prior year if they were declared in October, November, or December and a payment date was set at that time. These dividend distributions are considered to have been paid on December 31.

Capital Gain Distributions

Capital gain distributions are paid in January of the year following the year in which the gains were recognized and with few exceptions can be paid only once per year.[167] This is one of the few instances where income received after December 31 is taxed to the prior year. Although the long-term capital gains included in the distribution are treated as long-term capital gains to the investor, the same is not true for short-term capital gains. In this case, they are treated as nonqualified dividends. Note that in this case, the long-term status is independent of how long the taxpayer has held the investment company shares.

---

167. See *Investment Company Act of 1940*, 15 U.S.C. § 80a-1 through 15 U.S.C. § 80a-64. Rule 19b-1.

One of the drawbacks to an investment company holding is that capital losses are not passed through to the shareholders. Thus, in periods of extended down markets not only do most investment companies cease to make capital gain distributions because they have no net capital gains to distribute, but they also accrue capital losses that provide no immediate tax benefit to an investor. Once the markets turn up again and the investment companies start to generate capital gains on their trades, the initial capital gains are essentially tax free due to the capital-loss carryforward on the books of the fund.

In some instances, an investment company will opt not to distribute some of its capital gains. In this case, it must still report to the investor his or her share of undistributed capital gains and this is taxable income to the investor. However, the investor then adds the amount of undistributed capital gain to his or her cost basis.

EXAMPLE

As a financial advisor, you are considering recommending two mutual funds to your clients. The Knockout Fund is an aggressive growth, no-load fund with a $10 NAV. The Also-Ran Fund is also an aggressive growth, no-load fund with a $20 NAV, whose expense ratios and turnover activity are virtually identical to those of the Knockout Fund. You also note, however, that the Also-Ran Fund has an accumulated capital-loss carryforward equivalent to $2.00 per share, whereas the Knockout Fund has virtually no capital-loss carryforward. Which fund should you recommend?

The NAV is immaterial to the selection. You should probably recommend the Also-Ran Fund, because the first $2.00 per share of capital gains will be completely shielded from taxes–unless you believe the capital-loss carryforward is indicative of management's ability.

"Buying Taxes"

Buying shares in a taxable account shortly before a dividend or capital gain distribution is paid means that taxes will be payable almost immediately by the new investor. This is particularly a problem for capital gain distributions because they are made only once per year for most funds and in some years can be relatively large. Thus, although a mutual fund that holds a highly appreciated portfolio would certainly mean it has been successful, it also potentially means a capital-gains tax liability for the new investor.

An even more awkward situation that sometimes arises is when an investor buys some mutual fund shares where the portfolio has just taken a bunch of gains, the shares subsequently decline in value, and then at the end of the year the fund declares a capital gain distribution. Therefore, even though the investor has lost money at that point on his or her investment, he or she must still pay taxes on the capital gain distribution. The only saving grace in this situation is that after the capital gain distribution, the fund's NAV will adjust downward by the size of the capital gain distribution. This increases the investor's capital loss, so that if the investor sells the holding, he or she will be able to declare a capital loss on those shares that is larger than otherwise would have been the case, and the step-up in the loss equals the capital gain distribution.

Tax-Friendly Funds and the Turnover Ratio

Some funds are more tax friendly than others. The tax friendliness of a fund can usually be measured by the magnitude of its portfolio turnover ratio. The lower the turnover ratio, the more tax friendly the fund. This is because funds with low portfolio turnover ratios tend to generate fewer taxable capital gains on their portfolios, and thus will have smaller capital gain distributions. Furthermore, the lack of the fund's recognition and subsequent distribution of capital gains (that is, the lack of sales within the portfolio) means that the NAV can increase more rapidly, and the investor can control the timing of capital gains through the sale of the mutual fund shares. Remember, if a mutual fund pays a capital gain distribution of $2 per share, the NAV will drop at the time of payment by $2 per share.

By the nature of their objective, index funds are more tax friendly than traditional funds. They sell shares relatively infrequently, so there are fewer capital gain distributions. Also, unlike many traditional fund managers, index fund managers do not make end-of-quarter decisions to "dress up" their portfolios. Sometimes these decisions make no substantive change in the portfolio's risk-return characteristics but do trigger distributions that are taxable to the shareholder.

The concept of a fund's making one of its objectives to minimize capital gain distributions is actually relatively new; the first such fund marketed to the public was the Schwab 1000 fund.[168] It was at about this same time that Morningstar began producing tax-adjusted return numbers for funds.

---

168. Robert H. Jeffrey, "Tax-Efficient Investing Is Easier Said Than Done," *Journal of Wealth Management* (Summer 2001): 9.

Determination of Basis

Record keeping can get rather complicated for mutual funds[169]. If the investor buys mutual fund shares in a single purchase, and does not reinvest any dividends or capital gain distributions or buys any additional shares, determining the cost basis upon sale is like any other capital transaction. However, most investors end up acquiring mutual funds shares over time, from reinvestment of dividends or capital gain distributions, purchase of new shares, or all of the above. The cost basis can be based on specific share identification, FIFO (first in, first out), or average costs.

Specific Share Identification

If the investor adequately identifies the shares sold, he or she can use the adjusted basis of those particular shares to figure gain or loss. The investor will adequately identify mutual fund shares, even if he or she bought the shares in different lots at various prices and times, by doing both of the following:

- Specifying to the broker or other agent the particular shares to be sold or transferred at the time of the sale or transfer
- Receiving confirmation in writing from the broker or other agent within a reasonable time of the specification of the particular shares sold or transferred

First-in, First-out (FIFO)

If shares were acquired at different times or at different prices and the investor cannot identify which shares he or she sold, the investor should use the basis of the shares acquired first as the basis of the shares sold. In other words, the oldest shares owned are considered sold first. The investor should keep a separate record of each purchase and any dispositions of the shares until all shares purchased at the same time have been disposed of completely.

Average Basis

The investor can calculate gain or loss using an average basis only if he or she acquired the shares at various times and prices and left the shares on deposit in an account handled by a custodian or agent who acquires or redeems those shares. Once he or she elects to use an average basis, the

---

169. The information in this section is based on U.S. Department of Treasury, *Publication 564, Mutual Fund Distributions* (Internal Revenue Service, 2005).

investor must continue to use it for all accounts in the same fund. This does not preclude the use of a different cost basis for shares in other funds, even those within the same family of funds.[170]

EXAMPLE
Eve owns two accounts that hold shares of the Trustus Income Fund. She also owns 100 shares of the Trustus Growth Fund. If Eve elects to use average basis for the first account of the income fund, she must use average basis for the second account. However, she may use a cost basis for the growth fund.

The following two methods are used to calculate average basis:

- Single-category method
- Double-category method

Single-Category Method. Under the single-category method, the average basis of all shares owned at the time of each sale is computed, regardless of how the investor acquired them. This includes shares acquired with reinvested dividends or capital gain distributions, as well as those bought outright.

Even though all unsold shares of a fund are included in a single category to compute average basis, the investor may have both short-term and long-term gains and losses when he or she sells these shares. To determine the holding period, the shares disposed of first are considered to be those acquired first.

EXAMPLE
Trevor has bought 400 shares in the LJO Mutual Fund: 250 shares on May 15, 2009, at $10 per share, and 150 shares on May 15, 2010, at $15 per share. On November 11, 2010, he sold 300 shares. Under the single-category method, the basis of all 300 shares sold is the same—that is, Trevor paid $2,500 for the first batch and $2,250 for the second batch. The average cost is $11.875 per share [($2,500 + $2,250)/400]. With regard to the holding period, Trevor held 250 shares for more than one year, so the gain or loss on those shares is long-term. He held 50 shares for one year or less, so the gain or loss on those shares is short-term.

---

170. Tom Herman, "Calculating Stock Gains Need Not Be Too Taxing,"*The Wall Street Journal Online*, October 23, 2003.

Note that the cost basis of the shares the investor still holds after a sale of some shares is the same as the average basis of the shares sold. The next time the investor makes a sale, the average basis will still be the same, unless he or she has acquired additional shares (or has made a subsequent adjustment to basis).

Double-Category Method. In the double-category method, all shares in an account at the time of each disposition are divided into two categories: short-term and long-term. Shares held one year or less are short-term. Shares held longer than one year are long-term. The basis of each share in a category is the average basis for that category. This is the total remaining basis of all shares in that category at the time of disposition, divided by the total shares in the category at that time. To use this method, the investor specifies, to the custodian or agent handling the account, from which category the shares are to be sold or transferred. The custodian or agent must confirm the specification in writing. If the investor does not specify or receive confirmation, he or she must first charge the shares sold against the long-term category and then charge any remaining shares sold against the short-term category.

After the investor has held a mutual fund share for more than one year, he or she must transfer that share from the short-term category to the long-term category. The basis of a transferred share is its actual cost or other basis unless some of the shares in the short-term category have been disposed of. In that case, the basis of a transferred share is the average basis of the unsold shares at the time of the most recent disposition from this category.

An investor chooses to use the average basis of mutual fund shares by clearly showing on the income tax return, for each year the choice applies, that he or she used an average basis to report gain or loss from the sale or transfer of the shares. He or she must specify whether the single-category method or the double-category method was used to determine average basis. This choice remains in effect until the investor gets permission from the IRS to revoke it.

Taxation of Unit Investment Trusts

Unit investment trusts (UITs) hold fixed portfolios, which mature over time (if bonds are held) or are liquidated at a fixed point in time (if stocks are held). During the life of the UIT portfolio, the interest and dividend income are distributed to shareholders on a regular basis, as with any other investment company. As the bonds mature, the principal is distributed to the investors as a tax-free return of capital. Investors must adjust their cost basis for such returns. When a UIT equity portfolio is liquidated, investors usually have the choice of receiving the liquidating dividend, or rolling it over into the next such equity UIT that is being created. Regardless of which option is chosen, the investor must recognize the capital gain or loss for tax purposes at the time of the liquidation.

There is one exception to the mandatory recognition of capital gains upon liquidation of an equity UIT. Where the successor portfolio has the same securities as the terminating portfolio, the cost basis of those particular securities may be carried forward. If the entire successor portfolio is identical (in other words, the UIT is not really being liquidated), then there is no sale to be recognized.[171]

Wash-Sale Rule for Investment Companies

Although the wash-sale rule applies to investment companies the same way it applies to any other securities, there is one issue that is unique. It is, do the sale and purchase of two different index funds (or ETFs) within a 30-day window constitute a violation of this rule? The answer depends on which index is being tracked. If both index funds track the same index, such a trade would likely be considered a violation of this rule. As long as the two index funds track different indexes, the investor is not in violation of the rule.

TAX ISSUES FOR OTHER INVESTMENTS

Options

The tax treatment of options depends on the nature of the underlying asset. Because financial assets are capital assets, options on these assets are also capital assets.

If both the buyer and the writer of the option are initiating a new position, there are no tax consequences for either party. If the option lapses (that is, expires as worthless), the writer must treat the premium as a capital gain on the date of expiration, and the buyer claims a capital loss. The lapse of a call or put option is treated as if it were sold for zero.

---

171. For an example of this issue, see Morgan Stanley & Co., "FAQs: Unit Investment Trusts," *Morgan Stanley*, 2008. www.morganstanleyindividual.com/investmentproducts/unittrusts/faqs (accessed July 19, 2010).

If the writer of a put or call closes out the option by purchasing an identical put or call, he or she recognizes a short-term capital gain or loss equal to the difference between the amount paid to purchase the option and the amount received when the option was written. These gains or losses are short-term because the maturities of these instruments are less than one year. LEAPS® are an exception. The transactions could be long-term for these options.

If a call is exercised, the writer sells the underlying stock for the strike price. He or she recognizes a gain or loss as measured by the difference between the sum of the premium and the sales price, and the adjusted basis of the stock delivered to the purchaser. The holding period is measured from the date the stock was purchased to the date the stock was delivered under the terms of the option agreement. When a naked call is exercised, the writer, by definition, does not own the underlying stock required to cover the call at the time it was written. Thus, the writer will have to simultaneously buy and sell the underlying stock. Hence, this is clearly a short-term transaction.

EXAMPLE

Suppose Jason writes a call for 100 shares at a strike price of $40 per share; he also owns 100 shares purchased six months earlier at $30 per share and 100 shares purchased one month earlier at $35 per share. Jason receives a premium of $100 for the call. Nine months later, the owner of the call exercises the option. If Jason uses the first block of stock, he recognizes $1,100 of long-term capital gain ($4,000 exercise price + $100 option premium – $3,000 basis), because the call is exercised after the stock was held for 15 months. If he uses the second block of stock to cover the call, he recognizes a $600 short-term capital gain ($4,000 exercise price + $100 option premium – $3,500 basis), because the call is exercised after he held the stock for only 10 months.

If a put option is exercised, the writer purchases the underlying stock and has a basis equal to the net investment—that is, the strike price reduced by the option premium. The stock's holding period begins with the exercise of the option.

Annuities

The basic tax rule on the payments from an annuity during the distribution phase is that a designated portion of each payment is excludible from gross income as a tax-free recovery of the purchaser's investment, and the balance, which is income earned on the contract, is taxable as ordinary income.

If the annuity is part of a qualified plan, the usual tax treatment applies in that all of the payments during the payout period are fully taxable as ordinary income. This is because the premiums were tax deductible and the taxation of the earnings in the account (that is, interest, dividends, and capital gains) was deferred.

If the annuity is fixed and a nonqualified purchase, to determine the percentage of each payment that is tax exempt, one divides the total amount of premiums paid by the expected payout of the policy based on the annuitant's life expectancy. If the annuitant lives beyond this life expectancy, then the full amount of the payments become taxable.

EXAMPLE

Suppose Fred has paid $13,500 in premiums for a policy. Let's assume that when he is ready to start drawing monthly benefit payments his life expectancy is 15 years (i.e., 180 months). Let's also assume that the monthly benefit payment is $150. Over the next 15 years, Fred can expect to receive $27,000 ($150/month x 180 months) in benefits. In this case, one-half of each payment will be tax exempt, and the other half will be taxed as ordinary income. This one-half tax exemption is based on the ratio of $13,500 in premiums paid to the $27,000 in expected benefits. If Fred lives longer than 15 years, the entire monthly benefit must be taxed as ordinary income.

General, Limited, and Master Limited Partnerships

In general and limited partnerships, any income or loss is computed and allocated among partners based on the partnership agreement. The allocation is reported on a form known as Schedule K-1. Note that the allocation of income or loss is independent of any net cash flow achieved by the partnership and independent of any cash distributions. Thus, if the partnership elects to keep all of the cash generated by the business, the partners still have to pay personal income taxes on their shares of the partnership income.

The major advantage to partnerships arises when the partnership generates a loss. For a normal corporation, a loss results in no direct tax benefit to the shareholders other than any potential tax refunds due the corporation or any operating tax loss carry forwards the corporation can use. For partnerships, the loss can be allocated to the partners according to the same formula used to allocate gains. The individuals can then report these losses on their tax returns for the current year and thus reduce their taxable income.

As noted in an earlier chapter, the term master limited partnerships (MLPs) is used to denote a limited partnership that is publicly traded like shares of common stock. A special provision in the tax code allows MLPs to function as investment companies, and thus avoid the corporate income tax, provided they receive 90% of their income from natural resources and related activities. It is for this reason that the majority of the MLPs are in the gas, minerals, oil, and timber industries.

These investments can create quite complex tax treatments.[172] For example, suppose an investor has purchased an MLP unit (i.e., share) at $30. Next, suppose the MLP declares a cash distribution of $3 per unit. However, let's say that based on the income statement, only $0.60 of this cash distribution is a return of profits, and the rest, $2.40 is a return of capital. As discussed earlier, a return of capital is a tax-exempt event. Hence, the investor will have to declare the $0.60 per unit as a dividend on his or her tax return, and then reduce his or her cost basis by $2.40, the return of capital. Hence, the investor's cost basis is now $27.60, rather than the $30 originally paid.

Suppose the investor then sells the unit for $33. In this case, the difference between the original cost basis of $30 and the adjusted cost basis of $27.60 is now taxed as ordinary income. The balance would be taxed as a capital gain. Hence, this sale of shares produces $2.40 of ordinary income and $3 of capital gain per unit sold.

In some of the more successful MLPs that have been held for a long time period, the investors have found that the accumulated returns of capital exceed the original purchase price. As noted earlier, when a return of capital exceeds the adjusted cost basis, the excess return is taxed as a sale. At this point, if the unit is sold for more than the original cost, the entire amount of the original cost would have to be recognized as ordinary income. The only way to avoid this would be to hold the MLP until death and hope that estate tax laws still permit a step-up in cost basis at that time.

An investment in a MLP means a lot more attention to record keeping, and for some investors it would mean professional tax preparation. This means that for many, buying a few shares of an MLP would not make sense as the cost of the tax implications could easily exceed the tax benefits of this

---

172. The following material is based on Donald Jay Korn, "Mastering MLPs," *Financial Planning* (June 2004): 121-122, 124.

investment. Hence, MLPs should probably be purchased only when the combined investment in all MLPs in the portfolio is significant.

Futures Contracts

A few years ago, special tax rules were created for futures contracts where they are held as speculative positions. Such assets are capital assets and when the position is closed out, the capital-gain or capital-loss treatment would apply. However, as a special twist, any positions that are open as of December 31 of each year are treated as if they are closed out on this date. This includes both long and short positions. Furthermore, the gains and losses are arbitrarily allocated to being 60% long-term and 40% short-term. Naturally, after reporting these gains and losses on one's tax returns, the cost bases must be adjusted from that point forward.

If the futures position is held by someone who is hedging, then there are no tax consequences. Such a position is referred to as a "tax straddle." A tax straddle occurs when a person owns two positions such that the risk of loss from owning any one particular interest is substantially reduced by reason of the ownership of such other interest.[173]

INVESTMENT STRATEGIES FOR TAX-ADVANTAGED ACCOUNTS

In tax-deferred accounts, such as IRAs, 401(k), and 403(b) plans, there is no taxation as long as there are no distributions from the plan, regardless of whether the invested funds generate capital gain, dividends, and/or interest income. Taxes are assessed when funds are withdrawn from the account, which for most people is at retirement or during the retirement years.

The traditional investment strategy is to hold fixed-income investments in tax-deferred accounts and equity investments in ordinary accounts.[174] The reasoning for this rule-of-thumb is simple. Fixed-income investments pay interest, which is taxed as ordinary income anyway. Holding these investments in a tax-deferred account, therefore, does not change the marginal tax rate at which this income is taxed.

---

173. Tax straddles are discussed in U.S. Department of Treasury, *Internal Revenue Code*, Sec. 1077.

174. For example, see William Reichenstein, "Tax Efficient Investing: Picking the Right Pocket for Your Assets," *AAII Journal* (November 2005): 20-24.

Equity investments pay dividends and provide capital gains (assuming the investor is fortunate enough to own stocks that go up in value). As we have already seen, both qualified dividend income and capital gains are taxed at lower marginal rates. Furthermore, capital gains are not taxed until the investments are sold. By placing equities in tax-deferred accounts, the qualified dividend income and capital gains are eventually taxed as ordinary income (that is, a withdrawal from a tax-deferred account), rather than retaining their special tax status.

A second problem that arises if an investor buys equities in tax-deferred accounts is that most of these accounts have minimum required distributions (MRDs). Regardless of whether the investor wants to withdraw the MRD from a tax-deferred account each year, he or she must do so; the penalty for not doing so is rather severe. Hence, if the cash for an MRD that is not needed must be obtained by selling some of the holdings in the account, the capital gain effectively becomes taxed as ordinary income at that time. Had the securities been held in an ordinary account, there would be no MRD, and the investor could continue to defer the capital-gains tax. Remember, depending on the size of the estate, the year of death, and who the beneficiaries are, if the investor still holds the stock when he or she dies, the tax on the built-up capital gain might be completely avoided because the cost basis can still be stepped up to market value at the time of death for the beneficiaries under current tax law. If the securities are still held in a tax-deferred account at the time of death, the decedent's beneficiaries will have to pay ordinary income taxes on the withdrawals they are required to take.

Net Unrealized Appreciation

Withdrawals from qualified plans, such as ESOPs, 401(k)s, and qualified pensions, may be made in one of two ways.[175] The more common way is to have the holdings in the account sold and the cash rolled into an IRA account. There, it is invested until the individual starts to take his or her withdrawals. At that time, it is taxed as ordinary income. An alternative strategy, which is available when the investment in the qualified plan consists of the employer's stock, is that the stock can be directly distributed to the individual.[176] At the time of the distribution, the value of the stock consists of two parts. The first

---

175. Material in this section is based on John A. Nersesian and Frances L. Potter, "Revisiting Net Unrealized Appreciation: A Tax-Wise Strategy That May Realize More Benefits Than Ever," *Journal of Financial Planning* (February 2004): 55.

176. U.S. Department of Treasury, Internal Revenue Code, Sec. 402(e)4.

is the cost or tax basis, and the second is the net unrealized appreciation (NUA). The NUA is the difference between the market value of the stock and the cost basis. At the time of the distribution, the individual must declare the cost basis as ordinary income. The net unrealized appreciation is taxed as a long-term capital gain, but only when the stock is sold. Note that this holding period is long-term, regardless of how long the shares of the stock were held in the qualified plan. When the individual eventually sells the stock, any subsequent gain or loss is treated as a long-term or short-term gain or loss, depending on how much time elapses between when the stock is distributed and when it is sold, and whether the price has gone up or down during that period. In cases where there has been substantial price appreciation on the stock, the tax savings in taking the NUA approach can be substantial.

EXAMPLE

Roger Dean is getting ready to retire. The current fair market value of his employer's stock in his retirement plan is $1.3 million. He had been planning to take the cash and roll the money into an IRA account from which he plans to withdraw the money in 10 years. He believes he can earn 8% on this money. If that is the case, the account will grow to $2,806,602. Finally, if we assume his combined marginal tax rate on ordinary income at that time is 35%, he will owe taxes of $982,311 ($2,806,602 x 0.35) upon withdrawal, leaving him with $1,824,291. (To simplify the discussion, we are assuming all of the money is withdrawn as a lump sum on the date of retirement.)

Suppose, however, that the stock has a cost basis of $117,780, and that Roger takes the stock, uses the NUA treatment, holds the stock for 10 years, and receives an 8% rate of return on the stock. The following will occur: Roger will pay an immediate tax of $41,223 on the basis of $117,780 (35% x $117,780). The remaining value of the holding, $1,258,777 ($1,300,000 – $41,223), will then grow to $2,717,605. If the stock is sold at this time, there will be a capital-gains tax of $389,974 based on a 15% capital-gains tax rate and on the difference between the market value of $2,717,605 and the basis on which tax was already paid of $117,780. After payment of the taxes, Roger will be left with $2,327,631. This is $503,340 more then he would have if he had rolled the distribution into an IRA.[177]

. In a real-life application of this concept, the payment of the $41,223 in taxes creates a complication with respect to ending value. There are presumably two sources for the cash to make the tax payment. The first would be to sell some of the shares of stock, which then creates an additional capital gains tax, which is not covered herein. The second is to pay the tax from other savings. In this case, an opportunity cost is clearly created. The presentation here deals with this opportunity cost by subtracting the tax from the value of the stock at the time of the distribution.

Financial Planning Issue

Even in situations where the NUA strictly appears to be financially superior in terms of after-tax dollars, it may make more sense to take the IRA rollover. The reason is that the investment in the employer's stocks may represent such a substantial part of the employee's wealth, that it results in a substantial risk exposure. The IRA rollover provides a tax-free opportunity to convert the holing into an appropriately diversified portfolio.

---

income in respect of a decedent

If the NUA strategy in the above example is followed, we have to consider what will happen if Roger dies before the stock is sold. The bad news is that NUA is considered *income in respect of a decedent*. Thus, although assets passed to beneficiaries at the time of death normally have an automatic step-up in cost basis for the beneficiary to the current market value, this option is not available for NUA. The good news is that the beneficiary can still claim the NUA as unrealized appreciation and thus have it taxed as a long-term capital gain. In addition, the tax does not have to be paid until the stock is sold.

Traditional and Roth IRA Accounts

Earlier in this chapter we discussed the issues associated with a traditional IRA and whether or not a contribution is tax deductible. An alternative to the traditional IRA is the Roth IRA. The maximum contribution for 2010 is the smaller of taxable income or $5,000 per year, with an additional $1,000 contribution allowed for people who are 50 or older if they qualify. To qualify for the full contribution, one's adjusted AGI cannot exceed $167,000 for the MFJ status, and $105,000 for S status. There is a pro rata reduction in the allowable contribution if one's modified AGI slightly exceeds these limits. There are no age limits on contributing to a Roth IRA.

Contributions to a Roth IRA are never deductible. Withdrawals from a Roth IRA that reflect a return of contributions are always tax exempt. Any withdrawal of investment profits (capital gains, dividends, or interest) is also tax exempt provided it is a qualified withdrawal. A qualified withdrawal is one that has been in the account for at least 5 years and occurs on or after the investor reaches the age of 59½. There are, of course, special exceptions to these rules that also allow withdrawals to be qualified.

Tax Deduction for Losses in an IRA Account

Some IRA accounts have a cost basis associated with them.[178] This includes traditional IRAs in which at least some of the contributions were not deductible at the time they were made. It also includes Roth IRAs wherein none of the contributions are deductible. If the value of the IRA account is less than the cost basis, the account can be liquidated and some of the losses written off on the individual's tax return.

There are a couple of catches. First, all of the IRAs of the same type must be completely liquidated. Suppose an investor has two traditional IRA accounts; the value of one is $50,000 less than the cost basis, and the value of the other is $60,000 greater than the cost basis. Both accounts would have to be liquidated to obtain the tax break, and their combined market value actually exceeds the cost basis. Second, the loss is deducted as an itemized deduction subject to the 2% of AGI rule.

Most people are aware that there is a 10% penalty for premature withdrawals from an IRA account. In this case, the penalty does not apply because there is no income being generated, just a loss.

EXAMPLE

Your client, Peter Vergin, has only one traditional IRA. His investment selection has been poor, and the market value is $10,000, despite a cost basis of $50,000. His adjusted gross income this year is expected to be $60,000. What is his tax savings if he liquidates this account, assuming his marginal tax rate is 28%?

Peter has a loss of $40,000. If he has no other deductions that qualify under the 2% rule, he can take a deduction of $38,800 as the amount in excess of 2% (0.02 x $60,000 = $1,200) of his AGI. In a 28% tax bracket, this will save him $10,864 in income taxes. If he has other deductions that qualify under the 2% AGI rule, his tax savings will be slightly greater.

Note that in the above example, it is not clear that Peter would want to take this deduction. There are several other factors to consider. For example, once the money has been withdrawn, if it is reinvested in other securities, the returns on those securities will be subject to current income taxes. The

---

178. This section is based on Julia M. Brennan and David S. Hulse, "Evaluating the Tax Benefits of Deducting Stock Market Losses in IRAs," *Journal of Financial Service Professionals*, (September 2003): 45-55.

analysis can become quite complex, but it clearly starts with recognition of the tax savings that can be generated.

Conversions from Traditional to Roth IRA Accounts

Beginning in 2010, anyone can convert assets in a traditional IRA account to a Roth IRA. The transfer may occur in one of three ways. First, the individual can take a rollover from the traditional IRA and deposit the money in the Roth IRA within 60-day window. Second, the investor can request a trustee-to-trustee transfer, which avoids any potential complications when filing a tax return for that year. Third, the investor can request a same trustee transfer wherein the current trustee manages both the traditional and the Roth IRA account. If any of the necessary conditions for a conversion are not met in the year of the conversion, then there are rather serious penalties that would apply.

The one catch to this transfer process is that income tax is due on the amount transferred. Hence, one must consider a trade-off of paying taxes on the traditional IRA now versus paying taxes on the money when it is ultimately withdrawn, and how this expense compares with the benefit of having the money in a Roth IRA.

EXAMPLE

Charlene has $40,000 in a traditional IRA account. As her filing status is MFJ, her marginal tax rate is 25%. If she undertakes the conversion, she will owe $10,000 in income taxes this year.

Let's assume that this $10,000 is paid with part of the funds from the IRA. This leaves $30,000 to put into the Roth IRA. Let's further assume that Charlene will retire in 15 years, she will earn 8% on her assets, regardless of which IRA account the money is in. Finally, let's assume that her marginal tax rate during retirement will be 15%. To simplify the discussion, let's assume that the money is withdrawn as a lump sum on the date of retirement.

If Charlene leaves her money in her traditional IRA, the account would be expected to grow in value to $126,886.76. After paying 15% in taxes, she would be left with $107,853.75. If Charlene moves her money to the Roth IRA account, the $30,000 after taxes will grow to be $95,165.07. This is all tax free. In this case, Charlene is actually better off leaving the money in the traditional IRA. There are many calculators on the Internet that will solve these conversion problems.

REVIEW OF LEARNING OBJECTIVES

1. Personal taxation starts with summing up the gross income, subtracting the adjustments to obtain AGI, then subtracting the larger of the standard or itemized deductions and the personal exemptions to obtain taxable income. The tax liability is then based on one's filing status, with adjustments for such items as foreign tax credits, other taxes, and payments. An investor should always be aware of his or her effective marginal tax rate.

2. The taxation of the four basic types of investment income for federal tax purposes is provided in the following table.

Table 13-3 Tax Treatment of Investment Income	
Capital distributions on stock Interest on state and local (municipal) bonds	Not subject to federal income tax
Unrealized capital gains	Tax deferred until realized
Interest income (other than municipal bond interest) Nonqualified dividend income Payments from deferred-income plans, 401(k) plans, IRAs, and so forth Rents, royalties, and any other investment income payments Short-term capital gains and short-term capital gain distributions (from mutual funds)	Taxed at ordinary income tax Rate
Long-term capital gains and long-term capital gain distributions (from mutual funds) Qualified dividend income	Taxed at a 5% or 15% rate

3. The cost basis of an investment is the purchase price plus commissions and any other costs to acquire the asset. The cost basis is adjusted for such items as a capital distribution, stock splits, stock distributions, wash sales, and rights offerings.

4. A net short-term capital gain is taxed as ordinary income and a net long-term capital gain is taxed at 15% or 5% depending on the taxpayer's marginal tax rate on ordinary income. Net capital losses are first matched to capital gains, and then can be written off against ordinary income up to $3,000 per year, with additional amounts carried forward to the next year. Qualified dividends are also taxed at 15% or 5% rates, but nonqualified dividends are taxed as ordinary income.

5. Tax-harvesting involves using one's capital losses each year to provide reductions in one's ordinary income, as well as to provide the opportunity to take capital gains in order to rebalance one's portfolio. Tax efficient investing is the strategy of avoiding capital gains to the greatest extent possible.

6. The wash-sale rule disallows losses when a substantially identical security is bought 30-days prior to the sale of an investment up to 30-days after the sale of an investment at a loss. The losses that are disallowed may be used to adjust one's cost basis.

7. The after-tax yield on a bond is its internal rate of return based on the after-tax cash flows. There are no tax consequences when a convertible bond is exchanged for stock. Zero coupon and OID bonds require an imputed interest payment. Taxation of interest on EE and I savings bonds may be deferred.

8. Mutual fund investors should be familiar with the turnover ratio for a fund, and the likely implications for capital gains distributions in the future. Some funds focus on being tax efficient, while other funds have built up capital gains that an investor may want to avoid. There are several choices in tracking the cost basis of a mutual fund, including specific share identification, FIFO, and average cost basis using either the single-category or double-category method.

    Options are capital assets, but when exercised the premium becomes folded into the exercise price. Annuities usually provide a combination of taxable ordinary income and tax-free return of principal. LPs provide an investor the opportunity to write off operating losses that would not be deductible to a stockholder. MLPs provide the opportunity for tax-free returns due to write-offs by the partnership. Futures contracts that are held for speculative purposes must be treated as if they are liquidated on December 31, with part of the gain or loss treated as long-term and the rest as short-term.

9. An employee who is retiring and holds company stock in his or her qualified account has the choice to sell the stock and roll the proceeds into an IRA account, or to take delivery on the stock. In the former case, no taxes are due until distributions are taken from the IRA account, but all proceeds are taxed as ordinary income. In the latter case, income tax is due immediately on the cost basis, but all gains are potentially taxed as long-term capital gains. Losses in an IRA account may be deducted as a miscellaneous itemized deduction subject to the 2% of AGI limitation, if certain conditions are met. Finally, any investor may now convert assets in

a traditional IRA to a Roth IRA, although the amount transferred is taxed as ordinary income.

MINICASE

Your client, Rodney, indicates he is getting ready to retire. He is 61 years old and has accumulated $300,000 in his 401(k) plan, all of it is invested in his employer's stock. His cost basis in this stock is $100,000. Several of his colleagues who have retired recently have been in a similar situation, and all have liquidated this stock upon retirement and moved the money into IRAs. The reasons for this move have been to shield the money from current income taxes and to obtain diversification. This makes sense to Rodney, and he is planning to do the same. You would like to suggest an alternative strategy, namely that Rodney simply roll the stock over into a nonqualified account. Rodney was not planning on taking any cash from this investment until he turns 70. Assume that Rodney is in the 35% marginal income tax bracket today, and will likely be in the 28% marginal income tax bracket when he is in his 70's. Also, assume that the company's stock is expected to increase in value at a rate of 9% per annum during Rodney's holding period, but that alternative investments would grow in value at a rate of 10% per annum. Finally, assume the capital-gains tax in the future is the same as it is in 2010, and that the taxes are paid from other funds.

1. If Rodney follows his original plan, he will owe _____ in income taxes this year on his rollover of assets to his IRA. [8]

    (A) $0
    (B) $35,000
    (C) $65,000
    (D) $105,000

2. If Rodney has the securities issued directly to him, he will owe _____ in income taxes this year on this issuance. [8]

    (A) $0
    (B) $35,000
    (C) $65,000
    (D) $105,000

3. If Rodney follows his original rollover plan and liquidates the entire position when he is 70, he will owe _____ in income taxes at that time. [8]

    (A) $82,735
    (B) $84,000
    (C) $106,108
    (D) $198,068

4. If Rodney has the securities issued and liquidates the entire position when he is 70, he will expect to owe _____ in income taxes at that time (assuming there are no AMT complications and that none of the stock has been liquidated to pay taxes). [8]

    (A) $82,735
    (B) $84,000
    (C) $106,108
    (D) $198,068

5. The biggest single drawback to having the securities issued may well be

    (A) that the entire value of the holdings will be taxed as short-term capital gain upon liquidation. [8]
    (B) that had the IRA been used, a significant portion of the withdrawals would have eventually been tax exempt [8]
    (C) the transaction expense associated with having the stock issued directly
    (D) the continuation of a concentrated position in the employer's stock

CHAPTER REVIEW

Key Terms and Concepts

ordinary income
adjusted gross income (AGI)
net investment income
brackets
cost basis
short-term capital transaction
long-term capital transaction

tax-exempts
tax-equivalent yield
deep discount bonds
coupon tax effect
imputed interest
income in respect of a decedent

Review Questions

Review questions are based on the learning objectives for this chapter. Thus, a [3] at the end of a question means that the question is based on learning objective 3. If there are multiple objectives, they are all listed.

1. a. Define the basic model used for personal taxation, starting with total income and ending with the tax refund to be received or the tax due. [1]

    b. Your client is single. For 2010, she has wage income of $60,000, interest income of $2,000, nonqualified dividend income of $3,000, mortgage interest of $5,000, property taxes of $4,000, interest expense on margin loans of $6,000, and has paid $10,000 in withholding taxes during the year. Using Table 13-1, what does she owe in taxes, or what is her refund? [13-1]

    c. An investor has a federal marginal tax rate of 28% and a state marginal tax rate of 6%. What is his or her combined marginal tax rate if the investor [13-1]

    i. does not itemize his state income taxes?

    ii. does itemize his state income taxes?

2. Last year, Roy bought 100 shares of DEF stock for $2,000. Later, DEF declared a 5% stock dividend. If Roy sells 50 shares, what is their cost basis? [2]

3. a. What is the net short-term (ST) or long-term (LT) capital gain (CG) and capital loss (CL) for each set of trades? [3]

i.			ii.		
	STCG	$4,000		STCG	$2,000
	STCG	$2,000		STCL	$1,000
	LTCG	$1,000		STCL	$3,000
	LTCL	$5,000		LTCG	$500
iii.	STCL	$3,000	iv.	STCG	$2,000
	LTCG	$7,000		STCL	$4,000
	LTCG	$2,000		LTCG	$1,000
	LTCL	$4,000		LTCL	$5,000

    b. For each scenario in part a, compute the incremental taxes owed or the tax savings for someone in the 28% marginal tax rate for ordinary income. [3]

4. Explain the difference between tax-loss harvesting and tax-efficient investing. [4]

5.   Which of the following would be considered substantially identical securities to 100 shares of Class A common stock of the CDE Company, for purposes of the wash-sale rule, if Harold decides to sell and reinvest the proceeds? [5]
a.   Class B stock, which is convertible into Class A, at a 2:1 ratio
b.   Class A stock bought in his wife's Keogh account
c.   A call option on the Class A stock that is deep-in-the-money and has 30 days to maturity
d.   Convertible preferred stock that trades for $80 when the conversion value is $40
e.   Common stock in the company's closest competitor, where the two stocks tend to move together

6.   a.   Stephen buys some bonds for $1,050 on their coupon payment date. The bonds mature in three years, pay interest annually, and have a 10% coupon rate. If Stephen is in the 28% tax rate and any capital losses will be deducted from ordinary income, what will the after-tax rate of return be if he holds these bonds to maturity? [6]
b.   On July 1, James bought 10 bonds in EFG Company for $9,500 total. This included $50 in commissions and $125 in accrued interest. On September 30, the bonds paid their semiannual interest payment. They have a 5% coupon rate. If James sells the bonds on December 31, what is the impact on his interest income for the year? [6]
c.

        i. How much did Mac pay for a $1,000 par value, zero coupon bond that was sold with an 8% yield to maturity and had 30 years to maturity? [6]

        ii. What is his imputed interest income the first year? [6]

        iii. If Mac sells the bond at the market price of $200 after one year, what is his capital gain or loss? [2, 6]

7.   You are trying to decide between an AA rated municipal bond and an AA rated corporate bond for your client who is in the 28% marginal tax bracket. Both would be bought at par. If the yield on the municipal bond is 3%, and the yield on the corporate is 4.25%, which is the better deal? [6]

8.   a.   Explain how Joan would owe capital-gains taxes on a mutual fund at the end of a year even if the shares declined in price. [13-6]
b.   Elizabeth buys 100 shares of the GHI fund for $1,200, and later buys another 50 shares for $700. If she uses the single-category method to determine her average cost, what is her capital gain or loss if she later sells 60 shares for $780? [6, 8]

9.   Chad writes a naked call option (100 shares) on HIJ stock at a strike price of $50. He receives a premium of $5 per share, the option is exercised, and he must pay $60 to buy the stock in the open market for delivery. What is Chad's capital gain or loss? Is it long-term or short term? [2, 7]

10.   Your client, Richard, has two traditional IRA accounts. The first has a cost basis of $100,000 and a market value of $40,000. The second has a cost basis of $50,000 and a market value of $60,000. His AGI is $70,000, and he is in the 28% tax bracket. How much can Richard save on his taxes this year if he liquidates both IRA accounts? [8]

Learning Objectives

An understanding of the material in this chapter should enable the student to

1. Describe the nine-step investment process and identify the six common components of an investment policy statement.

2. Describe the relationship between the number of securities in a portfolio, the types of securities in a portfolio, and the riskiness of a portfolio.

3. Explain the key issues associated with portfolio rebalancing.

4. Discuss other aspects of investment selection including investment effort, minimum investment size, ethical and moral issues, different tax treatments, and concentrated portfolios.

5. Demonstrate how dollar-cost averaging plans work and describe examples of these plans.

6. Describe phenomena associated with behavioral finance and explain the implications of these phenomena for a financial planner.

7. Describe strategies for selling the client on a plan.

In an earlier chapter we looked at the theory of portfolio management. The theory is crucial, because without it, many of the processes and decisions may appear to be "voodoo investments" rather than professional applications of a rather complex theory. With this theory as background, let us now turn to the practical side of managing a portfolio. One does not have to be an investment whiz to be good at managing a portfolio. Remember, the majority of investments do well the majority of the time, and consequently the markets themselves will provide a reasonable rate of return over long time periods. It is up to the portfolio manager to: 1) do no harm, and 2) help the client understand what needs to be accomplished with his or her investments and how to stick to that goal through thick and thin. There are tricks of the trade, of which all planners should be aware, and we will review some of them in this chapter. However, before addressing those, we will begin with the fundamental issues associated with the investment process and how to create an investment policy statement.

WHAT SHOULD INVESTMENT ADVISORS BE DOING?

The investment planning process consists of nine steps. One of these nine steps involves writing an investment policy statement (IPS). It is actually more important to the investment planning process that the advisor and client agree on a written IPS and that the advisor follows this statement to the letter, than the results that are achieved. If the advisor achieves fabulous results, then it is unlikely that the client will be unhappy or will sue the advisor for malpractice. If, through no fault of the advisor, the process results in poor investment performance, then there is always the risk the client will take legal action. As long as there is an IPS and it has been followed to the letter, then the advisor should not be in legal jeopardy. Let us look at the nine steps of the investment process.

The Nine-Step Investment Process

The nine-step model for advising clients about portfolios is as follows:

1. Develop an understanding of the client's goals
2. Identify a target rate of return
3. Agree on the time horizon
4. Determine the client's tolerance for and capacity for risk
5. Define the asset classes
6. Determine an appropriate asset allocation
7. Create the IPS
8. Select the investments themselves
9. Monitor and adjust as needed

Let's now examine these nine steps of the IPS in detail.

Step 1: Develop an Understanding of the Client's Goals

Although goal setting is critical to creating a successful portfolio, few people actually set clearly defined goals. Financial service professionals should query the client to learn what he or she is trying to accomplish with various investments. Some clients may start with the simple goal of wanting to make some money. Other clients may have the slightly more developed goal of wanting a comfortable standard of living when they retire. While the second goal is better than the first, neither is adequate.

In cases such as these, the financial planner needs to help the client discover his or her goals and enunciate them in a clear manner. Such a process may take several visits with the client.

Many clients will have multiple goals and may have multiple accounts. Some accounts will be linked to specific goals, such as a Coverdell Educational Savings Account for financing a child's college education. Other accounts may be for general accumulation and not tied to a specific goal. Thus, multiple precise goals may need to be defined.

Going through the next few steps may make it clear to the planner (and client) that modification of the defined goals may be necessary, especially if the goals imply expected rates of return that the planner does not believe are achievable, or risk exposures that would make the client uncomfortable.

Step 2: Identify a Target Rate of Return

The financial planner needs to have the client develop a precise goal such as, "We want to retire in 20 years with an after-tax income of $60,000 per year in current dollars, and we want the income to continue as long as we live without depleting the principal." It is then incumbent upon the planner to translate this goal into a target rate of return. A target rate of return may be expressed as an absolute number, such as 8% per annum. However, it would be more appropriate to express the target rate of return in real rates rather than nominal rates. Thus, if the planner believes the inflation rate will be 3%, then stating the target rate of return as the inflation rate plus 5%, would imply a desired rate of return of about 8%. A desired nominal rate is equal to one plus the real rate times one plus the inflation rate, less one. So in this case, a desired real rate of return of 5% and an expected inflation rate of 3% would mean a target nominal rate of 8.15% $[(1 + 0.05)(1 + 0.03) - 1]$. When inflation rates are low, most people forget that what counts is real values and not nominal values. When inflation rates are high, everyone is acutely aware of the significance of real values. Consider the following complex example.

EXAMPLE

Mike and Beth Kasper approach you to help them develop a financial plan; their primary goal is retirement income. Mike and Beth plan to retire 20 years from today. Together they have wage and salary income of $100,000. They anticipate this will grow at the rate of inflation for the next 20 years. You project their social security and pension income will total $90,000 per year at retirement. The Kaspers have already accumulated $150,000 in financial assets. After extensive discussions about lifestyle issues, the couple agrees that they would like to retire with an income equal to 80% of their pre-retirement income. They plan to add $5,000 per year to their portfolio (assume the contributions are made at the end of each year) between now and retirement. What rate of return do they need to earn on their portfolio? Assume an inflation rate of 3% over the next 20 years, and that during the first year of retirement they want to draw out no more than 5% of the value of the portfolio.

Answer: The first step is to project what their income will be at the time of retirement. This is a simple future value calculation, which works out to $180,611 (SHIFT, C ALL, 100000, +/–, PV, 20, N, 3, I/YR, FV). Note that we assume that income will grow at the rate of inflation. The next step is to compute 80% of this value, which is $144,489 (0.8 × $180,611). This is the desired income during the first year of retirement. The third step is to subtract out the other projected retirement income, which means the Kaspers will have to plan on withdrawing $54,489 ($144,489 – $90,000) from their portfolio during the first year of retirement. If this is to represent 5% of the portfolio's value, then the portfolio itself will have to be worth $1,089,778 ($54,489/0.05). As we now know the beginning value of their portfolio ($150,000), the desired ending value ($1,089,778), the annual contributions ($5,000), and the time horizon, we can compute the required annual rate of return. It turns out to be 8.96% (SHIFT, C ALL, 150000, +/–, PV, 5000, +/–, PMT, 20, N, 1089778, FV, I/YR). In view of the projected inflation rate of 3%, the Kaspers need to earn a real rate of return of about 6% (8.96% – 3%).

Irreconcilable Differences?

An interesting issue frequently arises at this point. Suppose that the rate of return necessary to achieve the desired portfolio objective is, in the opinion of the planner, unachievable. Either it is just not realistically achievable or it is not appropriate given the client's risk tolerance and risk capacity (which will be discussed shortly). In other words, the client cannot achieve the desired goals. One of several things must happen:

1. The client can set lower, more achievable goals by targeting a lower-than-desired lifestyle during retirement.

2. The client can retain the goal, but make a commitment to set aside more money for savings in the intervening period. For example, if the client had been planning to contribute $5,000 per year between now and retirement, he or she may have to agree to set aside at least $7,000 each year.

3. The client can retain the goal, but accept more risk to try to achieve a higher rate of return. For example, if the client's risk tolerance calls for a maximum of 50% in stocks, and a weight of at least 75% in stocks is necessary to achieve the desired portfolio rate of return, then the client may have to reconcile to living with the added risk.

4. In the case of retirement planning, the client can make use of principal. Many clients adopt an income-only approach with no principal directed toward retirement income. Since they plan never to spend their principal, they must accumulate a larger portfolio to generate the necessary cash flow. Clients who are willing to spend down principal or to purchase a life annuity at retirement can lower their funding needs, sometimes significantly.

5. In the case of retirement planning, the client can delay the planned retirement date. A delayed retirement date not only allows personal assets to grow, there is a good chance that pension income will be higher, reflecting more service, shorter life expectancy, and probably a higher average income. Also, Social Security income will probably be slightly higher.[179]

Ethical Issue in Financial Planning

A widow has just received a life insurance settlement check of $500,000 from her husband's policy. She does not know how to use it most effectively, so she calls three financial planners. Planner A says he can get an 8% annual rate of return on her money. Planner B claims she will achieve a 10% rate of return. Planner C claims he will earn at least a 15% rate of return.[180] Which planner should the client use? The answer is none of them. Without learning more about the client, her risk tolerance, her resources, and her goals, a planner should not discuss what rates of return a client can achieve.

---

179. See, for example, Walt Woerheide, "The Impact of the Pension Fund on the Decision to Work One More Year," *Financial Services Review* 9, no. 1 (1999): 17–31.

180. This example is based on a true story told to the author by someone who called The American College seeking advice about which planner to use.

Ethical Issue in Financial Planning

A financial planner has ascertained a client needs a 12% rate of return to achieve his goal. This exceeds the rates of return the planner truly expects to achieve on any of his asset categories. The planner believes the client is unlikely to employ him if he suggests one of the five alternatives noted above. Rather, the client will likely seek another planner. In this situation, it is easy to see how a planner might be tempted into the unethical step of changing the numbers used in his or her projections (for example, change the expected return on stocks from 10% to 15%). If after a year or two the planner is unable to achieve these returns, he might then be able to convince the client to try one or more of the adjustments described above.

Step 3: Agree on the Time Horizon

In the above example, the Kaspers appear to have a well-specified time horizon of 20 years. However, it is not likely that they are planning to die within a few years of retirement. Many clients plan to live 30 years or more into retirement. So in the above example, one could also consider the relevant time horizon as 50 years (the 20 years till retirement, plus the 30 years after retirement). Other goals and portfolios may have much better defined time horizons. For example, the goal of saving for college likely consists of the time till a child goes to college, plus the amount of time spent in college.

Step 4: Determine Client's Tolerance for and Capacity for Risk

Determining a Client's Tolerance for Risk

There are actually two components to a client's risk tolerance. One is the level of risk the client can tolerate, and the second is the amount of risk the client is capable of tolerating. As mentioned earlier, it is critical that the financial advisor determine the client's tolerance for risk. Earlier, we defined the client's tolerance for risk by introducing the concept of indifference curves in a graph with axes showing expected return (vertical axis) and risk (horizontal axis). It is the slope (and shape) of the indifference curves that determine the optimal portfolio a client should hold.

Unfortunately, no one has figured out how to truly measure investment risk aversion in an individual and how to translate this into a portfolio recommendation. However, the fact that the perfect method of measuring risk tolerance has not yet been developed does not excuse the financial advisor from trying to determine how much financial risk a client is willing to tolerate. It is absolutely critical that every financial advisor make some formal, legitimate attempt to make as precise a determination as possible.

The most common practice is to have the client complete a risk tolerance questionnaire. An advisor could develop his or her own questionnaire, but unless the advisor holds advanced degrees in statistics and psychology, this could be dangerous. The reason is that there is a good chance that eventually a disenchanted client will sue the financial planner for investing funds inappropriately. A planner who cannot statistically prove the validity of the risk tolerance questionnaire could be in serious trouble. Thus, a planner gains an extra form of legal protection if he or she uses risk tolerance questionnaires that are developed by reputable professionals.

It should be noted that a person's degree of risk aversion is not a universally generalizable characteristic. People may be risk aversive in their investment decisions, and be comfortable taking risks in their driving, or vice versa. Thus, even if a financial planner has a client who goes to Atlantic City to gamble every weekend, this does not necessarily mean the client wants an aggressive portfolio. Perhaps the client views gambling as entertainment and is willing to pay the price for such entertainment, but wants a high degree of certainty with regard to retirement income. Similarly, clients who skydive as a hobby may nonetheless prefer conservative portfolios.

A risk tolerance questionnaire will produce some sort of "score." Low scores usually indicate a high degree of risk aversion, and a high score indicates a high degree of risk tolerance (i.e., a willingness to make risky investments). The developer of the questionnaire will then indicate how this score relates to a suggested asset-allocation model. Keep in mind that investors with low scores will be directed to highly conservative asset-allocation strategies, and those with high scores will be directed to aggressive asset allocations.

As a general concept, relating these scores to asset allocations is perfectly consistent with financial theory and highly appropriate. Nonetheless, the financial planner must always remember that there is no precision to this process. If a client's score produced a recommendation to hold 50% of assets in common stocks, this is a *guideline* and not a scientifically based factual statement.

Determining a Client's Capacity for Risk

The second element in assessing risk tolerance is determining the level of risk exposure a client is capable of accepting. There can be multiple reasons why clients expose themselves to more or less risk than what is suggested by their score on a risk-tolerance questionnaire. For instance, suppose in the previous example involving Mike and Beth Kasper, it turned out that they only need to earn a real rate of return of 2%, rather than 6%, to achieve their retirement objectives. This might be the case if the Kaspers had already accumulated more in the way of financial assets. Even though they have the temperament for handling more risk, the planner should consider advising them that there is a high probability of achieving their goals with a low-risk portfolio.

A second scenario might exist in which the clients can afford to, or even need to, take on more risk than the amount with which they are comfortable. In the case of the Kaspers, suppose that the amount of time until retirement is 35 years, rather than 20 years, and that the real rate of return they need to achieve given their savings plan is 7%. The combination of the long-time horizon in conjunction with the high rate of return they need to achieve (a 7% real rate combined with an expected inflation rate of 3%, meaning a nominal rate of return in excess of 10%) would certainly suggest they need to start off with an aggressive risk exposure. In this case, a portfolio allocation of 100% in equities would seem appropriate.

In cases such as these, where the advisor concludes the clients should take on a different level of risk exposure than is consistent with their risk tolerance, the task of the financial planner becomes one of educating the client, as well as advising the client. A critical element in helping people to accept risk is to ensure they understand the nature of the risk. People who skydive tend to have a solid understanding of how parachutes are packed, and the process for activating the chute. People who find the entire concept magical are highly unlikely to ever take a jump.

Step 5: Identify Asset Classes and Investment Vehicles

There does not seem to be broad agreement as to the number of asset classes that should appear in an IPS, the detail involved in specifying the asset classes, or the specificity of the investment vehicles. An appropriate number likely depends upon the size of the portfolio. Thus, small portfolios may specify as few as three to five asset classes, and truly large portfolios may specify 15 or more asset classes. The distinction in the number lies in the level of detail. For example, one asset class for the small portfolio may be equities. For the large portfolio, equities may be divided up into value, growth, international, and REITs, or may be further subdivided into large-cap value, large-cap growth, etc.

With regard to investment vehicles, the choices vary from being specific and listing securities by name, to providing broader groupings, such as ETFs, index funds, or actively managed mutual funds. While identifying investment vehicles, it might also be appropriate to identify the extent to which socially-responsible companies or funds will be utilized within the portfolio, and to specify what the criteria will be for the socially responsible investments.

Step 6: Design the Asset Allocation

Think of the previous step as producing a laundry list of asset classes. This next step involves assigning percentages to each item in the list. For example, the following table shows six asset classes that might be defined in the previous step. In the first part of this step, the actual percentage allocation is proposed. Note that some of the classes are listed as having a 0% allocation. The zeros indicate that an intentional decision has been made to omit investments in these categories. It is certainly possible that at a later date the advisor may recommend allocating some of the portfolio to these classes.

Table 14-1 Example of Asset Allocation			
Asset Class	%-Allocation	Expected Rate of Return	Standard Deviation
Large-cap stocks	30%	10%	12%
Mid-cap stocks	20%	11%	15%
Small-cap stocks	10%	12%	18%
Government bonds	0%	5%	6%
Corporate bonds	40%	6%	8%
Money mkt. fds.	0%	3%	1%

One of the key issues in defining the asset allocation is the extent to which it is intended to reflect the assets under management by the advisor, or the client's entire portfolio. For example, a client may have a large sum of monies invested in a 403(b) pension plan. These assets may be entirely invested in equities. There should be agreement as to whether the asset allocation should include these assets or not.

After defining the weights for each class, the planner should also define the expected rates of return and standard deviations of these rates of return. Expected rates of return and standard deviations should be based on expected future rates and variances. However, in practice, historical rates and variances are often used as proxies for future rates and variance, under the rather presumptuous assumption that these will not change over time.

Strategic Asset Allocation

What we have described so far in this step is known as strategic asset allocation.[181] For institutional portfolios such as endowment funds and pension funds—and even mutual funds—the board of directors or board of trustees should make the strategic asset-allocation decision. For an individual client, strategic asset allocation is the roadmap that should provide the constraints under which the portfolio will be managed. The purpose of strategic asset allocation is to determine the overall risk exposure of the portfolio and not to produce an allocation that will "beat the market" through factor selection.

Think of the strategic asset allocation as the vehicle to obtain the optimal portfolio on a simple efficient frontier. Remember, the efficient frontier in a world without a risk-free asset is a concave locus of points, an example of which is reproduced in *Figure 14-1*.

Figure 14-1
Efficient Frontier

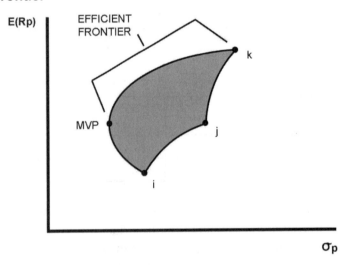

---

181. Several of the ideas in this section are from Mark Anson, "Strategic versus Tactical Asset Allocation: Beta versus Alpha Drivers," *The Journal of Portfolio Management* (Winter 2004): 8–22.

In strategic asset allocation, an efficient frontier is defined using just the asset classes as inputs. For example, suppose our asset allocation involved three asset classes, namely, stocks, bonds, and cash equivalents. Let's say we also define the following statistics for these three asset classes:

	Stocks	Bonds	Cash Equiv.
Expected return:	10%	5%	4%
Standard dev.:	18%	8%	2%
Covariances:	Covariance (stocks, bonds)		72.0
	Covariance (stocks, cash equivalences)		0.18
	Covariance (bonds, cash equivalences)		3.2

Based on this information, we can use any of several software packages to produce an efficient frontier that will look similar to *Figure 14-1*. The strategic asset-allocation decision is then a choice between which portfolio on this efficient frontier one wants to hold. As noted earlier, in theory it is simply a matter of imposing indifference curves on this graph to find the portfolio that lies on the highest possible indifference curve. In practice, it is frequently a case of looking at various combinations of expected rates of return and standard deviations of return to determine the combination with which the client is most comfortable.

When a client wants to follow a strict strategic asset-allocation approach, the ideal investments might well be index funds. Thus, the choice for stocks would be a stock index fund, the choice for bonds would be a bond index fund, and the choice for cash equivalents would be a money market mutual fund.

Strategic asset-allocation decisions must be long-term decisions. It is acceptable to change a strategic asset allocation, but such a change should be associated with a significant discussion as to why the new allocation is better. A change in *short-term* capital market expectations would almost certainly not have been an acceptable rationale for change in a strategic asset allocation.

EXAMPLE

The members of the board of trustees of the Dandy Manufacturing Corporation's Pension Fund have just met with their investment advisor, the Safe and Solid Investment Firm. Safe and Solid has proposed a set of expected rates of return, standard deviations, and correlation coefficients for use in analyzing potential portfolio allocations. Based on these inputs and prior discussions about probable strategic asset allocations, Safe and Solid makes the following proposal:

Portfolio Weights	Expected Return	Standard Deviation
70% Equity, 30% Bonds	9%	15%
60% Equity, 40% Bonds	8.5%	13%
50% Equity, 50% Bonds	8%	12%

After studying the above alternatives, the board opts for the 50-50 portfolio, as the one-percent reduction in expected return seems a small price to pay for the reduction in risk exposure achieved.

Step 7: Write the Investment Policy Statement

There are six components to an investment policy statement (IPS):

1. Key factual and account information, and summary of investor circumstances
2. Investment objectives, time horizon, and risk attitudes
3. Permissible asset classes, constraints, and restrictions
4. The asset allocation
5. Selection, monitoring, and control procedures
6. Signatures

Let's consider each of these in turn.

Key Factual and Account Information

This section should provide enough details about the account that a person walking in off the street would have all the basic account information. This statement begins by explaining the purpose of the account or accounts, and includes the identification of the values of the assets involved. It also lists the authorized decision makers, and provides the names and addresses of relevant parties. Next, it details the investor's key economic assumptions, and provides comments on the current investment environment. Finally, it should include the projected marginal tax rate for the investor and any other relevant tax information, a summary of current income and expenses of the investor, and, most importantly, the outlook for the investor's personal financial situation.

Investment Objectives, Time Horizon, and Risk Attitudes

The results of steps 2, 3, and 4 of the investment process, discussed above, are formally stated in this section. The investor's goals should include a statement addressing the desired rate of return, liquidity needs, net cash flow objectives, and income tax strategies. In most cases, the investor's time horizon will coincide with the investor's life expectancy. Many people might think that the primary goal should be the investor's retirement, which would mean the date the investor retires. However, given that many people now retire with projected retirement spans of 30 or more years, it must be remembered that nothing dramatic would be expected in the portfolio on the date of retirement. That is, there would not be much difference in an investor's risk tolerance one year prior to retirement (when he or she has one year of employment and 30 years of retirement in the future), versus at the time of retirement (when he or she is contemplating 30 years of retirement).

Although risk is traditionally expressed in terms of standard deviation of return on the portfolio, many clients will find this a meaningless concept. For this reason alone, it is valuable to consider additional measures of risk exposure, such as the potential magnitude of the portfolio's decline in any given year. Thus, a statement such as "declines of up to 5% or 10% in the market value of the portfolio in any one year can be tolerated," is a useful representation of risk exposure.[182] It is also important to recognize in the IPS that declines in value may occur, so that when they do occur, the advisor has documentation that the client was adequately advised about the possibility.

This section should also include evidence on the client's capacity to accept risk. This includes statements as to the adequacy of insurance coverage, dependents, nature of other income, and current degree of indebtedness.

Permissible Asset Classes, Constraints, and Restrictions

This section should be a summary of step 5 discussed above. It should identify both which assets are to be included, and which assets are to be excluded. There should be statements regarding pledging, hypothecating, lending securities, buying on margin, and short sales. There should also be a statement as to marketability requirements for the portfolio. In situations in

---

182. The concept of the maximum loss that can be tolerated is known as value at risk or VaR.

which there is a family business, or involvement or desired involvement in privately held companies, there should be a specification as to the percent of the portfolio that can be tied up in nonmarketable securities.

There should also be a statement regarding the extent of portfolio concentration, or the treatment of portfolio concentration. For example, an advisor may find that a client has inherited 100,000 shares of Exxon Mobile, and the stock currently trades at $90 per share. This means a holding of $9 million. Suppose the client's entire portfolio is valued at only $10 million. This represents a potential problem and it is clear that the IPS must address the issue of how this holding will be treated.

The Asset Allocation

This section should describe the asset-allocation model used in constructing the portfolio, as well as the statistical assumptions employed in the model. It should also indicate how the proposed asset allocation would have performed on a historical basis, or how it might be expected to perform in the future. Finally, it should lay out the rules for portfolio rebalancing (Step 9 of the investment process). Although we will discuss the issues associated with portfolio rebalancing later in the chapter, several issues must be discussed now.

The first issue involves establishing the frequency with which the IPS should be evaluated for rebalancing. Most people set a time interval for reviewing a portfolio, such as quarterly. The alternative is to rebalance as soon as one of the asset-allocation weights moves outside its target range (i.e., daily review).

The second issue involves defining the criteria that will determine when a portfolio is in need of rebalancing. The most common approach is to use fixed-percentage intervals. For example, if a portfolio's strategic asset allocation is 50% equity, 40% bonds, and 10% cash, the rebalancing triggers might be set at +/ 5% for each category. Thus, no rebalancing is needed as long as equities stay in the range of 45% to 55%, bonds in a range of 35% to 45%, and cash in a range of 5% to 15%. A more reasonable rebalancing trigger might be something like 10% of each target weight. Thus, the 50, 40, 10 portfolio would need rebalancing anytime the equity wondered out of the range of 45% to 55% (the same as above), but the bonds would rebalance outside the range of 36% to 44% (a variation of 10% of the 40% target), and the cash would rebalance outside the range of 9% to 11%.

Because the primary source of change in the value of a portfolio tends to come from the price changes in equities, rebalancing typically means selling bonds and cash to buy more stocks when stocks as a group have declined, and buying bonds and cash with the proceeds from the sale of stocks when stocks have been rising. Some people might call this strategy one of selling your "winners" and investing more in your "losers." Others would refer to this system as "buying low and selling high."

Selection, Monitoring, and Control Procedures

This section of the IPS deals primarily with the use of outside investment managers. The first part deals with the criteria for selecting a manager or managers. For example, it might specify how many managers should be used. It should certainly specify any quantitative criteria that should be utilized in selecting a manger. Naturally, it is likely that the final selection of a manager will rest not only on a set of quantitative criteria, but also upon the comfort level of the client and/or advisor in working with the specific managers.

There must be an agreement as to how frequently the investment managers need to report their results. Independent of their results, the portfolio managers should report certain events as they occur, including changes in their own financial condition, professional staff, investment strategy, and legal or regulatory issues that develop.

A second and different set of criteria should be developed for the removal of an investment manager. When managers are selected, it is usually the case that they are coming off stellar, or at least reasonable performances in recent years. Once selected, it should be understood that even the best managers can have off years. It is awkward to have to fire an investment manager, but easier to do if the criteria are set in advance.

EXAMPLE

What is the probability that an average manager will underperform his or her benchmark three years in a row? If we assume that the probability an average manager will underperform his or her benchmark is 50% percent (i.e., 0.50), then the probability of three consecutive years of underperformance is 0.50 x 0.50 x 0.50 = 0.125 or 12.5%. This means there is a one-in-eight chance such an event could be random.

What is the probability an above average manager will underperform his or her benchmark three years in a row? In this case, let's assume the probability of underperformance is 45%. This would mean that the probability of three consecutive years of underperformance is 0.45 x 0.45 x 0.45 = 0.0911 or 9.11%. This means there is about a 1-in-11 chance such an event could be random. Is it fair to fire what could be a superior portfolio manager when an event that has a 1-in-11 chance of happening randomly occurs?

Just as there are no surefire formulas for how to pick a "superior" investment manager, there are no surefire rules for when to get rid of a portfolio manager. Nobody advocates changing managers after only one year of poor performance. Similarly, few would argue that one should live with five or more years of poor performance. So, whether it is two, three, or four years of poor performance, and whether or not the investment manager should be given a year of probation, are items of debate that should be specified in the IPS.

The last item in this section should be the frequency with which the IPS itself is reviewed. Again, there is no definitive answer, and certainly no one would indicate a period of less than one year. One-, two-, or three-year intervals sound reasonable.

Signatures

As with all legal documents, this document needs to be signed. This signals its importance to BOTH the client and the portfolio advisor. The best protection an advisor has against disgruntled, and potentially litigious clients is an IPS signed by the client that has been followed. An IPS that has been signed by the advisor but not followed by the advisor is one of the best weapons for a disgruntled client.

Step 8: Select the Investments

Once the signed IPS is in place, then it is time for the advisor to pick the specific investments. If the investments are to be allocated to investment managers, then the criteria specified in section six of the IPS should be followed. If the advisor is going to select the investments independently, then there should be an understanding, if not a formal statement in the IPS, as to the criteria that will be followed.

It should be clear whether the advisor believes in efficient markets. If so, the strategy will be to buy index funds or construct portfolios that are designed to mimic large indices. If not, then the advisor's intention may be to engage in tactical asset allocation. Let's consider what is involved in this process.

Tactical-asset-allocation decisions differ from strategic decisions in several ways:

- Decisions are made for the purpose of beating the market rather than setting the desired level of risk exposure.
- These decisions are made more frequently.
- Decisions may include many more asset classes.

pure market timer   With regard to beating the market, a *pure-market timer* will be in the market when it is expected to rise and out of the market when it is expected to fall. The more common approach to market timing is to shift asset allocations within the guidelines of the ranges specified in the strategic asset allocation.

EXAMPLE

The strategic asset allocation for a portfolio might be specified as: 45%–60% in stocks, 40%–55% in bonds, and 0%–10% in cash equivalents. A bullish market timer would then change the portfolio to 60% in stocks and 40% in bonds. A bearish-market timer would put 45% in stocks, 45% in bonds, and 10% in cash equivalents. A neutral outlook might imply the following allocations: 50% in stocks, 45% in bonds, and 5% in cash equivalents.

Tactical allocation decisions may be made monthly, quarterly, or annually, or on an as-desired basis. Any changes in allocation weights that are not intended as long-term target objectives are, by definition, tactical allocation decisions.

Step 9: Monitoring, Managing, and Reporting

Just as monitoring and reporting requirements are established for investment managers, the advisor needs to also set requirements for reporting to the client. Portfolio evaluation techniques, which include the Sharpe ratio, the Treynor ratio, and Jensen's alpha, are the appropriate methods to use. For advisors with retail investment clients, calculating these values for each client's portfolio is rather daunting. It is quite easy to use these methods to evaluate mutual fund performance, however, because investor service firms perform these calculations regularly. While all the measures consider portfolio risk, the prudent advisor will compare performance results with mutual funds in the same generic class. For example, if the client's situation calls for an aggressive growth fund, comparing performance—even on a risk-adjusted basis—with income funds is not productive.

With regard to performance of the total portfolio, advisors should use benchmarks. Selecting market indices as benchmarks is tricky, because market indices do not have to pay transaction fees, management fees, or any other fees that normally accompany real portfolios that have real managers overseeing them. In addition, even the issue of computing the rate of return on the portfolio can become complicated when there is cash being added to and removed from the portfolio on an ongoing basis.

This last step of monitoring and reporting should, on a recurring basis, lead back to the first step. Remember, clients' situations may and do change. Clients age and as they do their risk tolerances change. Personal situations change as a result of marriage, divorce, birth of children, and death of parents. Dividends and interest accrue in a portfolio, and most clients make regular deposits into and withdrawals from their accounts, all of which create a continuous need for new investment decisions. In addition, changes in economic and market conditions will sometimes dictate that the portfolio be changed. For example, in recent years there has been a dramatic decline in yields on bonds and money market instruments. As a result, the expected rates of return on asset classes may no longer match the original assumptions. Finally, the portfolio itself will have performed better or worse than expected. Simply put, the advisor to an individual investor should repeat the prior eight steps periodically, noting in particular any change in the client's risk tolerance or goals.

Some advisors repeat this process on an annual basis, and others on a less frequent schedule. There appears to be no hard evidence supporting the selection of a particular interval for repeating the process. Certainly, anytime there is a major life event the process should be repeated. In the absence of such an event, the advisor should agree with the client on a schedule.

THE IMPACT OF PORTFOLIO SIZE ON RISK

A perennial question that financial planners must deal with is: What is the optimal number of securities for a portfolio? Unfortunately, there is no simple answer to this question—and it is important that the financial planner understand why there is no simple answer.

Evans and Archer published the classic research paper on optimal portfolio size in 1968.[183] They began their research study by randomly selecting 60 securities from a large database of stocks. For each of these 60 securities, they computed the standard deviation of returns over a fixed time period. They then computed the arithmetic average of the 60 standard deviations. They repeated the exercise by creating 60 portfolios, each of which contained two randomly selected securities. The standard deviations of returns for these 60 portfolios were computed and the arithmetic average again derived. This process was repeated for 60 portfolios of three randomly selected securities and repeated up to 60 portfolios of 40 randomly selected securities. For each portfolio size, the average of the 60 standard deviations was computed. Next, these 40 average standard deviations were graphed with the vertical axis showing the average standard deviation and the horizontal axis showing the size of a portfolio. Finally Evans and Archer computed the standard deviation for a portfolio consisting of every single security in their database. This was defined as the standard deviation of the market portfolio.

This exercise has been repeated many times using different data sets, different time periods, different holding periods, and so on. As one would expect, the actual numerical results differ slightly with each application, but the general principles that emerge are always the same. The typical graph that is produced is shown in the following figure. The general conclusions from these studies form some of the most important principles of investments today:

- On average, the total risk of a portfolio declines as additional securities are added to the portfolio.
- The total risk of a portfolio declines at a *decreasing* rate as additional securities are added. Thus, the addition of a third security to a two-security portfolio will reduce total risk by a substantially greater amount than will the addition of a 40th security to a 39-security portfolio.
- On average, the total risk of a portfolio converges downward toward the total risk of the market portfolio.

---

183. John Evans and Stephen Archer, "Diversification and the Reduction of Dispersion: An Empirical Analysis," *Journal of Finance* XXIV (1968): 761–769.

Figure 14-2
Portfolio Risk Declines as N Increases

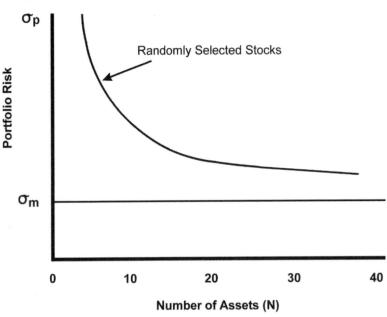

That is, diversification does not eliminate all risk. It only eliminates non-market or nonsystematic risk. This means that systematic risk becomes an increasing portion of the portfolio's total risk.

The Evans-Archer graph brings us to the crux of the optimal portfolio size question. If we assume that there is some cost to adding a security to a portfolio, then at some point the cost of adding a security to a portfolio is greater than the value of the reduction in risk from adding that security. Certainly for most investors the commission from buying 100 shares in each of two companies is more than the commission to buy 200 shares in one company. Some people would also argue that there is a monitoring cost. That is, a portfolio manager may have to spend more time monitoring stocks in a 50-stock portfolio than in a 10-stock portfolio. Hence, to the extent that each additional security necessitates additional time for monitoring, there is an implicit time cost when stocks are added to portfolios.

Let's ignore the monitoring cost issue by assuming that markets are efficient and therefore no monitoring is necessary. Let's also assume that the only transaction fee is the commission. If this were the case, then the optimal portfolio size is inversely related to the magnitude of the trading commission. This becomes our fifth principle:

- The lower the commission one pays per trade, the larger the number of securities that will be optimal.

If one paid no commission (for example, suppose one had a wrap account in which one paid an annual fee but did not pay any commissions per se), then in theory the optimal portfolio size becomes that of the market portfolio.

The Impact of Portfolio Composition on Optimal Portfolio Size

As one might suspect, the Evans-Archer graph can be quite sensitive to the composition of the portfolio. For example, suppose the securities that made up the portfolio were all mutual funds. Thus, each security would represent a portfolio of as many as several hundred or more securities. Hence, each security would already represent a highly diversified portfolio. In this case, the curve in *Figure 14-2* would converge much more quickly to the market portfolio than is the case when the securities represent individual stocks. This result can be easily seen by the drop in the risk exposure curve in *Figure 14-3*. Hence, the optimal number of holdings would likely be a much, much smaller number when one limits the holdings to only mutual funds.

Furthermore, if the mutual funds were load funds, then the optimal number of funds to hold would be limited. If they were no-loads, with no minimum investment requirement, then once again the optimal number of securities to hold would be potentially unlimited, even though there is negligible risk reduction as funds are added to the portfolio.

Figure 14-3
The Impact of Using Mutual Funds Rather than Individual Securities on Portfolio Risk

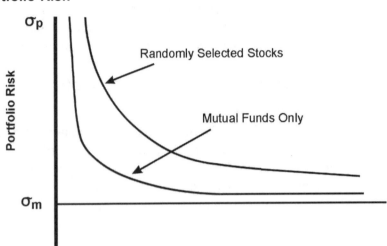

International Diversification

Another famous research piece looked at the effect of including securities of foreign companies in one's portfolio.[184] The stock markets in different countries appear to have a large component of independent variability. That is, a large part of the variability in their returns is unrelated to fluctuations in any one other country's domestic market. Thus, a strategy of adding foreign securities to a portfolio of domestic securities can be used to reduce the impact of the home country's business cycle. Investors can diversify internationally in a variety of ways. They can purchase shares in an international mutual fund, a U.S.-based multinational company, a foreign company's stock, or American depository receipts (ADRs) representing ownership of such securities.

Most advisors believe that at least some degree of international diversification is appropriate even though many U.S. corporations already have extensive international involvement. Although foreign stocks have, in recent years,

---

184. Bruno Solnik. "Why Not Diversify Internationally Rather Than Domestically?" *Financial Analysts Journal* 30 (1974): 48–54.

provided higher rates of return, the major benefit from international investing is diversification. The fact that foreign companies operate in markets in economies that do not coincide with the U.S. economy means that international investing reduces the variability—the risk—of the portfolio.

PORTFOLIO REBALANCING

An IPS should specify the frequency of rebalancing as well as the ranges to be tolerated. If the strategic allocation is 55%, with an acceptable range of 50%–60% for stocks, then as long as the stockholding is within this range, no trading is necessary. However, if during a bullish move, stocks increase to 60.1% of the portfolio, then should some stocks be sold? If so, then should the equity be repositioned to the original 55% target, or back to the edge of the target range?

Researchers have looked at some of the issues associated with the rebalancing process, and some of the results are actually counterintuitive to what most people would expect. One examination of the rebalancing process starts by assuming a cost function (e.g., a psychic cost) associated with a portfolio's asset allocation differing from the target asset allocation.[185] The rebalancing rules depend, in part, on the nature of the transaction fees. Two types are considered. One is where the transaction fee is always proportional to the size of the trade (e.g., the transaction fee is 5% of the value of the trade). The other type is a fixed dollar fee per trade (e.g., $20 per trade, regardless of the dollar value).

This research then shows how to compute the optimal range for the asset allocation, if the goal is to minimize the costs of the portfolio differing from the target ratio and to minimize the transactions fees. The calculation of the optimal range is rather complex, so let's assume the range is specified in the IPS. In the case where the transaction fees are proportional to the value of the trade, the optimal rebalancing scheme is to make no trades as long as the asset allocation is within the specified range, and then when it wanders outside of the range, to immediately adjust the portfolio just enough to move the actual allocation back to the limit, and not to the target. This produces superior results compared to a strategy of reviewing and rebalancing if necessary on a regular schedule, such as quarterly, and then resetting the allocation to the target percentage.

---

185. www.haas.berkley.edu/groups/finance/WP/rpf261.pdf, accessed July 19, 2010.

EXAMPLE

Suppose you are managing a portfolio for which the target asset allocation is 55% stock and the acceptable range is 50%–60%. In this case, if the commission is proportional to the size of the trade, then optimal rebalancing includes no trading as long as the stock allocation is within this range. However, if the percentage allocation were to end the day in excess of 60%, you would want to sell just enough stock and use the proceeds to buy other assets to move the stock allocation back to 60%. Similarly, if the portfolio were to end the day with less than 50% in stock, you would sell other assets and buy just enough stock to move back to 50%.

If there is an increase in transactions fees, then the size of the no-trade interval should also increase. Conversely, if the perceived variability in the returns on stocks were to decline, then the no-trade interval should decrease. The optimal no-trade interval is relatively immune to the differential between the expected rate of return on stocks and that of the other assets, and it is also relatively immune to changes in the risk-free interest rate.

If the transaction fees are viewed as fixed, rather than proportional to the value of trading, then optimal rebalancing changes only in the sense that there are now two trading ranges. There is a wider range that defines when trading takes place (as in the previous case), and there is also a narrower range, to which the adjustment is made.

EXAMPLE

Let's continue the previous example in which the acceptable asset allocation is 50%–60%, but in this case, let's assume there is also an inner range of, say, 52%–58%. The optimal rebalancing includes no trading as long as the stock allocation is within the 50%–60% range. However, if the percentage allocation were to end the day in excess of 60%, then you would sell just enough stock and use the proceeds to buy other assets to move the stock allocation back to 58%. Similarly, if the portfolio ends the day with less than 50% in stock, you would sell other assets and buy just enough stock to move back to 52%.

OTHER ASPECTS OF INVESTMENT SELECTION

Investment Effort

The monitoring of stocks, bonds, and cash equivalents can be a fairly straightforward process requiring minimal effort. This is particularly true when one holds actively traded securities. There is little to do because the market is quite efficient for highly marketable assets. By the time the financial advisor hears any news about General Electric, the news is incorporated into the stock price. As soon as the advisor starts to invest in securities that lack marketability, sets up hedged positions involving combinations of securities and options, or enters into futures contracts, then the need to monitor the portfolio goes up substantially. If a portfolio includes real assets, such as apartment buildings, racehorses, and so forth, then managing the assets will take a substantial amount of time. The investment advisor has to decide up front in conjunction with the client how much investment effort will be put into monitoring the portfolio. Presumably, the fees will match the effort.

Minimum Investment Size

Portfolios of some types of investments may be assembled with small sums whereas others require a much larger minimum commitment. Moreover, some investments have such low risk that a portfolio consisting of a single asset is an appropriate holding. For instance, a savings account can be opened for as little as $100 or less, and some higher-yielding bank certificates are available in $500 denominations. Some mutual funds will accept initial deposits of $1,000. Indeed, mutual funds offer an attractive way for investors to participate in the stock and bond market with relatively small sums of money. Many collectibles sell for a few hundred dollars or less. On the other hand, several thousand dollars are generally needed to purchase a single stock or bond position efficiently. If one believes that a minimum of 20 securities is needed for a well-diversified stock portfolio, and if an average investment of $3,000 is made in each holding, then the investor would need to commit at least $60,000 to create a diversified portfolio of 20 common stocks.

A single real estate purchase (to say nothing of a diversified real estate portfolio) is likely to require at least several thousand dollars (more likely tens of thousands of dollars) for just the down payment. Similarly, most brokers will not accept commodity accounts having less than $25,000 – $50,000 in investor capital.

Ethical and Moral Appeal

Investments may also differ substantially in their ethical and moral appeal, particularly to certain groups of investors. Some investors take the attitude that if an activity is legal, it is a proper area in which to invest. Other investors, however, want their investment dollars associated only with activities of which they personally approve. What is socially unacceptable for some, however, is not socially unacceptable for others. Social responsibility is largely in the eye of the beholder. No doubt, many investors would draw the line at pornography and prostitution even where these activities are legal. Others would refuse to become slumlords. Still others would object to investments in companies involved with one or more of the following types of products or activities: alcohol, tobacco, armaments, war toys, pollutants, non-unionized employees, unionized employees, child labor, misleading advertising, and poor safety records.

A decision not to invest in certain companies or industries always raises the question of whether this constraint on a portfolio means this portfolio is less likely to achieve an appropriate risk-adjusted rate of return. Most of the research in this field suggests that the answer is no. First, as noted above, there is no universal agreement as to what are inappropriate industries or companies in which to invest, so what one investor objects to may be perfectly reasonable to another. Hence, there are no industries or companies that are so objectionable that the few investors willing to invest in them are assured above-market rates of return. Second, most people have a relatively small list of industries or companies in which they would not invest. So this constraint typically has minimal impact on a portfolio recommendation list. In fact, the three screens most frequently cited by socially responsible mutual funds are to exclude companies in the alcoholic drinks, tobacco products, and gambling industries.[186]

Ethical Issue in Financial Planning

As a financial planner, you are meeting with some new clients, Joe Bob and Sallie Mae Jenkins. They are in their mid-30s, are both employed, have young children, and have a high tolerance for risk. They agree on a portfolio that is 80% stocks, 15% bonds, and 5% cash equivalents. You then suggest 25 of your favorite stocks, headed by the leading manufacturer of cigarettes in the country. This is a company you feel has been terribly undervalued in recent years and represents an excellent investment opportunity. Joe and Sallie Mae immediately object, because they believe smoking tobacco is a sin. Good financial planning means you will have to remove this stock from your list, as your objective is to help the clients achieve their goals in a manner satisfactory to them and not force on them what you think is in their best financial interest.

---

186. See Craig L. Israelsen, "The Wages of Sin: Are Investors Sacrificing Returns by Engaging in Socially Responsible Investing?" *Financial Planning* (February 2006): 100.

Splitting the Difference

If a client has only one investment account, then the strategic asset allocation applies to this account. However, many clients have multiple accounts. Furthermore, the investment income and capital gains in some accounts are either tax exempt or tax deferred provided certain conditions are met. The standard recommendation for tax efficiency is that one should hold assets with high current income (which usually means bonds) in one's tax-exempt or tax-deferred account, and investments with primarily capital gains (which usually means stocks) in one's regular accounts (that is, those without special tax treatment). If the percentage allocation between the non-qualified and qualified accounts exactly matches the client's optimal stock-bond allocation based on risk tolerance, then optimal tax-efficiency also produces optimal asset allocation. Invariably, this matching does not happen, which means that some sort of trade-off must be made between tax-efficiency and risk-tolerance. The amount of assets in a tax-exempt or tax-deferred account is usually not something one has much control over.

EXAMPLE

Drew and Annie Watson are new clients. They have accumulated $50,000 in their company's 401(k) plan and hold $100,000 in personal assets. Their 401(k) is invested entirely in stock mutual funds, and their personal assets are 50% stocks and 50% bonds. You and the Watsons decide on a strategic asset allocation for all of their investments of 50% stocks, 40% bonds, and 10% cash equivalents. In dollars, this translates into $75,000 in stocks, $60,000 in bonds, and $15,000 in cash equivalents. The obvious first step in executing the plan is to sell the stock funds in the 401(k) and replace them with bond funds. This provides $50,000 of the desired $60,000 investment in bonds, which means that the regular stock account will hold $75,000 in stocks, $10,000 in bonds, and $15,000 in cash equivalents. Note that since the purpose of the cash equivalents is to provide cash reserves, they must not be in the 401(k) plan, because this would make them inaccessible unless a steep penalty is paid. As a result of strictly following the asset allocation plan, the Watsons end up with bonds in their taxable account! Hence, the Watsons will end up sacrificing tax efficiency to achieve their strategic asset allocation. The alternative is to move away from their strategic asset allocation to achieve more tax efficiency.

To complicate the example, suppose that going forward the stocks have substantial price appreciation. This will likely mean that in order to stay close to the strategic asset allocation, the Watson's will have to sacrifice more tax efficiency.

Concentrated Portfolios

A particular problem arises when a client ends up with what is known as a concentrated portfolio. This is a portfolio in which one or a few securities have disproportionate weights. There is no mathematical definition as to what constitutes a concentrated portfolio and no precise description, but when it exists a capable financial planner will recognize it. Recognition is one thing, action is another since most of the time there is a price to pay to reduce the concentration. The problem with concentration is that it exposes the investor to non-market risk. Unless the investor has an incredibly strong reason to believe that the security (or securities) creating the undue concentration is (are) expected to have excess return, there is no reward for the concentration to compensate for the risk exposure.

EXAMPLE

Consider two portfolios, both valued at $1 million. In Portfolio A, one holding (a stock) is worth $800,000, and the other $200,000 is nicely diversified across various securities and asset classes. In Portfolio B, there are 200 different holdings, no one of which is worth more than $20,000. Portfolio A is a concentrated portfolio, and B is well-diversified. The problem is that the variability of returns for portfolio A is almost certain to be substantially larger than that for portfolio B. If the value of the one large holdings in A collapses, the portfolio will perform miserably. If the value of any one holding in B collapses, the overall rate of return may still be quite attractive.

There are two situations in which it is relatively easy to deal with a concentrated holding. The first is when the concentration occurs in a tax-deferred or tax-exempt account for which there is no restriction on selling the asset. In this case, part or all of the concentrated holding can be sold and replaced with a set of diversified holdings. The other situation occurs when the cost basis actually exceeds the market value of the asset. In this case the holding can be partially or completely liquidated, and with favorable tax consequences.

EXAMPLE

Last year, Andrew Jones inherited a $20 million stock holding in Rooster Corporation from his mother; this is his primary asset. Because it is an inheritance, the cost basis of the stock was stepped up to its market value at the time of his mother's death. Since the time of the inheritance, the stock has not performed well, and the holding is now worth only $16 million. Andrew seeks your advice. Serious consideration should be given to selling a significant portion of the stock to introduce needed diversification into his asset holdings. Such a move would also reap tax benefits from the capital loss.

The more common case is that the concentrated position occurs in a taxable account. The concentration usually comes about because one security has strongly outperformed the rest. In this case, there will be a substantial capital gain associated with the position. Selling the position creates a capital-gains tax, which will reduce the value of the account when the tax is paid. Nonetheless, this is sometimes the best course of action. Capital-gains tax rates are at historically low levels (the top capital-gains tax rate is 15%). It is, right now, a relatively cheap tax to pay. Some clients will have an aversion to paying a capital-gains tax. (After all, aren't they going to a financial planner to help them avoid paying taxes?) In these situations, the planner may have to give the client "permission" to take the profit and pay the taxes. If the client absolutely loathes the idea of paying any capital-gains taxes, then one strategy is to hold the stocks until the client dies, and obtain a step-up in cost basis. Of course, this may mean the client is only substituting an estate tax for a capital-gains tax, and depending on the size of the client's estate, the estate tax could be substantially more expensive.

An alternative is to set up some sort of hedge with the position. Usually, options would provide the best opportunity for hedging. The most common strategy is to set up what is known as a *collar*. A collar involves writing call options with strike prices above the current market price, and using the proceeds to buy put options with strike prices below the current market price.

EXAMPLE

Consider again Andrew Jones who now owns $16 million worth of Rooster Corporation. Andrew does not want to sell the stock, as he believes that would be an emotional betrayal of his mother's inheritance. The stock trades at $50 per share. You note that a call option with a strike price of $55 can be written for $3 per share. Similarly, a put option for $47.50 can be purchased for $3 per share. By writing the calls and using the proceeds to buy the puts, the collar can be established for only the cost of the commissions. Now, if the stock does well, Andrew has the opportunity to sell it at 10% above the current price (i.e., selling at $55 rather than $50). If the stock does poorly, he can limit any further losses to 5% of the current price (i.e., selling at $47.50, rather than $50). Thus, the collar allows Andrew to reap some price appreciation, and have the assurance of limited future loss. Although the collar doesn't deal with the emotional issue, it allows Andrew time to get used to the idea of selling the stock. If the idea of selling the stock is still repugnant, the collar can be unwound.

If the client is philanthropically inclined, then another solution is to give some of the holding to a favorite charity. This is particularly attractive if the stock has a low cost basis relative to the current market price. There are tax rules regarding how much charitable deduction a person can take in one year. If the value of the contribution exceeds this amount, the excess charitable contribution could be carried forward and used in subsequent years, again, with limits.

If the client wants some income from the holding, then the gift could be in the form of a charitable remainder trust (CRT). If the client wants some value of the holding to go to his or her estate and for the charity to have some immediate income, the gift could be in the form of a charitable lead trust (CLT).

It is certainly possible that the client may not have good documentation for the cost basis of at least some of the shares of the holding. An example might be where many of the shares were purchased through a dividend reinvestment program (to be discussed later). Shares with unknown cost bases make particularly good assets to give to charities.

If the client is not philanthropically inclined, but loves his or her family (or at least tolerates them), then another strategy is to give substantial blocks to family members. If the stock is valued at more than its cost basis, then the cost basis moves to the receiver of the stock. In addition, the holding period is reset to the date of the gift. A major benefit would be realized if the beneficiary could sell the gift (after one year), and be taxed in a lower tax bracket.

Another possibility is to give some stock to someone who would be expected to leave it back to the donor at the recipient's death. For example, the client gives $1 million worth of stock, which has a cost basis of $10,000, to a grandparent (let's assume no gift tax or estate tax implications), and there is no legally binding requirement to return the stock. The grandparent intends upon his or her death to will the stock back to the original holder. If the grandparent survives at least one year, as required under Sec. 1014(e) of the Internal Revenue Code, the stocks will have a step-up in basis to fair market value at the time of death. The stock could be immediately sold with no tax implication. Of course, there is always the risk the grandparent might give the stock to someone else, or sell it and spend the money.

Still another strategy is to use the equity value of the large holding to buy other securities on margin. Although the margin loan increases the risk of the portfolio, the additional securities would provide some diversification to reduce the risk of the portfolio.

There are multiple ways in which a client may come into a concentrated holding. Nonetheless, it is normally a "fly-in-the-ointment" type of problem that usually has no easy solution.

DOLLAR-COST AVERAGING

The most trivially obvious suggestion for investing is "buy low, sell high." The only problem with following this advice is that no one knows at the time whether the current price will later be viewed as a high price or a low price! Dollar-cost averaging is a strategy that attempts to put this advice into practice. In simple terms, dollar-cost averaging is the investment of a fixed amount of money at specified time intervals. For example, an investor might commit to buy $1,000 worth of a stock or mutual fund on the first day of each month for a period of one year. Investing a fixed dollar amount per period means that investors buy more shares when prices are low than when they are high. The benefit of such a strategy is that it frequently results in a lower average purchase price per share. It also helps some investors who are reluctant to invest a large sum of money in a single shot.

EXAMPLE

You have $9,000 to invest, but are afraid to plunk the money down all at once. So, you opt to dollar-cost in a mutual fund average over the next three months by buying $3,000 worth of shares today, and then another $3,000 at the end of each of the next two months. If the NAV of the fund (a no-load fund) is $20.00 today, $18.50 in one month, and $21.50 in two months, what is the total number of shares purchased and the average cost per share?

Answer: The number of shares purchased each month is $3,000 divided by the NAV at the time of purchase, or 150.000, 162.162, and 139.535. The total number of shares purchased is the sum of these three numbers, or 451.697. The average cost per share is $9,000 divided by the number of shares purchased, or $19.925. If you had purchased all the shares initially, you would have bought 450 shares ($9,000/$20.00), for an average purchase price of $20. If the example involved more purchase dates and if there were more volatility in the price of the security purchased, then the difference in cost basis and the number of shares purchased would be more dramatic.

Unless a stock goes into a persistent decline, dollar-cost averaging will accomplish its objective. It works best when the stock has an early decline and a later rise. It does not, however, protect the investor against losses in a steadily declining market.

EXAMPLE

Hernando DeSoto, a new client, has just found out that he has inherited $1,000,000 from a long-lost uncle. After a consultation, the two of you agree that his strategic asset allocation should be 80% stocks, 15% bonds, and 5% cash equivalents. You then present a list of 40 stocks that would represent an appealing diversified portfolio of common stocks. He immediately blanches when he realizes you are proposing to take $800,000 of his newly acquired wealth to buy stocks the next day. He says, "But suppose the market starts going down?" In this case, he would surely be better off waiting. You then remember that many investors fear regret more than they desire success. That is, they are more concerned that they will regret rushing into an investment than they are concerned about paying a higher price later. Of course, such an attitude could easily lead to perpetual postponement of the purchase of a stock.

To overcome this fear of regret, you suggest dollar-cost averaging, because if stock prices fall, he can buy more shares later. You propose to invest $40,000 per month over the next 20 months until the portfolio reaches its strategic asset allocation. Hernando is quite pleased with this plan and agrees immediately to begin the investment program.

The only problem with the above scenario is that research has shown that in terms of expected future wealth, Hernando would do best if he agreed to plunk down all $800,000 immediately.[187] However, getting investors to do what is best for them sometimes requires the use of suboptimal tactics, because it is the only way to get the job done.

Many people have no other option but to engage in dollar-cost averaging; often, they aren't even aware that is what they are doing. For example, employees who contribute a certain dollar amount of their paycheck each month to a defined-contribution plan in which they have specified certain investments for the account (usually mutual funds) are engaging in dollar-cost averaging. Employees probably think of this as a long-term savings program—and it is— but they are also using a dollar-cost averaging strategy.

---

187. Richard E. Williams and Peter W. Bacon, "Lump Sum Beats Dollar-Cost Averaging," *Journal of Financial Planning* (June 2004): 92–95.

EXAMPLE

Your clients, Larry and Eliza Baker, are a young couple who have come to you to create a financial plan that will allow them to enjoy a comfortable retirement. You note they have no accumulated savings. They indicate they are trying, but when they see money in their checking account toward the end of each month, they always think of something they really need to buy and promise themselves they will start their investment program next month. You are aware that one of the easiest ways to save is to invest some of each paycheck first, at the start of the month, and then feel free to spend what is left over at the end of the month. You suggest an automatic withdrawal plan, whereby the Bakers, who receive their paychecks on the first day of each month, can set up a plan to automatically transfer $500 on the first day of each month to an investment account. It could be a brokerage account, a mutual fund, or even a direct purchase plan (to be discussed shortly). Not only will this start the necessary savings plan, it will also likely establish a form of dollar-cost averaging.

Dividend Reinvestment Plans

One form of dollar-cost averaging is a dividend reinvestment plan (DRIP)—a program in which stockholders can reinvest their dividends directly into the company's stock. These plans may acquire either existing or newly issued stock. Typically the corporation sends the dividends of participating stockholders to the managing bank's trust department. This bank maintains an account for each shareholder. Each participant is credited with his or her shares less brokerage fees and administrative costs. Many DRIPs also permit additional stock purchases for cash. Large round-lot purchases by the plan tend to reduce the brokerage fees each participant would otherwise have paid. Some companies give discounts on their dividend reinvestments. Firms selling newly issued shares charge no brokerage fees on the transactions.

Dividend reinvestment plans have a number of advantages. From the firm's standpoint, the plans add to stockholder goodwill, increase demand for the firm's stock, save some dividend-related expenses, and encourage small stockholders to increase ownership. In addition, plans involving new share purchases reduce the firm's debt-to-equity ratio, provide a regular source of equity capital, and permit new equity to be sold without incurring underwriting fees or other flotation costs.

There is one drawback to dividend reinvestment plans, particularly for investors with larger portfolios. When investors have dividend income during the year, they can accumulate sufficient cash to purchase stocks in other companies, which increases the diversification of their portfolios. When one enrolls in a DRIP, one ends up buying more shares in the stocks held in the existing portfolio. Thus, DRIPs reduce the ability of an investor to increase the diversification of his or her portfolio by acquiring stock in other companies with cash accumulated from dividend income.

Direct Purchase Plans

Many companies now also offer a direct purchase plan (DPP). With a DPP the investor opens an account and arranges for a regular debit to a checking or savings account to purchase new shares. DPPs have the wonderful benefit of giving investors the opportunity to build a stock portfolio with what may be relatively small monthly purchases. They have the same drawback as DRIPs in that they limit diversification potential. However, DPPs are most attractive for new, younger investors who typically lack the resources to immediately build a diversified portfolio. In addition, after investors have accumulated a certain amount of shares in any one company, they can switch the DPP to other companies, thus building diversification over time.

An alternative to a DPP for one company is to set up an account with a firm that allows the investor to create what is essentially a direct purchase plan for a variety of stocks, index funds, and even closed-end bond funds. Some brokerage firms have even set up similar programs for their clients and at times have also allowed for reinvestment of dividends in the stock paying the dividends. From the stockholder's perspective, this ends up creating fractional shares.

Employee Stock Purchase Plans

Corporate employees will sometimes have the opportunity to participate in an employee stock purchase plan (ESPP). These plans are defined in Internal Revenue Code Section 423. They allow a company to sell stock to employees at a discount from the fair market price. To be approved for special tax treatment, the option to buy the stock must be offered to employees on a nondiscriminatory basis. The option cannot be transferred, that is, only the employee can use the option during his or her lifetime.

If all of the conditions of the plan are met, then the purchase price of the stock can be as low as 85% of the fair market value either on the offer/grant date or on the purchase date, whichever is less. Most plans allow employees to purchase stock every six months via payroll withholding.

The plans have good and bad features for both the company and the employee. They are a good deal for the company because it is able to raise equity capital without any transaction fees, other than the discount given to the employee. They are also good for the company because employees will presumably become more effective workers as an increasing amount of their financial assets become tied up in the company. The drawback for the company is that if the discount given is substantial, then wealth is effectively being transferred from the existing shareholders to the employees.

ESPPs can be quite attractive for the employee if the discount is substantial. In addition, they can act as a forced savings plan. Remember, many folks will not save out of their paycheck; they will save only when the money is transferred elsewhere. (This is the same reason the vast majority of people overpay on their income taxes.) Hence, an ESPP provides an opportunity to save that they might not otherwise have.

The drawbacks for the employee are twofold. First, if a company is struggling financially, then the employee is at risk of being laid off at the same time when the company's stock price may be hitting new lows. Hence, the employee has the double whammy of a significant drop in income occurring simultaneously with a significant drop in wealth. The other drawback is that if the employee accumulates a substantial amount of company stock through this plan, then he or she ends up with a concentrated holding, a potential evil we have already discussed.

BEHAVIORAL ASPECTS OF INVESTING

When we earlier introduced the topic of modern portfolio theory, we assumed that investors acted as economically rational people. Economists call this type of person the "economic man." Economic men (and women) base their investment decisions on the desire to hold portfolios on the highest possible indifference curve.

In the last 30 to 40 years, researchers have started to look at decision-making processes used by individuals, and have discovered that most individuals do not act like an "economic man." This study of the personal financial decision-making process is known as *behavioral finance*. Financial advisors need to understand the various characteristics of behavioral finance, so they can work more effectively with their clients in helping them make the best possible set of decisions.

Patterns and Predictions

A good first example of characteristics studied under behavioral finance is the desire to see patterns. The ability to spot patterns can be critically important to success and even survival. For example, those early hunters who noticed that certain animals would approach water holes at certain times of the day were more likely to be successful in their hunt for food than those hunters who failed to notice patterns in the behavior of their prey. In addition, people are more comfortable when they see patterns. No one likes to think that they live in a world that is completely random. An example of this is the saying that "tragedies come in threes." This can be comforting in that if two tragedies occur in quick succession, those affected can take comfort that there will only be one more tragedy, and then they will not have to suffer any more tragedies for a long time.

We talked earlier about the efficient market theory, and the fact that the implication of this theory is that stock price changes are like a random pattern. This pattern is random because investors establish an expected rate of return for a stock, based on their expectation of future news and events regarding that stock. If these expectations are unbiased, then whether the actual news or events turn out to be better or worse than expected will be random. If the price of the stock reacts to the difference between the expected news and events and the actual news and events, then the price changes will in fact be random. The randomness of stock price changes is difficult for many investors to comprehend, much less, believe. They are convinced there must be some sort of pattern in stock price changes that will predict future price changes. Hence, they look at charts until they believe they have identified patterns with predictive value, and then trade based on these patterns.

Because people are uncomfortable with randomness, we often seek to find causation, even when there is none and even when the effect of causation is absurd. For example, people often think, "if I take an umbrella, it won't rain!" In the stock market, when people place an order to buy a stock in the morning, and the stock price drops in the afternoon, they will attribute the decline to their having purchased the stock.

EXAMPLE

Suppose there is an aggregate consensus that the expected rate of return on a particular stock for the year is 10%; this is based on projections of the company's sales, net income, market share, and new product development, as well as the general trend in the economy overall and the industry in which the company is operating. The actual rate of return will turn out to be higher or lower depending on how actual events play out, compared to people's expectations. If events fall short of expectations, the actual rate of return might be only 5%, and if events turn out to be better than expected, the actual rate of return might be 15%. So it is both possible for a stock to steadily appreciate over time, and to have its price behavior on a day-to-day, week-to-week, month-to-month, or even year-to-year basis be random.

An offshoot of the desire to see patterns is the propensity to project past patterns into the future, even in the face of illogical consequences. If a company's income grows at a rate of 30% a year for 10 years, it is very easy to project such an increase in income for another 10 years. Thus, if a company had net income of $10 million, with a growth rate of 30% for 10 years, then the net income would be $137.86 million. If one projects that growth rate forward, then after another 10 years net income would be $1.90 billion. With an income of $10 million, this company would be considered really small. With annual income of $1.90 billion, it would be among the largest companies in our economy. Such growth is truly unlikely to happen in just 20 years.

In the face of uncertainty, people like to believe there are gurus who truly understand the world and can tell us the future. This is why some people make a living based on activities such as astrology, palm reading, and fortune-telling. Most of us think of ourselves as too sophisticated to be taken in by these charlatans, but then we turn around and listen with suspended disbelief to market forecasters who claim they know where the market is headed. Again, it is more comforting to our psyche to believe there are all-wise individuals who can figure out the future, rather than to accept that the future is random and unpredictable.

Many people incorporate hindsight bias. They like to believe that they would have predicted a certain event or bet on a certain team if they had only thought about it or taken action. Thus, after the Super Bowl is played, many people are convinced they would have bet on the winning team if they had actually taken the time to study the teams beforehand and placed a bet. Perhaps this is part of why so many analysts can tell us how clearly one should have seen certain emerging patterns. A discussion based on perfect certainty of how one should have invested in the past, makes it tempting to use that financial advisor for the future!

The Overly Optimistic Individual

In theory, the value of an asset should be the same, regardless of the way it is sold. However, in experiments, Dutch auctions consistently produce higher prices than sealed-bid auctions. In a Dutch auction, the seller sets a "high" offer price for an asset to be sold, and then starts the process of lowering this price until someone states he or she will buy at that price. A sealed-bid auction is one in which all prospective buyers submit bids simultaneously; when the bids are opened, the highest bidder buys the asset for that price.

A variation of this phenomenon can be observed in auctions in which everyone interested in bidding on an asset has only a rough idea of what it is worth. In this case, the ultimate buyer is likely to be a person who has erred on the high side of the true value.

Compounding the fact that at least some individuals have a tendency to overvalue an asset, is the fact that most people believe they are above average. Garrison Keillor has a standard line in which he says that all of the children in his fictional town of Lake Woebegone are above average. Research has shown that the vast majority of individuals believe they are above average in terms of driving skill, humor, and congeniality. Nearly everyone believes he or she will live longer than average. There is actually a reason why people conclude they are above average. It is that people attribute successes in life to their own talents and skills, and failures in life to bad luck, other people, or circumstances beyond their control.

Not surprisingly, during extended bull-market periods, self-confidence in trading skills grows, particularly among men. There is also a propensity for trading volume to increase. In other words, investors tend to attribute stock market profits to their own skills and not to the general level of rising prices, even in the face of the fact that people who trade more tend to underperform in the market. However, investors also attribute poor performance to bad luck.[188]

One recent study found that there is a high level of self-confidence among experienced investors. This shows up in the selection of portfolios made up

---

188. Shefrin, Hersh, *Beyond Greed and Fear: Understanding Behavioral Finance and the Psychology*, 2002, Oxford University Press.

of fewer securities (i.e., more investment in each individual holding), and a lack of consideration of the correlation of returns among the securities held.[189] Simply put, experienced, confident investors tend to act as if the rules of diversification do not apply to them.

To overcome these natural phenomena, bids should be made by groups of people, rather than individuals. In groups, it is more likely that there will be a pessimist to offset an optimist, thus leading to a compromise decision that is more likely to result in a reasonable bid. However, it should also be noted that group decisions tend to involve more risk than individual decisions. One likely reason for this is that in a group decision, an individual believes he or she can blame "the group" for a bad result, rather than be individually responsible if something goes wrong. Simply put, group decisions may result in fairer estimates of value, but also riskier choices of action.

The Law of "Small" Numbers

One of the classic laws of statistics is the law of "large" numbers. This law states that as a sample size gets larger, the mean of the sample will approach the mean of the population. As an example, consider a jar filled with 1,000 beads; some are red and the rest green. If a person does not know the percentage that is red, he or she can take a sample. If the sample is the entire population, i.e., the person looks at every bead in the jar, then the percentage is known with certainty. Most people would be happy to take a smaller sample, and if 60% of the sample is red, they will assume that 60% of all the beads are red. In some cases, the population is simply too large to count. For example, if a person wants to know how many adults in the U.S. feel they will be able to save adequately for retirement, it would be onerous to ask every single adult. Hence, we sample. Most public opinion polls now announce a margin of error along with their results. So, after sampling a large number of adults, one might say that 30% of people feel they will have adequately saved for retirement, with a margin of error of plus or minus 4%. The key point here is that the smaller the sample size, the larger the margin of error.

Even though this brief discussion of statistical sampling may seem obvious, most people, even well-trained professionals, will consistently ignore the reality of the importance of sample size, and will make inferences on really small samples. In the case of the jar filled with 1,000 beads, people may

---

189. Werner DeBondt, "A Portrait of the Individual Investor," *European Economic Review* 42 (1998): 831–844.

prefer to take out 10, as opposed to say 50 beads, and draw a conclusion about the percentage of red beads in the jar based on this small sample size. Generally, they will be just as confident as if they had sampled 50 beads.

Similarly, investors have a propensity to base expectations on small samples of rates of return. If asked what is a reasonable annual rate of return to earn in the stock market, most people will base their response on what the market has done in the last two or three years, rather than what it has done over the last 50 or more years. Investors want to buy more of the assets in their portfolios that have recently done well and sell those that have done poorly. However, doing so greatly diminishes the diversification of said portfolios.

It's All in the Packaging

Framing is a significant issue for investors. *Framing* is the manner in which an issue is presented. A good example can be found in an experiment recently conducted in the offices of a large tax-preparation firm in a large, Midwestern city. Some customers were given the opportunity to receive a 50% match on contributions to an IRA account made at the same time they filed their tax returns. Others were offered a 33 1/3% cash-back rebate on their contribution. In economic terms, the two offers were identical. If a person contributed $3,000, then a one-third rebate was $1,000, so the person ended up with a $3,000 IRA account, and was out-of-pocket only $2,000. Conversely, if the person contributed $2,000, then the 50% match gave them a $3,000 deposit for a $2,000 out-of-pocket expense. A larger percentage of people took the matching offer rather than the rebate offer, and those doing the matching offer were more likely to contribute.

An even better example of framing is provided by Benartzi and Thaler[190] who gave different groups of investors five funds from which to choose. Some funds were all-equity, others were balanced, and still others were bond only. The result was that the more equity funds presented among the choices, the higher the percentage of capital invested in equity.

In a similar study, the authors gave different investors combinations of portfolios from which to choose.[191] Invariably, the middle choices, in terms of risk exposure, were favored by investors. Thus, a portfolio of 90% equity and

---

190. Shlomo Benartzi and Richard Thaler, "Naïve Diversification Strategies in Retirement Savings Plans," *American Economic Review* 91(2001): 79–98.

191. Shlomo Benartzi and Richard Thaler, "How Much Is Investor Autonomy Worth?" *Journal of Finance* 57 (2002): 1593–1616.

10% bonds would likely be preferred if the alternative choices were 100% equity or 80% equity and 20% bonds. However, if the choices are 90%, 80%, and 70% equity, with the rest in bonds, then the 90% equity tends to be rejected as it is now one of the extreme choices.

EXAMPLE

After analyzing a client's risk tolerance and financial needs, a financial planner strongly believes the client should hold a portfolio of 70% equity and 30% bonds. The best way to ensure the client will agree with this recommendation is for the planner to present it to the client as the middle choice of three choices. One of the other two would be riskier, and the third would be safer.

A classic example of framing involves gains and losses, which are thought of relative to the size of an investment, rather than in absolute terms. If a person wants to buy something that costs $15 at the local hardware store, and notes that by traveling across town, he or she can save $5, that person is very likely to make the trip for the 33 1/3% savings. However, if the local purchase price is $500, and the same item is available across town for $495, the same buyer is unlikely to make the trip. Clients are more likely to haggle over a few dollars when they are tied to a small expense, as opposed to when they are associated with a large expense.

The "1/N" Approach to Investing

One of the classic examples of investing involves clients who, when given a relatively small menu of investment choices, generally invest equally in all of the choices.[192] Thus, if the planner recommends five funds to a client (that is, N equals 5) and lets the client allocate his or her money among the funds, the most common investment choice is for the client to put 20% (that is, 1/N) of his or her capital into each fund. One explanation is that people dread regret more than they love success. Hence, if given five choices, the client's primary fear will be that he or she will fail to put any money into the choice that performs best. Therefore, to assure that the best performing investment will be chosen, the client selects all of the investments.

There is a secondary effect that occurs when a client is given too many choices. The more choices a client is given, the more likely the client will

---

192. Bernartzi, Shlomo and Richard H. Thaler, "Naive Diversification in Defined Contribution Savings Plans." *American Economic Review* 91(1), 2001: 79–98.

do nothing. This is sometimes referred to as "analysis paralysis." Thus, a good number of good choices will likely assure a client will end up with a well-diversified portfolio. Too many choices, and the client will likely do nothing.

Mental Accounting

Investors have separate mental accounts, if not physically different accounts, for different goals; and they associate different risk tolerances with these accounts. Suppose an individual has $100,000 in an IRA account intended to support retirement, and another $20,000 in a Coverdell account. The former has a riskier asset composition than the latter. If there is a $1,000 gain in the IRA account, the individual is more likely to invest that money aggressively than if the $1,000 gain shows up in the Coverdell account. In either case, the individual is $1,000 richer, and can choose to apply it toward the retirement account or the college fund. In general, the individual will tend to keep the money in the account in which it accrued, and invest it with the risk tolerance of that account.

SELLING A CLIENT ON A PLAN

Earlier, we discussed how a planner may use the concept of dollar-cost averaging to move a client into a heavy-investment program and overcome the fear of regret the client may be experiencing with regard to buying all of the stocks today. This is just one example of how sometimes a financial planner has to create some type of story in order to give the client the confidence he or she needs to agree to set up a particular plan. In other words, the financial planner has a good sense of what the client needs to do, but explaining this with facts using such terms as expected return, standard deviation, covariance, correlation, and strategic and tactical asset allocations, may leave a client too confused to act. Hence, sometimes the financial planner needs to give the client a "common sense" way to look at the portfolio and the investment process. In this section, we will consider three stories that a planner can tell a client.

Building a Bond Portfolio

The planner and the client agree to invest $2,000,000 in Treasury bonds. The client is super conservative and would like to put all of it in short-term bonds. However, the planner appreciates that the yield curve is currently upward sloping and, to meet the client's income needs, the portfolio needs to be at least 50% in long-term bonds. The planner could simply explain to the client that 50% in long-term bonds is necessary for income purposes, and 50% can be put in short-term bonds to reduce the variability of the portfolio's return. A better story might be to tell the client to put 50% of the portfolio into 10-year bonds, and 50% into one-year bonds. If rates fall, the prices of the 10-year bonds will rise, and the portfolio will have a strong rate of return. If rates rise, the investor can hold onto the long-term bonds and take one-tenth of the short-terms bonds (i.e., 5% of the total portfolio) and use that to buy more 10-year bonds. If rates rise for each of the 10 years, the 10-year bonds will have matured and the client will still have his or her liquidity. Furthermore, the client will never have given up liquidity, as he or she will always have a substantial portion of the portfolio in short-term securities.

Portfolio Liquidation: Scenario #1

You are discussing strategic asset allocation with a newly retired client. He has $1,000,000 in assets and wants to generate $50,000 in income per year from the portfolio. As a financial planner you know that what he actually wants is not $50,000 in income but $50,000 in cash. There is a big difference. A plan to generate $50,000 in income would mean a portfolio dominated by long-term, fixed income securities. A plan to generate $50,000 in cash would mean that the money could come from maturing bonds or from the sale of securities, as well as from interest and dividends that accrue to the account. You know one of the greatest fears of retired clients is the concept of "liquidating the principal." You also know that, given the strong chance that this client may live for at least another 20 years or so, he or she must have a significant holding in equities or face substantial exposure to purchasing power risk.

You propose the following plan. Put $250,000 into cash equivalents and $750,000 into equities. If the stock market goes up, sell enough stocks to take out $50,000. For example, if the stock holdings go up 10% during the year, then at year-end they will be worth $825,000 [$750,000 x (1 + 0.10)]. Sell enough stocks to take out $50,000 in cash and start the next year with an equity portfolio worth $775,000. However, if the market goes down, take the $50,000 out of the cash equivalents. If the market goes up the second year, sell enough stock to take out the $50,000 cash and replenish the cash equivalents holding. If the market goes down the second year in a row, then again take the cash withdrawal from the cash equivalents and plan to replenish this account in the third year. The only way that the entire cash equivalents holding would be eliminated is if the market went down five years in a row, an event that has never occurred in our modern era. This approach allows the planner to adopt a 75% stock, 25% cash portfolio strategy, which would most likely serve the client better than a portfolio that generates $50,000 in income each year.

It should be noted that the actual application of such a strategy would also require the financial advisor to incorporate the effect of dividends into the cash that will be produced at the end of the year. For example, if the average dividend yield for the portfolio was 1%, then the portfolio would generate about $7,500 in dividends during the year. Hence, the planner only needs to come up with an additional $42,500 at the end of the year. In addition, there would likely be some tinkering to the portfolio that would be necessary to stay on target with the strategic asset allocation of 75% stock and 25% cash.

Portfolio Liquidation: Scenario #2

A variation of the above scenario would allow a planner to put the client into a bonds and stocks portfolio. Let's assume again a $1,000,000 portfolio and a desire to generate cash withdrawals of $50,000 per year. In this case, the planner could invest $50,000 in each of five categories of bonds. The bonds range in annual maturities from one year to five years. The remaining assets are invested in stocks. The strategy for the generation of cash is then much the same as before. If the market goes up the first year, the investor can take the cash from the stock market gains. In addition, he or she would take the proceeds of the one-year bond that has just matured and buy five-year bonds since each set of bonds would move up in maturity by one year. If the market goes down, the investor can take the cash from the one-year bond that has matured (less whatever dividends and interest income have been generated). At such time as the market goes up again, the bond holdings can be replenished.

REVIEW OF LEARNING OBJECTIVES

1. The nine-step investment process includes: understanding the client's goals, identifying the target rate of return, agreeing on a time horizon, understanding the client's tolerance for and capacity for risk, identifying asset classes and investment vehicles, designing the asset allocation, writing the IPS, selecting the investments, and monitoring, managing, and reporting. The IPS itself has six parts, which include: key factual and account information; investment objectives, time horizon, and risk attitudes; permissible

asset classes, constraints, and restrictions; the asset allocation; selection, monitoring, and control procedures; and signatures.

2.　On average, the total risk of a portfolio declines as additional securities are added, but at a decreasing rate. The optimal number of securities to hold depends on the size of the transaction fees and monitoring costs. Managed products, such as mutual funds, are much more efficient in achieving diversification. The inclusion of international investments plays a key role in minimizing portfolio risk. The number of the individual holdings within a portfolio also has a major impact on the degree of diversification.

3.　There is evidence that one should rebalance only to the edge of an acceptable asset range, and not to the midpoint of that range when commissions are fixed in nominal terms.

4.　Other aspects of investment selection a financial advisor should consider include the effort required to maintain an asset, minimum required purchase amounts, the ethical and moral appeal of various investments, reconciliation of the strategic asset allocation with the allocation of monies for optimal tax efficiency, and problems of a concentrated portfolio.

5.　Dollar-cost averaging is the process whereby a fixed-dollar amount of purchases are made at preset intervals, usually monthly. Some investors engage in different types of dollar-cost averaging because it is the only way they can accumulate the money to build a portfolio. Other investors engage in dollar-cost averaging because it provides a way to overcome the fear of regret if the investor makes a huge purchase all at once. Investors may dollar-cost average on their own, through a direct-purchase program or a dividend reinvestment program with a company, through an automatic-debit program with a mutual fund, or through employee stock purchase plans.

6.　An ongoing problem of investing involves human behavior. Namely, investors do not always follow the "economic man" approach to investment thinking. People have a tremendous capacity to see patterns where they do not exist. They are also more likely, at least when acting by themselves, to be overly optimistic. They are willing to place undue confidence in the "law of small numbers." Finally, they have a propensity to choose the middle option when several possibilities are offered, or to divide their money evenly over multiple choices.

7.　A good financial planner will note that often it is important to have a "story" to tell a client about how the portfolio will work. Technical presentations involving such terms as expected returns, standard deviations, covariances, and efficient frontiers will often overwhelm a client. A story about how money will move into and out of a portfolio may be easier for a client to understand.

CHAPTER REVIEW

Key Terms and Concepts

pure market timer

Review Questions

Review questions are based on the learning objectives for this chapter. Thus, a [3] at the end of a question means that the question is based on learning objective 3. If there are multiple objectives, they are all listed.

1.   Describe the nine-step model for investment advising. [1]

2.   Describe the differences between strategic and tactical asset allocation. [1]

3.   Why is it difficult to specify the optimal number of securities in a portfolio? [2]

4.   What are the two key issues associated with the rebalancing process? [3]

5.   Why would having multiple accounts with different tax treatments create a potential problem in matching a strategic asset-allocation scheme? [4]

6.   Why is the expected return on socially responsible portfolios not expected to differ from the expected return on other portfolios of equal riskiness? [4]

7.   Describe how to set up a collar to protect a client with a concentrated portfolio and give an example. [4]

8.   a.   Over the next three months, you will be transferring $100 from your end-of-month paycheck to the XYZ fund, for the immediate purchase of shares. What is the total number of shares purchased and the average cost per share if at the time of purchase the NAV of the fund (assume it is a no-load fund) has the following values: $10, $5, and $15. [5]
     b.   List some examples of dollar-cost averaging plans. [5]

9.   You show a client the two results from flipping a coin six times. The first result is H, T, T, H, H, T. The second is H, H, H, T, T, T. You ask the client which result is more likely to have actually occurred. The answer is that they are equally likely, but the client is almost certain to say the first is more likely. Why? [6]

10.   Give an example of how a plan could be pitched to a client without using the terms asset allocation, expected return, and standard deviation of return. [7]

The study and practice of investments requires the ability to work a variety of mathematical problems. If these problems had to be solved by long hand, or with a calculator that performed only the four basic arithmetic operations, many calculations would be tedious at best and in some cases impossible. Any financial calculator will make mince meat of most calculations nearly all practitioners encounter. Mastery of the material in this textbook does not mean memorizing the keystroke instructions for each type of problem. Mastery means understanding what is going on in the calculation so that you have a sense of what a right answer should look like, what the keystrokes should be (that is, which variables to enter), and how changes in inputs affect answers.

In this textbook, we provide the keystrokes only for the Hewlett-Packard HP-10BII calculator. Students who own other calculators are perfectly free to continue to use those calculators and may bring them to The College's exam (provided they meet The College's criteria as to appropriateness). However, when using other calculators, students are responsible for understanding how to use them. In many cases, there will be a great deal of similarity between the HP-10BII keystrokes and those of other calculators.

Basics of the HP-10BII

To turn the calculator on, press the ON key. To turn the calculator off, first touch the gold-colored key (left-hand column, third key from the bottom), hereafter referred to as SHIFT. Note that after you press the gold SHIFT key, the subsequent key you press will have the function marked in gold, not the function more prominently marked in white. Next, hit the OFF key (bottom row, left-hand-most key). Thus, the sequence to turn the calculator off is

SHIFT, OFF   (display turns off)

When you turn on the calculator, the display should be the number zero. What is important here is the number of zeros displayed after the decimal point. To adjust the number of decimal places in the display, hit SHIFT, then DISP (bottom row, second from the right), and then the number of decimal places to be displayed. For four decimal places, the following keystrokes are necessary:

SHIFT, DISP, 4   (display: 0.0000)

Whenever you are working on a problem that involves the use of decimal notation, you should set the display to four decimal places. Whenever you are working on a problem using percentages or dollars, you should set the display to two decimal places (because the smallest coin is the penny).

Remember that the actual number stored in memory retains as many decimal places as the calculator allows, regardless of what is displayed in the window. To illustrate this point, set the display to two decimal places (SHIFT, DISP, 2) and then divide 7 into 3 (3, ÷, 7, =). The display will be .43. Next, change the display to nine decimal places (SHIFT, DISP, 9), and the answer is now shown as .428571429. You may then switch back to two decimal places and the answer will show up as .43 again. If your answer on a problem differs only slightly from that shown in the book, the difference is frequently due to the number of digits displayed. Thus, if your answer to 3 divided by 7 is .43 and the book shows it to be .4286, then the difference is in the display level selected.

Another cause for differences in answers occurs when a series of calculations is required and you reenter some of the data. For example, suppose a problem involves dividing 3 by 7, and then multiplying the answer by 20. (Assume the calculator is set to display two decimal places.) You could first divide 3 by 7 to obtain an answer of .43, and then REENTER .43 and multiply it by 20 (.43, x, 20, =) to obtain the answer of 8.60. Alternatively, you could do the calculations in sequence (3, ÷, 7, x, 20, =) and obtain the answer 8.57. The difference in answers in this case is caused by rounding the answer to the division of 3 by 7 when it is reentered. When you have an answer that is quite close to the suggested answer and you have reentered data, consider this as a possibility for the variation.

Compounding Frequency

The single most common source of error, when students fail to obtain the same answer as that shown in the book, is the failure to adjust the compounding frequency. When you buy a new HP-10BII calculator, it is set at the factory for monthly compounding. Most problems in investments involve annual compounding or can be easily understood and solved using annual compounding even if the problem involves a different frequency of compounding. **It is highly recommended that you adjust the**

compounding frequency to annual (once per year) from the factory setting of monthly (12 times per year), as follows:

> 1, SHIFT, P/YR

The P/YR key is located in the top row, second from the right.

Sometimes, you may have occasion to change the frequency of compounding. If so, remember to change the frequency back to annual before you turn off the calculator—if you don't, when you turn the calculator back on, it will have the same compounding frequency as when you turned it off. If you then work on any problems that involve compounding frequency, you will get a wrong answer. To minimize the risk of this happening, it is an excellent habit to hit the sequence SHIFT, C ALL (this key is in the lefthandmost column, second from the bottom) immediately after turning on the calculator. You will then see the current frequency of compounding in the display window. If you are set for annual compounding, it will show

> 1 P_Yr

If you are set for monthly compounding, it will show

> 12 P_Yr

If you are set for annual compounding and you want to use monthly compounding, the keystrokes are

> 12, SHIFT, P/YR

Exponential Calculations

An exponential calculation involves taking a number to some power. There are two ways to do this. For geometric mean calculations, we use the exponent key (y^x). For example, suppose you want to calculate 1.05 to the eighth power (that is, 1.05^8). The long and tedious way to do this is to multiply 1.05 x 1.05 x 1.05 x 1.05 x 1.05 x 1.05 x 1.05 x 1.05, for a total of 1.4775. The quicker and cleverer way to solve for this answer is to use the exponent key as follows:

SHIFT, C ALL	(clears memory)
1.05, SHIFT, y^x, 8, =	(display: 1.4775)

This same key can be used to solve for roots. For example, suppose you want to ascertain the fourth root of 30. This can be written either as $30^{1/4}$ or $30^{.25}$. The keystrokes are as follows:

SHIFT, C ALL	(clears memory)
30, SHIFT, y^x, .25, =	(display: 2.3403)

Note that the power in this case is the value of one-fourth. The nth root of a number is that number to the power of $1/n$. Thus, a square root is entered as .5 (that is, ½).

Because the most common power and root calculations involve computing the square and the square root, those two computations are provided on the keypad. To square a number, use the x^2 key found in the bottom row, right-hand-most key. For example, to square 3, hit

SHIFT, C ALL	(clears memory)
3, SHIFT, x^2	(display: 9.0000)

To take the square root of 9, use the $\sqrt{x}$ key found on the second to bottom row, right-hand most-key. Thus, to solve for the square root of 9, hit

SHIFT, C ALL	(clears memory)
9, SHIFT, $\sqrt{x}$	(display: 3.0000)

Means and Standard Deviations

Investment analysis frequently involves the computation of means, or arithmetic averages, and standard deviations. Let's consider the computation of a mean, or arithmetic average, first. Suppose you want to compute the mean of five numbers: 14, 2, 12, –10, and –3. The old-fashioned way is to add up the numbers and divide by 5. The keystrokes are as follows:

14, +, 2, +, 12, +, 10, +/–, +, 3, +/–, =	(display: 15.0000)
÷, 5, =	(display: 3.0000)

The key +/– is located in the left-hand-most column, fourth row from the top.

A more efficient method to do this is to use the $\sum$+ key, which is located in the third row from the top, second key from the right. In this case, the keystrokes are as follows:

$$14, \ \Sigma+, \ 2, \Sigma+, \ 12, \ \Sigma+, \ 10, \ +/\text{-}, \ \Sigma+, \ 3, \ +/\text{-}, \ \Sigma+, \ \text{SHIFT}, \ (\bar{x}, \ \bar{y})$$

(display: 3.0000)

The $(\bar{x},\bar{y})$ key is located just to the right of the purple key (the statistics key). Note that in doing the entries this way, you do not have to divide the total by 5, because the calculator keeps track of the fact that there are five entries. Thus, when you solve for the mean in this computation, it automatically divides the total by 5.

Although there may seem to be as many keystrokes using the second method as the first, the major benefit arises if you want to compute the standard deviation. If you want to compute the sample standard deviation for these five numbers, then after the above data entries, the next keystrokes are

$$\text{SHIFT, } (S_x,S_y) \qquad\qquad\qquad \text{(display: 10.0995)}$$

The (S_x,S_y) key is located in the middle column, fourth row from the bottom (next to the $(\bar{x},\bar{y})$ key). For simplicity of presentation, we will frequently express this key as S_xS_y.

In some instances, you might want to compute the population standard deviation, rather than the sample standard deviation. In this case, the only necessary keystrokes, after entering the data as above, are as follows:

$$\text{SHIFT, } \sigma_x\sigma_y \qquad\qquad\qquad \text{(display: 9.0333)}$$

The $\sigma_x\sigma_y$ key is located in the second column from the right, the fourth row from the bottom (next to the S_xS_y key). Note that the population standard deviation is smaller than the sample standard deviation. This will always be the case because the sample standard deviation, as shown in equation 2-16 in the chapter, requires division of a sum of numbers by the term n - 1, where n is the number of data points, and the population standard deviation requires division of the same sum of numbers by n, as shown in equation C-3 in Appendix C.

Storing to and Removing from Memory

In some instances, you must do two separate calculations before combining numbers. To demonstrate this, let's consider the computation of the cube root of 30 (i.e., $30^{1/3}$). If you try to do this in sequence, the keystrokes are as follows:

SHIFT, C ALL	(clears memory)
30, SHIFT, y^x, 1, ÷, 3, =	(display: 1.0000)

You will find that when you hit the division key, the answer is presented as 30. In other words, the calculator is interpreting the keystrokes as if you are computing 30^1, or 30 to the first power, which is simply 30.

A better approach is to note that the cube root is the power of one-third, which is .3333. Thus, the keystrokes are as follows:

SHIFT, C ALL	(clears memory)
30, SHIFT, y^x, .3333 =	(display: 3.1069)

Although this is close to the correct answer, it is still not exactly correct.

The best way to do this calculation is to use the →M key. The →M key allows you to store a number in the calculator's memory. Any subsequent calculations will not affect the value in the memory unless the →M key is pressed or the SHIFT, C ALL sequence is pressed. Thus, the keystrokes are as follows:

SHIFT, C ALL	(clears memory)
1, ÷, 3, =, —>M	(display: .3333)
30, SHIFT, y^x, RM, =	(display: 3.1072)

This is, in fact, the correct answer. We can see that the approximation method in which we used .3333 as a substitute for storing the computation of 1 divided by 3 in memory is a really good approximation—but it is not perfect.

You can also keep a running total in memory. For example, suppose you want to add 3 and 7 and have the total in memory. Two ways to do this are

3, +, 7, =, M+	(display: 10.0000)

and

        3, M+, 7, M+   (display: 7.0000)

To verify the total is 10, hit RM as follows:

        RM   (display: 10.0000)

Regardless of which method you use to enter the total in memory, even after you remove the total from memory, the value is still stored there. This is known as "destructive read-in, nondestructive read-out." Thus, adding a new number to the total in memory will change the value in memory, but reading out (or removing) a number from memory does not alter the number in memory. To verify this point, after hitting the RM key as described above, add the number -2 to the total in memory, and read the new total in memory, as follows:

        2, +/-, M+, RM   (display: 8.0000)

Learning Objectives

An understanding of the material in this appendix should enable the student to

1. Compute the future value of a lump sum of cash.
2. Compute the present value of a lump sum of cash.
3. Compute the effect of compounding more than once per year.
4. Compute an effective annual interest rate.
5. Compute the future value of an annuity.
6. Compute the present value of an annuity.
7. Compute a net present value.
8. Compute an internal rate of return.
9. Value a perpetuity.

The primary tool in finance is the concept of the time value of money (TVM). TVM is used to calculate how much some lump sum or series of payments will accumulate to at a later time. This tool is also used to determine how much a future payment or cash flow is worth today. Finally, TVM is used to price securities by determining the present value of all cash flows expected to be paid to the owners of those securities.

Although many of these applications of TVM can be derived quickly and simply by using a financial calculator, a basic understanding of these concepts will help the user avoid errors of application and interpretation.

Basic Concepts of Time Value of Money

compound interest

Money grows over time to some future value as a result of compounding interest. *Compound interest* is interest on both the original principal and the interest that has been credited throughout the period. As a result of compounding, the future value will always exceed the present value, as long as the interest rate exceeds 0 percent.

opportunity cost

Interest accrues as compensation for delay in using the money. This compensation can be referred to as *opportunity cost*—the interest that could have been earned if the money had been invested elsewhere. For example, if you deposit $1,000 in a savings account and leave it there for 1 year, you expect your account to earn interest as compensation for your opportunity cost.

discounting   Conversely, some value in the future can be reduced to an equivalent value today using *discounting*. When a future value is discounted at some interest rate greater than 0 percent, the resulting present value is less than the future value. For example, in order to have $1,000 in 1 year from today, you would expect to be able to deposit less than that $1,000 in your bank account today.

There are two important variables you will need in order to determine the future value or present value of a cash flow. The first is the number of periods over which compounding or discounting occurs. The greater the number of periods an amount is compounded, the higher the future value or the lower the present value.

The second important variable is the interest rate used in the compounding or discounting process. The higher the interest rate for compounding, the higher the future value. Conversely, the higher the interest rate for discounting, the lower the present value.

Let's summarize these relationships. The future value is always higher than the present value. The future value *increases* when the number of periods (n) *increases* or the interest rate (i) *increases*. The present value has an inverse relationship with these variables-that is, the present value *decreases* when the number of periods (n) *increases* or the interest rate (i) *increases*.

So far, we have talked about relationships among variables for compounding and discounting. The four key variables in simple time-value-of-money problems are the number of periods, the interest rate, the present value, and the future value. Given any three of the variables, we can always solve for the fourth.

Relationship of Variables
• Future value is always higher than present value.
• Future value *increases* when number of periods (n) increases or interest rate (i) increases.
• Present value *decreases* when number of periods (n) increases or interest rate (i) increases.

Future Value of Single Sums

Let's consider a specific example of how to compute future value. Let's say that you deposit $100 in a savings account that earns 3 percent annually and leave it there for 4 years. Each year, the account will earn 3 percent on the principal sum of $100 plus the interest that has accrued on that principal. Each year your account will accrue interest as follows, starting from today, year 0:

Year 0	Deposit $100
Year 1	$100 + 3%($100) = $103
Year 2	$103 + 3%($103) = $106.09
Year 3	$106.09 + 3%($106.09) = $109.27
Year 4	$109.27 + 3%($109.27) = $112.55

This approach can quickly become tedious when it involves a lot of years. We can determine the future value more directly by using a general equation that takes into account each year of compounding. The general equation for future value is

$$FV = PV \times (1 + i)^n \qquad \text{(Equation B-1)}$$

where

	FV	= future value
	PV	= present value
	i	= interest rate for compounding
	n	= number of periods of compounding

Let's use the equation to verify the results of our example. In this case, FV is unknown, PV is $100, i is .03, and n is 4 years:

$$FV = PV \times (1 + i)^n$$
$$FV = \$100 \times (1.03)^4$$
$$FV = \$100 \times (1.1255)$$
$$FV = \$112.55$$

EXAMPLE

Calculate the future value of $8,000, invested for 19 years at 7 percent:

$$FV = PV \times (1 + i)^n$$

$$FV = \$8{,}000 \times (1.07)^{19}$$

$$FV = \$8{,}000 \times (3.6165)$$

$$FV = \$28{,}932.22$$

HP 10–BII Keystrokes:

SHIFT, C ALL, 1.07, SHIFT, y^x, 19, =, x, 8000, =

Solving for Future Value with the HP-10BII

The Hewlett-Packard HP-10BII will provide a precise answer to these types of problems with just a few keystrokes. After turning on the calculator, make sure the compounding frequency is set to once per year. (Appendix A provides a discussion of how to do this.) Because this particular problem involves an answer measured in dollars and cents, adjust the number of decimal places shown on the display to two by hitting

SHIFT, DISP, 2

Like most financial calculators, the HP-10BII is programmed to show opposite signs for present and future values. The convention is to enter outflows as negatives and inflows as positives. Let's consider once again the last example in which $8,000 is invested 19 years at 7%. In this problem, $8,000 is an investment—an outflow.

Now enter the data from the problem:

SHIFT, C ALL

8000, +/-, PV

19, N

7, I/YR

FV (display: 28,932.22)

Note that if you forget to enter the change of sign key (that is, the +/- key), the answer will be -$28,932.22. The calculator is programmed to analyze these problems with the assumption that at least one of the cash flows will have a sign opposite to the other. Hence, when you change the sign of the $8,000 to negative, you are telling the calculator that the investor is paying out (that is, investing) $8,000. Hence, it is a negative cash flow (a cash outflow) to the investor. The positive answer then indicates how much money comes back to the investor. By entering $8,000 as a positive number, you are telling the calculator that the investor is receiving the $8,000 today, and solving for how much the investor will have to pay back at the end of the time horizon. Hence, the answer will be a negative number that represents a payment by the investor.

One other item that we should mention is that when you are entering and reading display numbers that involve calculations using the financial calculator keys, the calculator is programmed to interpret all interest rates as being in percentage notation. Thus, the interest rate entered must be 7 and not .07, the decimal notation form of 7 percent.

Compounding More than Once Per Year

So far, we have assumed that compounding or discounting takes place annually, and you can assume so unless told otherwise. However, compounding or discounting may take place more frequently than annually. When that occurs, you can use the same equation, but the n and i variables must be adjusted. The following relationships apply to the frequency of compounding. First, the more frequent the compounding, the higher the future value. The more frequent the discounting, the lower the present value. Let's take a look at calculating a future value when compounding occurs more frequently than annually.

Let's say that your $100 deposit will receive 3 percent interest, but this time compounding will be on a monthly basis, or 12 times a year. You can expect that after a 4-year period, you will end up with more than $112.55—the amount you would receive when compounding is on an annual basis. Before we begin, remember that we will need to make adjustments both to n and to i. The adjustments can be expressed as follows:

> n = number of years multiplied by the frequency of compounding
>
> i = annual interest rate divided by frequency of compounding

In this case,

$$n = 4 \times 12 = 48$$
$$i = .03/12 = .0025$$

Now we can use our formula as usual, and when the results are rounded to the nearest penny, we get

$$FV = PV \times (1 + i)^n$$
$$FV = \$100 \times (1.0025)^{48}$$
$$FV = \$100 \times (1.127328)$$
$$FV = \$112.73$$

The HP-10BII keystrokes are

> SHIFT, C ALL
>
> 100, +/-, PV
>
> 4, x, 12, =, N
>
> 3, ÷, 12, =, I/YR
>
> FV (display: 112.73)

An alternative approach to solving this problem is to set the calculator to assume monthly compounding, then enter the number of months as 48 and the annual interest rate as 3 percent, and obtain the same answer. The keystrokes are as follows:

> 12, SHIFT, P/YR
>
> 100, +/-, PV
>
> 4, x, 12, =, N
>
> 3, I/YR
>
> FV (display: 112.73)

If compounding was semiannual, we would have multiplied the number of years by 2, and divided the interest rate by 2. If compounding was quarterly, we would have multiplied the number of years by 4 and divided the interest rate by 4. Adjustments to n and i are the same, regardless of whether you are calculating a future value or a present value. If you are working a series of problems (for example, on an exam), in which the frequency of compounding changes from one problem to the next, there is probably less chance for error if you select one compounding period (such as annual) and then adjust the time period and interest rate to reflect that programming selection than if you have to remember both to reset the compounding frequency and which interest rate to enter.

EXAMPLE

Determine the future value of $8,000 invested for 19 years at 7 percent compounded quarterly:

$$n = 19 \times 4 = 76$$

$$i = .07/4 = .0175$$

$$FV = PV \times (1 + i)^n$$

$$FV = \$8,000 \times (1.0175)^{76}$$

$$FV = \$8,000 \times (3.737797)$$

$$FV = \$29,902.38$$

Note that the quarterly compounding has increased the future value by $970.16 ($29,902.38 – $28,932.22), compared to the annual compounding in the earlier example.

The HP-10BII keystrokes are

SHIFT, C ALL

8000, +/-, PV

19, x, 4, =, N

7, ÷, 4, =, I/YR

FV (display: 29,902.38)

If you want to solve this problem by resetting the compounding frequency of the calculator, the keystrokes are

4, SHIFT, P/YR, SHIFT, C ALL

8000, +/-, PV

4, x, 19, = , N

7, I/YR

FV (display: 29,902.38)

Effective Annual Rate

nominal interest rate   In some cases, when compounding occurs more than once per year, we are interested in computing the effect of this process on the interest rate. When interest is compounded multiple times per period, it creates a distinction between what is known as the *nominal interest rate*—the stated rate-and the effective annual rate. The effective annual rate is the true annual interest rate in a problem.

The concept used in computing an effective annual interest rate requires breaking down the period of 1 year into the number of periods that interest is compounded. We then determine the compounding effect of these multiple periods. The formula for this is

$$r_{ear} = \left[1 + \frac{r_{nom}}{m} \right]^m - 1 \qquad \text{(Equation B-2)}$$

where r_{ear} = effective annual interest rate

r_{nom} = stated nominal annual interest rate

m = number of times per year compounding occurs

As an example, suppose you note that the interest rate on your credit card statement is 18 percent. Because the interest on credit cards is charged each month on the unpaid balance, the interest is being compounded monthly, or 12 times per year. The effective annual rate is then computed as

$$r_{ear} = (1+.18/12)^{12} - 1 = 1.015^{12} - 1 = .1956, \text{ or } 19.56\%$$

HP10-BII Keystrokes:

SHIFT, C ALL, .18, ÷, 12, +, 1, =, SHIFT, y^x, 12, =, –, 1, =

EXAMPLE

You are considering two different banks for your savings account. The first bank pays 4 percent compounded daily, and the second bank pays 4 1/4 percent compounded annually. Which bank offers the higher effective annual rate?

Answer: For the bank that pays interest compounded annually, no adjustment is necessary. Any interest rate compounded annually is automatically stated as an effective annual rate. To adjust the interest rate that is compounded daily, we start by noting that daily compounding means 365 times per year. We can thus compute the effective annual rate for the first bank as

$$r_{ear} = (1 + .04/365)^{365} - 1 = .0408, \text{ or } 4.08\%$$

This makes it clear that the bank that is offering 4¼ percent compounded annually has a much better deal in terms of the interest rate paid.

Any calculator with an exponent key (y^x) is capable of computing the effective interest rate. The following keystrokes are used to calculate the effective rate on the example above with the HP-10BII calculator:

SHIFT, C ALL

.04, ÷, 365, =   (this is $r_{nom}/365$)

+, 1, =, SHIFT, y^x, 365, =, -, 1, =   (display: 0.0408)

The calculation of the effective annual rate is also a programmed function. In the above example, 4 (not .04) is entered as the nominal rate (NOM%), and the number of periods per year (P/YR) is entered as 365. The EFF% key provides the effective rate. The keystrokes are as follows:

4, SHIFT, NOM%, 365, SHIFT, P/YR, SHIFT, EFF% (display: 4.08)

IMPORTANT: Remember to change the number of periods per year back to 1.

Present Value of Single Sums

So far, we've taken single sums of today's dollars and compounded them to various amounts in the future. Now we will work in the opposite direction, discounting future values back to the present. Let's say that 4 years from now you expect to receive $100 and you would like to discount it at 3 percent annually. You select that discount rate because you believe you could have earned this rate in an investment if the money were available to you now, rather than 4 years from now. We will discount the future value back to today, year 0, as follows:

Year 4	$100
Year 3	$100/(1 + .03) = $97.09
Year 2	$97.09/(1 + .03) = $94.26
Year 1	$94.26/(1 + .03) = $91.51
Year 0	$91.51/(1 + .03) = $88.84

We can obtain the same result using an equation based on the future value equation. Remember that FV = PV x $(1 + i)^n$. We can restate this equation for the present value by solving for PV:

$$FV = PV \times (1 + i)^n$$

$$\frac{FV}{(1 + i)^n} = PV$$ (Equation B-3)

$$PV = \frac{FV}{(1 + i)^n}$$

Let's use the equation to verify the results of our example. In this case, PV is our unknown, FV is $100, i is 3 percent, and n is 4 years. We will round our result to two decimal places.

$$PV = \frac{FV}{(1 + i)^n}$$

$$PV = \frac{\$100}{(1 + .03)^4}$$

$$PV = \frac{\$100}{1.125509} = \$88.85$$

The HP-10BII keystrokes are

SHIFT, C ALL

100, +/–, FV

3, I/YR

4, N

PV (display: 88.85)

You will notice that our answer is 1 cent different from our answer using the prior method. This difference is due to rounding.

EXAMPLE

Discount an asset promising $100 in 3 years back to today at a discount rate of 6 percent.

$$PV = \frac{\$100}{1.06^3} = \frac{\$100}{1.1910} = \$83.96$$

The HP-10BII keystrokes are

SHIFT, C ALL

100, +/-, FV

6, I/YR

3, N

PV (display: 83.96)

Determine the present value of $10,000 to be received 9 years from now, discounted semiannually at an annual rate of 5 percent.

$$n = 9 \times 2 = 18$$
$$i = .05 / 2 = .025$$
$$PV = \frac{FV}{(1+i)^n}$$
$$PV = \frac{\$10,000}{(1+.025)^{18}}$$
$$PV = \frac{\$10,000}{1.5597} = \$6,411.66$$

The HP-10BII keystrokes are

SHIFT, C ALL

10000, +/-, FV

9, x, 2, =, N

5, ÷, 2, =, I/YR

PV (display: 6,411.66)

Alternatively, you can set the calculator for semiannual compounding, in which case the keystrokes are

2, SHIFT, P/YR

10000, +/-, FV

9, x, 2, =, N

5, I/YR

PV (display: 6,411.66)

Periodic Cash Flows

So far, we have talked about compounding and discounting a single payment. We can also compound or discount a series of payments made at the end of each period. These cash flows may be of equal or different amounts. Let's consider first the case of the future value of a series of unequal cash flows.

Uneven Cash Flows

We can solve for the future value or series of cash flows by using the previous equations for each payment and totaling the results:

$$FV_n = CF_1 \times (1+i)^{n-1} + CF_2 \times (1+i)^{n-2} + \ldots + CF_{n-1} \times (1+i)^1 + CF_n \times (1+i)^0$$

(Equation B-4)

where FV_n = future value n periods from today of the cash flows

CF_t = cash flow in time period t

Note in the above equation that although the cash flows are numbered from 1 to N, the exponents of the interest rate terms are numbered from n-1 to zero. This is because the cash flow is invested at the end of each time period. Hence, a cash flow that is received 1 year from today will have only n-1 time periods in which to accrue interest. The cash flow that is received n periods from today will have no time to accrue interest because it is received at the same time we are determining the future value. When an exponent is zero, the value of the term is 1, regardless of what the expression might be. Thus, the last compounding term of $(1 + i)^0$ equals 1, and so the future value of the last cash flow is simply CF_n.

EXAMPLE

A client is considering funding a Coverdell IRA.[193] The client plans to set aside $500 the first year, $1,000 the second year, and $2,000 the third year. If you believe the client will earn 6 percent in this account, how much will the account be worth at the end of 3 years?

Answer:

$$FV_N = CF_1 \times (1 + i)^2 + CF_2 \times (1 + i)^1 + CF_3 \times (1 + i)^0$$

$$FV_N = \$500 \times (1 + .06)^2 + \$1,000 \times (1 + .06)^1 + \$2,000 \times (1 + .06)^0$$

$$FV_N = \$500 \times (1.1236) + \$1,000 \times (1.06) + \$2,000 \times (1)$$

$$FV_N = \$3,621.80$$

Unfortunately, there are no convenient keystrokes for computing the future value of a set of uneven cash flows. The most efficient way to use the calculator to do this would be first to compute the present value of the set of uneven cash flows (to be discussed next) and then to compute the future value of this present value number.

Let's now consider the present value of a series of uneven cash flows. The concept is basically the same as for the future value of such a series. Namely, the present value is the sum of the present values of each of the cash flows.

$$PV = CF_0 + CF_1 / (1 + i)^1 + CF_2 / (1 + i)^2 + \ldots + CF_{n-1} / (1 + i)^{n-1} + CF_n / (1 + i)^n$$

(Equation B-5)

In this case, the subscripts of the cash flows and the exponents of the interest rate term match up nicely. Note also that the first cash flow is identified as

---

193. A Coverdell IRA is for funding educational expenses. The profits in the account can accrue tax free and the withdrawals are tax free if they are used to pay for qualified educational expenses. The maximum contribution is $2,000 per year per recipient. People making the contribution are subject to certain income limits.

occurring at time period zero. Because it occurs immediately, there is no discount term associated with it. The present value of an immediate cash flow is the cash flow itself. Consider the following example.

EXAMPLE

Your client has a small, privately owned business. She is approached with a buyout offer. The offer is $1 million to be paid in one year, $2 million in 2 years, and $3 million in 3 years. You confer with your client and conclude that an appropriate discount rate is 10 percent. What is the value of this offer in today's dollars?

Answer (in millions):

$$PV = CF_0 + CF_1/(1+i)^1 + CF_2/(1+i)^2 + CF_3/(1+i)^3$$
$$= \$0 + \$1/(1+.10)^1 + \$2/(1+.10)^2 + \$3/(1+.10)^3$$
$$= \$0 + \$.9091 + \$1.6529 + \$2.2539 = \$4.8159$$

The keystrokes are as follows:

0, CFj

1, CFj

2, CFj

3, CFj

10, I/YR

SHIFT, NPV (display: 4.8159)

Note in the above keystrokes that a zero is entered as a cash flow at time period zero. That is, the calculator is programmed to assume that the first cash flow occurs immediately. Similarly, it is programmed to assume that all cash flows are entered consecutively by period. This means that if there is no cash flow in one of the periods, a zero must be entered for that cash flow.

EXAMPLE

Let's continue the previous example by assuming that your client makes a counteroffer that entails the payment of $3 million immediately, and a second payment of $3 million in 3 years. This involves the same total amount of cash payments, but there is an adjustment as to timing. How much has this adjustment altered the present value of the buyout offer?

Answer (in millions):

$$PV = CF_0 + CF_1/(1 + i)^1 + CF_2/(1 + i)^2 + CF_3/(1 + i)^3$$

$$= \$3 + \$0/(1 + .10)^1 + \$0/(1 + .10)^2 + \$3/(1 + .10)^3$$

$$= \$3 + \$0 + \$0 + \$2.2539 = \$5.2539$$

This has increased the value of the buyout by $.438, or $438,000. The keystrokes are as follows:

> SHIFT, C ALL
>
> 3, CFj
>
> 0, CFj
>
> 0, CFj
>
> 3, CFj
>
> 10, I/YR
>
> SHIFT, NPV (display: 5.2539)

Annuities

An annuity is a finite series of equal, consecutive payments. Annuities occur frequently in the investments world. For example, they can be sold as a product by themselves. Also, the sequence of interest payments on bonds is an annuity.

annuity due

regular annuity

When calculating annuity values, a critical factor is whether payments occur at the beginning of each period or at the end. An annuity with payments that occur at the beginning of each period is called an *annuity due*. An annuity with payments that occur at the end of each period is called a *regular annuity*. On the HP-10BII, the normal setting is for a regular annuity (that is, cash flows at the end of each period). To set the calculator for an annuity due, use the following keystrokes: SHIFT, BEG/END. The word BEGIN should appear in the display. To switch back to a regular annuity, use the same keystrokes and the word BEGIN will disappear from the display. Most problems in investments involve regular annuities rather than annuities due. When the term "annuity" is used without the timing references of "regular" or "due," assume it is a regular annuity.

Mathematically, one benefit of annuities is that we can use a simpler computation process than what is necessary for problems involving uneven cash flows. Consider first the future value of a regular annuity, using repeated applications of equation B-1. Because all of the payments are equal, we can replace the cash flow for each period with the common term PMT:

$$FV_n = PMT \times (1+i)^{n-1} + PMT \times (1+i)^{n-2} + ... + PMT \times (1+i)^1 + PMT \times (1+i)^0$$

(Equation B-6)

This equation can be manipulated by factoring out all of the PMT terms:

$$FV_n = PMT \times [(1+i)^{n-1} + (1+i)^{n-2} + ... + (1+i)^1 + (1+i)^0]$$

This produces an expression that says the future value of an annuity equals the payment per period times the sum of the future value terms for each payment. We can write the summation of terms in the brackets with the following short-cut formula:

$$FV_N = PMT \times \left[\frac{(1+i)^n - 1}{i} \right]$$

(Equation B-7)

EXAMPLE

Your client has just become a proud parent. He decides to fund a Coverdell IRA for his child with $2,000 per year for 18 years, starting 1 year from today. How much will the account be worth in 18 years if he earns 8 percent per year?

$$FV_N = PMT \times \left(\frac{(1+i)^n - 1}{i} \right)$$

$$FV_N = \$2,000 \times \left(\frac{(1+.08)^{18} - 1}{.08} \right)$$

$$FV_{18} = \$74,900.40$$

The HP-10BII keystrokes are

> SHIFT, C ALL, set for end-of-period payments
>
> 2000, +/-, PMT
>
> 8, I/YR
>
> 18, N
>
> FV (display: 74,900.49)

Next, let's consider the present value of a regular annuity. For the mathematics of this present value, we can substitute PMT for the cash flows in equation B-2:

$$PV = PMT / (1+i)^1 + PMT / (1+i)^2 ... PMT / (1+i)^{n-1} + PMT / (1+i)^n$$

(Equation B-8)

Because we are considering a regular annuity, we can omit the immediate payment from the equation. As with the future value equation, we can factor out the PMT terms. This produces the following expression:

$$PV = PMT \times [1 / (1+i)^1 + 1 / (1+i)^2 + \; . \; . \; . \; 1 / (1+i)^n]$$

We can then simplify the term in the brackets to the following:

$$PV = PMT \times \left(\frac{1 - \frac{1}{(1+i)^n}}{i} \right)$$

EXAMPLE

Your client has won a state lottery and is offered the choice between $800,000 cash in hand, and a payout of $60,000 per year for 20 years starting 1 year from today. After consulting with your client, you believe the appropriate discount rate to value the annuity is 6 percent. Ignoring taxes, is the lump sum payment or the annuity more valuable?

Answer: We need to determine the present value of the above annuity to see if its value is greater or less than the lump-sum payment.

$$PV = PMT \times \left(\frac{1 - \frac{1}{(1+i)^n}}{i} \right)$$

$$PV = \$60,000 \times \left(\frac{1 - \frac{1}{(1+.06)^{20}}}{.06} \right)$$

$$PV = \$60,000 \times \left(\frac{1 - \frac{1}{(3.2071)}}{.06} \right)$$

$$PV = \$688,195.27$$

The fact that the present value of the annuity is substantially less than the $800,000 lump sum award today indicates that your client should choose the lump sum, at least before taxes are considered.

The HP-10BII keystrokes are

> SHIFT, C ALL, set for end-of-period payments
>
> 60000, +/-, PMT
>
> 6, I/YR
>
> 20, N
>
> PV (display: 688,195.27)

Net Present Value

Virtually all investment decisions can be reduced to a simple question: Do the cash flows justify the price that would be paid for the investment? Two techniques that are commonly used to answer these questions are net present value (NPV) and internal rate of return (IRR). Let us consider the NPV calculation first.

For NPV purposes, an investment is defined solely in terms of the cash flows it is expected to produce. NPV generally is thought of as an expenditure of cash today followed by a series of cash inflows. A NPV calculation is quite similar to the present value of a series of uneven cash flows. The formula for NPV is

$$NPV = -Cost + CF_1 / (1+i)^1 + CF_2 / (1+i)^2 + ...CF_{n-1} / (1+i)^{n-1} + CF_n / (1+i)^n$$

(Equation B-9)

The first difference between equation B-5 (present value of a series of uneven cash flows) and equation B-9 (NPV) is that in the first equation the first term was defined as the cash flow at time period zero (CF_0), and in the second equation it is defined as the cost of the project or asset, which occurs at time period zero. The second difference is that in equation B-5, there is no assumption as to whether the time period zero cash flow is an inflow or outflow. In the NPV equation, the assumption is that there is a cash outflow at time period zero; hence the negative sign associated with cost. In practical terms, there really is no difference between the two equations.

The selection of the discount rate is critical in computing a net present value. The discount rate should be set at a value that reflects the riskiness of the cash flows being discounted. Many people like to use the capital asset pricing model to ascertain the appropriate discount rate.[194] Selection of an appropriate discount rate is invariably an art rather than a technical skill.

EXAMPLE

An investment offers the following expected cash flows: $CF_1 = \$110$, $CF_2 = \$121$, $CF_3 = \$133.10$. It costs $250. As a financial advisor considering whether or not to recommend this investment for your client, you review this investment and conclude that based on the riskiness of the cash flows, a 10 percent discount rate is appropriate. What is the investment's NPV?

Answer:

$$\begin{aligned} NPV &= -Cost + CF_1/(1+i)^1 + CF_2/(1+i)^2 + CF_3/(1+i)^3 \\ &= -\$250 + \$110/(1+.10)^1 + \$121/(1+.10)^2 \\ &\quad + \$133.10/(1+.10)^3 \\ &= -\$250 + \$100 + \$100 + \$100 = +\$50 \end{aligned}$$

Because the NPV is positive, the client should undertake the investment. The keystrokes for this calculation are

---

194. The capital asset pricing model is discussed in a later chapter.

SHIFT, C ALL

250, +/–, CFj

110, CFj

121, CFj

133.10, CFj

10, I/YR

SHIFT, NPV (display: 50.00)

Some people find the concept of net present value unclear because they are not sure how to interpret it. The easiest interpretation is that it tells a person the instantaneous impact on his or her wealth from undertaking that particular investment. In the above example, there is no difference between (a) walking down the street, finding $50 lying on the ground, picking it up, and putting it in your pocket and (b) purchasing the investment. In both cases, you are considered to be immediately wealthier by $50.

Many students like to argue this interpretation, saying there is a difference: The $50 on the ground is a perfect certainty, and the investment contains risk. Although this statement is true, it is also misleading. The reason is that in computing the NPV, an adjustment was made for risk, along with an adjustment for the timing of the cash flow. The sum of the future cash flows in the above investment is $364.10 ($110 + $121 + $133.10). To acquire these cash flows, the client has to pay only $250 today. Therefore, if we ignore risk and the timing of the cash flows, the investment will leave the client richer by $114.10 ($364.10 – $250). However, in analyzing the investment and adjusting for differences in the timing of the cash flows and allowing for risk, we have concluded that this investment will make the client wealthier by $50, not $114.10. The difference in these two numbers compensates the client completely for the fact that the investment is risky. Hence, it is equivalent in value to a perfectly certain $50. If you still feel that the $50 on the ground is a better deal, then you have not chosen the correct discount rate.

Internal Rate of Return

An alternative approach to valuing a project or an asset is to solve for the *internal rate of return (IRR)*. An IRR is the discount rate that causes the NPV of an investment to equal zero.

$$NPV = -\text{Cost} + CF_1 / (1 + IRR)^1 + CF_2 / (1 + IRR)^2 + ... CF_{n-1} / (1 + IRR)^{n-1} + CF_n / (1 + IRR)^n$$

(Equation B-10)

If the investment has only one or two cash flows, then we can actually solve for the IRR. But as soon as the investment has a life of 3 years or more, we cannot mathematically solve for the IRR.[195] However, IRRs are easily computed on a calculator.

EXAMPLE

An investment offers the following expected cash flows: $CF_1 = \$110$, $CF_2 = \$121$, $CF_3 = \$133.10$. It costs $250. As a financial advisor, you are not sure what the appropriate discount rate is to value this investment. So you decide to compute its IRR.

Answer:

$$NPV = 0 = -\text{Cost} + CF_1/(1 + IRR)^1 + CF_2/(1 + IRR)^2 + CF_3/(1 + IRR)^3$$

$$NPV = 0 = -250 + \$110/(1+IRR)^1 + \$21/(1\ IRR)^2 + \$133.10/(1+IRR)^3$$

$$IRR = 20.67\%$$

Note that there is no direct mathematical solution for the value of the IRR. Thus, you must solve the problem on a computer or with a financial calculator. The keystrokes for this calculation are

SHIFT, C ALL

250, +/–, CFj

110, CFj

121, CFj

133.10, CFj

SHIFT, IRR/YR (display: 20.67)

As with NPV, there is an intuitive way to interpret this value. The easiest way to interpret an IRR is that purchasing the investment is equivalent to putting your money into a savings account that pays an interest rate equal to the IRR. The proof is that if you did, you could exactly reproduce the cash flows of the investment.

---

195. There actually is a formula for solving for the IRR when there are three cash flows, but this formula is sufficiently complex that few people know it and how to apply it, and most have never heard of it.

As proof of this point, consider the investment in the previous example. Let's assume that a person could invest the $250 in a savings account that paid exactly 20.67 percent. If so, could the investor make withdrawals that would match the cash flows of the investment? *Table B-1* proves that this is the case.

Table B-1
Proof of Meaning of an IRR

Time Period (1)	Balance at Start of Time Period (2)	Interest Earned During the Period (3) = (1) x .2067	Withdrawal at the end of the Period (4)	Balance at the End of the Period (5) = (2) + (3)-(4)
1	$250.00	$51.68	$110.00	$191.68
2	$191.68	$39.62	$121.00	$110.30
3	$110.30	$22.80	$133.10	$.00

In *Table B-1*, the investor starts with $250. During the first year, this generates an interest income of $51.68 ($250 x .2067). At the end of the year, the investor draws out $110. The balance at the end of the year is then $191.68 ($250 + $51.68 – $110). This figure becomes the opening balance for the second year. In like manner, the investor is able to draw out $121 at the end of the second year, and $133.10 at the end of the third year. At that time, there is exactly nothing left in the account. Hence, investing $250 at 20.67 percent will permit a person to provide cash flows of exactly $110, $121, and $133.10 over the next 3 years. Thus, there is conceptually, no difference between saying this project has an IRR of 20.67 percent, and investing the cost of the project ($250) at a rate of 20.67 percent.

Unfortunately for the financial advisor in the above example, calculating that the IRR is 20.67 percent does not really determine if this is a good investment or not. The question remains whether or not this is a sufficiently good rate of return to compensate for the riskiness of the cash flows. If the investment is considered so risky that it should not be purchased unless the IRR is at least 25 percent, then you would have to turn it down because the IRR is inadequate. If the investment is considered moderately risky and it should not be purchased unless the IRR is at least 10 percent, then you would have to say that this is an attractive investment. In the discussion of NPV, we specified an appropriate discount rate of 10 percent for this investment.

Thus, we would reach the same conclusion after computing the IRR: The investment should be purchased.

Note that a decision maker will always reach the same conclusion whether he or she computes an NPV or an IRR, as long as the IRR is compared to the discount rate that is used in the NPV calculation. The point is that although some people prefer to compute an IRR rather than an NPV because they are uncomfortable selecting a discount rate for the NPV calculation, they are really not bypassing the problem. The reason is that they have to select a discount rate to determine whether or not an IRR is reasonably attractive.

Now, it is true that a negative IRR would mean automatic rejection of a project, and an extremely low IRR (such as 1 or 2 percent) would mean almost certain rejection. A negative IRR occurs whenever the sum of the future cash flows is less than the cost of the project, even before the discounting process. It is also true that unusually high IRRs such as 100 percent or more would likely mean certain acceptance. An IRR of 100 percent would mean you are doubling your money every time period! In truth, most investments do not produce such extreme values of IRRs, and thus the decision maker must still identify the appropriate comparison rate for an IRR calculation.

Perpetuity

perpetuity   There is a very simple formula in finance that occasionally has practical applications. It is the formula for valuing a perpetuity. A *perpetuity* is an annuity that goes forever. For example, if someone offers an investor the opportunity to receive $1,000 per year, forever, starting next year, the investor is being offered a perpetuity. The initial reaction to perpetuities is that they must be extremely valuable if they will pay forever. In fact, they are never as valuable as they might first seem.

So far, no individual has lived forever, and thus you might question whether there is any value to the receipt of cash flows after your death. In practice, this does not matter. The reason is that, in theory, a perpetuity can be sold at any time. As such, its value is not dependent on the life of the investor, but on the expectation that the payments will always be made.

The formula for valuing a perpetuity is

$$\text{Value of a perpetuity} = \text{PMT}/i$$

In the example mentioned earlier, if the annual payment were $1,000, and if the appropriate discount rate were 5 percent, then the value of this perpetuity would be $20,000 ($1,000/.05). This is easy to prove. Suppose a person has $20,000 cash in hand and invests it at a guaranteed rate of 5 percent forever. After 1 year, the interest income from this investment is $1,000. Let's assume the investor draws out the $1,000 accumulated interest and leaves the balance on deposit for another year at 5 percent. At the end of the second year, the investor can draw out another $1,000 and leave the $20,000 on deposit at 5 percent. This process can be repeated forever as long as the investor is willing to assume the interest rate on this investment pays 5 percent. Hence, as with our IRR example, the point is that if $20,000 invested at 5 percent can produce a perpetuity for its investor of $1,000 per year, then a perpetuity of $1,000 per year discounted (that is, valued) at 5 percent must be worth $20,000.

As we will see later, the most common example of a perpetuity in practice is preferred stock. Preferred stock has no expiration or termination date, and it usually promises to pay a fixed dividend forever. Some national governments have issued bonds that are perpetuities. They are promising to pay the bondholder interest forever. These are analogous to loans that never mature.

A final use of the perpetuity formula is that it always sets an upper limit on value. For example, suppose you are offered an investment opportunity that will pay $1,000 per year for 20 years. If a 10 percent discount rate is appropriate, how much is this investment worth? As seen above, you can value this as a present value of annuity. However, before any calculations are done, it should be clear to the analyst that the value of this annuity has to be less than $10,000. If the $1,000 per year were a perpetuity, then discounting these cash flows at 10 percent would make them worth $10,000 (that is, $1,000/.10). However, because the payments will run for only 20 years and not forever, they have to be worth less than the $10,000 value of the perpetuity.

A perpetuity can be converted to an internal rate of return number. This is accomplished by dividing the annual payment by the value of the perpetuity. For example, if you could buy a perpetuity that pays $1,000 forever for $20,000, your IRR would be 5 percent ($1,000/$20,000).

Appendix Review

Review Questions

Review questions are based on the learning objectives in this chapter. Thus, a [B-3] at the end of a question means that the question is based on learning objective B-3. If there are multiple objectives, they are all listed.

1. a.   A 35-year-old client just inherited $50,000. He wants to invest this money to finance his retirement. If you believe he can conservatively earn an average of 8 percent per year, and the client wants to retire in 30 years, how much should his account be worth at that time? [B-1]
    b.   Your client states that when he retires, he wants his portfolio to provide an income of $50,000 per year for 20 years. If you believe that the portfolio would be adjusted during his retirement years to earn a more conservative 6 percent, can he achieve this goal? [B-6]
    c.   Let's go back to part a. Suppose the client has no inheritance, but says he is willing to set aside $6,000 per year (at the end of each year) for the next 30 years. If you still plan to earn at least 8 percent on this portfolio, will the client be better or worse off in 30 years than if he had started with the $50,000 inheritance? [B-5]
    d.   After further consideration, your client indicates that he is willing to set aside $500 at the end of each month for the next 30 years. By how much will this change from annual investing to monthly investing be expected to increase his final portfolio? [B-3, B-5]
    e.   Finally, suppose you convince your client to make his contribution at the beginning of each month rather than the end. By how much will this be expected to increase his final portfolio? [B-3, B-5]

2. a.   A 25-year-old client tells you he wants to retire at age 60 with $1 million. He wants an aggressive portfolio, which means he wants to achieve at least a 10 percent rate of return, and he wants to fund this portfolio today with a single deposit. How much will he have to deposit today to expect to achieve his objective? [B-2]
    b.   The client in part a. suddenly realizes he has no cash with which to immediately fund his retirement plan. Instead, he will have to fund it with equal annual deposits, beginning 1 year from today. If he still wants an aggressive portfolio that will be expected to yield a 10 percent rate of return, what will the size of each deposit have to be to end up with $1 million? [B-5]

3.   As part of an overall portfolio recommendation, your client wants to put some money into a 5-year CD. You call four different banks and get the following rates. Which is the best deal? [B-4]

4% compounded daily

4.1% compounded monthly

4.15% compounded quarterly

4.2% compounded annually

4.   Your client's business is looking at three mutually exclusive projects. They can be described as follows: [B-1]
a.   The first costs $100,000, and is expected to produce net cash inflows over the next 3 years of $30,000, $40,000, and $50,000. The appropriate discount rate is 8 percent.
b.   The second costs $150,000 and is expected to produce net cash inflows of $30,000 at the end of each year for the next 10 years. The appropriate discount rate is 10 percent.
c.   The third costs $75,000 and is expected to produce net cash inflows of $10,000 at the end of each year, forever. The appropriate discount rate is 10 percent.
       i. What is the NPV for each project? [B-7]
       ii. Based on the NPVs, which of the three projects should the client accept? [B-7]
       iii. What is the IRR for each project? [B-8]

5.   You want to purchase an asset that is expected to provide an annual cash payment of $1,500 per year, forever, starting 1 year from now. If your discount rate is 15 percent, what is the maximum you would pay for this asset? [B-9]

The variability and covariability in security returns may be analyzed using historical data (ex post data) or a projected probability distribution. The nature of the data affects the formula that should be used to construct the variance or covariance statistic. Different formulas are used because historical data represent a sample, and projected data usually specify all possible outcomes. Statistical theory shows that variances and covariances estimated with sample data underestimate the true variance or covariance that is present in the data unless they are corrected in the formulas used to compute these values.

The formulas for the variance and covariance when using sample data are provided in chapters 2 and 3. This appendix provides the formulas to use when working with ex ante (forecasted) rates of return.

There are always two features to remember about forecasted data. First, each rate of return must have an associated probability. Second, these probabilities may be explicit or implicit. An example of an implicit probability distribution is a statement that the rate of return on an investment will be either 15 percent or –5 percent. Implicit in this statement is an assumption that the probability distribution is 50 percent for each outcome.

Variance

Let's start by looking at the formula for the variance when using forecasted data. In this case, the variance is derived first by taking the difference between each possible rate of return and the expected rate of return as calculated in equation 2-7. Second, these differences are squared. Third, the squared terms are multiplied with the associated probabilities. Finally, these products are added up, and the total is called the variance. In mathematical notation, the formula for the variance is

$$\sigma^2 = \sum_{t=1}^{n} P_i \times [R_i - E(R)]^2 \qquad \text{(Equation C-1)}$$

EXAMPLE

An investment offers a 30 percent probability of a –2 percent return, a 40 percent probability of an 8 percent return, and a 30 percent probability of an 18 percent return. The expected return is 8 percent, and the deviations from the mean are –10 percent, 0 percent, and 10 percent. The squares of these three differences are 100, 0, and 100 percent-squared. When these squared terms are multiplied by the associated probabilities and added up, the sum, which is the variance, is 60 percent-squared, computed as follows:

.30 x 100%-squared + .40 x 0%-squared + .30 x 100%-squared =

30%-squared + 0%-squared + 30%-squared = 60%-squared (or .0060)

Simple Example: Equal Probabilities

A financial planner will often encounter scenarios in which all of the potential rates of return are equally likely. When this type of problem occurs, the computations can be simplified. The expected return becomes nothing more than the arithmetic average, and the variance becomes the sum of the squared differences between each return and the expected return, divided by the number of observations, as shown in equation C-2:

$$E(R) = \overline{R} = \sum_{i=1}^{n} R_i / n = \frac{1}{n} \sum_{i=1}^{n} R_i \qquad \text{(Equation C-2)}$$

$$\sigma^2 = \sum_{i=1}^{n} \frac{[R_i - E(R)]^2}{n} = \frac{1}{n} \Sigma [R_i - E(R)]^2 \qquad \text{(Equation C-3)}$$

The reason for the simplification of these two equations over equations 2-8 and C-1 is that for n equally weighted returns, the probability of any return i is simply 1/n, so each P_i can be expressed as 1/n. If we substitute this into equations 2-8 and C-1, we get equations C-2 and C-3.

EXAMPLE

Assume equal probabilities of returns of -2 percent, 4 percent, 10 percent, and 16 percent:

$P(R_1) = P(R_2) = P(R_3) = P(R_4) = .25$

R_1	R_2	R_3	R_4
-.02	.04	.10	.16

The expected return is then computed as

$$E(R) = \left(\frac{-.02 + .04 + .10 + .16}{4} \right) = \frac{.28}{4} = .07$$

Next, compute the deviation of each possible return from these expected values:

$$X_i = R_i - E(R)$$
$$X_1 = (-.02 - .07) = (-.09)$$
$$X_2 = (.04 - .07) = (-.03)$$
$$X_3 = (.10 - .07) = (.03)$$
$$X_4 = (.16 - .07) = (.09)$$

These values are then squared:

$$(X_i)^2 = [R_i - E(R)]^2$$
$$X_1^2 = (-.09)^2 = .0081$$
$$X_2^2 = (-.03)^2 = .0009$$
$$X_3^2 = (.03)^2 = .0009$$
$$X_4^2 = (.09)^2 = .0081$$

The results are then totaled and averaged. The result of this computation is the variance (σ^2):

Sum = .0081 + .0009 + .0009 + .0081 = .0180

$$\sigma^2 = \frac{.0180}{4} = .0045$$

Finally, the standard deviation is the square root of the variance:

$$\sigma = \sqrt{.0045} = .0671, \text{ or } 6.71\%$$

Thus, this investment has an expected return of 7 percent and a standard deviation of 6.71 percent.

Note that equations C-2 and C-3 are built into the HP-10BII as follows:

Keystrokes when rates of return are entered as decimals:

SHIFT, C ALL, .02, +/-, T+, .04, T+, .1, T+, .16, SHIFT, $\sigma_x \sigma_y$ (display: .0671)

Keystrokes when rates of return are entered as percentages:

SHIFT, C ALL, 2, +/-, T+, 4, $\Sigma+$, 10, T+, 16, SHIFT, $\sigma_x \sigma_y$ (display: 6.71)

Covariance

The formula for covariance when ex ante data are used is

$$COV_{kl} = \sum_{i=1}^{n} P_i \times \left[R_{ki} - E(R_k) \right]\left[R_{li} - E(R_l) \right]$$ (Equation C–4)

where COV_{kl} = covariance of the returns on securities k and l

P_i = probability of R_{ki} and R_{li} occurring

EXAMPLE

Consider again two businesses at the beach, selling sunscreen lotion (business A) and umbrellas (business B). The rate of return on each business depends on the weather. Suppose that after listening to the weather forecast, you believe the following probabilities and rates of return apply to these businesses:

P_i	R_{Ai}	R_{Bi}	$R_{Ai} \times P_i$	$R_{Bi} \times P_i$
Probability	(Sunscreen)	(Umbrella)		
30% (rain)	–30%	40%	-9%	12%
50% (cloudy)	10%	2%	5%	1%
20% (sunny)	30%	–30%	6%	– 6%
		Total	2%	7%

The expected returns for each business are 2 percent and 7 percent. The covariance of returns between these two business is computed using equation C-4 as follows:

COV_{AB} = .30 x (–30% – 2%) x (40% – 7%)

+ .50 x (10% – 2%) x (2% – 7%)

+ .20 x (30% – 2%) x (–30% – 7%)

= –316.8% squared – 20% squared – 207.2% squared

= –544% squared

Notice that all three cross-products are negative, which is why the sum is a large negative number.

As with the variance calculations, if all possible rates of return are equally likely, equation C-4 can be simplified to the following:

$$COV_{kl} = \sum_{i=1}^{n}(R_{ki} - E(R_k)) \times (R_{li} - E(R_1))] / n \qquad \text{(Equation C-5)}$$

Appendix Review

Review Question

1. You have two securities, A and B. You believe in the coming year there are three economic scenarios: a strong economy, a normal economy, and a weak economy. The probability of each state of the economy and the rates of return for each security in each state can be summarized as follows:

Probability	Security A	Security B
.50	5%	4%
.30	3	6
.20	5	-1

    a.   Compute the variance and standard deviation for each security.
    b.   Compute the covariance for the two securities.

In chapter 6, we considered the case of the constant dividend growth rate model. The model has a wonderful simplicity to it, provides critical insights into stock pricing, but is not realistic in its scenario. That is, few companies are envisioned as having dividends that grow at a constant rate forever. In this appendix, we will consider complex dividend growth rate models. They are more realistic in terms of application, but create more mathematical complexity in terms of solutions.

Case I: Deferred Dividend

Let's start by considering the case of a company that pays no dividend today. For the stock to have value, there must be an expectation of a dividend some time in the future, even if it is only a liquidating dividend. So, let's suppose that the company plans to reinvest all of its earnings for at least 20 years. However, at that time, the opportunities for reinvestment will diminish, and the company will begin to pay out part of its earnings as dividends, although it will keep the rest to finance a slower rate of growth. Thus, the company expects to pay a dividend of $25 per share, beginning 21 years from today, and that dividend is expected to grow at a 4 percent rate forever thereafter. Finally, let's assume that an appropriate discount rate is 10 percent.

A two-step process is required to solve this problem. First, we have to value what the price of the stock will be in 20 years. Second, we must then value what that stock is worth today, given that there are no dividends to be paid over that time.

Step 1: $P_{20} = d_{21} / (r - g) = \$25 / (0.10 - 0.04) = \$416.67.$

Step 2: $P_0 = P_{20} / (1 + r)^{20} = \$416.67 / (1 + 0.10)^{20} = \$61.94.$

Keystrokes:

Step 1: SHIFT, C ALL, 25, ÷, 0.06, = (display: 416.67)

Step 2: 416.67, FV, 10, I/YR, 20, N, PV (display: –61.94)

In step 1, keep in mind that if you want to value the stock 20 years from today using the constant growth rate model, you have to use in the numerator the dividend that will be paid one year from the point in time to which you are valuing the stock. In step 2, you are simply discounting the price back

20 years. Note that $61.94 per share is a nice price for a share of stock that currently pays no dividend, and is not expected to pay any for 20 years.

Case II: Flat Dividend, Followed by Constant Growth

Next, let's assume that the company in question is expected to pay a constant dividend of $1.00 per share for three years. Beginning four years from today, the dividend will grow at a rate of 4% forever. Let's also assume a 10% discount rate.

A four-step process is now required to determine the price of the stock today. Step 1 is to compute the present value of the dividends during the flat years. Step 2 is to value the stock once the constant growth starts, step 3 is to compute the present value of this stock price from Step 2, and step 4 is to add together the present value of the dividends from step 1 and the present value of the stock price from step 3.

Step 1: $\$1/(1 + 0.10)^1 + \$1/(1 + 0.10)^2 + \$1/(1 + 0.10)^3 = \$2.49$.

Step 2: $P_3 = d_4/(r - g) = \$1.04 / (0.10 - 0.04) = \$17.33$.

Step 3: $P_0 = P_3 / (1 + r)^3 = \$17.33 / (1 + 0.1)^3 = \$13.02$.

Step 4: *Value of stock today* $= \$2.49 + \$13.02 = \$15.51$.

Keystrokes: Step 1: SHIFT, C ALL, 3, N, 10, I/YR, 1, PMT, PV (DISPLAY: –2.49), +/–, M+

Steps 2 & 3: 1.04, ÷, 0.06, = (DISPLAY: 17.33), FV, 10, I/YR, 3, N, PV (DISPLAY: –13.02), +/–, M+

Step 4: RM (display: 15.51)

Note that in the suggested keystrokes we are able to treat the first three payments as an ordinary annuity because they are all of equal value.

Case III: Irregular Dividend Followed by Constant Growth

The next situation to consider is where the initial dividends vary, rather than form a nice, smooth annuity. An example might be this: the projected dividends for the next three years are $1, $1.50, and $2. Thereafter, the dividends will grow at a constant rate of 4% forever. Assume a discount rate of 10%. Once again, to price the stock today requires the same four-step process that we used in Case II. That is, step 1 is to compute the present value of the first three dividends; step 2 is to value the stock in three years;

step 3 is to find the present value of the stock price in three years; and step 4 is to add together the results from steps 1 and 3. Here are the calculations:

Step 1: $\$1/(1 + 0.10)^1 + \$1.50/(1 + 0.10)^2 + \$2/(1 + 0.10)^3 = \$3.65$.

Step 2: $P_3 = d_4 / (r - g) = d_3 \times (1 + g) / (r - g) = \$2 \times (1 + 0.04) / (0.10 - 0.04) = \$34.67$.

Step 3: $P_o = P_3 / (1 + r)^3 = \$34.67 / (1 + 0.10)^3 = \$26.05$.

Step 4: *Value of stock today* $= \$3.65 + \$26.05 = \$29.70$.

Keystrokes: Step 1: SHIFT, C ALL, 0, CFj, 1, CFj, 1.5, CFj, 2, CFj, 10, I/YR, SHIFT, NPV (display: 3.65), M+

Steps 2 & 3: 2, x, 1.04, =, ÷, 0.06, = (DISPLAY: 34.67), FV, 10, I/YR, 3, N, PV (DISPLAY: –26.05), +/–, M+

Step 4: RM (display: 29.70)]

Note that in the above calculations, we are treating the first three cash flows as a series of uneven cash flows, and using the NPV function key that was discussed in Appendix A.

Case IV: Rapid Growth Followed by Slow (Constant) Growth

What is probably the most popular version of complex growth models is the one known as fast (or supernormal) growth, slow growth. What makes this model interesting is that the first growth rate is usually defined as being greater than the discount rate. The second growth rate, of necessity, must be less than the discount rate. There is only one way to solve this type of problem. The student must first define each of the dividend payments during the rapid growth period. Then the model is solved exactly the same way as in Case III. Consider the following situation: assume that the dividend just paid was $1.00, and that dividends will grow at a rate of 20 percent per year for three years. After that, they will slow to an annual growth rate of 4 percent. Finally, let us continue to use the 10-percent discount rate. This now becomes a five-step process. Step 1 is to project out the dividends during the rapid growth period. Steps 2–5 then become identical to what had been steps 1–4 in Case III. Here are the calculations:

Step 1: $d_1 = \$1 \times (1 + 0.20) = \$1.20,$

$d_2 = d_1 \times (1 + g) = \$1.20 \times (1 + 0.20) = \$1.44,$

$d_3 = d_2 \times (1 + g) = \$1.44 \times (1 + 0.20) = \$1.73,$

$d_4 = d_3 \times (1 + 0.04) = \$1.73 \times 1.04 = \$1.80.$

Step 2: $\$1.20/(1 + 0.10)^1 + \$1.44/(1 + 0.10)^2 + \$1.73/(1 + 0.10)^3 = \$3.58.$

Step 3: $P_3 = d_4 /(r - g) = \$1.80/(0.10 - 0.04) = \$30.00.$

Step 4: $P_0 = P_3 / (1 + r)^3 = \$30.00 / (1 + 0.10)^3 = \$22.54.$

Step 5: *Value of stock today* = $\$3.58 + \$22.54 = \$26.12.$

Keystrokes: Steps 1 & 2: SHIFT, C ALL, 0, CFj, 1, x, 1.2, = (DISPLAY: 1.20), CFj, x, 1.2, = (DISPLAY: 1.44), CFj, x 1.2, = (DISPLAY: 1.73), CFj, 10, I/YR, SHIFT, NPV (DISPLAY: 3.58), M+

Steps 3 & 4: 1.80, ÷, 0.06, = (DISPLAY: 30.00), FV, 10, I/YR, 3, N, PV (DISPLAY: –22.54), +/–, M+

Step 5: RM (display: 26.12)]

Review Question

1. Evaluate the stock of ZYX Corporation using the following information: [2]
   a. Prospective annual dividends over the next five years: $1.10, $1.20, $1.30, $1.40, and $1.50.
   b. Discount rate: 10 percent.
   c. Growth rate of dividends beginning with the dividend in year six is 4 percent.

Suggested Answer to Review Question

$PV = [\$1.10/(1.10)^1] + [\$1.20/(1.10)^2] + [\$1.30/(1.10)^3] + [\$1.40/(1.10)^4] + [\$1.50/(1.10)^5]$
= \$4.86,

$P_5 = (1.50 \times 1.04)/(0.10 - 0.04) = \$26,$

$P_0 = \$26/1.10^5 = \$16.14,$

Price = PV of dividends + PV of stock price in five years = $\$4.86 + \$16.14 = \$21.00.$

HP-10BII keystrokes: SHIFT, C ALL, 0, CFj, 1.10, CFj, 1.20, CFj, 1.30, CFj, 1.40, CFj, 1.50, CFj, 10, I/YR, SHIFT, NPV (display: 4.86), M+, 1.50, x, 1.04, = (display 1.56), ÷, 0.06, = (display 26.00), FV, 5, N, 10, I/YR, PV = (display –16.14), +/–, M+, RM (display 21.00)

There are a couple of nuances that make the analysis of investor-managed (i.e., investor-owned) real estate a little more complicated. The most important is the treatment of depreciation, and the other is the occupancy rate.

Depreciation

Accountants have long-recognized deprecation because it supports the matching principle, which is the idea that in figuring whether one made or lost money during the year, one should match the resources expended with the revenue generated during the year. Depreciation is easily demonstrated with an asset such as an automobile that wears out over time, but whose deterioration is neither readily visible nor easily measurable on an annual basis. Consider a business that buys a new car for $30,000, uses it for 5 years, and then finds that the car can only be sold for $5,000. The expenses for operating the car each year, such as gas, insurance, repairs, and tolls, are easily measurable. It is not appropriate to recognize the $25,000 decline in value when the car is sold, as there is understated usage in the first four years, and overstated usage in the fifth year. There needs to be some recognition on a year-to-year basis.

If each business were left on its own to ascertain the deterioration in the value of the car each year, then there would likely be a wide variety in depreciation expenses reported, and the process would be time-consuming. The facilitate fairness and uniformity, the IRS Code provides depreciation schedules for different types of assets, such as cars and investor-owned real estate. The schedule specifies the number of years an asset is to be depreciated, and the depreciation charge per year. Sometimes, there is little relationship between the IRS depreciation schedule and the actual decline in the value of a real asset. In addition, this schedule changes occasionally, but the schedule in place when a property is acquired is the one that applies for as long as the property is owned. For purposes of this discussion, let us assume that depreciation is charged on a straight-line basis. Specifically, let us assume real estate is depreciated over a 40-year useful life, and that the depreciation charge is 1/40th per year, which is 2.5 percent per year.

When investment real estate is acquired, the buyer must designate how much of the purchase price is for the land, and how much is assigned to the building or buildings on the land. The depreciation schedule is applied only to the buildings. Land is never depreciated.

EXAMPLE
In 2008, Don Tyler bought an apartment building for $2 million. Based on his realtor's professional opinion, Don assigned a value of $500,000 to the land, and the remaining $1,500,000 to the building. The depreciation charge for the first year would be 2.5 percent of the $1,500,000, or $37,500 per year.

The presence of depreciation charges creates a distinction between net income and net cash flow. When analyzing real estate, the net cash flow number is usually the more important number to consider. When computing net income, depreciation is one of the charges deducted from revenue, just like any of the expenses that are paid with cash. The most common method to compute the net cash flow is to first compute the net income number and then add back the depreciation charge.

EXAMPLE
Let us continue the previous example. Suppose that Don took in $48,000 in rental income during his first year. He paid $40,000 for utilities, maintenance, property taxes, and various other cash expenses. When combining his cash expenses with the depreciation charge, Don's net income for the year is a loss of $29,500 ($48,000 − $40,000 − $37,500). His net cash flow is $8,000 (−$29,500 + $37,500).

Note that when there are no income taxes involved, the net cash flow could also be computed by simply subtracting the cash expenses from revenue.

Because the reported net income is a loss, there could be some beneficial income tax implications in the above example. Income taxes are discussed in detail in chapter 13, but for purposes of this discussion, let us assume a tax rate of 25 percent. With taxes, the $29,500 loss would result in a tax-savings of $7,375 (.25 x $29,500), as it reduces Don's taxable income by that amount. Furthermore, when this tax savings is factored in, his net cash flow becomes $15,375 ($8,000 + $7,375).

Most people will note that as long as buildings are reasonably maintained, they usually appreciate rather than depreciate. Thus, the majority of real estate, the majority of times, is sold at gains relative to their purchase price. It is this ability to take depreciation charges that are in fact not really occurring that makes the tax treatment of real estate quite beneficial, and is part of what may make real estate an attractive investment, especially for people who have to pay taxes at high rates.

Occupancy Rates

It is rare to have rental property that is always fully rented. One of the major contributors to achieving good returns in real estate is to keep a property as fully rented as possible. This would mean that a new renter would always be taking possession of the property on the day after an old renter's lease ended and he or she vacated the property. In the case of a single rental unit (such as a single-family residence), the occupancy rate is the percentage of the year the house is occupied. In the case of a multiple unit building, the occupancy rate is the ratio of the number of actual rental days sold divided by the number of rental days available. To analyze the revenue implications for a given occupancy rate, simply multiply the occupancy rate by either the number of units that are available for renting, or by the revenue that would be generated if all units were rented at all times.

EXAMPLE
Let us continue the previous example. Suppose that Don's building has five units that can be rented, and his occupancy rate is 80 per cent. To make a revenue projection, assume that four units (.80 x 5) are rented all of the time and the fifth unit is unoccupied the entire year. Similarly, if Don's rental income would be $60,000 per year if all units were rented all of the time (i.e., the rental rate is $1,000 per month per unit), and his occupancy rate is 80 per cent, then his rental income is $48,000 (.80 x $60,000).

Review Question

1. You are considering buying a building on January 1. The building has 20 units that you believe you could rent each for $1,500 per month. The asking price for the building is $10,000,000, 20 percent of the purchase price would be allocated to the land, and the building would be depreciated over a 40-year life on a straight-line basis. The cash expenses would be about $200,000 per year. The projected occupancy rate is 90 percent. Your marginal tax rate is 40%.
    a. What is the projected net income for the first year?
    b. What is the projected net cash flow for the first year?

Suggested Answer to Review Question

a. Revenue = .90 occupancy rate x 20 units x $1,500 per month rental per unit x 12 months per year = $324,000

Depreciable Basis = $10,000,000 x (1 − .20) = $8,000,000

Depreciation Charge = $8,000,000 / 40 = $200,000 per year

Net Income = Revenue − cash expenses − depreciation = $324,000 − $200,000 − $200,000 = −$76,000

b. Tax Savings = 40% x $76,000 = $30,400

Net Cash Flow = Net Income + Depreciation + Tax Savings = − $76,000 + $200,000 + $30,400= $154,400

Consider the case of a client who has a 7-year time horizon. If the client wants to be immunized, then he or she should hold a bond portfolio whose duration is 7 years. The best candidate is a zero-coupon bond with a 7-year maturity. However, to make the example interesting, let's choose a bond with a maturity of 10 years, a coupon rate of 10 percent with annual payments, and a yield to maturity of 8 percent. The price of this bond is $1,134.20 (SHIFT, C ALL; 1000, FV; 1000, x, .10, =, PMT; 10, N; 8, I/YR; PV; display: –1,134.20). The duration statistic is 6.97 years, computed as

$$D_A = \frac{1 + .08}{.08} - \frac{(1 + .08) + 10(.10 - .08)}{.10[(1 + .08)^{10} - 1] + .08}$$
$$= 6.97$$

Although this duration statistic is not exactly 7.0, it is close enough for our purposes, and it makes for a more realistic example.

The first point to make is that if interest rates do not change, regardless of the holding period, the client will receive an effective rate of return of 8 percent. That is, if the yield to maturity stays at 8 percent and if all of the reinvested coupons earn 8 percent, the client's effective annual rate of return will be 8 percent, regardless of whether he or she sells the bond in 7 years or holds it for all 10 years.

What Happens When the Interest Rate Goes Up

Let's say that the day after the client buys the bond, interest rates rise to 10 percent. The immediate impact of this event is that the bond's price will fall to $1,000 (remember, whenever the coupon rate equals the yield to maturity, the price will equal par, regardless of any other conditions that apply). The bad news is the increase in interest rates has reduced the price of the bond. The good news is that the client can now reinvest his or her coupon payments at a higher interest rate. To see the effect of the higher interest rate, let's look at the value of the client's holding after 7 years. Remember, the client has a 7-year holding period, and thus intends to liquidate his or her investment at that time. Let's consider first the value of the coupon payments. The client will have received seven annual payments of $100 each, beginning 1 year from today and ending 7 years from today, and will have reinvested these at a rate of return of 10 percent. This is a future-value-of-annuity problem. To solve it on a HP-10BII calculator, use the following keystrokes:

> SHIFT, C ALL
>
> 1000, x, .10, =, PMT
>
> 7, N
>
> 10, I/YR
>
> FV (display: −948.72)

This next step is the tricky part. At the end of 7 years, the client will sell the bond. Therefore, we have to figure out what the bond's price will be at that time. Seven years from today, this bond will have 3 years to maturity and a 10 percent yield to maturity. The price will be $1,000, the same as it is today (for the same reason). The total value of the investment from the liquidation of the reinvested coupons and selling the bond is $1,948.72. The initial investment by the client is $1,134.20 (that is, the price of the bond today). The one question remaining is, what is the effective annual rate of return on an investment worth $1,134.20 today and $1,948.72 in 7 years? The keystrokes to solve this problem are

> SHIFT, C ALL
>
> 1134.20, +/−, PV
>
> 1948.72, FV
>
> 7, N
>
> I/YR (display: 8.04)

The answer is 8.04 percent. The yield to maturity at the time of the bond purchase was 8 percent. So the client has actually exceeded the expected HPR of 8 percent by 4 basis points. More important, however, is to understand why. The answer is that the bond chosen for immunization had a duration of 6.97 years, not 7.0 years exactly. Thus, the immunization was only near perfect, not perfect.

What Happens When the Interest Rate Goes Down

Let's now consider the other possibility, namely that market interest rates drop to 6 percent the day after the client buys the bond. In this case, the immediate impact of the interest rate decline is that the price will increase to $1,294.40 (SHIFT, C ALL; 1000, FV; 1000, x, .10, =, PMT; 10, N; 6, I/YR; PV; display: −1,294.40). This, of course, will make the client quite happy, but unfortunately the client now faces the prospect of reinvesting the coupon payments at a lower than expected rate (6 percent versus 8 percent). Once again, let us compute the future value of this annuity of $100 per year for 7 years. The keystrokes are

> SHIFT, C ALL
>
> 1000, x, .10, =, PMT
>
> 7, N
>
> 6, I/YR
>
> FV (display: −839.38)

Note that the future value of these reinvested coupons is about $109 less than their future value when the reinvestment rate was 10 percent.

Again, the tricky part is to determine the price at which the client can sell the bond in 7 years. As before, at that time, the term to maturity will be 3 years. But in this case, the YTM will be 6 percent. The price will be $1,106.92 (SHIFT, C ALL; 1000, FV; 1000, x, .10, =, PMT; 3, N; 6, I/YR; PV (display: −1,106.92)). The combined value of the reinvested coupon payments and the proceeds from selling the bond is $1,946.30 ($1,106.92 + $839.38). Finally, we again have to solve for the effective annual rate of return for an investor who starts with an investment of $1,134.20 and ends with $1,946.30. The answer is 8.02 percent, and the keystrokes are

> SHIFT, C ALL
>
> 1134.20, +/−, PV
>
> 1946.30, FV
>
> 7, N
>
> I/YR (display: 8.02)

Once again, the final answer is near perfect, but it is not exactly perfect because the bond selected did not have the perfect immunization number.

Implications for Portfolio Management

Note that the preceding analyses are simplistic in nature. They assume that interest rates change once during the client's time horizon, and that the change occurs before the next coupon payment. They also assume that the coupon payments can be reinvested at the same rate as the new yield to maturity on the bond. In fact, implicit in the analysis is the assumption that the yield curve is flat. This should be apparent because we assumed that after the initial change in interest rates, the yield to maturity on the bond and the reinvested coupons did not change, despite the fact the bond was moving toward maturity. Furthermore, we did not provide any specification as to the maturity of the instruments in which the coupons were invested.

Although all of these assumptions are highly unrealistic, they provide the basis for an immunization strategy. Clearly, an actual immunization strategy can work better for a large bond portfolio than for a single bond because the coupon payments would be of sufficient size to reinvest at the same yield and term to maturity as the client's holding period. Furthermore, immunization requires active monitoring. Because interest rates have the potential to change on a daily basis, an immunized portfolio must be adjusted regularly. Research on the optimal frequency of monitoring and adjusting the portfolio suggests that quarterly monitoring is sufficient.

Review Question

1.   Your client, Johanna Tyson, has an investment-planning horizon of 7 years. Current interest rates are 4 percent and she would like to minimize the risk of not receiving this rate of return. You are considering an immunization strategy that involves the purchase of a bond with a term to maturity of 9 years and a coupon rate of 8 percent. The YTM is, of course, 4 percent.
     a.   What is the price of this bond today?
     b.   What would her annual HPR be if interest rates jump to 6 percent immediately after buying the bond and she sells the bond after 7 years?
     c.   What would her annual HPR be if interest rates drop to 2 percent immediately after buying the bond?

Suggested Answer to Review Question

   1. Answer:

      a. HP-10BII keystrokes:

         SHIFT, C ALL,

         1000, FV, 4, I/YR, 9, N, 1000, x, .08, =, PMT, PV
         (display: –$1,297.41)

      b. Step 1: Determine the future value of the coupon payments.

SHIFT, C ALL,

6, I/YR, 7, N, 1000, x, .08, =, PMT, FV (display: –$671.51)

Step 2: Determine the selling price of the bond.

SHIFT, C ALL,

6, I/YR, 2, N, 1000, x, .08, =, PMT, 1000, FV, PV (display: –$1,036.67)

Step 3: Add the two ending values together.

$671.51 + $1,036.67 = $1,708.18

Step 4: Determine the HPR for this 7-year period.

SHIFT, C ALL,

1708.18, FV, 1297.41, +/–, PV, 7, N, I/YR (display: 4.00[%])

c. Step 1: Determine the future value of the coupon payments.

SHIFT, C ALL,

2, I/YR, 7, N, 1000, x, .08, =, PMT, FV (display: –$594.74)

Step 2: Determine the selling price of the bond.

SHIFT, C ALL,

2, I/YR, 2, N, 1000, x, .08, =, PMT, 1000, FV, PV (display: –$1,116.49)

Step 3: Add the two ending values together.

$594.74 + $1,116.49 = $1,711.23

Step 4: Determine the HPR for this 7-year period.

SHIFT, C ALL,

1711.23, FV, 1297.41, +/–, PV, 7, N, I/YR (display: 4.03[%])

The Black-Scholes formula[196] for pricing a call option is based on the following assumptions:

- The capital markets are frictionless—that is, there are no transaction costs or taxes, and all information is simultaneously and freely available to all investors.
- There are no short-sale restrictions.
- All asset prices follow a continuous stationary, lognormal, stochastic process.
- There is a constant risk-free rate of return over time, at which investors can borrow as well as lend.
- No dividends are paid.
- No early exercise is permitted (that is, European call options)

The resulting formula is as follows:

$$C_0 = S_0 N(d_1) - \frac{S N(d_2)}{e^{r_f t}}$$

$$d_1 = \frac{\ln(S_0/S) + (r_f + .5\sigma^2)t}{\sigma\sqrt{t}}$$

$$d_2 = \frac{\ln(S_0/S) + (r_f - .5\sigma^2)t}{\sigma\sqrt{t}}$$

where C_0 = option value

r_f = continuously compound riskless annual interest rate

S_0 = stock price

S = strike price of option

e = 2.718 (the natural logarithmic constant)

---

196. Knowledge of the Black-Scholes formula is not required for either the CFP™ exam or The American College course exam. The use of the Black-Scholes formula to estimate option values is appropriate for the more advanced student who is interested in examples of how option prices can be derived.

$t =$ time to expiration of option as a fraction of a year

$\sigma =$ the standard deviation of the continuously compounded annual rate of return of the underlying stock

$\ln (S_0/S) =$ natural logarithm of S_0/S

$N(d) =$ value of the standard normal cumulative distribution evaluated at d

Tables G-1 and G-2 are normal cumulative distribution tables that can be used to find the value of $N(d)$.

EXAMPLE

Given the following information:[197]

- The current market price of the stock (S_0) is $23/share.

- The option's strike price (S) is $25/share.

- The option has 3 months until expiration (t = .25).

- The standard deviation of the stock's return (σ) is .5 (50% per year).

- The risk-free rate of interest is 4 percent (r_f = .04).

We would estimate the value for a call option under the Black-Scholes model follows:

$S_0/S = \$23/\$25 = .92$

$\ln(S_0/S) = \ln(.92) = -.0834$

$(r_f + .5\sigma^2)t = (.04 + .5 \times .5 \times .5) \times .25 = .0413$

$\sigma\sqrt{t} = .5 \times \sqrt{.25} = .25$

$d_1 = (-.0834 + .0413)/.25 = -.1684$

Using table G-2 and interpolating, $N(d_1) = .4331$

$(r_f - .5\sigma^2) t = (.04 - .125) \times .25 = -.085 \times .25$

$= -.0213$

$d_2 = (-.0834 - .0213)/.25 = -.4188$

---

197. Calculators for pricing an option are available online. A particularly good one can be found at www.cboe.com. Click on "Options Calculator" under the Tools tab. Select "European" and then enter the following data: Index price, 23; Strike Price, 25; Volatility, 50; Annual Interest rate, 4; Annual Dividend yield, 0; and Days until Expiration, 91. The price of this call option should then be displayed at $1.5978. The calculator also shows the put option with the same terms to be valued at $3.3476.

Using table G-2 and interpolating, $N(d_2) = .3376$

$$r_f t = .04 \times .25 = .01$$
$$e^{r_f t} = e^{.01} = 1.01$$

The value of the call option (C_0) is

$$C_0 = (\$23 \times .4331) - (\$25 \times .3376/1.01)$$
$$= \$9.96 - \$8.36 = \$1.60$$

Review Problem

1. Using the Black-Scholes formula, estimate the value of a call option with 3 months to maturity and a strike price of $95 when the market price of the underlying stock is $100, the standard deviation of the stock's price is .5 (50% per year), and the risk-free rate is 10 percent.

Suggested Answer to Review Problem

1. The estimated value of the call option is $13.71, calculated as shown below:

$$S_0 = 100$$
$$S = 95$$
$$S_0/S = 100/95 = 1.0526$$
$$\ln(S_0/S) = .0513$$
$$\sigma = .5$$
$$.5 \times \sigma^2 = .5 \times .5 \times .5 = .125$$
$$r_f = .10$$
$$r_f + .5 \times \sigma^2 = .10 + .125 = .225$$
$$t = .25$$
$$(r_f + .5\sigma^2)\, t = .225 \times .25 = .0563$$
$$\sigma\sqrt{t} = .5 \times \sqrt{.25} = .25$$
$$d_1 = (.0513 + .0563)/.25 = .4302$$
$$N(d_1) = .6665$$
$$r_f - .5\sigma^2 = .10 - .5 \times .5 \times .5 = -.025$$
$$(r_f - .5\sigma^2)t = -0.25 \times .25 = -.0063$$

$d_2 = (.0531 - .0063)/.25 = .18$

$N(d_2) = .5714$

$r_f t = .10 \times .25 = .025$

$e^{r_f t} = e^{.025} = 1.0253$

$C = 100 \times .6665 - (95 \times .5714)/1.0253 = 66.65 - 52.94 = \$13.71$

Table G-1
For Values of N(x) When x ≥ 0

This table shows values of $N(x)$ for $x \geq 0$. The table should be used with interpolation. For example,

$N(0.6278) = N(0.62) + 0.78[N(0.63) - N(0.62)]$

$= 0.7324 + 0.78 \times (0.7357 - 0.7324)$

$= 0.7350$

x	.00	.01	.02	.03	.04	.05	.06	.07	.08	.09
0.0	0.5000	0.5040	0.5080	0.5120	0.5160	0.5199	0.5239	0.5279	0.5319	0.5359
0.1	0.5398	0.5438	0.5478	0.5517	0.5557	0.5596	0.5636	0.5675	0.5714	0.5753
0.2	0.5793	0.5832	0.5871	0.5910	0.5948	0.5987	0.6026	0.6064	0.6103	0.6141
0.3	0.6179	0.6217	0.6255	0.6293	0.6331	0.6368	0.6406	0.6443	0.6480	0.6517
0.4	0.6554	0.6591	0.6628	0.6664	0.6700	0.6736	0.6772	0.6808	0.6844	0.6879
0.5	0.6915	0.6950	0.6985	0.7019	0.7054	0.7088	0.7123	0.7157	0.7190	0.7224
0.6	0.7257	0.7291	0.7324	0.7357	0.7389	0.7422	0.7454	0.7486	0.7517	0.7549
0.7	0.7580	0.7611	0.7642	0.7673	0.7704	0.7734	0.7764	0.7794	0.7823	0.7852
0.8	0.7881	0.7910	0.7939	0.7967	0.7995	0.8023	0.8051	0.8078	0.8106	0.8133
0.9	0.8159	0.8186	0.8212	0.8238	0.8264	0.8289	0.8315	0.8340	0.8365	0.8389
1.0	0.8413	0.8438	0.8461	0.8485	0.8508	0.8531	0.8554	0.8577	0.8599	0.8621
1.1	0.8643	0.8665	0.8686	0.8708	0.8729	0.8749	0.8770	0.8790	0.8810	0.8830
1.2	0.8849	0.8869	0.8888	0.8907	0.8925	0.8944	0.8962	0.8990	0.8997	0.9015
1.3	0.9032	0.9049	0.9066	0.9082	0.9099	0.9115	0.9131	0.9147	0.9162	0.9177
1.4	0.9192	0.9207	0.9222	0.9236	0.9251	0.9265	0.9279	0.9292	0.9306	0.9319
1.5	0.9332	0.9345	0.9357	0.9370	0.9382	0.9394	0.9406	0.9418	0.9429	0.9441
1.6	0.9452	0.9463	0.9474	0.9484	0.9495	0.9505	0.9515	0.9525	0.9535	0.9545
1.7	0.9554	0.9564	0.9573	0.9582	0.9591	0.9599	0.9608	0.9616	0.9625	0.9633
1.8	0.9641	0.9649	0.9656	0.9664	0.9671	0.9678	0.9686	0.9693	0.9699	0.9706
1.9	0.9713	0.9719	0.9726	0.9732	0.9738	0.9744	0.9750	0.9756	0.9761	0.9767
2.0	0.9772	0.9778	0.9783	0.9788	0.9793	0.9798	0.9803	0.9808	0.9812	0.9817
2.1	0.9821	0.9826	0.9830	0.9834	0.9838	0.9842	0.9846	0.9850	0.9854	0.9857
2.2	0.9861	0.9864	0.9868	0.9871	0.9875	0.9878	0.9881	0.9884	0.9887	0.9890
2.3	0.9893	0.9896	0.9898	0.9901	0.9904	0.9906	0.9909	0.9911	0.9913	0.9916
2.4	0.9918	0.9920	0.9922	0.9925	0.9927	0.9929	0.9931	0.9932	0.9934	0.9936
2.5	0.9938	0.9940	0.9941	0.9943	0.9945	0.9946	0.9948	0.9949	0.9951	0.9952
2.6	0.9953	0.9955	0.9956	0.9957	0.9959	0.9960	0.9961	0.9962	0.9963	0.9964
2.7	0.9965	0.9966	0.9967	0.9968	0.9969	0.9970	0.9971	0.9972	0.9973	0.9974
2.8	0.9974	0.9975	0.9976	0.9977	0.9977	0.9978	0.9979	0.9979	0.9980	0.9981
2.9	0.9981	0.9982	0.9982	0.9983	0.9984	0.9984	0.9985	0.9985	0.9986	0.9986
3.0	0.9986	0.9987	0.9987	0.9988	0.9988	0.9989	0.9989	0.9989	0.9990	0.9990
3.1	0.9990	0.9991	0.9991	0.9991	0.9992	0.9992	0.9992	0.9992	0.9993	0.9993
3.2	0.9993	0.9993	0.9994	0.9994	0.9994	0.9994	0.9994	0.9995	0.9995	0.9995
3.3	0.9995	0.9995	0.9995	0.9996	0.9996	0.9996	0.9996	0.9996	0.9996	0.9997
3.4	0.9997	0.9997	0.9997	0.9997	0.9997	0.9997	0.9997	0.0007	0.9997	0.9998
3.5	0.9998	0.9998	0.9998	0.9998	0.9998	0.9998	0.9998	0.9998	0.9998	0.9998
3.6	0.9998	0.9998	0.9999	0.9999	0.9999	0.9999	0.9999	0.9999	0.9999	0.9999
3.7	0.9999	0.9999	0.9999	0.9999	0.9999	0.9999	0.9999	0.9999	0.9999	0.9999
3.8	0.9999	0.9999	0.9999	0.9999	0.9999	0.9999	0.9999	0.9999	0.9999	0.9999
3.9	1.0000	1.0000	1.0000	1.0000	1.0000	1.0000	1.0000	1.0000	1.0000	1.0000

Table G-2
For Values of N(x) When x ≤ 0

This table shows values of N(x) for x ≤ 0. The table should be used with interpolation. For example,
$N(-0.1234) = N(-0.12) - 0.34[N(-0.12) - N(-0.13)]$
$= 0.4522 - 0.34 \times (0.4522 - 0.4483)$
$= 0.4509$

x	.00	.01	.02	.03	.04	.05	.06	.07	.08	.09
0.00	0.5000	0.4960	0.4920	0.4880	0.4840	0.4801	0.4761	0.4721	0.4681	0.4641
0.10	0.4602	0.4562	0.4522	0.4483	0.4443	0.4404	0.4364	0.4325	0.4286	0.4247
0.20	0.4207	0.4168	0.4129	0.4090	0.4052	0.4013	0.3974	0.3936	0.3897	0.3859
0.30	0.3821	0.3783	0.3745	0.3707	0.3669	0.3632	0.3594	0.3557	0.3520	0.3483
0.40	0.3446	0.3409	0.3372	0.3336	0.3300	0.3264	0.3228	0.3192	0.3156	0.3121
0.50	0.3085	0.3050	0.3015	0.2981	0.2946	0.2912	0.2877	0.2843	0.2810	0.2776
0.60	0.2743	0.2709	0.2676	0.2643	0.2611	0.2578	0.2546	0.2514	0.2483	0.2451
0.70	0.2420	0.2389	0.2358	0.2327	0.2296	0.2266	0.2236	0.2206	0.2177	0.2148
0.80	0.2119	0.2090	0.2061	0.2033	0.2005	0.1977	0.1949	0.1922	0.1894	0.1867
0.90	0.1841	0.1814	0.1788	0.1762	0.1736	0.1711	0.1685	0.1660	0.1635	0.1611
1.00	0.1587	0.1562	0.1539	0.1515	0.1492	0.1469	0.1446	0.1423	0.1401	0.1379
1.10	0.1357	0.1335	0.1314	0.1292	0.1271	0.1251	0.1230	0.1210	0.1190	0.1170
1.20	0.1151	0.1131	0.1112	0.1093	0.1075	0.1056	0.1038	0.1020	0.1003	0.0985
1.30	0.0968	0.0951	0.0934	0.0918	0.0901	0.0885	0.0869	0.0853	0.0838	0.0823
1.40	0.0808	0.0793	0.0778	0.0764	0.0749	0.0735	0.0721	0.0708	0.0694	0.0681
1.50	0.0668	0.9655	0.0643	0.0630	0.0618	0.0606	0.0594	0.0582	0.0571	0.0559
1.60	0.0548	0.0537	0.0526	0.0516	0.0505	0.0495	0.0485	0.0475	0.0465	0.0455
1.70	0.0446	0.9436	0.0427	0.0418	0.0409	0.0401	0.0392	0.0384	0.0375	0.0367
1.80	0.0359	0.0351	0.0344	0.0336	0.0329	0.0322	0.0314	0.0307	0.0301	0.0294
1.90	0.0287	0.0281	0.0274	0.0268	0.0262	0.0256	0.0250	0.0244	0.0239	0.0233
2.00	0.0228	0.0222	0.0217	0.0212	0.0207	0.0202	0.0197	0.0192	0.0188	0.0183
2.10	0.0179	0.0174	0.0170	0.0166	0.0162	0.0158	0.0154	0.0150	0.0146	0.0143
2.20	0.0139	0.0136	0.0132	0.0129	0.0125	0.0122	0.0119	0.0116	0.0113	0.0110
2.30	0.0107	0.0104	0.0102	0.0099	0.0096	0.0094	0.0091	0.0089	0.0087	0.0084
2.40	0.0082	0.0080	0.0078	0.0075	0.0073	0.0071	0.0069	0.0068	0.0066	0.0064
2.50	0.0062	0.0060	0.0059	0.0057	0.0055	0.0054	0.0052	0.0051	0.0049	0.0048
2.60	0.0047	0.0045	0.0044	0.0043	0.0041	0.0040	0.0039	0.0038	0.0037	0.0036
2.70	0.0035	0.0034	0.0033	0.0032	0.0031	0.0030	0.0029	0.0028	0.0027	0.0026
2.80	0.0026	0.0025	0.0024	0.0023	0.0023	0.0022	0.0021	0.0021	0.0020	0.0019
2.90	0.0019	0.0018	0.0018	0.0017	0.0016	0.0016	0.0015	0.0015	0.0014	0.0014
3.00	0.0014	0.0013	0.0013	0.0012	0.0012	0.0011	0.0011	0.0011	0.0010	0.0010
3.10	0.0010	0.0009	0.0009	0.0009	0.0008	0.0008	0.0008	0.0008	0.0007	0.0007
3.20	0.0007	0.0007	0.0006	0.0006	0.0006	0.0006	0.0006	0.0005	0.0005	0.0005
3.30	0.0005	0.0005	0.0005	0.0004	0.0004	0.0004	0.0004	0.0004	0.0004	0.0003
3.40	0.0003	0.0003	0.0003	0.0003	0.0003	0.0003	0.0003	0.0003	0.0003	0.0002
3.50	0.0002	0.0002	0.0002	0.0002	0.0002	0.0002	0.0002	0.0002	0.0002	0.0002
3.60	0.0002	0.0002	0.0001	0.0001	0.0001	0.0001	0.0001	0.0001	0.0001	0.0001
3.70	0.0001	0.0001	0.0001	0.0001	0.0001	0.0001	0.0001	0.0001	0.0001	0.0001
3.80	0.0001	0.0001	0.0001	0.0001	0.0001	0.0001	0.0001	0.0001	0.0001	0.0001
3.90	0.0000	0.0000	0.0000	0.0000	0.0000	0.0000	0.0000	0.0000	0.0000	0.0000

Glossary

absolute-priority-of-claims principle • the principle in bankruptcy law that each class of liability claims is to be repaid in full before the succeeding category receives even partial payment

account maintenance fee • an annual fee charged by mutual funds, typically assessed to every account held by the investor

accumulation value • an annuity's value before any surrender charges

acid test ratio (quick ratio) • cash and accounts receivable divided by current liabilities; used to measure short-term liquidity

additional commitment risk • the degree to which an investment asset may require the buyer to put additional money into the investment

adjusted gross income (AGI) • the figure derived by subtracting certain adjustments from gross income

ADR • *See* American Depository Receipt.

advance-decline ratio • ratio of advancing stocks to declining stocks; high values are bullish if they persist

agency problem • the conflict of interests and disparity of goals between corporate managers and shareholders

agency security • a debt security issued by federal agencies such as the FNMA, GNMA, or Freddie Mac

AGI • *See* adjusted gross income.

all-or-nothing order • an order that must be executed in its entirety or not at all

alpha • the intercept term in the market model; in the arbitrage pricing model, the return that would be expected when all the independent variables equal their expected values

alternative minimum tax • tax that may be applicable to those with large amounts of otherwise sheltered income (preferences); applies when the tax liability computed by disallowing these preferences exceeds the liability when the tax is computed the normal way

American depository receipt (ADR) • a U.S.-traded security representing stock in a foreign corporation, priced in U.S. dollars

American option • an option that may be closed out or exercised at any time prior to or at its expiration date

American Stock Exchange (AMEX) • an organized stock exchange tending to deal in small- to mid-capitalization stocks; also known as the Curb Exchange

analyst neglect (neglected firm effect) • an alleged anomaly to the efficient market hypothesis that is characterized by the tendency of security analysts to overlook small or obscure firms in their security evaluations

annuity • a series of equal, consecutive, periodic payments. Also, an asset that usually promises to pay a fixed amount periodically for a predetermined period, although some pay a sum for an individual's lifetime.

annuity due • a series of equal, consecutive, periodic payments in which the first payment occurs immediately

anomaly • condition in the security markets that appears to allow for persistent abnormal returns after adjusting for risk

anxious trader effects • short-run price distortions caused by sales or purchases of impatient large traders

arbitrage • simultaneously buying in one market and selling equivalent assets in another for a certain riskless profit

arbitrage pricing model • a model used to explain stock pricing and expected return that introduces more than one factor in place of (or in addition to) the capital asset pricing model's market index

arbitrageur • a trader who attempts to exploit price differentials for equivalent investments or for the same investment in different markets

arithmetic mean return • the average return found by dividing the sum of the separate per-period returns by the number of periods over which they were earned

ask price (ask) • the price at which a dealer or market maker is willing to sell a particular security to an investor

asset allocation • the principal method of portfolio management by financial planners, based on the idea of dividing wealth among different types of assets

asset allocation fund • mutual fund that allows managers considerable flexibility in allocating the portfolio among the three major asset categories (stocks, bonds, and money market instruments) as market conditions change

asset turnover ratio • ratio of net sales to total assets

at-the-money option • an option whose strike price is equal to the current market price

average collection period (ACP) • net accounts receivable divided by daily sales

average tax rate • total amount of income tax paid divided by total income

back-end loads • fees assessed on a mutual fund account at redemption

balance of trade • the difference between a country's expenditures on imports and its proceeds from exports

balance sheet • a financial statement showing a firm's or individual's financial position that lists assets, liabilities, and net worth (equity) as of a particular point in time

banker's acceptance • a money market instrument usually arising from international trade and containing a bank's guarantee or acceptance

bankruptcy • a legal process for dealing formally with a defaulted obligation; may result in a liquidation or reorganization

bar chart • a type of graph that plots the price of the stock over time and typically contains data on the daily high and low prices, and volume

Barron's Confidence Index • a technical indicator based on the ratio of high-grade to average-grade bond yields, where a high value is bullish

basis • cash market price less price of a futures contract basis point one-hundredth of one percentage point; primarily used with interest rates

bear • one who expects a declining market

bear market • a declining market

bear raid • an attempt to drive prices down by massive short sales

bearish spread • an options strategy using two puts or two calls when a stock price decline is anticipated

benchmarks • standards of comparison used for portfolio performance goal setting and evaluation

Bermuda options • options that can be exercised on a multiple set of predetermined dates (the last being the expiration date)

best-effort basis • a securities offering in which the underwriter acts as an agent for the issuer and promises to use its best effort to sell the securities

beta • a parameter in the CAPM and APM models that relates stock or portfolio performance to market performance

bid-ask spread • the price difference between the bid price and the ask price for an asset

bid price • the price at which a dealer or market maker is willing to buy a particular security from an investor

Big Board • popular term for the New York Stock Exchange

binomial option-pricing model • a call option-pricing model that is an alternative to the Black-Scholes model

Black-Scholes model • the most commonly used call option-pricing formula

blind pool • a form of investment venture in which the precise purposes of the venture are not revealed to the pool of investors until later

block trade • a trade involving 10,000 shares or more, usually handled by a block trader

block trader • a member of the exchange who specializes in handling large trades in ways designed to minimize potential market disruptions

bond • a debt obligation (usually long-term) in which the borrower promises to pay a set coupon rate until the issue matures, at which time the principal is repaid

bond equivalent yield • a historic formula used for quoting prices on Treasury bills; BEY = [(10,000 price)/price] x (365/DTM)

bond fund • mutual fund that owns a portfolio of bonds

bond rating • a rating of a bond's investment quality and default risk, provided by a rating agency such as Standard & Poor's, Moody's, or Fitch

bond swap • a sale of one set of bonds and the purchase of another set to accomplish any one of several objectives

book value per share • the total assets of an enterprise minus its liabilities, minority interests, and preferred stock at par, divided by the number of common shares outstanding

brackets • the income ranges associated with different marginal tax rates

broker • an employee of a financial intermediary who acts as an agent (not a dealer) in buying and selling securities for customers

broker call-loan rate • the interest rate charged by banks to brokerage firms for loans that these firms use to support their margin loans to customers

brokerage firm • a firm that offers various financial services such as access to the securities markets, account management, margin loans, investment advice, and underwriting

bull • one who expects a rising market

bull market • a rising market

bullish call spread • an options strategy using two puts or two calls when a stock price increase is anticipated

business risk • the degree to which an enterprise's performance is subject to potential risk factors such as a change in consumer preference away from a particular good or service, ineffective management, law change, or foreign competition

buying on margin • the purchase of securities with borrowed monies

buying power • the dollar value of additional securities that can be purchased on margin with the current equity in a margin account

call feature • the provision that a bond is callable by the issuer. The call feature includes the call premium, the call price, and any timing constraints.

call-loan rate • *See* broker call-loan rate.

call option (call) • an option to buy stock or some other asset at a prespecified price over a prespecified time period

call premium • the additional amount above the face value that the issuer must pay to redeem a bond prior to its maturity date

call price • the price at which a bond, preferred stock, warrant, or other security may be redeemed prior to maturity. The call price is equal to the face value plus the call premium.

call provision • a provision in a bond indenture that gives the issuer the option of redeeming the bond prior to maturity

call risk • risk that a bond issuer may force redemption of its bonds prior to maturity

capital appreciation share • one of the two classes of shares in a dual purpose investment company. It promises no dividends during the life of the income shares.

capital asset pricing model (CAPM) • the theoretical model that seeks to explain returns as a function of the relationship between the risk-free rate, market risk premium, and beta

capital distribution • a dividend paid out of capital rather than from earnings. Such distributions are not taxed when received but do reduce the investment's cost basis.

capital gain (loss) • the difference between the market value of a holding and its cost basis, when the market value exceeds (is less than) the cost basis

capital market line • the line formed by combinations of the risk-free asset and the market portfolio

CAPM • *See* capital asset pricing model.

cash account • the most basic account for an investor, it is sometimes referred to as a Type 1 account. An investor must have sufficient cash already in the account to complete any purchases.

cash flow • sum of earnings plus depreciation

cash flow per share • the sum of after-tax profits and depreciation and other noncash expense divided by the number of shares of common stock outstanding

CD-type annuities • annuities that provide guaranteed rates over selected periods of time and a predetermined number of payments

Chapter VII • the chapter in the bankruptcy code that is used for the liquidation of businesses

Chapter XI • the chapter in the bankruptcy code that is used to allow firms the opportunity to reorganize under the protection of the bankruptcy court

characteristic line • the line defined by regressing the returns of a particular security against the return on a market index

charting • a graphical representation of stock price changes

chartist • technical analyst who uses price and volume charts to forecast prices

churning • trades that are made for the primary purpose of generating commission income for the broker

circuit breaker • a rule specifying conditions under which trading will be suspended

clearing firm • the firm that holds the customer's cash and securities and sends out statements describing the assets it holds as "on deposit" for the customer

closed-end investment company • a type of investment company whose shares are traded in the same markets as other stocks (the price varies from the fund's net asset value)

closing out a position • in options or futures trading, using an offsetting transaction to remove the investor from further exposure to the investment

CMO (collateralized mortgage obligation) • multiclass mortgage pass-through security that reduces uncertainty about prepayments by specifying time of repayment

coefficient of determination (R^2) • a parameter that measures how much of the variance of a particular time series or sample of a dependent variable is accounted for (explained by) the movement of the independent variable(s) in a regression analysis. With respect to portfolios, it is a measure of diversification.

coefficient of variation • the standard deviation of return divided by the mean return

coincident indicators • an economic series published by the National Bureau of Economic Research that is believed to track concurrently with the status of the economy in the normal business cycle

collectibles • assets accumulated by collectors, includes such items as coins, stamps, art, and antiques

combination position • any position in which more than a single put, single call, or single position in the underlying stock is held

commercial paper • short-term, nearly riskless debt instrument issued by large corporations with strong credit ratings

commodity-backed bond • debt security whose potential redemption value is related to the market price of some physical commodity

common stock fund • mutual fund that holds a portfolio consisting primarily of common stocks

company analysis • an examination of a firm's relative strengths and weaknesses

compound interest • interest earned on interest as a result of reinvesting one period's income to earn additional income the following period

compounding • the accrual of interest on interest

concentrated portfolio • a portfolio in which a disproportionately large percentage of the value is in one or a few securities

constant growth model (Gordon growth model) • form of the dividend discount model in which dividends are assumed to grow at a constant rate forever

contingent deferred sales charge • a fee, calculated as a percentage of net asset value, that investors might pay to redeem their shares of a mutual fund depending on how long the shares are held

contrarian rationale • the concept that certain investors are wrong more often than they are right, so one should ascertain what these investors are doing and do the opposite

conversion premium • the difference between the market price and the conversion value of a convertible security

conversion price • the face value of a convertible bond divided by the number of shares into which the bond is convertible

conversion ratio • *See* exchange ratio.

conversion value • the market price of a stock multiplied by the conversion or exchange ratio

convertible bond • a bond that can be converted into a specified number of shares of common stock

convertible preferred stock • a preferred stock that may be exchanged for a specific number of shares of the issuing company's common stock

convex • the curvature of the relationship is away from the horizontal axis

corporate bond • debt instrument issued by a corporation; its face value is usually $1,000

correlation coefficient • a measure of the comovement tendency of two variables, such as the returns on two securities

cost approach • a method of evaluating the value of a real estate investment in terms of the replacement costs of the property or the cost of equivalent land and construction

cost basis • the amount paid to purchase an asset

coupon effect • the lower a bond's coupon rate, the greater the percentage change in its price for a given change in interest rates

coupon rate • a bond's annual interest payments divided by its par value

coupon tax effect • before-tax yields-to-maturity on low-coupon, deep-discount issues are usually somewhat below yields on otherwise similar issues trading nearer to par

covariance • the correlation coefficient between two variables multiplied by each variable's standard deviation

covered call • a combination position of long the stock and short a call option

covered writer • an investor who owns the underlying stock at the time he or she writes a call option on that stock

credit balance • a positive cash balance in a brokerage account

cum-rights • the trading of common stock with rights attached

cumulative • a preferred stock for which any dividends in arrears must be paid before common dividends can be resumed

curb exchange • *See* American Stock Exchange (AMEX).

current assets • assets that are expected to be used up soon or quickly converted to cash (includes cash, accounts receivable, and inventory)

current liabilities • debts that will become due and payable in the next year (includes accounts payable, short-term bank loans, the current portion of long-term debt, and taxes payable)

current ratio • the ratio of current assets to current liabilities; a measure of short-term liquidity

current yield • a bond's coupon rate divided by its current market price

daily price limit (interday limit) • the rule established by the futures exchanges for the maximum range of price movement permitted between the closing price of the previous day and the opening price of the next day of trading for any given commodity

day order • an order that is canceled if it is not executed sometime during the day when it was entered

day trader • an investor who typically closes out his or her position daily, speculating on very short-term price movements

dealer • a security trader who acts as a principal rather than as an agent and who is considered a specialist or a market maker, not a broker

debenture • a bond that gives the lender no claim against any specific assets in the case of default

debit balance • a negative cash balance in a margin account—that is, a loan

debt capacity • a firm's ability to borrow money

debt-equity ratio • the ratio of total debt to total equity

debt management policy • the management of the maturity of the government's outstanding debt

debt ratio • total debt divided by total assets

decomposition analysis • the process of looking at combinations of other ratios that produce a particular ratio, such as the Du Pont analysis

deep-discount bond • a bond selling for substantially less than its par (face) value

default • a failure to pay principal and/or interest due on a debt obligation

default risk • the risk that a debt security's contractual interest or principal will not be paid when due

deflation • a decline in the prices of goods and services

depletion allowance • a 15 percent deduction that may be taken against royalty income from the drilling of oil when computing taxable income

depository institution • an institution, such as a bank, that accepts deposits

derivative security • a security whose value is derived from the value of another security or combination of other securities—for example, options, futures, rights, and warrants

dilution • reduction in value of stock of existing shareholders resulting from issuance of additional shares, exercise of rights or warrants, or conversion of convertible bonds or preferred stock

direct purchase plan • a plan by which a specified amount of money is automatically applied toward the purchase of a company's stock at specified intervals (such as once per month); a form of dollar cost averaging

discount rate (for income stream) • the interest rate applied to an expected income stream to estimate its present value

discount rate (monetary policy) • the interest rate charged by the Federal Reserve System on loans to member banks

discounting • determining the present value of expected future cash flows based on the discount rate and the time until the cash flows are expected to be received

discretionary account • account over which a broker is authorized to exercise discretion with regard to purchases and sales

disinflation • a slowing of the inflation rate

dividend capture • a strategy in which an investor purchases securities in order to own them on the day of record and then quickly sells them to capture the dividend but avoid the risk of a lengthy hold

dividend discount model • a model to evaluate stocks on the basis of the present value of their expected stream of dividends

dividend payout ratio • the percentage of net income (after preferred dividends) paid out as dividends on common stock

dividend reinvestment plan (DRIP) • a company program that allows dividends to be reinvested in additional shares

dividend valuation model • *See* dividend discount model.

dividend yield • a stock's annual dividend divided by the stock price

dividends • payments derived from profits that companies make to their stockholders

dogs of the Dow • a strategy for beating the DJIA, based on the concept of selecting the 10 stocks in the index with the highest dividend yields at the start of each year and then recasting the portfolio each year

dollar cost averaging • an investment approach requiring periodic (such as monthly) fixed-dollar-amount investments

dollar-weighted rate of return • a portfolio's annual rate of returns based on its internal rate of return

DOT (designated order turnaround) • a system on the New York Stock Exchange in which orders are routed electronically to the trading posts where the securities are traded (often used by program traders)

downtick • a trade at a price lower than the price of the immediately preceding trade

Dow theory • a charting theory based on identifying major trends that was originated by Charles Dow

dual listing • a security listed for trading on more than one exchange

Du Pont formula • a formula that breaks return on equity into its component parts

duration • a statistic that serves as an index for bond price volatility, and is the basis for an immunization strategy

earnest money • the margin deposit that serves as a security to guarantee that the buyer and the seller of a contract honor the terms of that contract

earnings before interest and taxes (EBIT) • earnings computed as gross profit less cash and noncash operating expenses

earnings per share (EPS) • the net income of a company, minus any preferred dividend requirements, divided by the number of common shares outstanding

effective annual interest rate • the annual interest rate calculated when the frequency of compounding is considered

efficient frontier • a set of portfolios, each of which offers the highest expected return for a given risk and the smallest risk for a given expected return

efficient market hypothesis (EMH) • the theory that the market correctly prices securities in light of the known relevant information. It is comprised of the weak form, semistrong form, and strong form.

electronic communications network (ECN) • organizations that provide networks in which customers trade securities directly with each other. ECNs make up the fourth market.

equity • ownership interest in a firm; sometimes used interchangeably with common stock or net worth

equity multiplier • ratio of a firm's total assets to equity; a measure of financial leverage

equity note (mandatory convertible note) • debt security that is automatically converted into stock on a prespecified date at a specific price or one based on a formula that is prespecified

equity REIT • a real estate investment trust that invests in office buildings, apartments, hotels, shopping malls, and other real estate ventures

equity value • the market value of all the securities in an account less the loan balance

Eurobonds • bonds that may be denominated in dollars or some other currency and are traded internationally. They are denominated in a currency other than that of the country in which they are issued.

Eurodollar deposits • dollar-denominated deposits held in banks based outside the United States. Most are located in Europe, but some are in Asia and other areas.

European option • an option that may be exercised only on its expiration date

ex ante • before the fact. Ex ante data refers to possible future values.

ex-dividend date • the first day of trading on which buyers of stock will not receive a declared dividend

ex-post • after the fact. Ex post data is historical data.

ex-rights • without rights attached. Stock trades ex-rights after the date of record for a rights distribution.

excess reserves • actual reserves less required reserves

exchange fees • a fee charged by many no-load fund families whenever the investor moves money from one fund to another within the family

exchange rate risk • the risk of loss in value associated with movements in currency exchange rates

exchange ratio • the number of shares of stock received upon conversion of a convertible bond or stock

exchange-traded fund (ETF) • a closed-end investment company that duplicates the portfolio of a particular stock market index such as the Dow Jones Industrial Average or the Standard and Poor's 500 Index

exercise price • *See* strike price.

expected HPR • the expected return on an investment over the holding period

expiration date • the date on which an option expires; in standard stock option contracts, the Saturday following the third Friday of the stated month

face value • *See* par value.

fallen angel • a name given to poorly rated bonds

family of funds • a group of mutual funds owned and marketed by the same company

Fannie Mae • *See* Federal National Mortgage Association (FNMA).

Fed • short for either Federal Reserve Board or Federal Reserve System

Fed call • a margin call based on the account's violation of the minimum maintenance margin rate as defined by the Federal Reserve Board

Federal Deposit Insurance Corporation (FDIC) • agency that insures deposits at depository institutions up to $100,000 per depositor

federal funds market • the market where banks and other financial institutions borrow and lend money on deposit at a federal reserve bank

Federal Home Loan Mortgage Corporation (Freddie Mac) • a government agency that assembles pools of conventional mortgages and sells participations in a secondary market

Federal Housing Administration (FHA) • a federal government agency that insures home mortgages

Federal National Mortgage Association (FNMA) • a corporation, now privately owned, that operates a secondary market in mortgages and issues its own debt securities to finance its mortgage portfolio; also called Fannie Mae

Federal Open Market Committee (FOMC) • the Federal Reserve Board committee that decides on open market policy

Federal Reserve Board (Fed) • the governing body of the Federal Reserve System

Federal Reserve System (Fed) • the federal government agency that exercises monetary policy through its control over banking system reserves

fill-or-kill order • a type of security market order that must be canceled unless it can be filled immediately

filter rule • form of technical analysis that advocates buying stock when the price rises by a given percent or selling when the price falls by that same percentage

firm-commitment basis • a public offering in which the underwriter purchases the securities from the issuer and then sells them to the public

fiscal policy • government use of taxing and spending to stimulate or restrain the economy

fixed asset turnover ratio • net sales divided by net fixed assets

fixed-income security • any security that promises to pay a periodic nonvariable sum, such as a bond paying a fixed coupon amount per period

flat • the trading of bonds without compensation for accrued interest

flexible-premium deferred annuity (FPDA) • an annuity contract in which the payout period is deferred and the premium is flexible during the accumulation period

flight-to-quality • the tendency of investors to sell risky investments and buy less risky investments when disturbing news is disseminated

floating rate note • a type of debt security whose coupon rate varies with market interest rates

floor trader • one holding a seat on an exchange who trades for his or her own account. Also known as a registered competitive market maker (RCMM).

forced conversion • the calling of a convertible security to effectively force the holder to exercise the conversion option

foreign exchange risk • the degree to which an investment is affected by movements in currency exchange rates in the country where the investment is located

forward contract • a customized, nonstandard contractual agreement to accept delivery (buy) and to deliver (sell) a specified commodity or financial instrument at an agreed-upon price, settlement date, quantity, and location

fourth market • direct trading of listed securities between institutions without using a broker

Freddie Mac • *See* Federal Home Loan Mortgage Corporation.

front-end load • a load (commission) on a mutual fund assessed at the time of purchase

full employment • the employment rate that is thought to be the maximum level before inflationary pressures accelerate

fundamental analysis • the evaluation of firms and their investment attractiveness based on the firms' financial strength, competitiveness, earnings outlook, managerial strength, and sensitivity to the macroeconomy and to specific industry effects

future value • the value that a certain amount of money today is expected to have at a specified time in the future

futures contract • a standardized commodities or securities contract to deliver a certain quantity of a commodity or security at a specified price at a specified future date

futures market • any regulated exchange in which standardized futures contracts are bought and sold—for example, the Chicago Board of Trade, Chicago Mercantile Exchange, and Commodity Futures Exchange

futures option • a call or put option on a futures contract

general obligation bond • a municipal bond secured by the issuer's full faith and credit and taxing power

geometric mean return • the effective annual rate of return over multiple time periods, computed as $GMR = [(1 + PPR_1)(1 + PPR_2) \ldots (1 + PPR_n)]^{1/n} - 1$

Glass-Steagall Act • a 1933 federal act that required the separation of commercial and investment banking; prevented competition between financial institutions in the banking, insurance, and securities industries

global fund • mutual fund that invests in the United States and in foreign markets

going long • buying an asset

go public • the process in which a start-up or heretofore private firm sells its shares in a public offering

good-'til-canceled (GTC) order • type of order that remains in effect until executed or canceled

Gordon growth model • *See* constant growth model.

Government National Mortgage Association (GNMA) • a government agency that provides special assistance on selected types of home mortgages

governments • U.S. government bonds issued by the Treasury Department and backed by the full faith and credit of the federal government

Gramm-Leach-Bliley Act • passed in 1999, this act repealed the Glass-Steagall Act (the Bank Act of 1933)

greenmail • the practice of acquiring a large percentage of a firm's stock and attempting to be bought out at a premium by threatening to take over the firm

gross domestic product (GDP) • the sum of market values of all final goods and services produced annually in the economy of a country

gross income • the taxpayer's total income as determined in the first section of Form 1040

growth fund • a common stock mutual fund that seeks price appreciation by concentrating on growth stocks

growth investing • investing in stocks that have above-average P/E ratios and whose earnings are expected to grow rapidly

growth stock • the shares of a company that is expected to achieve rapid growth in earnings

head-and-shoulders formation • a pattern of stock price trends that looks like a head and shoulders and is believed by some technical analysts to forecast a price decline

hedge fund • a type of pooled portfolio instrument organized for maximum investment flexibility. Hedge funds typically invest in derivatives, sell short, use leverage, and invest internationally.

hedge ratio • in the Black-Scholes model, that ratio of the number of calls written that would exactly offset the stock price movement of a number of shares of the underlying stock held

hedging • taking opposite positions in related securities to reduce or eliminate an existing risk—for example, purchasing put options on a stock one owns

histogram • a discrete probability distribution display

Holding Company Depository Receipts (HOLDRs) • analogous to sector funds—that is, they are ETFs that, instead of mimicking an index, hold selected stocks in a particular industry

holding period return (HPR) • the rate of return over some specific time period

holding period return relative (HPRR) • the end-of-period value relative to the beginning of-period value for a specific holding period; that is, the holding period return plus one (1)

house call • a margin call based on an account's violation of the maintenance margin rate as defined by the brokerage firm holding the account

hybrid convertible (exchangeable debenture) • a bond that is convertible into common stock of a company other than the company that issued the bond

hybrid REIT • a real estate investment trust that holds both equity and mortgage investments

immunization • the process of minimizing the interest rate risk on a bond portfolio by maintaining a portfolio with a duration equal to an investor's planning horizon

imputed interest • for a zero-coupon bond, the amount of interest income assigned to the bondholder each year

income annuity • *See* single-premium immediate annuity.

income bond • a bond on which interest is paid only if the issuer has sufficient earnings

income fund • a common stock mutual fund that concentrates on stocks that pay high dividends

income in respect of a decedent • if an investor takes a stock distribution from a qualified account and dies before selling the stock, the net unrealized appreciation would be treated as ordinary income on the investor's tax return for the year he or she died

income share • one of the two types of shares issued by a dual purpose investment company. An income share is like a preferred stock with a maturity date.

income statement • a financial statement that reports revenues and expenses over a specified period

indenture • the contract the company makes with its bondholders, including a commitment to pay a stated coupon amount periodically and return the face value (usually $1,000) at maturity

index arbitrage • a trading strategy involving offsetting positions in stock index futures contracts and the underlying cash market securities (stocks making up the index)

index fund • a mutual fund that owns a portfolio of either common stock or bonds that replicates a major market index such as the S&P 500 or the Lehman Brothers Aggregate Bond Index

index model • the model that expresses the return on a security as a function of the return on an index, that is $R_i = \alpha_i + \beta_i R_M + \varepsilon_i$

indifference curve • a locus of portfolios to which an investor is indifferent, on a graph that plots expected return on the vertical axis and risk on the horizontal axis

industry analysis • an assessment of the outlook for a particular industry

inflation • the rate of increase in the overall level of prices

inflation risk • the degree to which the purchasing power of an investment asset's future cash flows is affected by changes in the general level of prices in the economy

initial margin rate • the amount of equity that an investor must provide to purchase securities. If the initial margin rate is x, then the maximum amount that can be borrowed is 1 x.

initial public offering (IPO) • the offering to the public of securities in a firm that previously was privately held. *See* go public.

insider trading • buying or selling by investors with access to material nonpublic information relating to the company being traded

interest rate futures • a futures contract calling for delivery of a debt security such as a Treasury bill or long-term government bond. Because the value of debt securities varies inversely with market interest rates, people can speculate on interest rate changes by trading futures contracts on debt securities.

interest rate option • an option to buy or sell debt securities

interest rate risk • for debt securities, the risk associated with changes in the interest rates; consists of price risk and reinvestment rate risk

interim cash flow • cash added to or removed from a portfolio during a specified holding period

internal rate of return (IRR) • the discount rate that causes the NPV of an investment to equal zero

international fund • mutual fund that specializes in investments outside of the United States and helps the investor to further diversify his or her portfolio

in the money • for calls, when the current stock price is higher than the strike price; for puts, when the current stock price is lower than the strike price

intraday dependencies • nonrandom price movements of transactions taking place over the course of a single day

intrinsic value (call, right, warrant) • the price of the associated stock less the strike price of the option, or zero if the difference is negative

intrinsic value (put) • the strike price of a put less the price of the associated stock, or zero if the difference is negative

intrinsic value (stock) • the value that a careful evaluation would produce; generally takes into account both the going-concern value and the liquidation or breakup value of the company

introducing firm • the firm that employs the individual broker who takes the customer's order and sees that the order gets executed

inventory turnover ratio • the ratio of the cost of goods sold to average yearly inventory

inverted yield curve • a yield curve showing short-term interest rates higher than long-term interest rates

investment advisory fee • a fee paid to the mutual fund's management for portfolio supervision and other managerial activities

investment banker • a firm that advises on new security offerings and/or underwrites the offering on either a firm commitment or best efforts basis. For larger offerings, the investment banker may form a syndicate.

investment company • a company that only invests in other companies. The company may be either a closed-end company or an open-end company.

investment-grade • relatively high-quality corporate bonds

investment style • a description of a mutual fund's characteristics that typically considers company size and price-earnings ratio for stocks and time to maturity and quality rating for bonds

January indicator (January effect) • an anomaly detected in past studies of stock market performance that indicates that buying in the small-cap stock market in January tends to produce above-normal returns

Jensen's alpha • a risk-adjusted measure of stock or portfolio performance; the difference between the actual return to a stock or portfolio and the return that would have been expected, based on the capital asset pricing model

junk bonds • bonds rated lower than BBB or Baa that have significant default risk

Keynesian • one who believes in the efficacy of fiscal policy (government spending and taxing) for correcting problems of unemployment and inflation

lagging indicators • an economic series published by the National Bureau of Economic Research that is believed to trail the economy in the normal business cycle

leading indicators • an economic series published by the National Bureau of Economic Research that is believed to precede turns in the overall economy

lettered stock • newly issued stock sold at a discount to large investors in a private placement prior to a public offering of the same issue

Level 3, 2, or 1 • different levels of subscriptions to NASDAQ quotations

leverage • using borrowed funds to increase the return on equity

leveraged buyout (LBO) • the process whereby a firm is bought, new debt is issued by the acquired firm, and the proceeds of the debt offering are used to reimburse the acquiring firm for part of the cost of the acquisition

LIBOR • the London Interbank Offered Rate, which is the rate at which London banks are willing to lend money to each other

lifeboat provisions • provisions offered by some closed-end funds specifying that the funds take some action to bolster their shares if they sell at a discount exceeding 10 percent for a specified period

life-cycle fund • a mutual fund designed to appeal to investors in specific phases of the life cycle by providing appropriate asset allocations

limit order • an order to buy or sell at a prespecified price

limited discretionary account • an account in which the investor gives the broker the authority to make only certain types of trades without the investor's prior consent

limited partnership • a form of business organization that has the advantage of being taxed as a partnership, rather than as a corporation; however, like a corporation, the liability of limited partners generally consists only of their initial investment

liquid assets • assets that can quickly be converted into cash such as marketable securities or receivables

liquidating dividend • *See* capital distribution.

liquidity • the ease with which an investment can be converted to cash with little or no change from the previous trade

liquidity preference hypothesis • the term structure hypothesis that asserts that most borrowers prefer to borrow long-term and most lenders prefer to lend short-term

liquidity premium • the premium demanded by bond investors for holding bonds with longer terms to maturity

liquidity ratio • a financial ratio (for example, current ratio or quick ratio) that is a measure of the firm's ability to meet short-term obligations

liquidity risk • the risk of an inability to convert an asset to cash quickly at any time and without any loss of principal

liquidity yield option note (LYON) • a zero coupon convertible debt security that is both callable and redeemable at prices that escalate through time

load • a commission applied to mutual fund trades

load fund • any mutual fund that charges a load

long hedge • a hedging position in which the investor is long the futures contract and short the physical commodity

long-term capital transactions • any trade in which the purchase and sale are more than one year apart

Long-term Equity Anticipation Securities (LEAPS®) • options with expiration dates of up to 3 years, as opposed to maximum expiration dates of 9 months or regulator options

low-price effect • an alleged anomaly to the efficient market hypothesis that is characterized by the tendency for low-priced stocks to earn above-normal returns

M1 • the basic money supply that includes checking deposits and cash held by the public

M2 • a broader-based money supply definition than M1 that includes everything in M1 plus most savings and money market deposit accounts

Macaulay's duration • the value of the duration statistic that is computed by (1) multiplying each cash flow by the time period in which it is received, (2) discounting these products to the present using the bond's yield to maturity, and (3) adding up these terms and dividing the total by the price of the bond

macroeconomic analysis • an analysis of the overall economy, often performed prior to evaluating the prospects for individual firms

maintenance margin percentage • the minimum percentage of equity that an ongoing margin account is required to maintain at all times

management expense ratio • a mutual fund's operating expenses divided by its total assets

manufactured (synthetic) call • a call-like position generated by a combination of a put and a long position in the underlying stock; position with a profit function similar to a call

manufactured (synthetic) put • a put-like position generated by a combination of a call and a short position in the underlying stock; position with a profit function similar to a put

margin account • brokerage account partially funded with money borrowed from the brokerage firm; regulated by the Fed

margin call • a request to pay down part of the margin loan by adding cash to the account, selling some securities from the account, or adding marketable securities to the account

margin deposit • earnest money required to enter a futures contract

margin rate • the percentage of a securities purchase that must come from the investor's funds rather than from borrowing

marginal tax rate • the percentage that must be paid in taxes on any incremental income

mark to the market • to recompute the value of the equity position on a daily basis

market approach • approach to real estate valuation that considers the listing and selling prices of comparable properties

market maker • one who creates a market for a security by quoting a bid and ask price

market model • a model that relates a security's return to the return of the market

market order • an order that requires immediate execution to buy or sell at the best price available

market portfolio • a hypothetical portfolio representing each investment asset in proportion to its relative weight in the universe of investment assets

market risk • the degree to which a specific asset's return is affected by political, economic, demographic, or social events and trends; also, the degree to which an asset's return is affected by the investment market as a whole; also called systematic risk

market segmentation hypothesis • the theory that there are separate markets for bonds of different maturities, so the interest rates on bonds of one maturity should not be affected by the interest rates on bonds of another maturity

market timer • an investor who attempts to make a profit by the timing of moves into and out of the market

marketable assets • assets that can be quickly converted to cash without loss of value

married put • a put option held by an investor who also owns the underlying security

master limited partnership (MLP) • a method of organizing a business that combines some of the advantages of a corporation with some of the advantages of a limited partnership. Shares of ownership trade much like corporate stock, but the MLP is taxed like a partnership.

maturity • the length of time until a debt security must be redeemed by its issuer

maturity effect • the fact that the price of a bond is more volatile for a given change in interest rates the longer the term to maturity

May Day • May 1, 1975, the day on which brokerage commission rates were fully deregulated and became established by competition among firms

mean return • the arithmetic average return in a distribution of returns

mixed portfolio fund • a mutual fund that owns a portfolio of bonds, stocks, and other investment instruments

modern portfolio theory (MPT) • *See* portfolio theory.

modified duration • the duration number divided by one plus the yield-to-maturity

momentum • tendency for movement to continue in the same direction, such as a rising trend in stock prices

monetarist • one who emphasizes the significance of monetary (as opposed to fiscal) policy

monetary policy • government policy that utilizes the money supply to affect the economy and that is implemented by the Fed through its control of required reserves

money market • the market for high-quality, short-term securities such as negotiable CDs, commercial paper, bankers' acceptances, and Treasury bills

money market deposit account (MMDA) • a type of bank or thrift institution account that offers unregulated money market rates, requires a minimum deposit, and limits withdrawals G.22 Fundamentals of Investments for Financial Planning

money market mutual fund • a mutual fund that invests in short-term, highly liquid securities

money multiplier • the ratio of the change in the money supply to the purchase or sale of securities by the Federal Reserve Board

money supply • generally defined as the sum of all coin, currency (outside bank holdings), and deposits on which check-like instruments may be written.*See* M1.

Moody's Investors Service • a firm that rates bonds and publishes manuals containing extensive historical data on a large number of publicly traded firms

moral hazard • a situation that provides incentives to take inappropriate action, generally in the nature of unnecessary risks

mortgage • a loan collateralized by real estate

mortgage-backed security • a debt instrument representing a share of ownership in a pool of mortgages or backed by a pool of mortgages

mortgage bond • debt security for which real estate is pledged as collateral

mortgage REIT • a real estate investment trust that consists of a diversified portfolio of construction loans and/or mortgage loans

multi-class funds • mutual funds that have more than one class of shares. Usually the classes are A, B, and C.

multifactor asset pricing model • any asset pricing model with more than one factor or independent variable

municipal bond • a tax-exempt bond issued by a state or local government

municipal bond fund • a mutual fund that primarily holds municipal bonds

mutual fund • an open-end investment company

naked call • a call option written by an investor who does not own the underlying asset

naked writer • an investor who does not own the underlying stock at the time he or she writes a call option

National Association of Securities Dealers Automated Quotations (NASDAQ) • an automated information system that provides brokers and dealers with price quotations on securities that are traded over-the-counter

National Bureau of Economic Research (NBER) • a private nonprofit research foundation that tracks business cycles and sponsors economic research

national market issues (NMI) • selected NASDAQ securities that represent the largest firms listed on the quotation system

neckline • part of a bar chart pattern that resembles a person's head and shoulders

neglected-firm effect • *See* analyst neglect.

negotiable CD • a certificate of deposit that can be sold

net asset value (NAV) • the per-share market value of a mutual fund's portfolio; it equals the total net assets of the fund less any liabilities, divided by number of shares outstanding

net equity • with respect to a margin account, the total value of the account minus the amount of debt outstanding

net income • the number derived by subtracting net interest expense and taxes from earnings before interest and taxes (EBIT)

net investment income • investment income after the deduction of investment expenses

net profit margin (NPM) • net income divided by sales. This financial ratio is a measure of a firm's profitability.

net worth (equity) • the equity value of the balance sheet, computed as assets less liabilities

New York Stock Exchange (NYSE) • the largest organized stock exchange, based in New York City. Stocks listed tend to be large- to mid-capitalization stocks. *See also* Big Board.

no-load fund • a mutual fund for which no commission is required for purchase

nominal (interest) rate • the stated interest rate, not necessarily the effective interest rate

noncollectibles • unique, high price-tag items in which one might invest, including such items as a Broadway show, a movie, a racehorse, or a professional baseball team

nonmarket risk • risk not related to general market movements. This risk is diversifiable.

nonqualified annuity • an annuity that is purchased outside of any tax-sheltering program

normal distribution • a distribution corresponding to the shape of the normal (bell) curve

note • intermediate-term debt security issued with terms-to-maturity of one to 10 years

odd lot • a trade of fewer than 100 shares of stock

odd-lot activity • measure of the amount of odd-lot purchases or sales; said to reflect activity by less sophisticated investors

open-end investment company • a mutual fund; any pooled portfolio of investments that stands ready to redeem or sell its shares at their NAV (or NAV plus load if the fund has a load)

open market operations • Federal Reserve transactions (buying and selling) in the government bond market that are intended to influence the money supply, interest rates, and economic activity

open outcry • organization of futures trading on the futures exchanges in which traders shout their desire to buy or sell a contract, often using hand and finger signals

opportunity cost • implicit cost of an activity or course of conduct, based on forgone opportunities

option • a security giving the holder the choice to either purchase or sell a security at a set price for a specific period

option account • the account in which trades in puts and calls occur

Options Clearing Corporation (OCC) • the clearing house for listed options that facilitates options trading by guaranteeing execution of trades between options brokers and traders

ordinary income • income subject to the statutory marginal tax rates

out-of-the-money • for calls, when the current stock price is lower than the strike price; for puts, when the current stock price is higher than the strike price

over-the-counter (OTC) • the market in unlisted securities and off-board trading in listed securities

Pac Man defense • the process in which a company that is about to be acquired attempts to acquire the acquiring company

participating preferred stock • preferred stock that may pay an extra dividend in years in which the issuing firm pays unusually high dividends on its common stock

par value (bond) • the principal amount to be paid upon maturity of a bond or other debt instrument; sometimes referred to as the bond's face value

par value (preferred stock) • the value on which the security's dividend and liquidation value is based

pass-through • a share of a mortgage pool whose interest and principal payments flow through to the holders

payment date • the date on which dividend checks are mailed to investors

payment for order flow • the practice in which a dealer pays a firm or a particular broker for the number of orders that are sent to him or her

payout ratio • dividends per share as a percentage of earnings per share

P/E ratio • *See* price-earnings (P/E) ratio.

PEG ratio • the price-earnings ratio of a firm divided by the projected growth rate of its earnings

perfect hedge • a hedge in which there is a certainty that the basis will not change or a hedge in which the basis did not change

per-period return (PPR) • the return earned for a particular period (for example, an annual return)

perpetuity • an annuity that continues forever

pink sheets • quotation source for most publicly traded OTC issues

point-and-figure chart • a technical chart that has no time dimension. An x is used to designate an upward price movement of a certain magnitude, while an o denotes a comparable downward move.

political risk • the risk of losses on assets or investments located in foreign countries, where the losses are a result of such events as trade disputes, wars, political unrest, tariffs, corruption, or expropriation

portfolio insurance • a service in which the "insurer" endeavors to place a floor on the value of the "insured" portfolio. If the portfolio value falls to a prespecified level, the insurer neutralizes it against a further fall by purchasing an appropriate number of index puts or selling an appropriate number of index options.

portfolio theory • the combination of the capital asset pricing model (CAPM), efficient market hypothesis (EMH), and related theoretical models of security market pricing and performance

portfolio turnover ratio • the lesser of annual purchases or annual sales (excluding securities with less than one-year maturities) divided by the average monthly net assets

portfolio variance • a statistic that measures portfolio risk by quantifying the dispersion from the portfolio's average (mean) value

position trader • a commodity trader who takes and holds futures positions for several days or more

preferred habitat hypothesis • one of four hypotheses for explaining the term structure of interest rates, it is based on the idea of a tendency for borrowers and lenders to gravitate toward their preferred maturities

preferred stock • shares whose indicated dividends and liquidation values must be paid before common shareholders receive any dividends or liquidation payments

premium (option) • the market price of an option

premium over conversion value • the amount by which a convertible bond's price exceeds its conversion value

premium over straight-debt value • the amount by which a convertible bond's price exceeds its value as a nonconvertible debt security

present value • the value of an expected future sum or sums discounted by the appropriate interest rate or discount rate

price-book value ratio • the price of the stock divided by the book value per share

price-earnings (P/E) ratio • the share price of a stock divided by its actual or anticipated earnings per share. For trailing earnings, the P/E ratio is the stock price relative to the most recent 12-month earnings per share; for ex ante earnings, it is the stock price relative to the next 12-month expected earnings.

price risk • the risk of a bond's price changing in response to a change in interest rates

price stability • the absence of or low level of inflation or deflation. While the prices of specific goods would still fluctuate in response to market forces (supply and demand changes), the overall level of prices would be stable.

price-weighted index • an approach to calculating an investment index in which the relative effect of a security on the index is a function of the price of that security; larger prices have a larger effect

primary market • the market for the sale of new securities

prime rate • at one time, it was known as the borrowing rate that banks advertise as available to their least risky borrowers. Today, it is the rate banks use for pricing their loans.

principal • *See* par value.

private placement • a direct sale of securities to a small number of large buyers without the registration requirements of a public offering

probability distribution • a distribution of possible outcomes along with their associated probabilities

profitability ratio • a ratio, such as return on equity, that reflects the firm's profitability

program trading • a type of mechanical trading in large blocks by institutional investors that usually involves both stock and index futures contracts as in, for example, index arbitrage or portfolio insurance

promised yield • *See* yield-to-maturity.

prospectus • a document that all companies offering new securities for public sale must file with the SEC. It spells out in detail the financial position of the offering company, what the new funds will be used for, the qualifications of the corporate officers, risk factors, nature of competition, and any other material information.

proxy • a temporary transfer of one's right to vote

prudent investor • one who used the principles of modern portfolio theory to manage portfolios. A prudent investor focuses on the performance of the entire portfolio rather than the performance of individual securities.

prudent man rule • the selection of each security according to conservative investment standards. Thus a prudent man oversees each security separately rather than the entire portfolio.

purchasing power risk • the degree to which the purchasing power of an investment asset's future cash flows is affected by changes in the general level of prices

pure market timer • an investor who is in the market when it is expected to rise and out of the market when it is expected to fall

pure risk • risk that involves only the chance of loss or no loss

put-call parity • a theoretical relationship between the value of a put and a call on the same underlying security with the same strike price and expiration date

put option (put) • an option to sell a specified number of shares of stock at a specified price prior to a specified expiration date

qualified annuity • an annuity that is purchased through a tax-sheltered program

quick ratio • *See* acid test ratio.

R^2 • *See* coefficient of determination.

random walk • the random motion of stock prices that are as likely to move in one direction as another regardless of past price behavior

rating (bond) • a quality or risk evaluation assigned by a rating agency such as Standard & Poor's or Moody's

ratio analysis • balance sheet and income statement analysis that utilizes ratios of financial aggregates to assess a company's financial position, usually by looking for trends in financial ratios, by comparing a company's financial ratios with the industry average, or both

real estate investment trust (REIT) • closed-end investment company that buys and/or manages rental properties and/or real estate mortgages and pays out more than 95 percent of its income as dividends

real return • a return on an investment adjusted for changes in the price level. This amount equals the increase in purchasing power resulting from saving or investing money.

record date • the shareholder registration date that determines the recipients of that period's dividends

red herring • a copy of the registration statement that is filed with the SEC for a security offering. The front page of this statement contains a paragraph in red ink indicating that the company is not attempting to sell its shares before the SEC approves the registration.

regional exchange • any U.S. stock exchange other than NYSE or AMEX

registered competitive market maker (RCMM) • *See* floor trader.

registered representative • an employee of a registered brokerage firm who is qualified to serve as an account executive for the firm's customers. *See* broker.

registration statement • a statement that must be filed with the SEC before a security is offered for sale and that must contain all materially relevant information relating to the offering

regular annuity • a fixed number of equal, consecutive payments, with the first payment at the end of the first period

regular dividend • the distribution of dividend and/or interest income that a mutual fund has accrued

reinvestment load • a fee charged by some mutual funds for reinvestment of dividends

reinvestment rate risk • the risk associated with reinvesting coupon payments at unknown future interest rates

REIT • *See* real estate investment trust.

relative strength line • a line that plots the ratio of the stock's price to that of the S&P 500 Index or to some other appropriate average or index

RELP (real estate limited partnership) • a type of investment organized as a limited partnership that invests directly in real estate properties

replacement cost approach • *See* cost approach.

repurchase agreement (repo) • a type of investment in which a security is sold with a prearranged purchase price and the date is designed to produce a particular yield—in fact, an indirect form of borrowing

required rate of return • the rate of return on an investment required by investors to justify the degree of risk incurred; the risk-free rate plus the risk premium

reserve requirement • the percentage of reserves the Fed requires each bank to have on deposit for each increment of demand or time deposits

resistance level • a price or price range at which additional sellers enter the market, and thus would create the appearance of a barrier to additional price increases

return on assets (ROA) • net income after taxes divided by total assets

return on equity (ROE) • net income after taxes and preferred dividends divided by net worth

revenue bond • a municipal bond that is backed only by the revenues of the project that it finances

revenue sharing • the process whereby mutual funds pay brokers for promoting their funds' shares to investors

reward to variability ratio (RVAR) • *See* Sharpe ratio.

reward to volatility ratio (RVOL) • *See* Treynor ratio.

riding the yield curve • a bond portfolio management strategy that takes advantage of an upward-sloping yield curve by purchasing intermediate-term bonds and then selling them as they approach maturity

rights • securities allowing shareholders to acquire new stock at a prespecified price within a prespecified period, generally issued in proportion to the number of shares currently held and exercisable at a price that is usually below the current market price

rights offering • an offering of rights by a firm wishing to raise additional equity capital while avoiding dilution of existing shareholders' relative ownership

risk • the dispersion of possible returns from the expected return

risk-adjusted return • the return from an asset adjusted for the risk associated with the asset

risk averse • the degree of preference for less risky investments, even if they have somewhat lower expected returns

risk-free rate • the yield on a riskless investment, such as a Treasury bill

risk premium • the expected return in excess of the risk-free rate that is compensation for the investment's risk

round lot • the basic unit in which securities are traded, usually consisting of 100 shares

round-trip fee • the total commission costs of executing a transaction in the futures market paid at the time of the contract's formation

Rule 144 • an SEC rule restricting the resale of lettered stock

Rule 415 • an SEC rule allowing shelf registration of a security that may then be sold over a 2-year period without separate registrations of each part

run • an uninterrupted series of price increases or decreases

savings bond • a low-denomination Treasury issue designed to appeal to investors with minimal capital

scalpers • people who trade on the floor of the futures exchanges, seeking very quick turns in their holdings

seat • a membership in the New York Stock Exchange

secondary market • the market for already issued securities that takes place on the exchanges or OTC

secondary offering or distribution • a large public securities offering by existing investors made outside the usual exchange or OTC market

sector fund • a mutual fund that specializes in a particular segment of the market—for example, an industry (chemicals)

Securities Act of 1933 • securities law dealing with the issuance of securities and addressing the registration process, disclosure requirements, and related matters

Securities and Exchange Commission (SEC) • the federal agency with direct regulatory authority over the securities industry

Securities Exchange Act of 1934 • securities law dealing with existing securities, addressing the filing of periodic reports, regulating exchanges and brokerage firms, ongoing disclosure requirements, and prohibiting certain unethical practices such as market manipulation and insider trading

Securities Investor Protection Corporation (SIPC) • a federal agency that guarantees the safety of brokerage accounts up to $500,000, no more than $100,000 of which may be in cash

securitization • the process of turning an asset with poor marketability into a security with substantially greater acceptability—for example, a security that looks like a standard bond but is derived from real estate mortgage loans, auto loans, or credit card balances

security market line • the theoretical relationship between a security's market risk and its expected return under the capital asset pricing model. The equation form is as follows: $r_i = r_f + \beta_i (r_M - r_f)$ where r_i is security i's risk-adjusted expected return, r_f is the risk-free return, β_i is the beta measure for security i, and r_M is the return on the market portfolio.

self-regulatory organization • an organization regulated by the SEC under the authority of the Securities Act of 1934. SROs include the NYSE, the AMEX, and NASDAQ.

selling short • the act of borrowing and selling a security that belongs to someone else. The short seller covers by buying back equivalent securities and restoring them to the original owner.

semistrong form EMH • the hypothesis that current market prices fully reflect all publicly available information and react quickly to new information. An implication is that fundamental analysis of publicly available information and data cannot systematically yield superior returns.

semivariance • a measure of dispersion using only returns less than the mean

senior debt • debt that has priority over other (subordinate) debt

separation theorem • the idea that the decision of what portfolio of risky assets to invest in can be separated from the selection of an appropriate risk-return trade-off. In this scenario, all investors would select the market portfolio.

serial bond • a bond issue in which portions mature at stated intervals rather than all at once

Series 6 • a license that qualifies the broker to sell open-end mutual funds, initial offerings of closed-end investment companies, and such variable products as variable annuities provided the individual also holds the appropriate insurance license

Series 7 • a general securities registered representative license, which qualifies the broker to solicit, purchase, and/or sell all securities products, including corporate securities, municipal securities, options, direct participation programs, investment company products, and variable contracts

Sharpe ratio (reward to variability ratio) • a measure of risk-adjusted performance of an asset, calculated as the ratio of the asset's rate of return minus the risk-free rate divided by the asset's standard deviation

shelf registration • an SEC provision allowing preregistration of an amount of a security to be sold over a 2-year period without specific registration of each sale

short hedge • a combination position in which the investor is short on the futures contract and long on the underlying commodity or asset

short interest (stocks) • the number of shares sold short; sometimes used as a technical market indicator

short selling • *See* selling short.

short-term capital transaction • any trade in which the purchase and sale are less than or equal to one year apart

short-term trading index • the ratio of two ratios. The first ratio is the *number of* advancing stocks divided by the *number of* declining stocks, and the second ratio is the *volume of* advancing stocks divided by the *volume of* declining stocks.

single-premium deferred annuity (SPDA) • an annuity that is purchased with one payment, but the payout period is deferred for a period of time

single-premium immediate annuity (SPIA) • similar to SPDAs, but the benefit payments begin upon receipt of the single premium; also referred to as income annuities

sinking fund • a fund to which a borrowing company makes periodic contributions to ensure that the principal amount of its bond indebtedness will be repaid when due

skewed distribution • a nonsymmetrical statistical distribution that is spread out more on one side of its mode than the other; a nonnormal distribution

small firm effect • a possible anomaly to the efficient market hypothesis characterized by the tendency for small firms to earn above-normal rates of return after risk is taken into account

socially responsible fund • a mutual fund that invests only in corporations or other entities that maintain social and/or ethical principles that are consistent with those specified by the fund

sophisticated investor rationale • the concept that some investors are more sophisticated or knowledgeable than other investors. Thus, one should figure out what these sophisticated investors are doing, and do the same.

special offering • a large block of stock offered for sale on an exchange with special incentive fees paid to purchasing brokers (also called spot secondary)

specialist • an exchange member who makes a market in listed securities

specialty fund • a mutual fund designed for investors who seek special investment opportunities

speculating • the act of committing funds for a short period at high risk in the hope of realizing a gain

speculative risk • risk associated with speculation in which there is some chance of a gain and some chance of a loss

speculative value • *See* time value.

speculator • one who engages in risky transactions in the hope of a large return

spot market • the cash market for immediate delivery of a commodity

spread (bid-ask) • the difference between the bid and the ask price

spread (options) • purchasing an option and writing an option on the same security with different expiration dates or exercise prices

spreading • creating a combination trade such as both a long and a short position in the futures market

Standard & Poor's (S&P) Corporation • an important firm in the investment area that rates bonds, collects and reports data, and computes market indexes

standard deviation • a measure of the degree of dispersion of a distribution. The standard deviation is the square root of the variance. *See also* variance.

Statement of Additional Information • a statement that the mutual fund investor may request from the mutual fund manager that provides additional information about the mutual fund that is not found in the prospectus

statement of cash flows • financial statement showing cash flows into and out of a firm during the reporting period

stock certificate • document showing ownership of a specified number of shares of a company's stock

stock index option • an option on the value of a stock index

stock market index futures • a futures contract on a stock index that does not require delivery of the underlying stock index but is instead settled in dollars according to the difference between the strike price and the actual price of the index

stock market index futures • an analyst term used to describe the alleged tendency for the stock market to react more than is warranted to news, whether good or bad

stock split • the division of a company's existing stock into more shares (for example, 2 for 1 or 3 for 1)

stop-limit order • an order to implement a limit order when the market price reaches a certain level

stop-loss order • an order to sell or buy at market when a certain price is reached

straddle • a combination put and call option on the same stock at the same strike price and the same expiration date

straight bond • a bond that has no conversion feature

straight-debt value • the value of a convertible bond as a straight-debt (nonconvertible) bond, based on discounted present value of cash flows

strangle • similar to a straddle except that the options have different strike prices—that is, the strike price of the call option is above the strike price for the put option

street name • denotes a security held in a customer account at a brokerage house that is registered in the firm's name

strike price (exercise price) • the price at which the option holder can exercise the option to buy (call) or sell (put) shares

strip bond • a coupon bond (with its coupons removed) that returns only principal at maturity and thus is equivalent to a zero-coupon bond

strong form EMH • the view that market prices quickly and accurately reflect all public and nonpublic information (suggesting that even inside information will not consistently result in superior returns)

style drift • a portfolio that is drifting away from what had been an established style for a mutual fund

subordination • giving a bond issue a lower priority than other (senior) bond issues in bankruptcy

substitution swap • a type of bond swap in which an issue is sold to establish a loss and replaced with an equivalent issue, or a fairly priced bond is sold and replaced with an underpriced one

SuperDOT • advanced version of the DOT system

support level • a floor price that, according to technical analysis, tends to restrict downside price moves

surrender value • the value of an annuity contract after surrender charges have been deducted

switching • when an investor moves money from one fund in a family to another fund in the same family

synthetic call • *See* manufactured call.

synthetic put • *See* manufactured put.

systematic risk • *See* market risk.

taxable income • income on which an individual or corporation is taxed

tax-equivalent yield • the yield on state and local debt instruments after adjustment for the fact that the debt holder is not liable for federal income tax; calculated as $Y^{TE} = Y/(1-T)$ where

Y_{TE} is tax-equivalent yield, Y is nominal yield on state and local debt, and T is the investor's marginal federal tax rate

tax exempts • municipal bonds that are not subject to federal taxation

tax-loss harvesting • selling a security at the end of the year to establish a capital loss for tax reporting purposes

tax risk • the extent to which investment returns would be affected by changes in tax laws

technical analysis • a method of evaluating securities and forecasting future price changes based only on past price and volume behavior

technical default • a technical violation of a bond indenture provision such as failure to maintain certain financial ratios

technical market indicator • a data series or combination of data series said to be helpful in forecasting the market's future direction

tender offer • an offer to purchase a large block of securities made outside the general market (exchanges, OTC) in which the securities are traded (often as part of an effort to take over a company)

term structure (of interest rates) • the relationship between yield-to-maturity and term-to-maturity for bonds of like quality

term-to-maturity • the length of time to maturity of a debt instrument

third market • the over-the-counter trading of exchange-listed securities

thrift institutions • institutions other than commercial banks that accept savings deposits, especially savings and loan associations, mutual savings banks, and credit unions

ticker tape • the display of securities transactions shortly after their occurrence, typically electronically

tight money • restrictive monetary policy

times-interest-earned ratio • earnings before interest and taxes divided by interest expense (a ratio used to detect possible risk of default)

time value (option) • the excess of an option's market price over its intrinsic value

time-weighted rate of return • an approach to calculating rates of return that excludes the effect of additions to or distributions from the portfolio, and is computed as the geometric mean return

total asset turnover ratio • sales divided by total assets

trading stations (posts) • the spot on the floor of an exchange where a stock is traded

trail commission (trailer) • a fee not to exceed an annual rate of 0.25 percent that can be paid to mutual fund salespeople, presumably for providing ongoing service and information

tranches • classes of collateral mortgage obligation securities that have varying characteristics

Treasury bill (T-bill) • a short-term debt security issued by the U.S. Treasury

Treasury bonds • debt instruments issued by the U.S. Treasury with an initial maturity of more than 10 years

Treasury notes • debt instruments issued by the U.S. Treasury with an initial maturity of anywhere from one to 10 years

Treynor ratio (reward to volatility ratio) • a measure of risk-adjusted performance of an asset calculated as the ratio of the asset's rate of return minus the risk-free rate divided by the asset's beta

trustee • a bank or other third party that administers the provisions of a bond indenture or that, in general, holds property for the benefit of others

turnover • the relative frequency of trading securities within a mutual fund or other portfolio

turnover ratio • *See* portfolio turnover ratio.

12b-1 fee • a charge against the net assets of a mutual fund that has the ostensible purpose of compensating the management company for marketing costs. It cannot exceed an annual rate of 0.75 percent of average net assets per year plus another 0.25 percent service fee (trail commission or "trailer") that can be paid to salespeople for providing ongoing service and information.

two-name paper • a debt instrument, such as a banker's acceptance, that is issued by one source (for example, a corporation) and guaranteed by another (generally a bank)

unbiased expectations hypothesis • a theory explaining the term structure of interest rates, which states that long-term rates are a function of current and expected future short-term rates

underwrite • to agree to buy all or part of a new security issue, with the intention to sell the securities to the public at a higher price

underwriter • an investment banker who agrees to buy all or part of a new security issue for resale to the public

unemployment rate • the percentage of the workforce that is actually out of work and actively seeking employment

Uniform Principal and Income Act • the key law affecting the management of trust assets. First established the prudent man rule; later this was replaced with the prudent investor rule.

unit investment trust • a self-liquidating unmanaged portfolio in which investors own shares; a concept similar to a closed-end fund but with a specified liquidation date

uptick • a trade at a price greater than the previous trading price

utility function • a function that indicates the value (or utility) of incremental wealth for a specific individual

VA (Veterans Administration) • government agency that provides a variety of services for veterans and their dependents, including the guarantee of repayment of certain home mortgages

valuation • determining the value of an investment as the discounted value of all expected future cash flows

value investing • assembling a portfolio of stocks that sell at low P/E ratios

value stocks • stocks with below-average PE ratios

value weighted • any index in which each company's contribution to the index is based on its total market value

variable annuity • an annuity whose payment is tied to a benchmark such as a stock market index

variance • a measure of uncertainty or risk based on squaring the difference between each return and the mean return

venture capital • risk capital extended to start-up companies or small going concerns that usually requires an ownership interest, as distinct from a pure loan

versus purchase • a selling order that specifies the purchase date of securities to be delivered

warrants • certificates offering the right to purchase stock in a company at a specified price over a specified period. Unlike options, warrants are issued by the same company that issues the underlying stock

weak form EMH • the hypothesis that stock price movements and trading volume cannot be used to predict future price changes; implies that technical analysis cannot provide superior rates of returns

weights • the percentage of the portfolio invested in each security, based on market values

white knight • an alternative buyer for a company when management is attempting to avoid being acquired by a primary buyer

white squire • a third party to whom management sells a significant minority ownership in the company to avoid being acquired by a primary buyer

World Equity Benchmark Shares (WEBS) • index funds that replicate the stock market of a particular foreign country

wrap account • an account in which a single annual fee known as a wrap fee is paid. It is also known as a separate account or managed account.

wrap fee • a management fee charged by investment advisers that includes any brokerage fees incurred

writer • one who sells a put or call option and is therefore obligated to make the agreed-upon purchase or sale if the holder chooses to exercise the option

yield curve • *See* term structure (of interest rates).

yield to earliest (first) call • the holding period return with the assumption that the bond will be called as soon as the no-call provision expires

yield-to-maturity (promised yield) • a measure of bond yield that takes into account capital gain or loss as well as coupon interest payments; the discount rate that would make the present value of the bond's cash flows (interest payments plus face value at maturity) equal the purchase price of the bond

yield-to-maturity effect • the effect that for a given change in interest rates, bonds with lower YTMs have greater percentage price changes than bonds with higher YTMs, all other things being equal

zero-coupon bond (zeros) • a bond issued at a discount that matures at its face value and makes no interest payments prior to maturity

zero-sum game • situation in which total gains equal total losses among the players

zeros • *See* zero coupon bond.